GET THE MOST FROM YOUR BOOK

VOUCHER CODE:

H8H706XA

Online Access

Your print purchase of *Multicultural Counseling* includes **online access via Springer Publishing Connect**™ to increase accessibility, portability, and searchability.

Insert the code at https://connect.springerpub.com/content/book/978-0-8261-3953-5 today!

Having trouble? Contact our customer service department at cs@springerpub.com

Instructor Resource Access for Adopters

Let us do some of the heavy lifting to create an engaging classroom experience with a variety of instructor resources included in most textbooks SUCH AS:

INSTRUCTOR'S MANUAL

POWERPOINTS

TEST BANK

Visit **https://connect.springerpub.com/** and look for the **"Show Supplementary"** button on your **book homepage** to see what is available to instructors! First time using Springer Publishing Connect?

Email **textbook@springerpub.com** to create an account and start unlocking valuable resources.

Multicultural Counseling

LaTonya M. Summers, PhD, LMHC, LCMHC-S, is an award-winning assistant professor of clinical mental health counseling at Jacksonville University. There, she brings over 26 years of clinical mental health and addictions counseling experience and conducts research on multicultural issues in counseling and supervision. She has examined the impact of power, race, and gender on cross-racial interactions; natural hair bias and upward mobility in the workplace; clinical mental health needs of Black clients; and culturally specific professional development. Her work is featured in scholarly journals and at international and national professional conferences. Dr. Summers founded the national annual Black Mental Health Symposium, a conference aimed to equip mental health professionals with culturally specific skills to improve mental wellness in Black communities. She is the publisher of *Black Mental Health Today* magazine. Dr. Summers has been featured in *O* magazine on the subject of authenticity in the workplace and conducted a TEDx Talk entitled "Know Pain, Know Gain" (https://youtu.be/9b6pnlmR0-I).

Lotes Nelson, PhD, LCMHC-S, NCC, ACS, is clinical faculty at Southern New Hampshire University's Clinical Mental Health Counseling Program. Dr. Nelson is a Licensed Clinical Mental Health Counselor in North Carolina, a Board-Approved Clinical Supervisor, and a National Certified Counselor. She is also an award recipient of the prestigious National Board for Certified Counselor Doctoral Minority Fellowship. Dr. Nelson serves as a member of the Association for Creativity in Counseling Board of Directors and was previously a member of the Florida Counseling Association and the Licensed Professional Counselors Association of North Carolina Board of Directors, along with her many leadership roles in the mental health field and community at large. Notably, Dr. Nelson received The Samuel T. Gladding Inspiration and Motivation Award to recognize her inclusive practice through humility, collaboration, creativity, and expression through growth-fostering connections and cooperation. Dr. Nelson is vehement about the topic of multiculturalism as a first-generation immigrant herself. Her work has been focused on creating space for the minority, marginalized, and oppressed groups to be heard and belong. She has worked in various capacities dealing with diversity in people for over 25 years in both the corporate sector and mental health counseling discipline as a counselor, counselor educator, and supervisor. Her avid interest in diversity in people and counseling has been displayed in her research, scholarly writing, curriculum development, and academic work. Dr. Nelson was appointed and served as the Chair of the Anti-Racist Pedagogy Task Force of the Association for Counselor Education and Supervision (ACES) and served as a member of the National Board for Certified Counselors (NBCC) Ethics Task Force. Dr. Nelson enjoys spending quality time with her family.

Multicultural Counseling

Responding With Cultural Humility, Empathy, and Advocacy

LaTonya M. Summers, PhD, LMHC, LCMHC-S
Lotes Nelson, PhD, LCMHC-S, NCC, ACS

Copyright © 2023 Springer Publishing Company, LLC
All rights reserved.

No part of this publication may be reproduced, stored in a retrieval system, or transmitted in any form or by any means, electronic, mechanical, photocopying, recording, or otherwise, without the prior permission of Springer Publishing Company, LLC, or authorization through payment of the appropriate fees to the Copyright Clearance Center, Inc., 222 Rosewood Drive, Danvers, MA 01923, 978-750-8400, fax 978-646-8600, info@copyright.com or at www.copyright.com.

Springer Publishing Company, LLC
11 West 42nd Street, New York, NY 10036
www.springerpub.com
connect.springerpub.com

Acquisitions Editor: Rhonda Dearborn
Compositor: Exeter Premedia Services Pvt Ltd.

ISBN: 978-0-8261-3952-8
ebook ISBN: 978-0-8261-3953-5
DOI: 10.1891/9780826139535

SUPPLEMENTS:

A robust set of instructor resources designed to supplement this text is located at http://connect.springerpub.com/content/book/978-0-8261-3953-5. Qualifying instructors may request access by emailing **textbook@springerpub.com**.

Instructor's Manual: 978-0-8261-3955-9
Instructor's Test Bank: 978-0-8261-3954-2
Instructor's PowerPoints: 978-0-8261-3956-6

Voices From the Field Video Transcripts: 978-0-8261-3958-0

To access the *Voices From the Field* videos and their transcripts, log in to http://connect.springerpub.com/content/book/978-0-8261-3953-5 and enter the voucher code on the first page of this book.

22 23 24 25 26 / 5 4 3 2 1

The author and the publisher of this Work have made every effort to use sources believed to be reliable to provide information that is accurate and compatible with the standards generally accepted at the time of publication. The author and publisher shall not be liable for any special, consequential, or exemplary damages resulting, in whole or in part, from the readers' use of, or reliance on, the information contained in this book. The publisher has no responsibility for the persistence or accuracy of URLs for external or third-party Internet websites referred to in this publication and does not guarantee that any content on such websites is, or will remain, accurate or appropriate.

Library of Congress Cataloging-in-Publication Data

Names: Summers, LaTonya M., author. | Nelson, Lotes, author.
Title: Multicultural counseling : responding with cultural humility, empathy, and advocacy / LaTonya M. Summers, PhD, LMHC, LCMHC-S, Lotes Nelson, PhD, LCMHC-S, NCC, ACS.
Description: New York, NY : Springer Publishing, [2023] | Includes bibliographical references and index.
Identifiers: LCCN 2022030028 (print) | LCCN 2022030029 (ebook) | ISBN 9780826139528 (paperback) | ISBN 9780826139535 (ebook)
Subjects: LCSH: Cross-cultural counseling--United States. | Multiculturalism--United States. | Minorities--Counseling of--United States.
Classification: LCC BF175.4.C68 S86 2023 (print) | LCC BF175.4.C68 (ebook) | DDC 158.3089--dc23/eng/20220824
LC record available at https://lccn.loc.gov/2022030028
LC ebook record available at https://lccn.loc.gov/2022030029

Contact sales@springerpub.com to receive discount rates on bulk purchases.

Publisher's Note: New and used products purchased from third-party sellers are not guaranteed for quality, authenticity, or access to any included digital components.

Printed in the United States of America by Hatteras, Inc.

This book is dedicated to my late paternal grandmother, my first educator
Ethel L. Wallace.
You were the apple of my eye and I am the fruit of your labor!
—L. M. S.

This book is dedicated to my late father, Ricardo Gudez, who had an unwavering belief in my capabilities. Who used to say in his broken English, "You do good and show the world."
Likewise, I am dedicating this book to the immigrants in the world, who tirelessly work harder than they need, to show their worth.
My hope is that the world will begin to accept you for who you are.
To my son, Kris Stokes, for being the joy and breath that I take.
My desire is for this world to be gentler and kinder for your generations and beyond.
Lastly, to my husband, Frank Nelson, your steadfast support is one of a kind. Thank you for seeing me for who I am and always encouraging me to make the slightest difference in this world.
—L. N.

Contents

Contributors xvii
List of Videos xxi
Foreword Twinet Parmer, PhD, LPC, CST xxv
Preface xxix
Acknowledgments xxxiii
Available Resources xxxv

SECTION I. THE COUNSELOR'S WORLDVIEW

1. **The Counselor: Becoming a Culturally Responsive Counselor** 1
   Lotes Nelson

   Introduction to the Need for a Multicultural Counseling Approach 2
   What Is Multicultural Counseling and Why Is It important? 3
   The Counselor's Worldview 5
   Self-Awareness: Heritage, Values, Attitude, and Beliefs 7
   The Influence of Counselors' Sets of Beliefs and Therapeutic Relationships 8
   Developing Cultural Responsiveness for Counselors 9
   Ethical Consideration in Multicultural Counseling 11
   Summary 14
   Discussion Questions 14
   Key References 14

2. **Liberation Counseling as a Framework: Offering Anti-Oppressive Counseling** 15
   LaTonya M. Summers

   An Overview of Liberation Psychology 16
   Exploration of Intersectionality, Privilege, and Oppression 18
   Integration of Liberation Theory and Pedagogy and Counseling 18
   Liberation Counseling and the Oppressed 19
   Summary 22
   Discussion Questions 22
   Key References 22

3. **Counseling With Cultural Humility, Empathy, and Responsiveness** 23
   LaTonya M. Summers and Lotes Nelson

   What Is Cultural Humility and Empathy in Counseling? 23
   Enhancing Humility and Empathy in Counseling 25

Identifying and Utilizing Culturally Responsive Interventions   27
Summary   29
Discussion Questions   29
Key References   29

4. **Social Justice and Advocacy Readiness**   31
   Noreal F. Armstrong

   What Are Social Justice and Advocacy?   32
   The Intersectionality of Cultural Responsiveness and Social Justice   34
   Becoming an Advocate   38
   Using the Multicultural and Social Justice Counseling Competencies to Put Advocacy Into Action   41
   Summary   44
   Discussion Questions   45
   Key References   45

SECTION II. THE CLIENT'S WORLDVIEW

5. **Culturally Responsive Counseling for Clients of African American, African, and Afro-Caribbean Descent**   46
   LaVerne Hanes Collins and Alfonso L. Ferguson

   The Counselor: Exploration, Introspection, and Reflection   47
   What It Means to Be of African Descent in America   49
   Identity Development: Impact of White Privilege and Internalized Racism   50
   African Americans: Overcoming a Legacy of Slavery and Segregation   51
   African American Culture   54
   African Immigrants: Seeking More   56
   Afro-Caribbean Immigrant Groups: Struggling With Stereotypes   57
   Culturally Responsive Practices: Drawing From the Multicultural and Social Justice Counseling Competencies and Cultural Humility   59
   Crafting an Advocacy Agenda   60
   Counseling Children, Adolescents, and Young Adults   60
   Counseling Adults, Couples, and Families   62
   Implications for Clinical Practice   63
   Summary   66
   Discussion Questions   67
   Key References   67

6. **Culturally Responsive Counseling for Clients of Asian American and Pacific Islander Descent**   68
   Jung H. Hyun, John J. S. Harrichand, S Anandavalli, Yi-Wen Su, and Eunhui Yoon

   The Counselor: Exploration, Introspection, and Reflection   69
   Key Interpersonal Societal Issues Affecting Asian Americans   69
   Identity Development of Asian Americans   73
   Counseling Utilization and Help-Seeking of Asian Americans   74
   Culturally Responsive Practices: Drawing From the Multicultural and Social Justice Counseling Competencies and Cultural Humility   75
   Crafting an Advocacy Agenda   76
   Counseling Children, Adolescents, and Young Adults   79

Counseling Adults, Couples, and Families 82
Implications for Clinical Practice 84
Summary 86
Discussion Questions 87
Key References 87

7. **Culturally Responsive Counseling for Clients of Latinx Descent** 89
   George James Ramos and Antoinette Gines-Rivera

   The Counselor: Exploration, Introspection, and Reflection 89
   Latinx American History, Latinx Values, and Culture 90
   Mental Health Considerations and Perceptions 92
   Identity Development for Clients of Latinx Descent 92
   Counseling Utilization and Help-Seeking of Latinx Clients 94
   Culturally Responsive Practices: Drawing From the Multicultural and Social Justice Counseling Competencies and Cultural Humility 96
   Crafting an Advocacy Agenda 98
   Counseling Children, Adolescents, and Young Adults 100
   Counseling Adults, Couples, and Families 101
   Implications for Clinical Practice 102
   Summary 105
   Discussion Questions 106
   Key References 106

8. **Culturally Responsive Counseling for Clients of Native American Descent** 107
   Lynae S. Hemming and Julie A. Yliniemi

   The Counselor: Exploration, Introspection, and Reflection 107
   Cultural and Spiritual Values 108
   Acculturation Conflicts, Alcohol and Substance Abuse, Domestic Violence, and Suicide 111
   Identity Development and Acculturation for Clients of Native American Descent 114
   Counseling Utilization and Help-Seeking 117
   Culturally Responsive Practices: Drawing From the Multicultural and Social Justice Counseling Competencies and Cultural Humility 118
   Crafting an Advocacy Agenda 120
   Counseling Children, Adolescents, and Young Adults 121
   Counseling Adults, Couples, and Families 122
   Implications for Clinical Practice 123
   Summary 127
   Discussion Questions 127
   Key References 128

9. **Culturally Responsive Counseling for Clients of European American Descent** 129
   Paul H. Smith, Kelly King, and Catherine W. Hawkins

   The Counselor: Exploration, Introspection, and Reflection 129
   Definition of Terms 130
   White Racial Identity Development 131
   White Allyship 133

Identity Development for Clients of European American Descent   135
Counseling Utilization and Help-Seeking   138
Culturally Responsive Practices: Drawing From the Multicultural and Social Justice Counseling Competencies and Cultural Humility   139
Crafting an Advocacy Agenda   141
Counseling Children, Adolescents, and Young Adults   142
Counseling Adults, Couples, and Families   145
Implications for Clinical Practice   148
Summary   149
Discussion Questions   150
Key References   150

10. Culturally Responsive Counseling for Clients of Multiracial Descent   152
Victoria Austin, Karena Heyward, and Shanice Armstrong

The Counselor: Exploration, Introspection, and Reflection   152
Competencies for Counseling the Multiracial Population   154
Multiracial Identity Development Models   158
Stressors and Discrimination   160
Counseling Utilization and Help-Seeking   161
Culturally Responsive Practices: Drawing From the Multicultural and Social Justice Counseling Competencies and Cultural Humility   163
Crafting an Advocacy Agenda   164
Counseling Children, Adolescents, and Young Adults   165
Counseling Adults, Couples, and Families   166
Implications for Clinical Practice   167
Summary   168
Discussion Questions   169
Key References   169

11. Culturally Responsive Counseling for Lesbian, Gay, Bisexual, Queer++ Clients   171
Edward F. Hudspeth

The Counselor: Exploration, Introspection, and Reflection   172
Identity, Individuality, and Culture: Intersectionality   175
Gender Identities and Expression and Sexual Orientation   175
Intersectionality of Religion and Sexual/Gender Identities   178
LGBQ++ Prejudice, Discrimination, Oppression, and Stressors   179
Counseling Utilization and Help-Seeking   180
Educational Standards: Council for the Accreditation of Counseling and Related Educational Programs Standards and Association for Lesbian, Gay, Bisexual, and Transgender Issues in Counseling Competencies   181
Culturally Responsive Practices: Drawing From the Multicultural and Social Justice Counseling Competencies and Cultural Humility   182
Crafting an Advocacy Agenda   183
Counseling Children, Adolescents, and Young Adults   184
Counseling Adults, Couples, and Families   185
Implications for Clinical Practice   185
Summary   187
Discussion Questions   187
Key References   188

12. Culturally Responsive Counseling for Transgender Clients 189
Clark D. Ausloos and Lena Salpietro

The Counselor: Exploration, Introspection, and Reflection 190
Gender Identities and Sexual Orientation/Identity 191
Intersectionality of Religion and Sexual/Gender Identities 192
Stressors and Discrimination 193
Counseling Utilization and Help-Seeking 194
Culturally Responsive Practices: Drawing From the Multicultural and Social
    Justice Counseling Competencies and Cultural Humility 195
Crafting an Advocacy Agenda 198
Counseling Children, Adolescents, and Young Adults 200
Counseling Adults, Couples, and Families 203
Implications for Clinical Practice 208
Summary 209
Discussion Questions 210
Key References 210

13. Culturally Responsive Counseling for Women Clients 212
Natalie Arce Indelicato

The Counselor: Exploration, Introspection, and Reflection 212
Concepts of Gender Identity and Gender Expression Continuum and Gender
    Identity Models 213
Identities, Intersections, and Gender 215
Clinical Considerations for Counseling 216
Mental Health Disparities Related to Gender 216
Counseling Interventions Informed by Centering Gender and
    Intersecting Identities 218
Building Resilience and Activism 222
Counseling Utilization and Help-Seeking 223
Culturally Responsive Practices: Drawing From the Multicultural and Social
    Justice Counseling Competencies and Cultural Humility 223
Crafting an Advocacy Agenda 225
Counseling Children, Adolescents, and Young Adults 227
Counseling Adults, Couples, and Families 227
Implications for Clinical Practice 228
Summary 230
Discussion Questions 231
Key References 231

14. Culturally Responsive Counseling for Men Clients 232
Michael D. Hannon, Dae'Quawn Landrum, Guy J. Beauduy, Jr., and Fathiyyah F. Salaam

The Counselor: Exploration, Introspection, and Reflection 233
Contemporary Issues and Trends 234
Client Worldviews and Perspectives 237
Counseling Considerations, Stressors, Stereotypes, and Discrimination 239
Counseling Relationship and Self-Awareness 240
Culturally Responsive Practices: Drawing From the Multicultural and Social
    Justice Counseling Competencies and Cultural Humility 240
Crafting an Advocacy Agenda 241
Implications for Clinical Practice 242

Summary 245
Discussion Questions 245
Key References 246

15. Culturally Responsive Counseling Related to Religion, Spirituality, and Other Faiths 247
Janeé Avent Harris and Christine D. Gonzales-Wong

The Counselor: Exploration, Introspection, and Reflection 248
Religion and Spiritual Diversity: Beliefs and Practices 250
Discrimination and Oppression in Religion and Spirituality 253
Religion and Spirituality as the Source of Strengths 255
Culturally Responsive Practices: Drawing From the Multicultural and Social Justice Counseling Competencies and Cultural Humility 257
Crafting an Advocacy Agenda 259
Counseling Children, Adolescents, and Young Adults 260
Counseling Adults, Couples, and Families 262
Implications for Clinical Practice 262
Summary 266
Discussion Questions 267
Key References 267

16. Culturally Responsive Counseling for Clients of Jewish Descent 268
Kenneth D. Roach and Tzachi Fried

The Counselor: Exploration, Introspection, and Reflection 268
Individual Identities 269
Discrimination and Stereotypes 278
Challenges That Jewish Americans Experience 280
Counseling Considerations for Clients of Jewish American Descent 281
Identity Development for Clients of Jewish American Descent 282
Counseling Utilization and Help-Seeking 282
Culturally Responsive Practices: Drawing From the Multicultural and Social Justice Counseling Competencies and Cultural Humility 283
Crafting an Advocacy Agenda 285
Counseling Children, Adolescents, and Young Adults 285
Counseling Adults, Couples, and Families 287
Implications for Clinical Practice 288
Summary 290
Discussion Questions 290
Key References 291

17. Culturally Responsive Counseling for Clients of Muslim and Middle Eastern/North African Descent 292
Dana T. Isawi

The Counselor: Exploration, Introspection, and Reflection 292
Counseling Utilization and Help-Seeking 298
Culturally Responsive Practices: Drawing From the Multicultural and Social Justice Counseling Competencies and Cultural Humility 298
Identity Development for Clients of Muslim and Middle Eastern/North African Descent 304
Crafting an Advocacy Agenda 305

Counseling Children, Adolescents, and Young Adults *307*
Counseling Adults, Couples, and Families *308*
Implications for Clinical Practice *310*
Summary *314*
Discussion Questions *314*
Key References *314*

18. Culturally Responsive Counseling for Older Adults and Addressing Ageism *315*
Whitney George

The Counselor: Exploration, Introspection, and Reflection *316*
The Effects of Societal and Cultural Factors Relating to Ageism *318*
Ageist Ageism and Reverse Ageism *322*
Ethical and Counseling Considerations for Those Experiencing or Contributing to Ageism *323*
Implications for Counseling Students, Counselor Educators, and Clinical Practitioners *323*
Advocacy and Future Trends in Aging *325*
Counseling Utilization and Help-Seeking *325*
Competencies and Cultural Humility *327*
Crafting an Advocacy Agenda *328*
Counseling Adults, Couples, and Families *329*
Implications for Clinical Practice *330*
Summary *335*
Discussion Questions *336*
Key References *336*

19. Culturally Responsive Counseling for Clients With Disabilities and Addressing Ableism *337*
Damion R. Cummins

The Counselor: Exploration, Introspection, and Reflection *338*
Different Types of Disability *339*
Misconceptions About Individuals With Disabilities *340*
Differently Abled Identity Development Models *340*
Stressors and Discrimination *342*
Counseling Utilization and Help-Seeking *344*
Crafting an Advocacy Agenda *347*
Culturally Responsive Practices: Drawing From the Multicultural and Social Justice Counseling Competencies and Cultural Humility *348*
Counseling Children, Adolescents, and Young Adults *352*
Counseling Adults, Couples, and Families *353*
Implications for Clinical Practice *356*
Summary *358*
Discussion Questions *358*
Key References *359*

20. Culturally Responsive Counseling With Immigrant and Refugee Clients *360*
Claudia G. Interiano-Shiverdecker, Elvita Kondili, Cody McKenzie, and Ravza Nur Aksoy Eren

The Counselor: Exploration, Introspection, and Reflection *361*
Immigrants, Refugees, and Asylum-Seekers in the United States *362*

Client Worldviews and Perspectives 364
Stressors and Discrimination 366
Counseling Utilization and Help-Seeking 369
Culturally Responsive Practices: Drawing From the Multicultural and Social Justice Counseling Competencies and Cultural Humility 371
Crafting an Advocacy Agenda 373
Counseling Children, Adolescents, and Young Adults 374
Counseling Adults, Couples, and Families 376
Implications for Clinical Practice 376
Summary 377
Discussion Questions 378
Key References 378

21. Culturally Responsive Counseling for Military Clients and Families 380
Gigi Hamilton and Cori Marie Costello

The Counselor: Exploration, Introspection, and Reflection 381
Client Worldview and Perspectives 384
The Duality of Cultures 386
Liberation Counseling Framework for Military Service Members and Veterans 387
Life-Course Theory for Military Service Members and Veterans 390
Individual Identities 392
Culturally Responsive Practices: Drawing From the Multicultural and Social Justice Counseling Competencies and Cultural Humility 393
Stressors and Discrimination 393
Counseling Utilization and Help-Seeking 393
Crafting an Advocacy Agenda 394
Counseling Children, Adolescents, and Young Adults 395
Counseling Adults, Couples, and Families 395
Implications for Clinical Practice 396
Summary 399
Discussion Questions 399
Key References 400

22. Culturally Responsive Counseling Related to Poverty, Middle Class, and Affluence 401
Ami Camp and Merry Leigh Dameron

The Class of the Counselor: Exploration, Introspection, and Reflection 402
Ethical Mandates and Multicultural Counseling Competencies 407
Frameworks for Class and Classism 408
Application and Related Clinical Case Scenarios 413
Culturally Responsive Counseling, Social Justice, Advocacy, and Liberation Counseling 419
Summary 422
Discussion Questions 422
Key References 423

23. Culturally Responsive Counseling Related to Polyamory, Kink, and Taboo Culture 424
Eric Jett

The Counselor: Exploration, Introspection, and Reflection 425
Client Worldviews and Perspectives 426

Polyamory Versus Polygamy   *426*
Current Perceptions of Oppression and Challenges   *428*
Kink and Taboo   *429*
Stressors and Discrimination   *433*
Modern Theoretical Frameworks   *434*
Counseling Utilization and Help-Seeking   *442*
Implications for Clinical Practice   *442*
Summary   *445*
Discussion Questions   *446*
Key References   *447*

24. Culturally Responsive Counseling for Clients of the Gamer Culture, Fandoms, and Related Subcultures   *448*
Eric J. Perry

The Counselor: Exploration, Introspection, and Reflection   *449*
Client Worldviews and Perspectives   *450*
Gamer Culture and Gamer Identity   *450*
Fandoms and Fandom Identity   *453*
Applications to Conceptualization of Client Identity   *456*
Counseling Utilization and Help-Seeking   *458*
Current Research and Culturally Responsive Therapeutic Interventions and Approaches   *458*
Counseling Children, Adolescents, and Young Adults   *460*
Counseling Adults, Couples, and Families   *462*
Implications for Clinical Practice   *463*
Summary   *464*
Discussion Questions   *464*
Key References   *465*

SECTION III. PRACTICAL APPLICATION OF MULTICULTURAL COUNSELING

25. Broaching Race and Other Cultural Identities   *466*
Norma L. Day-Vines and Anita Young

The Counselor: Exploration, Introspection, and Reflection   *467*
Introduction to Broaching and the Continuum of Broaching Styles and Behaviors   *468*
Broaching Race and Culture Identities in Culturally Matched Therapeutic Alliances   *472*
Summary   *477*
Discussion Questions   *477*
Key References   *477*

26. Cultural Considerations for Assessment, Diagnosing, and Treatment Planning   *479*
Caroline Perjessy and Angiemil Pérez Peña

The Counselor: Exploration, Introspection, and Reflection   *480*
Cultural Insensitivity in Assessment, Diagnosis, and Treatment Planning   *483*
Appropriate Assessment and Treatment Tools   *485*
Current Research and Culturally Responsive Therapeutic Interventions and Approaches   *489*

Implications for Clinical Practice 490
Summary 493
Discussion Questions 493
Key References 493

27. Seeking and Receiving Culturally Responsive Supervision 494
Tonya Davis

The Supervisor and Supervisee: Exploration, Introspection, and Reflection 494
What Multicultural Responsiveness Looks Like in Clinical Supervision 496
Finding and Establishing a Healthy Working Alliance Within the Clinical Supervisory Relationship 496
Identifying the Potential Negative Impact of Power and Responsibility Held by Supervisors 499
Importance of Culturally Responsive Supervision 500
Best Practices: Drawing From the Multicultural and Social Justice Counseling Competencies 501
Summary 505
Discussion Questions 505
Key References 506

28. Cultural Considerations for the Counseling Workplace 507
Adrian Lira

Multicultural Counseling 508
Who Does Your Office Attract? 509
Introduction to a Culturally Sensitive Agency 510
Marketing Materials 516
Intake Forms: Readability, Translation, Paper and Pencil, and Using Computers 516
Accessibility 517
Distance Counseling 517
Summary 520
Discussion Questions 521
Key References 521

Index 523

Contributors

S Anandavalli, PhD, Assistant Professor, Clinical Mental Health Counseling, Southern Oregon University, Ashland, Oregon

Noreal F. Armstrong, PhD, LCMHCS, LPCS, NCC, LCDC, University Counselor, Student Life, Mars Hill University, Mars Hill, North Carolina; CEO and Executive Director, A Therapist Like Me

Shanice Armstrong, PhD, LPC, NCC, Clinical Faculty, Counseling Department, Southern New Hampshire University, Manchester, New Hampshire

Clark D. Ausloos, PhD, LPC, LPSC, NCC, Clinical Assistant Professor, Counseling Psychology, University of Denver, Denver, Colorado

Victoria Austin, EdD, Clinical Faculty, Counselor Education and Supervision, Counseling Department, Southern New Hampshire University, Manchester, New Hampshire

Guy J. Beauduy, Jr., MEd, NCC, CRC, Doctoral Fellow, Department of Counseling, Montclair State University, Montclair, New Jersey

Ami Camp, PhD, Assistant Professor, Department of Interdisciplinary Professions, East Carolina University, Greenville, North Carolina

LaVerne Hanes Collins, PhD, LCMHC, LPC, NCC, Owner and CEO, New Seasons Counseling, Training and Consulting, LLC, Atlanta, Georgia

Cori Marie Costello, PhD, LPC, LCPC, ATR-BC, Director of Student Support, The Family Institute at Northwestern University, Evanston, Illinois

Damion R. Cummins, PhD, LCMHC, Clinical Faculty, Clinical Mental Health Counseling, Southern New Hampshire University, Manchester, New Hampshire

Merry Leigh Dameron, PhD, Assistant Professor, Department of Human Services, Western Carolina University, Cullowhee, North Carolina

Tonya Davis, PhD, LCPC, Clinical Training Director and Core Faculty, Counseling@ Northwestern, Northwestern University, Evanston, Illinois

Norma L. Day-Vines, PhD, Associate Dean, School of Education, Johns Hopkins University, Baltimore, Maryland

Ravza Nur Aksoy Eren, MEd, Doctoral Student, Department of Counseling, Pennsylvania State University, State College, Pennsylvania

Alfonso L. Ferguson, PhD, LPC, LMHC, NCC, Assistant Professor, Graduate Counseling Programs, Social and Behavioral Sciences Department, Centenary University, Hackettstown, New Jersey

Tzachi Fried, PhD, Clinical Director, Dvir Institute for Behavioral Health, Jerusalem, Israel

Whitney George, PhD, LMHC, NCC, Dean of Applied Health Sciences and Associate Professor of Clinical Mental Health Counseling, Jacksonville University, Jacksonville, Florida

Antoinette Gines-Rivera, PhD, Dean, Alliance Graduate School of Counseling, Nyack College, New York, New York

Christine D. Gonzales-Wong, PhD, LPC, Assistant Professor, Texas A&M University–San Antonio, San Antonio, Texas

Gigi Hamilton, PhD, LCMHC-S, Personal Enrichment Counseling and Consulting Services, PLLC, Charlotte, North Carolina; Associate Professor, Northwestern University, The Family Institute, Evanston, Illinois

Michael D. Hannon, PhD, LAC, NCC, Associate Professor, Department of Counseling, Montclair State University, Montclair, New Jersey

John J. S. Harrichand, PhD, Assistant Professor, Department of Counseling, The University of Texas at San Antonio, San Antonio, Texas

Janeé Avent Harris, PhD, Assistant Professor, Interdisciplinary Professions, East Carolina University, Greensboro, North Carolina

Catherine W. Hawkins, APC, MEd, Counselor, Mindset Psychology, Atlanta, Georgia

Lynae S. Hemming, PhD, LPCC, NCC, Licensed Professional Clinical Counselor, Private Practice, South Fargo, North Dakota

Karena Heyward, PhD, Clinical Faculty, Counselor Education and Supervision, Counseling Department, Southern New Hampshire University, Manchester, New Hampshire

Edward F. Hudspeth, PhD, NCC, LPC-S, ACS, RPT-S, RPh, Chair and Associate Professor, Department of Counselor Education, Sacred Heart University, Fairfield, Connecticut

Jung H. Hyun, PhD, LMHC, NCC, Associate Professor, Department of Counseling, Nova Southeastern University, Fort Lauderdale, Florida

Natalie Arce Indelicato, PhD, Associate Professor, Clinical Mental Health Counseling, Jacksonville University, Jacksonville, Florida

Claudia G. Interiano-Shiverdecker, PhD, Assistant Professor, Department of Counseling, The University of Texas at San Antonio, San Antonio, Texas

Dana T. Isawi, PhD, Assistant Professor, Department of Counseling and Higher Education, Northern Illinois University, DeKalb, Illinois

Eric Jett, PhD, Clinical Faculty, Southern New Hampshire University, Manchester, New Hampshire

Kelly King, PhD, LPC, Lecturer, University of California, Davis, Davis, California

Elvita Kondili, PhD, Assistant Professor, Department of Counseling and Addiction Studies, University of Detroit Mercy, Detroit, Michigan

Dae'Quawn Landrum, MA, LPC, NCC, Department of Counseling, Montclair State University, Montclair, New Jersey

Adrian Lira, PhD, Counselor Education, Sam Houston State University, Huntsville, Texas

Cody McKenzie, MS, Doctoral Student, Department of Counseling, The University of Texas at San Antonio, San Antonio, Texas

Lotes Nelson, PhD, LCMHC-S, NCC, ACS, Clinical Faculty, Clinical Mental Health Counseling, Southern New Hampshire University, Manchester, New Hampshire

Angiemil Pérez Peña, Assistant Professor, Director of Clinical Training, National Louis University, Tampa, Florida

Caroline Perjessy, PhD, LMHC, LPC, Clinical Faculty, Clinical Mental Health Counseling, Southern New Hampshire University, Manchester, New Hampshire

Eric J. Perry, PhD, NCC, ACS, Clinical Faculty, Clinical Mental Health Counseling Program, Southern New Hampshire University, Manchester, New Hampshire

George James Ramos, PhD, Assistant Professor of Counselor Education and Supervision, Alliance Graduate School of Counseling, Nyack College, New York, New York

Kenneth D. Roach, EdD, Assistant Professor, Department of Counseling, Rocky Mountain University of Health Professions, Provo, Utah

Fathiyyah F. Salaam, MEd, MEdL, Department of Counseling, Montclair State University, Montclair, New Jersey

Lena Salpietro, PhD, LPC, NCC, Assistant Professor, Department of Public Health, University of North Florida, Jacksonville, Florida

Paul H. Smith, PhD, LPC, Assistant Professor, Mercer University, Atlanta, Georgia

Yi-Wen Su, PhD, Assistant Professor, Department of Counselor Education, Portland State University, Portland, Oregon

LaTonya M. Summers, PhD, LMHC, LCMHC-S, Assistant Professor of Clinical Mental Health Counseling, Jacksonville University, Jacksonville, Florida; Founder of the Black Mental Health Symposium and *Black Mental Health Today* magazine

Julie A. Yliniemi, PhD, MPHc, NCC, LPCC, Assistant Professor, Department of Psychology and Counseling, Arkansas State University, Jonesboro, Arkansas

Eunhui Yoon, PhD, Assistant Professor, Department of Educational Psychology and Learning Systems, Florida State University, Tallahassee, Florida

Anita Young, PhD, Associate Professor, Department of Counseling and Educational Studies, School of Education, Johns Hopkins University, Baltimore, Maryland

List of Videos

Organized by chapter, the *Voices From the Field* are available to support readers. A few chapters include a corresponding video that helps place the chapter content into perspective and provides practitioner perspective and real-world application. Readers would benefit from listening to and viewing the videos before reading each chapter. All videos are hosted by Dr. LaTonya M. Summers and Dr. Lotes Nelson. Transcripts are also available for each video. To access the videos, use the QR codes provided and enter the voucher code on the first page of this book.

Chapter 1
Video 1. The Counselor: Becoming a Culturally Responsive Counselor
Guest: Dr. Lotes Nelson

Chapter 5
Video 5. Counseling African Americans, Africans, Caribbean Blacks, and Immigrants of African Descent
Guests: Dr. LaVerne Hanes Collins and Dr. Alfonso L. Ferguson

Chapter 6
Video 6. Culturally Responsive Counseling for Clients of Asian American and Pacific Islander Descent
Guest: Dr. Jung H. Hyun

Chapter 12
Video 12. Culturally Responsive Counseling for Transgender Clients
Guest: Dr. Clark D. Ausloos

Chapter 13
Video 13. Culturally Responsive Counseling for Women Clients
Guest: Dr. Natalie Arce Indelicato

Chapter 14
Video 14. Culturally Responsive Counseling for Men Clients
Guest: Dr. Michael D. Hannon

Chapter 16
Video 16. Culturally Responsive Counseling for Clients of Jewish Descent
Guests: Dr. Kenneth D. Roach and Dr. Tzachi Fried

Chapter 19
Video 19. Culturally Responsive Counseling for Clients With Disabilities, Including Deafness and Blindness
Guest: Dr. Damion R. Cummins

Chapter 21
Video 21. Culturally Responsive Counseling Related to Military Personnel and Veterans
Guests: Dr. Gigi Hamilton and Dr. Cori Marie Costello

LIST OF VIDEOS | xxiii

Chapter 23
Video 23. Culturally Responsive Counseling Related to Polyamory, Kink, and Taboo Culture
Guest: Dr. Eric Jett

Chapter 24
Video 24. Culturally Responsive Counseling for Clients of the Gamer Culture, Fandoms, and Related Subcultures
Guest: Dr. Eric J. Perry

Chapter 28
Video 28. Cultural Considerations for the Counseling Workplace
Guest: Dr. Adrian Lira

Foreword

There are roads out of the secret places within us along which we must all move as we go to touch others.

—*Ralph Ellison* (King, 1981)

Initially, I was attracted to the title of *Multicultural Counseling: Responding With Cultural Humility, Empathy, and Advocacy*. Each chapter speaks to the relationship between multicultural counseling terminology and the significance and implications of the counselor's understanding of the role of cultural responsiveness, humility, empathy, and advocacy. These terms are grounded in the belief that they are significant core conditions in the process of helping. In a scholarly and insightful approach, concepts of multicultural counseling are presented in three sections: The Counselor's Worldview, The Client's Worldview, and Practical Application of Multicultural Counseling. The scope of topics contained within the 28 chapters of the text suggested that the editors adhered to the notion that all counseling is multicultural counseling. This notion serves as the unifying principle for their book, given the extent to which they articulated the intersectionality of a multitude of groups, worldviews, and perspectives. In doing so, Dr. Lotes Nelson and Dr. LaTonya Summers acknowledged that we live in a global society, influenced by diverse people whose worldviews dictate different ways of doing, being, and knowing for both counselor and client. As such, it is vital to acknowledge that counselors and clients travel different *roads out of the secret places within us along which we must all move as we go to touch others*.

Envision a pre-1960s counseling profession, absent a rainbow of diversity as a foundation for practice. Due to cultural shifts at all levels, counselors began to travel roads of secret places of certain populations. Specifically, counselors attempted to traverse into the clients' spaces and places lived, hearing unique stories of their lives and touching them with empathy. However, all was not well in the context of being a helper, because they possessed limited knowledge of these populations and the roads on which they traveled. Instead, helpers worked from the historical perspective supporting preconceived notions of clients as having minority status and being marginalized individuals who were perceived to be "culturally" disadvantaged. This suggested that difference was a deficit when compared to the many client populations. However, I would be remiss if I did not point out that throughout the world diverse people have always coexisted together while traveling roads out of secret places. It is gratifying to know that as global citizens, counseling professionals have embraced the need to know about those secret places of their clients. Fortunately, as we experienced the cultural shifts of the 1980s, multicultural counseling was beginning to be viewed as a valued approach in counseling.

At this juncture, we realized that if both client's and counselor's experiences are not understood in the context of their culture, little progress can be made in understanding issues. In preparation to touch others, significant milestones in research and techniques flourished. Specifically, in 1981 Sue published what he refers to as the "classic" textbook in multicultural counseling. Further solidifying a multicultural emphasis in counseling, a special edition of the *Journal of Counseling & Development* (Pedersen, 1991) was published. Accordingly, multicultural counseling came into its own and transformed the profession. As a result, multicultural counseling was proclaimed to be a theoretical perspective and designated to be the "fourth force" in counseling by Pedersen.

More personally, as a graduate student, and later entering the academy as a professor, I was privy to the evolution of this renaissance.

Over the last few decades, there has been a proliferation of books and related materials supporting a more expansive approach to understanding multicultural counseling. Nelson and Summers, inspired by the events of the pandemic, were compelled to venture down uncharted roads to examine social justice in a time of crisis that warranted a text entitled *Multicultural Counseling: Responding With Cultural Humility, Empathy, and Advocacy*. The authors were inspired to write an edited book that highlighted aspects of social justice and suggested that they were driven by "a great need to do our part to effect positive social change," especially in the context of the worst pandemic in a century. To meet this objective, such a compilation of edited chapters raised intriguing possibilities, supporting more expansive approaches to understanding multicultural counseling. Accordingly, Nelson and Summers noted that they considered "what was out there and was not." To that end, they were intentional in requiring that chapters be authored by individuals with specific lived experiences. According to the editors, "a lived experience approach ensured that we really touch on the nuances of that specific culture that may otherwise not be prominently addressed in the literature." Therefore, each of the 28 chapters offers a unique contribution written by individuals that reframed the narrative from a Eurocentric perspective to a more global understanding. Consequently, the authors undertook the ambitious task of conceptualizing multicultural counseling, as noted by Pedersen, as both an objective or narrow approach (Emic) and a subjective or broad approach (Etic) presentation of both the client's and counselor's worldviews and experiences within a particular culture.

In *Multicultural Counseling: Responding With Cultural Humility, Empathy, and Advocacy*, the first section, "The Counselor's Worldview," could be described as an attempt to answer the questions of "Who am I?" and "What is my duty?" In line with these questions, Chapters 1 through 4 present aspects of the counselor's worldview. The personhood of the counselor is addressed and the relevant terminologies (such as liberation, humility, empathy, and advocacy) are described in terms of cultural responsiveness. In addition, the professional responsibilities of the counselor relative to supervision, ethical practice, advocacy, and competencies are addressed in the context of culturally responsive interventions.

The second section, "The Client's Worldview," could be described as an attempt to answer the question of "Who is my client?" In Chapters 5 through 24, an expansive review of cultural considerations of various groups, the authors have made a unique contribution by exploring cultural groups beyond the concept of race and the counselor's preexisting orientations about the client. In organizing the chapters, each group is not only discussed in the context of new terminology, but also framed from a life span approach to be inclusive of counseling children, adolescents, young adults, adults, and even counseling with couples and families. In addition, existing models for professional responsibilities of the counselor relative to supervision, ethical practice, and competencies are addressed.

It is notable that in addition to the groups usually studied in multicultural counseling, the authors have expanded the boundaries to include additional cultural groups of color. Although the list is far too expansive to elaborate on here, I would be remiss to not mention some of these groups. For example, in addition to African American issues, Blacks in the diaspora, such as Africans, and Afro-Caribbean descent are explored. Other groups such as Muslims, people of Middle Eastern/North African descent (MENAs), people of Jewish descent, immigrants, and refugees are also discussed. Other cultural identities for special interest categories such as men, women, older adults, persons in the military, and the intersectionality of poverty, class, and affluence are addressed. The authors expanded the reader's notion of multicultural counseling by including emergent groups such as gamers, fandoms, and related subcultures. The authors were also intentional in including areas of gender and sexuality, such as transgender, queer++, polyamorous, kink, and taboo communities.

The third section, Chapters 25 to 28, considers "Practical Application of Multicultural Counseling" where the counselor may simply ask, "How?" Cultural responsiveness has been the mantra for this text. In line with this notion, the concern is how to achieve this in practice. At this point, two issues are central to being culturally responsive: how to talk about culture and the application in practice involving assessment, diagnosis, treatment, and supervision. It is gratifying to observe that the authors have a much-needed chapter on the workplace environment of the counselor as a factor in being culturally responsive.

Over the last five decades, our profession has actively been involved in the cultural imperative of infusing multicultural counseling across all specializations of counseling. Yet, much remains to be done given that we are witnessing a resurgence of barriers to social inclusion at all levels of society. As the old adage reminds us, "the more things change, the more they remain the same." Thus, it is vital that at this critical point, "we the people" of the counseling profession remain vigilant. Dr. Lotes Nelson and Dr. LaTonya Summers, in *Multicultural Counseling: Responding With Cultural Humility, Empathy, and Advocacy*, have created a body of work which suggests that they are vigilant as they envision advancing multicultural counseling to the "fifth force" in the counseling profession. As a former professor who taught multicultural counseling, I would be excited to introduce my students to this textbook. In terms of future directions of the profession, I would hope that we support the pronouncement that *"There are roads out of the secret places within us along which we must all move as we go to touch others."*

Twinet Parmer, PhD, LPC, CST
Professor Emeritus
Central Michigan University

REFERENCES

King, A. (1981). *Quotations in Black*. [Ralph Elerson. Notes. Date Unknown, #882, p. 181]. Greenwood Press.

Pedersen, P. (1991). Special Issue: Multiculturalism as a fourth force in counseling. *Journal of Counseling and Development*, 70(1), 5–12.

Pedersen, P. (1994). *A handbook for developing multicultural awareness*. American Counseling Association.

Sue, D. W. (1981). *Counseling the culturally different*. Wiley.

Preface

We are overjoyed to be able to present this resource to counselor trainees, counselors, and other mental health professionals. Our initial collaboration did not begin by discussing the essence of this book; however, our society dictated that a more critical resource be written. This project started at the onset of the COVID-19 pandemic, at about the same time as the tragedies of Breonna Taylor, George Floyd, and the anti-Asian shooting in Atlanta. It was almost a premonition to act upon the continued racial disparities that are taking place in the nation. The senseless racial acts that continue to strike were very challenging to watch, not just by the people domestically, but also internationally. Due to our futile environment, our focus shifted to the need to contribute to effecting positive change. As mental health counselors, we have the responsibility to continue to make room for advocacy for those who are not able to use their voice and to leverage the stage that we have, as professionals, to spread prolific messages to increase the knowledge related to our diverse identities amongst one another in order to attempt to decrease the ignorance that causes hurt, pain, and, for some, death in our communities.

To align with the objective of this multicultural book, and for the purpose of honoring each of our cultural experiences, we have each written short excerpts of our cultural journey.

DR. SUMMERS

It is only a surprise to me that I have come to do advocacy and anti-oppression work. As a young Black girl watching my father rebel against oppressive systems and barriers in the '70s and '80s, I decided early that I would not buck authority. His activism and resistance led him to jail many times, and, resultingly, I chose to not use my voice before I could even find it. I accepted the status quo and learned to navigate it well. If "you can't beat 'em, then join 'em" was a person, there you would find me. I joined *them* by leaving everything I knew and assimilating to dominant norms, values, communities, schools, and organizations. My dialect changed—I no longer pronounced words such as street as skreet, looked as look-ded, and I stopped inserting the word *be* where it did not belong, as in *I be writing the heck out of this preface*. My clothing style changed, as one of my childhood friends pointed out when I visited home from college. She said I dressed like a White girl, and when I asked her how a White girl dressed, she pointed at my outfit. I looked down at my linen Liz Claiborne shirt, Gap chinos, and Sam & Libby shoes and knew she was right. Just a year before and I would have been wearing the exact outfit she had on, because we traded clothes a lot. My vocabulary also changed, as I swapped words: photograph for picture, purse for pocketbook, cooking oil for grease, and washcloth for rag. The higher up in education I went, the bigger my words became. It's amazing how intersectionality and efficaciousness roll off my tongue with such ease.

I was a proud first-generation student to snag a graduate assistantship at a North Carolina PWI. I worked in the faculty development center where we facilitated training sessions to inform faculty. I was charged to do amazing things there, like review and fund faculty grant applications, coordinate monthly faculty development workshops, and award faculty who were considered "diversity champions." This was the mid-90s and looking back it was the beginning of my work in multiculturalism. Unfortunately, I was so busy trying to ascertain the power and privilege I saw in the folks around me that I never understood or accepted the power I already had.

I was an eager graduate, armed with an advanced degree and Whiteness. I was quickly recognized as a standout in every job I held and matriculated well through outpatient, inpatient, and private practice settings. It wasn't until I plateaued within the profession (translation: had gotten as far as I could go as a Black woman trying to be White) that I applied and was accepted into a doctoral program. There, I met myself. In the Advanced Multicultural Counseling course, where there was not a textbook, and the professor asked a question that I cannot recall. But I do remember the thought that unknowingly came out of my mouth. I asked the professor, "Do you mean I can bring my Blackness into this space as well as my intellect?" I cannot explain the cognitive dissonance I experienced in that moment. Whether it was self-imposed or inflicted upon me, I wish someone had told me that any part of me that was marginalized or minoritized was an asset and not a liability. And that is how I came to edit this book.

DR. NELSON

I was a young, courageous, 14-year-old, non-English–speaking Filipina girl who embarked on a plane from the Philippines to Reading, Pennsylvania, to begin my exchange student academic journey. In hindsight, I did not know what to expect nor was I really concerned about it. I did not know that my experience would be very different as a Filipina girl in the United States versus a native in my own country.

I was not very aware of "otherness" until I migrated to the United States from the Philippines. Sure, I was cognizant that my multifaceted cultural identities influenced the way I was treated, but the racial marginalization came to light when I arrived in the United States. As the 11th child of destitute parents in my home country, being othered was nothing new to me. I remember being embarrassed often because of the clothes I was wearing or because of my lunch which was typically fish and rice ("poor" people were commonly found to have more access to fish, if able to afford it), which was hard to ignore as soon as I lifted the lid of my lunch box. Being a "different" human was brought to light as an immigrant in the United States. Being a non-native English speaker was not very well received. The very notion that I occupied space here bothered some people, and I was countlessly advised to "go back to your own country," or being questioned whether I was legal to gain employment or was taking another American's job away from them. As I began dating and eventually married, many individuals questioned if my intention was to "get a green card." Being questioned if I am the "cleaning lady" for my own home when answering the door because someone cannot fathom that I may possibly live in "that" house. Fast-forward to the current climate, being looked at and feared because I may be a source of the coronavirus.

From these painful and diminishing experiences, my enthusiasm to help those who have been othered strengthened. My pursuit of higher education and receipt of my doctorate are all in the name of making a difference in the world. I continue to be afforded the opportunity to grow in my cultural awareness as an Asian American, and I aim to extend that same belief to other members of marginalized populations. I am committed to creating and encouraging equity in any space that I occupy, including my role as a counselor, counselor educator, and supervisor. My hope is that this multicultural counseling textbook will further assist others to continue to receive that sense of belongingness.

Writing this textbook was daunting, and we asked ourselves how we could write something additive, rather than something that puts people in a box as if groups are homogenous. We did our best to meet this aim by recruiting authors with lived experiences to write the respective chapters. Although this is not an absolute solution, we believe that representation matters. And we believe that a person who is armed with experience and research would contribute greatly to the instruction of counselors-in-training. Secondly, we used liberation counseling as a framework, an approach where counselors work to liberate their clients and are thereby themselves liberated through the process. Simply (though this is not a comprehensive description), liberation counselors believe in their clients' experiences (testimonials), and they work as if the clients rather than the counselors are the experts of their own lives, and they understand cultural capital and incorporate interventions from their clients' toolkits. Counselors are liberated from the savior complex, the need to have the answers, and an inclination to prescribe one-size-fits-all interventions.

We believed that the best way to respond to diverse people is with cultural humility, empathy, and advocacy. Thus, the major purpose of this book is to keep these factors acting as the engine that hums throughout each chapter.

THE BOOK

Each chapter opens with questions designed to have counselors consider their beliefs, attitudes, and judgments and how those might show up in their work with diverse clients. Each chapter includes clinical case scenarios where students can conceptualize cases using empathy, humility, and advocacy. A distinguishing feature of this book is that it includes cultures that may have been overlooked elsewhere. We believed it was important for students to prepare for clients who identify as gamers, and others who identify as polyamorous or kink. It was also important to us to prepare counselors to work with men. We did not believe that men should be excluded from the text just because they are not considered marginalized. Of course, we know this is not true for all men (e.g., men of color, gay men, etc.). We believe that counselors should be just as prepared to work with men, as we prepare them to work with women. We also sought to include various faiths in this text—such as agnosticism, atheism, and Indigenous spiritual practices—with hopes that counselors' first experience with such would be in this book rather than on their couches with clients. Moreover, we have dedicated a whole chapter to transgender people. Our goal was to give our learners the framework to really begin to understand who the people are that they will be serving.

The book is divided into three sections. The first section is comprised of four chapters and explores the counselor's worldview. The second section is made up of 20 chapters that encapsulate the client's worldview. The third section includes four chapters that demonstrate the application of multicultural counseling by broaching race and culture; providing culturally responsive assessment, diagnosis, and treatment planning; finding a supervisor who prepares advocates; and designing a culturally sensitive workplace. An Instructor's Manual and chapter-based PowerPoint presentations are available online from Springer Publishing for qualified instructors (see request access information in Available Resources); the Instructor's Manual includes sample syllabi for a semester-long course, along with discussion questions and activities for each chapter.

LaTonya M. Summers
Lotes Nelson

Acknowledgments

We wish to acknowledge Rhonda Dearborn at Springer Publishing Company, who saw our vision and understood the need for this work. She was the editor we needed to begin and complete this book. Secondly, we could not have gone the distance without the support of our families, friends, and colleagues. Lastly, there is no way this book would have come to pass without its amazing contributors. Thank you all!

Available Resources

INSTRUCTOR RESOURCES

 A robust set of instructor resources designed to supplement this text is located at **http://connect.springerpub.com/content/book/978-0-8261-3953-5**. Qualifying instructors may request access by emailing **textbook@springerpub.com**.

- **Instructor's Manual** containing discussion questions, activities and exercises, out-of-class assignments and/or activities, and practice-based resources for each chapter, as well as sample syllabi.
- **Instructor Chapter PowerPoints**
- **Test Banks** with over 275 multiple-choice and true/false questions. All questions include answers with full rationales and are available on Respondus®.

VIDEOS

Voices From the Field videos and accompanying transcripts are available for multiple chapters to provide practitioner perspectives and help the reader contextualize the chapters. To access the videos and their transcripts, log in to http://connect.springerpub.com/content/book/978-0-8261-3953-5 and enter the voucher code on the first page of this book.

SECTION 1: THE COUNSELOR'S WORLDVIEW

CHAPTER 1

The Counselor: Becoming a Culturally Responsive Counselor

LOTES NELSON

LEARNING OBJECTIVES

After reading this chapter, students will be able to:

- Recognize the need for multicultural responsiveness in the counseling profession given the United States' changing population.
- Summarize the counseling profession's historical beliefs and approach to counseling.
- Discover their own cultural identities and the roles they play in their counseling work.
- Evaluate the relationship between their cultural identities and their clinical approaches to their clients.
- Recognize schemes to help become a culturally responsive counselor.
- Identify the ethical and cultural obligations to becoming a culturally responsive counselor.

SELF-REFLECTION QUESTIONS

1. Think about your upbringing—the country, city, and state. Was it rural, urban? What about your family's traditions, norms, and values? What beliefs, biases, and judgments does your family hold against people who are culturally different from themselves?
2. All of these things show up with you in the counseling process. How might they affect your work with clients who are culturally different from you? With clients who are culturally matched?
3. What resources can you access to not inflict intentional and unintentional harm on your clients?

INTRODUCTION TO THE NEED FOR A MULTICULTURAL COUNSELING APPROACH

The Diverse Makeup of the United States

The makeup of the people in the United States continues to evolve. According to the U.S. Census Bureau (Jones et al., 2021), the United States is much more multiracial and more diverse than it had been when measured in the past. The 2020 Census showed that the White population remains the largest racial or ethnic group in the United States, with 204.3 million people, which represented a decrease of 8.6% since the 2010 Census (Jones et al., 2021). Likewise, the multiracial population changed considerably since 2010 and now stands at 33.8 million people compared to 9 million people, which embodies a 276% increase. The next largest racial populations are the Asian group at 24 million, the American Native and Alaska Native at 9.7 million, and the Native Hawaiian and Other Pacific Islander at 1.6 million. The Hispanic or Latino population was measured at 62.1 million in 2020, an increase of 23%, while the population that was not of Hispanic or Latino origin grew by 4.3% since 2010. The U.S. Census Bureau did note that these race data comparisons between the 2020 Census and 2010 Census should be used with caution, as they take into account the coding improvements that were made to the Hispanic origin and race questions. Nonetheless, these numbers are sufficient to paint a picture of the diversity of the people in the United States. With this diversity come the distinctions in which each person traverses through their life. These idiosyncrasies can be found in values and beliefs to live by, the languages spoken, the way one presents themself through their choice of clothing, their preferences in music, their traditions as determined by their regional locality, and overall composition of their familial influences.

The statistics just cited exemplify the need for multiculturalism in counseling. As these different groups appear in the clinical counseling setting, professional counselors must be cognizant of each person's multiple and varied cultural identities to provide utmost therapeutic care. Professional counselors must consider the client's cultural intersectional identities and their connection to their clinical concerns and ultimately the impact on the overall counseling process. Likewise, professional counselors are required to pay heed to their own cultural beings (e.g., beliefs, practices, traditions) and their influences in the counseling setting.

History of the Mental Health Counseling Profession

The historical roots of the mental health profession have been disparaging in nature. The formation of its care, from evaluation, to diagnosis, to intervention, has represented a White colonial pedagogy. The founding scientists in the profession have all been rooted in the White population's cultural philosophies. The natural consequence of this is that mental health work has historically followed the White cultural perspective. This means that the diversity in the people that it serves was not considered. The Black, Indigenous, and People of Color (BIPOC) communities were not at all represented at the start of the profession, thus outlining the necessity for a multicultural lens in mental health care. Benjamin Rush, often referred to as the "Father of American Psychiatry," described the concept of *Negritude*, which was said to be a "disorder" of a mild form of leprosy in which the only cure was to become White (Reilly, 2020). In 1851, renowned American physician Samuel Cartwright defined *drapetomania* as a treatable mental illness that caused Black slaves to run away from their owners and their services (Stahl, 2000). He explained that the disorder was a result of slave owners who made themselves familiar with the slaves, treating them as equals. As recently as 1914, drapetomania was still listed in the *Practical Medical Dictionary*.

Possessing knowledge of the historical systemic context of the mental health system delineates the need for culturally responsive counseling. Paying close attention to the racial disparities among the people that the counseling profession serves will help to bridge the present cultural gap. Giving attention and interest to the individual's cultural characteristics facilitates suitable mental health care.

American Counseling Association *Code of Ethics* and Council for the Accreditation of Counseling and Related Educational Programs Standards

According to its mission statement, the American Counseling Association (ACA), a not-for-profit organization, is dedicated to enhancing and "advancing the counseling profession, and using the profession and practice of counseling to promote respect for human dignity and diversity" (ACA, 2014, "About ACA"). The focus on diversity is outlined as central to the work of professional counselors. The ACA provides ethical guidance to counselors to promote client growth and preserve the client's welfare. In the spirit of fostering client well-being, professional counselors are obligated to provide culturally responsive care. The *ACA Code of Ethics* requires counselors to be "aware of— and avoid imposing—their own values, attitude, beliefs, and behaviors" onto the client (2014, A.4.b.). Counselors are to "respect the diversity of clients, trainees, and research participants" (ACA, 2014, A.4.b.). Likewise, counselors need to "maintain awareness and sensitivity regarding cultural meanings of confidentiality and privacy" (B.1.a.). Counselors need to demonstrate respect in determining different views toward disclosure of information. Counselors do not condone or engage in discrimination against prospective or current clients (C.5.).

The 2016 Council for the Accreditation of Counseling and Related Educational Programs (CACREP) Standards were written to promote a unified counseling profession. The CACREP accreditation denotes a commitment to program excellence. One of these standards is that "social and cultural diversity" is to be integrated throughout the program and the curriculum. Counseling programs are to embed theories and models of multiculturalism in counseling. CACREP accreditation signifies that the content and excellence of a program have been evaluated and meet standards set by the profession. The CACREP program accreditation is another layer to make certain that counselors meet the conditions of being able to demonstrate and apply cultural knowledge in their clinical work. At the time of this publication, the CACREP Standards are being revised and are expected to be implemented in 2024. The Standards Revision Committee was charged with examining issues related to infusing disability concepts into the core curricular areas, addressing social justice and advocacy, and providing specifications according to doctoral programs, to name just a few of their considerations.

WHAT IS MULTICULTURAL COUNSELING AND WHY IS IT IMPORTANT?

Multicultural counseling is an art in which the counselor engages in their work beyond themselves. Multicultural counseling is the counselor's ability to practice effective interventions that are culturally responsive through the context of the client's worldviews. Moreover, counselors can appreciate the cultural identities and intersectionalities of their clients through the recognition of the client's multifaceted cultural characteristics. Counselors can see who their clients are from their told and untold stories. They can gather rich information from the client's background: their race or ethnicity, their socioeconomic status, their overall cultural principle that makes them who they are as a person. The counselor works from a multicultural lens by considering each client's life circumstances and influences that have helped shape their unique attributes. Kuo et al. (2020) posited that successful integration of multicultural counseling practices establishes positive therapeutic relationships with their culturally diverse clients. The authors advised that counselor trainees and counselors need to stay vigilant to cultural concerns and issues as they arise. Moreover, being able to connect their cultural identities to the clinical presenting concerns can result in a richer conceptualization of the client's needs. As counselors learn more of the client's narrative, they are likely able to connect the factors that affect the client's mental health.

Culturally attentive counselors are mindful that the work is intricate. They are willing to pay attention to the cultural processes within the therapeutic dyad, meaning being aware of their own cultural background and the client's cultural background. Likewise, they must be able to recognize the connection of their cultural sense of self to the work they are doing with the client. They can recognize the impact related to the therapeutic relationship. Otherwise, when counselors are unable to distinguish the client's cultural factors tied to well-being, this can be harmful to the therapeutic alliance and further cause the client to never seek future counseling services.

Cultural Tunnel Vision

One of the common issues within the therapeutic work is the counselor's cultural tunnel vision. *Cultural tunnel vision* is the perception of reality based on a very limited set of cultural experiences. This phenomenon results in limiting counselors' ability to deeply understand their present circumstances due to their narrow awareness of the client's cultural values. The idea that counselor trainees or counselors may go into their work knowing only their own culture and may assume that all cultures are alike is, again, damaging to the client. As aforementioned, counseling is a multifaceted profession and requires counselors to consider the client's multilayered self. Counselors are to investigate the client's cultural background (e.g., what were they taught about gender role expectations?). Perhaps the client holds the belief that women are expected to perform the chores inside the home (e.g., cooking, cleaning, ironing, etc.), while men are expected to complete the chores outside of the home (e.g., mowing the lawn, automobile repairs, etc.). Moreover, considering the client's faith system can be an integral part of the therapeutic work. One's spirituality has been linked to assisting in decreasing older adults' symptoms of depression (Stearns et al., 2018). Those authors further suggested that an increased level of spirituality and religiosity can improve one's mental health.

The lack of cultural knowledge restricts the counselor in rendering appropriate counseling services to the client. Likewise, counselor trainees/counselors may impose their cultural values on the client by thinking that everyone shares the same cultural perspectives. The counselor's willingness to move away from cultural tunnel-vision phenomena can help in truly considering the best clinical care approach for the client.

Cultural Encapsulation

In 1962, the term *cultural encapsulation* was coined by Gibert Wrenn, one of the pioneers in the counseling profession (Heppner et al., 2012). The premise of the terminology is that culturally encapsulated counselors may believe in one set of standards. The consequence of this can promote cultural insensitivity toward their clients. Likewise, counselors can accept and exhibit inappropriate theories and fail to investigate the reasoning underlying those theories because it might not align with their existing assumptions, or fail to assess others' worldviews. Counselors may also make little or no attempts to understand others' beliefs and behaviors, and possess only one way of thinking with no motivation to investigate/acquire alternative cultural practices.

The trend of cultural encapsulation continues to be an issue for professional counselors today. An idea for moving away from this maladaptive notion is to gain perspective of one's cultural practices and learned assumptions, and be willing to compare them to others' viewpoints. The goal is to make room to identify shared beliefs and discover cultural uniqueness. Additionally, raising awareness of one's cultural biases and prejudices is a large part of the equation to dismantle cultural encapsulation. One must to be willing to be honest in one's self-investigation to gain knowledge of one's implicit or explicit biases. The challenge with cultural encapsulation is that counselors/trainees may inadvertently engage in discrimination and prejudice toward their clients (Corey et al., 2007).

Disregarding cultural variations in counseling is no longer acceptable and can really lead the counselor to experience ethical dilemmas and possibly even legal concerns. We hear "I don't see color in people"—and this very statement is a testament to the lack of cultural awareness and knowledge. *Colorblindness* is defined as a racial microaggression. This message conveys no regard to the racial challenges that folks in the BIPOC community experience. Colorblindness conveys that people with racial privilege are not in tune with what the BIPOC individual faces in their day-to-day life. For instance, when one says to a friend, "Oh, she is Asian but I don't see color," this communicates minimization of the Asian individual's negative racial experiences. This may include one's sexual orientation, gender, religion, and any other important dimensions of one's life. This notion supports the racial generalization that neglects to recognize the BIPOC person's race-based identities.

Colorblind counselors are ineffective in their role as clinicians; in fact, there is no room for dishonoring a person's individuality in counseling. This is where counselors' ability to be aware of their implicit and explicit biases and prejudices comes into play, to avoid causing damage to the client and continuing the message of racial generalization. Colorblindness is a deficiency in one's ability to be introspective of one's cultural values and the harm that they can cause to people.

THE COUNSELOR'S WORLDVIEW

Who Are You?

A large part of an aspiring counselor's role is to be contemplative of who they are as an individual and who they want to be as a counselor. Counselors will encounter clients from different cultural backgrounds, and thus require the skill to know not only their client's viewpoints, but also their own. Counselor trainees need to engage in the process of learning about themselves and their motivations to become counselors. The *ACA Code of Ethics* (2014) requires counselors to avoid imposing their beliefs and values onto their clients; therefore, the counselor must have strong knowledge of their cultural identities. Collins et al. (2010) posited that reflective practice is a valuable process to facilitate self-awareness. The counselor's self-knowledge promotes responsive cultural interactions between the counselor and the client.

An important idea to consider is to begin with the cultural beliefs that have been passed down within the family unit. Consider the beliefs, values, and customs that were taught to you at the beginning of your lifetime. For example, the counselor might consider the message regarding one's gender identity while growing up. Perhaps there's a strong belief that a person's assigned sex at birth is non-negotiable—meaning that a person with a vagina must therefore be a female, while a person with a penis must therefore be a male—and there's no other way of conceptualizing one's gender identity. Conceivably, consider the religious or spiritual messages or beliefs that the counselor has been practicing. Maybe it is the very idea of believing in "God" and the meaning assigned to what God is. Some believe that "God" is a protector and has been a constant part of their faith system, while others believe that "god" does not exist. As well, reflect on the messages that have been taught regarding lesbian, gay, bisexual, transgender, queer, questioning, ++ individuals. Additionally, imagine your comfort level in recognizing or talking about your racial/socioeconomic/gender/faith-based privilege. Define your cultural privileges. Are you aware of how your privilege(s) help you without even blinking an eye?

Ongoing self-examination of your cultural identities is an ethical obligation to continue to exercise cultural humility. Hook et al. (2016) defined *cultural humility* as one's ability to see another's perspective. Being willing to examine the influence of your own cultural beliefs on the therapeutic work is a beautiful beginning to respecting the client's cultural being. An awareness of any biases and prejudices and naming them in the moment (to self) will help you steer clear of imposing your values onto the client. Recognition of shared practices, as well as different sets of values, encourages cultural respect in the therapeutic setting. An unhelpful common phrase in counseling is "I understand" after hearing the client's difficult struggle. Do you really? Saying, "I understand" to the client negates their individual experience. Rather, explore the client's perspective of the experience. Connect their perspective to their cultural values and further investigate how this has contributed to the client's difficulties.

What Are You Bringing Into the Counseling Space That May Hinder the Cultural Process?

Implicit bias is when the counselor's actions are unconsciously influenced by their preexisting beliefs about certain groups of people (Banaji & Greenwald, 1995), whereas explicit bias is when those actions are intentional based on those preexisting beliefs. As a counselor, you must be willing to investigate what your beliefs are and their potential impact on the counseling process. Think back to the value systems that were given to you since your early childhood: for example, the value system that members in the BIPOC community are "up to no good." One may be hypervigilant when approached by a Black person, which is demonstrating unconscious bias or implicit social recognition. These unconscious attitudes can manifest into something bigger in the counseling session if the counselor is unaware. Explicit bias is the display of bias on a conscious level, such as overt racism and racist comments. The expression of explicit bias occurs as a result of deliberate thought. Again, there is no room for explicit or implicit biases in the counseling profession.

Existing stereotypical theories are detrimental to the counseling process. *Stereotypes* are overgeneralized beliefs about a particular group or class of people. What stereotypical beliefs do you hold about specific groups of people: for instance, beliefs related to Asian Americans and Pacific Islanders, Black people, Native American people, and so on? Keep in mind also that while negative stereotypes are more common, there are also positive stereotypes about particular groups of people. Either way, stereotypes about people are unhelpful. For instance, a person sees a group of Black teenage boys and assumes that they are going to break into someone's home or car. Another example of a stereotype is that Asian people are excellent at math. Such stereotypes can belittle the targeted race(s) while prioritizing the person who is making the stereotype.

Multicultural and Social Justice Counseling Competencies

Multicultural counseling is central to the counseling profession's ability to respond to each client's diverse needs. The client's conglomeration of cultural identities, values systems, privileges, or marginalized status requires culturally responsive therapeutic care.

Consequently, counselors need to attend to the client's cultural being. Due to this critical part of counselors' role, the Multicultural and Social Justice Counseling Competencies (MSJCC) document was developed by the Association for Multicultural Counseling and Development (AMCD), a division of the ACA. AMCD and ACA endorsed the competencies, thereby signifying the need to integrate multicultural and social justice competencies in all aspects of the counseling profession (Ratts et al., 2016).

The MSJCC provides a framework for counselors to address the multifaceted cultural identities of clients in the therapeutic relationship. The framework recognizes the need for counselors to speak to the issues around power, privilege, and oppression that the client may bring to the counseling session (Ratts et al., 2016). The conceptual framework of MSJCC was introduced in four quadrants to encourage counselors to consider counselor and client relationships: (1) counselor self-awareness, (2) client worldview, (3) counseling relationship, and (4) counseling advocacy interventions. The quadrants speak to the intricacy of the cultural intersectionalities that clients and counselors bring to the counseling relationship. Both the counselors and the clients are members of various religious/spirituality, economic class backgrounds, sexual identities, levels of psychological maturities, ethnic/racial identities, chronological/developmental challenges, threats to well-being and traumas, family backgrounds and histories, unique physical characteristics, and location of residences and language differences (RESPECTFUL model; D'Andrea & Daniels, 2001). It is also important to note that these cultural identities are classified into privileged and marginalized statuses. In the spirit of helping counselors implement multicultural responsiveness and being socially just, MSJCC encourages counselors to focus on the four domains of counselor self-awareness, the client's worldview, counseling relationship, and counseling and advocacy interventions (Ratts et al., 2016).

SELF-AWARENESS: HERITAGE, VALUES, ATTITUDE, AND BELIEFS

Self-Awareness

The counselor's cultural self-awareness is a vehicle to holding consciousness with one's cultural responsiveness for self and the client. Self-awareness is a form of consciousness that holds an understanding of one's personal self, including characteristics, behaviors, and feelings. Notably, developing self-awareness requires intentional examination of self, and sometimes demands the willingness to be vulnerable. Responsive cultural self-exploration requires facing the good, the bad, and the ugly of oneself.

Understanding One's Own Ethnic, Gender, and Cultural Heritage

Understanding of one's cultural influences upon values, beliefs, and judgment originates from the knowledge of one's ethnicity, cultural heritage, gender, religion, and many more cultural influences. Cultural self-awareness describes one's awareness of how one's culture has influenced oneself (Lu & Wan, 2018). In order to show empathy for our client's suffering, it is beneficial to have assessed our own cultural foundations. For instance, empathizing about a BIPOC client's racial suffering is difficult if you have not done the work on your own self to understand what race is and its role in our day-to-day living. Be informed on the cultural messages that you have been exposed to in your upbringing. Equally, be honest in owning and naming the beliefs that have been passed down to you. Some of these beliefs might be difficult to comprehend and acknowledge, but this is a very important part of the process. A starter self-exploratory activity could be identifying the originating countries your family is from. A person might also enjoy exploring their linguistic background to understand any potential differences from their current spoken language. Likewise, develop understanding of your own social class background. What was your family's historical socioeconomic status and what is it today? How does your socioeconomic level influence your privilege or not? Think about your religion: what values have been passed down to you related to your familial religion or spiritual background? Again, how does your religion or spirituality unfold in your current practice?

Your foundational cultural beliefs and values may consist of generational traditions that were passed down to you as long as you can remember, or they may consist of beliefs that you have acquired along the way as influenced by your environmental influences. Consider identifying the sets of values that you were taught for as long as you can remember, and take the time to evaluate what they are. Ask yourself if the beliefs still hold true today, or have they changed? Be reflective in this process, and again, reflect on how these attitudes are unfolded in your interactions with your clients.

THE INFLUENCE OF COUNSELORS' SETS OF BELIEFS AND THERAPEUTIC RELATIONSHIPS

The Influences of Counselors' Belief Systems in the Counseling Setting

The MSJCC encouraged counselors to be aware of their cultural stance, and especially to become familiar with the client's cultural value systems, because there are consequences in neglecting to do so. Counselors can cause harm when they fail to attend to the influence of their values on the work that they are doing with their clients. Likewise, they are not considering their client's needs, and are disregarding the requirement to put the client's best interest ahead of their own. For example, if the counselor is careless in talking about all of the luxurious things that they did over the weekend to their client who struggles economically, the client can internalize the message that the counselor is conveying and thereby the counselor causes intentional harm to the client. The concern with this reckless self-disclosure is that the client may elect to discontinue the counseling services. Similarly, if the client is discussing their political beliefs that diverge from the counselor's point of view, the counselor's response could define whether the client is going to feel safe or not to proceed in the counseling process. Self-disclosure is a phenomenon that must be cautiously exhibited in the counseling process. While the appropriate application of self-disclosure can augment the therapeutic alliance, careless and too much disclosure can be disadvantageous in the counseling relationship.

Transference and Countertransference

The counseling process is an emotion-filled experience. Clients bring different emotions into the counseling space, and counselors feel different emotions as well. The nature of the client–counselor relationship is intimate, in that clients share their emotions and thoughts that are private and may not have been shared with anyone else outside of the therapeutic setting. It is important to note the transference and countertransference phenomena that occur in the clinical setting.

Transference occurs when clients begin to have feelings, romantic or not, toward their counselor (Jenks & Oka, 2021). The client begins to associate the counselor with someone else in their past or present relationships. Consequently, the client starts to put unrealistic expectations and demands on the counselor. The client may also begin to exhibit emotions such as anger when the counselor broaches the topic of clinical termination because (as an example) it might remind the client of an abandonment experience with one of their parents.

Countertransference is the opposing side of transference. Countertransference is the counselor's unconscious feelings as a result of working with the client. Counselors may develop emotions toward the client, and begin to transfer their developed emotions to the client (Jenks & Oka, 2021). This may result in blurred boundaries in the clinical setting. For instance, the counselor may experience fondness for the client and begin to have more than casual conversations with the client in a way that is no longer therapeutically advantageous. The counselor begins to shift their approaches by allowing the client to bend the set guidelines a bit more; for example, allowing the client to cancel at the last minute without charging them the cancellation fee, or perhaps allowing the client to be consistently late to their appointment without addressing the concerns.

The ACA tasked counselors to apply the *Code of Ethics* to maintain respect for their clients (ACA, 2014). Understanding the client's cultural background and practices will help the counselor to avoid imposing their cultural values onto the client (ACA, 2014, A.4.b). Further, the ACA mandates that counselors manage and maintain boundaries and professional relationships (2014, A.6.). Therefore, when engaging in countertransference, the counselor could be in violation of the *ACA Code of Ethics*. The very principle of the *ACA Code of Ethics* should encourage counselors to really be mindful of their cultural beings and their influence on the clinical work. Neglecting to do so can lead to exhibiting harmful behaviors in the therapeutic work, such as lacking focus on the treatment plan because the counseling sessions are no longer clinical; rather, the counselor is talking about their weekend activities.

Value Conflicts in Counseling

The idea of value conflict is critical to take into account in the counseling process. When there are two or more individuals with varied sets of cultural values and beliefs, value conflict is bound to occur. Counselors must be attentive to the contrasting values between the client and themselves to avoid imposing their own values on their clients (ACA, 2014). Section A.1.a. clearly states, "The primary responsibility of counselors is to respect the dignity and to promote the welfare of clients" (ACA, 2014, A.1.a.). When counseling someone of a different religion than the counselor, for instance, it is the counselor's role and responsibility to resolve issues related to personal values.

Counselors are urged to acquire and enhance their knowledge of clients' values so as to formulate culturally responsive interventions and strategies. The counselor must demonstrate inclusive approaches in a way that honors the client's dignity and welfare. Counselors can seek consultation and supervision to help gain insight and perspective to avoid value conflict. The use of a client-centered theoretical approach is helpful in staying focused on the client's cultural needs. Doing so will allow the counselor to stay concentrated on the client's beliefs and minimize the risk of focusing on themselves.

DEVELOPING CULTURAL RESPONSIVENESS FOR COUNSELORS

Cultural Responsiveness

The deaths of George Floyd and Breonna Taylor and the Asian hate crime in Atlanta, among many other occurrences, have elevated the discussion of racism in the United States; for counselors, this means that they have to be equipped to have this conversation with their clients. Clients hear and experience these events in their communities, which may provoke negative emotions; for some it may be sadness, and anger for others. Counselors need to facilitate these sorts of racial and cultural conversations to help BIPOC people. So, how might counselors do this?

There is no more appropriate time than now for counselors to begin and/or further enhance their cultural knowledge. It is no longer enough to sit in silence or pretend that cultural conversations will not occur with our clients. Our clients are hurting and our BIPOC clients are re-traumatized, and it is the counselor's role to facilitate this crucial conversation. *Cultural competence*, introduced by Derald Wing Sue in the 1980s, was defined as a model of developing skills, knowledge, and self-awareness to be more effective in working with diverse populations. While cultural competence was a model that caused us to begin to think about our own cultural skills and knowledge, this author wants to invite readers to begin—or continue, for those who may have begun the journey—to exhibit cultural humility and responsiveness.

Cultural responsiveness includes the exploration of the client's cultural background and value systems. This means always investigating the client's personal beliefs related to religion, gender identities, sexual identities, socioeconomic status, level of psychological functioning, languages spoken, age, ableism, and more. In counseling, be proactive in embedding clients' cultural identities and intersectionalities with their clinical concerns. Examine how their cultural values connect to their mental health concerns. Ask clients about their cultural stance about mental health and mental health care. Applying culturally responsive clinical care shows that the counselor is being aware of their own sets of value systems and avoids inserting them in their client work. The counselor engages in reflexivity to constantly be aware of their own beliefs, judgments, and practice throughout the counseling process. Cultural responsiveness means the counselor is not taking a "one size fits all" approach. The counselor is being attentive to each of their client's cultural identities and needs and presenting treatment intervention approaches based on that.

Barriers to the Application of Cultural Responsiveness

Counselors who do not possess an awareness of their own cultural being will struggle in applying cultural responsiveness in their clinical work. Counselors who have not done the work to understand their own cultural values and beliefs will experience difficulty in deciphering the client's value systems. Additionally, the counselors' lower cultural knowledge acquisition will present a barrier in applying cultural responsiveness. For instance, a counselor who presents as being colorblind is not equipped to honor the client's cultural dignity and welfare. As aforementioned, colorblindness is harmful and minimizing to the BIPOC communities.

Counselors who are unwilling to delve into the client's cultural identities can do a disservice to the client and their healing or recovery process. Sometimes counselors are fearful about making a mistake or saying the wrong thing to their clients, and would much rather avoid broaching the topic of culture to avoid a mistake. Doing so prohibits growth and does not afford forward movement for the client in their clinical work. Therefore, counselors are encouraged to be courageous, while showing respect at all times, in broaching the topic of culture. It is imperative to note that counselors must also be willing to do their work to learn about the client's cultural practices through study of peer-reviewed literature outside of the counseling sessions. Do not rely on asking your client to teach you about their cultural being. Do not put a BIPOC person, who may experience marginalization often, in a space of having to educate you about their cultural standards; rather, do it yourself. Being proactive in researching the premise of your client's cultural background may also help the counselor to have this courageous cultural conversation with their clients.

ETHICAL CONSIDERATION IN MULTICULTURAL COUNSELING

Imposing Your Values Onto Your Clients

A counselor's principal role is to safeguard the client's dignity and promote the client's welfare (ACA, 2014, A.1.a.). In order to uphold the client's dignity and welfare, the counselor must have a good comprehension of the client's cultural backdrop. This includes the examination of the client's overall personhood to gain clarity on who the client is and what is important to them. As aforementioned, exercising a client-centered approach will help to place focus on the client rather than the counselor's agenda. This approach allows the counselor to receive the client's cultural identities and, likewise, continue to remind themself to keep the emphasis on the client to avoid inflicting their own values onto the client.

One common example of devaluing the client's cultural self is advice-giving. For example, the client shares with the counselor that their parents do not like their college major selection in psychology but rather want the client to study medicine because there are generations after generations of medical doctors in the family—and the counselor tells the client to change their major to keep peace within the family. The counselor's action is indicative of a lack of cultural responsiveness, as it neglects the exploration of the client's feelings and connection of the client's conceptualization to their cultural values. In this example, the counselor disregarded the ethical consideration of the client's morals and instead subjected the client to their opinion.

Counselor's Impairment

The ACA requires counselors to be aware of their professional responsibilities. Counselors are to periodically monitor their effectiveness to avoid harm to the stakeholders that they encounter. The ACA ethical standard, C.2.g., states that "counselors are to monitor themselves for signs of impairment from their own mental, physical, and emotional problems" (2014). This means that counselors are accountable for appraising their continued efficacy even when undergoing physical or psychological ailments. The ACA suggested that counselors seek support or assistance to navigate through challenges that may adversely affect their professional work.

Burnout

As rewarding as the work of a professional counselor is, counselors face challenges with burnout. The concept of burnout is the cost of caring. Prolonged exposure to trauma and other mental health concerns can cause a serious risk of mental health problems in the one exposed (i.e., the counselor; Padmanabhanunni, 2020). The author further stated that burnout is the consequence of a counselor's work. Burnout is the feeling of being at your wits' end. The counselor may feel like they are constantly upset, irritable, or have no more emotional or mental patience, and are therefore unable to empathize with the client's emotional state, leading to negligence.

Vicarious Trauma

Additionally, the counselor may experience compassion fatigue or vicarious trauma. *Vicarious trauma* is the absorption of a client's trauma or intense emotive manifestation.

The ACA (2022) describes vicarious trauma as the "emotional residue" from hearing repeated traumatic stories from clients. Counselors experiencing vicarious trauma may begin to exhibit trauma-like symptoms. When counselors reach this state, they may no longer be able to perform their professional duties and, therefore, will no longer be effective in their work. Counselors will begin to see a shift in their empathetic engagement with clients. Counselors are tasked with examining their own clinical usefulness. When they observe a shift in their treatment approaches or behavior or emotional reaction to clients, counselors are to raise self-awareness to gain understanding and/or obtain consultation or supervision to acquire transparency regarding their condition. Again, the *ACA Code of Ethics* outlines the counselor's obligation to monitor their impairment and seek assistance for repair (ACA, 2014). Counselors are to seek their own counseling to help to manage their symptoms and regain equanimity to provide optimal care for their clients.

Self-Care

The concept of self-care is commonly revealed throughout the counselor's training, so much so that it loses its luster after some time. Self-care is a multifaceted process in which one engages to foster healthy functioning and balance. As mentioned earlier, the counselor's work can be emotionally debilitating if one neglects care of themself. Without self-care, counselors cannot continue to demonstrate efficacy in their counseling work. Self-care aids sustainability.

The practice of self-care can vary from one person to another. It is important to note that self-care is as small or as big as you want it to be. The practice of self-care should align with the individual's capacities and abilities. For instance, it may be inappropriate to suggest to someone with a physical disability that they go for a walk as a form of self-care. Equally, getting a monthly massage may not be helpful for someone without the financial ability to afford such activity. The selection of self-care practice needs to be personal to the individual and one that is purposeful and reachable. These practices may look like reading (for those who are able), having quiet time (for those who may have the space to sit in quietness), or taking a shower to care for one's physical self. Self-care can also be specific to one's professional work: for instance, attending a peer-consultation group or sharing a break with a colleague to connect. The art of self-care lies in finding things that bring joy and peace to the counselor.

Gatekeeping and Supervision

Gatekeeping is a part of counselor educators' responsibility to meet the ethical consideration in keeping the client's dignity and welfare (ACA, 2014). *Gatekeeping* is the continued evaluation of a counselor's ability to be effective in their role as a professional counselor. The *ACA Code of Ethics* (2014) defined gatekeeping as "the initial and ongoing academic, skill, and dispositional assessment of students' competency for professional practice, including remediation and termination as appropriate" (p. 20). Counselor educators and supervisors will maintain an appropriate assessment of the counselor's professional efficacy. The counselor is given formative and summative feedback to ensure knowledge of their progress. Correspondingly, counselors are given the opportunity to remediate any shortfalls that may hinder their work with their clients.

Much like culturally responsive counselors, culturally responsive counselor educators and supervisors will note the supervisee's cultural considerations and aim to integrate them into their supervisory work. Counselor educators and supervisors will pay attention to the supervisee's learning style, communication style, theoretical abilities, and emotional disposition to make certain that they are guided accordingly in their developmental stages, and are therefore able to provide appropriate care for their clients. In instances where supervisees are ill-equipped to counsel their clients, counselor educators and supervisors have the ethical responsibility to help until the supervisee displays the appropriate professional proficiency, including up to dismissal from their role as a counselor. "Supervisors seek consultation and document their decisions to dismiss or refer supervisees for assistance" (ACA, 2014, F.6.b.).

CLINICAL CASE SCENARIO 1.1

Paola, a 32-year-old Latina female, is a professional counselor at a local community health agency. She specializes in working with immigrant couples who are newly getting acquainted with their new home country, the United States. Paola is providing clinical counseling services to a Vietnamese heterosexual couple who are experiencing relationship issues and are reporting that they are not seeing "eye to eye." The couple also reported that they are arguing and screaming at each other all the time. Paola is experiencing difficulties moving her clinical work forward. She reports being "stuck." She says she has been feeling stuck for about a month and a half now, and has not been able to offer any constructive clinical insight to her clients. She also shared that she and her partner are experiencing significant relationship issues, to the point that they recently separated to try to see if the distance will help their relationship. Paola is consumed with her own relationship concerns and feels like she can't offer anything to her Vietnamese couple clients. She feels tired and exhausted. She reports no longer understanding the clients' source of disagreements because Paola doesn't think they are a big deal. Paola is planning on going to her supervisor to discuss the case and her personal status to see if she can get clarity on her problem.

CLINICAL CASE SCENARIO DISCUSSION QUESTIONS

1. What are the counselor's cultural identities that need to be considered in this case scenario?
2. What are the clients' cultural identities that need to be considered in this case scenario?
3. Why are these cultural identities important to consider?
4. What does Paola need to consider about her own cultural beliefs and value systems as she counsels her Vietnamese clients?
5. What ethical consideration does Paola need to be concerned about related to her treatment effectiveness?
6. How might the clinical supervisee approach Paola's case during supervision?

END-OF-CHAPTER RESOURCES

 A robust set of instructor resources designed to supplement this text is located at **http://connect.springerpub.com/content/book/978-0-8261-3953-5**. Qualifying instructors may request access by emailing **textbook@springerpub.com**.

SUMMARY

The diverse makeup of the United States directs the need for counselors to be culturally responsive. In this chapter, you learned the elements of the intricate process of becoming a culturally responsive professional counselor. Counselors are to be aware of their own value system and ensure that the ethical mandate to avoid imposing one's values onto the client is honored. Applying multicultural responsiveness is a necessity in the counseling process, and the failure to do so can potentially cause damage to the client. Counselors are obligated to be informed of their ethical obligations that will ultimately lead to culturally appropriate clinical care for the client. This chapter also discussed the impairment of a counselor that can hinder the counseling process. Lastly, gatekeeping and supervision were covered as part of the counselor's significant ethical considerations.

DISCUSSION QUESTIONS

1. Why is it important for counselors to have awareness of their own cultural values and beliefs?
2. What should counselors do should they face inconsistencies in their clinical approach when counseling someone who is different from them?
3. What are transference and countertransference? What can the counselor do to minimize these?
4. What are the barriers to cultural responsiveness?
5. What is an example of a counselor's impairment? How do you mitigate this concern?

 THE COUNSELOR: BECOMING A CULTURALLY RESPONSIVE COUNSELOR

Guest: Dr. Lotes Nelson

https://connect.springerpub.com/content/book/978-0-8261-3953-5/part/part01/chapter/ch01

KEY REFERENCES

Only key references appear in the print edition. The full reference list appears in the digital product on Springer Publishing Connect: https://connect.springerpub.com/content/book/978-0-8261-3953-5/part/part01/chapter/ch01

American Counseling Association. (2014). *2014 ACA Code of Ethics*. Author. https://www.counseling.org/resources/aca-code-of-ethics.pdf

Ratts, M. J., Singh, A. A., Nassar-McMillan, S., Butler, S. K., & McCullough, J. R. (2016). Multicultural and social justice counseling competencies: Guidelines for the counseling profession. *Journal of Multicultural Counseling and Development*, 44(1), 28–48. https://doi.org/10.1002/jmcd.12035

CHAPTER 2

Liberation Counseling as a Framework: Offering Anti-Oppressive Counseling

LATONYA M. SUMMERS

LEARNING OBJECTIVES

After reading this chapter, students will be able to:
- Define concepts of intersectionality, privilege, and oppression
- Recognize tenets of liberation psychology
- Identify culturally responsive interventions by integrating liberation theory into counseling

SELF-REFLECTION QUESTIONS

1. Considering what you know now about intersectionality, privilege, and oppression, how would you define or describe them to one of your peers?
2. Whom should counseling liberate—the client, the counselor, both, or neither? Please explain your answer.

The counseling profession in America is predominantly White. Dollarhide and colleagues (2021) reported that 70.6% of U.S. counselors are White and 73.3% of them are women. When the profession hinges upon the norms and values of a predominantly White group, it becomes a reflection of the microcosm of U.S. race relations. Presumably, this predominant group of White women counselors has power as gatekeepers of the profession. They have the ability to "dictate acceptable counseling behavior, minimize diverse approaches, and restrict access to the profession by persons with historically oppressed identities, values, perspectives, and healing traditions" (Dollarhide et al., 2021, p. 104). Thus, a liberatory approach to counseling and its profession is vital to the diversity and wellness of the profession and diverse people.

If the counseling process does not liberate our clients, ourselves, and communities, then what is its purpose? When student counselors are trained in traditional theories of counseling and psychology they become adept at zeroing in on impairment at the individual, couple, and family level. Although this may be most suitable for mainstream clients, it inadvertently re-binds marginalized clients by placing blame for their pain and mental health experiences onto them. In contrast, immersing oneself in liberatory counseling approaches empowers counselors to examine suffering from within the context of the environmental factors that individuals, couples, and families endure (Domínguez et al., 2020). Rivera and Comas-Díaz (2020) assert that therapists who conduct liberation-based services "foster awareness of discrimination and inequality, fortify individuals' strengths, affirm cultural identities, and promote change to attenuate human suffering and improve people's lives" (p. 3). Counselors who utilize liberatory approaches believe in change: not just that their clients can change, but that they can change too and that they are agents of change against cultural, structural, and internalized oppression. Essentially, personal liberation begets collective liberation (Rivera & Comas-Díaz, 2020).

We invite students to this book and to work in the profession with openness, willingness to change, and a lack of inhibition. They will therefore have an ability to give clients what they themselves have gained and will continue to gain through liberatory counseling.

AN OVERVIEW OF LIBERATION PSYCHOLOGY

According to Burton and Guzzo (2020), the term *liberation psychology* may have first appeared in a 1976 book entitled *Psicologia de la Liberation* by Argentinian psychologists Caparros and Caparros. Yet, Ignacio Martín-Baró is credited with using the term as we know it today, as a distinct approach to combat oppression (Burton & Guzzo, 2020; Tate et al., 2013). It is important to note that liberation work predated Martín-Baró's 1986–1996 contributions, and such work may be known by other terms (Burton & Guzzo, 2020). For example, Dr. W.E.B. Du Bois's decolonizing work introduced the concept of double-consciousness and his conception of education as a transformative tool of equality for Black Americans included tenets used by succeeding liberation psychologists.

Nevertheless, Martín-Baró's development of liberation psychology was heavily influenced by liberation theology, a theological movement that stemmed from social action in the Christian church and the South American Catholic Christian tradition (Tate et al., 2013). Tate and his associates (2013) asserted that 20th century theologians rediscovered liberatory themes of the Bible and emphasized service to the poor and oppressed, which introduced the idea of religious leaders being social agents of change. Although early Christian theologians shifted their church work to community work, it was not until the 20th century in Spanish America that liberation theology became an "official school of theological thought and action" (Tate et al., 2013, p. 374). The Catholic Church had aligned itself with a sociopolitical movement that called for a New World and its priests violently worked to colonize Latin Americans. There arose priests who relied on biblical teaching to stand up against the savage colonizing forces for the civil rights of the indigenous peoples. Strategically, the priests set up base communities—gatherings of Catholics that met to worship and discuss Bible teachings as they related to their lived experiences and to work to improve their living conditions. When there was a shortage of priests, lay church members led the communities. Together, they built sewer systems and protested unfair land ownership laws (Tate et al., 2013).

It is important to note that Martín-Baró was a Jesuit priest, which undoubtedly influenced his development of the basic principles of liberation psychology. Along with other liberation theologians, Martín-Baró was murdered for his work in standing up against oppression. Since his death, his work has been further developed by other scholars and has been extended to address other forms of inequalities such as "disaster response, disability, cultures of violence and organized crime, and genocidal State crimes" (Burton & Guzzo, 2020, p. 33; Rivera, 2020). Following are some of the foundational concepts of liberation psychology, which you will find revisited in numerous chapters of this book: (a) reorientation of psychology, (b) recovering historical memory, (c) deideologizing everyday experience, (d) virtues of the people, (e) problemization, (f) conscientization, (g) transformation of the social scientist, (h) denaturalization, (i) power dynamics, and (j) praxis (Rivera, 2020; Tate et al., 2013).

Reorientation of psychology. This concept is essential to liberation psychology. It refers to Martín-Baró's argument that the Western norms and values underpinning psychology render it impotent against combatting severe and oppressive conditions (Rivera, 2020; Tate et al., 2013). In order to effect change among people who endure extreme conditions, psychology would need to reorient or shift its focus to the structural and sociopolitical oppression they endure.

Recovering historical memory. Another essential concept of liberation psychology is the recovery of historical memory, a process by which the counselor and client work together to find the client's "real" history. This is necessary because much of the history of oppressed people has been colonized, written from the oppressor's perspective (Rivera, 2020; Tate et al., 2013). Scholars assert that recovering history memory facilitates culturally responsive treatment planning and processes (Rivera, 2020).

Deideologizing everyday experience. When information about how people live comes through mediums such as church, media and social media, and governmental bureaucracies, we become blinded by the idealized views we develop about them. Martín-Baró called this phenomenon a "cultural stranglehold," and recommended that therapists peel back the layers of marginalized people's everyday experiences to reveal how violence, poverty, and other social injustices are created by dominant outlets in society (Domínguez et al., 2020).

Virtues of the people. A fourth tenet of liberation psychology is to identify and use the strengths of marginalized populations to help improve their lives. Using a strengths-based approach shifts the power differential of the therapeutic alliance with the oppressed client as the expert on the tools they have used to survive oppression. Yet, the clinician helps the client learn how to transform those tools for liberation.

Problematization. Understanding the problems clients face from their perspectives and not the practitioner's experience, professional opinion, or clinical lens is an important process in offering anti-oppressive counseling. This strengths-based step is conducted through discussion, questioning, and critical reflection, and its user presents inconsistencies between the lived experiences of oppressed people and the way it should be (Rivera, 2020).

Conscientization. This tenet of liberation psychology involves awakening and engaging the consciousness, or making one aware of a truth. It is activated and maintained by working through other tenets of liberation psychology. Liberatory counselors are able to lead clients to change with new knowledge and awareness (Rivera, 2020).

Transformation of the social scientist. Transformative justice is bidirectional—a counselor's walk alongside oppressed clients changes their lives as much as their clients'. Domínguez et al. (2020, p. 92) described this tenet in terms of participatory action research as a "cobeing and colearning" that disrupts power inequities and repositions the power of oppressed people. Growth occurs in the counselor, client, and community through an intentional unlearning

Denaturalization. Discrimination and oppression are rooted in normalized beliefs and assumptions. Denaturalization occurs when one questions and critically examines structures that lead to the creation of our erroneous assumptions. Denaturalization and deideologizing lead to problematization (Rivera, 2020).

Power dynamics. Liberation psychologists refer to the concept of power as the dynamics that marginalize and exclude, and those that resist oppression, attain wellness, and promote liberation. Power is active, creates change, and allows community involvement (Rivera, 2020).

Praxis. Praxis is the application of theory. Rivera (2020) asserts that theory cannot exist without application and vice versa.

EXPLORATION OF INTERSECTIONALITY, PRIVILEGE, AND OPPRESSION

Early diversity and inclusion efforts focused on the triad of oppression—race, class, and gender (Robinson et al., 2016)—but have been expanded by the application of intersectionality theory. Intersectionality, born out of law and critical race theory, was coined by Crenshaw (1991) and addresses multiple cultural identities, including race, ethnicity, gender, sexual identity, ability, social class, age, and spirituality. Essentially, Dr. Crenshaw explained that when we think about equality, we need to think beyond a person's race or gender because people often have more than one characteristic that is subject to discrimination. While a woman might experience sexism, an older Latina lesbian is at risk of experiencing ageism, sexism, racism, xenophobia, and homophobia. Attempting to understand a client's problem through only one lens is an exertion of privilege that promotes harmful counseling and perpetuates oppression. Such counselors generalize a client's experiences and do not honor the unique differences they bring to the counseling relationship.

The work of privilege has also expanded beyond race, class, and gender to explore special advantages granted based on age, religion, ability, and so on (Black & Stone, 2005). Oppression is found where privilege is unchecked. To assess dynamics of power, privilege, intersectionality, and oppression, counselors might conduct a power differential analysis, a process whereby counselors and clients consider areas of privilege (e.g., high educational level, good health, and religion) and areas of oppression (e.g., any marginalized factor such as gender, race, ethnicity, or poverty). This process might help counselors and clients find areas where they are culturally matched and culturally different. Such processes often help enhance therapeutic alliance (Comas-Díaz, 2020).

Counselors are advised to examine the unmerited favor that comes from maleness, youth, ability, and socioeconomic status and become sensitive to the fact that not everybody has these advantages. There is a direct impact on the counseling process and its outcome when counselors acknowledge intersectional identities of privilege and oppression between themselves and their clients (Cheshire, 2013).

INTEGRATION OF LIBERATION THEORY AND PEDAGOGY AND COUNSELING

Traditional counseling approaches seldom examine the experiences of oppressed people, and when considered those experiences are often pathologized. Counselors who use traditional counseling methods are viewed as the expert, leader, or guide and recovery comes from the top down. Liberatory therapists view their clients as the expert, leader, or guide and recovery is developed from the bottom up (Comas-Díaz, 2020). Most traditional methods are structured with pre-scripted interventions, whereas liberation counseling is "eclectic, syncretistic, and holistic" (Comas-Díaz, 2020, p. 170). Traditional theories assert that client recollections might not be accurate and might represent a theme, motivation, or goal. Liberation theory values client recollection as data, cultural capital, and a significant means to restore marginalized people's power and voices.

Thus, liberation theory is offered in this book to promote the recognition of within-group strengths and virtues to promote healing and wellness among marginalized communities. By unifying mainstream counseling approaches and liberation theory, counselors are able to respond with cultural humility, empathy, and advocacy. Through liberatory counseling, counselors work to better understand the individual domain within the social context. This includes conceptualizing an individual's problem by emphasizing the interconnection between self, other, and larger social structures such as the roles of power, oppression, and systemic barriers in psychological well-being.

Some scholars work to decolonize mental health professions by integrating liberation theory into pedagogy via immersion courses (Domínguez et al., 2020), or using testimonios research—first-person accounts of lived experiences as data (Domínguez & Noriega, 2022), or incorporating social justice-oriented service learning, community-based participatory research (CBPR), and practice-based evidence (PBE) approaches into their courses (Abe, 2020). Within a one-week-long immersion course with elementary school children in Huejotal, Huaque, Domínguez et al. (2020) found that 15 counseling psychology students reported increased critical consciousness, self-awareness, and cultural knowledge, and endorsed a commitment to social justice. Abe (2020) discouraged charity-oriented service learning projects because volunteer helpers see community members through a deficit-based lens; instead, Abe encouraged critical service learning projects where there is respect and reciprocity when volunteers work to understand community members' lived experiences. Power structures are shifted when community members, rather than the volunteers, are the experts.

Unlike the unidirectional approach to research, where researchers get what they need from community members without giving anything in return, CBPR is a reciprocal relationship in which researchers and community members use what they learn from each other for social change (Abe, 2020). Traditionally, researchers prefer empirically based interventions, but liberatory scholars permit community members to determine what is credible and effective. These are called practice-based evidence (PBE) approaches.

Testimonios research stems from Latin America and is often used to challenge oppression. Thus, to better understand "how to practice a responsible resistance to racist power structures" (Domínguez & Noriega, 2022, p. 146), two non-Black Latina psychologists thematically analyzed their responses to a question prompt. Four themes emerged from their research and emphasized that allies must question and challenge anti-Blackness, racist policies, and power systems, and decolonize psychology.

To respond with cultural humility, empathy, and advocacy, counselors could enhance their critical consciousness or employ any of the other seven tenets of liberation theory. Counselors could engage in an immersion course or a study-abroad program with the aim to better understand the lived experiences of marginalized people. Counselors view their clients as experts and use the clients' testimonios as data to recommend culturally appropriate interventions and PBE approaches. Counselors can also work with clients and community members to create social change by engaging in CBPR.

LIBERATION COUNSELING AND THE OPPRESSED

A counselor must first believe that racism and prejudice exist to know that people are oppressed. Such a counselor does not endorse racial colorblindness, nor do they turn a blind eye to any of the other isms (e.g., heterosexism, ageism, etc.). These counselors are also aware of their own biases, assumptions, and judgments and are culturally open. They are also attuned to clients' internalized oppression, where clients impose Eurocentric ideals upon themselves and other marginalized people. Like traditional counselors, liberation counselors promote wellness. However, liberation counselors practice wellness as fairness. They believe that "everyone has the right to be healthy, free, and with opportunities to fulfill their capacities" (Comas-Díaz, 2020, p. 173).

The liberation counselor works to gain the oppressed client's trust through radical humility and radical empathy. Comas-Díaz (2020) proposes that a counselor is radically humble when they work in a human-to-human relationship rather than a therapist-to-client alliance. They permit themselves to be mirrored in their clients, and vice versa, and value justice, equality, and love. A counselor who is radically empathetic "intuitively" feels the client's pain. Liberation counselors develop deep connections with their clients using "sensorial modes and connections and nonrational kinds of knowledge" (Comas-Díaz, 2020, p. 176). Liberation counselors do not sit in positions of neutrality, as traditional counselors do, because they use self-disclosure to acknowledge how social identities and social positions influence how one's world and life are understood. They regularly self-reflect to examine their contributions to injustice and inequality. When working as a liberation counselor who models service to humanity, social justice activism, and self-care, much self-work is required. Liberation therapists engage in their own therapy.

Knowing that society is designed for advantaged people, liberation counselors use intake forms or assessments that ascertain the strengths, cultural capital, creativity, and history of the oppressed client. When assessing a client's legal history, the counselor also considers the influence of privilege and oppression, such as racial profiling, mass incarceration, school-to-prison pipeline, detainment by immigration agencies, xenophobia, and so on. Liberatory counselors ask inclusive questions about gender and sexual orientation without othering clients, and ascertain a client's spirituality and religious practices without judgment when clients practice religion outside of Catholicsm and Christianity. Counselors provide a space where clients are free to speak about atheism, agnosticism, ancestral knowledge, and so forth. Liberation counselors are also able to identify adaptive and maladaptive means of spiritual and religious coping. For example, spiritual bypassing and buying into the prosperity gospel are maladaptive and oppressive. Counselors committed to liberatory work nurture clients' spiritual development and activism. Liberation counselors respect all people and believe that everyone has a right to make decisions about themselves and those things connected to them.

CLINICAL CASE SCENARIO 2.1: LIBERATION COUNSELING

Elaine, one of several clients on your caseload, is a 35-year-old White woman who came to see you because she believes she is having panic attacks. She walked into your office assisted by a cane and a large service dog that she did not mention when she telephoned your office. Elaine is married with two high school-aged children. She is a disabled military veteran who was honorably discharged at an E-6 rank. She now works as an office manager in the Reserve Officer Training Corps (ROTC) office at a local university. She has been reprimanded for excessive tardiness.

You remember your multicultural counseling training, so you do not assume that Elaine's presenting problem is related to being differently abled. You ask her about the physiological symptoms she called panic attacks. "It feels like a weight in my chest, like something's got its hand on my heart. My heart rate speeds up, and I feel like I can't catch my breath." You reflect content and Elaine confirms that you heard her correctly. You believe that Solutions-Focused Brief Therapy might be a good approach for this client, considering her military background and that a quick solution might be best. You ask Elaine to tell walk you through her day.

(continued)

CHAPTER 2: LIBERATION COUNSELING AS A FRAMEWORK | 21

CLINICAL CASE SCENARIO 2.1: LIBERATION COUNSELING (*CONTINUED*)

"I wake up in the mornings and I feel good. I'm up before my husband or children so I can have some me time. I make my coffee and take Luna, my service dog, out for a walk. I get home and wake up the girls before I get into the shower. I make my coffee while I get ready for work. I see the girls off and then I leave out the door shortly behind them. My husband works second shift so he sleeps through the morning. Almost as soon as I put my car in park when I get to the parking garage at work, it feels like I'm going to throw up. Sometimes I feel lightheaded. Mostly, I feel like I can't breathe. I get myself together and go inside and my coworkers are there. I know I'm late, but sometimes they are too. They halfway greet me. They don't listen to me at all, and usually are on their phones when I'm leading staff meetings. I don't feel like I belong there with those people." You then ask her one of the miracle questions: "If you went to bed tonight and woke up tomorrow and everything was better, what would be the evidence that a miracle occurred?"

"I would get to work and not feel panicky. I would feel respected at work, like I belong there." Your first inclination as a counselor is to give Elaine some anxiety management strategies. You feel that body scanning would be helpful, as would guided imagery and deep breathing or box breathing. While this is great, such interventions would be oppressive—you would be helping her cope with situations that cause her anxiety rather than considering the environmental factors that might be influencing her symptoms. Thus, as a liberation counselor you acknowledge the different identity markers that might overlap and be interdependent. For example, she is a woman who served in the military—what impact does this experience have on her presenting problem? She is also differently abled and has a service dog. How do these things influence her presenting problem or symptoms? You ask Elaine these questions, not from a deficit-based framework as if they were limitations, but from a strengths-based approach as assets.

Additionally, as a liberation counselor you ask questions about Elaine's workplace. You ask about her coworkers—their race, gender, age, and so on. You ask about their response to Luna. You also ask about the construction of the building—is there handicapped parking, how far is it from the building, are there elevators, and how far or close are they to Elaine's office? Asking these questions, you realize that Elaine's workplace may not be Americans with Disabilities Act (ADA)-compliant (parking is not close, the stairs are closer to her office than the elevator, and the time it takes her to get to the top of the stairs is equal to the time it would take her to get to the elevator on the other side of the building). Elaine's tardiness is strongly related to the fact that she has to work twice as hard as her able-bodied coworkers to get to work on time. Moreover, the panic attacks she experienced in the parking lot slowed her down. By Elaine's answers you recognize that her coworkers are discriminating against her because they believe she has special privileges because she brings her dog to work.

CLINICAL CASE SCENARIO DISCUSSION QUESTIONS

1. As a liberation counselor, how would you help Elaine, and why did you choose those interventions?
2. Your caseload is tight, and your work–life balance is near poor. How will you work Elaine's advocacy needs into your schedule?
3. What about being a liberation counselor might make you uncomfortable, and how would you manage that discomfort?
4. Describe how teaching Elaine anti-anxiety interventions further oppresses her.

END-OF-CHAPTER RESOURCES

A robust set of instructor resources designed to supplement this text is located at **http://connect.springerpub.com/content/book/978-0-8261-3953-5**. Qualifying instructors may request access by emailing **textbook@springerpub.com**.

SUMMARY

This chapter briefly introduced readers to the tenets of liberation theory and suggested ways for integrating it into counseling pedagogy and processes. Liberation counselors walk alongside oppressed clients, embody their pain, and recover the power and voices of the oppressed. Becoming a liberation counselor is a lifelong process, not an event or a destination of checkboxes for social justice. Counselors who work to free clients will free themselves, and liberated clients will liberate their communities.

DISCUSSION QUESTIONS

1. Describe the seven tenets of liberation psychology.
2. What are the differences between denaturalization and deproblematization?
3. Compare and contrast mainstream counseling and liberation counseling.
4. How is a counselor liberated by facilitating liberation counseling?
5. Explain the intersection between intersectionality, privilege, and oppression.

KEY REFERENCES

Only key references appear in the print edition. The full reference list appears in the digital product on Springer Publishing Connect: https://connect.springerpub.com/content/book/978-0-8261-3953-5/part/part01/chapter/ch02

Comas-Díaz, L. (2020). Liberation psychotherapy. In L. Comas-Díaz & T. Rivera (Eds.), *Liberation psychology: Theory, method, practice, and social justice* (pp. 169–185). American Psychological Association. https://doi.org/10.1037/0000198-000

Crenshaw, K. (1991). Mapping the margins: Intersectionality, identity politics, and violence against women of color. *Stanford Law Review, 43*(6), 1241–1299. https://doi.org/10.2307/1229039

Domínguez, D. G., Hernandez-Arriaga, B., & Paul, K. S. (2020). Cruzando fronteras: Liberation psychology in a counseling psychology immersion course. *Journal of Latinx Psychology, 8*(3), 250–264. https://doi.org/10.1037/lat0000148

CHAPTER 3

Counseling With Cultural Humility, Empathy, and Responsiveness

LATONYA M. SUMMERS AND LOTES NELSON

> **LEARNING OBJECTIVES**
>
> After reading this chapter, students will be able to:
> - Define cultural humility and empathy.
> - Assess the impact of one's own biases, assumptions, and judgments upon others.
> - Recognize how to develop culturally responsive interventions.

> **SELF-REFLECTION QUESTIONS**
>
> 1. What do you think it means to be a culturally responsive counselor?
> 2. Describe the difference between humility and empathy.

WHAT IS CULTURAL HUMILITY AND EMPATHY IN COUNSELING?

Being proud of who one is and where they came from is a strength. However, when culturally different people come together, dynamics of pride, power, and privilege might hinder their alliance. Counselors and supervisors are admonished to practice cultural humility (Hook et al., 2013; Jones & Branco, 2020; Sue & Sue, 2016; Watkins et al., 2019; Zhu et al., 2021). Although cultural humility has recently gained much scholarly interest in mental health professions, the construct was coined and defined as a "lifelong process of self-reflection and self-examination" by medical scholars Tervalon and Murray-Garcia in 1998 (Zhu et al., 2021). Cultural humility has been differentiated from cultural competence as "a way of being rather than a way of doing" (Sue & Sue, 2016), characterized as working from a humble stance by Watkins et al. (2019), and conceptualized by Hook et al. as "respect and lack of superiority toward an individual's cultural background and experience" (2013, p. 353). Zhu et al. proposed that a consensus conceptualization for cultural humility might be "an attitude of lifelong learning, a commitment to developing cultural awareness and questioning assumptions, respect, and an other-oriented stance to be open to new cultural experience" (2021, p. 74).

Using a liberatory framework, the first editor of this book posits that counselors who practice cultural humility show respect for clients and the various identities they hold—not just race and ethnicity, but including sexual orientation, religion and spirituality, age, gender, ability, military status, and so on. Culturally humble counselors also respect and acknowledge the cultural capital (strengths, resources, etc.) of their clients and use it in treatment plans and counseling processes. Counselors who are culturally humble trust their culturally different clients and believe their reports regarding harassment, discrimination, and oppression, rather than finding alternative (albeit clinical) ways to explain presenting problems. Counselors who practice cultural humility know they are not the experts in the room when they sit with clients whose lived experiences differ from their own. Lastly, culturally humble counselors are open, curious, flexible, and willing to walk alongside so they better understand their clients' needs (empathy), and they question their clients but mostly themselves to ensure that they are providing services that liberate their clients and themselves.

Empathy, a foundational concept among mental health professionals, has generally been defined as a vicarious response, such as Rogers's (1959) conceptualization of empathy as an ability to walk in another's shoes. Later, scholars characterized empathy as a character trait and found that some people are more empathic than others (Duan & Hill, 1996), and other scholars wondered if empathy could be enhanced (Batson et al., 1995, Batson et al., 1997). Hoffman (2000) was one of the first scholars to report that empathy could lead to social justice orientation. Though general empathy has been widely studied, Wang and colleagues (2003) studied empathy in cross-cultural settings and operationalized ethnocultural empathy with their Scale of Ethnocultural Empathy (SEE). SEE measures three domains of empathy: (a) intellectual empathy, where the culturally different client's thinking and feeling are sought to be understood; (b) empathic emotions, as the degree to which the counselor displays the culturally different client's emotional state; and (c) communicative empathy, where the verbal and oral expression reflects a client's intellectual empathy and empathic emotions. Liberation counselors describe that component of their work as radical empathy (Comas-Díaz, 2020). *Radical empathy* is the use of "sensorial modes of connection and other nonrational kinds of knowledge" to intuitively feel what their clients are feeling (Comas-Díaz, 2020, p. 176). The connection between liberation counselors and their clients is deepened by the counselor's ability to embody their client's suffering.

Cultural humility and empathy require counselors to use themselves as instruments of healing, and all the more in liberation counseling. Thus, self-care is mandatory for the counselor who engages in antidiscrimination and liberatory work. *Self-care* has been defined as "self-initiated behaviors that promote good health and well-being" (Christopher et al., 2006, p. 496) and should be intentional and routine. Oftentimes, self-care is touted as a luxury (bubble baths, aromatherapy, massages, skin and haircare, etc.), but Mitchell and Binkley argued that "self-care is not a luxury or a one-time act" (Mitchell & Binkley, 2021, p. 41). The authors recommended anti-racist strategies that counselor educators could use to help Black, Indigenous, and People of Color (BIPOC) and White students ward off burnout in their work toward social justice and advocacy. Anecdotal strategies for radical self-care include setting boundaries, saying no and not overcommitting, and practicing assertiveness. While engaging in liberation work, radical self-care might also include asking for help, delegating tasks, and working collaboratively in teams.

ENHANCING HUMILITY AND EMPATHY IN COUNSELING

Cultural competence is a common concept that is often used in the realm of multiculturalism. This phrase is often linked to one's level of cultural knowledge or the aspiration to reach that paramount cultural knowledge. The phrase speaks to the idea that there is a level at which one could attain the maximum cultural knowledge. This very notion can also perpetuate biases by sending the message that one can no longer expand on one's cultural learning, and implying that there is a pinnacle to one's cultural learning and knowledge and when that point is reached the person is deemed to be culturally competent. As we continue to evolve in our multicultural knowledge and development, the construct of cultural competence no longer matches the counseling profession's needs. The goal in the counseling profession and work is to continually progress in a way that is fulfilling the needs of the people whom we serve. Hence, the introduction of cultural humility.

Tervalon and Murray-García (1998), the originators of cultural humility, described the term as being a lifelong process of self-reflection and self-examination. This classification closely aligns with the need of our counseling clients and, consequently, should be the focus for counselor trainees and counselors. Cultural humility allows for recognition and continues to focus on the development of one's cultural identities and intersectionalities. The concept communicates the fact that there is no endpoint, but rather a sustained and prolonged assessment of one's intersecting cultural identities. For counselor trainees and counselors, cultural humility speaks to their willingness to examine themselves as well as the client's holistic cultural selves. Counselor trainees and counselors with cultural humility exemplify the attribute to ask questions about the person's ethnicity, gender, sexual identity, sexual orientation, social needs, socioeconomic status, and language. Cultural humility starts with one's willingness to explore one's cultural beliefs and values. As counselors understand their own cultural value systems, they are better able to see their client's cultural identities.

Principles of Cultural Humility

Lifelong Self-Exploration

Counselors are willing to continue to examine their own cultural identities. A large part of this is to be aware of their cultural privileges and their impact on their counseling work. The willingness to examine one's preexisting cultural value systems and be able to name the consequences in the event that beliefs are futile or hurtful to others. Self-reflective questions are helpful as a part of one's continued self-exploration. Examples of self-reflective questions are as follows:

- What are my foundational cultural value systems?
- What are my cultural identities and intersectionalities?
- How have I/do I experience power and privilege in my everyday living?
- How have I and do I experience marginalization?
- How do I present myself to others? How do I insert myself? How do I shield myself from cultural interactions?
- What am I comfortable with in terms of cultural discussions? What am I uncomfortable with in terms of cultural discussions?

Humility and Trustworthiness

The very essence of cultural humility in counseling is the counselor's willingness to be humble in the process. This process requires the counselor to realize who they are as a person and as a professional. To display humility is to hold comprehension of your own intentions and always honor the other individual's personhood. In the client–counselor relationship, this means the counselor will recognize what's theirs and what's of the client. The counselor will be willing to acknowledge their mistakes and always keep transparency at the forefront. For example, if the counselor is not familiar with the client's cultural practices, they are willing to own up to it and commit to doing the work to make progress in that area. Doing so will establish a bond of trust between the client and the counselor. The established trust can then be the foundation that allows for the counseling work to begin.

Acknowledging Power Dynamics and Biases

Counselor trainees and counselors acknowledge their power dynamic and biases within the counseling session. There is already a natural power dynamic between the client and the counselor such that the counselor can be seen to be in an authoritative position. Counselors with cultural humility recognize this and work to diminish the power differential in the counseling session. Counselors will work from the space of collaboration in order to lower the power discrepancy between client and counselor. This is even more imperative when counseling minoritized clients.

Counselors need to work on creating a safe and inviting space for the client. This may mean evaluating the counselor's workspace to have a less formal counseling office to create a hospitable atmosphere. Counselors function from a stance of partnership in their therapeutic work, inviting the client to collaborate rather than telling the client what to do, and communicating to the client that the counseling space is theirs to do what they see to be professionally appropriate. Likewise, counselors are to continue to examine their biases during their work with their clients, being aware of their existing biases and engaging in reflexivity to ensure damage control. Counselors need to be aware of their words and actions during the therapeutic work to avoid implicit bias.

Advocacy to Dismantle Systemic Barriers

Culturally humble counselors take actions beyond themselves. They make it a practice to examine and be aware of the systemic barriers that counseling clients face, especially our marginalized clients. The counselor makes advocacy work central to their role as a professional counselor. This also requires counselors to recognize their power and privilege and utilize their professional standing to let their voices be heard for those who are disfranchised. For example, a female transgender client expresses that she is prohibited from using the women's bathroom at school. The counselor advocates for the client by calling and writing a letter to ask for the school's policy to be changed to allow the female transgender client to be able to use the women's bathroom. Similarly, for an Asian single mother without access to mental or physical healthcare and treatment, a culturally humble counselor can leverage their position to advocate for this client to receive access to care. Culturally humble counselors will make advocacy a part of their routine work.

Counseling With Empathy

"Empathy is the ability to understand and respond to another person's experience and is an important skill for maintaining good relationships across the lifespan" (Kelly et al., 2022, p. 1). Therefore, counseling with empathy requires the counselor to put themself in another's position to comprehend their thoughts and feelings. This notion should not negate the client's experience, but rather *feel and hear* the client's experience. Counseling with empathy requires the counselor to be present and intentional in conceptualizing the client's narrative. In order for the counselor to be empathic in the counseling setting, the counselor must move away from their own values and beliefs and rather concentrate on the client. This supports the important notion that counseling sessions are *for* the clients and that the client should be the focal point of interest. Accordingly, the counselor will be able to hear the client's account of themself and naturally hear and learn of the client's cultural beings. A high level of empathy in the counseling session results in client motivation.

Counselor empathy can be shown in different forms throughout the counseling session. Counselors can practice Carl Rogers' unconditional positive regard as a way to show empathy in the counseling session (Velasquez & Montiel, 2018). Counselors see the client for who they are and believe that they are doing their best as a way to demonstrate empathy in the counseling session. Counselors can work from a nonjudgmental approach during the counseling session as a way to show empathy in counseling. Honoring the client's cultural beliefs and values demonstrates empathy in the therapeutic setting. Taking the client-centered approach allows empathy in counseling to organically emerge.

IDENTIFYING AND UTILIZING CULTURALLY RESPONSIVE INTERVENTIONS

Counselors who employ a racial colorblind and culture-blind approach apply mainstream techniques and strategies to every client, without recognizing or regarding the nuances of the client's experience. Turning a blind eye to the impact of racism and discrimination, the overrepresentation of marginalized people among the homeless and institutionalized, acculturation stress, and culture-related stressors is oppressive and harmful. Scholars call for counselors who prescribe culturally responsive interventions: strategies and techniques that are understood and accepted by clients (Ancis, 2004). Ancis reported that such interventions might reduce barriers associated with access to care and improve therapy outcomes.

Anecdotally, a White counselor conducted a biopsychosocial assessment on a young adult Black woman client and noticed that the client used the open palm of her hand to pat her head every now and then. The behavior was strange to the counselor so she watched intently as the client patted the crown of her head, then a few minutes later she patted the side of her head, and then the back. The pats seemed to be in a pattern of threes. The counselor also noticed that as the session went on, the patting increased. By the end of the appointment, the counselor was convinced that the client had an intermittent tic disorder.

Black counselors might have readily recognized the *pat* as the client's attempt to soothe an itchy scalp without messing up her hair. Counselors do not have to be culturally matched with their clients to deliver culturally responsive interventions. Counselors who practice cultural humility and empathy offer culturally responsive services. Such counselors would have asked the client about the behavior. Counselors who are hesitant to ask questions they think might make them look foolish or racist are at risk of inflicting harm upon their clients. Assessing and diagnosing clients without attention to culture and other contextual factors is culturally insensitive, oppressive, and harmful. Rather, a counselor might simply say to the client: "I noticed that you pat yourself on the head, tell me about that." Undoubtedly, bringing that to the client's attention (i.e., seeing the client or the client feeling seen) might be the beginning of a strong cross-cultural therapeutic alliance. When a counselor is willing to talk about things that are visible, they open the door to learn about things that cannot be seen. Of course, there are cultural factors that cannot be seen—ethnicity, religion, disability, and so on—but the observant counselor listens and watches.

Beginning counselors might want to know what culturally responsive interventions look like so they can employ them. However, including a list of strategies in this chapter would defeat the point of cultural responsiveness. Culturally responsive interventions are unique to each client. As stated before, such interventions are recognized and accepted by the client. If the counselor has to explain the intervention because it is foreign to the client, or long-term or consistent progress is not made, it means that the intervention is not culturally responsive. Offering clients boxed-up, one-size-fits-all, cookie-cutter strategies exacerbates the problems they seek help for. Walker (2020) asserted that the adoption of noncultural values and norms exacerbates mental illness.

To formulate culturally responsive interventions, counselors might ask the client, "When you think about the problem you're presenting today, can you think of how people in your family have managed or resolved it before?" or "Are there any family traditions or rituals you know of that worked to manage the problems you're dealing with today?" The counselor needs to ask about the cultural groups the client belongs to (e.g., socioeconomic status, religion, religion, etc.) and ascertain the values of those groups. What are the beliefs and assumptions of those groups, and are they primary in the client's life? How does the client feel about these beliefs and assumptions, and how do they influence the client's behaviors? The counselor would want to ask about the client's identity formation (where they are along the continuum of identity development) and where they would like to be. These and other strengths-based questions lead to culturally responsive interventions that teach, show, and remind clients that culturally different identities are assets, not liabilities.

CLINICAL CASE SCENARIO 3.1: CULTURAL HUMILITY

Your client is a 6-year-old Black boy named Sage whose mother brought him to counseling because he gets in trouble at school. Sage has been diagnosed with ADHD but is not medicated. His mother is single and informed you that she is struggling financially because she does not receive support from his father. You thanked his mother for trusting you and dismissed her to the waiting area. You brought Sage into your office where you learned that he wants a puppy. Sage tells you that he gets into trouble at school because he is bored, but if he had a puppy to come home to, he would be good. You determine that Sage does not need counseling and inform his mother that your recommendation for her sweet boy is a puppy.

CLINICAL CASE SCENARIO DISCUSSION QUESTIONS

1. Although you practiced empathy and humility as Sage's counselor, what might have you done differently to show cultural humility and cultural or radical empathy?
2. In what ways was your recommendation for a puppy not a culturally responsive intervention?
3. What would you do differently to help Sage and his mother?

END-OF-CHAPTER RESOURCES

 A robust set of instructor resources designed to supplement this text is located at **http://connect.springerpub.com/content/book/978-0-8261-3953-5**. Qualifying instructors may request access by emailing **textbook@springerpub.com**.

SUMMARY

Beginning counselors wonder if there will ever come a day when they enter their counseling sessions without anxiety. Our answer is twofold. Firstly, the more one practices as a counselor, the less anxious one becomes about their practice. However, should the day come that a counselor approaches their work with no anxiety, it might be an indicator that the counselor needs to leave the profession. Secondly, we believe that some anxiety is healthy and is a sign that the counselor considers their work with clients to be sacred, important, or bigger than themself. Such counselors are likely to consult with peers or supervisors, plan for their sessions, question themselves, read for knowledge, and not become overly reliant on self. Their counterparts are not able to practice cultural humility or empathy if they see themselves as the experts in the profession and over their clients' care.

DISCUSSION QUESTIONS

1. Using your own words, define cultural humility.
2. What will you use from this chapter to enhance your use of cultural humility and empathy with clients?
3. What might you use to develop culturally responsive interventions for your clients?

KEY REFERENCES

Only key references appear in the print edition. The full reference list appears in the digital product on Springer Publishing Connect: https://connect.springerpub.com/content/book/978-0-8261-3953-5/part/part01/chapter/ch03

Ancis, J. R. (2004). *Culturally responsive interventions: Innovative approaches to working with diverse populations*. Brunner-Routledge.

Hook, J. N., Davis, D. E., Owen, J., Worthington, E. L., & Utsey, S. O. (2013). Cultural humility: measuring openness to culturally diverse clients. *Journal of Counseling Psychology, 60*(3), 353–366. https://doi.org/10.1037/a0032595

Jones, C. T., & Branco, S. F. (2020). The interconnectedness between cultural humility and broaching in clinical supervision: working from the multicultural orientation framework. *The Clinical Supervisor, 39*(2), 178–189. https://doi.org/10.1080/07325223.2020.1830327

Tervalon, M., & Murray-García, J. (1998). Cultural humility versus cultural competence: A critical distinction in defining physician training outcomes in multicultural education. *Journal of Health Care for the Poor and Underserved, 9*(2), 117–125. https://doi.org/10.1353/hpu.2010.0233

CHAPTER 4

Social Justice and Advocacy Readiness

NOREAL F. ARMSTRONG

LEARNING OBJECTIVES

After reading this chapter, students will be able to:

- Discuss and evaluate the tenets of social justice and its application to the counseling profession.
- Demonstrate an understanding of the Liberation Model and Multicultural and Social Justice Counseling Competencies (MSJCC) and incorporate them into advocacy efforts.
- Reflect and develop a personal plan for advocacy and action.
- Analyze the success of current social justice initiatives toward cultural responsiveness.

SELF-REFLECTION QUESTIONS

1. What do social justice and advocacy mean to you?
2. How do social justice and advocacy fit in your role and work as a counselor?
3. What does the American Counseling Association (ACA) Code of Ethics say about social justice and advocacy?
4. How are social justice and advocacy alive today and what can you do to further the effort?

"Active involvement in advocacy, community outreach, and public policymaking are prime examples of interventions that can promote attention to social justice issues among practicing counselors and counseling psychologists" (Constantine et al., 2007, p. 25). Researchers Atkinson, Thompson, and Grant presented a framework that addressed eight potential helping roles in relation to working with diverse cultural populations. The following are four of the eight roles: adviser, advocate, consultant, and change agent key in the work of social justice and activism (Constantine et al., 2007). Social justice incorporates social issues that involve the individual, the family, the community, the wider society, and even the international community.

WHAT ARE SOCIAL JUSTICE AND ADVOCACY?

A common definition of *social justice* is the full and equal participation of all groups in a society that is mutually shaped to meet their needs. Social justice requires the equitable distribution of advantages, opportunities, and resources, as well as physical and psychological safety for all members of society (Mallinckrodt et al., 2014). Derald Wing Sue and his colleagues stated, "Multiculturalism is about social justice, cultural democracy, and equity" (Chung & Bemak, 2012, p. 33). As the fifth force in counseling and psychology, the social justice framework challenges mental health professionals to look beyond the individual and notice the larger influential factors in the clients' lives. By only focusing on what happens inside the therapy session, counselors may miss the larger issues of injustices that affect all individuals from diverse backgrounds; in contrast, the social justice focus aims to understand and advocate for equality and justice, thereby changing the systems. It has previously been argued that, before multiculturalism and social justice became the fourth and fifth forces, counselors and other mental health professionals who provided traditional services were not rocking the boat by following the status quo and were unintentionally helping to propagate various societal forms of oppression (Chung & Bemak, 2012). In addition, Martín-Baró asserted that helping professionals become agents of societal oppressive systems when oppressive power structures are ignored (Singh, 2016).

Steele (2008) mentioned a variety of definitions for social justice and advocacy while introducing the Liberation Model Framework. One definition described social justice as "scholarship and professional action designed to change societal values, structures, policies, and practices, such that disadvantaged or marginalized groups gain increased access to tools of self-determination" (Steele, 2008, p. 75). Another similar definition described social justice as promoting access and equity to ensure full participation of all people in the life of a society, specifically those who have been systematically excluded on the basis of race or ethnicity, gender, age, physical or mental disability, education, sexual orientation, socioeconomic status, or other characteristics of background or group membership. Ornstein (2017) stated, "the notion of social justice is based on the Christian doctrine of helping less fortunate people—the weak, sickly, and oppressed" (p. 545). For the United States, although similar ideas were shared with Western Europe on how to implement a more just society, ideally government would be used to bring about reform and legislation would right the wrongs of history (Ornstein, 2017).

Much of the literature about social justice discussed the concept of it being the fifth force in counseling. It was argued by some that the social justice counseling movement should be viewed as a "recurring wave" and requires more research to attain credibility and establish best practices (Ratts, 2009, p. 161). Despite the varying opinions, counseling professionals realized the importance of focusing on social justice to understand various factors influencing client well-being.

According to Ratts (2009), a theory of social justice counseling provides counselors with a theoretical framework for understanding the role oppression plays in shaping human behavior and the means to actualize advocacy in counseling. The idea is that social justice advocacy is an important counseling intervention that can alleviate oppressive conditions contributing to client stress. A social justice counseling perspective encourages counselors to develop a more balanced outlook between individuals and their environment. Viewing clients within the context of their environment helps counselors determine whether direct counseling or social justice advocacy is necessary.

Why Is It Important?

Counselors, counseling psychologists, and counseling students who are committed to principles of social justice must develop skills in creativity and courage in order to ameliorate the consequences of social injustice (Constantine et al., 2007). Counselors and counseling psychologists are situated in an optimal position to help society's inhabitants understand the undue effects of social injustices on the well-being of the larger society. Social justice is important because clients are individuals functioning within a set of intersecting systems that play a significant role in the stress and distress a client may face. Social injustices can occur across multiple levels and systems. They can be obvious and overt, such as pushing an older Asian American man to his death because he "could have something to do with the start of COVID-19." Or they can be subtle and covert, such as following a group of Mexican college students around in a store to prevent theft but not surveilling a group of White teenage males.

Researchers have argued that using direct counseling without attending to the social milieu may actually be harmful to clients because it forces individuals to "adapt to and cope with their environments, rather than change the social context, and in so doing, join the forces that perpetuate social injustice" (Ratts, 2009, p. 162). Additionally, it was reasoned that if the environment is the root of the problem, then maybe attention should be paid to community-based work and not just direct counseling. Community-based work could include offering mental health workshops at local churches to provide the community with information about health and mental health resources. Increasing awareness and access to resources may support what is happening in the counseling session. Theorizing social justice counseling as a paradigm unto itself also acknowledges that a shift has occurred in how services are provided. When counselors find that clients' problems are connected to living in an oppressive environment, they focus their efforts on changing social structures.

One structure in need of such change is the school-to-prison pipeline. Studies show that Black boys are four times more likely to be suspended than their White counterparts for similar actions (Washington, 2018) and that such actions are influenced by racial bias (Armstrong et al., 2021). Children and adolescents spend the majority of their waking hours at school, and when that environment is oppressive and prevents access to healthy cultural and social connections it can be detrimental to development (Armstrong et al., 2021). Counselors can offer training on a variety of concepts that can assist schools in providing quality care for diverse student populations and challenge them to review and change policies and procedures that may be rooted in historical bias.

Growth Through Liberation

Mental health professionals and counselors have an ethical and moral obligation to work toward social justice and address larger social problems within the therapeutic context (Chung & Bemak, 2012; Hailes et al., 2021). Traditionally, helping professionals have concerned themselves with wellness, health, and well-being. Helping people be well and enjoy is a great goal, "but as with any single value, wellness cannot stand on its own. Unless wellness is supported by justice, fairness, and equality, it is bound to fall. Wellness cannot thrive in conditions of inequality and injustice" (Prilleltensky & Prilleltensky, 2003, p. 276). To accomplish this, mental health professionals must be able to understand the relationship between their clients' cognitive and affective functioning, and their behaviors and interactions within their larger world. Liberation psychology, or the Liberation Model, is a tool to help counseling and psychology students, counselors, and psychologists engage social change principles that can be used to shift perspective and practice (Singh, 2016).

The Liberation Model is based on the work of theorist Paulo Freire and was developed for use with master's-level community counseling, school counseling, and counseling psychology students enrolled in introductory counseling courses (Steele, 2008). The Liberation Model's philosophy of education is grounded in and based on liberation pedagogy, liberation education, and liberation psychology, all derived from the philosophy of constructivism, with the primary goal of helping to facilitate "reflection and action upon the world in order to transform it" (Freire, 1993, as cited in Steele, 2008, p. 76).

The constructivist and problem-posing approaches used in the Liberation Model are effective for social justice advocacy training because they both have as their main concern the development of the kind of reflective and critical thinking skills determined by the profession to be necessary for social justice advocacy. The purpose of problem-posing education is to work toward ending oppressive societal practices, which is the goal of social justice advocacy.

Counselors and Social Justice Advocates

Counselors and counseling psychologists serve as advocates and change agents when they communicate or interface with structures, organizations, or institutions that marginalized or disenfranchised individuals or groups of people perceived as inherently oppressive to their well-being (Constantine et al., 2007). *Advocacy* is an umbrella term for a range of activities designed to change society by engaging individuals, employers, or the government. More broadly defined, psychology advocacy is the process of "informing and assisting decision-makers who promote the interest of clients, health care systems, and public and welfare issues and professional psychology" (Cohen et al., 2012, p. 152). Counselor education programs have taken active roles in preparing students to become advocates and to assess the systems and environments that influence clients' lives. From articles written in the early 2000s to now, multiculturalism and social justice concepts have evolved from theoretical frameworks to actionable steps that can foster positive growth in the counseling relationship and elicit change on a systemic level.

The American Counseling Association (ACA; 2014) mandates that, "when appropriate, counselors advocate at individual, group, institutional, and societal levels to address potential barriers and obstacles that inhibit access and/or the growth and development of clients" (p. 5). This ethical guideline is for all working as counselors, and it may mean stepping outside of one's comfort zone. As steps are taken to address social injustices, the ethical codes also state that counselors should obtain client consent before engaging in advocacy efforts on behalf of an identifiable client to improve the provision of services and to work toward the removal of systemic barriers or obstacles that inhibit client access, growth, and development.

THE INTERSECTIONALITY OF CULTURAL RESPONSIVENESS AND SOCIAL JUSTICE

Much of the literature on social justice and advocacy speaks to the positionality of counselors to globally help communities large and small understand the effects of social injustice, develop cultural competence, and help their peers provide support based on the cultural competence they have obtained. Responding to the needs of different cultures in this country and beyond is not new. Historically, counseling and psychology have focused more on the direct benefit of individual counseling (Constantine et al., 2007; Hanna et al., 2000; Steele, 2008). Over the last 40 years, counseling professionals have noticed a need to shift from a focus on the individual's psyche to study individuals' suffering and experiences within the context of their environmental conditions (Domínguez et al., 2020). This shift, highlighted in the Domínguez et al. (2020) article, gave credit to Martín-Baró, who saw the injustices and "advocated for marginalized communities and encouraged psychologists to move away from their focus on examining an individual's psyche to study the suffering of individuals' experiences" (p. 251).

For the purpose of this chapter, we discuss how historical conflicts are reflected in people's attitudes and emotional and behavioral responses years later. For example, legacies of injustice—histories of exclusion, marginalization, and oppression—are central to the formation of social identities, as is illustrated in the following situations. Consider the Tuskegee Airmen, for whom World War II was viewed as a fight against fascism abroad and racism at home. Just as historical conflicts reflect in people's attitudes and emotional and behavioral responses years later, efforts to address and change social injustices can reflect beneficial outcomes in the future.

An example of cultural responsiveness and social justice intersecting is how Filipinos fought in the early 20th century to become full American citizens and limit the discrimination they experienced (Hinnershitz, 2013). Filipinos were dedicated to improving their lives and those of others while in the United States. Filipinos who migrated and settled along the West Coast realized that their racial background overruled their rights to protection from harm and discrimination in America (Hinnershitz, 2013). Though technically not aliens, many Filipinos sought naturalization through the court system, with some successful court rulings. Hinnershitz (2013) highlighted that many Filipino men also fought for their rights of race, using their racial categorization as "Malays" rather than "Mongoloids" (p. 134), the category developed by anthropologists to describe the racial characteristics of Asians (Hays & Erford, 2018) to argue against anti-miscegenation laws in California and Oregon. Others decided to fight for social justice against discrimination in the workplace. From this example, we see the cultural influence of social justice by those who fight to change or correct policies aimed to separate and discriminate.

Counselors as Researchers

Counselors as researchers show another way cultural responsiveness and social justice intersect. Through research, counselors are not only able to assess the efficacy of evidence-based practices and assess the needs of clients, but we can also find where copious amounts of limited support and the infliction of dehumanization occur. For example, Campbell (2017) used her four-year action research study on sexual assault evidence going untested to highlight such disparities and to help support a change in the patterns of behavior by law enforcement in Detroit, Michigan. In 2009, there were approximately 11,000 sexual assault kits (SAKs) sitting in police custody. The majority of the kits were samples from African American women and girls, most of who were low-income. These untested kits meant there is "no opportunity for that evidence to aid in the prosecution of perpetrators, to give justice to survivors, to protect the safety of the community as a whole, and/or to exonerate those who have been wrongly accused" (Campbell, 2017, p. 315).

Additionally, Washington (2018) researched the benefits of integrating hip-hop in counseling with Black males. Washington posited that "through Hip Hop and rap music, social justice counselors could examine how the impact of zero-tolerance pre-K-12 disciplinary policies, hyper policing of Black neighborhoods … and mass incarceration impinge on the life chances of Black males" (2018, p. 96). As you continue to develop your counselor identity, what are your interests outside of counseling that could assist in how you combat social injustices or advocate for change?

Learning about the lives and stories of these women (mostly Black women, who have not been taken seriously because of the implicit bias woven into the mindset and fabric of our society) further demonstrates how much counselors and counseling students need to focus on advocating and working for social justice. Without counselors leading the charge with the therapeutic knowledge and skills we possess, how else will change take place? The officers and their superiors do not see there is a problem to solve (Campbell, 2017) and the women who have waited years for justice may not trust the system enough to speak up or have lost hope that any change will come. These stories are the catalyst for the development of more socially and culturally competent counselors who can step out of the counseling office and fight to see justice, equity, and equality across the systems of race, gender, ethnicity, socioeconomic status, religion, and ability.

Counselors and psychologists are also able to use research in concert with advocacy models to move the mental health profession forward through personal and professional introspection. Singh (2016) explored an idea proposed by Edwards in 2006 that an ally identity model emphasizes the value in being an aspiring ally rather than there being a specific endpoint. By doing so, anyone working as an ally does so with the intent to move from being an ally for self-interest to being an ally for social justice. This movement requires a shift in one's thoughts, beliefs, and values and the ability to challenge "the historical reality of prejudice and discrimination directly with the aim of transforming the structural systems of societies that uphold oppression" (Singh, 2016, p. 757). The Liberation Model or liberation psychology requires counselors and psychologists to assess how oppression is embedded in counseling and psychological theories, how those in dominant cultures have benefited from privilege, how possible past personal experiences with some form of oppression can help stimulate one to join those who are currently being oppressed, and how to take this knowledge and develop new culturally responsive practices. For example, Singh (2016) shared that cisgender psychologists interrogate the ways oppressive values are embedded in theories and work to develop theories that are culturally responsive to transgender and gender nonconforming (TGNC) people. Within liberation psychology, this process is called the "deideologization of psychology" (Singh, 2016, p. 757). The act of interrogating theories and working to develop culturally responsive practices is something you can practice during your time as a counseling student.

Advocates in All Places

Social justice and advocacy aren't only relegated to the counseling or helping professions. Musicians, rappers, entertainers, athletes, writers, journalists, and community members have provided examples of the many ways people can fight for social justice and advocate for change. Enraged and inspired after the 1963 16th Street Church bombing where four young Black girls were killed, Nina Simone wrote and performed "Mississippi Goddam" (1964). The song was Nina's way to take action, a way to protest against the violence happening across states to Black leaders such as Medgar Evers and others who were guilty of nothing other than being Black in America. Nina used the lyrics to highlight the past injustices, address the lack of action against the perpetrators, and express the concern for the state of America if things did not change soon. The song was one of the first written and used during the civil rights movement. Nina would change the name of the city in the lyrics as she traveled performing the song to provide significance for violence and injustices happening in those places (Fields, 2021).

In 1971, Gil Scott Heron rapped about the "no-knock" policy infamously established in New York that led to the murder of Black Panther leader Fred Hampton Sr. (Brooks et al., 2020). NWA, Rage Against the Machine, Tupac, and others rapped about the social injustices they witnessed in their communities in the 1980s and 1990s. In 2016, Beyoncé encouraged women to become advocates with her song "Formation" (Nadal, 2017), where she addressed the issues of police brutality, injustices behind the Hurricane Katrina devastation, and women's rights. She covered many themes related to race, gender, social class, and other intersectionalities. In the song's chorus, she sings, "Okay, ladies, now let's get in formation"—suggesting a call for communities (especially Black women) to organize politically to combat racial injustice and other inequities (Nadal, 2017, p. 936). Now, 57 years after "Mississippi Goddam," Lil Baby wrote and performed "The Bigger Picture," addressing the outcry of anger, frustration, pain, and continued social injustice toward people of color in America in the wake of the continued shootings of unarmed Black and Brown people.

Social Justice in a Pandemic

The year 2020 is etched in the memories of our global society as the year the coronavirus (COVID-19) changed the landscape of our lives. It also had a profound effect on social justice efforts. COVID-19, a virus with the title designated by the World Health Organization (WHO) in February 2020 (Centers for Disease Control and Prevention [CDC], n.d.), spreads primarily through droplets of saliva or discharge from the nose when an infected person coughs or sneezes. To lower the possibility of spreading the virus, scientists and researchers suggested that people stay six feet apart, wear masks, wash hands frequently, use a hand sanitizer with high alcohol content, and not participate in large gatherings (CDC, n.d.). Further, to follow health protocols, many places around the world went into lockdown. How we interacted and engaged with one another forever changed.

Suddenly, many people, except those deemed essential workers (i.e., healthcare personnel, first responders, and grocery store workers), were sequestered in their homes all day to read, work from home, navigate online communication systems, play games, and watch TV. Media outlets were the source of information about factors and statistics of the pandemic. Along with constant updates on the virus, other issues plaguing the world were also reported and more eyes were able to see. On May 25, 2020, the world watched as George Floyd was handcuffed, thrown onto the ground, and pinned in place with former police officer Derek Chauvin's knee on his neck until Floyd died. Millions of people around the world witnessed a man who was not resisting arrest get murdered on live TV. At a time in our society when information is disseminated within a matter of seconds, the televised death of George Floyd crashed into the lives of all who saw and disrupted the status quo. Continuous media coverage of COVID-19 made people aware of its causes, symptoms, confirmed cases by state, and fatalities. Each day there was an account of cases by state and lives lost. The longer we were in our the homes, the more we became aware of our mortality. There was time to talk, have family dinners, argue, laugh, cry, worry, be angry, feel frustrated, be creative, develop solutions, and learn to adapt. Time at home allowed personal defenses to come down. This author believes that the large number of people confined to their homes, finding connection through TV and media, finally saw *and understood* the social injustices that many have fought, marched, boycotted, and protested against. Now those previously blinded to or ignorant of the purpose for social justice activists were ready to take up arms, be allies, join the march, use their voices, and demand to be heard. Great! However, people were stuck at home or limited to very few places. How can someone advocate from their home?

Social Justice in the World of Social Media

The arrival of hashtags has a new meaning. Social media became a way for people to speak up and take action for causes that are important to them. During 2020, social media users witnessed celebrities, athletes, authors, politicians, nurses, and a host of other people using social media to make their voices heard or to support and promote the causes dear to them. Unfortunately, there was no lack of content for these newly minted advocates to pull from. On March 13, 2020, Breonna Taylor, an emergency medical technician (EMT), was shot five times and killed in her home during a police raid (Oppel et al., 2021). She was not armed. There were hashtags supporting mask-wearing, hand-washing, and social distancing alongside hashtags like Justice for Breonna, Justice for George Floyd, BLD PWR, Black Lives Matter, and Black Trans Lives Matter. People shared information on how to contact public officials and call for action to be taken and justice to be served. Citizens uploaded personal videos of police interactions, peaceful protests, and encounters with people in opposition to social change at high rates to monitor police actions in hopes that lives would not continue to be lost. Smartphones became tools used by those experiencing injustice or unfair treatment for documentation purposes. Through the use of social media, people were more informed of things happening and how they could participate in taking action.

As discussed earlier in the chapter, social justice, advocacy, and multicultural competence require knowing about the historical, political, and social injustices in society and within the helping profession. Cabrera et al. (2017) remind that college student activism has been at the center of higher education curricular, faculty, and student body diversification efforts—in particular along the lines of race and ethnicity. Learning this information includes giving time and energy to reading, having conversations, and deep self-reflection. Factors such as age, gender, race, socioeconomic status, and so on, may play a role in how people think activism and advocacy should look, but how much thought is put into what activism is? Cabrera et al. (2017) asked whether online displays of support can be seen as activism or seen as *slacktivism*—defined as "political activities that have no impact on real-life political outcomes, but only serve to increase the feel-good factor of the participants" (p. 1). At times, it may seem overwhelming.

For counselors and counseling students, social media can be a helpful tool as long as we remain ethical in our use. H.6.a. of the *ACA Code of Ethics* (2014) states that counselors' professional social medial presence should be separate from one's personal social media presence. The remaining codes, H.6.b, H.6.c, and H.6.d, can be summarized by admonishing counselors to be clear in the informed consent process about the benefits, limitations, and boundaries of social media; that they respect the client's privacy on social media; and that they do not disclose confidential information on public social media outlets.

BECOMING AN ADVOCATE

To become advocates, counselors must know what they stand for. What stirs your soul, what leaves an ache in your heart that can only be soothed by seeing real change happen? The answers to these questions are where you can start your process of becoming an advocate. The intersection of practice and advocacy involves moving outside the treatment setting to facilitate change at an organizational or systemic level, and to advocate for clients' needs with policymakers (Mallinckrodt et al., 2014). Constantine et al. (2007) shared that counseling programs could benefit from using educational, legal, and public policy institutions as experiential or applied learning sites for the development of critical social justice competencies.

Advocacy is taking action towards identified gaps that promotes or places emphasis on removing barriers to address cultural and social justice (Peters & Luke, 2021). Developing an advocacy platform as a counselor-in-training is just as important as developing one's counselor identity. Let us take each type of advocate and talk further about what that advocate looks like.

Pleading the case for another, specifically in front of a tribunal or judicial court. This type of advocate may show up to the family court to help plead for a client who is a single mother not to have to go to jail for a minor drug possession charge when she is the sole provider for her children. The advocate may point out other available support options. Another example could be a counselor sharing their assessment of an adolescent with behavioral issues, pleading for house arrest and counseling rather than placement in the juvenile justice system. It could also be a school counselor who advocates for students of color to receive the same punitive consequences as their White counterparts when there is inequality (Washington, 2018). In all of these instances, what remains constant is that counselors have to know the disparities that plague our social system and be familiar with unjust policies and systems to seek justice. Turning a blind eye or only looking at some issues perpetuate the status quo.

An advocate who defends or maintains a cause or purpose may include counselors lobbying for money to not be removed from the arts in schools because of the mental health benefits and impact of the arts on well-being. A counselor may help their client develop a memo or statement to share with the human resources manager as to why maternity leave is just as important for men as it is for women and why the amount of time off allowed should not be decreased.

One who supports or promotes the interests of a cause, or a group, may include advertising by social activist groups or causes on one's social media page or donating money to a cause that is working to bring change to a community in need. When using social media, it is important to abide by the ethical guidelines set forth by the ACA. As counseling students, supporting and promoting causes that have meaning can happen in classroom discussions, conversations with colleagues, and faculty meetings. Being an advocate means finding your voice and using it in places where change is needed.

Different Ways to Develop Advocacy

Another notion to introduce advocacy in the counseling program is for students to be encouraged to engage in an advocacy project to assess what they are passionate about, seek out needs in their area, and develop an advocacy event to bring awareness to the need. They can research local, state, and national resources; seek support, and develop a plan that one day they may implement. The idea of the assignment is to help students take what they have learned while in the counseling program, connect to community needs, and learn how to advocate on a midsize scale.

There is also advocacy within the intimate counseling setting. Driven by the Council for the Accreditation of Counseling and Related Educational Programs' standards (2016), students are to be aware of advocacy processes needed to address institutional and social barriers that impede access, equity, and success for clients (F.1.e), and strategies for identifying and eliminating barriers, prejudices, and processes of intentional and unintentional oppression and discrimination (F.2.h.). Specific concerns of social injustice within the school context, grounded in issues of race and ethnicity, gender, class, disability status, and sexual orientation, have negative effects on student outcomes (Williams & Greenleaf, 2012). Statistical results consistently show that racial-ethnic minority students are disproportionately represented in special education referral, assessment, and placement procedures; endure more severe punishments in response to misbehaviors in schools; are judged more harshly for minor infractions, and don't receive similar consequences as White students. These types of inequities and disparities within the U.S. school system "signify the need for professionals to make a more concerted effort at addressing environmental factors that serve as barriers to academic, career, and personal/social development" (Williams & Greenleaf, 2012, p. 143).

Advocacy Readiness

As counseling students, learning about the issues affecting the areas you live in and areas where you may one day serve is a way to find out what the need is and how you can help. Other examples may include looking for clinical sites serving populations that are out of your comfort zone, talking with your clients and asking them what changes they would like to see, attending city council or school board meetings, and assessing the interests you have from your own personal experiences. You may also wonder, as you have been reading, how you know if you're ready to take on social injustices and become an advocate. It is a process: one that happens over time, with personal exploration and a desire to learn about various systems of oppression. Advocacy scales have been developed to help counseling students and counselors determine their level of readiness. The Social Justice Advocacy Readiness Questionnaire (SJARQ) provides a means to advocate for social justice with persons of multiple cultural identities, including all sexual orientations and gender identities (Chen-Hayes, 2001). The SJARQ instrument contains three areas of self-assessment for social services staff: individual social justice advocacy awareness, comfort, and values; cultural social justice advocacy knowledge; and institutional/systemic social justice advocacy skills. Another assessment scale is the Advocacy Competencies Self-Assessment (ACSA) Survey. The ACSA Survey was developed as a tool to help social service and education professionals understand their level of advocacy competence (Ratts & Ford, 2010). Helping professionals can use the survey to assess their comfort level with being a social change agent as it pertains to the Advocacy Competencies framework. Haskins and Singh (2016) explained the development of the School Counseling Advocacy Assessment, which measures school counselor advocacy competency and includes the psychometric results regarding the reliability and factor structure. The authors also discuss implications for school counselors and school counselors-in-training.

Clark et al. (2020) presented three specific ways in which counselors and counseling students can engage in advocacy on behalf of their clients: (a) assist clients with problem-solving and finding resources; (b) increase client access; and (c) challenge poverty stereotypes. Counselors can also offer clinical services at a reduced rate or pro bono. Likewise, counselors can offer assistance in helping clients secure access to food, shelter, financial assistance, and so on.

While the continued engagement in social justice and advocacy on behalf of and with clients is essential, it is equally important to recognize that the journey toward cultivating multicultural and social justice competence is lifelong (Ratts et al., 2016). Washington (2018) posited that social justice counseling is a theoretical and pragmatic extension of multiculturalism's fundamental premises that seeks to engender a radical redistribution of vital resources among groups. As counseling students, use your time in your clinical courses to practice at sites that may have a social justice focus, emphasize less traditional helping roles, are community-based, and can push you out of your comfort zone (Constantine et al., 2007). Doing so may allow you to sharpen your "abilities to self-reflect about issues of race, ethnicity, oppression, power, and privilege relative to your own lives and to nurture your competence in working with a broader array of individuals" (Constantine et al., 2007, p. 28). Counseling programs and students can also benefit from taking a global perspective when addressing social justice issues. Much of the literature on liberation psychology and the liberation framework were rooted in global issues (Domínguez et al., 2020; Prilleltensky & Prilleltensky, 2003; Singh, 2016; Steele, 2008).

Self-awareness is an important part of the knowledge domain, which includes developing a critical awareness regarding one's own social identities and socialization. Self-awareness also includes a continual examination of one's own biases and areas for further learning and growth in relation to multicultural issues. Having conversations with others focused on social identities and social issues can help in self-examination and help identify one's "hot buttons" and emotional reactions when communicating with others about these issues (Mallinckrodt et al., 2014, p. 307).

USING THE MULTICULTURAL AND SOCIAL JUSTICE COUNSELING COMPETENCIES TO PUT ADVOCACY INTO ACTION

At its core, *multiculturalism* is the appreciation, acceptance, and promotion of multiple ethnic cultures in society. The multicultural counseling movement, which originated in the later 1960s, represented an effort to increase counselor educators' and practitioners' understanding of and support for the important impact that clients' racial, ethnic, and cultural backgrounds and worldviews have on their mental health and psychological functioning (Brady-Amoon, 2011). The formation of multicultural competencies dates back to 1982, when a task force was commission to develop a multicultural counseling competency. The birth of the Multicultural Counseling Competencies (MCC) took place in 1992 (Sue et al., 1992). In continuing the counseling profession's multicultural promise, two landmark articles were created: the "Multicultural Counseling Competencies and Standards: A Call to the Profession" (Sue et al., 1992) and "Operationalization of the Multicultural Counseling Competencies" (Arredondo et al., 1996). These competencies served as accountability "for counselor education, clinical practice, accreditation, and university programs and organization" to continue to shape the profession's multicultural focus (Singh, Nassar, et al., 2020, p. 239).

Building upon the original MCC, the Multicultural and Social Justice Counseling Competencies' (MSJCC's) added domain of counseling and advocacy interventions mirrors the aspirational competency of action as well as the systems-level change. Explorations would take place within the context of the counseling relationship (Singh, Nassar, et al., 2020). Attaining a broader conceptualization, the levels of awareness among self, other, and relationship would lead to intentional counseling interventions that are both multiculturally appropriate and socially just. Within the context of the counseling relationship, advocacy initiatives for and on behalf of the client would also be explored, such as connecting the client with advocacy groups within the community (Singh, Nassar, et al., 2020).

According to Ratts et al. (2016), the MSJCC are a theoretical framework to implement competency within counseling theories and practice. The MSJCC is a framework similar to Urie Bronfenbrenner's Bioecological model, with different systems that intersect and interact with each other across systems and time. Both models work in a circular and centric format where the systems in which we live influence our values, beliefs, traditions, attitudes, and behaviors. The MSJCC (Ratts et al., 2016) is focused on increasing counselors' awareness and knowledge of both their own culture and the cultures of their clients, allowing counselors to tailor their counseling approaches to their clients' cultural identities. Embedded in the first three developmental domains of the MSJCC model are "aspirational competencies: attitudes and beliefs, knowledge, skills, and action" (Ratts et al., 2015, p. 3).

Time is key in Bronfenbrenner's ecological systems because all of the systems function across time in the chronosystem. If you apply the same logic to social justice and cultural competence, it is clear that as time has changed, so has how we served our clients (Keum & Miller, 2020; Mallinckrodt et al., 2014). When investigating the external environments that have an influence on and over clients, we must consider that systems, people, and customs change over time. Referencing the ecological model when working with the MSJCC model will provide context to certain issues.

People standing up for the equal rights and privileges of others has been a longstanding action, dating back to the Women's Suffrage March in 1913. Marches, boycotts, sit-ins, peaceful protests, hashtags, and other outlets have been used to demonstrate solidarity in the fight for just and fair treatment of others. However, the counseling profession as a collective could improve its efforts by heeding the words of activist Senator John Lewis to "make some noise and get into good trouble, necessary trouble" (Bote, 2020). As mentioned throughout this chapter, counselors and counseling students are in a perfect position to sound the alarm, address the issues through a unique lens, and equip marginalized and unjustly treated people with tools to advocate for themselves. It is a common belief among counselors that the client is the expert in and on their life. Therefore, when thinking about supporting a cause or creating a plan to address a need, it is important to collaborate with clients. Finding out what is of interest to them is beneficial. For advocates intending to further such related causes, a better understanding of their target population may aid in the development of strategies and campaigns that will not only deliver messages but also increase the likelihood of recruiting additional adherents to client's causes (Rafi & Baunach, 2013).

Singh, Nassar, et al. (2020) mentioned that embedded within the fourth domain of counseling and advocacy interventions are six ecological layers: intrapersonal, interpersonal, institutional, community, policy, and global/international. Parallel with the call to action now included in the aspirational competencies, these six layers provide rich opportunities to develop and practice counseling advocacy. This component of the MSJCC is perhaps the most concrete and directly applicable. These competency layers guide counselors to connect the six developmental layers to one another and heed the feminist call to "make the personal political" (Singh, Nassar, et al., 2020, p. 247). Even if the advocacy initiatives that a counselor uses do not create immediate change at the policy level, it is important to know that the counselor is working on the client's behalf and on behalf of future clients with the same concerns.

The MSJCC asks counselors to be attuned to power in the following areas: (a) counselor self-awareness, (b) client worldview, (c) counseling relationship, and (d) counseling and advocacy interventions and use of power related to attitudes and beliefs, knowledge, skills, and action (Singh, Appling, & Trepal, 2020). There are four theories that provide practical examples of how to incorporate the MSJCC which counselors can use in everyday counseling interactions to address gaps in their training: Relational Cultural Theory (RCT), critical race theory (CRT), intersectionality theory, and liberation psychology. RCT derives from the premise that people grow through and toward relationships throughout their lives and that growth-fostering relationships are the source of meaning and empowerment (Singh, Appling, & Trepal, 2020). CRT is a framework that recognizes systemic racism as part of the American society and that racism is more than just an outcome of individual bias and prejudice—it is embedded in the law, policies, and institutions of the United States (Singh, Appling, & Trepal, 2020). Intersectionality theory affirms that people are often disadvantaged by multiple sources of oppression, such as their race, gender identity, religion, socioeconomic class, and so on. These identities do not exist on their own (Singh, Appling, & Trepal, 2020). Lastly, liberation psychology aims to understand the psychology of oppressed and disadvantaged communities by actively addressing the oppressive sociopolitical structure (Singh, Appling, & Trepal, 2020).

This information is a brief summary of four theories that can provide a roadmap for counseling students to become more aware of and engaged with social justice and advocacy. Each theory also offers space for the MSJCC competencies to be utilized in counseling. A common theme among the theories is collaborating with clients to disrupt and dismantle the status quo of oppressive attitudes, actions, and social injustices within the counseling and psychology profession and larger society. Advocacy takes self-awareness, self-reflection, and understanding of the social issues and their influence on you and your client's worldview, combined with a willingness to delve into the uncomfortableness with your clients as you both navigate change. As you continue on this journey, I encourage you to read more about each theory listed above and to seek knowledge on advocacy and social justice beyond your required reading and across different disciplines.

CLINICAL CASE SCENARIO 4.1: POWER IN A NAME

The following case study addresses one of many common social injustices that occur in our daily lives and provides context for how to be more aware of and argue for change as a way to bring social justice to the current and persistent issues.

Sterling is an African American woman in her mid-30s who works as an Assistant Dean of Student Services at a private college along the bible belt of the East Coast. Each month, Sterling treats herself to a massage, pedicure, and manicure as her self-care. Recently she had been thinking about taking on some new ventures to expand her knowledge and understanding of the world—she decided she wanted to learn a new language. Growing up, Sterling studied French because she wanted to be a famous fashion designer who worked and lived in Paris. She also took American Sign Language in college. However, she wanted to learn a language she would use, and she decided to take Vietnamese. Having gone to a nail salon for more than 20 years, she witnessed many things and often wondered what was being said when the nail technicians spoke in their native tongue. One Saturday as Sterling sat in the chair, thinking about learning a new language, she noticed that the customers called the nail technicians common American names rather than ethnocentric names. She wondered why the nail technicians did not use their native names, but she already knew the answer—it was easier for White customers. Sterling noticed that placating or operating from a Eurocentric focus had been the modality at every nail salon Sterling had visited across multiple states. She noticed that the nail technicians would use common names such as Jenny, Becky, Tony, and Tommy. They would offer White patrons water or wine and would provide hand massages for nail services other than manicures. Simultaneously, the offer of water or wine and an accompanying massage was not made to patrons of color, who often spent as much if not more money than their White counterparts. Sterling thought, "Is changing a key trait of who you are okay to do if it means you gain financial success?" The thoughts continued, "Do they see injustice in what they feel is necessary for them to do, and do they realize their actions are leading to harm? Do they care?" Sterling

(continued)

CLINICAL CASE SCENARIO 4.1: POWER IN A NAME (CONTINUED)

wanted to ask some of the questions swirling in her head, but she didn't know if that exact moment was the right time and if it was even an issue she wanted to be responsible for bringing awareness to.

CLINICAL CASE SCENARIO DISCUSSION QUESTIONS

1. How do you feel about Sterling's experience?
2. What would you do if you were in Sterling's position?
3. What social injustices happen around you that you have not paid much attention to? And why not?
4. Considering the MSJCC model, what do you believe to be your level of awareness regarding Sterling's case and other similar examples? What are you willing to do differently if you feel you could be more aware?
5. Moving into phase 2 of the Liberation Model, what voices are being heard in the counseling literature, and could any help Sterling navigate her next steps?

END-OF-CHAPTER RESOURCES

A robust set of instructor resources designed to supplement this text is located at http://connect.springerpub.com/content/book/978-0-8261-3953-5. Qualifying instructors may request access by emailing **textbook@springerpub.com**.

SUMMARY

This chapter aimed to explain multiple concepts of social justice and injustice while providing examples of why social justice is important. As the fifth force in counseling, social justice has been a key concept that the profession strives to attain and maintain. In recent years, a series of competencies developed and endorsed by different divisions within the ACA (MCC, MSJCC) have been utilized in our practice, pedagogy, and research. Members of the helping profession can address the injustices that demand resolution at different intersecting systems in a myriad of ways. The ACA encourages advocacy and provides guidelines for how counselors can advocate for and support their clients as they find the ability to advocate for themselves. Social justice awareness and action spiked during the racial and COVID-19 pandemics and presented novel ways in which counselors, counseling students, clients, and people seeking change can use our voices and talents to speak up and speak out about the injustice and inequities we see or experience. By utilizing the Liberation Model and MSJCC frameworks in conjunction with social justice-based theories to teach a culturally sensitive curriculum and challenge all students to acknowledge and address current and persistent societal issues, we can effect change on a large scale, thereby creating change in the lives of the individuals we serve. My aim as the author of this chapter was to advocate for sustained change within the profession by using counseling literature, pop culture, and different forms of media to highlight that people who have endured social injustices will use what they have to voice their lived experiences, hoping to bring awareness and change. As counseling students, you will keep the counseling profession moving forward; therefore, I challenge you to dive deeper into uncomfortable situations where social injustices find life. Small steps lead to big change. What will your first step be?

DISCUSSION QUESTIONS

1. What social injustices are you aware of and would like to help advocate?
2. How do you feel liberation psychology or the Liberation Model would be helpful in developing cultural competence and social justice awareness?
3. Reviewing the MSJCC Framework, what area would you work on to see continued growth?
4. How will you use any new self-awareness or new societal awareness to support client collaboration in reversing the status quo?
5. How will you challenge yourself to bring about societal change and sit in uncomfortable conversations with peers and clients?

KEY REFERENCES

Only key references appear in the print edition. The full reference list appears in the digital product on Springer Publishing Connect: https://connect.springerpub.com/content/book/978-0-8261-3953-5/part/part01/chapter/ch04

American Counseling Association. (2014). *2014 ACA Code of Ethics*. Author. https://www.counseling.org/docs/default-source/default-document-library/2014-code-of-ethics-finaladdress.pdf

Chung, R. C.-Y., & Bemak, F. P. (2012). *Social justice counseling: The next steps beyond multiculturalism* (pp. 25–52). SAGE Publications. https://www.doi.org/10.4135/9781452240503.n3

Constantine, M. G., Hage, S. M., Kindaichi, M. M., & Bryant, R. M. (2007). Social justice and multicultural issues: Implications for the practice and training of counselors and counseling psychologists. *Journal of Counseling & Development*, 85(1), 24–29. https://doi.org/10.1002/j.1556-6678.2007.tb00440.x

Mallinckrodt, B., Miles, J. R., & Levy, J. J. (2014). The scientist-practitioner-advocate model: Addressing contemporary training needs for social justice advocacy. *Training and Education in Professional Psychology*, 8(4), 303–311. https://doi.org/10.1037/tep0000045

Nadal, K. L. (2017). "Let's get in formation": On becoming a psychologist-activist in the 21st century. *The American Psychologist*, 72(9), 935–946. https://doi.org/10.1037/amp0000212

Ratts, M. J. (2009). Social justice counseling: Toward the development of a fifth force among counseling paradigms. *The Journal of Humanistic Counseling, Education and Development*, 48(2), 160–172. https://doi.org/10.1002/j.2161-1939.2009.tb00076.x

Ratts, M. J., & Ford, A. (2010). Advocacy competencies self-assessment (ACSA) survey©: A tool for measuring advocacy competence. In M. J. Ratts, R. L. Toporek, & J. A. Lewis (Eds.), *ACA advocacy competencies: A social justice framework for counselors* (pp. 21–26). American Counseling Association.

Ratts, M. J., Singh, A. A., Nassar-McMillan, S., Butler, S. K., & McCullough, J. R. (2016). Multicultural and social justice counseling competencies: Guidelines for the counseling profession. *Journal of Multicultural Counseling and Development*, 44(1), 28–48. https://doi.org/10.1002/jmcd.12035

Singh, A. A. (2016). Moving from affirmation to liberation in psychological practice with transgender and gender nonconforming clients. *The American Psychologist*, 71(8), 755–762. https://doi.org/10.1037/amp0000106

Singh, A. A., Appling, B., & Trepal, H. (2020). Using the multicultural and social justice counseling competencies to decolonize counseling practice: The important roles of theory, power, and action. *Journal of Counseling & Development*, 98(3), 261–271. https://doi.org/10.1002/jcad.12321

Singh, A. A., Nassar, S. C., Arredondo, P., & Toporek, R. (2020). The past guides the future: Implementing the multicultural and social justice counseling competencies. *Journal of Counseling & Development*, 98(3), 238–252. https://doi.org/10.1002/jcad.12319

SECTION II: THE CLIENT'S WORLDVIEW

CHAPTER 5

Culturally Responsive Counseling for Clients of African American, African, and Afro-Caribbean Descent

LAVERNE HANES COLLINS AND ALFONSO L. FERGUSON

LEARNING OBJECTIVES

After reading this chapter, students will be able to:

- Recognize the ethnic and cultural diversity within the African diaspora in the United States and discuss implications for clinical practice.
- Interpret the impact of heritage, attitudes, beliefs, understandings, and acculturative experiences when counseling people of African descent.
- Identify theories and models that may be applied when counseling people of the African diaspora in the United States.
- Describe the historical challenges and everyday stressors and challenges facing individuals of African descent in the United States

SELF-REFLECTION QUESTIONS

1. When assessing treatment readiness, how can a counselor distinguish between their own treatment biases and their clients' treatment barriers?
2. African Americans, Afro-Caribbeans, and African immigrants are often viewed collectively as Black. Why is it essential for counselors to understand the differences in each group's history?
3. How does a legacy of slavery and racial discrimination adversely affect African Americans' mental and physical health?

This chapter explores the major counseling considerations related to the African Diaspora in the United States. *Diaspora* refers to any individuals living away from their original homeland. In this discussion, the African Diaspora in America will include African Americans, Afro-Caribbeans, Black Africans (emigrants from the Sub-Saharan region of Africa), and Africans emigrating from other places. Throughout the chapter, we use the term "people of African descent" to refer to this collective. This also includes individuals who identified as Black or African American in combination with one other race (biracial) or in combination with more than one other race or ethnicity (multiracial) in the U.S. Census. According to the Pew Research Center (2021), between 2000 and 2019 these sectors of America's population increased from 36.2 million to 46.8 million people. Roughly 10% are foreign-born.

People of African descent in America have different lived realities that largely depend on the circumstances by which they or their ancestors arrived on U.S. soil. Despite their diversity, they find themselves broadly categorized into a collective racial identity. This chapter honors the diversity as well as the commonalities among them. Here, we discuss the cultures, worldviews, and historical considerations that are important for developing multicultural awareness in counseling. The goal is to prepare counselors to give culturally responsive attention to the psychological and relational needs of people of African descent.

THE COUNSELOR: EXPLORATION, INTROSPECTION, AND REFLECTION

Counselors do well to understand the beliefs and experiences of their clients and themselves as service providers. The beginning of the 21st century brought an awakened reality to America and the world. With the 2008 election and 2012 re-election of Barack Obama as the first U.S. president with direct African ancestry, America appeared to commence upon a new race narrative. The reality was that anti-Black racism had not been asleep and was adversely affecting the mental health of people of African descent (Williams, 2018). The 2020 report on hate crime statistics released by the Federal Bureau of Investigation (FBI) indicated that 63.6% of hate-crime victims in 2020 were targeted because of the offender's bias against race, ethnicity, or ancestry (FBI, 2021). The report stated that among single-bias hate crime incidents in 2020, there were 4,939 reported victims of race/ethnicity/ancestry motivated hate crimes. More than 55% of those were motivated by anti-Black/African American bias, a higher percentage than any other reported group.

A Harvard study on mental health and race-related stressors highlighted multiple ways racism can affect mental health risks for members of racialized groups (Williams, 2018). Mental health counselors are in a position to hear how clients of African descent have experienced bias, bigotry, discrimination, and other forms of trauma. The counselor's task is to listen without further victimizing clients with any bias of their own. That charge would be easy, except that the Eurocentric orientation from which many helping professionals serve can create blind spots and systemic bias, even within the context of counseling.

Counselor Bias Versus Treatment Barriers

In the mental health profession, clients are often seen as having a psychological or psychosocial barrier to treatment if their values or beliefs cause them to dismiss counseling as a solution to a problem. In this chapter, we suggest a paradigm shift. We do not refer to cultural, social, or individual values and beliefs as barriers to care. Consider a barrier to be present when someone *desires* access to something that they cannot easily acquire. Lack of transportation, finances, and childcare are some examples of barriers to care. Unchecked counselor bias is in effect when we persist with interventions that do not align with the clients' customs, preferences, or practices or when we label their preferred intervention as a barrier.

As we explore the worldviews of people of African descent, we encourage readers to challenge their definition of treatment barriers. For example, suppose an African American person wants to receive mental health care but lives in an area where the closest provider is two hours away, and internet access is spotty. That person has treatment barriers that limit their access to services. However, suppose that person has full access to mental health care but chooses to employ a religious or spiritual practice to manage their problem. In that instance, it is purely a matter of values and preferences, not a barrier. Section A.4.b. of the American Counseling Association (ACA; 2014) *Code of Ethics* says, "Counselors are aware of—and avoid imposing—their own values, attitudes, beliefs, and behaviors" (p. 5). Counselors refrain from imposing their values as the standard for how others receive help.

The Counselor's Race Narrative

One way for counselors to look introspectively at how their values have been influenced is to write their personal race narrative. The exercise of writing a race narrative allows the counselor to think about how their identity, perceptions, emotional reactions, behavior, and interpersonal interactions are affected by their experiences (Godsil & Goodale, 2013; Gooden, 2021). The following list provides examples of race narrative questions that assist a counselor in examining what they have learned about race and what they have done with race-based experiences.

Sample Race Narrative Questions

1. How do you self-describe racially? Ethnically? Has that changed over time?
2. When growing up, how did your family of origin self-describe racially/ethnically?
3. What were the messages (implicit or explicit) you took in growing up about *your* race? About *other* races?
4. Do you see yourself as marginalized or privileged? When responding, please consider whether you have race privilege, economic privilege, both, or neither.
5. What was your age and the first impression the first time you saw or met a person of another race?

Providers of mental health services are not immune to the cultural influences, biases, and stereotyped expectations of racialized populations. The power in a person's race narrative is in its promptings to recognize the origins of assumptions and beliefs (Godsil & Goodale, 2013; Gooden, 2021). The ethical practice of counseling demands this kind of exploration, introspection, and reflection.

The Influence of Colorblindness in a Counselor

"I don't see color" may be an innocent comment, but it may also reflect a lack of cultural awareness. It minimizes the reality of painful race-based experiences, excuses people from examining their own biases, and may even suggest that race-based differences do not matter. The truth is that America has *always* seen color but has not seen color *equitably*. "Skin color was and is a badge of difference" (Boyd-Franklin, 2003, p. 9).

Color was the basis of slavery in America (DeGruy, 2017), and chattel slavery set the context for treating people of African descent as inferior (Boyd-Franklin, 2003). Chattel slavery was a system of buying, owning, and controlling human beings—and their offspring—as property. Some historians estimate that between 20 and 30 million Africans were taken into slavery and transported over the course of about 400 years (DeGruy, 2017). Other estimates top 100 million, including those who died crossing the Atlantic

(Richards, 1980). Those who survived became unpaid laborers that could be bought, sold, killed, or traded at will (DeGruy, 2017). This kind of enslavement was legally practiced in America from the early 1500s until the ratification of the 13th Amendment in December 1865 (DeGruy, 2017; Gates & Yacovone, 2016).

From chattel slavery to today, being a person of African descent in America has brought unparalleled paradox. Black is still an identity that is experienced as *visible* and *invisible* at the same time because a person who says, "I don't see color" is making a statement about how they engage with a person of color. Black life can be *valued* and *devalued* by the same systems because while the life of a working slave in the fields was devalued and demeaned, the capture of an escaped slave brought a bountiful reward. Slaves could be involved in the construction of a building as laborers. Later, they could be denied the services offered in that same building, so their Black lives became *relevant* and *irrelevant* in the same space. Black is an identity that is *free* and *bound* at the same moment because the community-based burden of suspicion often overrules the Constitutionally based presumption of innocence until proven guilty. Clients may experience this and not have words to express the dichotomy and the incongruence.

Counselors must invite conversations about race to come from the background to the foreground of their clinical work. The way people of African descent have learned to respond to racial identity and discrimination issues is unconsciously woven into the fabric of their very lives. It can affect everything. The counselor's task is to personally seat themselves in a position of cultural humility and then seat their clients in a place of interpersonal dignity. It is like a seating arrangement in the counselor's mind. Counselors will more effectively serve people of African descent and other groups from this position. Rather than striving to be colorblind, counselors must strive for color-consciousness.

WHAT IT MEANS TO BE OF AFRICAN DESCENT IN AMERICA

"Due to the pervasive nature of structural racism in the United States, no Black person in America (regardless of their country of origin or ancestry) is immune from the effects of racism" (Lloyd et al., 2021, p. 1). Before healing work can begin, the counselor must understand the origins of anti-Blackness and have an awareness of the intergenerational trauma held by people of African descent. Intergenerational trauma is a phenomenon in which trauma is passed down from one generation to subsequent generations (American Psychological Association, n.d.). Survivors' responses to intergenerational trauma often show strong emotions, such as shame, increased guilt, anxiety, depression, suicidality, hypervigilance, relationship issues, and so on (American Psychological Association, n.d.). Counselors must be able to comprehend the ways that anti-Blackness and race-based trauma are perpetuated in contemporary society through interpersonal, institutional, and systemic racism.

America's Black/White Binary Paradigm

When addressing race relations in America, the automatic and initial reference point is the historically complex relationship between White and Black Americans. America's reductionist approach to race has served a long-standing purpose. "Race creates a caste-based system that positions certain people to be granted privileges and others not" (Archer, 2021, p. 13). "Race does the heavy lifting for a caste system that demands a means of human division" (Wilkerson, 2020, p. 18). Chattel slavery could not have been sustained without a delineation of the powerful versus the powerless. Race became the power broker's currency for end-to-end control over the lucrative slave trade.

A person who has not owned slaves or stolen directly from indigenous people may wonder what responsibility they have for that. Wilkerson (2020) suggests that America has inherited this caste system and compares its management to maintaining an old house. We may not have built it, but the deterioration in the form of cracks, ruptures, and other damage is now ours to repair. In the counseling room, counselors have the opportunity to initiate processes that bring healing and repair to the house we did not build but have inherited.

Wilkerson further notes that Europeans would not have identified themselves as White until coming to North America as much as they would have self-identified by their nationality. "They went from being Czech or Hungarian or Polish to being White, a political designation that only has meaning when set against something not White" (Wilkerson, 2020, p. 49). The primary classification of White came when they learned where they were positionally in the New World hierarchy (Roediger, 2006; Wilkerson, 2020). "It was in the making of the New World that Europeans become white, Africans become black and everyone else yellow, red, or brown" (Wilkerson, 2020, p. 53).

Similarly, Africans were not called Black in their homeland. They were historically and proudly known by their people groups such as Ewe, Akan, Igbo, and so on. In America, African slaves were denied the right to hold on to any sense of dignity or heritage. Their languages, customs, attire, rituals, religions, and names were banned. Slavery tore families apart; assigned ownership of children to plantation owners rather than to parents; and denied slaves the right to marry, the right to say "no," and the right to due process of the law. The system of the New World necessitated that people be separated, classified, and polarized based on what they looked like, and then ranked in a system called race (Wilkerson, 2020).

Whiteness is still positioned as the norm in unspoken ways, while other groups are racialized in the United States. In social conversations among Whites, people spoken of are usually presumed to be White unless described as Black or some other race. "Words such as 'ethnic' and 'race' are supposed to refer to the out-group rather than the in-group" (Archer, 2021, p. 14). "We may mention 'race' referring to people as Black or White or Latino or Asian or Indigenous when what lies beneath each label is centuries of history and assigning of assumptions and values to physical features in a structure of human hierarchy" (Wilkerson, 2020, p. 18).

IDENTITY DEVELOPMENT: IMPACT OF WHITE PRIVILEGE AND INTERNALIZED RACISM

Identity development is based on whom the individual believes they are in relation to the rest of the world. What are the aspects of self that a person thinks about? How do they psychologically position themselves relative to others? These types of internal questions are the basis of identity development. Several models of racial identity development have been theorized over the years. These models expand upon the concept popularized by Erik Erikson, whose seminal work considered race, ethnicity, and culture in his theorizing (Erikson, 1968; Phinney, 1989; Syed & Fish, 2018). Most models theorize movement from a negative or less desirable sense of self to a healthier sense of self.

The origination point in one's racial identity development is typically influenced by conscious or unconscious biases where White privilege, White norms, and internalized racism give power to negative societal messages that influence the individual's sense of self. The process of identity development may involve the undoing of anti-Black values, a progressive movement toward understanding, self-awareness, ownership, balance, and a healthier sense of self. In the following we highlight a few racial identity theories as an introduction and invitation for the reader to pursue independent learning in this vital field of study.

- William Cross conceptualized the People of Color Racial Identity Model, originally known as the Nigrescense Model of African American Identity. Cross focused on stages whereby he believed African Americans came to understand their identity (Cross, 2001; Cross & Fhagen-Smith, 2001).
- Jean Phinney developed the Multigroup Ethnic Identity Measure (MEIM). The MEIM is used to examine similarities and differences in ethnic identity among youths from different ethnic groups (Phinney, 1992). Poston (1990) theorized that biracial individuals experience conflict and periods of maladjustment in their identity development process.
- The Ethnic Minority Identity Development Model was developed by John Berry to look at ethnic minorities broadly. The first dimension concerns native culture retention or rejection. The second dimension concerns new culture adoption or rejection. Four possible acculturation strategies emerge: (a) assimilation, (b) separation, (c) integration, or (d) marginalization (Berry, 1992).
- Janet Helms (2020) conceptualized a White Racial Identity Development Model. In this model, the goal is for the White person to grow to feel safe and secure enough to nurture their Whiteness as they personally define it. From that position, they can proactively work to identify and actively confront racism.
- Joy and John Hoffman (1985) developed an integrated model addressing the identity development of People of Color and White people. This framework begins with the Conformity stage and moves to the final stage for both groups: Integrative Awareness. People of Color are believed to move from dissonance, as they experience discrepancies between racial idealism and reality, to a stage where, instead of seeing any particular group as the enemy, they see problems like racism and sexism as the object of their fight (Hoffman, 1985).

With Whiteness as the norm, people of African descent may experience a form of internalized racism. Internalized racism "leads people to internalize beliefs and stereotypes about their racial/ethnic (RE) group and/or about themselves because of their RE group membership" (Drexler, 2020, p. 785). Internalized racism results in disparaging beliefs about one's ethnic group based upon biases that occur in society. Disparaging beliefs often come from reproachful labels and nomenclature.

AFRICAN AMERICANS: OVERCOMING A LEGACY OF SLAVERY AND SEGREGATION

The 13th Amendment abolished slavery in the United States in 1865 (Gates & Yacovone, 2016). In 2020, people of African descent had been free for only 155 years. This means that most Americans in 2020 were only three generations away from slavery. So, the notion that slavery was "a long time ago" lacks relative accuracy. During the era of legalized slavery, slave-holding families built intergenerational wealth to which African Americans did not have access. Post-slavery, segregation continued to limit African American opportunity. Although slavery became illegal, brutality against people of African descent did not.

A 2020 report by the Equal Justice Initiative documented nearly 6,500 racial terror lynchings from the end of the Civil War to 1950 (Equal Justice Initiative, 2020). Almost one-third of those lynchings took place in the 12 years immediately after the Civil War, between 1865 and 1876. While these numbers are staggering, it is known that countless lynchings were never documented (Equal Justice Initiative, 2020; Taylor, 2019). Friends and relatives of victims were forced to watch or later find the bodies of their lifeless loved ones. Those who committed these acts went unpunished. For grieving families, it became a part of the family history.

In August 1955, Emmett Till was a 14-year-old African American Chicago native. While visiting family in Money, Mississippi, Till was accused of flirting with a White woman in a local store. Four days later, the woman's husband and brother-in-law abducted Emmett Till from his great uncle's house during the night. The men beat the boy until his face was unrecognizable, gouged out his eye, shot him in the head, tied a 75-pound cotton gin around his neck, and threw his body into the Tallahatchie River. An all-White, male jury acquitted Emmett's murderers after less than an hour of deliberation. His accuser later recanted her testimony, admitting that the boy had neither harassed, touched, nor threatened her.

In May 2020, 46-year-old George Floyd, an African American male, died on a Minneapolis street when a police officer held his knee on Mr. Floyd's neck for almost nine minutes. More than once, Mr. Floyd stated, "I can't breathe," before becoming unresponsive as onlookers begged the officer to stop. There were eyewitnesses and video recordings which showed that Mr. Floyd was unarmed and incapacitated. Mr. Floyd's death was one of many recorded incidents where an unarmed African American person died without due process. Security footage and witness videos revealed that there was no evidence of the police officers fearing for their lives, no evidence of a split-second decision in self-defense, no evidence of the need for excessive force in detaining Mr. Floyd. The image flooded social media and mainstream news media for the whole world to see. Floyd's death brought people of all races to the streets protesting police brutality against Black men and women. This time, there was a guilty verdict and a conviction.

The rate of fatal police shootings in the United States shows significant differences based on race. For people of African descent in America, the rate of fatal police shootings between 2015 and February 2021 stood at 35 per million of the population. For White Americans, the rate stood at 14 fatal police shootings per million of the population (Statista Research Department, 2021). A 2004 study found that subconscious stereotypes about African Americans influenced police officers' split-second decisions about the use of deadly force, resulting in a disproportionate number of Black victims of police shootings (Lee, 2017).

These are but a few of the race-based injustices and assaults that form the historical and contemporary backdrop of diasporic Africans. They are representative of the historical, intergenerational, and race-based trauma experienced by families from slavery to today. The residual effects of slavery are defined as "ways in which the racist treatment of African Americans, during and after slavery, has impacted multiple generations of African Americans" (Wilkins et al., 2013, p. 15). Yet, treatment systems typically do not acknowledge the intergenerational effects of slavery as targets for treatment (Mullan-Gonzalez, 2012).

African American Mental Health in America

Overall, mental health conditions for African American people occur at about the same or lower frequency as for White Americans (Substance Abuse and Mental Health Services Administration [SAMHSA], 2018). However, this can be easily misinterpreted if not considered within a historical context. The task of the mental health counselor is to remember that the historical experience of people of African American descent has been marked by trauma and violence at much greater frequency and prevalence rates than for their White counterparts. This trauma and violence have an adverse impact upon the mental and emotional health of African American adults, adolescents, and children. Counselors also need to understand how hope, resilience, and distinct cultural commitments serve as pillars upon which African Americans have survived through it all.

According to the National Survey on Drug Use and Health, 6.5 million Black adults (age 18 or older) reported having a mental illness and/or substance use disorder in 2019 (SAMHSA, 2020). This is an increase of more than 10% compared to 2018 (SAMHSA, 2020). Approximately 5.2 million Black people reported having a mental illness, and 23% of those (1.2 million people) reported a serious mental illness over the past year (SAMHSA, 2020). The rate of serious mental illness (SMI) rose among Black people of all ages between 2008 and 2019 (SAMHSA, 2020).

The rates of major depressive episodes for Black people in the United States between 2016 and 2019 were notably increased. For Black youth between 12 and 17 years of age, major depressive episodes increased from 9.1% to 11.4%. For Black young adults between 18 and 25 years old, major depressive episodes increased from 7.1% to 11.3%. In the age range from 26 to 49 years old, the rate of major depressive episodes increased from 5.7% to 6.9% during that same time period. For those 50 and older, the rate of major depressive episodes increased from 3.3% to 3.8% (SAMHSA, 2020).

The American Psychiatric Association (2017) report on African American Mental Health Disparities revealed that Black and African American people are more often diagnosed with schizophrenia and less often diagnosed with mood disorders, compared to White people with the same symptoms. Additionally, they are offered medication or therapy at lower rates than the general population. The same report showed that Black and African American people with mental health conditions, specifically those involving psychosis, are more likely to be in jail or prison than are people of other races. The fruit of that history is a general reluctance to accept services from a system that has not always engaged in beneficent and non-malevolent care.

Pandemic Effects on the Mental Health of African Americans

The World Health Organization (WHO) is the United Nations' agency that directs and coordinates the world's response to health emergencies (WHO, n.d.). On March 11, 2020, WHO declared the novel coronavirus known as COVID-19 to be a pandemic (WHO, 2020). COVID-19 brought sickness, death, and financial loss to people around the world. However, in the United States, due to multidimensional inequities and health disparities, African Americans were disproportionately impacted (Office for National Statistics, 2020), and the mental health effects of COVID-19 were notable in this historically resilient population.

The stresses and losses of the COVID-19 economic downturn, including losses of jobs, income, insurance, housing, health, loved ones, and support systems, hit low-income African Americans hard. As a result, they faced increased risks of depression, anxiety, substance use, and suicide (Snowden & Snowden, 2021). Stay-at-home orders, social distancing, and isolation during the pandemic limited a person's connection to their support systems, increasing the risk of developing stress- or grief-related response, and added to the vulnerability of those with preexisting mental health conditions.

Fears of infection and mistrust of vaccine protocols were high among African Americans. High representation as essential workers in transportation, fuel, food production, warehouses, grocery stores, delivery services, and healthcare impacted safety and created even greater susceptibility to burnout, mental illness, and substance abuse. Meanwhile, the African American community's reluctance to seek mental health treatment remained notable for historical reasons.

AFRICAN AMERICAN CULTURE

Family Life

Boyd-Franklin (2003) notes that although clients typically come to counseling for help with problems, it is important for counselors to adopt a strengths-based approach, rather than a deficit-based approach, to client care with African Americans. Some notable family and cultural strengths within African American communities include strong orientations toward kinship bonds and extended family relationships; work; education and achievement; and spirituality and religion (Boyd-Franklin, 2003). While these tend to be central themes in African American families, some of these attributes are unrecognized or overlooked by Whites whose expectations can be influenced by their own cultural experience or expectations.

Family constellations may look very different in African American homes. Kinship ties and collectivistic philosophy are at the heart of African American family life. African Americans inherited a legacy of families being torn apart on African soil and again on American soil through the slave trade. As a result, a culture of non-biological family relationships emerged, often including extended families and non-biological "just-like-family" relationships. Some literature refers to this last category as "fictive kin" or "play family," but the bond of a "just-like-family" relationship carries the same significance as biological family and plays an important role in the overall well-being of family members (Chatters et al., 1994).

Life at home often includes three or four generations, as well as extended family members such as cousins, aunts, and uncles. The U.S. Census Bureau reported that the percentage of African American grandparents living with children under 18 is 4.9%. Among those, 40.4% reported being responsible for their grandchildren (U.S. Census Bureau, 2021).

Economically speaking, a 2020 report released by the Joint Economic Committee revealed that the median wealth of Black families ($17,000) is less than one-tenth that of White families ($171,000; Joint Economic Committee, 2020). The report adds that during the majority of the past 50 years, if Black Americans' unemployment rates were experienced by the entire population, it would be recessionary. In other words, people of African descent experience recessionary times even when the rest of the country does not.

Despite the Black–White wealth gap, Black/African American families still have a full range of annual household income stratification: 19% are working poor/impoverished (under $15,000), 13% are working class and working poor ($15,000–$25,000), 25% are working class ($25,000–$50,000), 36% are middle class ($50,000–$150,000), 4% are upper middle class ($150,000–$200,000), and 3% are upper class ($200,000 and over; U.S. Census Bureau, 2019).

Boyd-Franklin (2003) also noted that unemployment rates and public assistance enrollments are unjustly used to suggest that a poor work ethic exists among African Americans. She points out that a number of researchers have discussed the emphasis on work and ambition in African American families. These studies found that much of the literature tends to overlook the strength of this attribute. "In truth, labeling African Americans as 'chronically unemployed' is just a way of blaming the victims for the economic and social situation that has created their victimization" (Boyd-Franklin, 2003, p. 21).

Life Expectancy and Health

Research shows that the experience of racism damages health and shortens one's life expectancy by promoting genes that lead to inflammation and illness (Thames et al.,

2019). The study found that "differential exposure to racial discrimination may contribute to racial disparities in health outcomes in part by activating threat-related molecular programs that stimulate inflammation and contribute to increased risk of chronic illnesses" (Thames et al., 2019, p. 277). "Racism leads directly or indirectly to greater poverty, a less healthful environment, poorer health, fewer physician visits, poorer pregnancy care, poorer nutrition, and poorer access to health care" (Rosenblatt & Wallace, 2005, p. 1).

In 2020, the life expectancy for the total U.S. population was 77.3 years. For non-Hispanic Whites born in 2020, the life expectancy was 77.6 years. For non-Hispanic Blacks born in 2020, the life expectancy dropped to 71.8 years, creating a life expectancy advantage of almost 6 years for Whites (Arias et al., 2021). The gap is widened for men, with African American men having a life expectancy 7 years shorter than White men (Arias et al., 2021). This shorter life span affects African American families in multiple ways, but most notably in the experience of grief and loss.

The shorter life expectancy often means losing parents, siblings, and spouses at a younger age than White Americans. The loss of a close relative at a young age can be devastating and carry lasting effects. Research suggests that early parental losses in childhood are tied to behavioral and emotional problems in adolescents and depression in adults (Pham et al., 2018). The emotional burden of the loss is further complicated if the bereaved family recognizes the impact of racism and concludes that their loved one may have lived longer in a world without health disparities and racial inequities (Rosenblatt & Wallace, 2005).

Expectation of Strength

For survival, members of all the African-related ethnicities have historically needed to sustain high levels of problem tolerance in response to their lived experiences. Consistent with that, the necessary and learned response of African Americans who face varying degrees of oppression and discrimination is one of inner resilience (DeGruy, 2017). Strength, not vulnerability, was the key to survival. Messages of hope historically suggested that "your ancestors were strong enough to survive slavery, and you're strong enough to survive this!" or "You'll never have to carry more than you can bear." High problem tolerance produces a mindset of "just wait it out," and "this, too, will pass" or simply, "I'm okay; I got this!" This self-ascribed strength has always been a part of Black communities (Office of the U.S. Surgeon General et al., 2001). The values of self-protective strength, privacy, and fortitude support the strong Black persona, but the stress of being strong is often overlooked. That makes religion and spirituality of utmost importance.

Religion and Spirituality

Churches have historically been a pillar of the African American community and an emblem of cultural independence (Gates, 2021). African Americans tend to report more religious influence than other racial groups, as indicated by the percentages who report that: they believe in God with absolute certainty, religion is very important to them, they pray daily, or they attend religious services at least once per week (Pew Research Center, 2014).

Studies also show that individuals experience shorter recovery times, fewer hospitalizations, and fewer relapses when faith is included in their wellness planning (Tarver, 2016). This may be of particular importance for African Americans. "A 2009 survey of individuals with mental health conditions and family members conducted by the California Mental Health and Spirituality Initiative revealed that 88% of African

Americans agreed or strongly agreed that faith is an essential component to their or their family member's wellness" (Tarver, 2016, para. 2).

There is great variety in religious affiliations of people of African descent in the United States, but regardless of denominational affiliation, the church continues to be the primary place to seek support, systemic change, and comfort (Gates, 2021). With the deep historical involvement of the Black Church in all aspects of the community and individuals' lives, many African Americans prefer their local churches as a viable alternative to professional mental health intervention. They may fear that a secular counselor will misunderstand what guides them, judge their beliefs, or perhaps even try to divest them of their faith (Rollins, 2009). Additionally, a small but growing number of African Americans are embracing the practice of African religions, as they seek to experience more of their African heritage (Boyd-Franklin, 2003).

AFRICAN IMMIGRANTS: SEEKING MORE

In 2018, there were more than 2 million Sub-Saharan immigrants in the United States. Echeverria-Estrada and Batalova (2019) noted that many African immigrants come to the United States with hopes of creating a different life and expanding the opportunities for their family members in the United States and family members still in their home country. They further noted that most of the Sub-Saharan African immigrants with lawful permanent resident status came either as immediate relatives of U.S. citizens, as refugees, or through the Diversity Visa Lottery (Echeverria-Estrada & Batalova, 2019). More than half of Sub-Saharan African immigrants were naturalized U.S. citizens in 2017.

Like African Americans and Afro-Caribbeans, the African immigrant is also subjected to racism and can be affected by discrimination, acculturation, and tokenization. Africans frequently combat assumptions that they migrated from underdeveloped countries and communities. They contend with questions like, "Did you live in a hut?" or "Did you have running water and electricity?" Though some Africans do migrate from rural areas, many originate from thriving economic communities and have acquired a competitive education. "Compared to the total foreign-born population in the United States, Sub-Saharan Africans are better educated, tend to participate in the labor force at higher rates, and are more likely to speak English at home" (Echeverria-Estrada & Batalova, 2019, p. 1). Although many African countries are considered underdeveloped based on Western standards of architectural advancement and community growth, questioning the civilization of the home country is a microaggression that can affect one's acculturation experiences and mental and emotional well-being.

The Meaning of Mental Health

To understand how Africans, particularly those with limited American acculturation, might explain mental health, it is beneficial to understand African explanations of common issues such as depression. Culturally conscious counselors will be aware that there is significant debate about the responsible use of the *Diagnostic and Statistical Manual of Mental Disorders* (5th ed.; *DSM-5*; American Psychiatric Association, 2013) symptomatology in other cultures. Diagnoses that are developed and tested in Western cultures may be invalid in different cultural settings.

Mayston et al. (2020) synthesized the results of 25 different qualitative studies conducted by different researchers on explanatory models of depression in nine Sub-Saharan African nations between 1995 and 2018. In 21 of the 25 studies from various African nations, the conditions described were seen as "mental disturbance," "sickness of the soul," or "burdened hearts." This is different from "madness," which was categorized as more severe with externalized, socially inappropriate, or destructive behaviors.

Generally speaking, Africans focus on causal factors in difficult life circumstances or events. The Mayston et al. (2020) synthesis found that cultural labels vary depending on the cause. In various African languages, there are specific words for the experiences of deep sadness, maternal child loss, and loss of loved ones (Mayston et al., 2020). Expressions such as "tired head" and "thinking too much" include many of the symptoms of major depression (Mayston et al., 2020). Other causes are associated with poverty and lack of resources for fulfilling basic needs; women being subjected to male control, dominance, or violence; possession by evil spirits (especially when the symptoms are chronic or persist over time); witchcraft; torment by ancestors who are angry because of one's conversion to Christianity or because one has failed to perform particular rituals; or curses imposed by somebody living, such as a jealous co-wife or community member (Mayston et al., 2020). Effective and culturally conscious interventions with African immigrants will recognize the culturally normative mingling of concepts associated with intrapersonal (self), interpersonal (social), and transpersonal (spiritual) worlds.

In many African cultures, mental health care and counseling specifically have not been known historically. Elders, traditional healers, spiritual leaders, and medical doctors provided care, but the very function of counseling and the role of a counselor are relatively new. As such, African clients unfamiliar with counseling as a profession may come for services at the suggestion of an American friend or associate. The counselor may find that the new client struggles to express why they are there and can only say that someone recommended they see a counselor. Counselors must be sensitive to the fact that the person may not know what to expect and may be reluctant to talk at all. They will likely view the counselor as the expert, like an Elder, rather than as the listener. As a result, the client may expect more directive assistance and less empathic listening.

People of African descent may also emigrate from other foreign countries such as Canada, France, and Great Britain, where they have had acculturation experiences. Their migration experience to the United States will be affected by the change in culture, status, and other race-based factors. Counselors who work from a place of cultural humility and cultural awareness will pay attention to how compound acculturation experiences affect the client's worldview, values, and coping strategies.

AFRO-CARIBBEAN IMMIGRANT GROUPS: STRUGGLING WITH STEREOTYPES

The Caribbean islands consist of 13 official countries and 21 territories and dependencies. "The Caribbean is the source of the U.S.'s earliest and largest Black immigrant group and the primary source of growth of the Black population in the U.S." (Frazier, 2005, p. 1). Afro-Caribbeans commonly migrate from countries where they have majority representation. Although Western ideologies of Black inferiority and socioeconomic hierarchy existed in their native lands, their racial identity did not carry minority status. Upon arriving in the United States, they must contend with a Black racial identity that carries imposed stigmas, assumptions, and beliefs.

Waters (1999) compared the differences between race relations in the Caribbean and race relations in the United States. "The Caribbean ... never had a large enough white population, nor a developed enough national culture based on that population, to develop the deep structures necessary to ingrain racism within the national consciousness" (Waters, 1999, p. 43). Deciding how to self-identify as a newcomer in a different society intersects with the question of how the new society will choose to identify the newcomer (Waters, 1999). Waters' research on West Indian immigrant identity in New York actually found that West Indians often prefer to distance themselves from the African American race label. "The immigrants did not regard having strong racial identity as meaning that they identified with black Americans. In fact, most immigrants distanced themselves from black Americans and wanted other people to know that they were not the same. They saw themselves as superior to black Americans, and they were disappointed and dismayed at the behaviors and characteristics they associated with black Americans" (Waters, 1999, p. 65). Some respondents in Waters' study preferred the term "Black" because in comparison to the term "African American" it left more room for ethnic distinctiveness within the racial collective. Others objected to the use of African American as a racial identifier simply because they did not come to the United States from Africa, and they resented the association (Waters, 1999).

In the three decades immediately following the 1965 immigration reform, West Indian immigrants had higher labor force participation rates, higher earnings, and higher educational goals and attainment than African Americans at that time (Deaux et al., 2007; Kalmijn, 1996; Model, 1991). The determination to achieve and perform gave rise to microaggressions and stereotypes.

Benjamin (n.d.) gives examples of common stereotypes such as Jamaicans having lots of jobs, living a Rastafarian lifestyle, practicing Voodoo, smoking marijuana, always being late, being skilled runners, and ending every sentence with "Mon." Gender role stereotypes portray Island men as womanizers and Island women as great sex partners. The Afro-Caribbean lifestyle is stereotyped as a carefree, leisurely, worry-free, celebratory approach to living (Benjamin, n.d.). This comes, in part, as a result of island vacation marketing. Images of beaches, marijuana, exotic umbrella drinks, and sounds of Caribbean music draw in tourists and create the impression that such a lifestyle is the experience of residents and immigrants.

Afro-Caribbeans are assumed to be more effective employees with a better work ethic than other groups (Logan, 2007; Thornton et al., 2013). Along with this stereotype comes great adulation from White employers. While many Afro-Caribbeans may feel successful as an ethnic community, some also have feelings of failure as Black persons due to feeling disconnected from the Black American community (Logan, 2007). As a result, Afro-Caribbeans in the United States may experience ambivalence in their belongingness in society because they are praised by their White counterparts for their hard work and drive while continuing to experience racism, segregation, and discrimination (Logan, 2007; Thornton et al., 2013). Like other people of African descent, Afro-Caribbeans are subject to demoralization and mental health challenges triggered by racism, economic disadvantage, sociopolitical unrest, and stereotype threat.

Deaux et al. (2007) pointed to research on stereotype threat which shows that negative stereotypes about a group's abilities and potential can undermine group members' performance. With a commitment to success and new possibilities in the United States, first-generation Afro-Caribbean immigrants thrived. Their drive gave rise to the work ethic stereotypes that became commonly accepted. Second-generation immigrants living with those stereotypes showed declines in measures of performance and economic success. This decline stands in contrast to the generational progression of earlier White immigrant groups (Deaux et al., 2007; Portes, 1995).

The Meaning of Mental Health for Afro-Caribbeans

Afro-Caribbean attitudes toward mental health are often influenced by experiences with individuals who struggled with severe mental illness before modern mental healthcare was available in the islands. Often these cases would have resulted in patients being institutionalized in highly stigmatized "insane asylums" (Mills, 2001). The harsh historical treatment of psychiatric patients in the Caribbean has reinforced a legitimate resistance to seeking mental health treatment. Mood disorders, psychosocial stressors, or trauma-induced mental health challenges may go unacknowledged and untreated.

Research conducted by Venner and Welfare (2019) suggested that Afro-Caribbean immigrants are often reluctant to seek counseling services due to stigmatization, stereotypes, and a strong belief that mental health or emotional challenges should remain private. While most of their participants denied any connection between their mental health and their ethnicity, most did highlight the importance of having space to discuss their heritage in counseling. Culturally conscious counselors will remember that for Afro-Caribbean clients, stigma may accompany a mental health diagnosis or treatment. Clients may fear bringing shame and ridicule to their family or community. Counselors will need to manage their biases about treatment-reluctant clients and help clients process any feelings of damage, inferiority, or embarrassment.

CULTURALLY RESPONSIVE PRACTICES: DRAWING FROM THE MULTICULTURAL AND SOCIAL JUSTICE COUNSELING COMPETENCIES AND CULTURAL HUMILITY

It is important for all counselors, both privileged and marginalized, to recognize how their positionality within society affects their work with the population they serve. Moreover, it is vitally important for privileged and marginalized counselors alike to continuously examine their attitudes and beliefs, knowledge, skills, and action (Ratts et al., 2015). A few African proverbs will be used to inform readers' understanding of cultural sensitivity as it relates to counselor self-awareness, the client worldview, the counseling relationship, and counseling and advocacy interventions.

Counselor Self-Awareness

"Man, know thyself" (Egyptian proverb). Privileged and marginalized counselors alike maintain ethical standards of care because they pay attention to how their own lived experiences, cultural background, and biases influence their interactions with clients. The counselor seeks an understanding of how social position informs their perception of marginalization and privilege. Culturally conscious counselors continually add to their cultural knowledge. They seek educational, consultative, and training resources to further understand how their lived experience influences their work with clients.

Client Worldview

"There can be no peace without understanding" (Senegalese proverb). Both privileged and marginalized counselors must remain cognizant of Black, Indigenous, and People of Color (BIPOC) worldviews. As discussed throughout this chapter, the Black identity is not culturally homogeneous. Counselors must consider how historical, intergenerational, and race-based trauma may affect a client's journey. Then the counselor must create a judgment-free space for African Americans, Afro-Caribbeans, and African immigrants to share their particular philosophy of life and their conception of the world.

Counseling Relationship

The counseling relationship will be heavily influenced by how the counselor presents in session. Counselors with unchecked biases will fail to communicate unconditional acceptance and empathy for the client's reality. Western or Eurocentric values must be laid aside when working with Africans in the diaspora. Process your biases as honestly as possible in clinical supervision.

Cultural Humility

"If you are filled with pride, then you will have no room for wisdom" (Tanzanian proverb). Wisdom and humility go hand in hand, just as pride and foolishness walk together (Exponencial Concursos, 2021). The humbler one is, the wiser one will be. In the counseling session, cultural humility is the antidote for viewing a client's value system as a treatment barrier. It is protection against a privileged counselor dismissing or questioning a marginalized person's experience of racism. Cultural humility recognizes the hazard of blurry vision that can only see situations from one's own perspective.

Counseling and Advocacy Interventions

"Prepare now for the solutions of tomorrow" (Congolese proverb). The last pillar of the Multicultural and Social Justice Counseling competencies focuses on how counselors advocate for their clients at the intrapersonal, interpersonal, community, public policy, and international and global affairs levels (Ratts et al., 2015). Advocacy takes the counselor's influence beyond the four walls of the counseling room, and into the halls of schools and institutions of higher education. Advocates go into city hall and community organizations and fight for equality. Advocates walk through halls where doors are closed to marginalized and disenfranchised clients to find the keys to justice. Advocates walk beside clients as they learn to use their voices that were muffled by discrimination and silenced by defeat. Every act of advocacy today sets the stage for empowerment and improvement tomorrow. While today's advocacy may only improve conditions for one, in due time, today's work will improve conditions for many.

CRAFTING AN ADVOCACY AGENDA

Culturally sensitive counselors are aware of the need to appropriately bring issues of race and culture from the background to the foreground of their clinical work. Compare that to color-blind or culture-blind counselors who do not consider contextual factors in the client's experience. For people of African descent, cultural sensitivity is often one of the most important characteristics of competence that a counselor can display (Gushue et al., 2017; Sue et al., 2019).

Counselors who gain credibility as advocates do so by acknowledging the oppressive structures affecting people of African descent. If the counselor is a member of a non-Hispanic White race or ethnicity, their credibility is strengthened when they acknowledge ways that they have benefited from a system designed to serve them and oppress others. From that position of cultural humility will come opportunities for advocacy initiatives, client empowerment, client advocacy, community collaboration, system advocacy, collective action, and social/political advocacy. As long as people of African descent continue to experience affronts to their dignity, the counselor's commitment to the client must extend beyond the counseling office.

COUNSELING CHILDREN, ADOLESCENTS, AND YOUNG ADULTS

When working with children and adolescents in families of African descent, there is a critical balance that must be attained between underdiagnosis and overdiagnosis.

Younger Black children tend to be overrepresented with emotional and behavioral diagnoses. Black adolescents tend to be overlooked regarding depression and suicide risk.

Black Children Disproportionately Diagnosed in Schools

Black children are particularly vulnerable to emotional/behavioral diagnostic disparities and can benefit from concerted advocacy efforts. Within that group, Black boys carry the greatest burden of disparate representation. This was noted as far back as the 1960s, when Dunn (1968) drew attention to the disproportionality of Black children in special education and presented a seminal work positing that special education programs may adversely affect the self-image of these children.

Townsend's (2018) study of school counselors' perceptions and effectiveness, regarding African American boys with disabilities in special education, built upon Dunn's work and sought to explain the processes leading to Black/African American boys being placed in special education from a counselor's perspective. Townsend noted that nearly 50 years after Dunn's hypothesis was presented, the African American overrepresentation that Dunn suggested was supported by data from the U.S. Department of Education's National Center for Education Statistics. The data show that among students ages 3 to 21 who are served by Individuals with Disabilities Education Act (IDEA) programs, emotional disturbance is documented as occurring at a rate of 7.4% among African American students, 7.0% among mixed-race students, and 2% to 5.5% for all other races/ethnic groups (NCES, 2016).

This data summary also suggests that Black boys are overrepresented in several disability categories. Showing that students receiving special education are likely to identify as African American, male, urban, and from low socioeconomic backgrounds (Artiles et al., 2010; Coutinho et al., 2002; Townsend, 2018). African American students have greater rates of reported emotional disturbance, cognitive disorders, learning disabilities, speech and language disorders (Townsend, 2018). The Civil Rights Data Collection (2010) reports that African American males make up 16.6% of special education students although they comprise only 8.5% of the total K–12 student population (Townsend, 2018). Therefore, school counselors need to be aware of biases within the system and must have tools for effective assessment and appropriate intervention.

Black Adolescents and Young Adults: Ring the Alarm for Suicide Risk

Black youth in the United States experience more illness, poverty, and discrimination than their White counterparts (Reeves et al., 2016). African American adolescents with mental health disorders are more likely to experience higher rates of depressive moods but are less likely to utilize mental health resources (Jon-Ubabuco & Dimmitt Champion, 2019). Unfortunately, some turn to suicide to alleviate their pain. Data from the Centers for Disease Control and Prevention show that the rate of suicide attempts for Black adolescents rose 73% from 1991 to 2017 (Lindsey et al., 2019). Suicide is now the second leading cause of death among Black adolescents (Price & Khubchandani, 2019).

In 2019, a Congressional Black Caucus report entitled "Ring the Alarm: The Crisis of Black Youth Suicide in America," from an Emergency Taskforce on Black Youth Suicide and Mental Health, noted the change in trend among Black adolescent suicide and called for action. While research has shown climbing rates for youth of other racial groups, this rate has historically been shown to be lower for Black youth, hence challenging the public perception that Black youth simply do not commit suicide (Emergency Taskforce on Black Youth Suicide and Mental Health, 2019). Suicidal ideation is often overlooked in youth, especially in families of African descent. "It was found that half of the caregivers were unaware that their child had thoughts of suicide, and rates of both parental unawareness and adolescent denial of suicidal thoughts were higher among racial minority families (most were Black)" (Lindsey et al., 2019, p. 19).

The SAMHSA (2020) reported that suicidal thoughts, plans, and attempts have also risen among Black and African American young adults. Although the rates are still lower than in the overall U.S. population between 18 and 25 years old, the SAMHSA study revealed notable increases from 2009 to 2019. Ten percent (456,000) of Black and African American 18- to 25-year-olds had serious thoughts of suicide in 2019, compared to just over 6% (303,000) in 2009. Nearly 4% (168,000) made a plan in 2019, compared to just over 2% (109,000) in 2009. Roughly 2.5% (108,000) made an attempt in 2019, compared to approximately 1.5% (74,000) in 2009. Such trends point to the need for culturally responsive counselors to be prepared to respond to the needs of these groups.

COUNSELING ADULTS, COUPLES, AND FAMILIES

Adult clients of African descent are often navigating multiple dimensions of life that are not typical or age-normative by Eurocentric standards. They may have experienced the early death of a family member. They may have grandparent guardianship or kinship care of a loved one. They may be managing some form of racial trauma or systemic racism. They may be trying to uphold the expectation to be strong at all times (Raheem & Hart, 2019).

Black men have different systemic challenges than Whites, such as disparate educational attainment and combatting the *"school-to-prison pipeline"* (Raheem & Hart, 2019, p. 1). Washington (2018) suggests that contemporary rap music provides Black males with a meaningful and relatable way of self-expression. He proposes that the introduction of hip-hop music into counseling can help Black males talk about their experiences of social injustice.

To provide descriptive language for the experience of Black female resilience, Woods-Giscombe et al. (2019) identified characteristics of females who see themselves as strong Black women. This research notes that strong Black women have, among other traits, a strong obligation to succeed, an obligation to manifest strength, and an obligation to help others even at their own expense. They found that the Strong Black Woman is a socially favorable and culturally expected persona with adverse effects on a woman's physical and mental health. Counselors are well-advised to keep these dynamics in mind when working with Black female adults.

Couples and Families

How does mental health affect marital satisfaction for Black couples over time? Jenkins et al. (2020) looked at the linkages between marital satisfaction, Black identity, and depressive symptoms in African American couples. The research showed that when wives normatively emphasize racial group membership as part of their overall self-concept (racial centrality), their depressive symptoms are associated with declines in their husbands' marital satisfaction. In contrast, when wives do not normatively emphasize racial group membership (racial lower centrality), their depressive symptoms did not affect their husbands' marital satisfaction. Culturally conscious counselors will give attention to the interdependence between spouses' mental health and relationship satisfaction, and the role of sociocultural factors in these linkages when working with heterosexual clients of African descent.

Boyd-Franklin (2003) identifies what she calls the Rage over Racism problem affecting African American couples. As couples struggle with racism and discrimination at every socioeconomic level, their mounting frustration about injustice, financial disparities, and other inequities can turn into rage that gets misdirected toward the family and couple relationships. What couples present as a marriage conflict can be reframed to help the couple see that they are both victims of racism. The couple often just needs to be invited to unite in the fight against racism's effects rather than fighting one another.

The Black lesbian, gay, bisexual, transgender, and queer (LGBTQ+) individuals who are in same-gender loving (SGL) relationships have unique challenges (Ferguson, 2020). The legalization of same-sex marriage heightened the risk of discrimination, victimization, and violence faced by many people who identify as LGBTQ+. While mainstream public visibility has increased for LGBTQ+ individuals, so has their susceptibility to traumatic experiences by way of hate crimes (Ronan, 2020). Sexual orientation hate crimes are "the third-largest category after race and religion" (Human Rights Campaign, 2020, as cited in Ronan, 2020, p. 1). In fact, gender-based hate crimes increased from 2.2% in 2018 to 2.7% in 2019 (Ronan, 2020). This is particularly true in Black communities where same-sex couples may feel ostracized or stigmatized for going against traditional, heterosexual values. In general, the intersection of race and sexuality creates circumstances unique to Black LGBTQ community members (Ferguson, 2020).

IMPLICATIONS FOR CLINICAL PRACTICE

Honoring Diversity

The American caste system called *race* affects the perceptions and experiences of clients and counselors, in ways big and small. Archer (2021) calls the solution Anti-Racist Psychotherapy, an approach designed to clarify the mental health effects of racism and provide a neuroscience-informed approach to resolve racial trauma. Anti-racist therapy brings matters of race from the background to the foreground, first in the counselor, and then in the therapeutic discourse. It is the counselor's professional responsibility and ethical obligation to confront and combat all forms of oppression, and that begins within each counselor. The clinical practice implications drawn from this chapter are many.

First, counselors must resist assumptions and generalizations about people of African descent. Avoid categorizing Black or African American as a collective and single racial identity. Honor the diversity among diasporic Africans and use the racial, ethnic, and cultural identifiers that the client prefers. Ensure that processes and procedures address the needs of clients through a culturally sensitive lens and provide culturally affirming forms, diagnostic assessments, interventions, and referrals using the preferred self-identification terminology of the client.

Counselors must recognize the historical considerations that may affect diasporic African clients' lives, their mental health, and their treatment perspectives. Specifically, counselors need an awareness of intergenerational, race-based trauma and how this type of trauma is expressed. Every counselor must consider how to apply trauma-informed care to the treatment of African American and other Black clients.

Withhold any judgment about family structures and roles or about spiritual practices. The flexibility and collectivistic approach to roles and relationships have served Black families well. When mothers fill the roles of both parents, when older children assist with parenting, when spiritual practices involve hearing from God, or when deceased ancestors are honored as living, the counselor should not be quick to pathologize or judge cultural norms as dysfunctional.

As Black adolescents are at higher risk for suicide attempts, counselors must be intentional about using effective methods for this population. Psychosocial interventions shown to have some level of effectiveness in the treatment of Black youth are multisystemic therapy (MST) for disruptive behaviors; peer resilient treatment for traumatic stress; and cognitive behavioral treatment (CBT) for disruptive behaviors. The counselor should always remember to culturally tailor these interventions to meet the needs of Black youth and their families. Although the field lacks sufficient evidence about individual and group CBT and individual interpersonal psychotherapy (IPT) with Black youth specifically, these are well-established depression interventions for adolescents in general (Lindsey et al., 2019)

This underscores the importance of the U.S. Preventive Services Task Force (USPSTF) recommendation to screen for depression in adolescents ages 12 through 18 in primary care settings. The American Academy of Pediatrics (AAP) has endorsed this approach. AAP recommends the use of a self-report screening tool to check for suicidal ideation and risk. Assessing youth presenting with significant depression symptoms is an important strategy. Counselors can also take action by understanding stressors and stress-related behaviors among African American adolescents, helping Black youth and families understand the path from suicidal ideations to suicidal attempts, developing prevention programs, and fighting against demoralizing and discriminatory practices that disadvantage Black youth.

Culturally Relevant Models

When providing counseling services to people of African descent, culturally conscious treatment providers understand the epigenetic transmission of trauma in the body, and they stay abreast of new research in this area. Several models have been formulated and published that help to theorize the enduring bio-psycho-social effects of slavery on the African American community. Among them are Post Traumatic Slave Syndrome, Segregation Stress Syndrome, and Racial Battle Fatigue.

Post Traumatic Slave Syndrome

The idea of Post Traumatic Slave Syndrome (PTSS) came out of the qualitative and quantitative research of Dr. Joy DeGruy (2017). It theorizes a condition that occurs when a group of people has experienced multigenerational trauma from past centuries of psychological and emotional enslavement, and then continues to experience *more* oppression through institutionalized racism in the present. It explains the etiology, or origin, of some of the adaptive survival behaviors of a people that survived slavery and was justified by the premise that African Americans were inherently genetically inferior to Whites. This was then followed by institutionalized racism, which continued to perpetuate injury upon African Americans. DeGruy uses the acronym M.A.P. to describe the result:

M: Multigenerational trauma together with continued oppression;

A: Absence of opportunity to heal or access the benefits available in the society; leads to

P: Post Traumatic Slave Syndrome (PTSS)

The theory suggests that PTSS produces vacant esteem, everpresent anger, and racist socialization, and then explores how African Americans can use the strengths gained in the past to heal in the present.

Segregation Stress Syndrome

Segregation Stress Syndrome is a lifelong reality where "the cumulative experiences with racially traumatic events caused long-lasting psychological consequences for

African Americans as individuals, families, and communities" (Thompson-Miller et al., 2015, p. 4). Racially traumatic events, such as rape/attempted rape, lynchings/loss of life, and loss of land during the Jim Crow Era resulted in long-term psychological consequences of witnessing, experiencing, or hearing of those traumatic experiences.

A key aspect of Segregation Stress Syndrome is the underlying fear that one or one's family could be killed or harmed without warning or reason (Thompson-Miller et al., 2015). The research reveals that African Americans have diverse emotions and strategies to cope with the event. They exhibited rage, shame, and anger. They coped using a wide range of reactions: obedience, resistance, denial, and collective forgetting. The symptoms varied based on the severity of the experience of the traumatic event, the time of earliest exposure, the length and frequency of exposure, and the severity of witnessing a racial traumatic event.

Racial Battle Fatigue

Racial Battle Fatigue (RBF) is a phenomenon studied and named by Dr. William A. Smith (Smith et al., 2020). Smith et al. (2020) explain RBF as the cumulative result of a natural race-related stress response to distressing mental and emotional conditions. As a framework for summarizing the effects of those lived experiences of racism and discrimination, RBF includes three major stress responses: physiological, psychological, and behavioral. The theory suggests that these conditions emerged from constantly facing racially dismissive, demeaning, insensitive, and/or hostile racial environments.

Multisystemic Approach to Cultural and Disability Awareness

Townsend's (2018) Multisystemic Approach to Cultural and Disability Awareness (MACDA) with Black boys is an ecological model for guiding school counselors in assessing needs and intervening at multiple levels. The MACDA model has infused theoretical tenets that are specific to working with African American boys with disabilities to address their behavioral and academic presentations (Townsend, 2018). Culturally aware counselors familiarize themselves with this type of culturally relevant model and develop a keen sensitivity to systemic bias and the resulting disparities affecting Black children.

CLINICAL CASE SCENARIO 5.1

Tasha is a 38-year-old married African American woman. She and her husband, Jeremy, are in marriage counseling. Tasha and Jeremy have two sons, ages 5 and 9. Jeremy is a respected senior pastor at a historical African American church in the heart of a major metropolitan area. As the "First Lady" of the church, Tasha has a variety of highly visible leadership roles that she describes as "fulfilling her calling as a pastor's wife," but she expresses that lately she's felt irritable, hasn't enjoyed her ministry role as much as she once did, and has had a hard time making decisions about how to balance life. Tasha grew up without economic privilege. Her grandparents who raised her were sharecroppers in a small rural Southern town. Jeremy grew up with a very different experience. He is a college graduate and third-generation pastor. Jeremy grew up attending private schools

(continued)

CLINICAL CASE SCENARIO 5.1 (CONTINUED)

and assisting his father and grandfather in ministry. Jeremy self-identifies as African American even though his maternal grandmother was German.

Their marriage counselor recommended that Tasha have some individual counseling to help manage symptoms of depression. In the first few sessions with Tasha, her counselor recognizes that Tasha experiences emotional and psychological abuse from Jeremy. Tasha reports that she doesn't sleep well, and her appetite has decreased so much that she has lost about 15 pounds without trying. Tasha reports that she feels tearful and overwhelmed a lot but says, "It's nothing. I just have to be strong because the ministry needs me." She explains that all the women in her family were strong Black women. Tasha had great respect for them, especially her mother, who passed away from complications of diabetes and COVID-19 at the age of 59. Tasha's mother had been a pillar in her life. "I was not able to say goodbye or give her the funeral that she deserved." Tasha briefly mentioned a history of childhood molestation and says, "If God could bring me through that, God can get me through anything!"

CLINICAL CASE SCENARIO DISCUSSION QUESTIONS

1. Do you think the treatment recommendation for Tasha to have individual counseling was a culturally sensitive one?
2. How does the Strong Black Woman Schema affect Tasha's presenting problem?
3. What goals would you address in Tasha's and Jeremy's couples counseling?

END-OF-CHAPTER RESOURCES

A robust set of instructor resources designed to supplement this text is located at http://connect.springerpub.com/content/book/978-0-8261-3953-5. Qualifying instructors may request access by emailing **textbook@springerpub.com**.

SUMMARY

Counselors who serve clients of African descent have the privilege of working with people with a legacy of resilience and survival. Their experiences are influenced by the way they or their ancestors arrived in the United States. Culturally relevant models of racial identity development and case conceptualization must inform the counselor's approach. For these populations, diversity-informed practice cannot be separated from trauma-informed care.

The client's values, approaches to help-seeking, etiology of problems, and experiences with bias or racism will affect their responses to interventions and outcomes. Without culturally informed care, the traumatic histories of the African diaspora remain overlooked and potentially invalidated. Effective counseling begins with the counselor's introspection and awareness. It continues with an intentional awareness of the trauma, identities, history, cultural values, and injustice that have been woven into the fabric of their lives. Counseling can be another strong thread in that tapestry.

DISCUSSION QUESTIONS

1. When working with clients of African descent, what are some fundamental behavioral health considerations and why?
2. Describe the ethnic and cultural diversity within the African diaspora in the United States and discuss implications for clinical practice.
3. Why are racial identity development models important when counseling people of African descent?
4. How do the challenges experienced by African Americans differ from those of African immigrants in the United States?
5. What are the challenges of living with collectivist values while inhabiting an individualistic society?

▶ COUNSELING AFRICAN AMERICANS, AFRICANS, CARIBBEAN BLACKS, AND IMMIGRANTS OF AFRICAN DESCENT

Guests: Dr. LaVerne Hanes Collins and Dr. Alfonso L. Ferguson

https://connect.springerpub.com/content/book/978-0-8261-3953-5/part/part02/chapter/ch05

KEY REFERENCES

Only key references appear in the print edition. The full reference list appears in the digital product on Springer Publishing Connect: https://connect.springerpub.com/content/book/978-0-8261-3953-5/part/part02/chapter/ch05

American Counseling Association. (2014). *2014 ACA Code of Ethics*. Author. https://www.counseling.org/docs/default-source/default-document-library/2014-code-of-ethics-finaladdress.pdf

Berry, J. W. (1992). Acculturation and adaptation in a new society. *International Migration, 30*, 69–85. https://doi.org/10.1111/j.1468-2435.1992.tb00776.x

Godsil, R.D. & Goodale, B. (2013). *Telling our own Story: The role of narrative in racial healing*. W.K. Kellogg Foundation. https://perception.org/wp-content/uploads/2014/11/Telling-Our-Own-Story.pdf

Phinney, J. S. (1989). Stages of ethnic identity development in minority group adolescents. *The Journal of Early Adolescence, 9*(1–2), 34–49. https://doi.org/10.1177/0272431689091004

Phinney, J. S. (1992). The multigroup ethnic identity measure: A new scale for use with diverse groups. *Journal of Adolescent Research, 7*(2), 156–176. https://doi.org/10.1177/074355489272003

Ratts, M. J., Singh, A. A., Nassar-McMillan, S., Butler, S. K., & McCullough, J. R. (2015). *Multicultural and social justice counseling competencies*. https://www.counseling.org/docs/default-source/competencies/multicultural-and-social-justice-counseling-competencies.pdf?sfvrsn=14

CHAPTER 6

Culturally Responsive Counseling for Clients of Asian American and Pacific Islander Descent

JUNG H. HYUN, JOHN J. S. HARRICHAND, S ANANDAVALLI, YI-WEN SU, AND EUNHUI YOON

LEARNING OBJECTIVES

After reading this chapter, students will be able to:
- List important historical aspects that affect Asian Americans and Pacific Islanders (AAPIs) in the United States.
- Identify general cultural characteristics of AAPIs.
- Recognize cultural wealth and intersectionality in working with AAPI clients.
- Apply the Multicultural and Social Justice Counseling Competencies (MSJCC) and critical lens for social justice and liberation to work with AAPIs.

SELF-REFLECTION QUESTIONS

1. What is your current perception of the AAPI population?
2. What biases do you hold in working with the AAPI group?
3. What cultural intersectional identities might an Asian American person have?

Asian Americans as a group are quite heterogeneous, with more than 20 subgroups (e.g., Chinese, Korean, Laotian, Taiwanese, Japanese, etc.), each made unique by linguistic, cultural, and sociodemographic backgrounds and immigration history in the United States (Sue & Morishima, 1982). We tried our best to provide overarching information as members of Asian American and Pacific Islander (AAPI) communities. However, readers should be mindful when drawing conclusions from this chapter and working with clients of AAPI descent. Rather than examining every ethnic group in the AAPI category, which is beyond the scope of this chapter, we focused on how to approach issues of mental health and systemic support for the AAPIs' experiencing discrimination and oppression.

In this chapter, following some brief comments on our reflexivity, key interpersonal social issues are discussed. Readers are then provided with a brief history of the racial identity development of Asian Americans, followed by the most recent approach to ethnic identity development of Asian Americans. Drawing from the Multicultural and Social Justice Counseling Competencies (MSJCC; Ratts et al., 2015), cultural humility, AsianCrit, counseling interventions, and practical action plans are suggested. The chapter concludes with a case scenario and discussion questions.

THE COUNSELOR: EXPLORATION, INTROSPECTION, AND REFLECTION

Professional counselors are expected to be attuned to their own sets of cultural values and beliefs. One's cultural identities dictate one's thinking patterns and behaviors; consequently, those principles are exposed to their clients in the clinical setting. Likewise, counselor trainees and counselors are required to have awareness of their cultural biases and prejudices that may negatively affect their interactions with their clients, resulting in maladaptive clinical interventions and rupturing their client relationships.

Counselor trainees and counselors are encouraged to pay close attention to their existing beliefs of the diversity of the people that they serve. Counselors must be fully attentive to a person's multicultural practices, especially those that are different from theirs, while also avoiding making assumptions that their similarities in values are "the same" rather than maybe sharing some fundamental beliefs but varied in many other ways. Clinicians must prevent imposing their own cultural values and beliefs unto their clients (American Counseling Association [ACA], 2014, A.4.b.).

In providing services to AAPIs, counselors must be willing to assess their own assumptions related to this ethnic group (e.g., model minority, etc.), investigating their conceptualization of the history of AAPIs in this country and the oppressive treatment that this group has experienced throughout the history of the United States. Counselors are encouraged to identify their existing biases that may present concerns in their therapeutic dealings with AAPIs. Additionally, counselor trainees and counselors are urged to be intentional in paying attention to the current events that continue to occur that have targeted the AAPI group. For instance, how do you feel about the social contract introduction that the coronavirus (COVID-19) was "caused" by the Chinese people? How might you help to debunk this notion in order to create an inclusive therapeutic environment for your clients? Moreover, how will you advocate for the AAPI communities to help eliminate their microaggression experiences due to the differences in their physical appearance and/or, for some, their linguistic challenges?

KEY INTERPERSONAL SOCIETAL ISSUES AFFECTING ASIAN AMERICANS

The acronym AAPIs includes a broad range of nationalities and cultural backgrounds. At least 43 distinct groups comprise the AAPI communities in the United States (Asian & Pacific Islander American Health Forum, 2011), so this acronym should not be used or taken to identify AAPIs as a monolithic group. The United States is home to approximately 24.5 million AAPIs, with 23 million identifying as Asian alone or in combination with one or more Asian or other race and 1.6 identifying as Native Hawaiian and Other Pacific Islander (U.S. Census Bureau, 2021a). Asian Indian, Chinese, Filipino, Japanese, Korean, and Vietnamese are six major ethnic groups within the AAPI diaspora accounting for 95% of the population, while Melanesian, Micronesian, Native Hawaiian, and

Polynesian ethnic groups comprise Pacific Islanders (Jones-Smith, 2019). Throughout this chapter, we use "Asian Americans" interchangeably with "AAPIs."

Key History of Asian Americans in the United States

Initially, Asian Americans were drawn to the United States by employment opportunities in low-skilled occupations (e.g., railroads, farming, laundry, etc.); however, anti-immigration laws and exclusionary immigrant policies motivated by racism and discrimination resulted in the Chinese Exclusion Act in 1882, the Geary Act in 1892, and the National Origin Act of 1924 that blocked AAPIs' immigration (Jones-Smith, 2019). Asian exclusion and gatekeeping in the United States were based on and resulted in the idea of "yellow peril": Western fears that "barbaric" Asians, specifically from China and Japan, would invade the United States and destroy civilized life. It was not until 1965, at the height of the civil rights movement, that the United States government reopened its doors to immigrants from around the world, including Asia, with the passage of the Immigration and Nationality Act of 1965. This Act of 1965 allowed Asian Americans to pursue employment opportunities as high-skilled workers (e.g., science, business, art, management, etc.), and the "yellow peril" label was transformed into the "model minority" label (Jones-Smith, 2019; National Endowment for the Humanities, n.d.).

The United States government established the Asian/Pacific American Heritage Week in 1978 to recognize the arrival of the first immigrants from Japan on May 7, 1843, and the significant contributions by Chinese railroad workers who helped construct the transcontinental railroad. However, in 1992 the United States Congress expanded the observance to a monthly celebration. In 2019, it was estimated that 88% of AAPIs 25 years and older were high school educated, and in 2018 approximately 554,500 owned their own business (U.S. Census Bureau, 2021a). Unfortunately, with the onset of the novel coronavirus (COVID-19), hateful political rhetoric, and biased media coverage, the AAPI communities continue to witness increased rates of racial discrimination, Sinophobia, and violence across the United States (Congressional Asian American Pacific American Caucus [CAPAC], 2020; Wen et al., 2020). In the following we identify some key issues spanning AAPI communities.

Collectivistic Worldview

Most Eastern cultures, that is, AAPIs, have collectivistic traditions (Triandis, 1995), which include strong family bonds and value the interests and goals of the group, family, or work over those of the individual (Duan & Wang, 2000). Solidarity is also valued and actively pursued within the family and work, especially when disagreements occur. The feelings of others are respected, which contributes to cohesiveness, and reciprocity is not only encouraged but actively promoted (Jones-Smith, 2019). According to Fuligni et al. (1999), there is an expectation of Asian American adolescents to respect, support, and assist their families and elders although they live in a society, the United States, where autonomy and independence are the norm. However, Sue, Sue, et al. (2019) noted that AAPI families differ in their adherence to collectivistic worldviews and should be assessed individually when working with members of the AAPI communities.

Family Structure and Parenting Styles

In addition to most AAPI families being collectivistic, they are usually patriarchal and hierarchical, that is, males and family members who are older hold greater power and status (B. S. Kim et al., 2020). A family member's actions reflect their family unit, and each family member is seen as the product of all generations of their family (E. Lee, 1997). Family rituals hold significance within AAPI communities, including ancestor worship, funeral rights, genealogy records, and family celebrations. Clearly defined roles and positions exist within the family based on hierarchy, age, gender, and social class (e.g., males are viewed with favor as they carry the family lineage and traditions and their primary duty is to their parents; Sue, Sue, et al., 2019). Traditionally, mothers fulfill a supporting role in the family while fathers discipline (Jones-Smith, 2019), and communication is usually top-down from parents to children (i.e., authoritarian and directive; Lau et al., 2009).

Five types of Asian American families have been proposed by E. Lee (1997), including (1) *The Traditional Asian American Family*: usually recent immigrants to the United States, have limited contact with U.S. society, and seek to maintain family traditions. (2) *The Cultural Conflict Asian American Family*: have different cultural values and conflict exists due to varying rates of acculturation to dominant United States values. Differences are also noted in parents' values and expectations, resulting in conflict related to school, work, and marriage, where children identify closely with U.S. culture compared to parents, and/or children have to assist parents in navigating the U.S. society. (3) *The Bicultural Asian American Family*: have well-acculturated parents who have lived in the United States for decades, and family members are usually bicultural and/or bilingual, well-educated with stable incomes, and live in multicultural communities. Parent–child relationships are defined as egalitarian with a nuclear family structure mirroring the dominant U.S. society. (4) *The Americanized Family*: is usually defined by having at least two generations of parents and children born in the United States, holding individualistic worldviews, communicating in English, and having an egalitarian family structure. (5) *The Interracial Asian Family*: differ in culture, values, religious beliefs, communication style, and relationships; when cultures are not integrated, conflict usually exists. It is important to note that parent–child conflicts are a common presenting problem for AAPI college students seeking counseling, which stems from an inability to reconcile the difference in acculturation (R. M. Lee et al., 2000, 2005).

Emotional Expression

Sue, Sue, et al. (2019) note that AAPI communities value self-control and emotional restraint when faced with pain and suffering. The ability to demonstrate self-control during a crisis is accompanied by reluctance to acknowledge strong emotions, that is, stoic demeanors, making it challenging for Western mental health professionals to understand and work with some AAPI clients (Kramer et al., 2002). In addition, humility is encouraged; for example, the contributions of others are valued over self-praise (Jones-Smith, 2019). Dishonoring one's family (name) is one of the worst offenses a family member can commit (Jones-Smith, 2019). In addition, sharing about one's family problems outside the family is highly discouraged; there is an unwritten rule that family problems are to be kept within the family. This practice is reinforced through the technique of shaming (e.g., discouraging behaviors that might negatively affect the reputation of one's family) and fear of "losing face" (i.e., having one's social status decline in relation to significant stakeholders; Leong et al., 2016). Respect for one's elders, that is, filial piety, is also valued in AAPI communities, which helps to maintain strong collectivistic family systems and emphasizes the fear of losing face and the expectation that children are responsible for caring for their parents/elders (Teon, 2016).

Model Minority Myth and Socioeconomic Challenges

In 2013, a Pew Research Center study found that Asian Americans had the highest income, were best educated, and, as a racial group, was the fastest-growing in the United States (Pew Research Center, 2013). Compared with other Americans, they placed more value on marriage, parenthood, career success, and hard work. Such findings have resulted in Asian Americans being labeled the "model minority" by researchers and White American society (Hsia & Peng, 1998), a development which continues to mask the historical and current discrimination, exclusion, and prejudice directed at them (Litam, 2020; Sue, Alsaidi, et al., 2019). Although support for the model minority stereotype is evident in their cultural values of diligence, frugality, educational and occupational achievement, and advancement, and maintaining "face" when met with adversity (Jones-Smith, 2019), AAPI researchers object to the use of the term (Litam, 2020; Sandhu et al., 2003). AAPIs in major United States cities (e.g., San Francisco and New York) experience problems of juvenile delinquency, and those from lower-income groups and recent refugees have limited access to healthcare stemming from cultural, financial, linguistic, and systemic barriers, a reality people outside these places seldom witness (Jones-Smith, 2019; Sue, Alsaidi, et al., 2019). The U.S. Census Bureau (2021a) documents that AAPIs have a higher rate of poverty even though they have a higher median income. Shah and Ramakrishnan (2017) documented the disparities within the AAPI communities in the area of education, noting that although Asian Americans are high achievers in education, most are undereducated, resulting in a bimodal distribution when averaged out, and thus resulting in misleading statistics. The model minority stereotype, according to Sandhu et al. (2003), prevents AAPI communities from accessing and receiving needed services, including government aid and resources.

Racism, Discrimination, Microaggressions, and Mental Health

AAPIs continue to experience explicit racism and physical and psychological discrimination because of their accent and physical appearance (Litam, 2020). In addition, Americans commit microaggressions toward AAPIs when they incorrectly assume that every AAPI they encounter recently arrived to the United States and/or cannot speak English well (Sue et al., 2009). In their study, Sue et al. (2009) participants identified eight major microaggressions Asian Americans experience: (a) being an alien in their own land, (b) attributing intelligence to them, (c) Asian women are exoticized, (d) interethnic differences are invalidated, (e) racial reality is denied, (f) cultural values and communication styles are pathologized, (g) viewed as second-class citizens, and (h) experiencing invisibility. Experiences of racism and discrimination may also depend on one's gender and immigrant status (Anandavalli et al., 2020), all of which have significant implications for the mental health and overall well-being of AAPIs (D. L. Lee & Ahn, 2011), especially when counseling may be viewed as a foreign concept (Sue, Sue, et al., 2019).

As COVID-19 continues to tally a death list that increases daily, it compounds the mental health needs of individuals and groups—particularly members of the AAPI communities. Counselors are encouraged to look for the effects of racial discrimination on AAPI clients stemming from COVID-19 not only in the workplace but also in educational institutions (for example, students bullied by peers). Many AAPIs may somaticize symptoms that mask mental health concerns. This includes symptoms of depression and anxiety, substance abuse, suicidal ideation, anger and shame, social isolation and avoidance, and overall psychological distress. It is therefore important to assess not only risk factors but also protective factors, and treatment options, when meeting with clients who are AAPIs (Litam, 2020).

IDENTITY DEVELOPMENT OF ASIAN AMERICANS

Ethnic Identity Development Models for Asian Americans

Tse (1999) developed a four-stage model after analyzing 39 published autobiographical accounts of Asian Americans: Ethnic Unawareness, Ethnic Ambivalence (childhood and adolescence), Ethnic Emergence (adolescence and early adulthood), and Ethnic Identity Incorporation (joined the ethnic minority American group). Similar to Atkinson et al.'s (1998) model, the first two stages feature unawareness and exploration of ethnic status. In the latter two stages, people start to recognize their minority status and explore other groups with whom they can share culture and common ground. In the last stage, Ethnic Identity Incorporation, people develop Asian pride and a greater understanding of their own identity as being of Asian descent while accepting who they are (Tse, 1999).

Based on the Erikson (1968) human development stages, models of identity development, including Cross (1971) and Helms (1990), appear to follow ego identity formation. For example, there is an assumption that conformity happens in early childhood, and dissonance may start from childhood. Resistance and immersion are more likely to happen in adolescence. However, many immigrants are not born in the United States. Their racial identity development does not necessarily start until they immigrate to the United States. These stage-like models (including those of Helms, Cross, and Atkinson) are not only linear but also bound to the individuals' minds (W. T. Jones, 1990). Furthermore, sociocultural impact or systemic oppressions do not seem to be considered in those models.

Recognizing that ethnic identity is formed during interactions with other racial groups, especially in the United States, researchers began paying attention to the Social Identity Theory and acculturation in the racial identity development of people of color. Phinney (1990) conceptualized the ethnic identity development based on Social Identity Theory and acculturation. Three stages proposed by Phinney (1990) consist of Unexamined Ethnic Identity (Diffusion and Foreclosure), Ethnic Identity Search (moratorium), and Achieved Ethnic Identity. The unexamined stage is characterized by a lack of exploration of ethnicity. Phinney (1990) suggested two categories, Diffusion and Foreclosure, under the unexamined stage. Diffusion means lack of interest in or concern with ethnicity. People with foreclosure hold a view of ethnicity based on the opinions of others. In the second stage, Ethnic Identity Search, people become involved in activities and experiences to find the meaning of ethnicity for themselves. In this process, rejection of the dominant culture may happen. In the final stage, Achieved Ethnic Identity, people come to a comprehensive deeper understanding of their ethnic identity by resolving issues between the dominant group and their own group (Phinney et al., 1990).

It is imperative to consider social context in ethnic identity development because humans are social beings. For Asian Americans, their identity development is intricate in relation to interpersonal relationships and interactions with external forces, such as customs and policies. To some extent, interactions with other people and external forces such as social context are major forces in AAPIs' ethnic identification, more than the internal forces, because the Asian concept of self is significantly affected by the community stemming from collectivistic perspectives (Yeh & Huang, 1996). This cultural aspect is demonstrated in "saving/losing face." For example, Asian Americans may conform to White society to avoid bringing shame to their family.

Factors Affecting Ethnic Identity Development

Aligned with the Social Identity Theory, empirical studies with Asian Americans have identified distinctive aspects in Asian Americans' ethnic identity development.

As suggested in Phinney's first stage, some Asian Americans are influenced by their parents' and caregivers' preferences. Especially for children from immigrant families, their identity development depends on their parents'/caregivers' attitudes toward the dominant culture. Another cultural aspect that may affect the Asian American's racial identity development is shame. Rooted in a collectivistic culture, Asian Americans consider themselves to be representatives of their nuclear and extended family, community, and society. It is frowned upon that individuals' behaviors as judged by others bring shame to their family and community. Therefore, avoidance of shame was found to be a strong motivating factor in making decisions on their thoughts and behaviors in ethnic identity development (Yeh & Huang, 1996). These cultural aspects, such as patriarchal family dynamics and saving face, may intersect with other social factors as children develop. From the collectivistic cultural perspectives, the social context changes when Asian American descendants reach college age. Their social context expands dramatically, so college-age years are key for ethnic minority youths' identity development (see Zhou et al., 2003).

History and social status in the United States should be considered. Southeast Asians are usually assumed to be the "unsuccessful" minority; rather than approaching AAPI clients from a deficit perspective, counselors need to be familiar with "refugee subjecthood" (Kwan, 2020), especially when working with the Hmong and Cambodian Americans. Defined as "the phenomenon in which refugees collectively and individually create, enact, and challenge subject positions shaped by social structure, such as law and education" (Kwan, 2020, p. 80), *refugee subjecthood* allows counselors to understand their issues deeply and contextually. Exploring transgenerational trauma as a common refugee experience, counselors can support clients' emotional experiences such as isolation or white-washing of Cambodian Americans (Kwan, 2020) that may be different from other AAPIs' experiences.

COUNSELING UTILIZATION AND HELP-SEEKING OF ASIAN AMERICANS

Literature has addressed that AAPI individuals utilize counseling services less compared to other racial/ethnic groups (J. E. Kim & Zane, 2016; Naito et al., 2019; Sue et al., 2012). Researchers have attempted to better understand factors related to the help-seeking of AAPI individuals, and then to reduce inequalities in access to mental health services.

Cultural stigma in the community and the model minority myth are commonly referenced factors that contribute to less counseling utilization by AAPI individuals in many studies. Lack of understanding or stigma related to psychological distress and mental health services can lead to neglect of their needs for counseling (N. Y. Choi & Miller, 2014; Naito et al., 2019). The stigma can have an impact at the individual level, by presenting their lack of self-control, and it is also connected to the shame of the whole family by bringing a negative reputation to the family and blaming poor parenting. The model minority myth discussed earlier is a false conception that AAPI individuals are academically, financially, and socially more successful than other ethnic and immigrant groups. It leads AAPI individuals to avoid their actual experiences of racism and strengthens the stigma attendant to experiencing struggle and seeking help (Woo, 2000). However, recent studies are focusing on systemic barriers.

Anticipating discrimination by authority figures, including health professionals and counselors, could be one of the systemic barriers for AAPI clients (Mereish et al., 2012). AAPI individuals' mistrust of cultural competencies of Western counselors (David, 2010) and previous experiences of racial discrimination are associated with reluctance to seek help (Burgess et al., 2008). Even after the COVID-19 outbreak, Asian populations are exposed to various forms of discrimination, which raised additional barriers to help-seeking behaviors in general and use of counseling services (Devakumar et al., 2020; Naito et al., 2020).

Lack of health insurance coverage is also considered a factor contributing to AAPI's lack of access to counseling services and help-seeking. According to the statistics, 7.2% of Asians, 12.7% of Native Hawaiian Americans and other Pacific Islanders, and 21.7% of American Indians and Alaskan Natives under 64 years old are uninsured, whereas 7.8% of White Americans are uninsured (Artiga et al., 2021). Lack of health insurance would lead AAPI individuals' mental health needs to be dealt with by primary care providers, especially when those individuals are experiencing somatization issues. Also, even when the individuals are aware of the need for mental health services, the lack of health insurance and concerns about the high cost of counseling services will raise barriers to help-seeking. Moreover, various forms of traditional treatment or indigenous healing from the AAPI communities are not covered by health insurance, thus exacerbating the delay in help-seeking by individuals.

The limited number of linguistically and culturally responsive counselors is yet another barrier to AAPI individuals' counseling utilization (Sue et al., 2012). Even though the numbers of AAPI counseling professionals are increasing, there are not enough counselors who sensitively understand the cultural background of the community. In addition, in the AAPI community, more than 50 ethnic groups and 100 languages and dialects exist; therefore, it is challenging to find certified interpreters for all the languages.

CULTURALLY RESPONSIVE PRACTICES: DRAWING FROM THE MULTICULTURAL AND SOCIAL JUSTICE COUNSELING COMPETENCIES AND CULTURAL HUMILITY

The MSJCC (Ratts et al., 2015) have provided a foundational framework for culturally inclusive practice. The MSJCC model addresses three dimensions that are required competencies: awareness, knowledge, and skills. Further, the quadrant encompassing these three competencies is useful for counselors to check in working with AAPI communities, especially because within-group differences are so apparent in the AAPI communities. For example, a female counselor who is of Vietnamese descent may belong to Marginalized Counselor and Privileged Client when she works with a Chinese-descent male older client. They may have to see themself as Privileged Counselor and Marginalized Client when they work with a transgender client. As another example, a White male counselor who identifies as queer may belong to Privileged Counselor and Marginalized Client when working with a Chinese immigrant male older client—but the same White male queer counselor may identify as the Marginalized Counselor and Privileged Client when working with the same Chinese immigrant male older client. Counselors working with AAPIs need not only be keen on their own privileges but must also take positionality into consideration. In addition, the meaning attributed to identity for an individual client and their identified ethnic group can play a critical role in building rapport. For example, a White male queer counselor may experience resistance earlier than expected from a Korean female client who is a conservative Christian, based on the client's religious values related to the LGBTQ+ community.

After counselors identify which quadrant they may belong to with their specific client, they need to examine themselves in relation to their awareness, learn about the client's worldview, build the counseling relationship, and develop counseling and advocacy interventions. Through this process, our hope is that the counselor will be culturally competent, and the client benefits from the counseling relationship with the counselor. While the steps seem to be clear, defining what it is to be multiculturally competent is quite complicated. One thing that may help is to practice three pillars, *Cultural Humility, Cultural Opportunities,* and *Cultural Comfort* (Hook et al., 2017). "Encompassing the intrapersonal and interpersonal spirit inherent in the multicultural orientation framework" (Hook et al., 2017, p. 29), *Cultural Humility* includes both concepts of cultural opportunities and cultural comfort. After they look into themselves and learn their identity and the impact of their identity on the counseling relationship (intrapersonal), counselors with *Cultural Humility* will be welcoming to clients who may not be familiar with the counseling space, while being open to learning their client's culture, values, and worldviews (*Cultural Opportunities*), and building the therapeutic relationship from there (interpersonal) rather than from an ethnocentric European counseling space. Recognizing the importance of addressing and juxtaposing culture and values in the counseling sessions, the culturally competent counselor can facilitate a relaxed and comfortable space for discussing culture, values, and worldviews, and improve their counseling skills and techniques when they experience discomfort.

In addition, it is important for counselors to understand the role of racism in Asian American experiences before working with this population. To do so, counselors can utilize the seven interrelated tenets of AsianCrit theory framework (Museus & Iftikar, 2014) to understand how White supremacy shapes the experience of Asian Americans. These seven interrelated tenets include Asianization; transnational contexts; (re)constructive history; strategic (anti)essentialism; intersectionality; story, theory, and praxis of Asian Americans; and commitment to social justice (for a complete description, see Museus, 2013). These tenets highlight the importance of understanding racism specific to Asian Americans, such as racialization of Asian Americans as foreigners and as a model minority (Ancheta, 2000; Wu, 2002); considering national and transnational context when understanding anti-Asian oppression; constructing a collective Asian American historical narrative; being aware of the intersection of the identities and systems of social oppression; listening to Asian Americans' stories and their experiences; and lastly, committing to social justice to eliminate the racism and oppression toward Asian Americans. In the following section, we discuss what counselors need to do, going beyond being culturally competent.

CRAFTING AN ADVOCACY AGENDA

Professional counselors, counseling supervisors, and counselors-in-training in the United States are expected to subscribe to and follow the guidelines outlined by the ACA (2014) *Code of Ethics* and Advocacy Competencies (Toporek & Daniels, 2018). The *Code of Ethics* mandates that we actively participate in social justice initiatives on behalf of and, when possible, with minoritized clients and communities in order to create a more equitable society. C. C. Lee (2007), one of the counseling profession's earliest writers on social justice, states "that all people have a right to equitable treatment, support for their human rights and a fair allocation of societal resources" (p. 1); "for [counselors and] educators ... [this implies] personal and professional conduct that opposes all forms of discrimination and oppression" (p. 1). For counselors to enact this definition of social justice, C. C. Lee (2007) provides counselors with five action steps that can be followed in our advocacy work with and on behalf of AAPI communities.

1. Explore Life Meaning and Commitment

As the counseling profession is rooted in the holistic-wellness model, counselors are responsible for listening and responding to the hurts and challenges of clients utilizing established best practices and empirically supported treatments in efforts to alleviate pain while providing clients with access to resources and allowing them to overcome and/or cope with difficulties in life. All clients (including AAPI clients and communities) are of inherent value and worth; developmentally, they come with certain preconceived beliefs and values that may differ from and/or contribute to their limited views of society. As counselors, part of our role is to inform them with the hope that their worldview will be expanded, allowing them to tolerate ambiguity and develop emotional complexity. Being active agents of change in society, we as counselors need to directly challenge and/or intellectually engage with the status quo while simultaneously equipping AAPI clients and communities with the tools necessary to do likewise. It is therefore important for us as counselors to broaden our worldview of society as we seek to establish equity for all people, including AAPI clients, while training them to become social justice advocates in furthering the call for equity. In so doing, we will be "committed to fostering and supporting a society that is more enlightened, just and humane through [our] life and work" (C. C. Lee, 2007, p. 1).

2. Explore Personal Privilege

In relation to personal cultural privilege, it is important for counselors, regardless of the intersections we embody, to be aware of the privileged (earned and unearned) and oppressed intersections we hold in society and how they may influence our work with AAPI clients and communities. As society continues to diversify, counselors can be powerful advocacy agents, exerting their influence on behalf of their AAPI clients and communities in opposition to a White, patriarchal, heteronormative society that often seeks to exploit them, with the intent of promoting "equity, human rights, and a fair allocation of societal resources" (C. C. Lee, 2007, p. 1). Counselors can encourage businesses and schools to intentionally hire and/or partner with AAPI people of different intersections, demonstrating their commitment to equity, diversity, and inclusion.

3. Explore the Nature of Oppression

According to C. C. Lee (2007), "counseling for social justice must be based on an understanding of the nature of oppression. Whenever people are denied access and equity that ensure full participation in the life of a society they experience oppression" (p. 2). It should be the responsibility of counselors to gain knowledge and awareness of the impact of oppression on AAPI communities (Chan et al., 2021). Counselors are also called to reflect on ways in which they may directly and/or indirectly further acts of oppression in their work with AAPI clients and actively work on developing ways to circumvent such acts, not only for their clients but also for the AAPI communities (Chan et al., 2021). As counselors are uniquely positioned to exert their authority/power in just and unjust ways, it is important for us to surround ourselves with and be open to feedback from respectable and loving mentors/peers to avoid abusing our power in relation to our AAPI clients and communities while being humble enough to take corrective action if this abuse of power does occur (Chan et al., 2021).

4. Work to Become Multiculturally Literate

Growing in our professional identity as counselors involves becoming "committed to living cultural diversity as a reality rather than experiencing it as an abstraction"

(C. C. Lee, 2007, p. 2). This involves adopting a lifestyle that challenges us to become multiculturally literate through experiencing with the intent of understanding the multifaceted nature of multiculturalism, especially as it pertains to AAPI communities (Chan et al., 2021). We can commit to increasing our multicultural literacy by seeking to actively gain knowledge of AAPI communities (past and present) and making it a priority to visit different places and meet and learn from various AAPI groups (nationally and internationally). Multicultural literacy should also involve the counselor spending time reviewing newspapers, periodicals, and literature from varied AAPI groups, and expanding our understanding by participating in different AAPI cultural experiences. Multicultural literacy might also involve counselors learning a new language or dialect and/or participating in the lifelong endeavor of encouraging religious/spiritual tolerance in relation to AAPI communities (C. C. Lee, 2007).

5. Establish a Personal Social Justice Compass

C. C. Lee (2007) encourages counselors to develop a set of personal principles and ideals expressing and guiding our commitment to social justice because they "provide a moral compass to guide both ... life and work" (p. 2). Some documents counselors could consider drawing from in developing their compass while working with AAPI clients and communities include the Universal Declaration of Human Rights (United Nations, 1948), which establishes universal principles founded on freedom, justice, and peace; the ACA (2014) *Code of Ethics*; the Advocacy Competencies initially developed by the ACA Counselors for Social Justice Division (Lewis et al., 2003) and updated by Toporek and Daniels (2018); and the MSJCC developed by the Association for Multicultural Counseling and Development (Ratts et al., 2015). Counselors can subscribe to these documents as part of their compass because they embody the essence of social justice ideals and principles (C. C. Lee, 2007). Our hope is for counselors to utilize these documents as guides in their personal and professional actions related to social justice and advocacy in the field of counseling generally, and especially in their work with AAPI clients and communities. In the following, we provide a brief systemic approach for counselors to advocate for and with AAPI clients and communities using Bronfenbrenner's (1979) bioecological systems theory as a framework.

Microsystem

At the microsystem level, a bidirectional relationship exists between the counselor and the AAPI client(s) with whom they regularly interact (Bronfenbrenner, 1979). Counselors working with AAPI communities can support AAPI clients, helping them identify and explore "safe" and "unsafe" relationships within the spaces where they exist (i.e., home, work, school, neighborhood). Next, counselors can empower AAPI clients by framing their concerns (e.g., anti-Asian hate) within larger systemic issues, thereby minimizing self-blame (i.e., personal sense of responsibility for their concerns; Sue & Sue, 1990). Here, the counselor seeks to empower AAPI clients toward engagement in self-advocacy within the spaces they exist (Haskins & Singh, 2015).

Mesosystem

At the mesosystem level, counselors working with AAPI clients reinforce microsystem interventions while exploring the mental health challenges that may emerge from interactions between AAPI clients and members within their community. By interacting with various social groups, counselors can leverage themselves to establish new relationships, and build support with spiritual, religious, and local/community leaders who are then able to directly or indirectly support AAPI clients (Sue, Alsaidi, et al., 2019).

Exosystem

At the exosystem level, the counselor examines social settings indirectly affecting AAPI clients, but where AAPI clients have no direct impacts (e.g., local politics, medical and social services; Bronfenbrenner, 1979). Interventions might focus on how Eurocentrism may further marginalize AAPI clients and negatively affect their overall mental health and well-being (D. L. Lee & Ahn, 2011). Working with AAPI clients requires counselors to shift their perspectives, focusing on systemic instead of interpersonal influences. Utilizing the MSJCC (Ratts et al., 2015), the counselor is encouraged to reflect on the intersecting ways in which their AAPI clients' privileged and oppressed identities uniquely affect their mental health.

Macrosystem

At the macrosystem level, the counselor examines the impact that cultural norms, values, and laws have on AAPI clients, without being directly influenced by them (Bronfenbrenner, 1979). Here, the counselor may collaborate with other health professionals (e.g., medical doctors, dentists, social workers) while exploring the impact of current United States political structures on the mental health and well-being of AAPI clients. By facilitating interprofessional collaborations, the counselor may be better positioned to participate in advocacy initiatives and address public policy issues on behalf of AAPI clients (Chan et al., 2019).

Chronosystem

At the chronosystem level, the counselor examines other societal systems directly and indirectly influencing their AAPI clients over time (e.g., anti-Asian bias and violence, xenophobia, the model minority myth; Bronfenbrenner, 1979). Interventions could address how the model minority myth has affected the way AAPI clients and communities are perceived by U.S. society. In addition, the counselor may consider how sociopolitical events (e.g., anti-Asian hate stemming from the COVID-19 pandemic) contribute to the disparaging attitudes toward AAPI communities, and actively dispel these harmful notions by facilitating workshops and training, while continuously engaging in state- and federal-level advocacy efforts to support the AAPI communities.

COUNSELING CHILDREN, ADOLESCENTS, AND YOUNG ADULTS

Asian Americans are identified as one of the fastest-growing student populations entering the American educational system. The number of Asian American children and adolescents in the United States has increased from 1.5 million to over 2.6 million since the 1980s (U.S. Census Bureau, 2021b). As of 2019, more than 2.7 million were enrolled in K–12 school settings (U.S. Census Bureau, 2021c). As a result, school counselors, school psychologists, and other mental health providers have a higher chance of encountering Asian American students who present clinical issues that are different from those in the mainstream culture. In this section, we present cultural aspects that might influence the mental health of Asian American children, adolescents, and young adults. We also discuss the barriers to Asian American youth's seeking mental health services and present some culturally responsive strategies for working with Asian American youth.

Factors Influencing Asian American Youth

AAPI youth have experienced many of the same developmental problems as other minority youth experience, such as strained social relationships with peers and discrimination, to name a few. Asian American youth have specifically experienced difficulties related to the model minority myth, acculturative issues, and parental expectations (Guo, 2017; S. Lee et al., 2009). The following section discusses the model minority myth, acculturation issues, and parental expectations in more detail and discusses how these factors affect Asian American youth.

Model Minority Myth

Asian Americans are often described as the "model minority." The model minority myth negatively affects Asian Americans, resulting in stress and negativity. According to one study (Thompson & Kiang, 2010), nearly 100% of Asian American youth surveyed had reported experiencing this stereotype. Although the model minority image sometimes is viewed with pride by some Asian American adolescents and college students, others feel that this image forces them into an unrealistic social identity (Oyserman & Sakamoto, 1997; Thompson & Kiang, 2010). Even with the positive aspects of the model minority myth, Asian American youth often suffer from having a negative image of this stereotype, such as excessive competition and social awkwardness (Lin et al., 2005). In addition, Asian American children were shown to have higher rates of clinical depression, suicidal thoughts, and anxiety disorders compared with peers from other pan-ethnic groups (Austin & Chorpita, 2004; Chang et al., 1995; H. Choi et al., 2006; D. L. Lee & Ahn, 2011; Nguyen et al., 2004; Okazaki, 2000). The model minority image also creates a wide range of psychological problems in Asian American youth (Zhou et al., 2003). For example, many Chinese American youths have reported ethnic discrimination due to the model minority image (Rosenbloom & Way, 2004). Historically, the children of Asian immigrants tend to perform better than Hispanics, non-Hispanic Blacks, and non-Hispanic Whites on achievement tests and levels of educational attainment. Higher academic performance has become a pattern for Asians (Jiménez, 2017). This high academic performance expectation also affects how teachers perceive Asian American students. Teachers with stereotypical ideas about Asians tend to hold high expectations toward Asian American students and expect them to perform better academically. However, teachers' high expectations of Asian American youth may trigger discrimination from peers who did not receive the same level of attention (Louie, 2008). The unreasonably high expectations can also contribute to youth's fear of failure (Tang, 2008). This perceived discrimination stimulates depressive symptoms, substance use, poor mental health, and self-esteem and anxiety issues (Gee, 2002; Gee, Delva, et al., 2007; Gee, Spencer, et al., 2007; Mossakowski, 2003).

Acculturation

In addition to unrealistic images of the model minority, acculturation levels play another important role in the mental health of Asian Americans. *Acculturation* is defined as the process whereby members of an immigrant group slowly adopt the behaviors and attitudes of the host society (Gordon, 1964). Portes and colleagues developed a typology to explain the process of immigrant children learning the host country's language and culture. This typology includes consonant, dissonant, and selective acculturation (Portes &

Rumbaut, 2001, 2014; Portes & Zhou, 1993). *Selective acculturation* indicates that immigrant children are in the process of learning the host country's language and culture without abandoning their parents' culture and their ethnic community. *Consonant acculturation* refers to immigrant parents and their children learning and adapting to the host country's culture and language at the same pace. *Dissonant acculturation* refers to the process through which immigrant children lose their ethnic culture and language, which can result in conflicts between parents and children. These levels of acculturation affect Asian American children, adolescents, and young adults. Asian American youth with selective acculturation would have more positive educational outcomes; in contrast, dissonant acculturation leads to more negative outcomes (Portes & Rumbaut, 2014).

High identification with the Asian culture of origin is crucial in relation to acculturation. Fuligni et al. (2005) found that high Asian identification was associated with high academic motivation and achievement among Chinese high school students. Korean American youths' low levels of acculturation were predictive of poor social skills for peer interaction, resulting in psychological stress (Rhee et al., 2003). Researchers also found that Korean American students aged 18 to 29 have reported negative mental health outcomes associated with the pressure of balancing their Korean identity while limiting their Korean background to fit into the culture of the United States (Hovey et al., 2006). The culture of the United States values more individualistic behaviors. In a study of 217 Korean American students (ages 13–18), ethnic identity (a sense of belonging and positive attachments to one's ethnic group) was a significant predictor of internalizing and externalizing problems. Students' perceived discrimination also correlated with adolescents' externalizing problems (Shrake & Rhee, 2004).

The levels of acculturation also influence willingness to seek help from mental health professionals. Individuals with low levels of acculturation may continue to perceive stigma around seeking mental health services. In contrast, people with high levels of acculturation are more open to help and services for their mental health and are more likely to seek professional help for psychological problems. Santiago (2005) has found that individuals with high levels of acculturation are more likely to seek professional help for psychological problems. High levels of acculturation are also associated with higher tolerance of the stigma relating to seeking help for psychological issues (Atkinson & Gim, 1989). Matching value is another important factor influencing satisfaction with the counseling experiences (B. S. K. Kim & Atkinson, 2002). This also speaks to the influences of levels of acculturation on help-seeking behaviors regarding mental health services and youths' experiences with mental health supports.

Parental Influences

Culture influences many aspects of an individual's life, including parenting style, parental expectations, and the ways parents communicate to their children. Many Asian countries are influenced by Confucian teachings, which emphasize hierarchical relationships (Rothbaum et al., 2000; Triandis, 1995). Parents from Confucian cultures are comfortable with directly communicating their expectations to their children even after their children become young adults. In contrast, parents in middle-class North American culture value more equal relationships between adults and children. As a result, Asian children are more easily influenced by their parents and their parents' expectations. The downside of being easily influenced by parental expectations is that Asians and Asian Americans have a higher chance of being less satisfied with their lives because they may feel that they have not attained their parents' standards (Oishi & Sullivan, 2005).

In addition to the influences of parental expectations, Asian Americans have a tendency to highly value education. People of Asian descent have positive achievement-related attitudes and behaviors, which might result from traditional beliefs about education in their cultures (Ng & Wang, 2019). This belief might be influenced by Confucianism, but this value placed on education can also be seen in those without a Confucian heritage, such as East Indian Americans (Sue & Okazaki, 1990; Xie & Goyette, 2003). Parental expectations regarding education and other aspects of a child's life can have a strong impact on a youth's mental health. Oishi and Sullivan (2005), having explored the relationship between perceived parental expectation and young adults' well-being, found that fulfillment of parental expectations is associated with higher levels of life satisfaction and self-esteem. However, Japanese college students had lower levels of life satisfaction and self-esteem than did American college students. Japanese college students also reported lower levels of fulfilling parental expectations than did American students.

COUNSELING ADULTS, COUPLES, AND FAMILIES

Asian communities within the United States continue to grow at an exponential rate. As discussed earlier, various intersecting identities exist within the Asian communities, which consequently have a unique impact on their mental health. Crenshaw (1989) points out that our unique intersecting identities of privilege and oppression have a dramatic impact on how we navigate this world. Intersectionality theory is an offshoot of the larger critical race theory. According to Crenshaw, human experiences are rarely one-dimensional. Thus, per the theory, human experiences are not solely dictated by gender, race, or age. Instead, they are transformed by a unique confluence of sociocultural identities that dictate our experiences of power, privilege, and oppression. Therefore, instead of providing generalized recommendations for counseling adults, couples, and families who identify as Asian, we offer an intersectional perspective that is imperative to providing a culturally responsive counseling experience for AAPI communities. Specific benefits of adopting an intersectional perspective are:

1. More thorough case conceptualization of the clients' presenting concerns.
2. Consideration of power, oppression, and privilege, and their consequent impact on a client's worldviews, the therapeutic alliance, and counselors' self-awareness as outlined in the MSJCC (Ratts et al., 2015).
3. A shift from a symptom reduction perspective to the holistic well-being of the client, as clients' behaviors are understood in the context of their culture.
4. Moving away from Eurocentric, monolithic consideration of AAPI clients' experiences to a deeper understanding of the heterogeneity within the community.

For a long time, mental health literature about Asian communities has been one-dimensional and homogenizing (Anandavalli, in press; Chan et al., 2021). Popular media and academic textbooks were alike in describing Asian community members as docile, obedient, submissive, and so on. In other words, mental health literature grounded in Eurocentrism and White supremacy may inevitably include or recast notions of model minority myth and other forms of stereotypes, as they are not founded on a critical and social justice perspective (Cho, 1997). In a previous section of this chapter, AsianCrit theory was discussed, drawing attention to how Asianization in itself was a racial experience. Asianization rests on a supremacist notion of what attributes are inherently Asian. Typecasts and racist tropes are used to reduce the complexity and heterogeneity of AAPI communities. Adopting a critical perspective, this section delineates how clinicians can work with individuals, couples, and families in the Asian community.

Nevertheless, counselors working with AAPI communities must recognize that while there are some common Asianizing experiences, their adult, couples, and family clients will also present idiosyncratic features in counseling. Adopting the intersectionality theory, three specific intersections are examined in this section. They are racialized sexual harassment experienced by women, queer communities and the discrimination faced by them, and lastly academics, particularly counselor educators who identify as Asian.

Racialized Sexual Harassment Experienced by Asian American and Pacific Islander Women

Racialized sexual harassment refers to the weaponization of sexual harassment to communicate messages of racial inferiority and submissiveness to the larger Asian community (Anandavalli, in press). Scholars have indicated that Asian women continue to be fetishized under the dominant gaze wherein they are caricaturized as sexually deviant and submissive. Furthermore, sexualized racist tropes such as "yellow face," "geisha sex," and "mama san" are popular categories in pornography, consequently normalizing violent and harmful attitudes and behaviors against Asian women (Azhar et al., 2021; Fritz & Paul, 2017). Unfortunately, counseling literature on this topic is limited, despite a significant proportion of Asian women reporting harassment (Cho, 1997; Ho et al., 2018; Sue et al., 2007). Thus, adopting an intersectional approach may help counselors observe how various identities compound the oppression faced by various sectors of the Asian population.

In a recent article exploring the concept of racialized sexual harassment faced by Asian women, Anandavalli (in press) examined how race, gender, and social class intersected to perpetuate a denigrating attitude toward Asian women. Anandavalli (in press) adopted the Multidimensional Model of Broaching Behavior (MMBB; Day-Vines et al., 2020) to identify specific strategies that counselors can use when working with Asian women who have experienced this specific form of victimization. Day-Vines et al. (2020) note that MMBB has four main broaching domains. These are: (a) intracounseling (intersecting identities occupied by clinician and AAPI client, and the consequent impact on power in the counseling relationship); (b) intraindividual (by actively broaching AAPI clients' intersecting identities such as race, age, and gender, counselors may create an opportunity to acknowledge the compounding nature of oppressive social hierarchies); (c) intra-racial, ethnic, and cultural (in this domain, professional counselors examine how within-group [i.e., the client's cultural group] differences affect the individual's mental health); and (d) interracial, ethnic, and cultural (counselors examine how power differences between groups along the dimension of race, ethnicity, gender, class, and other social dimensions amplify inequity in society and have a damaging impact on clients' mental health). Day-Vines and colleagues observe that based on clients' needs, counselors may have to flexibly move among various domains. Thus, counselors working with AAPI women who may have been victimized based on their gender and race can be supported using the MMBB's intentional approach to broaching.

Queer Communities

Another specific intersection of AAPI communities is the queer community. A confluence of model minority myth, sexism, and xenophobia often result in compounded oppression faced by queer folks from AAPI communities. Patel (2019) discussed in her recent inquiry that South Asian queer women experience racial discrimination and demands for assimilating to the Western norms of what constitutes queerness. Patel discussed how White queer folks leverage their racial privilege and discredit the intersecting experiences of queer South Asian women. Scholars have also discussed how queer South Asian women are the perpetual outsiders, and constantly "othered" through the narrow colonial lens as "conservative" and "traditional" (L. Jones, 2016). Patel notes that despite several scholars identifying discrimination faced by queer South Asian women, little has changed in the past two decades.

Counseling Considerations and Interventions for Couples and Families

Although the above-mentioned concerns affect individuals' mental health, the systems approach to well-being makes it evident that individual mental health has an impact on couple and family mental health as well. This statement may stand especially true for AAPIs, as AAPI communities are especially known for valuing the collective well-being and harmony in the community. Here, three key considerations are offered as counselors seek to work with relational units (e.g., couples and families).

1. **Acculturation stress:** Irrespective of their immigration status, AAPI families and couples frequently experience othering and messages of being "perpetual foreigners." Positioned against dominant White standards, AAPI communities may face the continual pressure of acculturating to White heteronormative standards. Counselors must be culturally responsive and trauma-informed as they invite relational units to examine their own White proximity-seeking behavior and its impact on their well-being.
2. **Stereotypes and anti-immigrant sentiment:** In the context of xenophobia, and heightened Sinophobia, families and couples may experience significant stress on their mental health. Counselors must address systemic inequities in their clinical work and explicitly invite clients to process their trauma.
3. **Cultural strengths and community wealth:** AAPI communities have faced several waves of trauma, oppression, and discrimination. However, AAPI communities are also resilient and leverage their unique cultural capitals to support their mental health. Counselors are strongly recommended to examine the unique strengths of AAPI relational units (e.g., ambition, resilience, resourcefulness) and incorporate them into treatment planning.

IMPLICATIONS FOR CLINICAL PRACTICE

Within Group Differences

The within-group differences should be taken seriously when it comes to AAPIs. AAPIs are one of the minority groups that are extremely diverse in history, culture, and language. However, historically and sociopolitically, AAPIs are considered one ethnicity in the United States. Although AAPIs may share some traditional cultural aspects, such as collectivistic worldviews and patriarchal family dynamics, the impact of historical, regional, social-political, and generational differences on identity development and mental health makes generalization impossible. It is wise to take this chapter as a guide in understanding and advocating for AAPIs rather than overgeneralizing and applying methods without caution. For ethnic identity development, it is recommended that counselors learn more about the historical and cultural uniqueness of AAPIs, as scholars have contributed in the literature (see Ibrahim et al. [1997] on Indian and Pakistan Americans' identity development and Nadal [2019] on F/Philippine Americans').

Contextualized Intersectionality

AAPIs are one of the minority groups that have been silenced and ignored regarding discrimination and oppression throughout United States history. Unfortunately, their pain and experience of violence and crimes received some attention during the COVID-19 pandemic. However, AAPIs' mental health issues are less understood, misunderstood, and sadly forgotten compared to those of their White counterparts. Counselors working with AAPIs should apply intersectionality in their practice, as it is apparent that each AAPI individual experiences discrimination and oppression differently. Further, the history among Asian countries, their immigrant history, and the United States history using AAPIs as a model minority for political purposes make intersectionality more critical in understanding the experiences of AAPIs. In addition, AAPIs' concept of self significantly depends on the society's perception of their collective identity due to their collectivistic perspectives. Therefore, it is imperative for counselors to have a deeper understanding of how AAPI clients' experiences are positioned and contextualized within the community to which they belong.

Strengths-Based, Cultural Asset Approach

Deficit- and damaging-centric narratives about minoritized communities have been a dehumanizing weapon in human history, wherein denigrating stories about the culture and intellectual potential of certain cultural communities have been perpetuated, and perhaps even normalized (Tuck, 2009). An insistence that racial and ethnic minority communities are culturally impoverished, devoid of any redeeming attributes is based on White supremacist notions. Such narratives eventually give birth to harmful racist tropes and stereotypes (Tuck, 2009; Yosso, 2005). However, a strengths-based approach that draws attention to cultural strengths such as resilience, aspirations, familial support, spirituality, and community can offer a counter-narrative to such damaging narratives (Anandavalli, 2021). Critical race theorist Tara Yosso (2005) has written extensively about the importance of adopting a strengths-based approach in working with racially minoritized communities. Her theoretical framework, known as Community Cultural Wealth, draws attention to six different types of cultural strengths. These are familial capital (support from a family network), aspirational capital (the desire and motivation to maintain hope and ambition despite systemic injustices), social capital (networks of communities and people that to provide emotional and instrumental support in the face of injustices), linguistic capital (intellectual and social strengths developed through the use of various languages), resistant capital (knowledge and skills developed through defiant behavior challenging inequitable structures), and navigational capital (skills of maneuvering through systems that are inherently unfair to Black, Indigenous, and People of Color [BIPOC] communities).

Given the numerous sociopolitical challenges the AAPI community in the United States has suffered through, damage-centric narratives may be especially harmful to this community. Clinicians are invited to adopt a strengths-focused approach, examining the unique cultural assets and legacies that support AAPI communities. For instance, counselors may ask their clients, "As the U.S. society is becoming increasingly anti-Asian, what are some cultural and familial strengths that help you navigate?" Thus, a strengths-based and cultural capital-affirming approach to counseling may help in shifting damaging narratives and offering culturally affirming counseling to AAPI communities.

CLINICAL CASE SCENARIO 6.1

John Doe was referred to you (a mental health counselor) upon the recommendation of the school counselor. John Doe is a Korean American, male 10th grader, with symptoms of depression. His grades started dropping when he began high school. He was a swimmer and played violin until he moved to a new high school that is ethnically diverse. His previous school was predominantly White. He is quiet and shy, and he does not talk much in the first session. His parents immigrated to the United States before he was born. John's father is a manager of a luxury car dealership, and his mom is a housewife. Both parents are college graduates from Korea. He has a younger sister who is in seventh grade and excels academically. His family attends a Presbyterian Korean church. While John was referred to you, his mom disclosed that she has issues in her marriage and is considering counseling for herself.

CLINICAL CASE SCENARIO DISCUSSION QUESTIONS

1. What other information would the school and mental health counselors need to know to better assist John?
2. What cultural considerations are relevant to this case?
3. As a counselor, what interventions would you choose in working with John? Why?
4. Which MSJCC quadrant would you identify in working with John and his family?
5. Working with John's mom, what kinds of social and interpersonal cues would you utilize in building rapport with her?
6. How will you advocate for John within the school system? Within his family?

END-OF-CHAPTER RESOURCES

A robust set of instructor resources designed to supplement this text is located at **http://connect.springerpub.com/content/book/978-0-8261-3953-5**. Qualifying instructors may request access by emailing **textbook@springerpub.com**.

SUMMARY

Many concepts have been introduced throughout this chapter to consider in counseling AAPIs. It is important to note the history of AAPIs in the United States as well as the racism, discrimination, and microaggressions that have been inherently a part of their experiences. These encounters are also very much continuing to be a part of their present-day cultural concerns as AAPIs in the United States. Culturally responsive counselor trainees and counselors must pay close attention to the cultural makeup of AAPI communities, as this will result in productive clinical interventions. Counselors need to pay attention to the collectivistic worldviews of AAPIs and explore how these views emerge in their interactions with the family unit and the collective AAPI communities. It is also important to attend to AAPIs' cultural values as it relates to their mental health help-seeking behaviors. Counselors are advised to do their utmost to employ culturally responsive clinical approaches in order to provide optimal care for AAPI people.

DISCUSSION QUESTIONS

1. What cultural challenges do AAPI groups experience?
2. What are the different acculturation stages that an AAPI individual might experience?
3. How do queer members of AAPI communities define and make meaning of their intersection?
4. What is a model minority myth?
5. What is the "saving face" phenomenon?

▶ CULTURALLY RESPONSIVE COUNSELING FOR CLIENTS OF ASIAN AMERICAN AND PACIFIC ISLANDER DESCENT

Guest: Dr. Jung H. Hyun

https://connect.springerpub.com/content/book/978-0-8261-3953-5/part/part02/chapter/ch06

KEY REFERENCES

Only key references appear in the print edition. The full reference list appears in the digital product on Springer Publishing Connect: https://connect.springerpub.com/content/book/978-0-8261-3953-5/part/part02/chapter/ch06

American Counseling Association. (2014). *2014 ACA Code of Ethics*. Author. https://www.counseling.org/resources/aca-code-of-ethics.pdf

Anandavalli, S. (2021). Strengths-based counseling with international students of color: A community cultural wealth approach. *Journal of Asia Pacific Counseling*, 11(1), 111–124. https://doi.org/10.18401/2021.11.1.7

Anandavalli, S., Harrichand, J. J. S., & Litam, S. D. A. (2020). Counseling international students in times of uncertainty: A critical feminist and bioecological approach. *The Professional Counselor*, 10(3), 365–375. https://doi.org/10.15241/sa.10.3.365

Atkinson, D. R., & Gim, R. H. (1989). Asian-American cultural identity and attitudes toward mental health services. *Journal of Counseling Psychology*, 36(2), 209–212. https://doi.org/10.1037/0022-0167.36.2.209

Atkinson, D. R., Morten, G., & Sue, D. W. (1998). *Counseling American minorities: A cross cultural perspective*. McGraw Hill.

Chan, C. D., DeDiego t, A. C., & Band, M. P. (2019). Moving counselor educators to influential roles as advocates: An ecological systems approach to student-focused advocacy. *Journal of Counselor Leadership and Advocacy*, 6(1), 30–41. https://doi.org/10.1080/2326716X.2018.1545614

Chan, C. D., Harrichand, J. J. S., Anandavalli, S., Vaishnav, S., Chang, C. Y., Hyun, J. H., & Band, M. P. (2021). Mapping solidarity, liberation, and activism: A critical autoethnography of Asian American leaders in counseling. *Journal of Mental Health Counseling*, 43(3), 246–265. https://doi.org/10.17744/mehc.43.3.06

Crenshaw, K. W. (1989). Demarginalizing the intersection of race and sex: A Black feminist critique of antidiscrimination doctrine, feminist theory and antiracist politics. *University of Chicago Legal Forum*, 140, 139–167. https://chicagounbound.uchicago.edu/cgi/viewcontent.cgi?article=1052&context=uclf

Helms, J. E. (1990). *Black and White racial identity: Theory, research, and practice*. Greenwood Press.

Kim, B. S. K., & Atkinson, D. R. (2002). Asian American client adherence to Asian cultural values, counselor expression of cultural values, couselor ethnicity, and career counseling process. *Journal of Counseling Psychology*, 49(1), 3–13. https://doi.org/10.1037/0022-0167.49.1.3

Litam, S. D. A. (2020). "Take your Kung-Flu back to Wuhan": Counseling Asians, Asian Americans, and Pacific Islanders with race-based trauma related to COVID-19. *The Professional Counselor*, 10(2), 144–156. https://doi.org/10.15241/sdal.10.2.144

Ng, F. F. Y., & Wang, Q. (2019). Asian and Asian American parenting. In M. H. Bornstein (Ed.), *Handbook of parenting: Social conditions and applied parenting* (3rd ed., Vol. 4, pp. 108–169). Routledge. https://doi.org/10.4324/9780429398995

Phinney, J. S. (1990). Ethnic identity in adolescents and adults: Review of research. *Psychological Bulletin, 108*(3), 499–514. https://doi.org/10.1037/0033-2909.108.3.499

Phinney, J. S., Lochner, B., & Murphy, R. (1990). Ethnic identity development and psychological adjustment in adolescence. In A. Stiffman & L. Davis (Eds.), *Ethnic issues in adolescent mental health* (pp. 53–72). SAGE.

Ratts, M. J., Singh, A. A., Nassar-McMillan, S., Butler, S. K., McCullough, J. R., & Hipolito-Delgado, C. (2015). *Multicultural and social justice counseling competencies*. Association for Multicultural Counseling and Development. https://www.counseling.org/docs/default-source/competencies/multicultural-and-social-justice-counseling-competencies.pdf?sfvrsn=20

Sue, D. W., Sue, D., Neville, H. A., & Smith, L. (2019). *Counseling the culturally diverse: Theory and practice* (8th ed.). Wiley.

CHAPTER 7

Culturally Responsive Counseling for Clients of Latinx Descent

GEORGE JAMES RAMOS AND ANTOINETTE GINES-RIVERA

LEARNING OBJECTIVES

After reading this chapter, students will be able to:

- Recognize the sociocultural, racial, and historical issues that influence multiracial clients, to increase counselor awareness and reduce cultural insensitivities.
- Develop a deeper awareness of multiracial identity development and competencies so as to address the needs of multiracial clients.
- Identify ways to advocate for improved learning and address the ongoing needs of multiracial clients.
- Review culturally responsive strategies and techniques that will support multiracial populations.

SELF-REFLECTION QUESTIONS

1. Consider what your own interactions with Latinxs have been across the span of your life. What common values, if any, have you observed?
2. How have the media and government affected how people have viewed immigrants from Latin American counties?
3. What role does family play in Latinx families?
4. What do you think some of the common attitudes about mental health are in Latinx communities?

THE COUNSELOR: EXPLORATION, INTROSPECTION, AND REFLECTION

The counseling profession is unique. It is a field wherein practitioners often are challenged to go beyond what they were merely taught within their educational journeys so they can constantly update their knowledge about therapies and strategies that help their clients, the demographics of which are constantly changing. Through the years, it has been made clear that this profession requires a healthy dose of self-awareness to be successful. Although this principle is taught in many graduate-level counseling programs, not all professional counselors adhere to this standard. The Council for the Accreditation of Counseling and Related Educational Programs (CACREP) 2009 standards define competent professionals as individuals who have acquired the knowledge and skills necessary to practice their profession correctly while at the same time building their own professional identity (Liles & Wagner, 2010). A well-developed professional identity helps a person operate with integrity, adhere to established ethical standards, and gain a complete understanding of clients and their problems. However, let us not disregard that developing into a well-rounded professional counselor requires time, skill acquisition, and self-introspection.

Counselors must be aware of themselves to be competent in their profession because self-awareness can lead to more effective practice (Field, 2017; Watson & Schmit, 2019). A self-aware counselor is someone who works professionally and competently, and who can demonstrate that they can identify and accept their limitations when receiving supervision or referring clients to more competent or more suitable professionals when needed (Liles & Wagner, 2010). A healthy awareness of one's limitations also leads to seeking additional training and understanding. This includes being aware that one can hold certain biases and prejudices about a particular client of color based on one's upbringing, experiences, or simple unfamiliarity (Cook et al., 2019; Matthews et al., 2018).

Even though self-awareness is not innately acquired, emerging counselors studying this profession are expected to monitor their limitations and biases to decide how to use appropriate counseling treatments in specific settings. According to Hansen (2009), four requirements must be met to establish the concept of self-awareness. The self must (a) be authentic, (b) be open to reflection, (c) have a permanent essence, and (d) be able to be articulated in words. These existential criteria suggest that a person has higher-order cognitive abilities to self-regulate their thoughts and activities. Being a counselor requires metacognition for introspection, exploration, and reflection. *Metacognition* is the process through which a person thinks about how they think (Martinez, 2006). Higher levels of metacognition have been related to improved problem-solving ability, as well as goal-setting capacity. Metacognition is described as knowing and understanding one's thinking, as well as knowing when and how to use metacognitive techniques to enhance awareness and understanding of one's own thought processes (Byars-Winston & Fouad, 2006; Wilkinson, 2011).

Counselors must learn to recognize how they think or feel about their own thought processes so that they can develop appropriate counseling therapies that will benefit the client. Responding to unexpected events is aided by one's prior experience or the comprehension of a scenario, and an understanding of how one reacts to unfolding events. When presented with actual issues that cannot be solved by prior knowledge or intuitive responses, a responsible counselor will defer to metacognitive activity (Byars-Winston & Fouad, 2006; Wilkinson, 2011). Counseling situations can be intricate, challenging, and puzzling (Ziomek-Daigle & Curtis, 2017). To contextualize their clients' idiosyncrasies, metacognitive processes can be instrumental in processing the matter at hand. Metacognitive techniques may be utilized effectively in counseling sessions using here-and-now processing and detecting countertransference (Wilkinson, 2011).

LATINX AMERICAN HISTORY, LATINX VALUES, AND CULTURE

Hispanic ethnicity in the Americas dates to the Spanish discovery of Nueva España and the subsequent early encounters with indigenous peoples. Later, the addition of

Africans contributed to the development of a unique Hispano legacy (Gann et al., 2019; Martínez & Gonzalez, 2021; Rumbaut, 2019). Hispanic culture in North America is often associated with Spanish colonial history and Mexico. However, individuals from South and Central America and the Caribbean have been altering the nature of Hispanic culture since the second half of the 20th century. Recent scholarly studies have researched the landscape's effect on Hispanic-inspired architectural, agricultural, and mining activities. Simultaneously, researchers' interest in Hispanic self-identification and the site of new communities is growing (Gann et al., 2019; Martínez & Gonzalez, 2021; Rumbaut, 2019).

Hispanics have become the largest minority group in the United States, according to the United States Census of 2000, up 57.9% from the previous census (Guzmán, 2001). Congress passed legislation in 2000 that allowed for multiple ethnic identities in the census. Hispanic ancestry is primarily associated with large populations in the western United States (Gann et al., 2019; Martínez & Gonzalez, 2021; Rumbaut, 2019). However, emigration and intermigration figures from the 2000 census show Hispanics settling in new areas across the country, with significant increases in the south and northeast.

Mexicans have traditionally been the largest nationality among the Hispanic community in the United States, followed by Puerto Ricans and Cubans. Mexicans account for 58.5% of the Hispanic population, Puerto Ricans 9%, and Cubans 3.5%, according to census data from 2000 (Acuña, 2017). The numbers have significantly increased through the years, with Dominicans accounting for 2.2% of the Hispanic population, Salvadorans for 1%, and Colombians for 1%. The remaining 23% of the 35.3 million Hispanics in the United States are from Latin America, the Caribbean, and Spanish immigration (Acuña, 2017). Despite the influence of the Latin American group, there is no Pan-Hispanic identity. Pan-Hispanic identity is a political neologism used to group ethnic groups based on their related cultural origins (e.g., all Spanish-speaking groups). According to Licea (2020), it was only in the late 1960s that individuals from former Spanish colonies in the Americas and Spain emerged to represent a distinct ethnic or racial group. Only 24% of this group's members use a pan-ethnic moniker to identify themselves, while 60% believe they do not have a shared cultural background.

Research on the Hispanic culture in the Americas conceptualizes the culture as a multivalent model revolving around some areas of convergence, rather than viewing the Hispanic culture as a monolithic entity. The earlier monolithic models included having a Spanish linguistic legacy, genetic and cultural creolization, observing a Catholic tradition, and possessing a shared history of the national independence story from being conquered and oppressed by Spanish rule (Fernández-Armesto, 2014). However, this familiar narrative excluded the hundreds of thousands of Indian and *mestizo* ancestors who were already residing and settling in the North American Spanish possessions before the United States took over the country. *Mestizo* is defined as a racial identification of European and Indigenous American ancestry. Latin American countries use the word *mestizo* (mixed) to designate persons of mixed European and indigenous origin. Spain's past dominion established touchstones for numerous nations and areas, but these touchstones are insufficient to characterize all Central and South American and Caribbean states' peoples (Fernández-Armesto, 2014).

The Emergence of Latinx

The term *Latinx* emerged during the early 2000s when some individuals of Latin descent did not want to be identified by gender (Salinas Jr & Lozano, 2019). Therefore, Latinx replaced the terms *Latino* and *Latina* so that individuals would not have to be identified through the expression of gender. Latinx, being a gender-neutral term, is very much supported by members of the Latin lesbian, gay, bisexual, and transgender (LGBT) communities (Salinas Jr & Lozano, 2019.). This is because the male and female binary is deeply rooted throughout the Spanish language; the Spanish tend to lack neutral nouns, as terms are either masculine or feminine (Beatty-Martínez & Dussias, 2019). Therefore, the creation of Latinx has broken away from many of the Spanish language's traditional grammar rules. Latinx has become used more regularly throughout social media and academic writing, but not all members of the Latin community have heard or have even used the term. For example, approximately one in four American Hispanics have heard of the term Latinx, but only 3% of their population has used it (Noe-Bustamante et al., 2020). Therefore, throughout this chapter, the traditional terms Latino and Latina will be used where appropriate.

MENTAL HEALTH CONSIDERATIONS AND PERCEPTIONS

A study by Aguilar-Gaxiola et al. (2002) engaged Latinos in discussions about mental health. Latinos from 13 California towns and two high schools were included. The research revealed impediments to healthcare access and service users and made recommendations for addressing inequalities (Aguilar-Gaxiola et al., 2002). Moreover, acculturative stress, poverty, bad housing, inadequate transportation, abuse, trauma, language hurdles, social isolation, and prejudice were among the identified obstacles faced by Latino people. Most obstacles were discovered to lead to mental health issues such as despair, anxiety, and alcohol and substance abuse (Benuto et al., 2018; Tineo et al., 2020; Verile et al., 2019). However, many Latinos throughout the study revealed that they did not seek treatment because of the associated stigma, a lack of understanding about the significance of mental health, a lack of access to resources for managing mental health issues, and treatments that were not culturally or linguistically appropriate (Benuto et al., 2018; Tineo et al., 2020; Verile et al., 2019). Latino Americans need to know that mental health and social services are available and can be easily accessed if they are willing to press through the existing barriers (Benuto et al., 2018; Tineo et al., 2020; Verile et al., 2019).

IDENTITY DEVELOPMENT FOR CLIENTS OF LATINX DESCENT

Minority groups have a unique experience in developing a sense of self or self-concept. Unlike White Americans, Latinos in the United States have a different experience as a minority group. Identity development is important because it affects a person's sense of self-connection to inner beliefs and others (Umaña-Taylor et al., 2002). A sense of self is a complicated system of beliefs that individuals have about themselves, each of which has a corresponding value (Umaña-Taylor et al., 2002).

Counseling with Hispanics in the United States from different ethnicities is not without challenges, and requires an understanding of both their political and economic status (Acosta et al., 1990). One challenge for the counseling profession is to maintain anonymity; as many Hispanics are of undocumented status, counselors must protect "even to the point of keeping no records" (Acosta et al., 1990, p. 34). Consequently, the attempt to provide culturally balanced counseling poses an additional dilemma: that of the practitioner's competence level of cultural literacy and ability to respect and understand clients' cultural beliefs and values without conceding to "stereotypical evaluations that rob clients of their individual histories and choices" (Falicov, 1998, p. 6). Falicov further attested, "While they may acknowledge that clients are deeply connected to their cultural roots" (1998, p. 5), therapists may be unaware of what cultural heritage and social context have to do with human suffering and mental health care. Consequently, recent literature affirms that perhaps the most obvious hindrances to improving cultural sensitivity in counseling are the limitations of theories, models, and research in addition to the need for consensus on an accurate definition of *cultural sensitivity* (Herman et al., 2007).

The prevailing ideas and concepts of Americanization change people's conceptions of themselves over time. Generational disparities within the Latino community cause variations in cultural identification. In areas such as self-esteem, depression, ethnic pride, and academic performance, each generation will meet distinct experiences that boost and impair identity development and well-being (Ma-Kellams, 2021). It is more possible to comprehend the influence of assimilation, acculturation, enculturation, and biculturalism on Latinos' adaptation process and identity formation by analyzing and characterizing these processes (Huynh et al., 2018). Individuals who are identified as Latino or Hispanic cannot be considered a homogenous group of people. This goes for most racial groups, as there are various people within the Latino community or people of Latino descent (Cervantes & Bui, 2017). Recognizing this is critical for the readiness of counselors to serve this community properly.

Acculturation and *assimilation* are terms used to describe the processes that occur when two different cultures interact (Ferreira, 2014). When one culture influences another, it causes alterations in attitudes, values, behaviors, ethnic label identification, and language. Assimilation is an outcome of acculturation where the original culture is replaced by the host culture. Instead, the local culture is preserved, and parts of the new culture are adapted (Ferreira, 2014). Due to physical proximity to the host country, language, continual immigration, and prejudice, Latino immigrants are less likely to integrate (Ferreira, 2014). Because their native language, Spanish, is still spoken by other immigrants, such as their family and neighbors, there is less temptation to forsake their culture. Furthermore, they are familiar with Spanish terms in American society (Ferreira, 2014). Acculturation entails the creation of new identities based on interactions and environment (Ferreira, 2014). However, in the bid to adhere to and observe American cultural standards, it can sometimes come at the cost of sacrificing a portion of one's own culture (Quintana & Scull, 2009). Finding the right balance to manage the acculturation and enculturation processes might lead to a level of biculturalism that combines the two cultures (Ferreira, 2014). *Enculturation* is the gradual process in which the individual learns and acquires the accepted norms and values of a culture. The entire development of both cultures is greatly influenced by individuals' experiences as children.

One in every five children currently living in United States urban areas is either an immigrant or born to immigrant parents, with the majority being South American (Artico, 2000). Each day, nearly 1,000 immigrant students are entering schools throughout the United States (Rong & Brown, 2002). Magdaleno (2006) posits that California's public school system alone currently is comprised of 2.96 million students, 47% of whom are Latino immigrants. Language learning is one of the most common examples of the acculturation and assimilation processes. In the United States, English is necessary for daily communication, job searching, and revenue generation (Ferreira, 2014). These conditions force immigrants to develop skills in speaking and understanding English as a second language. With newer generations, English becomes the dominant language, making it impossible to speak Spanish 100% of the time to maintain Latino identity and engage in cultural practices.

Because the original language is no longer spoken, children who reject the Spanish language might be regarded as exhibiting assimilation. Around 95 of 1,222 Latino people polled in the United States felt it was critical for future generations to communicate in Spanish, even though 51% of Latinos born in the United States are English dominant and 38% are bilingual (Taylor et al., 2012). Despite the loss of the Spanish language and a lack of understanding of Hispanic culture, there was still a sense of cultural pride among succeeding generations of Latinos (Taylor et al., 2012).

COUNSELING UTILIZATION AND HELP-SEEKING OF LATINX CLIENTS

Based on the statistics provided by the United States Census Bureau, a fifth of the U.S. population by 2060 is likely to be foreign-born (Colby & Ortman, 2015). Among these foreign-born individuals, Latin Americans or those with Hispanic ethnicity will increase two-fold and account for as much as nearly 29% of the overall national population (Colby & Ortman, 2015). This is likely to have many implications for various aspects of society. If predictions were to come true, and the population increased from 55 million from 2014 to 119 million by 2060, this would make it the third fastest-growing minority group in the United States (Colby & Ortman, 2015).

Despite the rapid growth of Latinos, culturally appropriate therapy for mental health disorders and issues that this group encounters is relatively scarce, and largely ineffective (Vespa et al., 2020). A pattern can be seen in how Latinos utilize healthcare and counseling services, depending on their generations. First-generation immigrants used mental health services less frequently, particularly for anxiety and mood disorders (Bauldry & Szaflarski, 2017; Szaflarski et al., 2017). Even when they had recently suffered a problem, Mexican immigrants in the late 1990s were hesitant to seek mental health treatment (Barrera & Aratani, 2017; Gonzales et al., 2011; Rosales & Calvo, 2017). Mexican-Americans and other Latinos born in the United States were more likely than first-generation immigrants to have access to healthcare (Barrera & Aratani, 2017; Gonzales et al., 2011; Rosales & Calvo, 2017).

Unlike first- and second-generation Mexican immigrants, both men and women in Puerto Rico were likely to receive mental health care (Barrera & Aratani, 2017; Gonzales et al., 2011; Rosales & Calvo, 2017). There were no follow-up studies involving Puerto Rican islanders or those living in the United States to track their use of mental health services. Nonetheless, because there were no ethnic or cultural obstacles to Western treatment theories in the Alegria et al. (2004) study with Puerto Rican islanders, it might be extrapolated that they were more likely to use and be offered mental health care.

Families, stigma, and socioeconomic factors are cultural and social attitudes that can lead to treatment rejection or low motivation for therapy (Torrero, 2021). Latino, both in Latin America and in the United States, is a varied ethnic community. However, some basic ideas characterizing Latinos and Latino culture endure. *Familismo*—a strong affiliation, affection, and devotion to one's family, and the belief that family is essential in one's life—is a prevalent cultural attitude (Torrero, 2021). It is feasible to think of Latino families as entangled (Torrero, 2021) rather than interdependent, and as valuing collaboration and cohesiveness above competitiveness and dependency (Torrero, 2021). For Latinos, family is likely to be their first or primary source of assistance, leading to them not seeking therapy or delaying treatment (Torrero, 2021). This cultural mindset could be viewed as potentially interfering with Western treatment theories (e.g., psychotherapy).

Families, a significant role in Latino culture, can also influence mental health access for this group (Villatoro et al., 2014). Culturally, Latinos are known for their vows to keep family secrets to themselves, never violating the family's trust by disclosing family matters to an outsider except in the case of a priest, minister, or pastoral counselor (Acosta et al., 1990). It is important to understand that, historically, Latinos are not known to seek outside counseling services and generally designate one person within the family to whom everyone goes for advice (Acosta et al., 1990). According to Falicov (1998), traditionally, it is only the psychotic (*los locos*) who need mental health care. In fact, a request for outside counseling and/or attending mental health services are looked upon as "shameful," and the person who does so is considered "complicated and problematic" (Falicov, 1998, p. 39). Still, when the elected counselor's attempts fail to remediate a problem, individuals may then resort to their neighborhood religious leaders (Acosta et al., 1990; Falicov, 1998; Sells et al., 2007). The National Latino and Asian American Study (NLAAS), a household survey that examined the incidence of mental illnesses and services used by Latinos, was employed. According to epidemiological research, nearly 60% of Latinos satisfy diagnostic criteria for mood, anxiety, or drug use disorder at least once in their lives (Alegria et al., 2004).

Institutional and linguistic obstacles discourage Latinos from accessing services (Torrero, 2021), and alternative resource theory argues that enmeshment in society acts as an alternative resource for these services (Torrero, 2021). Family members and friends close to the family who are commonly relied upon for coping with emotional discomfort and other mental health-related difficulties are included in social enmeshing, an aspect of *familismo* (Villatoro et al., 2014). *Behavioral familismo* is described as the inclination to resort to close family and friends rather than mental health providers when facing mental health difficulties, as well as to the sense of family support (Villatoro et al., 2014). Latinos with high levels of behavioral *familismo* were less likely to seek official mental health treatments and more likely to use informal services such as religion, according to the findings (Villatoro et al., 2014). Another element is the usage of religious services or suggested folk healers.

A literature review revealed a link between low socioeconomic status (SES) and greater rates of depression, aggression, and stress exposure (Adler et al., 1994; Torrero, 2021). Further study indicates a link between poor socioeconomic status and depression in Latinos (Torrero, 2021). This is more likely to be seen among immigrant, undocumented, and first-generation Latinos who have moved to economically and psychologically complex areas (Torrero, 2021).

The stigma associated with mental illness among Latinos may also lead to the underutilization of treatment. According to studies, Latinos are more prone to seek medical help for psychological issues (Olcoń & Gulbas, 2018; Zvolensky et al., 2020). However, depending on age and acculturation levels, this inclination to suffer somatization may be inconsistent. On the Personality Assessment Scale (PAI), Latino students were less likely than European American students to report somatic symptoms, according to Estrada and Smith (2019). It is conceivable that younger Latinos who have been more acculturated to the mainstream United States are better at recognizing psychological stress and distinguishing it from physiological issues. Nonetheless, to avoid the stigma of visiting a mental health practitioner, medical providers are likely to be selected (Gonzales et al., 2011). Stigma should be viewed as a barrier to treatment, particularly in the case of psychotherapy.

When a majority cultural group sets the tone for mental rehabilitation, non-belonging individuals' treatment options and psychological experiences are limited and excluded. Viladrich's ethnographic research in New York City, in which she used qualitative methods to explore Argentine immigrants' access to health providers, illustrates the importance of knowing a client's perspective (Abramson et al., 2002). Argentinians, unlike other Latino individuals, believe in the efficacy of Western medicine and have a reasonable opinion of psychotherapy. According to Viladrich's research, they disrupted U.S. providers and formed informal networks that provided them access to Argentinian health professionals they considered compassionate and trustworthy. The client-therapist relationship and the use of therapeutic services are influenced by views about the disease and mental health, in addition to treatment options (Lombana, 2021).

Getting Latino clients to participate in treatment is a process that should not—and, in some cases, cannot—be hurried (Lombana, 2021). Respect for cultural etiquette (the socially and culturally acquired set of unstated standards for interacting with strangers) is essential to the therapeutic interaction. For engaging and establishing a connection, Delgado-Romero's (2001) idea of *Conocimiento* (knowledge) urges the therapist to depend on naturally occurring cultural etiquette. When a connection contains aspects of mutuality and reciprocity, Latino clients will see it as favorable. Expectations of mutual conduct such as "responsiveness," *respecto* (respect), *confianza* (trust), and *dignidad* (dignity), as well as adequate space and time, are all part of the *compromiso* (commitment) that develops (Lombana, 2021).

As these examples show, *dichos* may be applied to the therapeutic process in a variety of ways. They might also be chosen to aid in the resolution of specific problems (Santiago-Rivera, 2003). According to Aviera (2002), *dichos* refers to the use of Spanish-language proverbs and *refranes* (sayings) in the treatment of a regressed population of Hispanic/Latino, usually psychiatric inpatients.

Certain *dichos* work with couples and families, as well as with anger management and as a cognitive restructuring tool, to assist clients to become more flexible in their life approach (De Rios, 2014). They are also used in therapy work with battered women to identify feelings and address culturally based challenges and other types of resistance (Cohrssen-Hernandez, 2020). The therapist could transform what could be a foreign experience for the client into a culturally appealing and less alienating service by using dichos (Cohrssen-Hernandez, 2020). When discussing the consequences of utilizing *dichos* in treatment for Latino and non-Latino therapists, it is advised that non-Latino (and non-Spanish-speaking) clinicians use *dichos* in therapy with Latino clients and seek advice from a Latino clinician (Lombana, 2021).

One of the aims—or rather, prerequisites—of therapy, is establishing a trusting connection and healing atmosphere. Clients may expose themselves and engage in challenging and demanding work. When dealing with Latino clients, it is essential to understand and respect their expectations, which are influenced by culture and worldview, and incorporate this knowledge into the therapeutic approach. The usage of *dichos* is one example of how this may be assisted, and it works similarly to a spoon in that it can help bring out what is in the pot (Lombana, 2021).

CULTURALLY RESPONSIVE PRACTICES: DRAWING FROM THE MULTICULTURAL AND SOCIAL JUSTICE COUNSELING COMPETENCIES AND CULTURAL HUMILITY

One foundational researcher on the topic of multicultural counseling competency (MCC) is D. W. Sue (D. W. Sue et al., 1992). D. W. Sue's seminal work described the realities at that time of a profession struggling to identify the needs of the *"minority client"* as well as meet the counseling challenges of that era (D. W. Sue et al., 1982). Researched over decades (Caldwell et al., 2008; Patterson, 1996), the theory of MCC continues to subsist within the margins of ambiguity (Caldwell et al., 2008; D. W. Sue et al., 1982). Counseling's multicultural interest was set in motion roughly 50 years ago when clinicians took notice of the underrepresentation of various minority groups in mental health services and how poorly the services were rendered (Patterson, 1996).

D. W. Sue et al. (1992) created the MCCs to assist mental health professionals in meeting the care and counseling needs of individual clients who came from different cultural backgrounds, organizations, and communities. Multicultural viewpoints have become entrenched in many facets of the counseling profession since their emergence and acknowledgment. The MCCs influenced the development of the American Counseling Association's (ACA's) *Code of Ethics* (ACA, 2014) and other ACA divisions' ethical codes. The incorporation of the MCCs and these related abilities into the counseling profession has resulted in a more comprehensive understanding of historically marginalized groups' experiences and, more importantly, in incorporating multicultural conceptions into counseling practice. The primary premise of this idea is that counselors must be multiculturally competent to assist every individual in society effectively. Three essential criteria of multicultural competency explain the three elements of intercultural counseling. Multicultural counseling competency, according to this idea, has three features. The first is that the counselor is conscious of their assumptions, attitudes, and prejudices. Incorporating the culturally varied client's perspective is the second factor. Finally, in the practice of therapy, the counselor develops methods and approaches in line with culture (D. W. Sue et al., 1992). Each of these qualities has three dimensions: (a) attitudes and beliefs (awareness), (b) multicultural counseling competency knowledge, and (c) abilities (D. W. Sue et al., 1982). Collins and Arthur (2010) and D. W. Sue et al. (1992) mentioned these dimensions-based features.

First, to be actively aware of one's assumptions, the counselor must see themself as a cultural creature, and admit one's proclivity to see the world through one's own cultural lens. Awareness also entails understanding how one's cultural background, experiences, attitudes, beliefs, and prejudices may influence the counseling process (Collins & Arthur, 2010; D. W. Sue et al., 1982). Ultimately, this means being at ease with variations in race, ethnicity, values, and beliefs of one's clients. Apart from these attitudinal factors, it means possessing a clear understanding of your own ethnic and cultural history and understanding how that cultural identity may affect the counseling process. It also means that recognizing the standard stages in forming personal cultural identity, and understanding how oppression, racism, discrimination, and stereotyping can influence everyone in a diverse community, are essential (Collins & Arthur, 2010; D. W. Sue et al., 1982). Counselors can gain insight into their own social impact on others and how their communication style affects the counseling process with individuals from various backgrounds.

Apart from having the right attitude and knowledge, counselors should also have the skills to determine opportunities that can help their clients recover, regardless of their background, and to manage conflicts and prejudices. These skills include seeking educational, consultative, and training opportunities to increase one's understanding and effectiveness in servicing clients from various cultural backgrounds. In addition, counselors should confront adverse emotional reactions, prejudices, or value judgments directed toward specific groups (Collins & Arthur, 2010; D. W. Sue et al., 1982).

Seeing oneself as a cultural and racial person searching for a nonracist identity is another crucial skill to have. The second dimension of having a good understanding of how ethnically varied a client's point of view could be also entails a set of attitudes, knowledge, and skills. Concerning the counselor's attitudes, it is important to be conscious of negative sentiments against various groups that might sabotage the therapy process while also being committed to altering such thoughts and attitudes (Collins & Arthur, 2010; D. W. Sue et al., 1982). It also necessitates being open to other points of view that are appropriate for a culturally varied client. To meet this second significant dimension of this framework, the counselor should have detailed knowledge and information about their culturally varied clients (Collins & Arthur, 2010; D. W. Sue et al., 1982). Counselors should strive to gain knowledge of sociopolitical effects on minorities' lives, which may have an impact on the counseling process. Along with these attitudes and knowledge, counselors should have the skills to seek educational opportunities to improve their knowledge, understanding, and skills in multicultural counseling and stay up to date on the newest research on a variety of groups. They must also be adept at becoming connected with various people (Collins & Arthur, 2010; D. W. Sue et al., 1982).

The third dimension is developing counseling tactics and procedures that are culturally appropriate. Counselors should have the attitude of respecting clients' religious or spiritual beliefs, values, and native helping traditions that they believe are beneficial in the psychological or counseling process, as well as valuing and accepting the use of a different language in the therapy process (Collins & Arthur, 2010; D. W. Sue et al., 1982). In line with this, counselors should know and understand the cultural aspects of counseling and how these aspects may conflict with the ideals of various cultural groups.

Counselors should acquire skills in identifying methods to assist social change within the society through learning about the family structures, values, and beliefs of the culturally varied clientele. They must also have the ability to recognize an issue with a minority client that is caused by racism or bigotry directed toward that client. Allowing a client who speaks a different language to participate in therapy sessions using a translator or sending the client to a bilingual counselor is also needed (Collins & Arthur, 2010; D. W. Sue et al., 1982).

CRAFTING AN ADVOCACY AGENDA

Social justice was included as one of the essential professional principles by the ACA in 2014. As evidenced by the Advocacy Competencies; *Code of Ethics* (2014); CACREP; and 2001, 2009, and 2016 editions of the Multicultural and Social Justice Counseling Competencies (MSJCC) standards, social justice has become an increasingly present inclusion in the counseling profession (Lewis et al., 2002; Ratts, 2011).

While social justice is a constant in the counseling profession's abilities and standards, the key elements contributing to social justice growth remain a topic of study across disciplines. Identifying essential elements, particularly non-static ones like training, training supports, and racial views, can offer data to training programs that can guide curriculum creation and program practices to orient students toward social justice. In addition, examining students' pro-multicultural/social justice behaviors (attending classes, attending conferences) and beliefs (perception of being in a supportive training environment, colorblind awareness) on social justice interest, commitment, and self-efficacy helps determine whether the profession is preparing students to honor diversity, embrace a multicultural approach, and promote social justice (Singh, Appling, et al., 2020).

Singh, Nassar, et al.'s (2020) study examined the degree to which counseling students self-identified having a pro multicultural/social justice attitude through reported social justice interest, commitment, and self-efficacy. In addition, whether students expressed colorblind racial attitudes, received training, or sought academic assistance about social justice was evaluated to aid in developing training program suggestions (Singh, Appling, et al., 2020). Counseling programs can examine how social justice is incorporated into their curriculum and how instructors are visible, offer, and involve students in social action practice and research by measuring students' views of training support. Training programs can examine the advantages of incorporating diverse training techniques into the curriculum to elicit good social justice results by investigating the link between training constructs and social justice variables of interest, commitment, and self-efficacy (Singh, Appling, et al., 2020).

Advocacy working with and on behalf of people, groups, communities, and systems is what social justice counseling includes (Singh, Nassar, et al., 2020). At the individual level (working with clients), social justice in counseling involves one-on-one treatment. It also includes counselors who see clients and client concerns from an ecological viewpoint (Greenleaf & Williams, 2009). According to the ecological approach, clients' lives and issues occur in an environment that might have a direct impact on their well-being (Bemak & Chung, 2011a, 2011b; Greenleaf & Williams, 2009; Singh, Appling, et al., 2020).

The counselor may support clients by recognizing external impediments, recognizing client strengths, and encouraging clients to develop and participate in self-advocacy as part of advocacy therapy (Crumb et al., 2019; Farrell & Barrio Minton, 2019; Kozan & Blustein, 2018). Counselors are in a unique position to learn about difficulties that may be present that obstruct clients' access to services because they work with those clients. As a result, counselors may have a "unique knowledge of repeating themes" that influence client lives (Lewis et al., 2002, p. 2). Within the counseling profession, advocacy can be completed on behalf of a specific client or address issues that affect the well-being of people or groups (ACA, 2014; Lewis et al., 2002).

The awareness and gaining of an understanding of culture and diversity and how they affect oneself, clients, and communities are referred to as multicultural competency (ACA, 2014). Multicultural competency is now a prerequisite across all counseling specialties in the *2014 ACA Code of Ethics* (see section C.2.a), a change from the 2005 ethical code (ACA, 2005). Counselors' knowledge, skills, attitudes, and beliefs (KSA) concerning dimensions of their own and their clients' racial or ethnic identity are included in the framework for the Multicultural Counseling Competencies (Crumb et al., 2019; Farrell & Barrio Minton, 2019; Kozan & Blustein, 2018).

Multicultural counseling recognizes clients' many identities as well as oppression's impact on their lives. Counselors and counselors-in-training must be aware of injustices surrounding social identities such as race and ethnicity to transition from conventional counseling duties to the practice of social justice advocacy (Crumb et al., 2019; Farrell & Barrio Minton, 2019; Kozan & Blustein, 2018).

To educate counseling students to be social justice advocates, social justice must be included in all curricula and programs, with faculty/mentor assistance (Crumb et al., 2019; Farrell & Barrio Minton, 2019; Kozan & Blustein, 2018; Sullivan, 2019). Experiential training could serve as a method for skill development and a chance for learners to acquire exposure to social concerns and overcome their reluctance (Burnes & Singh, 2010). The social justice development paradigm emphasizes awareness and involvement as a change catalyst. Exposure to conflict or injustice, whether direct or indirect, is one of their proponents for eliciting transformation (Moeschberger et al., 2006).

Researchers who discovered exposure to injustice as a predictor of social justice interest have added to the evidence (Hage et al., 2020; Swartz et al., 2018). Exposure to injustice was regarded as one of the two most significant elements in establishing a social justice perspective by participants in Caldwell et al.'s (2008) qualitative study. One of three mediating factors (exposure to injustice, formal diversity experiences, and strong interracial friendships) found to have a significant negative association with colorblind racial attitudes was exposure to injustice (Hage et al., 2020; Swartz et al., 2018).

Intercultural awareness, knowledge, skills, and social justice have been infused into ethics and competencies. Counseling programs must ensure that students are prepared to engage in social justice advocacy and action. Embodying a social justice orientation necessitates continual efforts to recognize, examine, and question one's knowledge of oppression, discrimination, stereotyping, and racism, as well as how they influence a counselor's personal and professional life (Ratts, 2011; Singh, Appling, et al., 2020). Acknowledging one's racist attitudes, actions, and beliefs is aided by increasing knowledge and awareness of how these ailments influence self, client, and counselor–client relations (Ratts, 2011; Singh, Appling, et al., 2020).

Individuals who advocate for a colorblind approach may struggle to recognize client and systemic concerns connected to race, or they may dismiss racism as a factor in social inequity (Neville et al., 2014). According to studies on undergraduate psychology students (Miller et al., 2009) and school counselors, having a colorblind ideology negatively affects social justice interests (Singh, Appling, et al., 2020). Researchers concluded that being aware of White privilege, institutional discrimination, and racial concerns is critical for school counselors interested in and committed to social justice. This claim is in line with the profession's requests for more growth and involvement in social justice counseling (Ratts, 2011; Singh, Appling, et al., 2020). Furthermore, understanding the training variables that influence social justice interest, commitment, and self-efficacy might help counselor education programs design strategies to support students' social justice growth (Ratts, 2011; Singh, Nassar, et al., 2020).

COUNSELING CHILDREN, ADOLESCENTS, AND YOUNG ADULTS

While counseling agencies have extended their services and are reaching more children and adolescents with mental health issues than ever before, minority students, particularly Latino students, have historically been ignored. Their unique needs have been overlooked (Kearney et al., 2005). Minorities may need counseling services at lower levels due to a lack of knowledge of multicultural concerns, resulting in more severe and uncontrolled emotional and academic challenges (Turner & Llamas, 2017). More ethnic minorities are pursuing higher education today than at any other period in history (Turner & Llamas, 2017). It can be expected that when more minority students enroll in college, more minority students will need counseling services, making it even more necessary for counselors to pay attention to the needs of minority students. Although empirical research on Latino youth development is limited, interest in the Latino immigrant adolescent continues to grow as debates and views continue to be expressed (Sands & Plunkett, 2005). Concurrently and according to Norrid-Lacey and Spencer (2000), few studies have truly investigated the social world that these individuals enter and create; thus, better insight is needed to enhance understanding of the familial, social, and academic experiences of the adolescent Latino immigrant in our schools. Such information could very well benefit not only the families, but also those making decisions concerning policy, curriculum, and instructions in the schools and districts these students attend (Norrid-Lacey & Spencer, 2000). Padilla and Lindholm (1984) posit that most of the research concerning adolescent Latinos that has been conducted is related to delinquency, substance abuse, high school dropout rates, teen pregnancy, and gang-related activities. To address these and many more concerns regarding this group, future research is needed to identify key predictors that affect Latino adolescent immigrants. More research must be conducted to determine the processes involved in migration, separation at early childhood, and the effects this may have on the adolescent as far as placing them at risk for psychological problems. Researchers can also determine, from the Latino adolescent's perspective, what major stressors are being experienced during this stage, as well as what types of support systems can be mobilized in addressing such stressors. Researchers can also explore methods for making diagnosis and treatment more culturally appropriate in counseling this group. Portes and Zady (2002) put forward studies of social and psychological phenomena in periods of change and transition that are particularly attractive for developmental researchers. These authors emphasize the significance of specific beliefs, values, and activity patterns and describe how these constructs cross from the social to the psychological plane, facilitating the understanding of relinquishing of "self" (Portes & Zady, 2002). Concerning the immigrant adolescent, whose development is clarified very often through the opposing forces in an intercultural context, this study is a unique opportunity for this writer to uncover significant factors contributing to the questions of the Latino immigrant's early childhood separation and its effect on adolescence.

When it comes to going to the United States for education, international Latino students confront the same obstacles as native-born Latino individuals. Due to the unique circumstances of international study, additional challenges such as language barriers, immigration documentation, guilt over being away from family, homesickness, learning a new culture, conflicts with identity or culture norms, and financial and academic concerns are all present (Arredondo, 1991; Atkinson et al., 1992; Romero, 2009; S. Sue & Chu, 2003; Wilton & Constantine, 2003).

One of the challenges in offering stronger and more culturally aligned counseling services to Latino children is that the variety of the Latino community has long been overlooked. Even though the problems and challenges that Latino and foreign Latino students experience differ, the existing literature tends to mix these two groups. Because key predictive themes like acculturation, gender roles, treatment expectations, and history differ among different groups, we lose valuable information that might help us understand user trends and obstacles for Latinos seeking mental health care. S. Sue (1998) emphasized the significance of within-group distinctions by stating that dynamic sizing, or "knowing when to generalize and be inclusive and when to individualize and be exclusive" (p. 446), is a crucial aspect of cultural competency.

Treating diverse Latino student subgroups as a single entity limits information about differences between international Latino students (IBs) and U.S.-born Latino students (USBs) and may leave out valuable information about a third group: international Latino students who have obtained U.S. citizenship (IBUSs). While data on this third group are limited, we may presume that their college stresses differ from those of the other two groupings in ways that may influence counseling usage.

Undocumented Latino youth face a far more difficult position. Undocumented Latino children may feel obliged to contribute financially to their family once they reach a particular age. When family obligations and educational obligations conflict for attention, issues arise. Family conflict may have a factor in Latino children's high dropout rates and demand for mental health services (Benuto et al., 2018; Ríos Vega, 2020; Roth, 2017). Many undocumented Latino teenagers have been socialized in American society and have lived in the United States for most of their life (Benuto et al., 2018; Ríos Vega, 2020; Roth, 2017). When they graduate from high school, they are confronted with the harsh reality of limited job opportunities and methods to support themselves. According to the Immigration and Nationality Act of 2008, undocumented Latino individuals who are 18 years old or older and residing in the United States without legal documentation breach federal law. Undocumented Latino youngsters throughout the country are terrified of being deported. Deportation orders for high school and university students have lately been issued in California, Florida, New Jersey, New Mexico, and Washington (Benuto et al., 2018; Ríos Vega, 2020; Roth, 2017).

COUNSELING ADULTS, COUPLES, AND FAMILIES

Latinos have unique obstacles compared to other migrant groups. Due to various potentially complicated contextual circumstances, Latinos are at a higher risk of social isolation. Distance from family, a collectivist culture, social marginalization, immigration rules, and difficulties accessing care are just a few of them. These difficulties can have a significant impact on both clients' and therapists' sessions. Families are a cultural value connected with Latino households; in which close family relationships are valued highly (Ayón, 2020; Ayón et al., 2018, 2020). Grandparents, cousins, aunts and uncles, and other relatives beyond the nuclear family are frequently included in these ties. Furthermore, *familismo* prioritizes the care of one's family over one's own needs (Ayón, 2020; Ayón et al., 2018, 2020).

Many Latino families in the United States are alienated from close relatives, causing cultural customs to shift and feelings of isolation to increase (Ayón et al., 2018, 2020). Depressive symptoms have been related to family separation (more so among females) because this can cause them to lose a significant amount of support from their relatives (Ayón et al., 2018, 2020). Meanwhile, regular family reunions, a sense of positive social support, and *familismo* have all been shown to protect Latino individuals against feelings of isolation, anxiety, and depression (Ayón et al., 2018, 2020).

Among many minority groups, Latino individuals experienced the most emotional separation from other family members, given their strong sense of family and community ties. They strive to survive in a foreign land by acculturating in various ways. For example, many parent–child conflicts arise as children learn English, attend school, and consume English-language media faster than their parents. These variables can lead to a disconnect in cultural beliefs between parents and children, causing family rifts and increasing isolation. Previous research has discovered a link between acculturative stress and family cohesion (Dillon et al., 2013). Researchers have recommended that therapists address family culture conflict as part of treatment because of the significant impact of acculturation on Latino families' processes (Darghouth et al., 2015).

In a culture based on collaboration, Latino individuals may be more vulnerable to isolation because most families share a collectivist culture that emphasizes family and interdependence among family members (Oyserman & Lee, 2008). Latino cultural norms and backgrounds are disrupted by separation from family and isolation from the community, making these losses particularly upsetting. In a culture that values individuality and autonomy over unity and cohesiveness, many people may feel like they are breaking new ground when forming connections (Oyserman & Lee, 2008).

IMPLICATIONS FOR CLINICAL PRACTICE

The chapter highlighted how critical it is to teach practitioners-in-training to be skilled at working from multisystemic frameworks that support Latino clients' mental health. Practitioners-in-training, for example, should be taught to recognize multisystemic variables that may be linked to a client's mental health experiences and know-how to help. This chapter should be utilized to aid in the development of culturally sensitive and ecologically appropriate evaluation instruments and treatments for the Latino community in the United States.

This might lead to an increase of Latino individuals utilizing mental health services in the United States. Because greater information about mental health problems may not by itself result in changes in health-seeking behaviors, it is essential to recognize and address personal, familial, community, and systems-level barriers to help-seeking (Christensen et al., 2021). As a result, identifying multisystemic variables might be a way to boost Latino mental health care utilization rates. In addition, the previous studies identified in this chapter point to multisystemic factors and themes in Latino-focused literature produced between 2006 and 2015 (Christensen et al., 2021).

Community-oriented counselors dealing with Latinx individuals, particularly Mexican Americans, must recognize social support and relationships (Shah & West-Olatunji, 2019; Thomas et al., 2018). Continued parental and community support for Mexican American teenagers should be promoted to assist the clients in developing a feeling of belonging. Counseling services begin with high school admission and continue throughout their high school career; therefore, a holistic approach to counseling can be seen as both developmental and progressive. Throughout high school, therapy services evolve and increase in tandem with the clients' growth and development (Shah & West-Olatunji, 2019; Thomas et al., 2018). The *Holistic Approach for Counseling Mexican American Adolescents* can be used by professional counselors in several contexts, including community organizations, private offices, and schools.

This technique, for example, may be used as part of a family-school partnership project in which counselors use group therapy in an after-school program. Counselors can also use group therapy in community centers, after-school programs, or faith-based organizations. When describing the operational principles of action research, Stringer and Dwyer (2005) stressed relationship, communication, involvement, and inclusion. Implementing a holistic approach when counseling Mexican American adolescents should be influenced by research and wraparound counseling. This includes establishing connections, conducting research, developing treatment plans, and utilizing culturally centered interventions (Stringer & Dwyer, 2005).

Additionally, formalism (*formalismo* in Spanish) is a notion in which proper respect is exhibited (e.g., using formal titles at first and expressing *respecto* [respect] depending on age, social standing, and gender; Miller et al., 2009). It might be beneficial to consult with Latino therapists to balance them in therapy (Ferreira, 2014; Ma-Kellams, 2021). Initially, a Latino client, particularly an individual who is not well acculturated to the American society, may adopt a "talk to when spoken to" attitude and avoid direct eye contact, both of which might be signals of respect.

When evaluating their clients, counselors can undoubtedly see the importance of religion in their lives because many Latinos have strong religious views, which may significantly affect how they view mental illness and treatment, and therefore on how they regard the therapist. *Fatalismo* (fatalism) is a term that relates to the notion that divine providence rules the universe and that no one can control or avert disaster (Paniagua, 2013). Exploring a person's potential religious or supernatural explanations for mental or emotional difficulties is also essential. Some people tend to focus on these religious or supernatural explanations, such as emotional disorders being caused by malevolent spirits or witchcraft. Mental health is largely viewed and treated by many Latinos in terms of their spirituality and religiosity.

CLINICAL CASE SCENARIO 7.1

Matilde is a 17-year-old Mexican American female. She moved to the United States two years ago from Mexico City and currently lives in San Diego, California, with her mother, Rosa; her father, Jorge; and her brother, Vinny. Matilde's mother and father have noticed that over the past year she has become withdrawn, speaking less with her family, and communicating less with her relatives who still live in Mexico City. Matilde has been close to her brother throughout her life and has even lessened the time spent with him, choosing to spend more time in her room at home, alone.

Jorge, Matilde's father, doesn't like Matilde to go out with her friends and appears controlling as to what she can and can't do. Matilde has reported that she doesn't have many friends, except the two girls whom she met at school. Her friends, Cathy and Helen, are the same age as Matilde, and they identify as Caucasian. Rosa, Matilde's mother, is more supportive of Matilde, and often lets

(continued)

CLINICAL CASE SCENARIO 7.1 (CONTINUED)

her see her friends when her father is at work. However, these times are limited, and Matilde can only talk to her two friends over the phone.

Matilde's parents have tried to help Matilde with her withdrawal behaviors. Jorge suggested that she go to church with them on Sundays and perhaps join a youth group. Matilde has not shown any interest in this. Furthermore, both Rosa and Jorge have called a spiritual advisor in Mexico for advice, who says that they should take a trip back to Mexico City so that Matilde can be treated spiritually there. The spiritual advisor has said that Matilde's withdrawing behaviors could be due to unseen evil forces that need to be eliminated. Jorge and Rosa have said that they cannot afford to take this trip for at least six months as they would need to save up money.

Rosa has been talking to her sister, Anna, who lives in Mexico City. Rosa has been telling Anna how Matilde seems sad and is withdrawing from the family and they don't know what to do. Anna has recommended that perhaps Matilde should visit with a counselor to talk about any problems until they can afford the trip back to Mexico. Rosa is reluctant but agrees to see if this is something that Matilde would want to do.

Rosa talked with Jorge about having Matilde go to a counselor, but he is against it. Jorge reported that he doesn't want his family's business to be heard by a stranger. Jorge reported that they should just wait to see the spiritual advisor in six months and that Matilde will be okay until then. When Rosa talked with Matilde about seeing a counselor, Matilde was receptive to the idea and agreed to go. To not upset Jorge, Rosa made the appointment when he was at work.

This will be Matilde's first time seeing a therapist. After reviewing the background from the intake assessment as noted here, discuss how you would approach Matilde's case by answering the following questions.

CLINICAL CASE SCENARIO DISCUSSION QUESTIONS

1. Discuss how you would approach Matilde's case from a culturally responsive perspective.
2. Discuss the importance of the terms familisimo, respecto, and simpatia in relation to Matilde's case.
3. How does Sociosoma play a role in this case?
4. Discuss ways in which Matilde could be struggling from an acculturation perspective.
5. Discuss ways in which Matilde could be struggling from an assimilation perspective.
6. How differently would you treat Matilde versus a client who identified as White or Caucasian? Why?
7. How are Matilde's generational differences important in this case in relation to her ethnicity?
8. What would be your course of treatment for Matilde? Why?

END-OF-CHAPTER RESOURCES

 A robust set of instructor resources designed to supplement this text is located at **http://connect.springerpub.com/content/book/978-0-8261-3953-5**. Qualifying instructors may request access by emailing **textbook@springerpub.com**.

SUMMARY

Based on statistics and academic research, it can be safe to assume that the Latino community is presently one of the largest ethnic and racial minorities in the United States (Gann et al., 2019; Martinez & González, 2021; Rumbaut, 2019). This population is slated to grow further, even doubling to 120 million by the year 2060. Even though that year seems far away, one must be aware that the counseling profession is also unlikely to change overnight. If the profession is to transform into culturally sensitive work and counselors become advocates for the Latino community, specific changes must be facilitated. There is now a need to take serious stock of how counselors can work with Latino clients and encourage more to utilize available mental health and counseling services.

Working with different clients, in general, can serve as a great learning experience, especially if they come from a cultural background different from the counselor's. Many master's programs in counseling require students to take a multicultural course to prepare for working with clients from other cultures. However, textbooks can only provide so much broad information. Competent multicultural counseling is not likely to result from a term or two of studying, nor can it be restricted to a single chapter in a textbook.

In addition, more than multicultural competence, counselors can meet the unique needs of the Latino community if they also recognize the need for social justice and advocacy. Over the past decade, the acknowledgment of advocacy and social justice in the profession of psychology has grown. The American Psychological Association has urged psychologists to take on their role as change agents in promoting social justice. Suppose social justice is defined as a vision of society in which resources are distributed equally, and all members of society are guaranteed to function in a safe and secure environment (Villenas et al., 2019). In this case, a similar vision may be realized inside companies (e.g., schools, colleges, and hospitals). After all, the organizational environment, which includes norms, procedures, and structures, influences policy direction and focus and the duties and responsibilities of mental health and educational experts, both directly and indirectly. As a result, rather than confining psychological treatments to the individual, personal level, counselors should work together as change agents to strive to promote structural transformation at a systemic level for addressing the counseling needs of the Latino community.

Social justice efforts of group psychologists could include but not be limited to only facilitating a counseling group as a supportive environment for Latino individuals to help them solve their myriad of developmental, situational, and academic concerns. Group counseling can serve as a strong milieu for promoting long-term social change, primarily because of its capacity to instill hope and even universality while imparting information and concrete mental health help.

DISCUSSION QUESTIONS

1. What are some considerations that must to be taken into account when working with Latino families?
2. What could be some cultural differences between a Latino client who was born in the United States versus a client who migrated from Latin America to the United States from the same country?
3. How does the term Latinx seek to be inclusive within the Latino population?
4. How are adolescent males and females treated differently within families?
5. How can a lack of information and understanding on the part of a counselor be harmful to Latino clients?

KEY REFERENCES

Only key references appear in the print edition. The full reference list appears in the digital product on Springer Publishing Connect: https://connect.springerpub.com/content/book/978-0-8261-3953-5/part/part02/chapter/ch07

American Counseling Association. (2005). *2014 ACA Code of Ethics*. Author.

Arredondo, P. (1991). Counseling Latinas. In C. C. Lee, B. L. Richardson, C. C. Lee, & B. L. Richardson (Eds.), *Multicultural issues in counseling: New approaches to diversity* (pp. 143–156). American Association for Counseling.

Falicov, C. J. (1998). *Latino families in therapy: A guide to multicultural practice*. Guilford Press.

Ferreira, A. M. (2014). *A look into the Latino experience: The process of identity formation for Latinos in the United States* [Senior thesis, Claremont McKenna College]. https://scholarship.claremont.edu/cmc_theses/886/

Gann, L. H., Duignan, P., & Gann, L. H. (2019). *The Hispanics in the United States: A history*. Routledge.

Gonzales, Nancy A, Coxe, S., Roosa, M. W., White, R. M. B., Knight, G. P., Zeiders, K. H., & Saenz, D. (2011). Economic hardship, neighborhood context, and parenting: prospective effects on Mexican-American adolescent's mental health. *American Journal of Community Psychology*, 47(1–2), 98–113. https://doi.org/10.1007/s10464-010-9366-1

Kozan, S., & Blustein, D. L. (2018). Implementing social change: A qualitative analysis of counseling psychologists' engagement in advocacy. *The Counseling Psychologist*, 46(2), 154–189. https://doi.org/10.1177/0011000018756882

Lewis, S., Tarrier, N., Haddock, G., Bentall, R., Kinderman, P., Kingdon, D., Siddle, R., Drake, R., Everitt, J., Leadley, K., Benn, A., Grazebrook, K., Haley, C., Akhtar, S., Davies, L., Palmer, S., Faragher, B., & Dunn, G. (2002). Randomised controlled trial of cognitive-behavioural therapy in early schizophrenia: Acute-phase outcomes. *The British Journal of Psychiatry*, 181(S43), s91–s97. https://doi.org/10.1192/bjp.181.43.s91

Ratts, M. J. (2011). Multiculturalism and social justice: Two sides of the same coin. *Journal of Multicultural Counseling and Development*, 39(1), 24–37. https://doi.org/10.1002/j.2161-1912.2011.tb00137.x

Torrero, A. (2021). *The Impact of Acculturation of Latinos on PAI Profiles* [Doctoral dissertation]. Alliant International University.

CHAPTER 8

Culturally Responsive Counseling for Clients of Native American Descent

LYNAE S. HEMMING AND JULIE A. YLINIEMI

LEARNING OBJECTIVES

After reading this chapter, students will be able to:
- Identify the impact of historical and generational trauma of Native Americans, both in the past and present.
- Categorize the unique complexities experienced by Native Americans and the impact on their well-being and culture.
- Interpret their own cultural humility as it relates to counseling Native American clients.
- Develop the incorporation of traditional cultural healing practices into clinical practice with Native American clients.

SELF-REFLECTION QUESTIONS

1. What knowledge do you have about the historical and generational trauma within the Native American population?
2. What is your competence and knowledge level to be able to provide clinical services to Native American people?
3. How might you incorporate traditional healing as part of your clinical interventions?
4. What biases might you have toward Native American people?

THE COUNSELOR: EXPLORATION, INTROSPECTION, AND REFLECTION

Currently, there are 574 different Native American tribes in the United States, each with its own history and traditions (Bureau of Indian Affairs, 2021). Approximately 3 million people identified themselves as Native American or Alaska Native during the 2010 Census. This represents approximately 1.7% of the total population of the United States. Another 2.3 million people identify as Native American or Alaska Native in combination with one or more races. Seventy-eight percent of Native Americans and Alaska

Natives live outside of American Indian reservations or Alaska Native villages. The remaining 22% of the Native American and Alaska Native population live on American Indian reservations or Alaska Native Village lands (U.S. Census Bureau, 2011).

Native Americans have a rich cultural tradition of storytelling and are by practice oral societies. Storytelling is a core practice of Native American culture (Eder, 2007). It is the primary means of transmitting information, nurturing values, and educating in the Native American culture. Stories provide both direction and a sense of cultural pride. Stories are woven into ceremonies, chants, and other important occasions (Toelken & Tacheeni, 1981). The Navajo Nation, the largest Native American tribe in the United States, encompasses parts of Utah, New Mexico, and Arizona. Within the Navajo community, stories are treated as the highest form of capital. A person who knows the stories, legends, folktales, and ceremonies is considered the wealthiest in the community (Toelken & Tacheeni, 1981).

The oral tradition of Native American societies has resulted in scattered and sometimes unaligned narratives of Native American history. In contrast, European history, and the subsequent history of European settlers in the United States, have a vast historical written record. Throughout time, there have been many peaceful interactions between the Native Americans and the European settlers; however, there has also been turmoil and conflict. The upheaval has cost many lives on both sides and has resulted in the loss of cultural and spiritual identity to several generations of Native Americans.

CULTURAL AND SPIRITUAL VALUES

Native American culture has its foundations in spirituality, harmony, and connection. There is diversity in the beliefs and practices of each tribe and across levels of acculturation (M. T. Garrett & Wilbur, 1999). In this chapter, the authors present information that is generalizable to Native Americans of many tribes and areas but will provide examples and specifics of the Anishinaabe traditions, as one of the authors is a member of this community. Anishinaabe tribal community is located in the Midwest of the United States and parts of Canada. Like most other tribal groups in the United States, it experienced severe loss of land, culture, and language throughout history. The community the second author grew up in is rural and comprised of both Native and non-Native community members. It has tribal housing, tribal centers, casinos, and other tribally owned businesses (Brissette et al., 2020).

Spirituality

The foundation of Native American spirituality is honoring the connection between all things through harmony and balance (M. T. Garrett & Wilbur, 1999). All the parts of the universe are connected with continually flowing energy and deserve respect and reverence. Native American culture believes that all things have life and spiritual importance because they all have a specific role and purpose. The goal of personhood is to find one's purpose and role (J. T. Garrett & Garrett, 1994). Several other commonly held traditional beliefs include the following as compiled and described by Locust (1988):

1. There is one higher power known as the Creator, Great One, or Great Spirit.
2. Plants, animals, and human beings are all a part of the spirit world. The spirit world exists in tandem with the physical world.
3. Humans are composed of spirit, mind, and body. These are all interconnected parts and illness affects all three.
4. Wellness is harmony among the spirit, mind, and body. To be unwell is to be in disharmony in mind, body, and spirit.

5. Natural unwellness is caused by violating a natural or sacred social law.
6. Unnatural unwellness is caused by conjuring from those with destructive intentions.
7. Each of us is responsible for our wellness. We do so by attending to the self, relationships, and universe.

Grandfather Teachings

The seven grandfather teachings are another foundational belief of the Native American way of life in many Anishinaabe communities. According to Benton-Banai (1988), they were given to the seven grandfathers by the Creator as a guide for respect and sharing. These grandfather teachings provide a framework for understanding Anishinaabe wellness (Kading et al., 2019).

Nibwaakaawin—*Wisdom*

To cherish knowledge is to know Wisdom. Wisdom is given by the Creator to be used for the good of the people. In the Anishinaabe language, this word not only expresses "wisdom," but also means "prudence" or "intelligence."

Zaagi'idiwin—*Love*

To know peace is to know Love. Love must be unconditional. When people are weak they need love the most. In the Anishinaabe language, this word with the reciprocal theme /idi/ indicates that this form of love is mutual. In some communities, *Gizhaawenidiwin* is used, which in most contexts means "jealousy" but in this context is translated as either "love" or "zeal." Again, the reciprocal theme /idi/ indicates that this form of love is mutual.

Minaadendamowin—*Respect*

To honor all creation is to have Respect. All of creation should be treated with respect. You must give respect if you wish to be respected.

Aakode'ewin—*Bravery*

Bravery is to face the foe with integrity. In the Anishinaabe language, this word's literal meaning is "state of having a fearless heart"—to do what is right even when the consequences are unpleasant. Some communities use either *Zoongadikiwin* ("state of having a strong casing") or *Zoongide'ewin* ("state of having a strong heart").

Gwayakwaadiziwin—*Honesty*

Honesty in facing a situation is to be brave. Always be honest in word and action. Be honest first with yourself, and you will more easily be able to be honest with others.

Dabaadendiziwin—*Humility*

Humility is to know yourself as a sacred part of Creation. In the Anishinaabe language, this word can also mean "compassion." You are equal to others, but you are not better. Some communities instead express this with *Bekaadiziwin*, which in addition to "humility" can also be translated as "calmness," "meekness," "gentility," or "patience."

Debwewin—*Truth*

Truth is to know all these things. Speak the truth. Do not deceive yourself or others.

Ancestors

Ancestors are not considered people of the past, who were once here. They are considered Spirit beings that are with us today and have a strong reverence within the Native American culture. Ancestors are here to help and to guide the living. When we get still, when we get silent, through meditation and spiritual groundedness, we can feel their presence, which is why Ancestors sometimes come when we are sleeping, we are still.

When people see Spirits, also known as "orbs," it is not looked upon by people of Native American descent as a pathological problem. Instead, it is looked upon as the ancestors communicating a message. One Anishinaabe author worked with several students who would talk about seeing orbs that were dark in color, almost black energy forms. It seemed that in most cases the dark orbs were seen where death had occurred. For example, the dark orbs were reported to have been seen at the local casino and the tribal school; both had a suicide take place there. Students also talked about seeing white or light-colored orbs; these were associated with purity and joy. The students explained that they could tell if someone was trustworthy by the energy color they could see around that person.

Healers

Native American healers are honored and respected. They study for several years to acquire their knowledge, skills, and abilities. Typically, their qualifications are based on their studies and who their teachers are or have been. Unlike many university-educated helpers who live outside of the community, these healers live in the community and their lives are transparent to those they work with (Day et al., 2014).

Women

Women are the backbone of the Native American culture. Women have been respected and honored throughout Native American history (L. T. Smith, 2012). Honoring women is embedded in many tribal languages. For example, in Anishinaabe, *Ikwe*, the word for woman, is connected to *Aki*, which is the word for Earth; both givers of life. The word for "old woman" is *mindimoove*, which translates to "the one who holds it all together" (Livesay & Nichols, 2021).

Traditional Names

In many Native American tribes, traditional names are given. These are also known as "Indian names" or "Spirit names." Some names are given at birth and others at milestones in a person's life. It is believed that we are all born with Spirit names that will guide us during our time on earth. In the Anishaabe community, the person who names another person becomes their We-eh. The We-eh gives the person they have named part of their spirit and will be connected to that person for eternity. The We-eh becomes a source of guidance, advice, and support for that individual throughout their lifetime.

The Anishinaabe author of this chapter has her traditional name, Ogema Anungikwe, which translates to Chief/Lead Star Woman. She was told by the medicine man/We-eh who named her that she would be called upon to be a leader at times. Her name has helped guide her life and find purpose in what she does both personally and professionally.

Animals

Animals are considered sacred and honorable. Animals, such as wolves, buffalos, and bears, are used within stories to help develop identities and explore one's worldview (Magoulick, 2017). Animals are here to teach us things. If we watch animals carefully, and with intent, they will teach us lessons on how to live life. For example, the beaver teaches us that we need to use our gifts. If the beaver did not gnaw, its teeth would continue to grow and cause problems in its life. Just like the beaver, we need to use the gifts that the Creator has given us.

Smudging

Smudging is a cleansing ceremony that includes burning plants, herbs, and resins while prayers are being said. The resulting smoke cloud is believed to cleanse the air and those within it. Smudging is one of the most popular rituals used to clear people and places of negative elements. Smudging is used in nearly every Native culture within the Western hemisphere and has played an active role for centuries (Powwows.com, 2020).

Drums

Drums are another powerful and important piece of Native American culture. Native Americans use hand drumming as a way to connect with themselves and their culture, and as a guide to reveal their intrinsic knowledge. A drum, once made, is considered to have a spirit of its own. It has its own life and needs respect and caring for. The person who carries the drum must take great care of it. Drums are found at almost all Native American events, celebrations, and ceremonies (Pedri-Spade, 2016).

Eagle Feathers

Eagles are considered one of the United States' greatest national symbols (Breining, 2008). The eagle feather is also a widely used symbol in Native American culture. Eagle feathers are considered sacred and are used in a variety of religious practices to heal and create balance (J. Smith, 2016). They are considered medicine to promote well-being and allow one to function in harmony with others and with the environment (Kinoshameg & Robson, 2018). The U.S. government law prohibits anyone from possessing eagle feathers; however, this prohibition has one exception, which is to allow federally recognized Native American tribes to use eagle feathers for religious purposes (J. Smith, 2016).

ACCULTURATION CONFLICTS, ALCOHOL AND SUBSTANCE ABUSE, DOMESTIC VIOLENCE, AND SUICIDE

Historical Background

At one time in history, the United States was known as Mother Earth to more than 5 million Indigenous people (Warren, 2009). The Indigenous people who inhabited North America lived in harmony with the land and the cycle of the seasons. Men, women, children, and Two-Spirited (LGBTQ) beings all had roles in their communities and within their tribes. A strong sense of community and family permeated their culture, and a sense of identity was woven into their daily lives through their cultural practices.

The colonization of the United States, or Mother Earth, began in 1492 by the Europeans. Many of these first colonists believed that their expansion was saving the barbaric inhabitants by spreading Christianity. Throughout the 16th century into the 19th century, the Native American population sharply declined for several reasons (Pritzker, 2000). The spread of violence between Natives and colonists and between rival tribes led to a significant loss of life. The enslavement of Native Americans and epidemics of the diseases brought by new settlers also contributed to the significant loss of life among Native Americans. Following this rapid decline, some Native American groups realigned themselves and became new cultural entities (Pritzker, 2000). This sharp decline and reorganization had a cascade of effects on the generational exchange of culture.

Native Americans' lands were progressively and systematically removed through a multitude of means, but most famously through the "Manifest Destiny" movement of the 1840s. This infamous period was aimed at expanding the territory of the United States westward and progressing civilization. It removed Native Americans from their land, and in some areas, extreme force and murder of these Native Americans were allowed with impunity (Pritzker, 2000). In 1851, the United States Congress voted to require Native Americans to stay on plots of land designated to each tribe, which are known today as reservations.

Thousands of Native American children died while at boarding schools. Surviving children were eventually allowed back into their communities as young adults full of unresolved trauma and grief. Their language was lost, and their cultural ways were forgotten. The young women were taught in these boarding schools that what happened to their bodies was decided by others and their voice was not heard. Additionally, the young men learned that physical violence was the answer to conflict and a tool for communication (M. T. Garrett & Pichette, 2000).

The influx of colonization robbed Native Americans of their connection with some of their primary cultural beliefs, including their connection to the land, their connection to each other, and their connection to their cultural and religious practices. The combination of the unsteadying loss of their cultural beliefs, coupled with the trauma of violence and death brought about by epidemics, war, and the boarding schools, has created a disparity for Native Americans that is still present today.

Native American Health Disparities

One of the primary areas of disparity experienced by Native Americans today is in their health. *Healthcare disparities* are differences in access to or availability of facilities and services. Health disparities among Native Americans have existed for well over 500 years. Jones (2006) states that since the time of colonization the major genocidal weapons used against Native Americans include the following: smallpox, measles, influenza, malaria, STDs, murder, mind control, rape, dehumanization, removal, hepatitis, plague, chickenpox, and diphtheria. These tactics have affected the health and well-being of the Native American population. Jones found that New England tribal nations' populations declined by 90% to 95% during the first century after the first contact with the Europeans. For example, the Arawak Nation population decreased from roughly 400,000 members in 1496 to 125 individual members in 1570 (Jones, 2006).

The medical community is just beginning to see the impact of the violent and generational trauma on the physical and mental health of Native Americans. The widening gap in health disparities is also believed to be tied to factors such as inadequate education, poor access to services, and economic adversity. Native Americans suffer from among the worst disparities in the nation and a disproportionate death rate compared to their non-Native cohort (Espey et al., 2014).

An example of this disparity and its persistent impact can be explored in conjunction with the 2020 COVID-19 pandemic. Native Americans across New Mexico died of COVID-19 at rates 19 times that of all other populations combined, according to data provided by the New Mexico Department of Health. The majority that lost their lives lived on remote tribal lands. They accounted for 57% of the state's cases, despite being only 11% of the population, and had infection rates 14 times that of the rest of the population. Other states also had disproportionately high rates of COVID-19 in Native communities (Kaplan & Davis, 2020).

Nutrition

Traditionally, Native Americans lived off the land; they had gathering and hunting practices in place to keep them nourished throughout the year, even during the toughest of winters. Due to the loss of land available to Native Americans when they were forced onto reservations, they began to experience nutritional concerns. Native Americans did not have access to nutritious foods and relied on heavily processed foods. Today, Native American communities have disproportionate burdens of diabetes and obesity, with an estimated 29.7% of youth being obese (Bullock et al., 2017). In recent years, programs have been created to help communities reconnect with Mother Earth. Johns Hopkins Center for American Indian Health and three rural Indigenous communities launched the "Feast for the Future" (FFF) to promote access to healthy foods and the transfer of traditional food-based knowledge from elders to youth (Cueva et al., 2020).

Mental Illness and Substance Use Among Native Americans

Unfortunately, far too few studies have been conducted to accurately examine mental health and substance use among Native Americans. Access to rigorous statistics is limited and is indicative of a system that has been overlooked and underfunded. It is estimated that approximately 4 million Native Americans are struggling with mental illness. Approximately 9.2% of Native American adults endured serious psychological distress in the past 30 days, compared to 3.7% of non-Hispanic White adults (U.S. Department of Health and Human Services [DHHS], 2018).

The second author of this chapter vividly remembers that mental illness in her reservation community was prevalent and ongoing. She reflected, "It seems like with all the loss and grief that is complex and ongoing we have a tough time getting mental illness under control. Just as someone is starting to heal, they are hit with another traumatic experience to try and process, it feels like a revolving door."

Native Americans experience posttraumatic stress disorder (PTSD) more than twice as often as the general population of the United States (DHHS, 2018). Children and adolescents who are Native American have the highest likelihood of developing major depressive disorder during their lifetime compared to any other ethnic or racial group. The incidence of postpartum depression is over 23% among Native American women.

Substance use and abuse are higher among Native Americans. The rate of substance abuse among Native American students is 3.4 times the United States national average for the same peer group (DHHS, 2018). Recent findings from a 2018 National Survey on Drug Use and Health found that 10% of Native Americans meet the criteria for a substance use disorder (Substance Abuse and Mental Health Services Administration [SAMHSA], 2018). Almost 25% of Native Americans reported binge drinking in the past month, and 17% report drug abuse in the past month. Native American adolescents have regularly had the highest substance use rates compared to other United States racial or ethnic groups since 1974 (SAMHSA, 2018).

Suicide, Domestic Violence, and Violent Crimes Among Native Americans

The overall death by suicide rate is 20% higher for Native Americans than for non-Hispanic Whites. Suicide is the second leading cause of death for Native Americans ages 10 to 34 (Centers for Disease Control and Prevention, 2013). Violence, unintentional injury, homicide, and suicide account for 75% of deaths for Native Americans aged 20 to 29 years. According to the Centers for Disease Control and Prevention (2013), 16% of students enrolled in a Bureau of Indian Affairs school have attempted suicide within the past year.

The U.S. Department of Justice, Office of Justice Programs (2016) reported that approximately four in five Native American adults have experienced some form of violence in their lives. This includes intimate partner violence, stalking, community violence, or sexual violence. Eighty-four percent of Native American women have experienced violence and 81% of Native American men report experiencing violence. This is 1.2 times higher than their White counterparts. In 2016, there were 5,712 known incidents of missing and murdered Native American women (Native Womens Wilderness, 2021). In one of the few longitudinal studies about Native American women, Robin et al. (1997) found that across their lifetime 67% experienced physical violence from a partner, 40% reported experiencing adult sexual assault, 40% reported childhood sexual assault, and 27% report childhood physical abuse.

Elder Abuse

Elders in tribal communities are people who carry wisdom and traditional Native American knowledge and medicine, regardless of age. Traditionally, elders were respected and protected. However, it cannot be assumed that this is the modern-day norm due to mental health issues, substance abuse, and violence within the communities. Crowder et al. (2019) found a high occurrence of abuse among Native American elders, a group already experiencing disproportionately high health and socioeconomic disparities.

IDENTITY DEVELOPMENT AND ACCULTURATION FOR CLIENTS OF NATIVE AMERICAN DESCENT

Acculturation is described by Garcia and Ahler (1992) as the cultural change that occurs when two or more cultures interact closely and persistently. The change occurs in varying degrees and frequently, and one culture changes more than the other. The process can happen voluntarily or can be deliberately enacted by a dominant group to maintain control over a conquered people. Native American acculturation was forcibly enacted by United States government policies from approximately 1890 to 1970 (Lomay & Hinkebein, 2006). Many policies that were enacted were culturally destructive, such as boarding schools and land redistribution. They were intended to eradicate cultural ideologies (Whitbeck, 2006). Some laws prohibited Native Americans from using their language and spiritual practices. Separating generations through boarding schools and redistributing tribal groups through reservations accelerated the acculturation of Native Americans to Western ideologies (Whitbeck, 2006).

Acculturation for people of Native American descent can be defined as "the degree to which the individual accepts and adheres to both majority and tribal cultural values" (Choney et al., 1995, p. 76). Researchers and clinicians struggle to apply current models of acculturation to Native Americans because Native Americans have the unique experience of forced removal from their lands, forced acculturation through governmental policies, and the complete restructuring of their traditional ways. This experience contrasts with the experiences of other cultural groups that were not historical residents of the United States. Like other cultural groups, however, Native Americans experience discrimination, microaggressions, and race-related stress that lead to difficulties with identity development (Reynolds et al., 2012).

In contrast to acculturation, which is focused on the adoption of mainstream beliefs, enculturation is the inculcation of tribal culture in Native Americans (Little Soldier, 1985). For many years it was illegal to practice and teach Native American cultural traditions; luckily for many Native Americans, this is no longer true. Values and traditions can be passed on and taught in a variety of settings, such as local clubs for the youth, schools, and community gatherings.

Some tribal nations, including the one where the second author is from and the first author worked, hire a cultural coordinator within their government. This person is utilized for many different purposes. One example is when the first doses of the COVID-19 vaccinations came to the community: the cultural coordinator conducted a community ceremony and blessed the vaccines that were about to be used. If counselors at the school want to do a Sweat Lodge ceremony with a group of students, they will reach out to the cultural coordinator, who will help prep and run the Sweat Lodge ceremony. Anyone who is in a helping position and wants to incorporate a traditional healing component has access to the cultural coordinator, who can either directly help them or point them in a direction where they can get assistance.

Levels of acculturation and enculturation differ among tribes, regional groups, and individuals. Each Native American tribe varies in its level of acceptance of tribal values, practices, variations of these customs, language, and relationship norms. M. T. Garrett and Pichette (2000) adapted the work of previous scholars such as R. D. Herring (1996) and LaFromboise et al. (1990) and identified a combination of five levels of acculturation for Native Americans.

1. *Traditional:* May or may not speak English, but think and speak in the Native language; follow traditional values and practices.
2. *Marginal:* May speak both English and the Native language; may or may not fully accept the cultural practices and beliefs of their tribe nor fully identify with mainstream cultural values and behaviors.
3. *Bicultural:* Accepted by dominant culture generally and tribal society simultaneously; able to know and accept both mainstream values and traditional values of their tribe.
4. *Assimilated:* Accepted by the dominant culture; endorse and practice only mainstream beliefs and values.
5. *Pantraditional:* Assimilated Native Americans who have chosen to return to their traditional beliefs, values, and practices; are generally accepted by mainstream culture but are seeking to embrace the previously lost traditional cultural heritage.

These levels of acculturation can be conceptualized as a continuum on which individuals may fall. However, in-group identification of "Indian-ness" can vary greatly (M. T. Garrett & Pichette, 2000). This categorization generally relies on a person's life experiences and life choices. For example, is it okay for a person to work and live in the city during the week and return to the reservation during the weekend? Is it okay for a person to practice some traditional practices and not others? Can a person who was not raised on the reservation adopt the "old ways" despite having lived most of their life with the mainstream, modern ways (J. T. Garrett & Garrett, 1994)? Offensive terms such as "apple" illustrate the conundrum that Native Americans experience when they are caught between two cultures. A no-win situation is created in which they are considered "red" on the outside and "white" on the inside (LaFromboise et al., 1993).

These identity conflicts can lead to negative outcomes for Native Americans who are caught between cultures and struggling to find a sense of identity. Little Soldier (1985) created an acculturation continuum with monocultural/traditional values on one extreme and monocultural/assimilated values on the other. Individuals who are in the middle are considered bicultural and have been indoctrinated with traditional values but have acquired the behaviors needed to function in mainstream American culture (Little Soldier, 1985). The "danger zone" occurs when an individual is caught between monocultural and bicultural. The individual has the traditional or mainstream values but lacks the knowledge, skills, or behaviors to function in the opposite culture, resulting in feelings of being out of place, stuck between two worlds, and not belonging (Little Soldier, 1985).

Native Americans who do not have an identity that is established as monocultural or bicultural can experience an identity conflict that leaves them feeling out of touch with their culture of birth and not connected to or comfortable in the mainstream culture. This battle for a place in the world can lead to negative outcomes such as higher rates of dropouts in school; feelings of rejection, depression, and/or anxiety; and higher incidence of substance use. Native Americans who have an established identity as bicultural or monocultural have fewer difficulties academically, personally, and socially (Gone, 2009; Lomay & Hinkebein, 2006; Rees et al., 2014). Potential ways for counselors to address this "danger zone" are discussed in the later parts of this chapter.

Addressing Acculturation With Clients

It is imperative that counselors working with Native American clients address and assess their acculturation and enculturation level, given the diversity within the Native American community. Counselors must avoid making assumptions about the identity of their clients without asking for more information. Counselors can achieve this informally through targeted questions, and formally through the clinical interview and assessments.

Assessment of Acculturation

There is a scarcity of research on Native American acculturation measures, and the established appraisals for other cultural groups do not always include Native Americans as part of their evaluations (Kim & Abreu, 2001; Zane & Mak, 2003). Some assessments exist that are specific to certain tribes, such as the Rosebud Personal Opinion Survey (Hoffmann et al., 1985), which is a 32-item measure of language use, customs, social behavior, religious practices, identification of traditional culture, ancestry, or blood quantum specific to the Rosebud Sioux tribe. The Navajo Community Acculturation Scale is a one-item measure that assesses acculturation from low to high acculturation within the Navajo community (Boyce & Boyce, 1983).

LaFromboise (1999) created the Living in Two Worlds Survey (LTWS) to assess the socialization of adolescents into Native culture and the dominant White culture. It consists of 50 items divided into two scales: adeptness at Indian culture and adeptness in White culture. The LTWS was developed to operationalize biculturalism and identify skills needed to exist effectively in both cultures and behavioral deficits regarding those skills. M. T. Garrett and Pichette (2000) created the Native American Acculturation Scale (NAAS), which is not tribe specific and is designed for a wide range of adult ages. It is a 20-item measure used to assess involvement in Native American culture across three domains: core self, cultural self-expression, and cultural and community engagement.

Winderowd et al. (2008) developed the American Indian Enculturation Scale (AIES), which also is non-tribe specific and is aimed at assessing the balance between White cultural beliefs and Native cultural beliefs and practices. The AIES has 17 items that participants rate based on their participation in each potential facet of American Indian life, such as attending Indian church or seeking help from elders. Counselors and counselor trainees may use the AIES at the beginning of the counseling relationship to identify appropriate interventions and means for incorporating Native American culture into the therapeutic relationship and treatment plan. These assessments explore topics such as language, relationships, media consumption, food choices, and religious practices. Counselors can use these assessments or informal questions to determine the client's place on the acculturation continuum.

Through both informal and formal assessment of the client's cultural identity, counselors can more accurately work with their client and choose appropriate interventions that incorporate the person's cultural identity (M. T. Garrett & Pichette, 2000). It will also convey interest in the client's culture, which Thomason (2012) found in their research was a factor in gaining and sustaining trust between a Native American client and a non-Native counselor.

COUNSELING UTILIZATION AND HELP-SEEKING

Harmony and healing are universal themes in the literature and practices of Native Americans (J. T. Garrett & Garrett, 1994). Native Americans view illnesses as stemming from being out of harmony within the self and environment. Locust (1985), as cited in J. T. Garrett and Garrett (1994), described this viewpoint: "If one stays in harmony, keeps all the tribal laws and all the sacred laws, one's spirit will be so strong that negativity will be unable to affect it" (p. 14).

When experiencing this type of disharmony, a Native American person may choose to visit a Medicine Man or Woman. They will sit together, and collaboratively they will decide what the problem is. The Medicine Man or Woman will suggest ways of dealing with the illness or assign the person a specific task. They will also include a support system for the person and a ceremony or ritual to help restore harmony within the person (J. T. Garrett & Garrett, 1994).

Rates of Utilization

Previous studies have implied that Native Americans are less likely to seek medical services and mental health services (Dana, 1986), but current studies, though limited, are showing minimal differences between Native and non-Native rates of help-seeking. Help-seeking rates vary across tribes, regions, and gender. In some areas, help-seeking among Native Americans is higher than in the general population (Beals et al., 2005).

Treatment Preferences

Many Native Americans pursue mental health in combination with traditional healing. In a study by Evans-Campbell (2008) of Native American women who had experienced violence in their lifetimes, 70% of the women accessed traditional mental health services. An additional 75% of the participants in their study had accessed a traditional Native American intervention such as visiting a traditional healer, participating in a sweat lodge, or offering tobacco to cope with their distress. Often, the reason for seeking help dictates the method of help pursued (e.g., traditional or mental health). Disorders such as substance use, anxiety, and depression may be viewed as best healed by traditional practices (Beals et al., 2005).

Native Americans have a slight preference for Native American counselors and mental health professionals (Scheel et al., 2011). However, this preference does not indicate a lack of openness. Scheel et al. (2011) found that American Indian college students are open to seeking help from non-American Indian counselors regardless of their level of enculturation to their tribal traditions.

Barriers to Help-Seeking

Some Native Americans view counseling and mental health treatment with suspicion due to past assimilation tactics used during colonization (Hartmann & Gone, 2012). Still, others drop out or do not seek services due to a lack of cultural congruency between the providers, lack of knowledge about services for them, and financial constraints (King, 1999; Roh et al., 2017). Additionally, there is a dearth of providers who are trained to meet the unique needs of Native Americans.

Accessibility is a barrier for Native Americans seeking mental health treatment. The federal government provides healthcare to the members of federally recognized tribes through the Indian Health Services (IHS); however, only one in five Native Americans reports having access to these services. This can be due to the location of the services; these services are typically located on reservations, but the majority of Native Americans do not live on reservations (Brown et al., 2000). Only about 50% of Native Americans have health insurance provided through an employer, while another 25% rely on Medicaid and another 25% have no health insurance (Brown et al., 2000).

The traditional methods of counselors are individualistic and emphasize the role of the individual in their healing. This viewpoint is in direct contrast to the traditional Native American beliefs of community and humility. Clients generally do not respond well to these methods due to this incongruency (McCormick, 1997). Native Americans benefit from counseling services that include sources of support and/or methodologies that are inclusive of others (e.g., family therapy), as this is more in line with the traditional healing practices and beliefs.

CULTURALLY RESPONSIVE PRACTICES: DRAWING FROM THE MULTICULTURAL AND SOCIAL JUSTICE COUNSELING COMPETENCIES AND CULTURAL HUMILITY

To be a culturally responsive practitioner when working with Native American clients, a counselor must blend traditional cultural values and practices within the existing theoretical clinical framework. Counselors need to identify the client's level of acculturation on the continuum of cultural commitment and establish a blended approach that meets the needs of the client. The approach may include traditional healing practices and traditional healers, the incorporation of Native American values, or simply an awareness of cultural differences. Fundamental to all of this is the practitioner's own need for cultural humility and understanding of the psychology of liberation when entering the therapeutic relationship with a client of Native American heritage.

Cultural Humility

Hook et al. (2013) defined *cultural humility* as a stance one assumes in a relationship. The stance is open to the other person, their identity, and the aspects of their identity that are most important to them. For example, a Native American client may request to start a counseling session with a smudging ceremony, a traditional cleansing ceremony. A counselor practicing cultural humility will approach this ceremony with an engaged and open heart. They will be fully present and curious throughout the ceremony. In contrast, a counselor may simply allow the client to engage in their cultural practice but may not be fully engaged or open to learning and participating in the ceremony. The latter conveys a lack of openness, while the former demonstrates sincerity and humbleness.

To move toward cultural humility, a person makes a lifelong commitment to continuous learning and evaluating themselves (Tervalon & Murray-García, 1998). Practicing cultural humility involves working toward the resolution of power imbalances and developing partnerships with advocacy groups (Tervalon & Murray-García, 1998). J. T. Garrett and Garrett (1994) advise counselors to come first as students, and second as professionals, to facilitate this sharing of knowledge and the correction of power imbalances.

Liberation Psychology

The term *liberation psychology* refers to the use of an approach to psychology that aims to understand and address the experiences amongst the marginalized and oppressed individuals (Aron & Corne, 1994). Counselors who use this model and approach seek to foster awareness of discrimination, affirm cultural identities and promote changes that ameliorate suffering (Aron & Corne, 1994). Steele (2008) recommends beginning this process as counselors-in-training by investigating and deconstructing the dominant cultural and political ideas. This includes examining theories of psychology and counseling to identify the ways in which privilege and oppression manifest in them. Learners can ask questions such as "Whose perspectives are represented in the counseling literature? Who is allowed to speak? Whose voices are not heard?" (Steele, 2008, p. 80). This practice of awareness and scrutiny should be continued throughout a counselor's training and work with clients by continually asking: How does the internalized dominant culture show up in me in counseling (Singh, 2019)? The internalization of the dominant cultural characteristics and the subsequent inactivation of this are critical to counseling because it is only when counselors reflect on their own internalized oppression and dominant cultural values that we can all heal individually and collectively (Singh, 2019).

Traditional Values in the Theoretical Framework

There is a dichotomy between traditional Native American values, which emphasize cooperation, groups, harmony, present living, and respect for elders, and the dominant culture, which emphasizes individuality, competition, scientific explanations, and rigid adherence to time (J. T. Garrett & Garrett, 1994). These contrasting values can be obstacles for Native Americans today, both within society and within the counseling relationship. Many of the dominant counseling theoretical frameworks are modeled on traditional European or European/American values.

Modesty

Native American culture traditionally values modesty. Behaviors that draw attention to oneself, such as loud voices or boasting, are discouraged. When a person receives individualized recognition or attention, it is common for that person to put their head down and avert their eyes in deference (J. T. Garrett & Garrett, 1994). Counselors and other individuals who are not familiar with these practices may misinterpret this behavior as evasive, withdrawn, or evidence of lying. The mental status exam widely recognized and utilized by mental health professionals to evaluate the psychological well-being of all individuals relies on the "appropriate" use of eye contact as part of its exam (Trzepacz

& Baker, 1993). A counselor or other clinician who is not knowledgeable about this cultural trait may pathologize behavior that is made consciously as a sign of respect to the interviewer.

The value of modesty can also create discomfort for Native American clients in counseling environments that rely heavily on direct conversation. Good Tracks (1973) identified that Native American clients experience greater discomfort with invasive questioning and the requirement for self-disclosure. Culturally responsive counselors allow space for clients to gather their thoughts and will match their client's tone and rate of speech (J. T. Garrett & Garrett, 1994).

Being Over Doing

Another area of potential discord or misinterpretation can be the mainstream culture's emphasis on accomplishments, tasks, and work. This is in opposition to the traditional Native American value of *being* over *doing* (J. T. Garrett & Garrett, 1994). This concept states that the goal of life is to develop the inner self, not simply to accomplish tasks or gather material wealth. For example, mainstream culture asks, "What do you do for a living?" whereas Native American culture asks, "Where do you come from?" A counselor may misconstrue this mindset as a lack of motivation or direction, and thus may unknowingly try to move the client toward gaining a sense of identity through their work or other life milestones.

Connection

Native American culture has an emphasis on community through tribes, family, and connection. The tribe is an interdependent system that gains its value through the whole rather than the sum of its parts. The meaning of family for Native Americans goes beyond blood relationships and the nuclear family. Native American children may grow up in numerous households, sometimes simultaneously. The entire universe can be thought of as a family, each member having a particular role and purpose (J. T. Garrett & Garrett, 1994).

Because of this emphasis on connection, Native Americans may not respond well to individual counseling services that emphasize an individualistic worldview (McCormick, 1997). The mainstream culture views health and counseling as a private relationship between the provider and the patient. However, Native Americans emphasize healing through connection: connection with the earth, and connection with others (Dufrene & Coleman, 1994). How can one heal mentally if there is no connection in the treatment? Counselors are encouraged to include sources of support in counseling such as family members, elders, or traditional healers.

CRAFTING AN ADVOCACY AGENDA

Learn About the History and Disparities

As one of the most marginalized racial groups in the United States, Native Americans face many challenges, such as high rates of poverty, violence, and substance abuse (Duran, 2006; Reynolds et al., 2012).

It is important to gain an understanding of the current challenges facing the local community, tribe, and nation where the counselor is located, and the advocacy efforts that are already underway. White et al. (2020) encourage non-Native counselors to attend meetings or community sessions on a particular topic affecting the community to deepen their understanding of the issue. A counselor can then use their skills and time, with the permission of the appropriate Native leader, to make progress on this issue. Native Americans have historically been mistreated by outside groups coming into their communities, and therefore counselors offering support may encounter hesitation and/or resistance. To respect this and allow Native Americans to have agency over their communities, counselors may need to wait for an invitation to participate or assist (White et al., 2020).

To become an ally and a culturally responsive counselor, counselors are encouraged to become a physical presence within their local Native American community (R. Herring, 2000). This means being present for community events such as powwows, rodeos, and dances, and participating in ceremonies when invited. Counselors can learn more about these ceremonies and customs by visiting reservations, cultural centers, and interacting with members of the tribe (Richardson, 1981). The first author, who is not Native American, has engaged in this learning process and was honored by the warmth and openness she encountered at every event or ceremony she attended. Counselors who approach these opportunities with humility and respect will likely experience the same welcoming environment from Native American communities.

Learn About Movement for Rights/Protection

Native Americans often have a vested interest in their communities, wanting it to be a better place for future generations. A teaching that is habitually given by elders is that when we are in pain, we have two choices on what to do with it: use it as a weapon or use it as a tool. Native Americans have taken the pain and used it to launch movements such as the "Missing and Murdered Indigenous Women and Girls" movement, aimed at raising awareness of violence against Native American women (Lucchesi & Echo-Hawk, 2016). Likewise, there is the "Indigenous Environmental Network" which represents several Indigenous groups in their fight to protect the land and its spiritual significance from threats such as the Keystone XL Pipeline project (Indigenous Environmental Network, 2021).

COUNSELING CHILDREN, ADOLESCENTS, AND YOUNG ADULTS

Native American youth under the age of 18 comprised 33.9% of the total population of Native Americans in the United States at the time of the last United States census. The next largest age group for Native Americans is those individuals between the ages of 25 and 44, and the overall population has a median age of 31 years old (U.S. Census Bureau, 2011). These youth and young adults face many unique challenges across several domains. Their risk is prominent for a multitude of adverse outcomes, including maltreatment, mental health diagnoses, death by suicide, and both accidental and violent deaths (Beals et al., 1997; Fitzgerald & Farrell, 2012). Native American youth are also at the highest risk on numerous outcome measures, such as high school dropout rates, teen pregnancy, and poverty (M. T. Garrett & Portman, 2011). In their communities, they experience poverty, malnutrition, substance abuse, domestic violence, and health disparities.

Like many other areas related to Native Americans, there is a scarcity of research on the mental health concerns and therapeutic needs of Native American youth. Beals et al. (1997) conducted a study with Native American youth between the ages of 13 and 17 and found that the four most common diagnoses for these youth were: attention deficit hyperactivity disorder, marijuana use disorder, major depressive disorder, and other substance dependence or abuse. When compared to nonminority children, Native

American youth were more likely to be diagnosed with attention deficit hyperactivity disorder, conduct disorder, oppositional defiant disorder, and substance abuse or use (Beals et al., 1997). Kenney and Thierry (2014) projected that 56.7% of American Indian and Alaska Native youth have experienced anxiety or depression. This contrasts with White youth at 43.6% (Kenney & Thierry, 2014). Differences in prevalence between populations have been ascribed to political, relational, and historical factors (West et al., 2012). These factors include experiences of racism and historical trauma resulting from forced assimilation and genocide (Manson et al., 2005; Swan & Sanitorium, 2013).

Implications for Counseling

R. Herring (1999) compiled a list of common presenting issues for Native American children and adolescents that reflect both the developmental needs of youth and adolescents, as well as the unique cultural challenges imposed upon Native American youth. This list includes:

- Failure to develop a positive self and ethnic identity
- Poor academic achievement
- Substance use
- Lower academic achievement after fourth grade
- Adverse effects of discrimination, racism, and misperceptions of Native Americans
- Conflicts resulting from the discrepancy between peer expectations and familial expectations
- Generational conflicts resulting from varying degrees of acculturation

R. Herring (1999) goes on to offer recommendations for addressing these and other areas of concern with Native American youth:

- Address cultural identity and the degree of acculturation of the client
- Allow time for trust to develop before focusing on a problem
- Allow extended family or other important persons (e.g., Indigenous healers) to participate in the session
- Allow flexible session start and end times
- Match the client's nonverbals
- Respect silence
- Use strategies that create practical solutions to problems
- Demonstrate respect for the client's culture

Additionally, the enculturation of cultural values is a protective factor for Native American youth (Gone, 2009; Lomay & Hinkebein, 2006). Ponce-Garcia et al. (2019) theorized that social support, particularly from elders and grandparents, promotes resilience among Native American youth because it also serves to instill cultural values and overall enculturation. Counselors can encourage the client to connect with elders, grandparents, or other individuals who can foster cultural pride and inculcate the client with cultural values. Clients can also be encouraged to participate in cultural events, programs, and other activities that foster community and cultural values.

COUNSELING ADULTS, COUPLES, AND FAMILIES

Adults

Few studies and even fewer longitudinal studies are assessing the specific needs of Native Americans. One study conducted by Kinzie et al. (1992) followed approximately

131 Native American adults on the east coast, and upon follow-up 20 years later, 70% of participants had received a mental health diagnosis during that time. One of the most significant factors affecting Native American adults is substance use. Native Americans have a higher rate of substance use disorders than any racial group (SAMHSA, 2008). When working with Native American adults, Harper (2011) recommends that counselors stay cognizant of these issues and other topics that are affecting Native Americans, as they may also affect diagnosis and treatment planning and matters such as substance abuse, trauma, depression, and suicide (Harper, 2011).

Couples and Families

Family is an essential piece of many Native Americans' lives, and counselors can anticipate that this may be reflected in the counseling process. The definition of a family can vary by individuals, areas, and tribes. It can include extended relations, family friends, community members, or other important people in the client's life, so it is important for counselors to avoid labeling or imparting their definition of a family onto clients (SAMHSA, 2020). Similarly, each family has its own unique rules, traditions, roles, and protocols. Counselors must approach this with curiosity and without assumptions. It is also necessary to explore the impact of acculturation, enculturation, tribal affiliation, and historical context on the family or couple in its past and present (SAMHSA, 2020).

IMPLICATIONS FOR CLINICAL PRACTICE

Stately and Waltman (2016) recommend the "3 Cs" method when working with clients of Native American descent. The 3 Cs are *context* (counselors understand the story of Native Americans and its impact on the client), *comfort* (counselors build safety within the therapy setting), and *communication* (counselors use techniques to build relationships and foster growth). These concepts will be explored in detail in this section.

Context

As previously discussed, it is imperative to understand the historical trauma of Native Americans to conceptualize their present needs and circumstances and approach the therapeutic relationship with empathy. Native American clients may benefit from the counselor labeling and addressing historical trauma and helping the client to contextualize their own experiences. Sotero (2006) simplified the major historical phases that have affected Native Americans into seven phases that counselors can use to address this topic with clients.

1. *Phase 1: Manifest Destiny (1492–1776):* Colonization occurred and introduced disease and alcohol into Native American communities.
2. *Phase 2: Economic Competition (ongoing):* The introduction of colonization brought about competition for resources that has resulted in widespread poverty and economic loss on an individual and a tribal level.
3. *Phase 3: Invasion/War Period:* The genocide of Native Americans began on a widespread level with events such as the Wounded Knee Massacre, mass lynching, and government-sanctioned executions.
4. *Phase 4: Reservation Period (1887–1943):* Native Americans were confined and relocated to reservations. They were forced to depend on their oppressor for resources and experienced a lack of security due to being forced to give up traditional means of meeting their needs.

5. *Phase 5: Boarding School Period (the 1880s–1930s):* Thousands of Native American children were forcefully removed from their families and placed into boarding schools to be inculcated with Christian values. At the end of this period, young adults returned to their homes having experienced years of violence. The traditional family system was destroyed.
6. *Phase 6: Relocation and Termination Period (the 1950s and 1960s):* Native American people were removed from reservations and moved to urban areas after being promised economic opportunities that were not delivered. People who moved into these urban cities experienced extreme racism, poverty, and a loss of community.
7. *Phase 7: Child Welfare Policies (through the 1970s):* A large number of Native American children were removed from their homes and placed into non-Native foster or adoptive homes. It is estimated that in the early 1970s, approximately 25% to 35% of all Native children had been removed from their homes.

Clients of Native American descent may be slow to warm up to and build trust with a non-Native counselor due to the historical trauma. However, studies have shown that Native American clients feel increased comfort when working with non-Native counselors if the counselor is open to and shows interest in their cultural history and the historical context of their story (Trimble, 2010).

Comfort

Counseling clients of Native American descent may require increased patience as counselors build safety in the therapeutic relationship. Thomason (2012) recommends that counselors offer water, coffee, or tea to Native American clients to foster comfort and respect. Thomason further recommends that counselors minimize intake paperwork before an in-person meeting, as invasive questioning can be harsh or threatening to clients who may have been affected by historical trauma or have feelings of mistrust of the helping system.

Counselors may want to model appropriate self-disclosure by sharing information about themselves, who they are, and where they came from. As previously discussed, Native American culture focused on *being* rather than *doing*, and therefore there is an emphasis put on understanding a person's background (J. T. Garrett & Garrett, 1994).

The traditional Native American concept of time is focused on the present and does not strictly adhere to clocks. This is sometimes referred to by in-group members as "Indian time" and implies the mindset that things will happen at the time they are meant to happen (J. T. Garrett & Garrett, 1994). Counselors can attempt to accommodate this in a variety of ways, such as having an open-door policy during particular times of the day or having drop-in times built into the daily or weekly schedule (SAMHSA, 2018). Counselors can be prepared to have some clients arrive late or call outside of business hours. This should be handled with understanding and creativity to find solutions that meet both parties' needs (SAMHSA, 2018).

Confidentiality must also be included in comfort building. Counselors who work with a client of Native American descent may be in communities that are close-knit or small, resulting in opportunities for clients to potentially know one another or for the counselors to see clients outside of the therapeutic setting (SAMHSA, 2018). Counselors need to be thorough when giving informed consent for the counseling process and specifically address these dual relationships and potential areas that may affect or compromise confidentiality (J. T. Garrett & Garrett, 1994).

Communication

The counseling skills and techniques used with Native American clients are largely the same as those used universally. Trimble (2010) emphasizes the importance of relationship-building over any specific theoretical orientation or technique. Native Americans traditionally learn through observation rather than verbal analysis. Techniques such as modeling and role-play have been endorsed by research as effective with clients of Native American descent. The following recommendations are also made by J. T. Garrett and Garrett (1994):

- Ask permission
- Give thanks
- Be patient
- Do not interrupt clients
- Allow time for thinking
- Allow space for clarification
- Use descriptive statements, metaphors, and imagery
- Allow for silence

Cultural Customs

In addition to the 3 Cs recommended by Stately and Waltman (2016), the incorporation of cultural values and traditional healing is also recommended. Non-Native counselors should not attempt to perform these ceremonies or rituals themselves in treatment, but rather be open to the inclusion of these in the treatment planning, intervention, or evaluation processes.

Traditional healing is often holistic and is based on the understanding of the interconnectedness of all areas of life and the importance of balance and harmony. The traditional healers who conduct these ceremonies can be allies in the treatment process. Healers are usually knowledgeable about resources in the community and may be able to connect clients with additional support services and programs. Counselors can ask clients who are working with traditional healers if they would like the healer to be involved in helping to plan treatment or ask if clients would like to work with a traditional healer if they are not already (SAMHSA, 2018). There are no organizations to certify traditional healers, but by reaching out to elders, community members, and supervisors, counselors can identify and integrate authentic, reliable healers into mental health treatment.

The specific activities that may be included as a part of this will vary depending on the community, tribe, area, or group. The activities may be individual activities that happen outside of mental health treatment (e.g., spirit camp, ceremonies, traditional hunting) or can be incorporated into treatment (e.g., smudging, traditional crafting, talking circles). It is a collaborative effort between the treatment providers and the client(s) to determine what will be best (SAMHSA, 2018).

CLINICAL CASE SCENARIO 8.1

Dakota is a 15-year-old Native American female living on a rural reservation. She is currently attending a K–12 tribal school. Her teachers referred her to the counselor after her grades started to drop in her classes. When visiting with

(continued)

CLINICAL CASE SCENARIO 8.1 (CONTINUED)

the counselor, she revealed that she had been seeing ghostly shapes that are dark and near her bed at night so she cannot fall asleep. Dakota has seen these images before in her childhood, but none as dark as these. Her lack of sleep, she believes, has led to difficulty in concentrating, causing her grades to drop.

Dakota's mother was diagnosed with bipolar disorder, PTSD, and substance use disorder. As a teenager, she worked for a local pimp on the weekends, to help her single mother pay the bills and buy groceries. Dakota's mother became addicted to meth when Dakota was seven years old. Dakota explained to her counselor that there was a time when her mother was present and took her to school almost every day. However, after her mother began abusing meth and stopped taking her medication, her mother's behaviors changed dramatically. Later, her mother was imprisoned for selling meth.

Additionally, Dakota's father was an alcoholic. However, when her mother went to prison and he had to care for all of the children in the home, he went to substance abuse treatment. At treatment, he was exposed to traditional Native American ceremonies such as sweat lodges. This helped him feel connected to his culture, which he never had before when growing up off the reservation. This connection to his culture helped him stay sober and raise his children.

Dakota attended a tribal school on her reservation and was able to participate and learn about her culture while in school. Dakota started each Monday morning at school with a Pipe Ceremony conducted by a Native American school employee or a local elder. She learned a great deal of her Ojibwe language by taking courses in school. She learned how to harvest traditional Native American wild rice during her science class. She even got to go on the lake in a canoe to gather the wild rice before she harvested it.

Dakota is experiencing cultural identity difficulties because of being raised by parents and loved ones who have mixed levels of acculturation. Dakota struggles to balance her desire to fit in with her Native American peers at school and her home life. Dakota feels stuck in the middle and unsure where she belongs.

Dakota was in disharmony when she was seeing the orbs and could not sleep, as both her physical and mental health were simultaneously being affected. The medicine man came to her counselor's office and collaboratively created a plan with Dakota and her counselor. He also gave her the task of collecting cedar boughs from the cedar tree at the school. She needed to make little bundles to hang over the windows in her bedroom. This would offer protection when she was falling asleep. She later confirmed that this task did help her. Dakota later confirmed that doing these tasks helped her sleep through the night and feel rested in the morning. This in turn translated to improved engagement and performance at school.

CHAPTER 8: CLIENTS OF NATIVE AMERICAN DESCENT | 127

CLINICAL CASE SCENARIO DISCUSSION QUESTIONS

1. Name Dakota's cultural identities that are important to note in your counseling work.
2. What traditional healing practice might you explore with Dakota to supplement your treatment interventions?
3. What is your advocacy plan to ensure that Dakota is provided with well-rounded and culturally responsive clinical care?

END-OF-CHAPTER RESOURCES

A robust set of instructor resources designed to supplement this text is located at http://connect.springerpub.com/content/book/978-0-8261-3953-5. Qualifying instructors may request access by emailing **textbook@springerpub.com.**

SUMMARY

There are approximately 3 million people who identify as Native Americans in the United States, descended from more than 562 different tribes. These individuals have unique and complex needs due to the trauma and historical oppression of the past coupled with the health and economic disparities and generational trauma of the present. Counselors must be knowledgeable of the history of Native Americans, including genocide, wars, and biased government laws, if they are to understand the context of the present challenges affecting clients of Native American descent. Counselors working with these clients must also educate themselves on the cultural and spiritual values of those they are working with, including how to assess individual clients for their level of acculturation and enculturation to the dominant cultural group and their Native American tribe cultural group. Many Native American clients view mental health treatment with distrust due to historical assimilation practices; therefore, it is imperative for counselors to use cultural humility to build connection and comfort and establish context within the counseling relationship. Counselors are encouraged to blend traditional cultural values and practices into the existing theoretical counseling framework as part of the individualized treatment planning process. Weaving in the strengths, resiliency, and wisdom of the culture can lead to a strengthened therapeutic bond and improved counseling outcomes.

DISCUSSION QUESTIONS

1. How will you integrate Westernized counseling modalities with traditional Native American practices to enhance counseling outcomes?
2. What aspects of colonization, genocide, and social injustice of Native American populations are most salient to cultivate cultural humility in the therapeutic relationship?
3. What are your experiences, conceptualizations, and beliefs about family? How might they differ or share similarities with clients of Native American descent on relevant topics (e.g., family member roles, the definition of a family member, dynamics of addiction)?
4. How can counselors incorporate the cultural value of community when working with Native American clients (e.g., session structure, treatment planning, assessing and evaluating progress)?
5. What impact could any Westernized values you may hold have on the therapeutic process, relationship, and client when working with a client of Native American descent?

KEY REFERENCES

Only key references appear in the print edition. The full reference list appears in the digital product on Springer Publishing Connect: https://connect.springerpub.com/content/book/978-0-8261-3953-5/part/part02/chapter/ch08

Aron, A., & Corne, S. (Eds., Trans.). (1994). *Writing for a liberation psychology: Ignacio Martín-Baró*. Harvard University Press.

Beals, J., Manson, S. M., Whitesell, N. R., Spicer, P., Novins, D. K., Mitchell, C. M., & AI-SUPERPFP Team. (2005). Prevalence of *DSM-IV* disorders and attendant help-seeking in 2 American Indian reservation populations. *Archives of General Psychiatry*, 62(1), 99–108. https://doi.org/10.1001/archpsyc.62.1.99

Boyce, W. T., & Boyce, J. C. (1983). Acculturation and changes in health among Navajo boarding school students. *Social Science & Medicine*, 17(4), 219–226. https://doi.org/10.1016/0277-9536(83)90119-3

Choney, S. K., Berryhill-Paapke, E., & Robbins, R. R. (1995). The acculturation of American Indians: Developing frameworks for research and practice. In J. G. Ponterooto, J. M. Casas, L. A. Suzuki, & C. M. Alexander (Eds.), *Handbook of multicultural counseling* (pp. 73–92). Sage Publications.

Crowder, J., Burnett, C., Laughton, K., & Dreisbech, C. (2019). Elder abuse in American Indian communities. *Journal of Forensic Nursing*, 15, 250–258. https://doi.org/10.1097/JFN.0000000000000259

Evans-Campbell, T. (2008). Historical trauma in American Indian/Native Alaska communities: A multilevel framework for exploring impacts on individuals, families and communities. *Journal of Interpersonal Violence*, 23(3), 316–338. https://doi.org/10.1177/0886260507312290

Garrett, M. T., & Pichette, E. F. (2000). Red as an apple: Native American acculturation and counseling with or without reservation. *Journal of Counseling & Development*, 78(1), 3–13. https://doi.org/10.1002/j.1556-6676.2000.tb02554.x

Kenney, M. K., & Thierry, J. (2014). Chronic conditions, functional difficulties, and disease burden among American Indian/Alaska Native children with special health care needs, 2009-2010. *Maternal and Child Health Journal*, 18(9), 2071–2079. https://doi.org/10.1007/s10995-014-1454-7

Kinoshameg, R., & Robson, P. (2018). Culture of encounter: Reconciliation and integration of the Anishinabe and the Catholic. *Religious Studies and Theology*, 37(2), 241–258. https://doi.org/10.1558/rsth.37605

LaFromboise, T. D., Coleman, H. L. K., & Gerton, J. (1993). Psychological impact of biculturalism: evidence and theory. *Psychological Bulletin*, 114(3), 395–412. https://doi.org/10.1037/0033-2909.114.3.395

LaFromboise, T. D., Trimble, J. E., & Mohatt, G. V. (1990). Counseling intervention and American Indian tradition: An integrative approach. *The Counseling Psychologist*, 18(4), 628–654. https://doi.org/10.1177/0011000090184006

Pritzker, B. (2000). *A Native American encyclopedia: History, culture and peoples*. Oxford Press.

Richardson, E. H. (1981). Cultural and historical perspectives in counseling American Indians. In D. Wing Sue (Ed.). *Counseling the Culturally Different: Theory and Practice* (pp. 216–255). John Wiley & Sons.

Singh, A. A. (2019). *The racial healing handbook: Practical activities to help you challenge privilege, confront, systemic racism, and engage in collective healing*. New Harbinger.

Smith, J. (2016). Reflections on the NBCC-I White Earth Institute. In *Substance Abuse and Mental Health Services Administration Minority Fellowship eNewletter*.

Smith, L. T. (2012). *Decolonizing methodologies: Research and indigenous peoples* (2nd ed.). Zed Books.

Stately, A., & Waltman, J. (2016). *Working with Native American patients and clients: The 3 C's*. Minnesota Psychological Association. https://www.mnpsych.org/index.php?option=com_dailyplanetblog&view=entry&category=event%20recap&id=161:working-with-native-american-patients-clients-the-3-c-s

CHAPTER 9

Culturally Responsive Counseling for Clients of European American Descent

PAUL H. SMITH, KELLY KING, AND CATHERINE W. HAWKINS

LEARNING OBJECTIVES

After reading this chapter, students will be able to:
- Recognize the sociocultural context and factors present when counseling clients of European American descent.
- Develop a deeper awareness of identity development models and competencies to address the needs of clients of European American descent.
- Identify ways to practice advocacy when working with clients of European American descent.
- Review culturally responsive strategies that will support clients of European American descent.

SELF-REFLECTION QUESTIONS

1. What cultural factors comes to mind in working with European American clients?
2. What intersectional identities might be present in working with European American clients?
3. What are the appropriate intervention considerations for European American clients?
4. What advocacy efforts are needed for this client group?

THE COUNSELOR: EXPLORATION, INTROSPECTION, AND REFLECTION

Reflecting on the counseling process, oneself, and the client are central to the work of counseling. Embedded in that reflection is exploring the intersection of the ethnic and racial background of oneself and the client. This chapter explores the multifaceted considerations necessary for counseling clients of European American descent. The group designated as *clients of European American descent* refers to clients who identify their ethnic heritage as being connected to both the continents of Europe and America. Those of

European American descent encompass people who have ancestors who arrived in the United States at various points in the history of the country, from before the formation of the country to the modern day. The U.S. Census Bureau does not inquire about European American identity, so numbers of Americans that identify with this ancestry and heritage are unclear. Fused with the term *American* is racial Whiteness (Tran & Paterson, 2016). 76.3% of people in the United States racially identify as White and 60.1% identify as White, not Hispanic or Latino (U.S. Census Bureau, 2019). Many people of European American descent racially identify as White and profit from the privileges embedded in American Whiteness. White supremacy is the notion and experience of benefiting from a system that assumes the superiority of White people (Archer, 2021). The superiority inhabits every aspect of society at the expense of non-White people. Importantly, within the histories of both the counseling and psychology professions, in the United States and globally, is a systematic and persistent bias toward counseling White people, based largely on the United States' history of White supremacy.

So, how has the counseling profession been biased for clients of European American descent? As any student of the history of psychology will know, the origins of the modern system of helping emerged in the early 20th century through figures such as Sigmund Freud in Europe and Frank Parsons in the United States (Gladding, 2018). Numerous others contributed to this professional development, but, importantly, the patients or clients in this era were primarily White and European or European American. As counseling theories and approaches were developed within this largely racially homogenous environment, and as people of color (POC) were historically excluded from higher education, White mental health concerns were not only privileged but also normalized.

Because of the bias toward White clients and counselors, many researchers in the mental health professions invite a reexamination of this history that includes internationalizing or decolonizing (Goodman & Gorski, 2016; Mills, 2014) the profession. This reconceptualization invites a deeper reflection on how these therapeutic approaches were developed and who was therefore ignored in the conceptualization. As a result, much of the multicultural counseling literature has focused on non-White clients or POC to expand knowledge about counseling these groups (Goodman & Gorski, 2016; Haskins et al., 2015). These professional initiatives emerged in the latter half of the 20th century to create standards around multicultural competence because the profession had not effectively considered or addressed counseling non-White clients.

DEFINITION OF TERMS

When referring to clients of European American descent, many other words or concepts might be attached to this group of people. In this section, those terms will be explored to give sociocultural context and to illustrate the challenge of discussing the ever-changing complexities embedded in race and ethnicity. Clients who identify as *European American* associated their ethnicity and primary ancestry with the continent of Europe.

Although this chapter refers to a group of people as European Americans, there remain nuances to this category. For example, a client might trace their ancestry to numerous European countries and be able to recount a patchwork of immigrant stories that were passed down for generations. Another client might have been born in a European country, then recently immigrated to the United States. These two clients might identify as European American but have different cultural backgrounds and worldviews, indicating heterogeneity within the ethnicity.

Caucasian is a fading racial term within modern society due to the unclear reference and inaccurate definition. Caucasian refers to an 18th-century definition of a group of people coming from an area that spanned from parts of Asia, Europe, and North Africa

(Bhopal & Donaldson, 1998). Over time, this term began to be used for people with lighter skin and/or of European descent. Due to the nonspecific and inaccurate use of the term in modern society, this term will not be used in this chapter.

The racial descriptor of *White* has been cultivated over time to delineate one group of people in contrast to another, primarily Black people. Race is a socially constructed phenomenon that embeds privilege and oppression to increase the power of one group over another. Within the United States, race has been codified and administered to rationalize slavery, extend slavery and oppression in other forms post-abolition, and enable the profiteering off of people not considered White. Ta-Nehisi Coates argues that "the elevation of the belief in being white was not achieved through wine tastings and ice cream socials, but rather through the pillaging of life, liberty, labor, and land" (Coates, 2015, p. 8). The racial Whiteness in the United States must be understood and conceptualized through the origin of the enslavement of Black people. Throughout the chapter, there will be fluidity between the use of the terms *European American* and *White* due to the overlapping references within professional literature and modern usage. Although the terms are not equivalent, the focus of this chapter aims to illuminate the common counseling implications when working with people who identify with both of these labels.

People of Color (POC) or *Black, Indigenous, and People of Color* (BIPOC) are people who do not racially identify as White. These terms label the person in the context of a diverse collective. POC/BIPOC experience discrimination and marginalization in various ways, but the collective identity can help with organizing against systems of power to advocate for positive change for all POC. BIPOC as a descriptor centers the experiences of those most marginalized in society, Black and Indigenous people, within the label to highlight their struggles and experiences in the United States. There remains some hesitancy or critique about the overuse of these terms, especially when it might be more accurate to refer to a specific racial or ethnic group rather than the collective.

As this chapter unfolds, it is important to reflect on your own experiences with White people or people of European American descent. For some readers who identify with this group, this reflection might involve exploring other groups of people that also identify as White to consider not only the similarities but also the differences within this group. Exploration might also involve reflecting on how you understand this ethnic group based on your lived experience and subsequent biases. For others who do not identify with this group, your reflection might involve a process that analyzes your experiences with this ethnic group and how you think about this group relative to the counseling profession. These moments of exploration are essential in counselor training to develop insight into how biases might affect the counseling relationship. You are encouraged to explore your experiences and biases with this group individually and collectively. Individual exploration could include activities such as journaling about your biases or researching more about the ethnic group of your client. Collective exploration could include activities such as bringing up your prior experiences or biases in supervision or talking with a peer about their European American heritage. What ways seem most relevant for you to explore this ethnic group?

WHITE RACIAL IDENTITY DEVELOPMENT

As with other cultural identities, White racial identity develops over time, represents varying levels of complexity, and influences social interaction within and across racial/ethnic group lines. However, within a socially stratified society wherein White people occupy a dominant, privileged position, White racial identity development is also distinct from other cultural identities. Two major differences include the invisibility and false sense of superiority that define Whiteness. Given that institutions and the mainstream worldview in the United States are representative of White norms, White people often have difficulty recognizing the benefits they receive by virtue of their (socially constructed) race. Without recognition of their privilege, individuals of European American descent might view the world as fair and objective. In this way, the ease with which White people move through the world—particularly White people who also receive class, gender, and other privileges—can lend itself to internalized superiority.

Against this backdrop of historical and present-day inequality among racial/ethnic groups, White racial identity development involves recognition of racial realities and progression toward an authentic, integrated, non-racist White identity. In this section, we examine Janet Helms's leading White Racial Identity Development Model (WRID). It is important to note that the context surrounding when these models were developed, as well as how they were received, exemplify how Whiteness works: Whiteness both positions non-White people as distinctly worthy of study (i.e., "Othered," viewed from a deficit-based approach), and avoids more rigorous self-examination of European Americans (i.e., the default or "above" culture; Helms, 2017). Thus, models of racial minority identity predated the WRID, and researchers at the time scrutinized Helms's ideas (see Helms [1993] for her description of these events).

The WRID is comprised of two overarching processes: (a) internalization of racism and (b) evolution of a non-racist White identity (Malott et al., 2015). Within each process, there are three racial-identity schemas (pattern of thoughts and behaviors) that indicate the individual's degree of complexity. Under Internalization of Racism are Contact, Disintegration, and Reintegration statuses. Contact is marked by a lack of awareness or acknowledgment of racialization and its effects. In this stage, White individuals may believe that everyone is treated equally, regardless of race, and may believe themselves to be colorblind. Disintegration involves internal conflict surrounding racial disparities that bring about disorientation or criticism of White race socialization. In the disintegration phase, a White individual may be confronted for the first time with racial disparity and may feel guilt or shame. Finally, reintegration involves affirming oneself as White and the view that White individuals are superior to non-White individuals. Reintegration can be viewed as bringing resolution or "equilibrium" to the disorientation of the disintegration status (Utsey & Gernat, 2002). In the reintegration phase, White individuals may choose to "blame the victim," or believe that White people ultimately deserve the privileges they have. Some individuals may remain in the Reintegration phase for their whole lives.

Beyond the internalization of racism comes the Evolution of a non-racist White identity. These stages include Pseudo-Independence, Autonomy, and Immersion-Emersion statuses. Pseudo-Independence is associated with the intellectualized view that White individuals benefit from privilege; analysis is often focused on disadvantages faced by non-White people as opposed to self-examination of Whiteness (Helms, 2017). People within this status might be taking steps to change personally held racial attitudes. The Autonomy stage represents both identifying as White and occupying a non-racist stance, whereas Immersion-Emersion features more proactive efforts toward an antiracist White identity, including ongoing interrogation of Whiteness (Carter et al., 2004). Autonomy is the first status where being White is integrated as an aspect of the person's own identity. Immersion-Emersion deepens this awareness of self and involves meaningful interactions with people cross-racially.

Helms's model provides a way to conceptualize a White person's level of racial complexity. *Racial complexity* refers to the ability to understand racial qualities and experiences of self and others (Helms, 1993). Importantly, the statuses just identified are not necessarily progressed through linearly (step by step). Instead, these statuses reflect different cognitive styles related to race and the nature of the person's surroundings (racially homogenous versus heterogeneous; Helms, 1993). In other words, Helms's statuses represent an approach to self and others as racial beings that can be fluid and context-specific. In theory, a person could evidence multiple dimensions at the same time, although people often have a primary or most-preferred dimension. Helms also notes that European Americans can remain static within a single status for much of their lives, particularly if it is reinforced by people around them and not directly challenged through cross-racial interactions; other people may have a more dynamic and evolving racial identity across the life span (Helms, 2020).

After considering the stages of WRID, take a pause here to consider a White person in your life (If you are White, you could reflect on yourself!). What stage of White racial development best describes you (or the White person in your life) at this current moment? How do you imagine they (or how do you) view people based on their race? Unaware of race or "colorblind" (the view that "race should not and does not matter"; Neville et al., 2000, p. 60; the impact of which is the harmful denial of race and racism as a reality for POC)? Having a preference for members of their group? Having a superficial idea or intellectual preoccupation about members of other racial groups? If they (or you) consider yourself to be anti-racist, what work do you still have left to do? You may also want to consider how these various identity statuses are expressed or acted out in day-to-day life by listing examples.

WHITE ALLYSHIP

A White ally is "a person who consciously commits, attitudinally and behaviorally, to an ongoing, purposeful engagement with and active challenging of white privilege, overt and subtle racism, and systemic racial inequalities for the purpose of becoming an agent of change in collaboration with, not for, people of color" (Ford & Orlandella, 2015, p. 288). Becoming a White ally is an ongoing process and should be understood as continuous and growth-based. Additionally, White allyism is most closely associated with Helms's stage of Autonomy described earlier. Using the Multicultural and Social Justice Counseling aspirational competencies of attitudes and beliefs, knowledge, skills, and action (AKSA) developed by the American Counseling Association (ACA) Governing Council as a framework, four important tenets of White allyship are outlined. The tenets of White allyship are self-reflexivity (attitudes and beliefs), understanding White supremacy and systemic racism (knowledge), a commitment to promote equity (skills), and coalition building with BIPOC (action).

The first tenet of White allyship is self-awareness. White allies will have taken significant steps toward interrogating their own biases, positionality, and participation in White supremacy culture. In a 2005 study by Nosek et al. (2005), 88% of White people were found to have a pro-White or anti-Black unconscious bias. Because this unconscious bias affects the majority, if not all, of White people, White allies must take steps to challenge their internal biases. Accompanying this interrogation will include an acknowledgment that there is a widespread privilege associated with being White in America.

Part of the process of self-awareness will include understanding oneself as a racial and cultural being (a process many White Americans have bypassed because Whiteness often remains invisible to the dominant group). This process of interrogation may include questions like:

- What judgments or biases have I learned and/or adopted based on my Whiteness?
- How does my Whiteness affect the way I show up in the world?
- What was I taught, both overtly and implicitly, about my racial identity?

- Was my racial identity discussed when I was growing up? If so, how was it discussed? What messages did I receive about my racial identity?
- How has my relationship with my Whiteness evolved over time?
- How is my identity linked to the history of White supremacy in the United States?

White allies will consider the process of self-reflexivity and self-exploration as continuous and ongoing, including the acknowledgment that, despite their desire toward allyship, sometimes their White privilege may have a blinding effect on their ability to recognize or understand the perspectives of BIPOC and/or the interplay of systems that uplift a culture of White supremacy. Edwards (2006) studied social justice allies and cautioned: "Individuals who are supportive of social justice efforts are not always effective in their anti-oppression efforts. Some who genuinely aspire to act as social justice allies are harmful, ultimately, despite their best intentions, perpetuating the system of oppression they seek to change" (Edwards, 2006, p. 39). In this way, sometimes a White ally will need to acknowledge their failures (particularly in the form of implicit or explicit participation in White supremacy) and take steps to repair these failures when necessary, including utilizing these failures as tools to learn how to move forward. White allies will ideally arrive at a place wherein they "seek critique as a gift" because critique will best enable them to move forward in their social justice work (Edwards, 2006, p. 47).

The second tenet of White allyship is the ongoing pursuit of knowledge as it pertains to White supremacy, systemic racism, and the nuances of privilege and oppression. White allies will understand that the ongoing pursuit of knowledge is integral to their work. In particular, White allies will be willing to listen in a spirit of cultural humility to the experiences of BIPOC individuals. Evans et al. (2019) warn about a certain type of White ally, calling them someone who might want to help, but is ignorant of the racist sociopolitical environment, thereby furthering racism. In this way, a sociopolitical understanding of the depths of racist structures, knowledge production, and ideology that are ubiquitous both currently and historically in American culture is integral to the work of White allies. White allies will acknowledge that the work falls on *them*, not on their relationships with BIPOC individuals to provide them with this knowledge or understanding.

Additionally, White counselor allies, in particular, will recognize that more research must be pursued in the area of White counselors in the field, specifically around addressing race-based trauma and the impact of White privilege in the practice of counseling (Evans et al., 2019). In light of the need for more research and the fact that the profession has been historically biased toward White clients and counselors, White ally counselors should be willing to seek out new research and/or, if possible, add to the research themselves. Additionally, White counselor allies may discover the importance of emphasizing multicultural counseling theories within their practice, especially those theories that are attempting to re-imagine traditional and highly popularized Eurocentric models.

The third tenet of White allyship is the commitment to promote equity within the profession. Edwards's (2006) conceptual model for social justice ally development outlines a trajectory for allyship development that ideally evolves from (a) aspiring ally for self-interest to (b) aspiring ally for altruism to, finally, (c) an ally for social justice. Edwards's model highlights an important argument that White allies, through the course of their development, will have understood to be true: racism hurts everyone! White allies will understand that although the harm done to the dominant group is not comparable to the harm done to the oppressed group, the collective cost on society is vast and significant (Edwards, 2007). When White allies understand that racism and White supremacy are hurting everyone (including themselves), they understand that their role is to promote equity at the systems level to promote liberation for all. As

Edwards says, a White ally for social justice seeks to "escape, impede, amend, redefine, and destroy the system" (2007, p. 47). Heather McGhee, in her book *What Racism Costs Everyone and How We Can Prosper Together,* discusses the problematic and widespread belief among White Americans that if racial equity were to exist, it would come at a personal cost to White Americans: "the narrative that white people should see the well-being of people of color as a threat to their own is one of the most powerful subterranean stories in America. Until we destroy the idea, opponents of progress can always weather it and use it to block any collective action that benefits us all" (McGhee, 2021, p. 15). White allies will come to see the psychic costs of White supremacy culture not just as a threat to POC but also as a threat to themselves.

Arguably the most important tenet of allyship is the fourth: coalition-building with BIPOC. As you may remember from the definition of White allyship that starts this section, White allyship means working to be "an agent of change with, not for, people of color" (Ford & Orlandella, 2015, p. 288). Coalition building does not include working *over* or *for* BIPOC but rather *with* BIPOC. White allies will have worked through potential motivations for allyship, such as the White Savior Industrial complex (which is the desire to provide help to BIPOC out of self-serving interests) or tokenism (believing that racism is a problem based on one relationship with a BIPOC individual). White allies should be careful to understand the implicit effects of their privilege, which may include feeling like their ideas are superior and/or should always be respected and/or listened to. White allies will practice listening and sometimes will resist the urge to speak in favor of listening. Additionally, White women should be aware of the urge to falsely equate their experiences of gendered oppression with racial oppression.

White allies may find that they are ostracized or shunned by other White people (Evans et al., 2019) because they are pushing back against a system that many White people subscribe to and believe in. White allies should make sure to practice self-care as they pursue the important work of acting as agents of change.

IDENTITY DEVELOPMENT FOR CLIENTS OF EUROPEAN AMERICAN DESCENT

Messages about one's own and other people's racial group membership are exchanged within families, schools, media, and other community and educational settings. Identity development for people of European descent occurs in the context of sociopolitical movements in the United States as well as historical legacies (e.g., immigration stories, participation in slavery, and the Civil War). Frameworks such as critical race theory (CRT) increasingly call attention to how history can be skewed to emphasize narratives of progress or accomplishments of European Americans as well as exclude the stories and contributions of POC (Dixson & Anderson, 2018). As a result, the way we learn about and discuss sociopolitical movements and historical legacies can be fraught with disagreement and distortions, reflective of different worldviews. For example, Civil Rights-era campaigns for equity and the Black Lives Matter* movement's push for accountability and investment in Black communities were/are viewed through different lenses. One lens could position such movements as divisive or disrespectful of institutions that White Americans might view as "working well." Another lens could emphasize how our history of racial injustice persists into the present day and requires continued advocacy until safety, freedom, and opportunity are available to BIPOC. Ask

---

*Black Lives Matter is a highly visible advocacy organization formed in 2013 after the vigilante killing of a Black teenage boy, Trayvon Martin; their mission is to oppose White supremacy and anti-Black violence in communities (blacklivesmatter.com).

yourself: How do I make sense of these movements? How is that response affected by my racial identity or developmental phase?

Additionally, at the level of the family, identity development could include information about family origin and ties to Europe. Some White clients may have more developed connections to their European heritage, perhaps through language, food, or other customs. Indeed, during early periods of migration in the 1800s, the European country of origin created many more divisions than it does (for most) in the present day (see McMahon & McMahon, 2002 for a discussion of the Irish American experience and additional reading). Identification with a country of origin could also be influenced by the recency of immigration (e.g., differences between first-, second-, or third-generation immigrant experiences) or the depth of contact they have with people or places (e.g., communication with relatives abroad, travel). Often, identification with a European country of origin can also provide a more positive affiliation or offer a more distinct set of cultural practices. Both might be comforting to White clients if they are wrestling with the meaning and impact of Whiteness or feel adrift or "uncultured" in a society where they represent the "mainstream." As implied in the WRID, being able to acknowledge one's identity as White, without also claiming superiority, is an important marker of identity development. Emphasis on a European country of origin, to the exclusion of considering Whiteness, could suggest that a client has bypassed or avoided addressing some of the more difficult thoughts and feelings surrounding their race (e.g., guilt, sadness, grief, "In what ways am I responsible for human rights abuses against POC?" "What does it mean to be White in a country where White supremacist groups exist?"). Pause again: To what extent does a White person in your life (or do you personally) identify with the European country of origin versus their (your) White racial status? What factors might inform this choice?

The Role of Socialization

Racial socialization is the process by which people come to learn about their racial identity and what it means for their interactions with others, including comparisons or views about superiority (Bartoli et al., 2015). Researchers describe White racial socialization as happening implicitly in the sense that White norms inform many environments (e.g., schools, workplaces) and involve restraining racist impulses. In other words, the goal of White racial socialization is to develop a positive view of members of the in-group and to promote smooth interactions with out-group members. Unfortunately, this can take the form of promoting colorblindness as a way of being or deny the ongoing relevance of race in social problems we face today. Examples include instructing children on how *not* to appear racist (e.g., if a White child comments on the skin color of a non-White child, a typical response would be to shut race talk down and encourage politeness; Sue, 2015).

Consider when and how you first realized what your racial group membership was. Relative to POC in the United States, research suggests that White people hold more positive attitudes about their racial group and have less explicit preparation for the existence of racial bias (Baron & Banaji, 2006; Hughes et al., 2009). Both of these findings reinforce how implicit messages that circulate in our culture (e.g., media, education) present more positive images of people of European descent and downplay the role of race in stratifying our society. The degree to which a person accepts racial realities and seeks interaction with people who are non-White informs what that person comes to believe about themself and others. Next, we examine values commonly held by people of European descent, including how those values inform worldview and develop in the context of inequality.

Values and Worldview

Values, or the qualities and principles that people regard as important, can be influenced by cultural and racial/ethnic group membership. As noted earlier, the centrality of Whiteness in the United States context means that values held by White individuals are elevated as the norm or even most desirable for all people. It is important, then, to understand what some of these values are and how we, as counselors, and our clients relate to them. This set of nine values presented by Helms (2020) and developed by Katz (1978) offers a view of mainstream values that have their roots in White cultural norms: (a) rugged individualism, the view that independence and self-sufficiency are more important than interdependence, community, or collectivism; (b) nuclear family is assumed to include two parents and children; (c) rationalism and logic are valued over emotion; (d) time is strictly observed in terms of efficiency and punctuality; (e) European beauty standards are considered most attractive; (f) action-orientation, or the perspective that people have control over their behaviors and thus should be able to control their circumstances; (g) universalism of European American history and culture to the exclusion of other histories and cultures; (h) competition and working to better oneself or secure more resources; and (i) history is filtered through the experience of White Americans.

In another list, Jones and Okun (2001) identify norms that reflect White supremacy culture in organizations (e.g., workplaces). A sample of these norms includes: (a) perfectionism, which includes emphasis on deficiencies and views work output as a measure of worth; (b) sense of urgency, such that there is pressure to take grand, decisive action rather than acknowledging uncertainty or developing more thoughtful, long-term views; (c) defensiveness related to constructive feedback, especially for those at the top of the hierarchy, or protecting against liability; (d) individualism, demonstrated by a lack of cooperation and shared responsibility or reward; and (e) objectivity, the view that people can be detached, unemotional, rational, and unbiased at all times.

Additionally, values and worldviews for people of European descent may vary based on ancestry. The family's country of origin before the United States could have a stronger influence on a person's values if immigration was relatively recent (e.g., a first- or second-generation Italian American would likely have more ties to Italian culture than someone who is a third- or fourth-generation Italian American) or if they are embedded in a community where these values are widely reflected (e.g., Irish Americans living in Boston or Israeli Americans living in Miami, where they have proximity to others with shared culture). Considering Italian Americans as an example, Italian cultural values around family and togetherness (Luciano et al., 2012) may promote more collectivist norms and behaviors (e.g., intergenerational family households) compared with other European Americans living in the United States. Similarly, region, socioeconomic status, or prominent subcultures in the United States (e.g., Queer communities) can also shape or alter the expression of values associated broadly with White cultural norms. As another example, members of the Queer community would likely not affirm the value of the nuclear family, under the assumption that this family represents a heteronormative ideal.

You might notice that many of these values involve exclusion and have a narrow, Eurocentric focus on what is desirable or superior. Additionally, descriptions of these values and norms emphasize the potential harms they produce. Using beauty standards as an example, this value, and surrounding messages (e.g., preferences displayed in advertising and mass media) and actions (e.g., the pursuit of thinness through dieting and restriction), have harmed people within and outside of the White racial/ethnic group (e.g., promotes colorism and skin lightening, diet culture and disordered eating). People of European American descent may not be aware of the beauty standards that they hold or how those implicit standards shape behavior (e.g., filtering potential partners by race on popular dating apps). Developing such awareness could allow the holder of the value to inventory its impact in their life and make a more informed, intentional decision about their values moving forward. Discarding values that are related to White supremacy can be viewed as a meaningful step in racial identity development.

Other values in the preceding lists, such as rugged individualism or the emphasis on an action orientation, share ties with sociopolitical views. A prominent example in the United States is the notion that "pulling oneself up by one's bootstraps" or applying "hard work" and assuming "personal responsibility" can result in financial or status benefits. This view persists despite abundant evidence exposing how institutions and policies systematically benefit some (e.g., wealthy, White, cisgender, heterosexual, males) over others (e.g., impoverished, POC, women, queer individuals); in other words, barriers to upward mobility exist for marginalized members of American society. Instead of acknowledging and remedying these, the bootstrap viewpoint recommends harder work and assuming more personal responsibility, obscuring systemic classism, racism, heterosexism, sexism, and so on.

Finally, some of the above values could theoretically be held more neutrally and not be accompanied by negative views about out-group members. Two such examples are values for rationalism and relationship to time. An individual could value logic over other kinds of knowledge and punctuality or having an order to time over more fluid and flexible approaches to time without also devaluing others. Insights from counseling theory, such as Acceptance and Commitment Therapy (ACT; see Harris [2009] for a fuller understanding of ACT and values), show us how even as values might represent a personal ideal to strive for, they are not meant to be attained. In other words, values have limitations and should be pursued with flexibility. Further, we can have value conflicts, as in when a value for rationalism is overridden by a value for kindness in responding to a loved one's emotional experience that points to the contributions of other values and worldviews. Thus, if we view all of our values, including racial and ethnically informed values, as personal ideals that do not apply in every context and should not be adopted uniformly by every person, then they become more personalized and help us represent our unique worldview and positionality.

COUNSELING UTILIZATION AND HELP-SEEKING

White adults have reported consistently higher rates of using counseling and therapy services, relative to Asian, Black, and Latino/a/x adults (Dobalian & Rivers, 2008; Substance Abuse and Mental Health Services Administration [SAMHSA], 2015). In one study of mental health service use within the past year, this rate was 16.6% for White respondents (SAMHSA, 2015). Variation in the use of services by people of European descent exists across other demographics: (a) women reported higher participation, at 21.5% compared with 11.3% of men; (b) adults in age brackets 26 to 34 and 35 to 49 used services at higher rates (18.1% and 19.3%, respectively) compared to age brackets 18 to 25 (14.3%) and 50+ years old (15.2%); and (c) White adults below the federal poverty level used services at a rate of 23.3%, with a descending rate as percent above the poverty level increased (18.3% for 100%–199% of poverty level, 15.5% for 200% or more of the poverty level). Such trends suggest that mental health service use is far from ubiquitous, even for groups that report relatively more access. Additionally, within-group differences in the use of counseling could suggest something about how those subgroups (e.g., White women, White adults, White people who are under-resourced) view counseling or their path to accessing it. For instance, women, often socialized to be more expressive and emotion-oriented, may find the prospect of counseling more comfortable than men if they have been socialized to be emotionally restrained (Young, 2017). When and how someone is referred (by themselves or someone else) could also be related to their developmental phase, health insurance status, or use of other health services.

With respect to the prevalence of various mental health conditions, roughly 20% of people of European descent reported having symptoms (within the past year) of mental illness, and a larger share reported general distress compared to all other racial/ethnic groups, excepting Native Americans (SAMHSA, 2012). The most frequently diagnosed disorders among White Americans include major depressive disorder (MDD), bipolar type I disorder, social phobia disorder, and generalized anxiety disorder (GAD; SAMHSA, 2012). Researchers have compared the prevalence of GAD and MDD across racial/ethnic groups, with people of European descent having a marked increase in these two diagnoses relative to Black and Latino/a/x populations (the difference being an average of 40%) and Asian populations (60% difference; Grant et al., 2005; Hasin et al., 2005; SAMHSA, 2014). Other research has pointed to lower prevalence of psychotic disorders, such as schizophrenia, among White Americans compared with Black Americans, as well as lower rates of inpatient substance abuse treatment; both trends should also be contextualized in terms of overdiagnosis and overreliance on more restrictive, higher levels of care experienced by Black Americans (Gara et al., 2019; SAMHSA, 2014).

Patterns of substance use disorders among people of European descent have also emerged, with alcohol use generally more accepted than illicit drug use. In fact, despite similar rates in illicit drug use among White and non-White Americans, White Americans have reported less concern that someone within their family could be affected (Pew Research Center, 2001, March 21; SAMHSA, 2014). This finding suggests that there is less understanding of the scope and prevalence of drug addiction among White Americans. The substance with the highest rates of abuse among White Americans is heroin, followed by cannabis (SAMHSA, 2014). Additionally, people of European descent generally report greater trust or comfort with the use of potentially addictive prescription medication relative to other racial groups (Hadjicostandi & Cheurprakobkit, 2002; Hamid, 1998; SAMHSA, 2014). Research into the type of mental health services used by racial/ethnic groups in the United States demonstrated that White people reported more use of prescription medication as their treatment type (at 14.4%) compared to other groups (ranging from 3.1% for Asian Americans to 14.1% for multiracial people; SAMHSA, 2014). Taken together, the relative comfort of people of European descent with prescription medication could indicate greater trust in the medical field in general or a preference for this route of treatment over other routes (e.g., talk therapy, holistic interventions).

CULTURALLY RESPONSIVE PRACTICES: DRAWING FROM THE MULTICULTURAL AND SOCIAL JUSTICE COUNSELING COMPETENCIES AND CULTURAL HUMILITY

Within the counseling profession, guidelines and standards have been established to guide professional practices that address and respond to cultural differences. As with any ethnic group, it is important to explore heterogeneity within the group as well as larger trends or common experiences within the group. Countless intersecting identities exist within the group of European Americans. Therefore, counseling a European

American client necessitates a reflexive and adaptive process that involves the various other identities of that individual. For example, although a European American might experience social privilege in one area of their life (e.g., race), they might experience oppression in another area of their life (e.g., gender, disability status).

Lacking in much of the professional literature is guidance on counseling White or European American clients. In much of the literature, there is the assumption that "diverse" clients are synonymous with clients of color (Haskins et al., 2015). Not only does this assumption further support the White supremacist notion that Whiteness is the norm and, therefore, need not be interrogated, but it also limits learning about unique elements present when working with a White client.

To help counselors best respond to these client and counselor differences of identity and social positioning, the Multicultural and Social Justice Counseling Competencies (MSJCC) were created (Ratts et al., 2016). These competencies outline and highlight practices and behaviors to create a more just, equitable, and multiculturally responsive counseling profession.

The MSJCC builds on the original Multicultural Counseling Competencies (Sue et al., 1992) by integrating the importance of social justice in the work of counseling, centering the experiences of oppression and privilege, and understanding that identities are intersectional (Ratts et al., 2016). These competencies provide a framework for training and accountability for responsive counseling practice with culturally diverse groups.

European Americans have social privilege compared to other ethnic groups due to the history of this country (e.g., slavery, voting, opportunities for wealth creation). The MSJCC provides a framework for describing variants of the counseling relationship based on a continuum of privilege and oppression. For example, a counselor of European American descent might be working with a Latinx client. This differential of privilege in the counseling relationship must be considered by the counselor. Importantly, both the counselor and the client also inhabit other identities that must be considered and might affect the relational experience of privilege or oppression. The European American counselor might be transgender and the Latinx client might be cisgender. These other intersectional identities would affect how each of those individuals would experience the counseling relationship.

Despite the reality that European Americans inhabit social privilege associated with Whiteness, it is important to consider the other identities that might be oppressed in society (e.g., gender, religion, sexuality). These identities in totality can inform the felt experience in the counseling relationship and, more generally, in society.

The MSJCC also outlines domains that inform multicultural and social justice practice in counseling. These areas are (a) counselor self-awareness, (b) client worldview, (c) the counseling relationship, and (d) counseling and advocacy interventions (Ratts et al., 2016). Counselors need to become aware of their assumptions and biases when working with a client of European American descent. These reflections might include previous interactions or portrayals in media and pop culture. Reflecting on these biases can enable the counselor to be more intentional when working with these clients, and not respond automatically based on prior assumptions.

Next, the client's worldview is an important consideration. What are the features of their belief system, outlook on life, and driving values that inform their decision-making? Counselors should understand the racial identity development of their clients. Recognizing how embedded and historical privileges affect the view of themselves and others can illuminate ways in which the client has been socialized. Other intersecting identities, such as gender, also deserve full exploration within the client worldview. Counselors might also seek out external information about the client's worldview to enhance their knowledge of the client.

The counseling relationship is the third domain that explores how the identities of the counselor and client intersect, especially related to the ways that privilege and oppression show up in the relationship. For example, a client of European American descent might experience more power in the counseling relationship with a counselor of color. This power might help and/or hinder the client's experience in counseling. Haskins et al. (2015) explored the experience of Black counseling students working with White clients. One finding of this research was that these students felt pressure to act as a model minority in the counseling relationship so as to be perceived as more professional. Due to limited educational and supervisory support, many did not feel they had space to discuss their experience and challenges when working with a White client. If both the counselor and client are of European American descent, then other differing identities might become more pronounced in relation to power and privilege in the counseling relationship (e.g., age, gender).

Lastly, counseling and advocacy interventions refer to how a counselor can provide relevant and multiculturally competent services to a client based on the counselor's unique attributes and background. Some of these interventions might be systemic in approach. A counselor might help a client understand how their heritage affects certain beliefs and values. Expanding client awareness about their racial or ethnic identity development can give them insight into how these social influences have affected their life and decision-making. This process could involve exploring unearned privileges and systemic supports due to their racial and ethnic identity (see McIntosh, 1989).

Cultural humility emerged in the counseling field as a way to conceptualize and measure an interpersonal stance that is open and curious about a client's culture (Hook et al., 2013). In contrast to cultural competencies, cultural humility embodies a relational process that does not assume a priori knowledge or skills. Relevant to working with European American clients, it would be important to practice openness and curiosity about the client's background and worldview. It might not be initially apparent what the client's experience of their ethnic background is and/or how significant that background is to the client's presenting issues. When working from a culturally humble stance, the counselor does not take an "expert" stance as to the client's culture (Hook et al., 2013). This process might begin with asking: What are the features of your cultural background? What is your experience being White in today's society? Tell me important aspects of your family history. All of these questions invite a position of humility when exploring the client's ethnic and racial identities. Both the MSJCC and the stance of cultural humility are central to ethical practice when working with European American clients.

CRAFTING AN ADVOCACY AGENDA

Advocacy in the counseling profession is inextricably linked to social justice and is a way to work toward a more equitable world for our clients (Ratts et al., 2010). The initiatives for advocacy in the counseling profession emerge from the very onset of the profession. Frank Parsons, often considered to be the first American counselor, helped advocate for struggling workers in Boston through vocational guidance programs in the late 1800s (Gladding, 2018). Since then, advocacy has reemerged as a central feature in the profession, as displayed in the MSJCC and the ACA Advocacy Competencies (Lewis et al., 2003; Ratts et al., 2016). Because clients from marginalized groups live with systems of oppression and because the systems of oppression affect clients in multifaceted ways, advocacy is a way through which to acknowledge both the specific and generalizable effects of marginalization and to assist the client in ways that are not solely limited to individual psychological change. In many ways, change on an individual level for a client is deeply reliant upon the social structures and ecosystem within which the client participates. Advocacy can be understood as a continuum, involving the ever-present and evolving shifting between person-centered and community-centered work (Gladding, 2018).

Advocacy for White and European American clients might seem illogical or even immoral due to the reality of White clients' privileged racial status in the United States. Nevertheless, taking an intersectional assessment of our clients might uncover other identities that are marginalized within their lived experience. For example, a White male college student might come into counseling expressing frustration with some of his class assignments and social interactions. Once the counselor explores the situation further, the counselor might discover that despite the student's persistent academic challenges, he has never been assessed for a learning disability and that he has limited resources at home due to his family's financial distress. Advocating for and with this client might involve helping the student access available school supports and psychological testing. Additionally, it might be important to consider how the intersection of the client's socioeconomic status (SES) is affecting the client's relationship to his education and his peers. Perhaps the client feels isolated based on his lack of financial resources and his inability to participate in certain activities because of this. Thus, advocating for this student would not revolve around his White identity or ethnic background, but instead could focus on areas where there might be marginalization or oppression at a systemic level, such as a potential learning disability or low SES.

In this way, crafting an advocacy agenda for clients of European American descent would not be relative to that identity in isolation, but would focus on intersectional identities (e.g., immigrant, transgender, physical disability). As the ACA Advocacy Competencies outline (Lewis et al., 2003), it is important to base advocacy on the client's needs and resources. There will be situations where it will be more helpful to act on behalf of the client (for example, helping the student client to connect with school-based testing). Other times, it might be more beneficial to act with the client to seek solutions (for example, empowering the student to develop more meaningful relationships with his peers).

COUNSELING CHILDREN, ADOLESCENTS, AND YOUNG ADULTS

It is important when counseling and developing interventions for White children and adolescents to remember that, historically, counseling literature about children has tended to focus on White children and their needs. Although the following considerations may feel applicable to children from many races and ethnicities, and while there are certainly common issues that children across races and ethnicity face, the counseling field nevertheless has a continued responsibility to incorporate various racial identities into the research about counseling children so that the literature continues to explore how race uniquely affects a child's identity and development.

Many counseling theorists have stressed the importance of the ecological model, originally developed by Urie Brofenbrenner, especially in relation to counseling children, adolescents, and young adults (Bronfenbrenner, 1992). The ecological model emphasizes the idea that children and adolescents are the product of intersecting systems that together affect the development of the child. The *microsystem* is the specific environment in which the child develops. A child's microsystems may include family, peers, school, and/or religious institutions. The *mesosystem* refers to the interplay between two or more microsystems. For example, what happens to a child at home is likely to affect how the child shows up at school. The *exosystem* refers to various environments in which the child may not be directly involved but that nevertheless affect the child's development. Some examples of the exosystem are the neighborhood, the parent's workplace and/or friends, and the media. In particular, because the media has historically favored, highlighted, and glorified the stories, ideas, and experiences of White Americans, a White child may unconsciously develop an inflated sense of superiority based on their Whiteness—a bias that is likely to affect the White child's self-concept and their relationship to others.

The *macrosystem* is the overarching belief system or culture in which the child develops. For a White child, the values of White supremacy culture that were discussed earlier are likely to play an important role in the identity and formation of the child, even if the child's racial identity is rarely discussed or if the concept of White supremacy is deliberately excluded from the child's understanding. In this way, a White child may believe that they "don't have a culture," or that they are colorblind, and may find themself without a productive context through which to explore their racial identity. Additionally, White children may experience guilt or shame regarding their racial identity once or if they develop an understanding of privilege and oppression. Simultaneously, a White child might have important cultural ties that originate from a European American identity. As has been discussed throughout this chapter, the specific elements of that cultural identity will have to be explored to understand how those traditions and beliefs might affect the client and their counseling concerns.

When counseling White children, you may notice the various ways in which the child's macrosystem (or overarching cultural values) may be affecting the child's growth and development. For example, because of the strong emphasis on individualism for White individuals, sometimes the good of a family may be sacrificed for the pursuit of an individual within that family, particularly if the individual holds the most power within the family system. Conversely, individual struggles may be overlooked to protect the family's overall reputation. For example, a child may be suffering from severe anxiety, but the family may not want to share this information because it might reflect poorly on their family system as a whole. Another effect of the focus on individualism among White Americans tends to be that individuation from the family is widely valued, which may lead some children or adolescents to feel ignored or disconnected from their family system too quickly. White children may be expected to "grow up fast" and to "pick themselves up by the bootstraps," just as their parents did.

Although a child's intersecting systems are important for the counselor to consider, the child's stage of development is equally crucial for the counselor to understand. A popular developmental model is Piaget's four stages of cognitive development (Huitt & Hummel, 2003). Children ages 0 to 2 are in the *sensorimotor stage*, wherein children gain knowledge and make discoveries through sensory experiences and the manipulation of objects. In this dramatic stage of growth, children find language and begin to learn object permanence (the idea that objects exist even when the child cannot see them). Children ages 2 to 7 are said to be in the *preoperational stage*, in which children are learning how to explain and remember their feelings, engage in pretend play, and use words and pictures to represent objects. During this stage of development, children are often egocentric and may struggle to understand someone else's viewpoint. Counseling during this developmental stage may be most successful utilizing play so that the child can express their feelings most appropriately. Children ages 7 to 11 are in the *concrete operational stage*, wherein they develop literacy, the ability to use logic, and the ability to understand something from another person's point of view. During this developmental period, peer relationships become especially important, and counselors may want to focus on helping their clients work on interpersonal skills. The final stage of development according to Piaget's model is for ages 12 and up and is called the *formal operational stage*. In this stage, adolescents are beginning to think abstractly and to consider both morality and social/political issues. During this time, adolescents are often struggling with identity formation, especially with how to distinguish themselves from their peers and family systems. Counselors during this developmental time may be focused on helping their clients navigate the complexities of relationships, sexuality, and family dynamics.

The developmental model and the ecological model can both be helpful frameworks through which to consider the unique challenges White children and adolescents may bring to counseling. The rest of this section focuses on various difficulties White children and adolescents may face throughout their development. As you reflect on these challenges, you may want to consider the extent to which some of these challenges may feel both "universal" and/or "specific" to White children and adolescents. Perhaps the answer will be somewhere in the middle.

A common challenge White children may face is dealing with the repercussions of divorce. Even as the two-parent nuclear family is often idealized in White culture, divorce rates among White Americans fall between 36% and 38% for White men and women throughout their lifetimes (Swanson, 2016). Thus, counseling children postdivorce is one of the most common reasons that counselors work with younger people (McClure & Teyber, 2003). Often, children with divorced parents face difficult adjustment periods, especially as they acclimate to moving between two different households. Finley and Schwartz (2010) call this period "the divided world of the child," and the adjustment period can sometimes lead to negative psychological, behavioral, and academic consequences for the child (Wallerstein, 2008). It is important to note, however, that not all children adjust negatively to divorce, especially if the family system before the divorce was full of conflict. It is also important to consider the child's developmental stage when considering the impact of divorce on the child. For example, older children may be more likely to feel anger and anxiety and to participate in blaming, whereas younger children may feel rejection and may feel as if the divorce is their fault. When helping a child deal with divorce, counselors will want to help the child through the process of acknowledging and accepting the divorce, resolving the feelings of anger and self-blame that may show up for the child, and disengaging from any parental conflict that may arise in the home as a result of the divorce.

In general, because White culture places less emphasis on emotions and more emphasis on rationalism and logic, some White children may find themselves struggling to understand or deal with their feelings that may be less "acceptable" or may appear to other people as negative. In particular, White boys are told to dismiss their feelings, especially those of sadness. This cultural value may make it particularly difficult for children or adolescents who are struggling with a depressed mood or depression. Depression is characterized as a mood disorder that can have negative effects on how a person feels, thinks, and acts (American Psychiatric Association, 2013). For children or adolescents, depression can have significant effects on academic performance, sleep, appetite, and self-esteem. Depression is considered to be one of the most common psychological problems in adolescence, and depression often manifests in adolescence from ages 13 to 19 (Costello et al., 2006). Depression is a risk factor for both suicide attempts and completions, and suicide is the second leading cause of death for 15- to 24-year-olds in the United States (National Institute for Mental Health, 2021). Successful treatment strategies for depression may be utilized in the group, individual, and family systems. Additionally, cognitive behavioral therapy (CBT) has been shown to be an effective, evidence-based treatment for children and adolescents struggling with depression. CBT helps individuals recognize and acknowledge negative automatic thought structures and replace the negative thought structures with more realistic interpretations. Antidepressant medication is often effective alongside traditional psychotherapy, and, if it is used, coordination with a medical provider is crucial.

In addition to depression, many White children and adolescents will be affected by death at some point in their upbringing. Death might include the loss of a grandparent, a sibling or parent, a friend, or a pet. The counseling relationship can be incredibly important as a child or adolescent comes to terms with the reality of death and deals with the aftermath of the death itself. It is important to note that the experience of death during childhood or adolescence can sometimes resurface later in life as well. When children are grieving, they must receive clear and age-appropriate information about the death so that the child understands that they did not cause the death and so that the child or adolescent finds appropriate ways to memorialize their loved one (Worden, 2018). Family interventions centered around making meaning out of the loss and the potential restructuring of familial roles can be helpful, and helping the child maintain routine and structure may also be helpful. Individual psychotherapy may be focused on allowing the child to openly express their feelings and thoughts about the death and helping the child commemorate their loved one. Play therapy or bibliotherapy may also be beneficial.

As usage of the internet, social media, and cell phones has become ubiquitous in American culture, children and adolescents are dealing with the impact of social media, online social relationships, and sometimes cyberbullying. In a 2010 study looking at technology usage in adolescents ages 15 to 18, adolescents were said to be using technology for 53 hours a week (around 7 hours a day; Rideout et al., 2010). While some research has indicated some positive effects of social media on adolescents, much of the research shows that extensive use of technology can lead to negative outcomes (Tao, 2014). Importantly, many adolescents are engaging in identity formation in an online setting at the same time that they are forming their identity in a "real-life" setting. Rather than dismiss or minimize the relevance of social media usage and online presence for children and adolescents, counselors should make sure to engage with the emotional experiences of adolescents online, particularly the repercussions of relationship loss and/or bullying in the online sphere (Tao, 2014).

COUNSELING ADULTS, COUPLES, AND FAMILIES

As mentioned throughout this chapter, much of the development of counseling theories and approaches have emerged from White therapists for White clients. Based on this history, one could argue that most counseling theories are suited for White, European American adults, couples, and families. There is some truth to this argument. For example, in the same way that White Americans are often connected to the value of individualism and the search for personal meaning, traditional counseling models often have a bias toward a similarly individualistic approach to help and healing. Additionally, humanistic and cognitive behavioral theories also center change on and through the individual. Because of the individualistic focus of traditional counseling, many counseling theories, therefore, might be helpful and productive for White clients. Missing from such a broad approach, however, is the recognition of heterogeneity within European American communities and some of the cultural features that are distinct from other cultural groups. Ignoring the unique client differences and heterogeneity in European American communities belies the spirit of being a multiculturally competent counselor. Being aware and knowledgeable about some of the cultural values that are predominant in European American communities, such as individualism and success orientation, might assist in conceptualizing and intervening appropriately. However, assessing for and understanding the unique client worldview is imperative for effective treatment.

Alongside the recognition of the heterogeneity within White America is the recognition that the various intersecting identities White Americans inhabit will inevitably affect the individual's experience of the counseling relationship. Some of these identities include sexuality, relationship status, age, gender, socioeconomic class, immigration status, and mental health. Because a person does not just inhabit one identity (i.e., simply a White person) but rather is a product of many intersecting identities (i.e., a cisgender White lesbian from a rural Southern state), the counselor needs to recognize the various ways that identity plays a part in the client's presentation and/or their conceptions or ideas about how they want to change. Additionally, a client may experience privilege through one area of their identity (i.e., white skin) but may experience oppression based on another part of their identity (e.g., gender and sexuality).

Even as there is a need for appreciating the intersecting identities of clients as well as the heterogeneity of White Americans, there are nevertheless certain patterns or issues that many White American clients undergo and/or face within the counseling setting. One such pattern is what Nancy Schlossberg refers to as the *transition model* (Schlossberg, 1984). Schlossberg's model, rather than emphasizing clear developmental milestones (as in Piaget's developmental model outlined earlier), emphasizes the idea that life transitions have important effects on adults throughout their life span. In particular, sometimes transitions are anticipated (e.g., a move or graduation), whereas other transitions may be unanticipated (e.g., the loss of a job or the death of a loved one). Personal expectations around certain transitions play an integral role in the client's response to the transition. For example, while one person may face graduation from college with excitement and positive expectation, another person may experience anxiety and dread. In other cases, transitions can turn out to be *nonevents* (e.g., an individual remaining single when she wanted to get married and start a family by a certain age), and nonevents can cause pain or anxiety for some clients.

The transition model helps contextualize the complexities associated with *acculturation*, which is the changes people experience during cross-cultural transitions or contact (Sam & Berry, 2010). Many White Americans may experience or have recently experienced immigration to the United States and may encounter difficulty with the transition. For example, there might be a recent adult immigrant from Poland who has moved to a Polish community within the United States. Their ties to the Polish community and culture will influence how they identify with American values versus Polish values. They might be confused or even disturbed by the White American's focus on individualism, especially if their cultural context emphasized a more collective, family-centered approach. As immigrants participate in the process of acculturation, people might use various strategies to maintain (or not) their heritage and participate (or not) in the other culture. Preservation of heritage can be expressed in cultural values (e.g., collectivism, centrality of family), practices (e.g., language or religion), or through material representation (e.g., food or dress). Also, the recency of immigration can inform the cultural values that feel most important to them. Counselors need to assess for and respond to the acculturation patterns of recent European immigrants and European Americans with strong cultural ties to their European ancestry.

Other experiences by some White people have been the felt experience of a loss of status or privilege due to an increasingly diverse and globalized world. Despite the current reality of White supremacy, some White people have a sense that their social power and/or culture is being lost or reduced. It can be helpful for counselors to explore their felt experience while also challenging irrational beliefs or misplaced blame if such emerges. The Day-Vines et al. (2020) broaching model can help the client explore their racial and ethnic identities, as well as other identities, as they relate to a presenting concern. *Broaching* is when a counselor intentionally brings the client's racial, ethnic, or cultural identity into the conversation as it relates to the client's concerns. Although the literature primarily focuses on broaching with marginalized clients (Day-Vines et al., 2020; King & Borders, 2019), broaching with White or European American clients could enhance their insight into their own identities and identity development. For example, a European American student might move to a college located in a large metropolitan area from a small town where there was limited racial and ethnic diversity. The student might experience a feeling of isolation and loneliness due to this significant transition. If the student went to counseling, the counselor might invite the client to explore how the feelings of isolation relate to their own ethnic identity and the different sociocultural environments at college versus the home.

The intersecting identity of gender can also play a role in the experiences of White clients. For example, White men are often socialized from a very young age to adopt the rules of masculinity, including the focus on competition, aggression, and independence. Some social theorists refer to this enculturation as *toxic masculinity* because this socialization can lead to harm to society at large, especially through its promotion of violence and its connection with misogyny and homophobia (Parent et al., 2019). Toxic masculinity may be one of the reasons why men commit the vast majority of crimes and why men have much higher rates of substance abuse than women do. Additionally, because White boys are often discouraged from practicing help-seeking behaviors, this difficulty or inability to ask for help can lead to distrust or a dismissal of the counseling relationship later on, even when the White male is struggling. Another important mental health issue that can show up for White men is depression. Estimates suggest that more than 6 million men experience depression in the United States every year (National Institute of Mental Health, n.d.). Additionally, middle-aged White men have the highest rate of suicide in America (Centers for Disease Control and Prevention, 2019). When working with White men, individual psychotherapy may want to focus on helping the man express himself within a safe, nonjudgmental space, and in a place that allows the man to explore his feelings and vulnerabilities on his terms and within his timeline. Group counseling can also be helpful, as it can allow men to connect with others who are feeling similar emotions and to practice emotional connection and vulnerability.

For White women, their gender may also be an important element of their identity. Although the feminist movement has, in many ways, improved the lives of women in America, there still exist vast disparities today. One example of this is the wage gap. On average, White women only earn 79 cents to every White man's dollar, while Black women only earn 62 cents and Hispanic women only earn 54 cents (Bleiweis, 2020). This gap, though much less pronounced for White women, may nevertheless mean that White women may be struggling to balance career and family roles, including maintaining financial stability. Additionally, White women may be dealing in counseling with the balancing of multiple roles, including but not limited to childcare, eldercare, and career. Feminist theory may be helpful to utilize when counseling women because feminist theory emphasizes the idea that the personal is political, meaning that a woman's problems are likely connected to a political solution (Enns, 2012). For example, if a mother is struggling to return to work after having a baby, perhaps the problem is not "within" the woman but rather because the woman does not have enough paid leave to successfully transition into new motherhood. While there are many issues unique to women, White women in particular may feel compelled to universalize their experience of being a woman to include women of other races and ethnicities. This universalization of experience has had damaging effects on the feminist movement because the struggles and desires of White women have historically been prioritized over the struggles of women of color.

Substance abuse or substance dependence are other important challenges that can show up for White clients. White men and women engage in some of the highest-risk drinking patterns compared to other groups (Chartier & Caetano, 2010). Additionally, substance abuse issues often co-occur with other mental health issues, resulting in a *dual diagnosis*, which is the coexistence of substance abuse and a mental health disorder. Importantly, substance abuse is the number one cause of preventable death in the

United States. Because substance abuse is such an important issue within the counseling context, many counselor education programs are offering specialties in addiction counseling. Counselors working with people with substance abuse disorder should be cognizant of the possibility that their clients may need a higher level of care, including residential facilities or outpatient treatment centers. Counselors working with clients with substance abuse disorder may also find it helpful to apply a developmental framework to their client's recovery journey. One such developmental framework is Gideon's Developmental Model of Recovery (1975), which emphasizes four stages of recovery: the isolation stage, the relatedness stage, the transformation stage, and the self-actualization stage. These stages emphasize the process of recovery, starting with the isolation stage during which the addict is participating in the addiction behaviors and simultaneously experiencing loneliness, feelings of guilt and shame, and irrational fears (Brooks & McHenry, 2015). As the client moves through the other phases, including stopping the addiction behaviors, they will develop an increased connection to others, and fear and anxiety will be reduced. Eventually, the client may reach self-actualization, in which they have integrated themself with their present moment and their relationships to self and others. Thinking about addiction through the lens of a developmental model such as this one can help the counselor to understand recovery as a multi-step process, and, just as in development, a process that may include lots of starts and stops.

Developing knowledge around what mental health issues European Americans face in your community, especially due to the heterogeneity of this population, is critically important. Besides the issues surrounding acculturation, gender identity, ageism, and substance abuse, other factors that might affect specific mental health needs in your community might include urban versus rural location, age patterns, sexuality, unemployment, tightness of local community, natural disasters, and religiosity of the population.

IMPLICATIONS FOR CLINICAL PRACTICE

On the surface, counseling clients of European American descent seems to be straightforward and the assumed norm in counseling due to the history of the profession. Although aspects of this notion are true, it remains important to consider the intersectional identities of these clients and the unique lived experience of their racial and ethnic identity. Whiteness and what it means to be "American" have been fused (Tran & Paterson, 2016), which raises a question: What does it mean to be European American outside of or distinct from Whiteness? Although this chapter does not answer such systemic and sociological questions, it does help counselors navigate issues of race and identity with White and European American clients. The overlapping features of these groups point to important influences and considerations of White privilege in counseling, as well as heterogeneous cultural features dependent on the specific client.

This population might have less awareness about their racial and ethnic identity because it is the assumed norm in our society (Adams, 2016). Helping clients raise their awareness of their racial and ethnic identity might help them better contextualize their experience with others. It could be useful for counselors to share information with clients about White racial identity development. In doing so, clients could be prompted to determine their status(es) and reflect on its function, both internally (thoughts and feelings associated with it) and interpersonally (its impact on relationships and interactions). Understanding certain features or common counseling concerns within the population can give counselors a better ability to respond to these clients' mental health needs. Lastly, the MSJCC and a culturally humble stance in counseling can provide a therapeutic environment where clients' needs are understood and addressed in a culturally responsive way.

CLINICAL CASE SCENARIO 9.1

Ryan is a 17-year-old White male who is currently in his junior year of high school. Ryan's mother and father have recently finalized their divorce, and Ryan has chosen to live with his mom. Ryan is at counseling under his parents' insistence. Ryan says that his parents are "furious at him for not wanting to go to college, and it's about the only thing they agree on these days." Ryan's father has worked his entire adult life as an insurance salesman, and Ryan describes him as "pathetic" and "racist" and he says that if he goes to college, he will turn out just like his dad. When asked to speak further about his father's worldview, Ryan says that his father is a "privileged man who has never given a thought about what it's like to be anyone else." In addition, Ryan says that he and his father have opposing political views. When asked about his racial or ethnic identity, he says that he is White and is not sure when his European ancestors came to America. "Maybe sometime in the 1800s," he said. Ryan is talented at art and wants to pursue a career in the arts, but Ryan's parents have told him that if he doesn't go to college, they will "cut him off financially."

CLINICAL CASE SCENARIO DISCUSSION QUESTIONS

1. What are Ryan's primary concerns at this time? What counseling approaches do you believe will be most beneficial for Ryan?
2. Using Helms's White Racial Identity Development Model, what stage might you place Ryan in? What strategies would you use as his counselor to help him interrogate his relationship to his identity?
3. What values might be especially important in Ryan's family system, and how might these values be connected to Ryan's racial or ethnic identity?

END-OF-CHAPTER RESOURCES

A robust set of instructor resources designed to supplement this text is located at http://connect.springerpub.com/content/book/978-0-8261-3953-5. Qualifying instructors may request access by emailing **textbook@springerpub.com**.

SUMMARY

"Clients of European descent" refers to clients who identify their ethnic heritage as being connected to both the continents of Europe and America. The counseling profession has historically been centered around the needs of clients of European descent, resulting in the privileging and normalization of White client concerns.

White racial identity development models reflect the range of statuses European American clients might present with and have implications for their views about themselves and others as racialized people. White allyship is an ongoing process that includes self-awareness, the pursuit of knowledge, the promotion of equity within the profession, and coalition building with BIPOC.

Socialization into White racial identity and European American values is informed by factors such as exposure to diverse others, surrounding sociopolitical climate, family worldview, and immigration history. These factors can influence client concerns in counseling across the life span. European Americans tend to seek counseling services at higher rates than other racial/ethnic groups, which can be understood in the context of structural advantages. When considering advocacy for White clients, it is important for counselors to take an intersectional approach to client concerns that considers the whole self and context.

DISCUSSION QUESTIONS

1. What are your primary concerns when working with White clients? How might you navigate these concerns when working with this group?
2. How could a counselor help support their clients of European American descent toward becoming White allies?
3. How might a counselor explore identity with a client of European American descent if the client does not see their ethnic background as having a distinct "culture"?
4. What are some examples of White cultural values and how could they be observed or changed to reduce harm to non-White individuals?
5. How does a White person's racial complexity change as they apply different schemas in Helms's WRID?

KEY REFERENCES

Only key references appear in the print edition. The full reference list appears in the digital product on Springer Publishing Connect: https://connect.springerpub.com/content/book/978-0-8261-3953-5/part/part02/chapter/ch09

American Psychiatric Association. (2013). *Diagnostic and statistical manual of mental disorders.* https://doi.org/10.1176/appi.books.9780890425596

Archer, D. (2021). *Anti-racist psychotherapy: Confronting systemic racism and healing racial trauma.* Each One Teach One Publications.

Carter, R. T., Helms, J. E., & Juby, H. L. (2004). The relationship between racism and racial identity for white Americans: A profile analysis. *Journal of Multicultural Counseling and Development, 32*(1), 2–17. https://doi.org/10.1002/j.2161-1912.2004.tb00357.x

Evans, A. M., Williams, B., Staton, A. R., Green, D., & Shepard, C. (2019). Allyship: The responsibility of white counselor education allies in addressing racism and discrimination. *International Journal on Responsibility, 4,* 27–42. https://commons.lib.jmu.edu/ijr/vol3/iss2/4

Helms, J. E. (1993). I also said, "White racial identity influences White researchers." *The Counseling Psychologist, 21*(2), 240–243. https://doi.org/10.1177/0011000093212007

Helms, J. E. (2017). The challenge of making whiteness visible: Reactions to four whitenessarticles. *The Counseling Psychologist, 45*(5), 717–726. https://doi.org/10.1177/0011000017718943

Helms, J. E. (2020). *A race is a nice thing to have: A guide to being a White person or understanding the White persons in your life* (3rd ed.). Cognella.

Hook, J. N., Davis, D. E., Owen, J., Worthington, E. L., & Utsey, S. O. (2013). Cultural humility: measuring openness to culturally diverse clients. *Journal of Counseling Psychology, 60*(3), 353–366. https://doi.org/10.1037/a0032595

Lewis, J. A., Arnold, M. S., House, R., & Toporek, R. L. (2003). *ACA advocacy competencies.* https://www.counseling.org/docs/default-source/competencies/aca-advocacy-competencies-updated-may-2020.pdf?sfvrsn=f410212c_4

Ratts, M. J., Lewis, J. A., & Toporek, R. L. (2010). Advocacy and social justice: A helping paradigm for the 21st century. In M. J. Ratts, R. L. Toporek, & J. A. Lewis (Eds.), *ACA advocacy competencies: A social justice framework for counselors* (pp. 3–10). American Counseling Association.

Ratts, M. J., Singh, A. A., Nassar-McMillan, S., Butler, S. K., & McCullough, J. R. (2016). Multicultural and social justice counseling competencies: Guidelines for the counseling profession. *Journal of Multicultural Counseling and Development*, 44(1), 28–48. https://doi.org/10.1002/jmcd.12035

CHAPTER 10

Culturally Responsive Counseling for Clients of Multiracial Descent

VICTORIA AUSTIN, KARENA HEYWARD, AND SHANICE ARMSTRONG

LEARNING OBJECTIVES

After reading this chapter, students will be able to:

- Recognize the sociocultural, racial, and historical issues that influence multiracial clients, to increase counselor awareness and reduce cultural insensitivities.
- Develop a deeper awareness of multiracial identity development and competencies to address the needs of multiracial clients.
- Identify ways to advocate for improved learning and address the ongoing needs of multiracial clients.
- Review culturally responsive strategies and techniques that will support multiracial populations.
- Review the value of using intersectionality and a liberation framework when working with clients.

SELF-REFLECTION QUESTIONS

1. What does it mean if a counseling client describes themself as multiracial?
2. What cultural factors do you need to consider when working with multiracial individuals?
3. How will you show cultural responsiveness in your clinical intervention approach for multiracial clients?
4. What advocacy efforts will you engage in to benefit your multiracial clients?

THE COUNSELOR: EXPLORATION, INTROSPECTION, AND REFLECTION

Multiracial identity cannot be "defined" without first discussing what "race" means. Honestly, there is no "coherent, fixed definition of race" (Coates, 2013, para. 5). There is the acknowledgment that people in Europe, Sub-Saharan Africa, Asia, and the early

Americas lived isolated from one another and developed differing physical traits (Coates, 2013). Put plainly, race is a social construct resulting from social and historical processes that tends to construct groups into opposing binaries (e.g., Black and White), create otherness, determine one's location in systems of power and inequality (Andersen & Hill Collins, 2016), and widen existing division between White people and people of color (Kivel, 2017). The U.S. Census Bureau (n.d.) classifies race into five major categories: White, Black or African American, American Indian and Alaska Native, Asian, and Native Hawaiian and Other Pacific Islander. Respondents can also note Hispanic or Latino ethnicity (of any race).

What does it mean to be multiracial? Let's start with the basics; put simply, the authors of this chapter define *multiracial* as holding two or more racial identities based on your biological ancestors' identities. Often confused with or overly simplified to being of both Black and White descent, multiracial identity can include any combination of racial and/or ethnic identities. As mentioned earlier, it is challenging to define multiracial identity because identifying as multiracial defies current constructions of race (Shih et al., 2007; Shih & Sanchez, 2005).

Currently, there are 16,875,542 self-identified multiracial Americans, making up 5.2% of the total population in the United States (U.S. Census Bureau, n.d.). The number of people who identify as multiracial continues to grow (Henriksen & Maxwell, 2016). The U.S. Census numbers may not be accurate, as some multiracial people choose to identify with a monoracial category on demographic forms (Townsend et al., 2012). The Pew Research Center (Parker et al., 2015) took a different approach for determining how many multiracial people exist in the United States by considering parents' and grandparents' racial backgrounds. By their estimate, 6.9% of the adult American population is multiracial, with half of this population being of White and American Indian background. It is important to note that this group also reported being the least likely to identify as multiracial (Parker et al., 2015). People with Black and American Indian backgrounds make up 12% of the multiracial adult American population, while 11% of the U.S. multiracial population are White and Black; 11% are multiracial Hispanic; 6% are White, Black, and American Indian; 4% are White and Asian; and 5% are "some other combination" (Parker et al., 2015). Nearly half of all multiracial Americans are younger than 18 years old and between the 2000 and 2010 censuses, the number of Black and White biracial Americans doubled (Parker et al., 2015). This increase of multiracial people in the United States is projected to increase in the 2020 census results (Crane, 2020). The increased number of multiracial people in the United States leads people to believe that racism has declined, but "racism is resilient" (Kivel, 2017, p. 182). That racial hierarchy still exists where White is at the top, and lighter skin tones are favored (Kivel, 2017). The population of multiracial people seeking mental health services continues to grow, creating an ethical mandate to ensure that counselors are informed and trained correctly to work with multiracial clients.

With that, we will leave you with several points of reflection:

- How does your clinical paperwork allow space for multiracial clients to identify authentically?
- How do you discuss racial identity with your clients?
- How have you internalized the typical understanding of race?
- What race-based stereotypes were/are upheld in your family of origin? How do you perpetuate them now?
- What is your relationship to multiracial people (historically through your family lineage and in the present time)?
- What are your intentions in working with this population?
- What motivations do you have for serving multiracial clients?

COMPETENCIES FOR COUNSELING THE MULTIRACIAL POPULATION

Multiracial clients embody diversity and intersectionality (Crenshaw, 1991; Nicolas et al., 2019). Clients who hold multiple heritages have lived experiences and face challenges that require clinicians to think complexly about race and ethnicity, hierarchies of inequality, systems of oppression, privilege, historical contexts, life span development, socialization, acculturation, and identity politics, among other issues (Albuja et al., 2020; Zou & Cheryan, 2017). A person with a multiracial identity can include any combination of racial and/or ethnic identities with divergent traditions and cultures. There is, therefore, a wide range of diverse issues that could be presented in the counseling process that clinicians must be prepared and trained to address (Henriksen & Maxwell, 2016; Kenney et al., 2015; Nishina & Witkow, 2020).

In 2015, the American Counseling Association (ACA) adopted and endorsed the Multiracial/Ethnic Counseling Concerns (MRECC) Interest Network's *Competencies for Counseling the Multiracial Population* (CCMP) "to serve as a resource and provide a framework for how counseling and other helping professionals can competently and effectively work with and advocate for members of the multiracial population" (Kenney et al., 2015, p. 2). The CCMP are organized in accordance with the 2009 Council for the Accreditation of Counseling and Related Educational Programs (CACREP) Standards (CACREP, 2009) and bring recognition to the experiences and needed practice standards for "interracial couples, multiracial families, multiracial individuals, and transracial adoptees and families" across the affectional spectrum (Kenney et al., 2015, p. 2). Within their praxis working with multiracial clients, culturally competent counselors will adapt strategies, seek training, and understand issues of human growth and development, social and cultural diversity, helping relationships, group work, career development, assessment, research and program evaluation, and professional orientation and ethical practice as those issues affect clients. In the following sections, some of the directives of the CCMP will be outlined.

Human Growth and Development

Internal and external forces (e.g., self-identification, phenotype, location and community demographics, and interpersonal relationships) greatly influence the process of developing, establishing, and maintaining identity development for biracial individuals (Henriksen & Maxwell, 2009; LaBarrie, 2007). Messages that multiracial children receive and internalize about themselves can be affected by their caregiver's ethnic identity status (monoracial or multiracial), identity development conflicts, and the use of racial labels. Avoidance and inability to discuss race, White supremacy, and racial discrimination within interracial and transracial families contribute negatively to the emotional well-being of biracial youths. Further, a lack of strong supportive relationships, diversity within the community, and positive racial messages can contribute to multiracial children feeling isolated, marginalized, and struggling to establish a healthy identity (Henriksen & Maxwell, 2009; LaBarrie, 2007; Nadal et al., 2013; Root, 1994). Family generational and immigration status, and the observations of racial power within the family, additionally contribute to identity development as they provide an avenue for introduction to color consciousness, social ignorance, and shared racial patterns (Radina & Cooney, 2000).

Among the charges in the CCMP in the core domain of human growth and development, counselors are instructed to appreciate and understand: developmental tasks of multiheritage populations; fluid processes of identity development; the uniqueness of identity connection and inter- and intragroup differences; generational and geographic differences in acceptance of multiracial communities; and the impact of oppression and discrimination (Kenney et al., 2015). To accomplish these charges, counselors are encouraged to increase their knowledge of diverse lived experiences of multiracial communities across the life span by examining research, literature, and media. Counselors should engage in consultation, supervision, and targeted continued education. Furthermore, counselors are encouraged to consider the intersections of biological, familial, and psychosocial factors on developmental concerns as they conceptualize and understand client presenting issues (Kenney et al., 2015).

Social and Cultural Diversity

The knowledge and awareness needed to understand the complexities of social and cultural diversity among multiracial individuals, couples, and families is staggering. As multiracial populations include a broad and growing constellation of groups and individuals from a combination of racial and ethnic backgrounds, mental health professionals are challenged to increase their knowledge of the micro, meso, and macrosystemic factors to understand clients (Henriksen & Maxwell, 2016; Root, 2002, 2003). Social and cultural factors that affect the lived experiences of multiracial communities include racial and ethnic, gender, and affectional identity development models, the family-of-origin cultural customs, historical events, legislation, and racial trauma (Henriksen & Maxwell, 2009). In consideration of these factors, counselors must understand the salient experiences and themes when working with multiheritage clients. Counselors must be able to navigate cultural discussions and dynamics, repair ruptured alliances, identify advocacy opportunities, and become aware of and challenge their own assumptions and biases about their client and their client's intercultural status (Kenney et al., 2015).

Counselors seeking to address the changes proposed by the CCMP (Kenney et al., 2015) might educate themselves about historical and present-day experiences of oppression, prejudice, and discrimination that affect multiracial communities. This knowledge might be attained through research, literature, or discussion with leaders of the multiheritage community. Counselors can also work to incorporate and develop skills in broaching: "deliberate and intentional efforts to discuss those racial, ethnic, and cultural concerns that may impact the client's presenting concerns" (Day-Vines et al., 2020, p. 107). Day-Vines et al. (2020) proposed the Multidimensional Model of Broaching Behavior, which calls upon counselors to be skillful in acknowledging similarities, differences, and misunderstandings within the counselor–client relationship and implementing social justice and advocacy interventions to address the client's encounters of racism, discrimination, and oppressive events.

Helping Relationships

Monoracialism is a common stereotype experienced by clients from multiracial backgrounds. Microaggressions centered around the othering, oversimplifying, and confusion that multiracial communities experience as they seek to affirm themselves and explore their identities contribute to psychological and social stressors (Fisher et al., 2014). Mental health professionals are charged to be mindful to establish safe, empathetic, and supportive therapeutic relationships wherein multiracial communities can freely affirm, vent, and explore the intricacies of their identities. Culturally competent counselors "maintain an orientation of wellness," "understand that multiracial identity may not be the reason for seeking counseling" (Kenney et al., 2015, pp. 11–17), and are careful not to impose their own agenda and assumptions on clients. Clinicians across settings are charged with being intentional in creating spaces where multiracial clients can identify and externalize their experiences free from internalized societal messages (Sebring, 1985).

To accomplish tasks set forth in the domain of helping relationships, counselors are encouraged to use intake and interviewing materials that are inclusive, allowing individuals from diverse backgrounds to self-identify. Counselors should be sure to "assess the degree to which clients experience resilience and oppression related to their multiracial background" (Kenney et al., 2015, p. 17). Counselors should avoid making assumptions or generalizations about multiheritage clients, taking time to reflect and address their own internalized biases, prejudices, and discriminatory beliefs (Ratts et al., 2015). Additionally, in working collaboratively with clients to identify strengths, challenges, and the focus of the session, counselors are encouraged to utilize anti-oppressive theoretical perspectives, which will be discussed later in this chapter.

Group Work

While there is diversity in the experiences, racial identity development, and attitudes among multiracial communities, there also exists a commonality of themes that can be addressed, strengthened, and affirmed in group settings (Narvaez & Kivlighan III, 2021). Group counseling can facilitate universality, experiences of cohesion, belongingness, and hope (Burlingame et al., 2004; Narvaez & Kivlighan III, 2021). Culturally competent counselors who facilitate group counseling with clients from multiple heritages are therefore charged by the CCMP (Kenney et al., 2015) to adeptly translate and bridge high- and low-context communication interactions. High-context communication is characterized, for example, by the use of more indirect, implicit, and nuanced speech, wherein sensitive messages might be more carefully coded to avoid giving offense. In contrast, low-context communication is more explicit and direct, and messages are more literal. Mental health professionals must also be prepared to broach culture and moderate conversations of cultural identity, oppression, and inter- and intragroup prejudices, and appreciate the impact of White supremacy, colorism, and monocultural identification among members of multiracial groups.

Narvaez and Kivlighan III (2021) propose the following facilitator preparation strategies for counselors seeking to display competencies in group work with multiheritage clients: engage a multicultural orientation, consult with mental health professionals specializing in work with multiracial populations, and investigate the literature. Counselors should increase facilitation proficiencies (e.g., discussing and establishing safety for members, encouraging member self-advocacy and support-seeking skills, and attending to group dynamics; Narvaez & Kivlighan III, 2021). Group counselors should be prepared to use counseling skills and interventions that explicitly support, validate, and process distress with multiracial members (Kenney et al., 2015; Narvaez & Kivlighan III, 2021).

Career Development

Multiracial communities are inclusive of a spectrum of identity configurations, such as those who hold multiple minority statuses or belong to racialized and historically oppressed groups (e.g., Black-Hispanic, queer, lesbian, disabled, large-bodied). In a qualitative exploration of multiracial students' experiences during their college careers, participants reported being subject to discrimination and prejudice both because they were perceived to be monoracial and because of their multiracial heritage (Museus et al., 2016). Common themes of multiracial discrimination and prejudice included "(a) racial essentialization, (b) invalidation of racial identities, (c) external imposition of racial identities, (d) racial exclusion and marginalization, (e) challenges to racial authenticity, (f) suspicion of chameleons, (g) exoticization, and (h) pathologizing of multi-racial individuals" (Museus et al., 2016, p. 680). This research demonstrates the interdependent experience of inequality that multiracial individuals face and undergirds the necessity of culturally competent counselors being prepared to advocate for the unique career development needs of multiracial communities. The CCMP recognize and encourage mental health clinicians to be knowledgeable about the impact of privilege, power, oppression, and discrimination within the workplace. Career counselors should assess inter- and intrapersonal dynamics, and assist in countering stereotypical and restrictive career development and decision making practices for sexually, ethnically, gender, and physically diverse groups of multiracial populations (Kenney et al., 2015).

Assessment

When it comes to assessment and multiracial communities, several challenges exist that mental health practitioners, researchers, and students must be aware of. One emerging challenge is the self-identification trends of multiracial Americans. According to the U.S. Census Bureau (n.d.), multiracial populations have continued to rise. However, there exist challenges in adequately measuring and identifying multiracial populations, as demographic surveys do not allow for appropriate identification. Additionally, Henriksen and Maxwell (2016) highlight that some individuals with multiple heritages may choose monoracial categories on demographic forms in accordance with their multiracial identity status (Townsend et al., 2012). Assessment tools normed for multiracial communities are few. Additionally, as there does not exist a "coherent, fixed definition of race" (Coates, 2013, para. 5), fundamental difficulties result in inconsistent measurement of demographic factors. Therefore, culturally competent counselors are called to be especially considerate in their use and selection of ethically appropriate and comprehensive assessments. Further, in using assessments, mental health stakeholders must recognize individual differences among multiracial populations and understand and address systemic inequities that might influence the assessment and its interpretation (Kenney et al., 2015). Mental health professionals should work to familiarize themselves with the Association for Assessment and Research in Counseling (AARC) Standards for Multicultural Assessments (O'Hara et al., 2018). Further, standards provided by the Substance Abuse and Mental Health Services Administration (SAMHSA; 2014) provide a greater foundation for culturally responsive assessment.

Research and Program Evaluation

As multiracial populations grow and become more represented, a need for research that can sustain and inform policy, public health, and evidence-based treatment practices has emerged (Museus et al., 2016; Sanchez et al., 2020). Culturally competent counselors facilitate this process by being aware of current multiracial research and literature and its limitations, conducting research, and formulating "questions that include interracial, interethnic, and diverse sexual orientations and gender identity/expression couples and include these couples in research" (Kenney et al., 2015, p. 14). Culturally competent counselors also refrain from comparing monoracial and multiracial communities in reductive language and avoid presenting skewed research (Kenney et al., 2015). The CCMP encourage administrators and counseling clinicians to conduct research, asking questions that allow a thorough exploration of multiracial and intersectional identities and differences in acculturation and cultural identity development status. Administrators and program evaluators should be sure to include careful discussion which prevents generalizations and over-stereotyping of multiracial populations (Kenney et al., 2015).

Professional Orientation and Ethical Practice

Clients from multiracial heritages bring with them a complex array of concerns and histories for culturally competent counselors to consider. Culturally competent counselors must attempt to familiarize themselves with the unique and shared "interracial, interethnic and diverse sexual orientations and gender identity/expression" of individuals, couples, families, and communities from multiheritage communities (Kenney et al., 2015, p. 15). Simultaneously, culturally competent counselors must acknowledge that it may not be possible to have a thorough grasp of all issues facing multiracial populations and must have access to research, supervision, and consultation strategies to address deficits and provide non-stigmatizing and affirming mental health care and advocate across ecological systems (Kenney et al., 2015). These tasks are further fundamental to the professional and ethical guidelines established and supported by principles within the *ACA Code of Ethics* (2014) and related professional training standards (CACREP, 2015). A professional counseling identity demands lifelong learning and commitment to clients. Counseling professionals should seek to develop and maintain cultural competence, avoid maleficence, promote justice, and support client autonomy (ACA, 2014). These professional values are especially important when working with multiracial populations.

MULTIRACIAL IDENTITY DEVELOPMENT MODELS

Multiracial identity development is a complex process affected by internal and external factors (Chao, 2012; Henriksen & Maxwell, 2009; LaBarrie, 2007; Root, 2003). As multiracial children experience a more nuanced and culturally diverse introduction to concepts of ethnic and racial awareness than their monoracial peers, the multiheritage population's identity development must be approached from unique frameworks (Umaña-Taylor et al., 2014). Further, due to the pluralistic nature of multiracial subgroups and the differences in their sociopolitical and cultural experiences, racial identity development often differs between multiple heritage communities (Berry, 2006; Harris & Sim, 2002; Lou et al., 2011; Sue & Sue, 2003). For this reason, in this section, we focus on four multiracial identity development models, which will provide a framework for understanding racial awareness and self-identification of diverse multiracial groups, not limited to Black-White individuals. It is worth mentioning that these models are not exhaustive of the literature and there exist specific ethnic identity models for understanding configurations of multiheritage clients.

Stage Models of Multiracial Identity Development

Recognizing the inability and inefficiency of monoracial racial identity development models to explore and capture the developmental processes for multiracial communities, one of the earliest stage models of biracial identity development was developed by Poston (1990). Poston's five-stage model outlined biracial identity development through the following stages: *Personal Identity*, *Choice of Group Categorization*, *Enmeshment/Denial*, *Appreciation*, and *Integration*. In the *Personal Identity* stage, a biracial individual's sense of self is based on personality constructs identified within the family rather than society at large. At this stage messages about cultural differences and awareness are low, and the individual may not be aware of their multiheritage. During the *Choice of Group Categorization* stage, individuals are pressured by social and situational contexts to identify an ethnic heritage, often monoracial, and based on phenotype. Consequences of this stage are often exhibited in the *Enmeshment/Denial* stage, wherein individuals face negative emotional and psychosocial consequences as a result of choices made in the previous stage. In the *Appreciation* stage, individuals are primed and positioned to explore the historical and cultural meanings of their multiple ethnicities. Finally, in the fifth stage, *Integration*, a sense of wholeness is developed as multiracial individuals integrate the complexities of their identities (Poston, 1990).

Kerwin and Ponterotto (1995) based their model of multiracial identity development on empirical data, creating an age-stage–based model wherein racial awareness and integration are affected by personal, social, and environmental considerations. This model follows the identity development of multiracial individuals across the life span. Multiracial children's burgeoning awareness of differences and similarities between skin color and hair texture characterize the *Preschool* stage. During this stage, multiracial children are not likely to have a strong identification with their multiple heritages. However, in the *Entry to School* stage, multiracial children often face pressure to ascribe to a monoracial ethnicity based on phenotype, in a process similar to Poston's (1990) *Choice of Group* identification. In the *Preadolescence* stage, multiracial youth become more aware of social meanings, prejudices, and biases ascribed to their ethnic identity membership. This awareness, alongside developmental tasks of identity formulation and construction and societal pressures, assists and contributes to the self-selection of a chosen cultural identity in the *Adolescence* stage. Next, in the *College/Young Adulthood* stage, multiracial youths continue to explore and embrace their chosen monoracial identity and gain more capacity for an expanded sense of self, inclusive of their multiracial heritage. It is in the *Adulthood* stage that multiracial individuals have the increased flexibility in the construction of their identities and interpersonal relationships to develop a more complex understanding of self, which incorporates and explores their full culture (Kerwin & Ponterotto, 1995).

Ecological Models of Multiracial Identity Development

Ecological models posit that identity development is a fluid and complex process affected by multiple interacting factors. Root's Multiracial Identity Model (1998) and the Multidimensional Model of Biracial Identity Development (Rockquemore & Brunsma, 2002) are two such ecological models which specifically address the identity development of multiheritage populations. Root's Multiracial Identity Model (MIM; 1998) is one of the earlier ecological models of multiracial development and has been revisited by a number of scholars (Reens, 2008). The MIM recognizes the impact of intersectional, ecological, sociocultural, historical, political, inter/intrapersonal relational exchanges, and racial and ethnic background as contributing to identity development. Root (1998) posits that individuals can resolve marginality inherent in their multiheritage identities in one of four healthy ways. First, *accept the identity assigned by society*; second, *identify with both groups*; third, *choose a single racial identity*; or fourth, *accept a mixed-race heritage identity*. Root's model proposed that a person's racial identity status can be situational, varying in public and private spheres, and flexible to the needs and demands of the individual.

The Rockquemore and Brunsma (2002) Multidimensional Model of Biracial Identity also proposes four options of racial identification for individuals: (a) "Singular Identity," wherein the individual recognizes one race; (b) "Border Identity," wherein an individual acknowledges both racial heritages, perceiving "their position as one of both oppression and advantage" (p. 200); (c) "Protean Identity," wherein an individual recognizes racial identities jointly or separately, creating space for a possible third identity, and shifting "their identity according to the context of any particular interaction" (p. 201); and (d) "Transcendent Identity," wherein individuals choose not to consider racial classifications as a part of their status.

Awareness of multiracial identity development models provides counselors with a framework for appreciating and normalizing the lived experiences and within-group differences of multiracial communities. Counselors need to be prepared to address the unique challenges and experiences of multiracial clients and to integrate affirming interventions that support the developmental tasks of racial identity development. As presented by these models of ethnic identity development, multiracial individuals must contend with critical incidents, people, and periods in their lived experiences that affect the formulation of a positive sense of self (Miville et al., 2005).

STRESSORS AND DISCRIMINATION

Multiracial clients face stressors and discrimination that parallel those of other Black, Indigenous, and People of Color (BIPOC) groups. However, this population faces some unique challenges, a prominent one being that discrimination comes from both White communities and communities of color (Dalmage, 2013). They endure racial microaggressions with questions such as "What are you?" "But where are you *really* from?" "You're not from around here, are you?" and "How did you get your hair like that?" Moreover, discriminatory remarks that sexualize multiracial people are constant reminders that they are not a part of the dominant race or racial norms. They often feel pressure to disclose their racial identity due to the intrusiveness of others.

Many people of multiracial descent ask themselves, "Where do I belong?" First, there is often pressure from monoracial people to choose one race with which to identify. For many multiracial people, society sees them as the identity that they most outwardly resemble (Swanson, 2013). In other words, stereotypes of racial constructs are used to assume one's identity. When the world sees you as one identity and you see yourself as another, an internal conflict can occur. "Do I choose others' assumptions as to my identity?" one might ponder. There is also societal pressure that a person cannot claim more than one racial group to align with. This links back to White supremacist values which demand that a bloodline must be "pure." Multiracial folks who have European lineage are often not accepted into White circles because their multiracial identity demotes them to a lower social classification of the race (Deters, 1997). A sentiment that multiracial people might feel due to societal pressure to fit into one racial "classification" is that "I'm not X enough for X people, and I'm not Y enough for Y people." For example, I'm not Black enough for the Black people, and I'm not White enough for White people. This notion causes negative impacts on one's racial identity development (Root, 1994).

Additionally, those who identify with more than two racial identities may feel that they are not X enough to claim that identity. For example, "My grandmother is Chinese, but I'm only 25% Chinese. Can I even claim that?" Related to questioning one's identity, multiracial families may even ask folks in their family to hide parts of their racial identities because of injected biases that stem from their own internalized acceptance of elevating dominant racial groups. This hiddenness might lead their family members to an "easier" life and the ability to find a partner who might have overlooked them if their true identities were revealed, or other "benefits" from being more closely aligned to dominant racial norms. Multiracial people are subjected to social consequences and mental health challenges when they do not conform to societal norms of understanding racial classifications (Coleman & Carter, 2007; Miville et al., 2005; Sanchez & Bonam, 2009; Townsend et al., 2009).

Second, there are societal reminders related to these values that you are an "other" and belong nowhere. When White is the norm (or there is a dominant race at all) and your multiracial identity puts you outside of that norm, there are constant reminders of it, such as microaggressions, struggling to find products that market to your complete identity, noticing that your racial identities are not considered in decision-making, and so on. Being told repeatedly that you are "other" has consequences, such as internalizing messages from people, groups, systems, and so on that outcast you and seemingly inform you of "what you can and cannot do" (Reicherzer, 2021, p. 8). These survival methods dictate how we live our lives and result in a "heavily edited version of ourselves" (Reicherzer, 2021, p. 9).

Third, you may not know the actual identities of your ancestors. This can be due to family secrets (as mentioned earlier, but another example are secrets that mask the shame of a cut-off or distant relationship), historical events affecting the lives of ancestors (e.g., colonization, wars, enslavement, etc.), or having little information on a parent's or parents' lineage(s). Having little information may occur when a person is adopted into a family with little documentation on their background. Another example is when a person does not know the identity of their biological parent or fore parent. This makes the already painful question of "What are you?" hit in a completely different way.

COUNSELING UTILIZATION AND HELP-SEEKING

As noted earlier, multiracial populations are growing rapidly in the United States (Parker et al., 2015). Advancements for this population within the counseling field are visible with the inclusion of interest groups such as the Multiracial/Ethnic Counseling Concerns Interest Network of the ACA, and the development of the CCMP in 2015 (Kenney et al., 2015). However, even with the rise of discussion within our society and improved efforts in the counseling field, it still exposes the lack of proper training of counselors currently and those who will be working with multiracial clients (Greig, 2015). According to Henriksen and Maxwell (2016), there continues to be a growing need to ensure that counselors are trained on multiracial identity development and understand the importance of multiracial competencies to provide the best care for this population (Bray, 2015). A Pew Research Survey conducted a national survey of 1,555 multiracial adults who identified with two or more races; the results showed that many multiracial adults experienced racial discrimination, racist slurs, and unfair treatment by police (Parker et al., 2015). Additionally, multiracial individuals may experience issues with the social invalidation of identity, lower self-esteem, and depression (Salahuddin & O'Brien, 2011).

As counselors, it is essential that we explore the challenges, issues, and cultural components of multiracial clients and families, and the barriers that affect help-seeking behaviors. In general, there is limited research that focuses explicitly on counseling utilization by multiracial clients. This may be due to limited research that explicitly explores this population's concerns—also, acknowledging that it would depend on these individuals' diverse cultural and racial identities (Greig, 2015).

In 2017, the American Psychiatric Association (APA) reported that 24.9% of individuals who identified with two or more races were most likely to report mental health issues than any other race. Multiracial adults, Whites, and American/Indian/Alaska Natives were also more likely to seek prescription medication and utilize outpatient mental health services (APA, 2017). According to the SAMHSA (2022) National Survey on Drug Use and Health, 43% of multiracial individuals received mental health services in 2019.

However, these same organizations still acknowledge the disproportionate inequality for marginalized groups, including multiracial populations. When multiracial individuals choose not to seek counseling, that choice ultimately may be due to their beliefs, morals, and messages related to mental health they may have received from their cultural group. Racial groups, such as Latinx (a gender-neutral alternative describing people of Latin origin or descent), Hispanic, African American, and Asian Americans, are more likely to avoid mental health services due to being negatively labeled within and outside of their communities (Schatell, 2017). These populations are typically taught that family business and problems must be protected. For Latinx, African American, and Indigenous People, one's spiritual and religious faith may also affect whether one chooses to seek mental health services (Schatell, 2017). If part of one's multiracial identity is within one of these groups, it could contribute to one's negative thoughts about counseling and influence the choice to seek treatment.

As mentioned earlier in the chapter, racial discrimination and prejudice may play a significant role in whether clients choose to participate in any form of mental health treatment. If members from a particular racial group already feel marginalized in society, they may fear that a mental health diagnosis will present even more challenges. A national survey conducted across the United States of 2,137 adults reported that 72% experienced discrimination more than once in the healthcare system (Nong et al., 2020). With a preexisting lack of trust in providers, such experiences could play an active role in a person's lack of desire to pursue treatment (Hardeman et al., 2016).

With the increased attention on multicultural counseling, the counseling field has recognized that there have been, and continue to be, different treatment barriers for multicultural clients. One of the first issues is the lack of counselor cultural self-awareness (Schatell, 2017). As the opening vignette illustrated, counseling programs are required to teach at least one multicultural counseling class in their program. One class is not enough to fully encompass the multifaceted elements of working with multiracial clients (Bray, 2015). Even when students are introduced to cultural humility and awareness, there remains hesitancy to acknowledge that every individual has their own cultural biases. Counselors who can identify and express their implicit biases, prejudices, and assumptions will be able to explore ways to improve (Jones-Smith, 2019). Those who engage in regular self-reflection are more likely to be sensitive to their clients' needs, thus lowering the risk for potential harm or ruptures in the counseling relationship.

Considering that some multiracial clients may struggle with embracing their racial identity, it may be hard for them to locate a counselor who understands and is trained on multicultural and multiracial concerns. Multiracial clients may seek counseling to explore their multiple intersecting identities; however, this may not be the presenting concern for every client. When counselors are not cognizant of their own beliefs and values, they may make assumptions about their clients or inadvertently commit microaggressions while working with them. For example, a counselor from a Westernized culture may create goals for their clients that are more aligned with American culture than with the roles and expectations of clients from other cultures. In some cases, multiracial individuals may even make initial assumptions about multiracial counselors based on their appearance, which could mirror their experience in society (Jones-Smith, 2019).

Nevertheless, counselors may instinctively feel that a client's mixed heritage may be the reason they have come to counseling, potentially ignoring the actual needs of the client (Wilt, 2011). A counselor committed to practicing cultural humility will work closely with the client to learn more about them based on the client's worldview, values, and beliefs rather than assuming that the counselor knows the clients' "real issues." Counselors must recognize that this population's presenting concerns and needs are just as diverse and unique as the clients are.

As the multiracial population continues to rise in the United States, counselors will need to equip themselves with proper training, improve their cultural awareness, and advocate for the needs of this population (Cornish et al., 2010). As counselors, we must continue to advance the profession to identify any additional barriers to help-seeking while finding effective ways to empower multiracial clients and families to seek counseling (Kenney et al., 2015). Our commitment to the profession requires us to advance our support of, and appropriately address, this population's unique needs. Most importantly, counselors need to continue to dispel the myths surrounding multiracial individuals, interracial couples, and multiracial families while advocating for and celebrating the unique identities, resiliency, and strengths of this population.

CULTURALLY RESPONSIVE PRACTICES: DRAWING FROM THE MULTICULTURAL AND SOCIAL JUSTICE COUNSELING COMPETENCIES AND CULTURAL HUMILITY

Counselors have shifted from pursuing cultural competency to incorporating more culturally responsive interventions and practicing cultural humility with clients. This is highly pertinent when working with multiracial individuals, interracial couples, and multiracial families. It would be virtually impossible for anyone to consider themself culturally competent in the various rich multiple heritages of any group. Practicing cultural humility with this population allows counselors the opportunity to explore more about their own existing beliefs concerning multiracial individuals while learning more about the unique values, experiences, and cultural elements of their presenting clients.

Before working with a multiracial client or family, a counselor would want to consider their own beliefs about multiracial individuals and families (Hays & Erford, 2017; Jones-Smith, 2019). Reviewing the Multicultural and Social Justice Counseling Competencies (MSJCC) would be an excellent starting point, mainly focusing on counselor self-awareness and thereby assessing and exploring their attitudes and beliefs about this population. It is common for newer counselors to believe that they already have a nonjudgmental stance and that they will provide unconditional positive regard to anyone they encounter. Acting with cultural humility means one would accept that all individuals have their own assumptions, worldviews, values, beliefs, and biases as members of privileged and marginalized groups (Kenney et al., 2015). It may be beneficial for counselors to consider the following questions before working with multiracial clients:

- How do I feel about multiracial individuals?
- What are my assumptions or beliefs about this population?
- What are my thoughts about interracial couples and interracial marriage?
- What do I think about multiracial children?
- Do I immediately assume that multiracial clients struggle due to their racial identity?
- What are some of the potential barriers that could arise for me when working with multiracial populations?

These are only brief suggestions of self-reflective questions to explore; they do not fully capture all the potential elements that a counselor would want to reflect upon before working with this population. Please take note: To truly practice cultural humility with multiracial populations, one must open oneself up to a lifelong commitment of self-reflection, willingness to honor and respect the value others have in this world, and accept that this journey of growth is ongoing (Jackson, 2020).

Just as one prepares for one's sessions each week, practitioners should make sure to devote the same effort and energy to learning more about culturally responsive practices with multiracial clients. The ongoing process of practicing cultural humility is one of the central elements of utilizing culturally responsive techniques. After participating in preparatory work, it is essential to expand one's awareness around issues concerning discrimination and racism, and how these issues may affect multiracial clients (Sue et al., 2019). When feeling stuck, seek additional training or clinical supervision to broach this topic with multiracial clients.

Another healthy practice of a culturally responsive counselor would be to utilize the multiracial competencies mentioned earlier in this chapter, along with the MSJCC, when working with this population. Referencing both sets of competencies will help counselors evolve as professionals by enhancing their self-awareness as a counselor and deepening their understanding of their client's lived experiences and worldviews (Ratts et al., 2016). Additionally, it will improve the counseling relationship, and help the counselor explore appropriate ways to advocate for multiracial clients (Ratts et al., 2016). One of the best ways to support multiracial clients is by finding ways to empower them to advocate for themselves. Some ways a counselor may do this are by (a) identifying a client's strengths, (b) supporting the client with the creation of a self-advocacy plan, and (c) role-playing scenarios with the client on how to communicate their needs to different individuals (Donald & Moro, 2014). At the same time, counselors must do their part for the community and the profession overall (Hays & Erford, 2017).

CRAFTING AN ADVOCACY AGENDA

The ACA Advocacy Taskforce (2020) defines *professional advocacy*, an essential piece of counselor identity, as "taking action to promote the profession, with an emphasis on removing or minimizing barriers to the counselors' ability to provide services" (para. 3). Counselors must define advocacy for themselves. Take into account your strengths and abilities. Perceived strengths are different from strengths that others have noted and/or strengths that you can provide evidence for. For example, if you have been excellent in a lobbying role for a different cause in the past, maybe lobbying makes sense for you regarding your clients' needs. Some may not even know where to begin in a lobbying role, so a different role makes more sense for them. The idea here is not to recreate the wheel (unless you want to try something different) and tap into areas where you already find meaning, passion, fulfillment, or expertise. It is important to note that ending systemic injustice that affects multiracial clients requires systems-level advocacy to dismantle systems, laws, policies, or procedures at the national, state, community, and organization levels (Ratts & Greenleaf, 2018). Counselors will need to decide what role they will play.

It also makes sense to reflect upon what you are willing to risk as you define an advocacy agenda for your multiracial clients. For some folks, calling out discrepancies, misinformation, or exclusionary practices in their place of employment is acceptable because they are willing to assume the associated risks. For others, this may feel like too big of an ask. When speaking out against societal norms in some way, whether that is writing letters to your representatives or marching in solidarity at protests, the risk is part of the equation. We can rarely challenge the status quo without some pushback. Thus, it is important to consider this upfront and to be mindful of the associated risks as you develop an advocacy plan.

COUNSELING CHILDREN, ADOLESCENTS, AND YOUNG ADULTS

At first glance, children in a multiracial family may have varying physical features and complexions. Consider how this could affect the way a child may see themself and the role it may have in their racial identity development. It may shift how they are treated in school, at home, and by other family members (Cornish et al., 2010). When multiracial children are empowered to embrace their multiracial identity, then they tend to be well-adjusted, high achievers, and have a strong sense of themselves (Shih & Sanchez, 2005). As a counselor, paying attention to these parts of the child's lived experience is vital. Additional considerations for multiracial children are their varying family dynamics, familial relationships, and alternating lived experiences with racial groups if they have siblings. Children at a young age seek a sense of belonging, and it is necessary to consider how these elements may affect their view of themselves (Phillips, 2004).

Multiracial children may feel pressured to identify with one particular racial group among their peers. In some cases, they may identify one way socially, then shift when they are at home or with other family members. According to Johnston and Nadal (2010), the denial of one's multiracial heritage is another microaggression that they face in school and in their community, which can be detrimental to their functioning. Please be mindful not to make assumptions about the child or potentially minimize their experiences based on their appearance. One way of empowering children who have felt dismissed is by validating their experiences and allowing them the space to be heard (Greig, 2015). Focusing on their strengths and assets may also encourage multiracial children to have a greater belief in themselves and their identity (Pedrotti et al., 2008). Multiracial children who learn to embrace and identify with their multiracial heritage have high levels of self-esteem (Lusk et al., 2010). Being open and allowing them a space to express themselves will help multiracial children feel heard and supported.

The period of adolescence is a critical part of development, and multiracial adolescents may have difficulty navigating their dual or multiple heritage because of others' pressure to determine who they are and where they fit (Henriksen & Maxwell, 2016). One of the best practices a counselor can use is to allow the teen to explore who they are from their racial perspective (Henriksen & Maxwell, 2009), keeping in mind not to force them to celebrate, explore, or embrace parts of their culture if they choose not to. This allows the adolescent freedom and control over who they are and how they see themself; in prior interactions, they may have felt robbed of this. Henriksen and Maxwell (2016) also noted that multiracial teens might be asked numerous questions about their cultural background and how they identify, and attention may be drawn to their physical features.

As multiracial individuals age, any lingering identity issues and concerns could become amplified as they navigate early adulthood. When working with this group, consider exploring their self-esteem, cultural background, friendships, relationships, and sense of belonging (Hays & Erford, 2017; Narvaez & Kivlighan III, 2021). Counselors will need to focus on building a strong therapeutic alliance. To do this, consider using creative techniques such as journaling, role-playing, and the use of narrative therapy to explore what may be happening in their life (Pedrotti et al., 2008). Creating a supportive and nonjudgmental therapeutic relationship is vital. However, the key component with these groups is finding ways to help them navigate their multiracial heritage without pressuring them to conform to social norms or expectations, remembering that you can help them safely explore who they are and how they can develop a sense of belonging within their family, school, workplace, and community.

COUNSELING ADULTS, COUPLES, AND FAMILIES

Counseling multiracial adults may draw upon similar elements as work with young multiracial adults. A counselor would want to allow the client to share their presenting issues and implement culturally responsive practices to build rapport. Potential issues that may arise could be related to racial identity development, peer relationships, depression, problem behaviors, and self-esteem (Dixen-Peters, 2010). Counselors may want to start by exploring their ineffective and effective ways of functioning and consider how this may influence their overall functioning, societal interactions, and relationships.

Using a cultural genogram could give the client the freedom to explore more about themselves and family dynamics, and help the counselor understand more about the client's background (Blount & Young, 2015).

Kenney and Kenney (2018) recommend using both ecomaps and cultural continuums when working with multiracial adults. The counselor can use an ecomap to help the client explore and consider their relationships with families and with external networks (Kenney & Kenney, 2018). The counselor can then guide the client through their varying experiences while supporting them on who within their support system they can go to for comfort and support. In addition, the cultural continuum can help a client consider their coping skills and reactions to events in their life that challenged their multiracial background (Kenney & Kenney, 2018).

Blount and Young (2015) indicated that multiracial couples might encounter the following obstacles: lack of support, opposition to their relationship by family and friends, societal pressures, and negative stereotyping of the relationship/marriage. Blount and Young (2015) also noted that multiracial couples tend to bring their diverse backgrounds, cultures, spiritual practices, and lived experiences into the relationship, which assists them in being able to adjust to ambiguous situations. Counselors will need to explore each partner's different cultural worldviews and how those relate to their presenting issues, thereby helping them understand how their lived experiences due to their culture have shaped who they are, how they see the world, and the way they function in the world and with each other (Jones-Smith, 2019). Incorporating narrative therapy elements with couples may empower them to share their story with their partners (Edwards & Pedrotti, 2004). Counselors may even want to consider utilizing the Multiple Heritage Couple Questionnaire (MHCQ), which can help counselors address the varying challenges multiracial couples may face (Henriksen et al., 2007). Cultivating an environment where the multiracial couple can be true to their cultural experience, values, background, and worldview will help them gain better insight into how they each approach different problems. In turn, it helps multiracial couples to respond with empathy, understanding, and compassion.

When working with multiracial families, a counselor will need to explore more about each member's culture and how they identify; this will help build therapeutic trust between the family and the counselor. Next, a counselor would need to know some of the common obstacles that families may face (e.g., multiracial families may experience rejection and discrimination). Some of the common challenges they may face are feeling rejected or excluded within their community and extended family (Nadal et al., 2013). In some cases, family members may feel pressure to deny who they are or only identify with one racial group. Based on these experiences, families may choose to deny their children the opportunity to learn more about their culture. If family members do not embrace their multicultural unit, they may encourage their children to only identify as one race and encourage them to assimilate into mainstream society. If one partner is White, they may not feel confident discussing race with their children (Dixen-Peters,

2010). It will help if the counselor can provide education around the need to discuss these topics while assisting them with resources to do this successfully. In working with monoracial parents of color, counselors may need to empower families to explore racial identity, ethnicity, colorism, racism, and discrimination at a healthy age with their kids. By doing so, the family will learn how to bond together to support one another (Blount & Young, 2015).

IMPLICATIONS FOR CLINICAL PRACTICE

Counselors are conditioned to utilize treatment strategies that teach people to cope within oppressive systems rather than implementing healing methods that acknowledge and attempt to dismantle those systems. Both are needed. Being a professional counselor requires advocacy and concerted efforts to engage in your community to call attention to problematic structures and systems that continue to oppress multiracial clients. Related to this, when race-based trauma happens on the national or community level, counselors must not turn a blind eye. Acknowledge these events, process them with your multiracial clients, and refrain from going on with "business as usual." An example of such an event may include the murder of an unarmed African American person at the hands of police or the discovery of an unmarked mass grave of Native American children. For clients with African American lineage or Native American lineage, it is worth exploring how these events are affecting them rather than checking in on their typical presenting concerns.

It is essential to explore other ways of dealing with your clients. This might be through spiritual practice, rituals, music, dance, vocalization, community or group healing, or other traditional or indigenous ways of knowing and healing from their cultures. Again, this is where openness is critical. French et al. (2019) offer some great insights into helping multiracial clients heal rather than teaching them how to cope. According to the authors, healing for BIPOC individuals happens through gaining "critical consciousness about their oppression" and seeking "to resist the associated racial trauma" (French et al., 2019, p. 19). The authors challenge counselors to focus on healing within the community instead of focusing on individualistic healing. French et al. assert that effective counseling with clients of color and indigenous clients should also focus on radical hope, strength, cultural authenticity, and self-knowledge (French et al., 2019). These ideas should be considered by those working with multiracial clients as a means to move away from traditional coping skills that pacify rather than bring about true healing.

Microaggressions are very real, and counselors are not immune to them. Counselors have to do some deep self-reflection to serve multicultural clients, but it does not stop there. Consider how one might work to become a racial ally, "an individual who works as an advocate for all people of color facing racism" (Singh, 2019, p. 170). Singh (2019) suggests that characteristics of racial allies include staying humble, apologizing when one is wrong, being a good listener, believing the experiences of people of color, continuously educating oneself about racism, and connecting with other racial allies. Allies should avoid appointing themselves as a racial ally, pausing racial allyship, participating in "call-out" culture, talking about being a racial ally too frequently, thinking one has all the answers or that one's answers are best, and avoiding the feeling of grief and loss (Singh, 2019). Additionally, avoid making assumptions: be honest about when you are not knowledgeable. With a foundational knowledge of the world that multiracial clients navigate, explore the world through your clients' perspectives adding their individual nuances, understanding, values, and so on.

CLINICAL CASE SCENARIO 10.1: AN ADULT MULTIRACIAL FEMALE WITH RACIAL IDENTITY ISSUES

Daniel is an Asian male counselor-in-training who is starting his first day at his practicum site. Jackie, his first client, is a 20-year-old multiracial female seeking counseling because of a recent breakup and challenges at work. She does not feel like she will ever find a partner who will understand her. She reports she is of African, Indian, and Italian descent, and was born in the United States. She reported that her ex-partner, who is a White American male, and previous partners of varying ethnicities had pursued her based on her "exotic looks," and she feels like she has been fetishized rather than treated as a true partner in relationships. She indicated that her partner lashed out at her before the breakup and called her a "mutt." Her ex-partner had complained that she did not stand up enough for the rights of people of color. Jackie reported that this reminded her of her childhood struggles with her own identity. She expressed feeling hurt by his comments but also conflicted about how she should see herself. Jackie indicated that although she knows all parts of her racial background, she grew up primarily with her Italian mother, and she was raised heavily in her mother's culture. Her mother's family disowned Jackie's mother because she was in an interracial relationship. Jackie has a limited relationship with her father's family for similar reasons. Her father was inconsistently in her life, so she does not feel as connected to his culture. She expressed being bullied throughout her childhood and never feeling like she belonged anywhere. Jackie initiated counseling because she wants to learn how to be more confident in herself and her identity. Daniel feels nervous because, although he took a multicultural counseling course in his graduate program, he still feels uncomfortable talking about race with clients.

CLINICAL CASE SCENARIO DISCUSSION QUESTIONS

1. Identify Jackie's many complex multiracial issues.
2. Where would you start in exploring Jackie's multiracial background?
3. What would your therapeutic intervention look like?

END-OF-CHAPTER RESOURCES

A robust set of instructor resources designed to supplement this text is located at http://connect.springerpub.com/content/book/978-0-8261-3953-5. Qualifying instructors may request access by emailing **textbook@springerpub.com**.

SUMMARY

The number of multiracial people in the United States continues to rise and is projected to increase after the 2020 U.S. Census results are reported (Crane, 2020). Counselors must become informed of how to meet the needs of this unique population that is made up of different heritages. This chapter aims to provide counselors and others in the helping professions with historical background information that is pertinent to working with multiracial groups. The readers will become more knowledgeable about the CCMP (Kenney et al., 2015), how culturally appropriate assessment tools can be utilized with this population, and get introduced to multiracial identity development models to consider when trying to understand racial identity development among multiracial communities. Additionally, those in the helping profession will become familiar with barriers to treatment, ways to advocate successfully for multiracial clients, and therapeutic interventions/approaches to consider when counseling multiracial individuals, children, couples, and families.

DISCUSSION QUESTIONS

1. How are you normalizing oppression in your interactions with clients? (In your diagnostic process, in your treatment planning, in the theoretical orientation you prioritize, etc.)
2. What harm might you have caused to past clients? What can you do about it now?
3. How are you adequately prepared to provide space for clients who hold the dominant culture's identities and a historically marginalized racial group?
4. How can you continue to honor and hold space for multiracial clients without bias?
5. How will you explore and incorporate healing methods (not coping) congruent with your clients' identities?
6. What are you willing/able to risk to be a racial ally for all people of color?

KEY REFERENCES

Only key references appear in the print edition. The full reference list appears in the digital product on Springer Publishing Connect: https://connect.springerpub.com/content/book/978-0-8261-3953-5/part/part02/chapter/ch10

American Counseling Association Advocacy Task Force. (2020, June 3). Professional advocacy: A call to the profession. *Counseling Today*. https://ct.counseling.org/2020/06/professional-advocacy-a-call-to-the-profession/

Hays, D. G., & Erford, B. T. (2017). *Developing multicultural counseling competence* (3rd ed.). Pearson.

Henriksen, R. C., & Maxwell, M. J. (2009). Multiple heritage students and social justice in schools. *Counseling Interviewer, 41*, 1–8.

Henriksen, R. C. Jr., & Maxwell, M. J. (2016). Counseling the fastest growing population in America: Those with multiple heritage backgrounds. *Journal of Mental Health Counseling, 38*(1), 1–11.

Henriksen, R. C. Jr., Watts, R. E., & Bustamante, R. (2007). *The multiple heritage couple questionnaire*. PsycTESTS. https://doi.org/https://doi-org.ezproxy.snhu.edu/10.1037/t03080-000

Kenney, K. R., & Kenney, M. E. (2018). Individuals and families of multiracial descent. In D. G. Hays & B. T. Erford (Eds.), *Developing multicultural counseling competence* (3rd ed., pp. 471–502). Pearson.

Kenney, K. R., Kenney, M. E., Alvarado, S. B., Baden, A. L., Brew, L., Chen-Hayes, S., Crippen, C. L., Harris, H. L., Henriksen, R. C., Jr., Malott, K. M., Paladino, D. A., Pope, M. L., Salazar, C. F., & Singh, A. A. (2015). *Competencies for counseling the multiracial population*. American Counseling Association. https://www.counseling.org/docs/default-source/competencies/competencies-for-counseling-the-multiracial-population-2-2-15-final.pdf?sfvrsn=c7ba412c_16

Nadal, K. L., Sriken, J., Davidoff, K. C., Wong, Y., & McLean, K. (2013). Microaggressions within families: Experiences of multiracial people. *Family Relations, 62*(1), 190–201. https://doi.org/10.1111/j.1741-3729.2012.00752.x

Ratts, M. J., & Greenleaf, A. T. (2018). Counselor-Advocate-Scholar model: Changing the dominant discourse in counseling. *Journal of Multicultural Counseling and Development, 46*(2), 78–96. https://doi.org/10.1002/jmcd.12094

U.S. Census Bureau. (n.d.). *ACS demographic and housing estimates: 2020: ACS 5-Year estimates data profiles.* Retrieved March 20, 2020, from https://data.census.gov/cedsci/table?q=DP05&tid=ACSDP1Y2019.DP05

CHAPTER 11

Culturally Responsive Counseling for Lesbian, Gay, Bisexual, Queer++ Clients

EDWARD F. HUDSPETH

LEARNING OBJECTIVES

After reading this chapter, students will be able to:

- Explore their readiness for work with lesbian, gay, bisexual, queer++ (LGBQ++) clients.
- Recognize the impact of discrimination, oppression, and stressors on the lives of LGBQ++ clients.
- Analyze ethical codes as to how they apply to work with LGBQ++ clients.
- Select evidence-based, affirmative practices for work with LGBQ++ clients.
- Formulate and advocacy plan for work with LGBQ++ clients.

SELF-REFLECTION QUESTIONS

1. Think about biases, prejudices, and assumptions you might have about LGBQ++ clients. How do these help and hinder your ability to provide culturally sensitive counseling?
2. What hesitancies, if any, do you have about working with clients who are LGBQ++?
3. What attributes do you have that will enable you to work with LGBQ++ clients?

The counseling profession has made great strides over the past few decades. We came from a place of needing to demonstrate our worth, to the mental health community as well as society, to being a leader within mental health fields. Our associations and their codes of ethics and practice guidelines have guided us in becoming well-trained, ethical, and accountable. The American Counseling Association (ACA) and its divisions along with the National Board for Certified Counselors (NBCC) and the Council for the Accreditation of Counseling and Related Education Programs (CACREP) have made licensure possible in all states and the District of Columbia as well as recognition by entities such as the federal Department of Veterans Affairs. Our associations and educational standards act as a foundation when teaching and practicing. The resulting framework supports the development of culturally responsive counseling for lesbian, gay, bisexual, queer++ (LGBQ++) clients.

This chapter highlights some of the necessary components of culturally responsive counselor training recommended for those who work with LGBQ++ clients. Combining a philosophy of liberation counseling (Fanon, 1961/1963; Freire, 1968/2000; Martín-Baró, 1994); a beneficial developmental framework (RESPECTFUL; D'Andrea & Daniels, 2001), codes of ethics (ACA, 2014; American Mental Health Counselors Association [AMHCA], 2020; National Board for Certified Counselors [NBCC], 2016), practice competencies (Association for Lesbian, Gay, Bisexual, and Transgender Issues in Counseling [ALGBTIC; Harper et al., 2013]; Association of Multicultural and Counseling Development [AMCD; Arredondo et al., 1996; Ratts et al., 2016]), and educational standards (CACREP, 2015), a solid pathway to teaching, competency, and advocacy emerges.

In an article about liberation psychology's application to LGBT clients, Russell and Bohan (2007) make the statement, "In dealing with LGBT clients, we are charged to address not only questions of individual identity and psychological functioning but also matters of political power and social oppression" (pp. 64–65). Liberation psychology, and thus liberation counseling, developed from the philosophy and work of Fanon (1963), Freire (2000), and Martín-Baró (1994). The primary tenets of liberation psychology include (a) the importance of helping oppressed people develop a critical awareness of oppression and (b) recognizing the connection between individual and sociopolitical factors as they contribute to oppression. A central philosophy of liberation work is to prevent the problem from being conceptualized as the individuals and instead seeing the problem as one of the collective. Counseling focused on liberation conceptualizes that the problems of individuals cannot be understood in isolation from all the economic, political, cultural, and historical conditions which gave rise to them.

Therapeutically, goals of liberation counseling are (a) to help individuals, groups, and communities understand the personal, cultural, and institutional factors that contribute to their problem(s), (b) act to change these conditions, and (c) to liberate themselves from both internal and external oppressions. To read more about liberation psychology and counseling, see G. Adams et al. (2015), French et al. (2020), Hanna et al. (2000), and Tate et al. (2013).

THE COUNSELOR: EXPLORATION, INTROSPECTION, AND REFLECTION

As counselors are trained, they are exposed to significant amounts of information, guided in their application of this information, and asked to self-evaluate and reflect. Exploration, or learning, begins the process, but the process and its outcome are not fully realized without introspection and reflection. In the end, one of the goals of counselor training is the realization that exploration-introspection-reflection is a cycle that should be repeated throughout one's training and career.

Exploration

Though there are many topics to consider when a counselor-in-training (CIT) begins their personal journey of exploration, one of the first should always be reviewing the ethical codes related to one's practice. Counselors are guided by multiple organizations through ethical codes, competencies, and educational standards, which include (a) the *2014 ACA Code of Ethics* (ACA, 2014), (b) the *AMHCA Code of Ethics* (AMHCA, 2020), and (c) the *NBCC Code of Ethics* (NBCC, 2016). Ethical codes offer significant guidance;

yet, at times, as counselors, one falls short in acting on this guidance. For many, codes of ethics are adhered to (a passive action) rather than used as guidelines that can be actively applied.

Ethical Codes Connected to Culture, Competency, and Advocacy

CITs, like all members of the counseling profession, are guided by codes of ethics from multiple professional associations (ACA, 2014; AMHCA, 2020; NBCC, 2016). As part of their training, they should learn about and engage in a dialogue about the purpose of ethical codes. Throughout counselor training, multiple courses, if not all, include and demonstrate how ethical codes are applied within specific topics and with specific populations. As CITs become familiar with ethical codes, they should come to realize that ethical codes add practice parameters to aspects from counseling relationships to assessment and research to professional responsibilities. As CITs are developing the knowledge, skills, and dispositions necessary to become effective counselors, they should also be developing awareness and insight into the importance of ethical codes. As CITs are trained and supervised to become culturally responsive counselors for LGBQ++ clients, they should be diligent and look for ways to practically apply ethical codes related to culture, competency, and advocacy (see Table 11.1). Above all other codes, these ethical codes form the foundation for ethical practice with LGBQ++ clients.

Use of clinical case scenarios provides an opportunity for CITs to use ethical decision-making and explore how ethical codes can be applied across diverse situations. Stay clear of clinical case scenarios that lack reality and are monotonous and unidimensional.

TABLE 11.1 ETHICAL CODE LOCATION

	ACA CODE OF ETHICS	AMHCA CODE OF ETHICS	NBCC CODE OF ETHICS
Culture	**Section A:** The Counseling Relationship **Section C:** Professional Responsibilities **Section E:** Evaluation, Assessment, and Interpretation **Section F:** Supervision, Training, and Teaching	**Section C:** Counselor Responsibility and Integrity	**Directives** 4, 26, and 48
Competency	**Section C:** Professional Responsibilities **Section F:** Supervision, Training, and Teaching	**Section B:** Counseling Process **Section C:** Counselor Responsibility	**Directives** 13, 26, and 63
Advocacy	**Section A:** The Counseling Relationship	**Section F:** Other Roles	None

ACA, American Counseling Association; AMHCA, American Mental Health Counselors Association; NBCC, National Board for Certified Counselors.
Source: American Counseling Association. (2014). *2014 ACA Code of Ethics*. Author. https://www.counseling.org/Resources/aca-code-of-ethics.pdf; American Mental Health Counselors Association. (2020). *Code of Ethics*. Author. https://www.amhca.org/HigherLogic/System/DownloadDocumentFile.ashx?DocumentFile Key=24a27502-196e-b763-ff57-490a12f7edb1&forceDialog=0; National Board for Certified Counselors. (2016). *Code of Ethics*. Author. https://www.nbcc.org/Assets/Ethics/NBCCCodeofEthics.pdf.

When clinical case scenarios are used to developed scripts that can be role-played, then the clinical case scenarios come alive and are more engaging. Also, news reports and media can be used to explore real situations and the individuals involved.

Previously mentioned was the passive action of adhering to ethical codes versus actively applying them. To conceptualize ways to actively apply ethical codes, consider the following example. Within the *ACA 2014 Code of Ethics*, Section C: Professional Responsibility: C.5. Nondiscrimination, is the following code:

> Counselors do not condone or engage in discrimination against prospective or current clients, students, employees, supervisees, or research participants based on age, culture, disability, ethnicity, race, religion/spirituality, gender, gender identity, sexual orientation, marital/partnership status, language preference, socioeconomic status, immigration status, or any basis proscribed by law. (ACA, 2014, p. 9)

If one were to personalize this code and actively apply the code, it might look like the following:

> *I will explore ways in which I may unintentionally discriminate* against prospective or current clients, students, employees, supervisees, or research participants based on age, culture, disability, ethnicity, race, religion/spirituality, gender, gender identity, sexual orientation, marital/partnership status, language preference, socioeconomic status, immigration status, or any basis proscribed by law.

This active application personalizes the essence of the ethical code and challenges CITs to take responsibility, be accountable, and become aware of and explore their implicit biases. During exploration, a next step might be to encourage CITs to self-assess for implicit bias (see the Implicit Association Test [IAT]; Greenwald et al., 1998).

Introspection and Reflection

As a result of exploration and finding ways to practically apply what has been learned, CITs are trained to evaluate what they (personally) bring to counseling relationships. Application of knowledge is affected by one's history, values, biases, and worldview. One's utilization of counseling skills and application of counseling theories are channeled through one's personal lens. Nothing can be free of what one consciously or unconsciously brings to a therapeutic relationship without introspection and reflection. The processes of introspection and reflection should bring about self-awareness and insight.

From an organizational (viz., the university and counseling program) as well as individual perspective, CITs can be encouraged to view and discuss the Multidimensional Model for Developing Cultural Competence (Sue, 2001), the Multicultural and Social Justice Counseling Competencies Figure (Ratts et al., 2016, p. 4), and The Continuum of Cultural Competence (Center for Substance Abuse Treatment, 2014). CITs can also be encouraged to complete self-assessments of cultural competency (see the Multicultural Awareness/Knowledge/Skills Survey [MAKSS], D'Andrea et al., 1991; the Cross-Cultural Counseling Inventory-Revised [CCCI-R], LaFromboise et al., 1991; the Cultural Competency Self-Assessment Questionnaire [CCSAQ], Mason, 1995; the Multicultural Competency Assessment [MCA], Mitchell, 2018; the Multicultural Counseling Knowledge and Awareness Scale [MCKAS], Ponterotto & Potere, 2003; the Multicultural Counseling Awareness Scale [MCAS], Ponterotto et al., 1996; and the Multicultural Counseling Inventory [MCI], Sodowsky et al., 1994).

Many classroom discussions, activities, and assignments offer CITs an opportunity to practice, in controlled environments, components of culturally responsive counseling for LGBQ++ clients. As a means of understanding a client's worldview, a CIT can explore clinical case scenarios and film characters, and conduct practice sessions with classmates (see Conner & Walker, 2017). CITs can read about and practice using the RESPECTFUL framework (see D'Andrea & Daniels, 2001), as well read about and incorporate tenets of liberation counseling (Hanna et al., 2000). By practicing specific interventions and review codes of ethics, CITs can become familiar with counseling and advocacy interventions.

IDENTITY, INDIVIDUALITY, AND CULTURE: INTERSECTIONALITY

How many *nondiscrimination statements/policies* have you read this year? Based on the entity making the statement and location of that entity, the routine public disclosure includes: [*Name of Organization, Business, Educational Institution, etc.*] does not and shall not discriminate based on race, color, religion (creed), gender, gender expression, age, national origin (ancestry), disability, marital status, sexual orientation, or military status (Age Discrimination Act of 1975; Age Discrimination in Employment Act of 1967; Americans With Disabilities Act of 1990; Civil Rights Act of 1964; Rehabilitation Act of 1973).

As is, the statement/policy contains multiple categories and demographics that relate to various facets of groups. However, these facets barely scratch the surface of all that makes up one's identity, individuality, and culture. Identity, individuality, and culture are more than a collection of characteristics. Identity, individuality, and culture are an intricate interweaving of characteristics that require significant research and practice to capture, understand, and competently address. There are many definitions of identity, individuality, and culture. As counselors, we have seen these definitions and (it is hoped) could, if asked, define them. Thus, there is no need to define them here; rather, here we consider how the three terms come together in the sense of intersectionality. In 2017, Columbia Law School published an interview with Kimberlé Crenshaw, who coined the term *intersectionality*. In the interview, Crenshaw offers a description of intersectionality that is practical, making it useful for practitioners and their education of clients and/or supporters of clients: "Intersectionality is a lens through which you can see where power comes and collides … . It's not simply that there's a race problem here …, or an LBGTQ problem there" (Columbia Law School, 2017, para. 4).

It is an individual's multiple layers of identity, intersecting through a cultural context, that define the individual's experience of intersectionality. When training counselors, it is important to understand intersectionality without failing to acknowledge everyone's experience. Recognition of group and individual intersectionality, when working with LGBQ++ clients, is paramount to competent training.

GENDER IDENTITIES AND EXPRESSION AND SEXUAL ORIENTATION

Over time, the concepts and terminology associated with gender identity, gender expression, and sexual orientation have changed. However, like other aspects of identity and culture, not all terminology is accepted or used by each subgroup within the LGBQ++ community. Older members may accept and use terminology that younger generations would not use. Likewise, the range of terms used by some generations may be more restrictive, while others have a more expansive range. Regardless, there are terms that all counselors should know. Therefore, understanding the terminology related to gender identity and expression and sexual orientation begins with reviewing the terms used to describe each. Numerous organizations (e.g., HRC, n.d.) provide lists of terms and definitions related to gender identity and expression and sexual orientation. One will also find useful lists of terms and definitions on news websites (e.g., C. Adams, 2017; Wamsley & Nett, 2021).

Gender Identity

Gender identity, as defined by the HRC (n.d.), is an individual's personal concept and perception, and the terminology they use to define themself as male, female, a blend, or neither. According to the HRC (n.d.), specific terms and definitions related to gender identity include:

- **Agender:** A term that represents a neutral gender identity and expression.
- **Androgynous:** Appearance that is indeterminately male or female.
- **Bigender:** Term used to describe someone who identifies as both man and woman.
- **Cisgender:** Describes people whose gender and identity are congruent with the sex they were born with.
- **Gender Binary:** A system in which gender is constructed into two strict categories of male or female. Gender identity is expected to align with the sex assigned at birth and gender expressions and roles fit traditional expectations (HRC, n.d.).
- **Gender-Expansive:** A person with a wider, more flexible range of gender identity and/or expression than typically associated with the binary gender system. Often used as an umbrella term when referring to young people still exploring the possibilities of their gender expression and/or gender identity (HRC, n.d.).
- **Gender Fluid:** Describes a person whose gender identity and/or expression is not static and may change based on context.
- **Gender Nonconforming:** A broad term referring to people who do not behave in a way that conforms to the traditional expectations of their gender, or whose gender expression does not fit neatly into a category. While many also identify as transgender, not all gender nonconforming people do (HRC, n.d.).
- **Genderqueer:** Genderqueer people typically reject notions of static categories of gender and embrace a fluidity of gender identity and often, though not always, sexual orientation. People who identify as "genderqueer" may see themselves as being both male and female, neither male nor female, or as falling completely outside these categories (HRC, n.d.).
- **Gender Questioning:** A term used to describe a person who is not sure about their sexual orientation, gender, and/or expression and are exploring.
- **Nonbinary:** An adjective describing a person who does not identify exclusively as a man or a woman. Nonbinary people may identify as being both a man and a woman, somewhere in between, or as falling completely outside these categories. While many also identify as transgender, not all nonbinary people do. "Nonbinary" can also be used as an umbrella term encompassing identities such as agender, bigender, genderqueer, or gender-fluid (HRC, n.d.).
- **Queer:** A term people often use to express a spectrum of identities and orientations that are counter to the mainstream. Queer is often used as a catch-all to include many people, including those who do not identify as exclusively straight and/or folks who have nonbinary or gender-expansive identities. This term was previously used as a slur but has been reclaimed by many parts of the LGBTQ movement (HRC, n.d.).

- **Transgender:** An umbrella term for people whose gender identity and/or expression is different from cultural expectations based on the sex they were assigned at birth. Being transgender does not imply any specific sexual orientation. Therefore, transgender people may identify as straight, gay, lesbian, bisexual, and so on (HRC, n.d.).
- **Transsexual Person:** A term used to describe a person who has physically changed the sex they were assigned to at birth (i.e., from male to female, or female to male).
- **Two-Spirit:** A cultural term used by First Nations people to describe a person who identifies as having both a male and female spirit.

Gender Expression

Gender expression, as defined by the HRC (n.d.), refers to an individual's external appearance of one's gender identity that is expressed through their behavior, the way they dress, and their mannerisms and/or voice. WHO defines gender expression as "the way in which an individual outwardly presents their gender. These expressions of gender are typically through the way one chooses to dress, speak, or generally conduct themselves socially" (WHO, 2016, p. 1).

Sexual Orientation

Sexual orientation, as defined by the HRC (n.d.), is "an inherent or immutable enduring emotional, romantic or sexual attraction to other people." WHO (2016) describes sexual orientation as "a person's physical, romantic, and/or emotional attraction towards other people. Sexual orientation is comprised of three elements: 'sexual attraction, sexual behaviour, and sexual identity'" (WHO, 2016, p. 1).

According to the HRC (n.d.), specific terms and definitions related to sexual orientation include:

- **Asexual:** Often called "ace" for short, *asexual* refers to a complete or partial lack of sexual attraction or lack of interest in sexual activity with others. Asexuality exists on a spectrum, and asexual people may experience no, little or conditional sexual attraction (HRC, n.d.).
- **Bisexual:** A person emotionally, romantically or sexually attracted to more than one sex, gender, or gender identity though not necessarily simultaneously, in the same way or to the same degree. Sometimes used interchangeably with *pansexual* (HRC, n.d.).
- **Gay:** A person who is emotionally, romantically or sexually attracted to members of the same gender. Men, women and nonbinary people may use this term to describe themselves (HRC, n.d.).
- **Intersex:** Intersex people are born with a variety of differences in their sex traits and reproductive anatomy. There is a wide variety of difference among intersex variations, including differences in genitalia, chromosomes, gonads, internal sex organs, hormone production, hormone response, and/or secondary sex traits (HRC, n.d.).
- **Lesbian:** A woman who is emotionally, romantically or sexually attracted to other women. Women and nonbinary people may use this term to describe themselves (HRC, n.d.).
- **Pansexual:** Describes someone who has the potential for emotional, romantic, or sexual attraction to people of any gender, though not necessarily simultaneously, in the same way, or to the same degree. Sometimes used interchangeably with *bisexual* (HRC, n.d.).

- **Questioning:** A term used to describe people who are in the process of exploring their sexual orientation or gender identity (HRC, n.d.).
- **Same-Gender Loving:** A term some prefer to use instead of lesbian, gay or bisexual to express attraction to and love of people of the same gender (HRC, n.d.).

Terminology is just a part of the beginning as one tries to understand how each LGBQ++ client describes and conceptualizes themself. Though individuals may have similarities, one cannot generalize. As part of building the therapeutic relationship, it is the counselor's responsibility to explore each client and their story. Textbooks, research, and training are helpful when establishing one's foundation of knowledge. However, as a CIT, one must be willing let clients teach about themselves, because a client will always be the best source of information regarding themself.

INTERSECTIONALITY OF RELIGION AND SEXUAL/GENDER IDENTITIES

Over the past decade, there have been several survey reports about religion and LGBQ++ individuals (see Conron et al., 2020; Newport, 2014; Schwadel & Sandstrom, 2019). Each report indicates that LGBT individuals are significantly less religious than non-LGBT individuals. In essence, about half of LGBT adults indicate that they are religious or indicate that religion is an important aspect in their life (Conron et al., 2020; Newport, 2014; Schwadel & Sandstrom, 2019). Schwadel and Sandstrom (2019) report that LGB Americans are less likely to see the Bible as the Word of God, but nearly 77% believe in God. These authors note that LGB individuals are "less likely than straight adults to say they feel a deep sense of spiritual peace and well-being at least once a week, and are somewhat less likely to say they regularly feel a strong sense of gratitude or thankfulness" (Schwadel & Sandstrom, 2019, para. 9). Schwadel and Sandstrom (2019) also state that "LGB adults are as likely as straight adults to say they think about the meaning and purpose of life at least weekly, and meditate at least once a week" (para. 7). Newport (2014) hypothesizes that there are multiple reasons why LGBT individuals are less religious. Among these, he asserts that they may not feel welcomed in services where same-sex relationships are condemned, or they may not live in geographical areas (i.e., Bible Belt) where church-going is common, and may not be as old as the religious community (research shows that younger people are less religious).

Over the past two decades, there have also been a number of studies about religion and LGBQ++ individuals (Paul, 2019; Rodriguez et al., 2013). One of the first counseling studies, by Schuck and Liddle (2001), served as a foundation for later studies. These authors found that nearly two-thirds of participants had experienced conflict between religion and their sexual orientation. They identified the sources of conflict as "denominational teachings, scriptural passages, and congregational prejudice" (Schuck & Liddle, 2001, p. 63).

Paul (2019) identified higher levels of sexual identity exploration and higher levels of fundamentalism as connected to higher levels of religious and spiritual struggles. Rodriguez et al. (2013) indicated "that higher lesbian, gay, and bisexual self-esteem scores and openness about sexual orientation correlate with higher levels of spirituality" (p. 1).

Schuck and Liddle (2001) stated that resolution of the conflict between religion and sexual includes "identifying as spiritual rather than religious, reinterpreting religious teachings, changing affiliations, remaining religious but not attending, and abandoning religion altogether" (p. 63). Though none of these are suggestions for, nor should they be specific goals of, therapy, as part of processing their experiences, LGBQ++ individuals may arrive at these resolutions.

LGBQ++ PREJUDICE, DISCRIMINATION, OPPRESSION, AND STRESSORS

To conceptualize the impact of prejudice, discrimination, and oppression on LGBQ++ individuals, it is helpful to define each. Definitions appear in the following individual sections. Understanding these factors is key to conceptualizing their impact on LGBQ++ individuals, because the three are connected. Discrimination is an externalization of a prejudice, and oppression is the impact of prejudice and discrimination on the people who experience it (Everyday Feminism, 2017).

Prejudice

The NCCJ (n.d.) defines *prejudice* as a "judgment or belief that is formed on insufficient grounds before facts are known or in disregard of facts that contradict it. Prejudices are learned and can be unlearned" (para. 3). Prejudice has been studied in many projects. If considering prejudice and LGBQ++ individuals, Meyer (2003) is worth reviewing. Though this article is nearly two decades old, it provides a foundation for understanding the impact of prejudice on the lives of LGBQ++ clients.

Discrimination

Discrimination is experienced by many, and with every layer of one's individuality comes the potential for discrimination. Discrimination is a fact, across the world, for LGBQ++ individuals. A recent article, "Discrimination in the United States: Experiences of Lesbian, Gay, Bisexual, Transgender, and Queer Americans" (Casey et al., 2019), provides evidence of how common discrimination is against LGBTQ Americans. Numerous reports describe the discrimination faced. Discrimination and inequalities are experienced in education, healthcare, access to services, employment, families, and society in general. In the report, "Discrimination in America: Experiences and Views of LGBTQ Americans," National Public Radio et al. (2017) describe the personal experiences of LGBTQ Americans, perceptions in communities, and national beliefs and politics. The report summary indicates that LGBTQ Americans experience significant personal, institutional, and local community discrimination.

Hudson-Sharp and Metcalf (2016), in their report, "Inequality Among Lesbian, Gay, Bisexual and Transgender Groups in the UK: A Review of Evidence," note that nine areas were identified regarding differences seen in LGBT groups compared to non-LGBT groups. These *differences* were areas of discrimination and included:

> education; safety; health and access to healthcare; access to services; employment; adoption and fostering; homelessness and access to housing provision; participation in civic society; and 16–19 year olds' education, employment or training (NEETs). (Hudson-Sharp & Metcalf, 2016, p. i)

The authors also noted that the "evidence base for an effective assessment of inequality and relative disadvantage by sexual orientation and gender identity is deficient and has major gaps" (Hudson-Sharp & Metcalf, 2016, p. i).

In a summary of mental health disparities for LGBTQ Americans, the Division of Diversity and Equity Health (2017) described the increased prevalence of depression, anxiety, substance abuse, and suicide attempts in the LGBTQ population.

Oppression

The NCCJ (n.d.) conceptualizes oppression as:

> When an agent group, whether knowingly or unknowingly, abuses a target group by institutional/systematic discrimination, personal bias, bigotry, and social prejudice. (para. 6)

Some federal and state laws provide protection against LGBQ++ discrimination (hence limiting systematic oppression). However, upon review of prominent federal antidiscrimination laws (e.g., Civil Rights Act of 1964, etc.), only *sex discrimination* is mentioned.

Review of state laws demonstrates that only 22 states have laws that prohibit discrimination based on sexual orientation and gender identity (see HRC, 2021; Movement Advancement Project, 2021).

Considering the facts presented here, oppression is evident in the lack of a universal law that protects against LGBQ++ discrimination.

Stressors

The prejudices, discriminations, and oppressions experienced by LGBQ++ individuals produce stress. Therefore, one can define them as stressors. Friedman (1999) describes stigma, prejudice, and discrimination as the initiating events that lead to a stressful social environment, which could lead to mental health issues.

It is powerful for CITs to hear about these stressors in the lives of their clients. Clients' willingness to identify the prejudices, discriminations, and oppressions that affect them requires courage and trust. It is not likely that a client will automatically disclose what has affected them. For this reason, CITs must take the necessary time to develop a trusting therapeutic relationship and create a safe space for their client to take the risk of disclosure.

COUNSELING UTILIZATION AND HELP-SEEKING

The help-seeking behaviors of individuals has been a routine topic of research for decades. A search of the internet will yield many articles related to the help-seeking behaviors of many populations and age groups. As for LGBQ++ individuals, several studies have been published over the last few years (see Alberts & Rohrsetzer, 2020; Hta et al., 2021; McNair & Bush, 2016; Spengler & Ægisdóttir, 2015). Though each of these studies considered different aspects of LGBQ++ help-seeking and in different settings and locations, each yielded beneficial information. Quantitative and qualitative studies are represented. Findings suggest that the more open and "out" one is with their sexuality and gender, the more likely one is to be affected by societal stigma, as well as to seek help from various resources (Alberts & Rohrsetzer, 2020, p. 47). Hta et al. (2021) found that barriers to seeking help included internal resistance, lack of resources and information about mental health, limited availability of and accessibility to services, negative perception of mental health services, and stigma against LGBT communities. In a McNair and Bush (2016) study, the most common barriers to help-seeking were found to be discrimination and lack of LGBTI sensitivity of services, particularly for gender-diverse, queer, and pansexual participants. Help-seeking increased when there was mainstream community connectedness, a trustworthy primary care physician, and encouragement by friends. Moreover, Spengler and Ægisdóttir (2015) found that the more negatively an individual views their LGB identity, the higher their intentions to seek psychological services.

From these studies, CITs can list the factors that lead to LGBQ++ individuals seeking help. Also, and from an advocacy perspective, CITs can identify potential barriers to help-seeking. As advocates, CITs can help reduce the barriers to help-seeking by (a) engaging in personal exploration, introspection, and reflection (see the "Counselor: Exploration, Introspection, and Reflection" and "Cultural Humility" sections in this chapter); (b) empowering clients through their therapeutic work; and (c) creating an advocacy plan.

Competencies, Educational Standards, and Cultural Humility

In conjunction with the multiple ethical codes that guide counselor training and practice, there are also competencies and educational standards. These include (a) competencies developed by ALGBTIC (now named the Society for Sexual, Affectional, Intersex, and Gender Expansive Identities [SAIGE]), and AMCD; (b) educational standards set forth in the 2016 CACREP Standards (CACREP, 2015); and (c) affirmative practices (Ginicola et al., 2017).

Similarly, practice competencies are often used as benchmarks rather than guidelines for action. These statements are made to parallel the multitude of things that have been written about culturally responsive counseling for LGBQ++ clients in that they are passively adhered to rather than actively applied. The educational standards set forth by CACREP in the 2016 CACREP Standards (CACREP, 2015) provide guidelines for curriculum development. The standards create a foundation for what all counselors need to know. However, it is up to counseling programs, through teaching and learning, to add context and connect the standards to age groups and populations and provide opportunities for CITs to apply them. Within affirmative practices, theories, models, and interventions focus on the recognition of and advocacy for LGBQ++ populations.

Association Competencies and Counselor Training

Of the competencies available to guide CIT training, counseling programs have the (a) ALGBTIC Counseling Competencies (Harper et al., 2013), (b) AMCD Multicultural Counseling Competencies (Arredondo et al., 1996), and (c) Multicultural and Social Justice Counseling Competencies (Ratts et al., 2016). Though not specifically educational standards, the ALGBTIC Counseling Competencies will be discussed in the educational standards section of this chapter.

The original AMCD Multicultural Counseling Competencies (Arredondo et al., 1996) were added to and revised in creating the Multicultural and Social Justice Counseling Competencies (Ratts et al., 2016). Across these competencies are the foci of (a) counselor self-awareness, (b) client worldview, (c) counseling relationship, and (d) counseling and advocacy interventions. Each of these foci can be used to guide the education of CITs.

EDUCATIONAL STANDARDS: COUNCIL FOR THE ACCREDITATION OF COUNSELING AND RELATED EDUCATIONAL PROGRAMS STANDARDS AND ASSOCIATION FOR LESBIAN, GAY, BISEXUAL, AND TRANSGENDER ISSUES IN COUNSELING COMPETENCIES

The educational standards set forth by CACREP in the 2016 CACREP Standards (CACREP, 2015) provide guidelines for educating CITs. Within the 2016 CACREP Standards Section 2: Professional Counseling Identity, eight core areas provide specific education and learning components that must be covered in a counseling curriculum. In each of the core areas, educators will find an interwoven thread of culture and ethics. The overall goals of the educational standards and potential CACREP accreditation are to systematically expose CITs to topics, assess their learning, and demonstrate their development of competency. Though developed with the 2009 CACREP Standards in mind, the ALGBTIC Counseling Competencies can be adapted and update to mirror 2016 CACREP Standards.

In unison, the 2016 CACREP Standards and ALGBTIC Counseling Competencies provide guidelines for developing and conducting culturally responsive counseling training for those working with for LGBQ++ clients. Curriculum that is aligned to both would provide an opportunity for CITs to (a) be introduced to concepts, (b) have their learning reinforced with activities that demonstrate learning, and (c) apply their learning in mock sessions followed by application to actual clients. As mentioned in the 2016 CACREP Standards, CITs must be exposed to the educational standards across the curriculum and with increasing depth as CITs move from foundational courses to clinical practice. For lists of resources useful in counselor training, see Singh and Gonzales (2014), Troutman and Packer-Williams (2014), and Wynn and West-Olatunji (2009).

Cultural Humility

In the *Counseling Today* article "Practicing Cultural Humility," author Sidney Shaw (2017) notes that little research has explored counselors' multicultural competency from the perspective of the counselor and the client. In these studies, counselors have rated their cultural competency higher than they were rated by their clients. Shaw (2017) goes on to state that when counselors rate their multicultural competency high, they are less willing to explore and grow in this area. In essence, these counselors demonstrate lower levels of cultural humility. *Cultural humility*, as defined by Tervalon and Murray-García (1998, p. 2), is "a lifelong process of self-reflection and self-critique whereby the individual not only learns about another's culture, but one starts with an examination of her/his own beliefs and cultural identities." Mosher, Hooks, Farrell, et al. (2017), as cited in Mosher, Hooks, Captari, et al. (2017), state that across research, cultural humility includes "(a) a lifelong motivation to learn from others, (b) critical self-examination of cultural awareness, (c) interpersonal respect, (d) developing mutual partnerships that address power imbalances, and (e) an other-oriented stance open to new cultural information" (p. 223). To develop cultural humility and practice it, Mosher et al. (2017, pp. 225–228) indicate that the necessary components are "(a) engaging in critical self-examination and self-awareness, (b) building the therapeutic alliance, (c) repairing cultural ruptures, and (d) navigating value differences."

Cultural humility provides the foundation through which multicultural competencies can be applied. During their training, CITs have an opportunity to learn about cultural humility, explore their level of cultural humility, and begin to apply multicultural competencies. There are useful assessments that can be used to develop self-awareness related to one's cultural humility.

CULTURALLY RESPONSIVE PRACTICES: DRAWING FROM THE MULTICULTURAL AND SOCIAL JUSTICE COUNSELING COMPETENCIES AND CULTURAL HUMILITY

The text *Affirmative Counseling With LGBTQI+ People* (Ginicola et al., 2017) provides a comprehensive overview of affirmative practices. The chapters of the text provide information on topics ranging from identity development to best and evidence-based practices to working with subsets of the LGBTQI+ population. The information included is specifically focused on practitioners with a counseling identity. Ramírez (2018) notes that a literature review of Gay Affirmative Practices (GAP) yields five common categories that include types of competencies, organization/job policies, appropriate terminology, and skills. The categories are: (a) emotional competency,

(b) intellectual competency, (c) practice environment, (d) respectful language, and (e) open-ended questions.

As noted in the "Association Competencies and Counselor Training" section of this chapter, counselor educators can teach competencies, engage CITs in practicing competencies (viz., with clinical case scenarios and role-plays), and encourage self-assessment. In addition to the self-assessments mentioned in that section, counselor educators can incorporate assessment of social empathy (see the Social Empathy Index [SEI]; Segal et al., 2012), advocacy competencies (see the Advocacy Competencies Self-Assessment [ACSA]; Ratts & Ford, 2010), affirmative practices (see the Gay Affirmative Practice Scale [GAP]; Crisp, 2006) and attitudes, competencies, and skills specific to LGBQ++ clients.

The RESPECTFUL Framework for Exploration and Conceptualization

The RESPECTFUL framework (D'Andrea & Daniels, 2001) provides a way to conceptualize all the factors that interact to influence an individual's mental health development. According to D'Andrea and Daniels (2001), the framework focuses on two assumptions: (a) counseling is a means to client development and growth and (b) development is multidimensional. This multidimensionality is defined as all the factors that influence mental health development (D'Andrea & Daniels, 2001). D'Andrea and Daniels (2001, p. xvii) list the 10 elements of RESPECTFUL as: (R) religious/spiritual identity, (E) economic class background, (S) sexual identity, (P) psychological maturity, (E) ethnic/racial identity, (C) chronological/developmental challenges, (T) various forms of trauma and threats to well-being, (F) family background and history, (U) unique physical characteristics, and (L) location of residence and language differences. The 10 elements of RESPECTFUL can be used to process how each contributes, in a positive sense or negative sense, to a client's mental health development, and the RESPECTFUL framework offers a developmental lens for understanding many of the aspects of identity, individuality, culture, and intersectionality. For more thorough definitions and examples of each of the elements of the framework, see D'Andrea and Daniels (2001).

CRAFTING AN ADVOCACY AGENDA

As CITs develop their foundation of knowledge and skills and begin to apply these in role-plays and with clients, a natural next step is to begin to consider how they can advocate for their LGBQ++ clients. Advocacy, in terms of ethics, is described in the "Ethical Codes Connected to Culture, Competency, and Advocacy" section of this chapter. These codes do not give specific examples of how to advocate. In the *ACA 2014 Code of Ethics*, Section C: Professional Responsibility: Introduction (ACA, 2014), is the following: "Counselors are expected to advocate to promote changes at the individual, group, institutional, and societal levels that improve the quality of life for individuals and groups and remove potential barriers to the provision or access of appropriate services being offered" (p. 8). To accomplish what this statement requires, action is needed. A first action step might be to create an advocacy plan and agenda.

Numerous articles describe counselor advocacy for LGBQ++ clients (see Sandman et al., 2014; Simons & Cuadrado, 2018; Stark & Crofts, 2019). However, no specific article gives a format or template for an advocacy agenda or plan. On the internet, it is easy to find guidelines for developing an advocacy agenda or advocacy plan. These can be extrapolated and applied for counselor advocacy. The "Designing an Advocacy Strategy" toolkit from Knowledge SUCCESS (n.d., p. 5–8), lists the following six steps for developing an advocacy plan: (a) "Define the issue"; (b) "Set a clear advocacy goal and objectives for policy action"; (c) "Identify target audiences who can either make the necessary change or influence decision makers"; (d) "With the target audiences in mind, plan a set of activities and design communication materials using the most reliable, relevant, and current information"; (e) "Expand the base of support and raise resources (both human and financial) to carry out planned activities"; and (f) "Design a monitoring and evaluation (M&E) strategy."

Creating an advocacy agenda and developing a plan does not have to be complicated. Planning can begin by completing a needs assessment and identifying the need within one's community. Once needs are identified, goals can be set that address the needs. Goals can be further subdivided into objectives that make the efforts accomplishable. As goals or objectives are met, evaluate the outcomes. If the outcomes are not being met, reevaluate, and modify the plan. Small accomplishments and successes can be the foundation for significant change.

COUNSELING CHILDREN, ADOLESCENTS, AND YOUNG ADULTS

As CITs are trained, they learn a set of foundational skills and techniques that can be used with varying age ranges. However, these skills must be adapted based on the age of the individual client. As a CIT, one must remember three things: (a) children and adolescents are not adults; (b) in most states, children and adolescents cannot not consent to therapy (they can only assent); and (c) whatever method you select to use to help a child or adolescent must be developmentally appropriate.

CITs will not likely have access to clients with ages that range across the life span. What works for a 11-year-old will not be as successful with a 5-year-old. Further training, supervision, and practice are necessary to become competent. Likewise, knowing and using affirmative, evidence-based practices with adult LGBQ++ clients does not make one competent to work with youth.

Though many of the practice guidelines for working with LGBQ++ youth are dated, they still provide a foundation for ethical and affirmative practice. Adelson (2012), in the article "Practice Parameter on Gay, Lesbian, or Bisexual Sexual Orientation, Gender Nonconformity, and Gender Discordance in Children and Adolescents," describes nine principles that should guide practice. These are:

Principle 1. A comprehensive diagnostic evaluation should include an age-appropriate assessment of psychosexual development for all youths.

Principle 2. The need for confidentiality in the clinical alliance is a special consideration in the assessment of sexual and gender minority youth.

Principle 3. Family dynamics pertinent to sexual orientation, gender nonconformity, and gender identity should be explored in the context of the cultural values of the youth, family, and community.

Principle 4. Clinicians should inquire about circumstances commonly encountered by youth with sexual and gender minority status that confer increased psychiatric risk.

Principle 5. Clinicians should aim to foster healthy psychosexual development in sexual and gender minority youth and to protect the individual's full capacity for integrated identity formation and adaptive functioning.

Principle 6. Clinicians should be aware that there is no evidence that sexual orientation can be altered through therapy, and that attempts to do so may be harmful.

Principle 7. Clinicians should be aware of current evidence on the natural course of gender discordance and associated psychopathology in children and adolescents in choosing the treatment goals and modality.

Principle 8. Clinicians should be prepared to consult and act as a liaison with schools, community agencies, and other healthcare providers, advocating for the unique needs of sexual and gender minority youth and their families.

Principle 9. Mental health professionals should be aware of community and professional resources relevant to sexual and gender minority youth.

These principles make a strong foundation for working with LGBQ++ youth and their families. Other resources that are useful include "A Guide for Understanding, Supporting, and Affirming LGBTQI2-S Children, Youth, and Families" (Poirier et al., 2014); "Family and Social Development" in *Counseling LGBTQ Adults Throughout the Life Span* (Iarussi, 2017); and "Providing Services and Support for Youth Who Are Lesbian, Gay, Bisexual, Transgender, Questioning, Intersex, or Two Spirit" (Poirier et al., 2008).

COUNSELING ADULTS, COUPLES, AND FAMILIES

Most of what one learns (e.g., skills, techniques, theories, interventions) as a CIT was developed through research on adult populations. Therefore, most CITs should have a significant foundation for working with adults. When specifically working with adult LGBQ++ individuals, multiple resources are helpful (see ACA, n.d.; American Psychological Association [APA], 2011; Mental Health America [MHA], n.d.; National Alliance on Mental Illness [NAMI], n.d.). Linville and O'Neil (n.d.-a, n.d.-b) provide suggestions for working with LGBQ++ couples and families, and the National Resource Center on LGBT Aging (2020) provides resources for working with LGBQ++ older adults. Each of these resources provides suggestions for working with members of the adult LGBQ++ population.

The following section contains suggestions for how CITs can take all of what they learned and apply it in practice with LGBQ++ clients.

IMPLICATIONS FOR CLINICAL PRACTICE

Over time, the conceptualization and view of LGBQ++ individuals have changed from one of deviance and pathology to one of acceptance. Though the counseling profession has a long way to go on this journey toward understanding and cultural competency, overall attitudes toward LGBQ++ individuals are changing. Specific research may not yet point this out, but other indicators are present. These include (a) an increased number of research articles that focus on LGBQ++ clients as clients and (b) more textbooks with chapters that describe socially just and culturally competent work with LGBQ++ clients (e.g., this textbook). Regardless, LGBQ++ individuals encounter internal and external barriers that affect their mental health (Grella et al., 2009), and though there is a need for LGBQ++ competent mental health services, such services are not readily available in all areas of the country.

LGBQ++ Competent Counselor Training

As counseling professionals, we have a unique opportunity to experience a client's worldview, beliefs, perspectives, and intersectionality. This opportunity requires counselors to engage in an ongoing examination of their own attitudes and belief systems to develop and remain culturally competent and skilled counselors. To that end, counselors can (a) review empirical literature on attitude formation, (b) review scholarly publications on societal and counselor attitudes toward LGBQ++ individuals and couples, and (c) engage in reflection, introspection, and conversations about the variables influencing their attitudes toward LGBQ++ individuals and couples. From this, it is hoped, will come a well-rounded understanding of potential counseling implications and ways to enhance one's counselor self-efficacy with members of this community.

CLINICAL CASE SCENARIO 11.1

Ben is a 31-year-old biracial (White and Latino) male who grew up in the rural, southeastern part of the United States. Growing up, his mother, Joan, who is White, worked in a factory, and his father, Thomas, who was Latino, worked on a farm. Ben's father died in an accident when Ben was 8. Ben's mother remarried when he was 10, and he has two younger siblings. Ben's stepfather, Mitchell, is a mechanic and the father of his younger brother, Sam (age 21), and his younger sister, Tina (age 18).

Ben has a good relationship with all the members of his family. His family was never well-off, but they also never lived in poverty. Ben's mother attends a Baptist church, his biological father was Catholic, and his stepfather grew up in the Methodist church, but now attends a Baptist church with Ben's mother. Ben, like his siblings, attended church with his mother while living at home. Since graduating from college Ben has infrequently attended church. As an adult, he explored many different religious denominations, but never found a belief system that aligned with his.

Ben was the first in the family to attend and graduate from college. He attended a state university about three hours away from where he grew up, and he graduated magna cum laude with a degree in accounting. For more than 7 years, Ben has been an accountant at a midsize firm in a city four hours away from where he grew up. His brother is about to enter his last year of college at the same school Ben attended, and his sister will begin college soon, at an art school nearly eight hours away from their hometown.

In high school, Ben never dated much. In college, he came out, and around his friends, then and now, he is openly gay. Ben's partner of 3 years, Caleb, is 29 and works as a chef in an upscale restaurant. The two have considered marriage. Caleb is out and accepted by his family. However, Ben's family is unaware of his sexual orientation. As the two have grown closer, Ben has experienced stress and mild depression as he contemplates coming out to his family. Caleb convinces Ben to speak to a counselor.

CLINICAL CASE SCENARIO DISCUSSION QUESTIONS

1. Based on Ben's case, how would you utilize the RESPECTFUL framework to guide your conceptualization and treatment?
2. There is a lot that you do not know about Ben's coming-out process. Concerning this, what would you want to explore with him?
3. When conceptualizing Ben, his life, and his current situation, what aspects of intersectionality are important to consider?
4. If you were to craft an advocacy agenda for Ben using the six steps outlined in the respective section of this chapter, what would it include?

END-OF-CHAPTER RESOURCES

 A robust set of instructor resources designed to supplement this text is located at http://connect.springerpub.com/content/book/978-0-8261-3953-5. Qualifying instructors may request access by emailing **textbook@springerpub.com**.

SUMMARY

There are numerous articles that conceptualize and describe implementation of multicultural competencies, social justice tenets, ethical standards, and affirmative practices within a counseling curriculum (Bemak et al., 2011; Cates et al., 2007; Celinska & Swazo, 2016; Killian et al., 2019; Riggs & Fell, 2010). In the article "Implementing Multicultural Social Justice Strategies in Counselor Education Training Programs," Bemak and Chung (2011) describe infusing multicultural and social justice tenets through programmatic changes, faculty recruitment, and student learning. Cates et al. (2007) present research findings by comparing multicultural competency and general counseling knowledge and skill competency. Celinska and Swazo (2016) describe implementing a multicultural curriculum design and present evidence of how the curriculum enhances CITs' openness to diversity. Killian et al. (2019) describe how CITs feel underprepared for working with LGBQ++ clients and make recommendations for bringing together the competencies developed by multiple divisions of ACA, ethical codes, and educational standards through an experiential learning framework. Finally, Riggs and Fell (2010) describe and report the findings of a workshop developed to teach cultural competency for working with LGBQ++ clients.

As counselor educators work to incorporate liberation counseling tenets; multidimensional, developmental models such as RESPECTFUL; ethical codes; competencies; educational standards; and affirmative practices into meaningful and beneficial educational practices, focus and attention are needed to research and report the outcome of these educational practices. Though the progress is encouraging and evidence of the benefits of culturally responsive counselor training for those working with LGBQ++ clients exists, more is needed. Effort is needed to incorporate all the components into best practice, clinical practices, or expectational practice guidelines.

In the medical field, practice guidelines offer the highest level of evidence of utility and benefit (Ackley et al., 2008). For the counseling profession, randomized controlled trials are seen as the gold standard. The question here is: Who is right? Randomized controlled trials provide good outcome data; however, practice guidelines are developed from the data of countless studies. Can we advocate for more studies with the eventual goal of practice guidelines? The answer is, yes.

DISCUSSION QUESTIONS

1. After reading this chapter, including the case of Ben, what concerns do you have about working with LGBQ++ clients?
2. If you were intentionally introspective and reflective to understand your level of cultural humility, where should you begin to prepare your work with LGBQ++ clients?
3. Knowing the obstacles, prejudices, and discrimination that LGBQ++ clients face, what can you do to help eradicate such barriers?

KEY REFERENCES

Only key references appear in the print edition. The full reference list appears in the digital product on Springer Publishing Connect: https://connect.springerpub.com/content/book/978-0-8261-3953-5/part/part02/chapter/ch11

American Counseling Association. (n.d.). *Resources: Clients in the LGBTQ+ community*. https://www.counseling.org/knowledge-center/mental-health-resources/lgbtq

Arredondo, P., Toporek, R., Brown, S. P., Jones, J., Locke, D. C., Sanchez, J., & Stadler, H. (1996). Operationalization of the multicultural counseling competencies. *Journal of Multicultural Counseling and Development*, 24(1), 42–78. https://doi.org/10.1002/j.2161-1912.1996.tb00288.x

Casey, L. S., Reisner, S. L., Findling, M. G., Blendon, R. J., Benson, J. M., Sayde, J. M., & Miller, C. (2019). Discrimination in the United States: Experiences of lesbian, gay, bisexual, transgender, and queer Americans. *Health Services Research*, 54(Suppl. 2), 1454–1466. https://doi.org/10.1111/1475-6773.13229

Council for the Accreditation of Counseling and Related Educational Programs. (2015). *2016 CACREP standards*. http://www.cacrep.org/wp-content/uploads/2018/05/2016-Standards-with-Glossary-5.3.2018.pdf

Ginicola, M. M., Smith, C., & Filmore, J. M. (2017). *Affirmative Counseling With LGBTQI+ People*. American Counseling Association. https://doi.org/10.1002/9781119375517

Ratts, M. J., Singh, A. A., Nassar-McMillan, S., Butler, S. K., & McCullough, J. R. (2016). Multicultural and social justice counseling competencies: Guidelines for the counseling profession. *Journal of Multicultural Counseling and Development*, 44(1), 28–48. https://doi.org/10.1002/jmcd.12035

Singh, A. A., & Gonzales, M. (2014). *ACA counseling brief: LGBTQQ-affirmative counseling. The center for counseling practice, policy, and research*. https://isucounselingresources2017.weebly.com/uploads/1/1/3/4/11344496/aca_practice_brief_lgbtqq_coun.pdf

CHAPTER 12

Culturally Responsive Counseling for Transgender Clients

CLARK D. AUSLOOS AND LENA SALPIETRO

LEARNING OBJECTIVES

After reading this chapter, students will be able to:
- Recognize the diverse, persistent challenges faced by transgender and gender-diverse people and how these challenges deeply influence health, well-being, and life functioning.
- Recognize how the counselor's own identity, and reflection on that identity as it relates to others, is essential to ethical, affirming, and supportive care with transgender clients.
- Use affirming, celebratory, and liberating counseling approaches that promote resilience and strength in clients.
- Assemble with other professionals, stakeholders, and families to advocate for inclusive and transgender-affirming policies, practices, and curricula in institutions.
- Evaluate the unique and important factors of intersectionality and how these factors affect clients and the therapeutic alliance.

SELF-REFLECTION QUESTIONS

1. When did I first become aware of my gender? What do I first remember about experiencing a gender identity and expressing it?
2. What are my earliest memories of adhering or not adhering to socially prescribed gender roles?
3. Have I ever been chastised for not prescribing to social ideas of how others perceive my gender?
4. How might my perceptions of gender be influenced by my upbringing, family, friends?
5. What message have I heard from others regarding my gender identity? Was this congruent with my perception of my gender? With others' perceptions?
6. Presently, how do I express my gender? Does this expression change based on who or what is around me? Have I ever experienced being misgendered (assumed you were a different gender)? If so, what was this experience like for me?

7. How do other cultural factors (e.g., race/ethnicity, age, ability/disability status) influence the privilege, power, and oppression I experience due to my gender identity?
8. Do I know transgender people in my personal or professional life? How do I perceive them and engage with them?
9. How can I continue to work on my own biases and prejudices throughout my life?

Pervasive in society is a binary concept of gender (i.e., males and females). When we are born, medical providers determine and assign sex based on biological and genetic factors. Commonly, families raise children as the gender congruent with the assigned sex. For example, a baby assigned male at birth is often raised as a socially stereotypical male, made to wear blue, and given toy trucks as gifts. Ultimately, one's sex-assigned-at-birth (i.e., male, female, intersex) may or may not be congruent with one's gender identity. A person who experiences a congruence with their gender identity and their sex-assigned-at-birth (SAAB) is referred to as *cisgender*, whereas someone whose gender identity is different from their SAAB is referred to as *transgender*, or *trans* (O'Hara et al., 2013). Although these various identities share some common understanding, each identity and personal narrative is unique to each client.

While there is still much progress to be made, there has been an increase in visibility and representation for transgender and gender-diverse people in society, both through media and popular culture. Although there is a hesitancy among gender-diverse people to seek mental health treatment, professional counselors need to be prepared to work with gender issues, and transgender and gender-diverse clients, in a culturally responsive way. This chapter introduces readers to foundational elements when working with transgender clients, as well as more nuanced interventions and action items, within and outside of the counseling session.

THE COUNSELOR: EXPLORATION, INTROSPECTION, AND REFLECTION

Clinical Case Scenario 12.1 introduces Carson, a counselor-in-training (CIT), and his new client Max. Unfortunately, Max's experience in counseling is all too common. Clinicians and helping professionals lack awareness, knowledge, training, and skills in working with transgender and gender-expansive clients. An important skill in the work of helping professionals is self-reflection and increasing one's awareness of deeply held biases and beliefs. Exploring all parts of oneself positions the counselor with curiosity and openness in session, allows the clinician to be more transparent with their clients, and increases the strength of the therapeutic alliance. In counselor education programs, diversity and multicultural courses often introduce the Multicultural and Social Justice Counseling Competencies (MSJCC; Ratts et al., 2016). Outlined in the competencies are foundations of attitudes and beliefs, knowledge, skills, and action, nested within the praxis of Counselor Self-Awareness, Client Worldview, Counseling Relationship, and Counseling & Advocacy Interventions (Ratts et al., 2016). Attitudes, beliefs, and self-awareness are foundational in the practice of culturally sensitive and inclusive counseling. Additionally, counselors need to be aware of and able to broach issues related to identity with clients, and how these identities relate to the constructs of privilege, power, and oppression (Salpietro et al., 2019). *Implicit bias* is a term often used to describe the automatic and unintentional reactions that contribute to discrimination and marginalization (Devine et al., 2012). To mitigate implicit bias, counselors must be both aware of and concerned with the consequences of their actions, using deep reflection and exploration (Plant & Devine, 2009). Counselors must also understand the limits and challenges of using standard psychotherapeutic approaches with marginalized clients, and work to raise critical consciousness of oppressive systems and move towards liberation (Domínguez et al., 2020).

Gender is often the first part of identity that children develop and is highly influenced by family and peers (Brooks-Gunn & Lewis, 1979). Starting as young as two or three years of age, children begin to associate dress and behavior with gender; and, around age five, children understand the stable nature of gender (gender constancy; Kohlberg, 1966). Many of us may recall early life memories associated with certain toys or events that are, in fact, gendered. Binary gender stereotypes (e.g., females playing with dolls, males playing with cars and trucks) are deeply ingrained in the Western culture. Families are often found to host gender reveal parties, to announce the child's sex-assigned-at-birth, releasing pink balloons for a girl or blue balloons for a boy. Our world is deeply entrenched in a binary, cisnormative culture.

We, the authors, feel strongly that cultural responsiveness, particularly when working with transgender people, is a dynamic and fluid process, and requires intentionality (Salpietro et al., 2019). In reflecting on gender, gender identity and expression, and the intersection of these concepts within ourselves, we invite you to reflect on the following questions, not only prior to your work but also throughout the counseling process with transgender clients. These questions are created to start the reflection process and are not exhaustive. You might find that you want to use these reflections before and/or after a session with a client, in discussion during supervision, before or after a course, or even with your own family and friends.

GENDER IDENTITIES AND SEXUAL ORIENTATION/IDENTITY

Our biological *sex* is determined by our chromosomes, our gonads (ovaries, testes), secondary sex characteristics (developed during puberty), and behavior (Tannenbaum et al., 2016). When society celebrates at gender reveal parties, they are in fact celebrating the sex-assigned-at-birth, *not* gender. This practice further conflates that one's sex assigned at birth *must* be the same as one's gender identity. *Gender identity* (GI) describes one's own unique, deeply understood internal sense of gender (Ginicola et al., 2017). *Gender expression* (GE), however, describes one's way of expressing their gender externally, through dress, hair, clothes, makeup, piercings, tattoos; as well as voice, mannerisms, and behaviors (Killermann, 2017). It is important for counselors not to make assumptions about clients, noting that a client's GI may or may not be "congruent" with their GE. For example, a transwoman may express their gender in different ways than what is expected by society. She may choose to paint her nails but dress in clothing that society typically associates with men. In the United States, there are deeply embedded gender and social norms which often dictate behaviors, mannerisms, and dress (Cislaghi & Heise, 2020).

Often, GI is conflated with affectional and sexual identities, meaning people may assume that someone who is transgender is also gay, or that a gay man who acts in a more stereotypical feminine way must also be a transwoman. GI falls along spectra of "male-ness," "female-ness," more than one gender, or no gender at all (Killermann, 2017). Sexual identities also fall along a broad spectrum of attractions and non-attractions. Focusing solely on sexual identity (historically called *sexual orientation*) severely limits the broad array of types of attractions a person may or may not experience and is reductionistic. *Affectional identity* is a holistic, inclusive term encompassing other types of attractions and bonds, romantic or not (Ginicola et al., 2017). *Demiromantic*, for example, is a term used to describe someone who must form a strong emotional bond with another person before experiencing romantic attraction (Ginicola et al., 2017). Broadly, affectional/sexual identities refer to the bonds and attractions that one might or might not have; these bonds may be romantic in nature, sexual, a combination of the two, or neither.

Sam Killermann (2017), an educator and author who has written extensively about gender, gender identity, and gender expression, highlights the importance of looking at gender as less of one spectrum (male to female), as this excludes diverse gender identities outside of the binary view of gender (e.g., nonbinary, gender fluid, agender). Instead, he encourages us to use continuums of both male-ness and female-ness. This way, an individual can correctly identify their own identity based on degrees of male-ness, female-ness, neither, or both. While ultimately counselors use the language and labels that clients use for themselves, the following section highlights terminology that may be used or discussed in the session.

INTERSECTIONALITY OF RELIGION AND SEXUAL/GENDER IDENTITIES

Religion has an important role in shaping ideas around GI and assigned sex identity (ASI) in culture and can be both harmful and protective for transgender people. Historically, there has been a strong relationship between religion and people experiencing prejudice; and some religions have doctrines that may promote cisnormativity (i.e., Judaism, Christianity, Islam, among others) which declare that "their respective deity create[d] mankind with individuals ... entrenched in the gender binary" (Campbell et al., 2019, p. 23). When compared to non-religiously affiliated people, individuals who are religious report more interpersonal discomfort (Kanamori et al., 2017) and negative attitudes toward transgender people (Solomon & Kurtz-Costes, 2018). Religiously affiliated people do not conceal these attitudes, as one-third of transgender people reported that they left their religious community for fear of rejection, with transpeople of color being more likely to leave their communities (James et al., 2016). Nearly one in five respondents indicated that they were rejected by their religious community (James et al., 2016). Transgender people may be more at risk for religious prejudice and discrimination, as they may have both nondominant gender and nondominant affectional and/or sexual identities. Counselors should be prepared to work with clients on issues related to religious acceptance and/or rejection, as well as internalized transmisia (also called transphobia). Counselors are encouraged to use tenets from liberation psychology to dismantle power and oppression at multiple levels in their work, and help clients recognize societal forces outside their control, while building support, suggesting strategies, and empowering clients.

Little is known about the relationship between religious affiliation and the experiences of transgender people, but research suggests that religious affiliation and acceptance could be a protective factor (Grossman et al., 2016; James et al., 2016; Levy & Lo, 2013). Of those who recently engaged with a religious community, 96% reported that they experienced acceptance from community leaders and members or were told that their religion accepts them (James et al., 2016). Grossman et al. (2016) found that more frequent attendance at religious services in transgender youth was related to decrease in suicidal ideations. Some literature has been dedicated to religious identity development in Christian transgender people. In one study, Christian transgender women's experiences were explored, and participants identified how exploration into their gender identity was at times strengthened by their faith (Yarhouse & Carrs, 2012). Dual-identity development, in both gender identity and religious identity, was found in a small sample of transgender people who indicated that this process was painful and conflicting, but also promoted comfort, acceptance, and joy (Ghazzawi et al., 2020). Findings suggest that exploring both gender identity and religious identity in counseling could be helpful for religiously affiliated transgender people. Counselors should find ways to integrate the client's religious identity, such as the utilization of prayer, sacred text, or incorporating religious identity into existing models of practice.

STRESSORS AND DISCRIMINATION

Meyer (2003) proposed that discrimination and stigma related to nondominant gender, affectional and/or sexual identities are associated with increased mental health problems. This stress can be compounded by additional, intersecting factors of one's identity. For example, a transman with a disability or a transwoman of color reportedly experiences significantly more stress than their transgender counterparts (James et al., 2016). Much of this stress is the result of structural cissexism or the idea that cisgender identities are superior to transgender identities (LeMaster & Johnson, 2018), which is seen in both covert (language, gendered dress), and overt ways (verbal, physical, and/or sexual assault and abuse; Nadal et al., 2012). Cissexism reinforces hatred toward and disgust at transgender people. Sadly, when transgender people do seek support from law enforcement, they experience high levels of mistreatment and harassment (almost 60% of respondents), particularly Black and Brown transwomen (James et al., 2016). This mistreatment is also seen in prison and jail populations, with transgender people who have offended often being placed either in isolation, or with populations that share the same sex-assigned-at-birth designations, and experience discrimination and harassment from inmates as well as prison offers and staff (Brömdal et al., 2019).

Of all affectionally, sexually, and gender-diverse identities, transgender students face the greatest risk for harm at school (Becerra-Culqui et al., 2018). In schools, transgender students experience harassment and discrimination in the classroom by peers and teachers, confusion and discomfort among teachers, and a general lack of knowledge and respect for personal pronouns and ways of identifying (Kosciw et al., 2018). It is no surprise, then, that transgender students have lower self-esteem and lower grade point averages, and ultimately may drop out of school (Kosciw et al., 2018).

Transgender people face overt and covert discrimination, marginalization, assault, and abuse in communities, including at home (often being kicked out of their homes), in the workplace (high rates of job loss and employment discrimination), while traveling, and in social spaces (e.g., stores, restaurants, hotels, gyms; James et al., 2016). Even more alarming is the disproportionate amount of physical abuse and murder of Black and Latinx transwomen between the ages of 15 and 35 (Dinno, 2017). There continues to be an array of anti-transgender legislation passed by states; however, in March of 2021, the U.S. House of Representatives passed the Equality Act, which, if fully passed into law by the U.S. Senate, would provide non-discrimination protections for transgender and queer people (employment, housing, credit, education, public spaces; Human Rights Campaign [HRC], 2021a).

Concerningly, due to cissexism, discrimination, and isolation, transgender people have increased mental health concerns (e.g., depression, anxiety, posttraumatic stress disorder [PTSD]; Martinez-Velez et al., 2019; Meyer, 2003), substance use disorders (Reisner et al., 2014), and suicide rates (Herman et al., 2017). Particularly salient for professional counselors is the fact that transgender people have had historically negative experiences with medical providers and mental health professionals, and avoid seeking care altogether (James et al., 2016). Transgender people often report that they are misgendered by their providers, blatantly discriminated against, and experience provider confusion and lack of understanding, leading to transgender people having to educate their medical providers (Grant et al., 2011).

COUNSELING UTILIZATION AND HELP-SEEKING

Transgender people may present to counseling for concerns related or unrelated to their gender identity, and are often faced with significant barriers to care (including negative experiences with providers; Salpietro et al., 2019). Clients may seek support as they begin to explore their gender identity, and counselors can help transgender clients prepare for social transitioning or gender-affirmative medical procedures, both emotionally and factitively, through referral letters. Transgender people may need help addressing adverse experiences, including discrimination and stigma, as well as the lasting psychological impact these adversities can have. Counselors can help transgender people identify and address internalized transmisia and assess the influence of cultural and societal norms on their gender identity and expression. Presenting concerns may also include navigating interpersonal relationships, such as those with partners, family, friends, or colleagues. Not all transgender people present to counseling seeking to explicitly explore gender identity; however, it is important for counselors to utilize a social justice framework in considering how client problems could be influenced by experiences of prejudice, discrimination, and stigma. In a national survey, 77% of transgender people indicated that they wanted counseling or therapy services, but only 58% had ever engaged in services (James et al., 2016). Despite experiencing disproportionate rates of mental health problems compared to their cisgender counterparts, transgender people face significant barriers to mental health treatment, including lack of access to competent, affirmative providers, and affordability.

Counselors are mandated to provide affirmative and ethical treatment to all people (American Counseling Association [ACA], 2014); however, research shows that professional counselors may not be adequately prepared to meet the needs of transgender people. Transgender clients have reported that they often feel as if their mental health providers are not knowledgeable about transgender issues (Benson, 2013; Hunt, 2014; McCullough et al., 2017; Mizock & Lundquist, 2016), stating that they have had to educate their providers about gender identity, and the political, medical, and cultural aspects of being transgender (Benson, 2013; McCullough et al., 2017; Snow et al., 2019). This invalidation by providers often leaves transgender people feeling misunderstood and unsupported in therapeutic settings (Hunt, 2014). Provider lack of competency in working with transgender people may lead to an over- or underemphasis on gender identity, creating significant barriers for clients and promoting increased irritation and dissatisfaction with care (Hunt, 2014; Mizock & Lundquist, 2016). The experiences of transgender people in counseling are not unfounded, as CITs and professional counselors have reported that they were not prepared to meet the needs of transgender people (O'Hara et al., 2013; Salpietro et al., 2019; Whitman & Han, 2017).

Transgender people have reported that previous bad experiences with providers (e.g., being misgendered; McCullough et al., 2017), fear of poor treatment, and stigma were common barriers to seeking mental health services (Benson, 2013; Hunt, 2014; Shipherd et al., 2010). One in 10 transgender people reported that a mental health professional "tried to stop them from being [transgender]" (James et al., 2016, p. 109), and three-fourths of them had experienced such microaggressions before the age of 25. Transgender persons of color and transgender persons with disabilities are more likely to report negative experiences with providers and healthcare avoidance. Transgender people who identify as American Indian (50%), Middle Eastern (40%), Multiracial (38%), or with a disability were more likely to have had a negative experience with a healthcare provider in the last year compared to those who are White, Black, or Asian (James et al., 2016). Additionally, transgender persons of color are more likely to avoid healthcare due to fear of mistreatment than are transgender people without an intersecting nondominant identity (James et al., 2016).

The cost of counseling and mental health care are systematic barriers that often make these services inaccessible for transgender people, especially for transgender people of color and transgender people with disabilities. Transgender people are less likely to be insured compared to the general population (James et al., 2016), and those without insurance are significantly less likely to see a mental health professional (Carter et al., 2020). Transgender persons of color, including those who identify as Black, American Indian, and Latinx, are more likely to be uninsured (James et al., 2016). A national study indicated that access to mental health care varied by income, and transgender people with no income or significantly low income (i.e., $1–$9,999) were far less likely to have received counseling than those who earned $50,000 or more (James et al., 2016). Transgender persons of color and transgender people with disabilities are more likely to not see a healthcare provider due to the cost of services (James et al., 2016).

CULTURALLY RESPONSIVE PRACTICES: DRAWING FROM THE MULTICULTURAL AND SOCIAL JUSTICE COUNSELING COMPETENCIES AND CULTURAL HUMILITY

The MSJCC (Ratts et al., 2016) include aspirational competencies of attitudes and beliefs, knowledge, skills, and action. These are interwoven into the praxis of working toward multicultural and social justice competence (Ratts et al., 2016). We use the same competency headings to highlight culturally responsive practices when working with transgender people.

Attitudes and Beliefs

We started the chapter with a discussion of the importance of counselor self-reflection, and the authors highlight the concept again here. Exploring, learning (and sometimes unlearning), and processing the counselor's views of diversity is a foundational element of working with any client. In addition to intentional self-reflection (with or without the use of prompts), it can be valuable to discuss these concepts with others who may or may not be similar to you. This could include formal consultation with colleagues, seeking supervision, or through more informal dialogues with colleagues, or people not involved in helping professions. When reflecting on gender, counselors must assess their privileges. Cisgender counselors may consider using privilege lists or statements (e.g., www.itspronouncedmetrosexual.com/2011/11/list-of-cisgender-privileges) to deepen introspection and reflection. Having a deeper understanding of our own privileges and those of our clients can help counselors strengthen therapeutic alliances and outcomes.

Knowledge

An important part of culturally responsive counseling is having strong knowledge of how best to meet the needs of transgender clients. Counselors must know common terminology, pronouns, and names used by transgender clients, as well as other important foundations of mental health risk factors, significant challenges faced by transgender people, resilience factors, and knowledge of social and medically affirming transition care. Counselors must also have knowledge of and access to allied, affirming providers (such as physicians, endocrinologists, and speech-language pathologists), and transgender-affirming social support groups.

The Importance of Language

Asking about, recognizing, and using a client's pronouns is foundational to a trusting relationship. Allowing clients to self-identify their gender identity, the name they use, and their pronouns in intake forms is one small but important step in fostering a safe, liberating environment. In session, it is important to ask, "What pronouns do you use?" regardless of working with a transgender or gender-expansive client, to demonstrate respect and validation. If a counselor misgenders a client, recognizing the mistake, apologizing, and taking intentional steps to not misgender again are essential in repairing a possible therapeutic rupture.

While understanding the use of pronouns is fundamental, counselors must remain vigilant in their quest to seek knowledge above and beyond basic gender concepts. Counselors should not assume a client's gender, and if unsure, should use neutral pronouns such as they/them. Intake paperwork should include a fill-in-the-blank option for self-identification of gender identity (as compared to checkboxes), and SAAB (if this information is required to know). If checkboxes are used, make sure to include options for diverse gender identities (i.e., gender-fluid, nonbinary). In addition, counselors must work ethically to respect client confidentiality, and honor the client's chosen names whether written or in spoken form. While this chapter highlights terminology a transgender client may use, we advise readers to learn from your clients what language is most congruent with them.

Social and Medical Gender-Affirming Transitions

While transgender people may or may not choose to affirm their gender in any way, counselors must be prepared to have discussions with clients about the transition processes, potential barriers, supportive skills and strategies, and other providers and resources. Often, transgender clients will start to dress in a way that is congruent with their gender. A transman may choose to bind their chest using a binder; a transwoman may choose to tuck their genitals or use a gaff. Counselors should understand what these gender-affirming interventions are and how clients can access them. Counselors should stay up-to-date with changing terminology and interventions, by learning from such organizations as the World Professional Association for Transgender Health (WPATH), Society for Sexual, Affectional, Intersex, and Gender-Expansive Identities (SAIGE), or the National Center for Transgender Equality (NCTE). Counselors must also understand the risks and benefits of affirming gender through clothing for the client, including assessing safety at home and engaging in problem-solving with the client. Imagine you have a client who is a transwoman starting her gender-affirming transition but lives in an environment where she does not feel safe overtly wearing feminine clothing. You may determine with your client that she is able to wear affirming undergarments and paint her nails, which can be masked while at home, but still affirms her gender. Counselors are often called to write letters of support for hormone therapies and medical treatments. Depending on the age of the client (among other factors), hormone blockers may be used, or masculinizing/feminizing hormones (WPATH, 2012). Clients may also have breast/

chest surgeries, genital surgeries, or other interventions, like voice surgery, liposuction, or hair reconstruction (WPATH, 2012).

Understanding Context

It is essential for counselors to recognize that a transgender client may be coming to counseling for issues not related to gender. Transgender clients may present with minimal or no gender dysphoria at all (WPATH, 2012). Counselors must also recognize the social and political context that surrounds clients and their stories, including the historical gender/sexual prejudice, based on embedded cisnormativity and pervasive discrimination, and collaboratively work to mitigate these factors (Ausloos, in press). Counselors must also understand the context of suppressive and harmful legislation, and how this affects clients' human rights, and physical and mental health.

Skills

Building upon awareness of our attitudes and beliefs, and transgender-specific knowledge, counselors must have skills to work affirmingly with transgender clients in individual counseling. Counselors must also be skilled in working with family systems and relationships, and in supporting clients with community referrals (Ginicola et al., 2017). The following section introduces best-practice approaches in working with transgender clients, including using an affirmative, celebratory, and trauma-informed lens, increasing support and resilience factors, and empowering the client. Counselors need to know the ways in which clients affirm their gender socially (e.g., clothes, hair, speech), ways to support clients through these experiences, and work with clients to navigate expectations when they encounter challenges in life. Mindfulness-based techniques (e.g., new-wave cognitive behavioral therapy [CBT], dialectical behavioral therapy [DBT], Acceptance and Commitment Therapy [ACT]; for examples, see Iacono, 2019) can be combined with other techniques, including emotionally-focused therapy (EFT; Chang et al., 2018).

Affirmative Counseling

A pantheoretical approach, affirmative counseling, involves affirming and validating gender identity and expression as normative and diverse, with several key components, including acknowledgment of societal biases and oppression, mutual problem-solving, collaborative crisis planning, empowerment, and advocacy (Ausloos, in press). Counselors should work at the local and national level toward abolishing harmful reparative or sexual orientation change therapies, which are not effective, and more importantly, can be extremely traumatizing and harmful for transgender clients (Movement Advancement Project, 2017). Celebratory and strengths-based strategies are recommended, which recognize and celebrate positive aspects of the client's life and empower the client (Lytle et al., 2014).

Trauma-Informed Lens

Transgender people face pervasive discrimination, from microaggressions to overt physical violence. These experiences, in addition to possible previous negative interactions with providers, can result in trauma for transgender clients. Counselors should use a trauma-informed approach whether or not a transgender person directly reports trauma. Counselors should acknowledge and validate the clients' trauma and foster a safe space for clients to heal (Chang et al., 2018).

Action and Advocacy

Counselors should reflect upon their own and the client's attitudes and beliefs, possess critical knowledge in the history of oppression of transgender people and work in actionable ways to move systems, organizations, and people toward more diverse, inclusive, and equitable ways of being. Counselors can take action in each of the MSJCC domains of attitudes and beliefs, knowledge, and skills (Ratts et al., 2016). Counselors take action by actively seeking resources and spaces that work to dismantle systemic oppression. This may include reading, writing, self-reflection, or spiritual practices. Counselors can take action by engaging with transgender people in their communities, in more informal ways, and learning about transgender experiences directly from transgender people (Salpietro et al., 2019). It is imperative that counselors ask questions of and include the transgender communities in their advocacy and research, which may require counselors to increase personal connections with transgender people in the community. Counselors take action in learning affirming, inclusive practices and advocating for these practices with other counselors and professionals. See the "Crafting an Advocacy Agenda" section of this chapter to learn more pragmatic ways to empower, take action, and advocate for and with transgender clients.

Affirming Providers and Ancillary Services

An important factor in affirmative, competent care is having knowledge of and access to regional and national providers and resources. Providers should include not only medical providers and endocrinologists, but also speech-language pathologists, psychologists, and legal resources (WPATH, 2012). It is important that counselors consider accessible resources, including online group support and other online resources.

CRAFTING AN ADVOCACY AGENDA

Counselors should engage in advocacy efforts with or on behalf of transgender clients on individual, community, and public levels. We pose a list of potential individual-, school/community-, and public area-level advocacy efforts that counselors can implement to ensure the health and well-being of transgender people (Toporek & Daniels, 2018). These suggestions are not comprehensive, and counselors are encouraged to adapt advocacy interventions to best meet the needs of the individual and community.

Individual-Level Advocacy

Individual-level advocacy focuses on issues faced by the individual client or within a counselor's direct purview. Counselors can ensure that their office policies and procedures are gender affirmative. This includes gathering feedback from GE clients and working with agency administration to institute change. Counselors may revise paperwork to ensure that it includes expansive identities and opportunities to identify names and pronouns and create inclusive bathroom policies. Providing transgender-affirmative training to agency employees can also contribute to creating a transgender-inclusive environment. Counselors can also create a list of local transgender-affirmative resources that can be provided to clients and display resources in locations around their agency and within the community to increase accessibility and visibility of affirmative care. Directly intervening in situations of discrimination, cissexism, harassment, and so on is another way counselors can engage in individual-level advocacy. Numerous bystander intervention training programs are available (e.g., *Hollaback!*: www.ihollaback.org/), but the major tenets of intervention include making your presence known, naming the problematic behavior, and getting the victim to a safe location. Encouraging transgender clients to get involved or start their own local community group can help counselors empower clients to be advocates. Groups such as a local or state branch of *Equality*, which are organizations that work to achieve equality and eliminate discrimination against LGBT people, can help transgender clients find community and advocate for themselves.

School/Community-Level Advocacy

School- and community-level advocacy include interventions that aim to address issues faced by a group of people either in an academic or community setting. Counselors should be involved in their community by engaging in or creating community advocacy teams or committees. These teams/committees bring community members from different arenas (e.g., community mental health, education, public service) together with the goal of creating more affirmative and inclusive spaces for transgender people. Potential areas of focus for advocacy teams/committees are ensuring the safety of public facilities for transgender people or advocating for policy change in public schools (e.g., policies to allow students to identify the name they want to be called, gender-based extracurricular policies). Counselors can also provide direct services to their community by facilitating support or counseling groups for transgender people and providing transgender-affirming education in the community in places such as local schools and businesses.

Public Arena-Level Advocacy

Public arena-level advocacy focuses on systematic social change through law and policy. Counselors must familiarize themselves with local, state, and national laws and work to raise awareness about them to engage in public arena-level advocacy. Visiting local, state, and national government websites as well as utilizing resources such as the American Civil Liberties Union (ACLU) are a few of the many ways to stay informed. To lobby for change against anti-transgender legislation, counselors can write letters or meet with or call their local, state, or national representatives. In these interactions, counselors should identify themselves as professional counselors, express their concerns about specific policies and legislation, citing relevant literature when appropriate, and request a follow-up response. The ACA has a Governmental Affairs and Public Policy team that provides counselors with an overview of relevant state and federal legislation as well as tips and strategies for advocates (www.counseling.org/government-affairs). Advocating for insurance companies to cover transgender-specific care is another way counselors can engage in public arena-level advocacy. Counselors should be familiar with the rights of transgender people in healthcare and be prepared to articulate why affirming healthcare is vital for transgender people. For more information on transgender rights in healthcare, please review state and federal law or utilize resources from advocacy groups, such as the NCTE (https://transequality.org/know-your-rights/health-care).

Counselors should also be familiar with national, state, and local organizations that advocate on behalf of transgender people. National organizations such as the NCTE and the Transgender Law Center (TLC) both have advocacy and policy agendas that aim to protect the rights of transgender people. Counselors can get involved by assisting with community-level events or making monetary donations. State-level organizations such as Equality Florida or Equality Ohio engage in education, lobbying, and grassroots organizing to increase the safety and well-being of transgender people in their state. Local organizations, or local chapters of larger organizations such as PFLAG, provide counselors with the opportunity to engage in advocacy and education in the area in which they reside.

COUNSELING CHILDREN, ADOLESCENTS, AND YOUNG ADULTS

As children progress through childhood, it is developmentally normal and healthy to explore gender identities and expressions. Children as young as 2 or 3 years old begin to recognize their gender, use gendered pronouns, and may wear gendered clothing; toward the ages of 6 and 7, children develop gender constancy (Kohlberg, 1966). Counselors need to understand that early expression of gender diversity does not necessarily guarantee the person will be transgender or gender-diverse later in life (Nealy, 2017). It is best practice for counselors to meet children and families where they are, embrace and celebrate diversity, and foster a safe space for clients while providing psychoeducation to parents about gender identity development and ways to support their children (Chang et al., 2018). Additionally, parents and clients may need strong psychoeducation on various meanings of identity and terminology, and connections to resources and community support. In these stages, counselors may work with children on nonmedical gender-affirming interventions, like dress, hair, and other ways of gender expression. In some cases, clients and their families may work with medical providers and endocrinologists in considering puberty-suppressing hormones (Coleman et al., 2011).

Adolescents

As adolescents near puberty, they may experience increased gender dysphoria or extreme distress with their bodies related to the incongruence with their expected gender identity. This is particularly true as youth develop secondary sex characteristics, which create additional stressors for those transgender youth who are interested in "blending" or "passing" (i.e., attempting to appear cisgender). Adolescents who otherwise felt stable may now have to bind their developing breasts, for example, or may experience discomfort in developing facial hair, which can increasingly distance an adolescent from their authentic gender identity. It is during this time that counselors may have increasing sessions with parents or guardians, to support, provide education, and, ultimately, foster a safe and supportive environment at home. However, it is also important for counselors to remember that not all clients present and work through gender in the same way. Therefore, it is imperative counselors work with adolescents to learn from *them* what challenges they face, their sources of resilience, and how they want to navigate their gender (remembering that not all transgender adolescents are in counseling to work on gender-related concepts).

Young Adults

Young adults often experience a combination of life changes: moving to a new school, starting a new job, adjusting to new social supports, or changes in support by parents or guardians. As young adults increasingly enter social spaces, they may experience discrimination, marginalization, and stigma, and counselors must be prepared to process and validate these experiences, while empowering, problem-solving, and advocating for and with clients. Young adults may also experience new and/or changing romantic or non-romantic partnerships and bonds. Counselors working with young adults must have knowledge of the types of partnerships and bonds, including consensual nonmonogamous or polyamorous relationships. *Polyamory* refers to relationships or bonds with multiple partners. At this stage, counselors must also understand transgender clients' unique experiences with autonomy and being considered legal adults.

Historical Pathologizing

Counselors must recognize the long history of gender-related pathologizing in the medical and psychiatric communities. Not too long ago (in the 1980s), Gender Identity Disorder (GID) was added to the *Diagnostic and Statistical Manual of Mental Disorders* (*DSM*; Houssayni & Nilsen, 2018). This diagnosis was given to clients who presented with an incongruence with their gender identity and their SAAB. In the most recent version of the *DSM* (Fifth Edition; *DSM-5*; American Psychiatric Association, 2013), there has been a movement toward de-pathologizing gender diversity, and clients can now be diagnosed with gender dysphoria (Houssayni & Nilsen, 2018). Remember that transgender and gender-diverse clients may or may not present with gender dysphoria, and counselors should recognize when the diagnosis of gender dysphoria is required for other treatments. For example, a client who identifies as a transman may present to counseling to work through trauma or interpersonal issues unrelated to gender; the a counselor must meet the client where they are without assumptions. These concepts are important to note for counselors working with children and adolescents, who may already feel disempowered and disenfranchised. Working through an affirmative counseling lens, it is important to have shared discussions of social and historical discrimination against transgender people and how this might affect young transgender clients (Chang et al., 2018).

Navigating Privacy and Confidentiality

Balancing the needs of the client and the therapeutic relationship with a legal obligation to parents/guardians is an additional unique challenge when working with transgender youth. First and foremost, counselors must honor and empower clients. It is also important to remember the legal obligation to parents or guardians if the client is under the age of consent (ACA, 2014, Section B.5.b). This could be challenging, for example, if the family is unaware of the child's transgender identity and use male pronouns at home, while the client has requested for you to use female pronouns in the counseling session. This is one example of the unique, contextual nuances of working with transgender youth and their families. A counselor must balance promoting client autonomy and honoring the needs of the child (ACA, 2014) with understanding the needs, feelings, and reality for parents or guardians. The following example outlines dialogue between a counselor and client addressing this situation.

> **Counselor:** As you know, we are meeting with your parents later in the session—I know you have mentioned your parents do not use your name or pronouns at home. I want you to be comfortable, but I also want you to know I am here to advocate for and with you, however that looks.
> **Client**: I know... I think it's best if you just call me my birth name for today's meeting. Honestly, they probably won't be able to talk about it if I use my authentic name.
> **Counselor**: They may be resistant to hearing information, in general. My hope is to provide a safe space so they can have their concerns heard and validated. I will also have separate sessions with them, to

provide them more education on how they can better support you at home. But ultimately, your safety is my primary concern.
Client: I get it. It's an uphill battle—but they will probably listen to you more than they listen to me. I just want them to hear it from someone "official."
Counselor: I want you to know that we will work towards a place of shared understanding and respect with your family—it may not be easy, but I will be here for support, and we will always problem-solve together to determine what to do.

Exploring Relationships and Feelings

Transgender people, particularly transgender youth, navigate a "coming out" process, through identity development, and eventually "reveal" their authentic selves to others. Although this can be empowering and an important step in healthy development, youth are often invalidated when they come out as transgender to parents. Often, parents might think their child is too young to know their gender and may worry about the welfare and safety of their child (Russell & Fish, 2016). Counselors may wish to work with families separately, providing support and psychoeducation. Often underlying parents' anger and confusion is fear for their child, and this should be explored and validated. Concurrently, it is important to both validate and support the client, while also providing alternative perspectives, helping to negotiate the feelings of both client and parents (Salpietro et al., 2019). Counselors work with clients and their families to navigate coming out to extended family members and friends, at work, and at school (Russell & Fish, 2016). While there are biological processes linked to gender identity development, much of the process is influenced by caregivers, their responses, and a transgender child's access to resources (Katz-Wise et al., 2017).

Advocating for Change

As we previously discussed (see the preceding section, "Creating an Advocacy Agenda"), it is important for counselors to take action and advocate for their clients when they encounter barriers to healthcare, inequities at work and schools, or systemic discrimination. First, counselors work with clients to find out what their rights are as transgender people, under the law (ACLU, 2021; NCTE, 2021). Counselors working with transgender youth and adolescents must work within systems where they collaborate with school counselors and families to best support the client. An integral part of advocacy is visibility and representation. Counselors should promote and engage in agency- or community-wide programming. *The Day of Silence*, for example, is a national student-led initiative where people all across the world take a vow of silence to protest discrimination against queer and transgender people Gay, Lesbian, and Straight EducationNetwork (GLSEN, n.d.). *Solidarity Week* (historically called *Ally Week*) centers advocacy, awareness, support, and visibility for transgender and queer people, and highlights intersecting identities, specifically Black, Indigenous, and Persons of Color (BIPOCs; GLSEN, n.d.; Henry & Grubbs, 2016).

Increasing visibility and highlighting transgender people and relationships as normative and healthy is important in reducing stigma and increasing understanding. Emerging research highlights a relationship between having personal relationships with transgender people and feeling more competent and comfortable to work with transgender clients in a clinical setting (Salpietro et al., 2019).

COUNSELING ADULTS, COUPLES, AND FAMILIES

While gender identity is developed at a young age (Olson & Gülgöz, 2018), a majority of transgender people do not begin affirming gender through social or medical transitioning until they are adults, with most indicating that they began transitioning between the ages of 18 and 24 (James et al., 2016). Whether they are currently living as their gendered self or considering a physical or social transition, transgender adults may need assistance in navigating various stages of life, including social relationships and experiences, employment and career concerns, education, identity, family development and maintenance, intimacy, or other relevant psychological concerns. Being a transgender person can have a significant impact on development across the life span as a result of discrimination and oppression. Counselors should be knowledgeable about how negative social beliefs, such as cisnormativity and transmisia, affect the different areas of transgender peoples' development. Utilization of a developmental approach when working with transgender people can ensure positive identity development across the life span. While we chose to highlight one approach, please note that other approaches and models could be equally efficacious.

The Gender Affirmative Lifespan Approach (GALA) is a psychotherapy framework that utilizes therapeutic interventions aimed at combating internalized oppression in nonbinary clients (Rider et al., 2019). The authors of the framework postulate that addressing internalized oppression can lead to positive mental health outcomes, and therefore offer improvement in health and well-being (Rider et al., 2019). The GALA framework addresses the complexity of gender health across the life span and is grounded in five philosophical foundations and five core components. Although this model was created for use with nonbinary clients (non-cisgender and binary transgender people, i.e., male-to-female [MTF], female-to-male [FTM]), we feel it can be an inclusive framework for work with all transgender and gender-diverse clients. The five philosophical foundations of GALA are: (a) transgender-affirmative care; (b) intersectionality; (c) transparency; (d) developmental differences in care across the life span; and (e) an interdisciplinary approach. *Transgender-affirmative care* refers to the centering of transgender voices and experiences in healthcare, and gender navigated as an identity as opposed to a disorder. Clinicians must acknowledge and integrate intersectionality in their practice, attending to culture, age, ability status, class, affectional and sexual identities, and other relevant client identities and experiences. In sum, counselors must be attuned to the various factors of their clients' identities and how these factors ffect client experiences. For example, a Latinx transwoman who uses a wheelchair faces specific and unique barriers that must be understood by a counselor. In addition to discrimination due to having a non-cisgender identity and identifying as a nondominant racial/ethnic identity (Latinx), this client may face additional barriers because of their ability/disability status.

Transparency in the therapeutic relationship mitigates power differentials between clinician and client by equal sharing and accessibility (e.g., lacking clinical jargon) of information. The philosophical attention to developmental differences across the life span attends to the fluidity of gender identity and expression over time, and the intentional selection of interventions based on the developmental age of the client (e.g., child, adolescent, adult, elder). Critical to competent care for nonbinary and transgender clients is an interdisciplinary approach that promotes interaction across disciplines to ensure continuity of care. The philosophical foundations of GALA inform the core components of the framework. The five core components of GALA include: (a) developing gender literacy; (b) building resiliency; (c) moving beyond the binary; (d) exploring pleasure-oriented positive sexuality; and (e) making positive connections to medical interventions. The core components guide the primary topics for clinical application and intervention and were developed as a way for clinicians to enact the philosophical foundations. Developing gender literacy involves helping clients identify how a binary view of gender leads to societal oppression and discrimination, and that gender expression and identity are not defined by one's body. Clinicians help build resiliency by encouraging clients to find and create safe spaces, identify support systems, and develop coping skills. Clinicians and clients move beyond the binary by accepting and celebrating all gender identities and expressions. Therapeutic intervention surrounding pleasure-oriented positive sexuality promotes healthy gender and sexual development. Clinicians should also be able to make appropriate referrals to medical interventions and be knowledgeable of different medical interventions and affirmative providers.

Older Adults

Counselors must be knowledgeable about the unique experiences of transgender older adults and be able to help clients address barriers and build resilience. Transgender older adults are a highly marginalized population (Fredriksen-Goldsen et al., 2014) as they experience the intersection of transmisia and ageism, leading to an overall lack of information about the population. Many transgender older adults aged during decades in which transgender identities were "heavily stigmatized and pathologized," leading some to hide their gender identity and transition later in life (Auldridge et al., 2012, p. 1). Transgender older adults are at a higher risk for poor physical health, disability, depressive symptoms, and perceived stress when compared to cisgender LGB older adults (Fredriksen-Goldsen et al., 2014). They also reported more lifetime incidences of discrimination, including verbal insults, threats of physical assault, and employment and healthcare discrimination, as well as limited social supports and higher rates of internalized stigma (Fredriksen-Goldsen et al., 2014). Transgender older adults are fearful of accessing healthcare due to fear of discrimination by providers or internalized stigma (Fredriksen-Goldsen et al., 2014; James et al., 2016). Even when transgender older adults decide to access healthcare, they may face financial and insurance barriers. Unemployment rates for transgender people are three times higher than the U.S. national average (James et al., 2016), resulting in disparities in health insurance access and affordability of care (Fredriksen-Goldsen et al., 2014; Persson, 2009). Discrimination and disparities in access to care are especially alarming, as transgender older adults who accessed gender-affirming care were more likely to report a high quality of life compared to those who did not receive care (Cai et al., 2019). Competent counselors are able to advocate on behalf of their transgender older adult clients and will need to be able to collaborate effectively with other medical providers and caregivers to ensure optimal health. Counselors should be familiar with transgender-specific healthcare and prepared to address misconceptions that one is too old for transgender-affirming care. Older adults may need additional assistance navigating experiences with transmisia and coming out, especially if they chose to physically transition later in life, as visual and auditory cues may limit their ability to control who they come out to. Helping transgender older adults identify safe spaces and people is a vital component of counseling, as transgender older adults may have limited options due to medical or financial restrictions (e.g., need for assisted living, in-home caregivers). Counselors should be familiar with local gerontological providers that are affirming and be prepared to educate providers on the unique needs of transgender older adults.

Couples

Transgender partners may present to counseling for a myriad of issues, and counselors should recognize that issues may be unrelated to one or more of the partners' gender identities. They may need help managing common concerns that couples report, including parenting, intimacy, and finances (Lev, 2004). Couples may also present to counseling to better deal with concerns that develop because of incessant discrimination, stigma, and multiple stressors related to their identities. In these cases, counselors should focus on how societal influences may have affected the couple's presenting concerns, but not make the partner's gender identity the focal point of counseling (Giammattei, 2015).

Transgender couples present in many different configurations of gender identities and ASIs. All partners may identify as transgender or gender nonconforming, and the ASIs of partners may remain constant or shift through transition or the course of their life span. Transgender partners may or may not transition physically, and therefore their gender identity may be visible or invisible. Gender identity may have been known before the onset of the relationship, or a partner could be coming out within the relationship.

When couples present for issues related to partner gender identity, it is important for counselors to understand the unique challenges and strengths that couples with a transgender partner may experience to provide competent care and reduce harm. Additionally, counselors must understand the diversity of gender and sexuality and the impact of cisnormativity, heteronormativity, and transmisia on individuals and society. As identified by Giammattei (2015), issues related to safety, coming out, and redefining the relationship may be prevalent in couples counseling.

Safety

Transgender people experience shocking amounts of violence and discrimination in public and intimate settings, and the effects of this violence may have to be addressed in couples counseling. A national study of transgender people found that in the past year, 48% of respondents reported that they were "denied equal treatment or services, verbally harassed, and/or physically attacked because of being transgender" (James et al., 2016, p. 199). Transgender people are at a higher risk for negative interactions in public if their gender identity is visible or they are perceived by others to be transgender (James et al., 2016). Partners of transgender people have reported fear for their physical safety (Motter & Softas-Nall, 2021; Platt & Bolland, 2018), which may affect decisions to go out in public or disclose gender identity to others (Platt & Bolland, 2018). Counselors should help couples develop safety plans and identify safe spaces, communities, and people. Interventions may include having the couple inform others of when and where they are going or familiarizing themselves with an area prior to going (e.g., knowing the exits, location of non-gendered public restrooms).

Interpersonal safety may also become a concern when working with couples with a transgender partner. Fifty-four percent of transgender people reported that they experienced some form of intimate partner violence (IPV) in their lifetime (James et al., 2016). Transgender people of color and individuals with disabilities are more likely to experience IPV (James et al., 2016). From 2013 to 2020, 85% of transgender people who were murdered were people of color and 78% were transgender women of color and a significant portion of these murders were IPV (HRC, 2021b). In 2020, nearly 70% of transgender persons who were murdered were killed by an acquaintance, friend, family member, or intimate partner (HRC, 2021b). Nearly half of the respondents reported IPV that involved coercive control, such as intimidation or emotional abuse (James et al., 2016). Microaggressions from partners are reported by transgender people, including microaggressions that minimize their identity, project gendered expectations, misgender, or question the status of their relationship (Pulice-Farrow et al., 2017). It is important that counselors screen partners separately to assess for IPV before the onset of couples counseling. Microaggressions or other abusive behaviors should be addressed in counseling and individual safety plans should be created as needed.

Coming Out

The coming-out process for a transgender person in a relationship presents both challenges and celebrations for the individual and their partner(s). Counselors should be prepared to navigate the needs of all partners individually and conjointly. The transgender partner may be acknowledging their gender identity for the first time, or their gender identity could be known, but they are now choosing to come out or transition socially (Giammattei, 2015). Partners of transgender people may feel confused, hurt, or betrayed, shifting between anger and denial (Giammattei, 2015; Lev, 2004). Partners may also experience strong emotions related to grief, loss, or pain (Motter & Softas-Nall, 2021) and counselors should be prepared to help partners navigate these feelings. Counselors should help the transgender partner clearly communicate their gender identity and needs to their partner(s), as well as what their gender identity may mean for the couple (Lev, 2004; Malpas, 2012). All partners must decide whether they can support each other through the potential changes. Couples with a transgender partner who chose to physically transition have reported improved communication, affirming sexual relationships, support from communities and loved ones, passing privilege, and improved awareness of social issues (Motter & Softas-Nall, 2021). Counselors should focus on helping couples learn effective communication strategies and consider integrating role-playing techniques to help transgender clients and their partner(s) communicate with each other and other important people in their lives.

Redefining the Relationship

Relationship dynamics are likely to shift when a partner comes out as transgender, especially if they are medically transitioning. Counselors will need to address concerns related to the ASIs of partners, intimacy, and social experiences. It is not uncommon for all partners to have a shift in how they label their ASI when one partner is transgender (Malpas, 2012; Platt & Bolland, 2018). In these situations, counselors must be open to a spectrum of identities, and must be aware of their own heteronormative and gender role expectations; counselors must not assume ASIs based on heteronormativity (Giammattei, 2015). Partners may decide to continue a sexual relationship, decide to pursue only a romantic relationship, or explore nonmonogamous experiences; counselors should help couples communicate and define their sexual or affectional desires (Malpas, 2012; Motter & Softas-Nall, 2021). Couples with a transgender partner may have to adapt to changes in their social experiences, including relationships with others and social privilege. The couple may experience the loss of relationships with families and friends or membership in communities (e.g., a formally cisgender lesbian couple in which one partner identifies as transmale; Motter & Softas-Nall, 2021; Platt & Bolland, 2018). Couples may also struggle to label their relationship as their identities shift (Motter & Softas-Nall, 2021). Depending on the gender and ASIs of partners, a partner's transition may result in a loss of heteronormative and cisnormative privilege, or the acquisition of passing privilege (Giammattei, 2015; Malpas, 2012; Motter & Softas-Nall, 2021). This may be perceived as a benefit of transition by couples, with some reporting that it led to more familial acceptance or resulted in increased concerns over safety (Motter & Softas-Nall, 2021; Platt & Bolland, 2018).

Families

Familial acceptance and support have a significant influence on the health and well-being of transgender people; therefore, it is important to engage families when counseling transgender people. A majority of transgender people (60%) report that their families are generally supportive of their transgender identity (James et al., 2016). Those who indicated support from their family were less likely to experience homelessness, attempt suicide, or experience significant psychological distress (James et al., 2016). Familial rejection is associated with poorer outcomes related to housing, economic stability, and attempted suicide (James et al., 2016). Transgender people who were rejected by their immediate family were two times more likely to have experienced homelessness and engaged in sex work, especially Black and Latinx transgender women. Additionally, they were more likely to have tried to kill themselves (49%) than transgender people who were not rejected (33%; James et al., 2016). It is essential to note the disproportionate amount of discrimination and marginalization of transgender POC, particularly Black transwomen, who experience higher rates of rejection, discrimination, overt abuse, assault, and suicide (HRC, 2021c; Whitman & Han, 2017).

Just as with couples, the composition of families can be diverse. Families can consist of parents, siblings, grandparents, or other close relatives or nonrelatives. Counselors may also find themselves working with the family of a child or adolescent who is transgender. Sometimes, families can present for counseling to seek support for a parent or adult family member who is transgender. Families of transgender people may present to counseling due to the distress of the transgender family member, distress of family members, or both.

Regardless of whether the transgender person in the family is a child, an adolescent, or an adult, counselors must first assess familial acceptance, support, and/or opposition to the transgender family member's gender identity and expression (Coolhart & Shipman, 2017). Ensuring a safe space for transgender people is vital, and if family members are not affirming, separate sessions may be required in the beginning stages of counseling (Coolhart & Shipman, 2017). As acceptance and safety are established, counselors will often have to take on an educative role when working with families, including educating parents and other family members about gender identity, expression, and gender-affirming interventions. This may involve deconstructing various social constructs (e.g., the binary conceptualization of gender), providing guidance on affirming language, and highlighting the stress, oppression, and discrimination transgender people experience. For example, a parent may struggle with using their child's authentic pronouns and may misgender their child at home or in the counseling office. Counselors should provide safe spaces for families to learn about the importance of using proper pronouns, as this reduces suicide and leads to increased well-being (Durwood et al., 2017). Counselors must decide if sharing relevant scholarly, scientific data and/or published literature with families will support the therapeutic process and their transgender clients. Using information from the United States Transgender Survey (2015), for example, may elucidate for parents the extreme mistreatment of and violence toward transgender people, and the harmful effects on physical and mental health (James et al., 2016). Additionally, counselors should understand and validate the difficulty for some parents, as they may have their core beliefs challenged, feel isolated, must learn a new language, and may feel the loss of a role as a parent to their child (O'Doherty, 2018). As your transgender clients spend most of their lives outside the counseling environment, it is essential to support and strengthen a client's social support system (whether that is their family, friends, coworkers, etc.). Themes of grief and loss are prominent in family counseling (Harper & Singh, 2014), and counselors should be prepared to make appropriate referrals and hold space for the emotional responses of family members (Giammattei, 2015). Referrals for parents may include individual counseling, couples counseling for parents, or support groups for families of transgender people (Giammattei, 2015).

IMPLICATIONS FOR CLINICAL PRACTICE

Intentionality

Counselors who work with transgender clients are required to intentionally seek out specific training for transgender-specific issues and must stay current with changing terminology and societal trends, legal and ethical issues, and affirming best practices (Salpietro et al., 2019). Additionally, informal, personal experiences with transgender people foster better relationships with transgender clients in counseling sessions (Salpietro et al., 2019). Counselors should seek to learn from transgender-identifying people who have lived experience when possible; and invite transgender people to serve on local committees, task forces, and advisory boards. Counselors should also be familiar with competencies and best practices for counseling transgender people.

Consultation, Supervision, and Referrals

Counselors are guided by ethical codes which admonish counselors to not practice outside the bounds of their competence (ACA, 2014, Section C.2.a). Counselors must consult with other counselors who have had more experience working with transgender clients. If seeking supervision, counselors must first determine if the supervisor is competent and knowledgeable (this can be accomplished through prior questions). Counselors must work with allied mental health professionals, medical providers, and community organizations, and should model using affirming and inclusive language of transgender people and issues (e.g., pronouns, names, nuanced terms).

Inclusive Practices

Counselors can engage in advocacy and create a safe space for transgender clients by ensuring inclusivity in their practice. Intake and other relevant forms should be gender-affirming and free of cisnormativity and heteronormativity, by creating open-ended questions that do not pose a dichotomy (e.g., male/female). Forms should also have spaces for clients to indicate their pronouns and their chosen name. Counselors can create transgender-affirmative physical spaces in many ways, including the visibility of transgender flags or stickers, literature in the waiting room created by or for transgender people, and offering gender-neutral or all-gender restrooms. Counselors should also advocate for policies that are affirming of transgender people, including those that prohibit discrimination based on gender identity or expression.

Social Supports

As transgender people are often marginalized and ostracized, an important part of treatment, healing, and growth is helping transgender clients establish (and possibly rebuild) healthy relationships and navigate unhealthy ones. Social support is a strong protective factor for transgender people, and counselors should work with clients to facilitate and strengthen family relationships, if appropriate (Ginicola et al., 2017). Counselors provide psychoeducation, facilitate divergent perspectives in session, promote client assertiveness, and help connect families and clients to other transgender families (Salpietro et al., 2019). Counselors should connect transgender clients to local community transgender-affirming organizations and/or support groups (see "Creating an Advocacy Agenda" section). When connecting clients to resources, it is important to make sure they are current and accessible.

CLINICAL CASE SCENARIO 12.1

Carson, a counselor-in-training, is beginning his field placement work at a local mental health agency, seeing clients with a variety of presenting issues. When his first client of the day, Max, age 17, enters the room, Carson begins his usual discussion of informed consent, confidentiality, and the initial assessment. After some time, Max admits that he has been out of his home for 2 weeks after his parents kicked him out for coming out as transgender. He reports he has been staying at a friend's house, with people coming in and out of the house, through all times of the day and night. He also shares that he has been self-harming to release some of his pain. In the session, Carson uses active listening, reflection, and validation skills, but is unsure where to go from there. Carson has not had experience working with transgender clients and urges the client to reconcile with his parents so that he can be in a "safe home." Carson also asks Max to give him all the items he uses to cut himself before leaving. Max leaves the session feeling invalidated and misunderstood, feeling as if Carson lacks comfort, confidence, and skills in working with transgender clients. Carson returns to his office and consults with his supervisor. He realizes he has much more to learn about working with transgender clients and wants to learn more about the lived experiences and historical marginalization of transgender people to better support them. His supervisor informs him of the importance of safety and security and reminds Carson of the statistics for suicidality among transgender youth, especially if they are not supported at home. They also discuss the unique nuances in working with a minor client and balancing the needs of the client with those of their parents and/or guardians. They develop a plan to reconnect with Max, provide additional resources, establish effective coping responses, and work toward repairing the therapeutic relationship in a collaborative way.

CLINICAL CASE SCENARIO DISCUSSION QUESTIONS

1. What things did Carson do well with Max?
2. In what ways were Carson's recommendations and interventions culturally insensitive?
3. How could Carson have practiced cultural humility and empathy?

END-OF-CHAPTER RESOURCES

A robust set of instructor resources designed to supplement this text is located at http://connect.springerpub.com/content/book/978-0-8261-3953-5. Qualifying instructors may request access by emailing **textbook@springerpub.com**.

SUMMARY

This chapter highlights the diverse, persistent challenges faced by transgender and gender-diverse people throughout the life span, and how these challenges deeply influence health, life-functioning, and help-seeking behaviors. The chapter stresses the importance of counselor self-reflection and exploration of strongly held beliefs, in service of transgender clients. Readers learn about affirming, celebratory, and liberating counseling approaches that promote resilience and strength with transgender youth through older adults. Additionally, this chapter discusses the importance and impact of systems such as families, schools, and partnerships/relationships, and how to navigate complex situations with minors and legal guardians. Lasty, this chapter highlights important factors of intersectionality (race/ethnicity, age, social class, ability status) and how these factors affect a client and the client–counselor relationship.

DISCUSSION QUESTIONS

1. What are three ways you can stay up to date with current trends, issues, and best practices in working with transgender clients?
2. How might you navigate a situation in which you have disapproving and invalidating family members of a minor child, who insist you tell them if their child expresses any ideas about their gender?
3. How would you work with an older adult, who is coming to terms with their gender identity, and wants your help in coming out to their current partner and family?
4. Why is it important to address societal stigma, discrimination, and oppression with transgender clients?
5. What are some creative interventions you might use with transgender children or adolescents who may not feel comfortable with talk therapy?

  CULTURALLY RESPONSIVE COUNSELING FOR TRANSGENDER CLIENTS

Guest: Dr. Clark D. Ausloos

https://connect.springerpub.com/content/book/978-0-8261-3953-5/part/part02/chapter/ch12

KEY REFERENCES

Only key references appear in the print edition. The full reference list appears in the digital product on Springer Publishing Connect: https://connect.springerpub.com/content/book/978-0-8261-3953-5/part/part02/chapter/ch12

Ausloos, C. (in press). LGBTQI+ affirmative counseling. In S. Dermer & J. Abdullah (Eds.), *The SAGE encyclopedia of multicultural counseling, social justice, and advocacy*. SAGE.

Ginicola, M. M., Smith, C., & Filmore, J. M. (Eds.). (2017). *Affirmative counseling with LGBTQI+ people*. https://doi.org/10.1002/9781119375517

Henry, H. L., & Grubbs, L. (2016). Best practices for school counselors working with transgender students. *Ideas and Research You Can Use: VISTAS 2017*, 1–20. https://www.counseling.org/docs/default-source/vistas/article_4557cd2bf16116603abcacff0000bee5e7.pdf?sfvrsn=6

James, S. E., Herman, J. L., Rankin, S., Keisling, M., Mottet, L., & Anafi, M. (2016). *The report of the 2015 U.S. transgender survey*. https://transequality.org/sites/default/files/docs/usts/USTS-Full-Report-Dec17.pdf

Killermann, S. (2017). *A guide to gender: The social justice advocate's handbook* (2nd ed.). Impetus Books.

Kosciw, J. G., Greytak, E. A., Zongrone, A. D., Clark, C. M., & Truong, N. L. (2018). *The 2017 national school climate survey: The experiences of lesbian, gay, bisexual, transgender, and queer youth in our nation's schools*. Gay, Lesbian, and Straight Education Network. https://files.eric.ed.gov/fulltext/ED590243.pdf

Nealy, E. C. (2017). *Transgender children and youth: Cultivating pride and joy with families in transition*. W. W. Norton.

Ratts, M. J., Singh, A. A., Nassar-McMillan, S., Butler, S. K., & McCullough, J. R. (2016). Multicultural and social justice counseling competencies: Guidelines for the counseling profession. *Journal of Multicultural Counseling and Development*, 44(1), 28–48. https://doi.org/10.1002/jmcd.12035

Salpietro, L., Ausloos, C., & Clark, M. (2019). Cisgender professional counselors' experiences with trans* clients. *Journal of LGBT Issues in Counseling*, 13(3), 198–215. https://doi.org/10.1080/15538605.2019.1627975

Toporek, R. L., & Daniels. (2018). *American Counseling Association advocacy competencies*. American Counseling Association. https://www.counseling.org/docs/default-source/competencies/aca-advocacy-competencies-updated-may-2020.pdf

CHAPTER 13

Culturally Responsive Counseling for Women Clients

NATALIE ARCE INDELICATO

> ### LEARNING OBJECTIVES
>
> After reading this chapter, students will be able to:
> - Identify examples of gender disparities related to mental and physical health, educational attainment, and wage earnings across development.
> - Define concepts such as gender identity, gender expression, and gender-affirming counseling.
> - Summarize ways in which gender intersects with other identities to affect mental health and wellness.
> - Recognize empowerment and advocacy strategies to implement with women clients.

> ### SELF-REFLECTION QUESTIONS
>
> 1. Think about biases, prejudices, and assumptions you might have about women clients. How do these help and hinder your ability to provide culturally sensitive counseling?
> 2. What hesitancies, if any, do you have about working with women clients?
> 3. What attributes do you have that will enable you to work with women clients?

THE COUNSELOR: EXPLORATION, INTROSPECTION, AND REFLECTION

Gender disparities related to mental health, educational attainment, career satisfaction, and wage earnings arise in large part as an outcome of sexism (World Health Organization [WHO], n.d.), and mental health consequences of sexism occur across race and ethnicity, age, and nationality. Counselors who practice with cultural humility understand the limitations of their worldviews due to cultural conditioning, historical and thriving systems of oppression, and sociopolitical contexts. This extends to their understanding of the role that gender and sexism play in their lives, the lives of their clients, and how these factors affect the therapeutic relationship. Counselors must be aware of their attitudes and beliefs about women who are cisgender, transgender, and gender nonconforming as a critical step in providing culturally responsive, nonsexist, gender-affirming care.

What does culturally responsive, nonsexist, gender-affirming counseling look like? It is mental health care, focused on working with clients to identify their strengths, increase awareness of their gendered identities, and become change agents in their own lives and in the lives of others. Counselors using this approach work toward social justice, improved well-being, and equity for all people, while also recognizing the impact of sociopolitical forces on mental health and challenging the status quo related to gender. Providing culturally responsive counseling for women clients means centering the client's experiences related to gender and gender expression, sexism, and sociopolitical factors, and working to critically analyze cultural influences on thoughts, feelings, and behaviors (Substance Abuse and Mental Health Services Administration [SAMHSA], 2014). Additionally, as counselors we must intentionally create space for the multiple and intersecting identities that clients bring to counseling by knowing and noticing racial, class, gender, ability, and race/ethnic advantages and disadvantages. It means intentionally asking clients which identities are salient for them and how those inform their lives. It means seeking peer supervision and consultation, engaging in personal counseling, journaling, and conducting periodic gender and power analyses of one's life to stay connected to one's values and assumptions concerning gender and power. In practice, it helps inform therapeutic interventions and increases empathy for counselors who are working with women who have perspectives and experiences different from their own.

CONCEPTS OF GENDER IDENTITY AND GENDER EXPRESSION CONTINUUM AND GENDER IDENTITY MODELS

Gender refers to the characteristics of women, men, girls, and boys that are socially constructed, including norms, behaviors, and roles (WHO, n.d.). The term *gender* is often used to emphasize that social learning and social context are important influences on what cultures define as "male" and "female." Gender and gender identity represent complex constructs that have vacillated over time.

Sex refers to the biological characteristics distinguishing male and female that are assigned at birth (American Psychological Association, 2018), which include biological differences in chromosomes, anatomy, hormones, reproductive systems, and physiology (Lindsey, 2015). *Gender* refers to social, cultural, and psychological differences between males and females that are socially constructed and associated with masculinity and femininity. To simplify, sex is the biological assignment of male or female, while gender is the socialized masculine or feminine characteristics (Lindsey, 2015).

Cisgender refers to individuals whose gender identity and/or expression matches the sex they were assigned at birth (Tate et al., 2015), and the term *transgender* broadly describes individuals who self-identify with a gender other than that assigned to them at birth (American Psychological Association, 2015). These terms are deeply rooted in a gender binary, which inadequately represents the vast spectrum of gender identities embraced by individuals. In recent years, there have been calls to reject the gender binary, or the idea that males and females must be classified into two distinct, oppositional categories defined as masculine or feminine (Bittner & Goodyear-Grant, 2017). Gender is now often described as nonbinary and fluid, viewed on a continuum of characteristics people may act on regardless of their biological sex (Lindsey, 2015).

The term *transgender and gender nonconforming* (TGNC) has been used to describe individuals who do not adhere to societal pressures to conform to gender norms and roles. *Transgender* is a term that refers to persons whose gender identity is different from that normatively expected based on assigned sex (American Psychological Association, 2015). The term *nonbinary* (also known as gender-expansive, gender creative, gender independent, genderqueer, bigender, and/or agender) is used to refer to gender-nonconforming people who may not identify with a male/female binary system of gender categorization, or a person whose gender identity and/or gender expression is outside of what is expected based on assigned sex, but may be more complex, fluid, multifaceted, or otherwise less clearly defined than a transgender person (American Psychological Association, 2015). Approximately 25% to 35% of TGNC individuals identify as nonbinary or gender nonconforming, indicating a gender identity and/or expression outside of the dichotomous male/female binary (James et al., 2016).

As early as 1968, Robert Stroller coined the term *gender identity*, and claimed that individuals experience threats to their gender identity as a threat to their overall sense of self. In other words, when a person's gender identity is challenged or insulted (e.g., a man being told he has a "feminine handshake" or a woman being told that she is "manly"), it can threaten their sense of self. This often happens to individuals who are gender nonconforming who often feel forced to select binary categories in daily life (e.g., "male" versus "female" on a job application). Individuals can identify as both transgender in identity and expansive or fluid in gender expression. For example, a person who was assigned male at birth has a gender identity of a girl and gender expression consisting of mainly those ascribed as masculine, that is, a masculine trans girl. Ty is a good example. Assigned male at birth, Ty, then Tyler, knew she was born in a body that did not match her gender, and by age 14 was living in her affirmed gender identity—a girl. She maintained her short hair and masculine-style clothes as she lived her life as a girl named Ty.

Like gender identity development, gender roles can fluctuate over the course of a person's development. Gender roles are societal expectations based on gender for the way a person should behave, speak, dress, and interact in the world. Every society and cultural group has gender role expectations, and they can vary from group to group. Gender roles are performed according to social norms, which are shared rules that guide people's behavior in specific situations. For example, girls and women are generally expected to be nice, nurturing, caretaking, and emotionally expressive, while boys and men are generally expected to be strong, aggressive, risk-taking, and emotionally withdrawn. Research has shown that children are aware of gender roles by age two or three and can label others' gender and sort objects into gendered categories (Martin & Ruble, 2010). By kindergarten, most children are well-aware of and subscribe to culturally appropriate gender roles (Meland & Kaltvedt, 2019). They may face negative consequences such as being criticized, bullied, marginalized, or rejected by their peers when they do not conform. A boy who takes dance classes instead of playing sports or a girl who plays with trucks instead of dolls may be ridiculed and face difficulty gaining acceptance from peer groups. Boys tend to be subject to more intense ridicule for gender nonconformity than girls (Kreis, 2019). According to O'Neil (2015), men's gender role conflict is a psychological state where limiting definitions of masculinity restrict men's well-being and human potential, and lead to behavioral problems such as sexism, violence, homophobia, depression, substance abuse, career dissatisfaction, and relationship issues. He argued that gender role conflict does not just harm boys and men, but also girls and women, TGNC people, and society at large due to its direct and indirect effects.

Sexism is the belief that the status of women is inferior to the status of men (Lindsey, 2015). Sexism is reinforced in systems of patriarchy, male-dominated social structures, leading to the oppression of women. Patriarchy values male-centered norms throughout social institutions and becomes the standard by which all persons are expected to abide. Although men are not impervious to the negative consequences of sexism, women and TGNC individuals are more likely to experience its negative effects.

IDENTITIES, INTERSECTIONS, AND GENDER

Understanding the influence of how gender shapes our client's lives, attitudes, and behavior, as well as our own, is critical to culturally responsive practice. This understanding is enhanced by integrating key concepts such as race, social class, sexuality, religion, ability, and other salient identities and statuses along with gender. This idea is known as intersectionality (Crenshaw, 1989). Intersectionality is grounded in the work of Black feminist thought (Collins, 2000; Lewis et al., 2018), and describes how interrelated systems of oppression intersect to marginalize individuals (Crenshaw, 1989). Intersectionality is pivotal to understanding gender patterns in counseling. Attention to intersectionality is central to developing counseling interventions that consider the multiple oppressions of people with distinctive combinations of disadvantages based on gender, race, and social class (Hancock, 2016). Intersectionality is focused on exploring the ways that systemic, institutional, and structural oppression and privilege affect individuals and communities (Lewis et al., 2016). Additionally, there is a focus on individual- and community-level transformation through social action. Researchers have pointed to acknowledging the role of intersectionality as an important component of radical healing in communities of color (French et al., 2020). While race, class, and gender have been the basis for intersectionality inquiry, inquiry and research on intersectionality continue to expand to examine additional salient identities, such as sexuality, ethnicity, religion, and ability.

Intersectionality in feminist theory explains how interrelated categories help define a person's identity and status (American Psychological Association, 2017). While some categories, such as Whiteness, come with advantages or privileges, others, such as poverty, come with risks. For example, when the issue of poverty is only examined by gender—women are at increased risk of living in poverty compared with men—it ignores the interconnectedness between race, social class, health, age, employment, and education that puts certain women at higher risk than others (WHO, n.d.). For example, a 30-something-year-old cisgender White woman living in poverty with no health issues and a high school diploma has different levels of risk and marginalization than an unemployed lesbian of color in her 60s with chronic health issues and housing instability. Black sexual minority women have been described as experiencing "triple jeopardy" on account of their multiply marginalized social status (Bowleg et al., 2003, p. 88). Therefore, to get a clearer picture of the client, the counselor must also consider other forms of oppression that the client faces that intersect with her gender. Attention to intersectionality highlights the privilege, which is the right to unearned benefits granted to specific people or groups, or lack of privilege that come with various identities. When White middle-class feminists focus on the oppression of women, they may not recognize the privileges that come with their race and class. Women are better served when interventions and counselor conceptualizations consider an intersectional approach. Attention to the diversity of women clients as it relates to their intersecting identities is a source of building the therapeutic relationship because it allows the client to be seen and understood as a whole, unique person. It highlights the notion that there is a synchronistic effect when multiple marginalized statuses are at play (Collins, 2000).

CLINICAL CONSIDERATIONS FOR COUNSELING

The identities of the counselor and client are salient aspects of the therapeutic relationship; therefore, counselors should be aware of how dynamics of race/ethnicity, gender, age, class status, ability level, and sexual orientation are at play within themselves as individuals, within the client, and in the interplay between the two. Providing affirmative therapy for girls and women and developing a strong therapeutic relationship requires the counselor to have a congruent sense of self, which involves awareness of negative or false beliefs about gender, gender identity, and gender expression. Counselors risk upholding dominant, damaging narratives of gender if this work is not prioritized. Cultural responsiveness begins with cultural humility. Both are the foundation to understanding our clients and the counselors' selves and providing support on a deeper level. Cultural humility is a continuum of inward self-awareness, outward valuing of others, and upward growth (Hook et al., 2013). To practice *cultural humility*, counselors must have both an accurate view of themselves and respect for others without an attitude of supremacy or superiority (Davis et al., 2011). It is an orientation that is based on self-reflexivity (i.e., reflecting on your own process as a counselor), appreciation of clients' expertise, and openness to sharing power with and learning from clients and others (e.g., colleagues, community members, friends; Lekas et al., 2020). It is like feminist approaches in that it is a career-long commitment to self-reflection, a lens by which the counselor views the world rather than a set of interventions to implement.

Culturally responsive counselors continually examine the counseling process, paying attention to potential bias and not inadvertently perpetuating the status quo or further marginalizing clients. Culturally responsive counseling requires empathy to truly understand and conceptualize how the client's social identities interact and influence the client's distress. Barriers to this practice include feelings of fear and inadequacy, subscribing to colorblindness, discomfort with emotionally charged conversations and conflict, and being polite. These clinical considerations are important when counseling girls and women because they serve to model for clients the value of self-examination and challenging gender stereotypes and roles.

MENTAL HEALTH DISPARITIES RELATED TO GENDER

Disparities in mental health disorders related to gender have been identified in regard to risk, prevalence, presentation, course of illness, and treatment (American Psychiatric Association, 2017). Gender affects critical determinants of mental health and health outcomes (WHO, n.d.) such as socioeconomic status, rates of interpersonal violence, and role-strain/caretaker responsibility. For example, higher risk and prevalence of sexual violence for women correspond to higher prevalence of trauma-associated mental health issues. Globally, women are approximately twice as likely to experience mental illness compared to men (WHO, n.d.). Researchers have found a significant correlation between gender inequality and gender disparities in mental health, often tied to a country's wealth such that gender inequality was associated with increased gender disparities in depressive disorders. Additionally, men suffered from more mental health problems compared with women when dealing with situations of high wealth inequality (Yu, 2018). Significant gender differences are consistently found to exist for depression, anxiety, and somatic complaints (WHO, n.d.). This is not independent of gender inequality in the prevalence of domestic violence, sexual abuse, unpaid caring work, higher hours of work, low social status, and lack of access to reproductive rights and education for women. Current patterns of morbidity and mortality in physical and emotional health show gender differences as narrowing for some behaviors (such as alcohol use, smoking, and sexuality), while diverging for suicide and violence, with women experiencing increased levels of both. Depression is almost twice as common among women versus men, and the proportion of adults with depression increased with decreasing family income levels (Brody et al., 2018).

Likewise, significantly more women are affected by eating disorders compared to men (T. A. Brown et al., 2020). The etiology of eating disorders is a combination of biology, psychology, and culture (Malson & Burns, 2009). Risk factors for eating disorders include having a relative with an eating disorder, chronic dieting, poor body image, anxiety disorder, bullying experiences related to weight, and having characteristics of perfectionism and rigidity (Bakalar et al., 2015). Eating disorders with onset in adolescence are reported for females of all racial groups (Cheng et al., 2019). Self-esteem is fragile during adolescence for girls of all races, and weight issues contribute to their insecurity. Anorexia has the highest mortality rate of any psychiatric disorder, and more than two-thirds of individuals do not seek mental health support (Arcelus et al., 2011). Cultural beliefs significantly influence the development of eating disorders, which are often described as culture-bound disorders, first associated with norms of dieting and rigid beauty ideals in American society (Banks, 1992).

Women experience sexual and physical violence at higher rates, which puts them at greater risk for mental health consequences (Marcus et al., 2012). Gender-based violence affects women at significantly higher rates than men and is highly predictive of the severity of negative mental health outcomes (WHO, n.d.) such as posttraumatic stress disorder (PTSD) and depression (Nathanson et al., 2012). Women wait an average of 4 years after the onset of PTSD symptoms before seeking help (Breslau, 2001) and develop PTSD after a traumatic event at a higher rate compared to men (Valentine et al., 2019).

Risk factors for common mental health issues that disproportionately affect women include wages, poverty rates, violence, and caregiver burden (American Psychiatric Association, 2017). Women who work full-time earn about 82 cents for every dollar that their male counterparts earn each year (Bleiweis, 2020), and women (11%) are more likely than men (8%) to live in poverty (U.S. Census Bureau, 2020). An estimated 60% of caregivers are women (AARP, 2020), and they spend 50% more time providing care than male caregivers (Sharma et al., 2016). The COVID-19 pandemic has increased the risk for women falling into poverty in the United States, as they face greater economic insecurity, due in large part to unprecedented unemployment that has disproportionately affected women (Shierholz, 2020).

The type of work women do is correlated to their health. For example, employed women and those with less traditional gender role orientation and higher gender equity have better physical and psychological health (WHO, n.d.). Professional women frequently describe their jobs as stressful, but workers in entry-level jobs are more likely to report stress-related illnesses such as insomnia and headaches. This pattern is often traced to cultural expectations for women to meet others' needs before their own (Baiocchi-Wagner & Olson, 2016). Associated with the Strong Black Woman Schema, this pattern is prevalent in women of color who are socialized for strength and resilience that valorize their caretaking at the expense of their well-being (Abrams et al., 2019). In *Black Macho and the Myth of the Superwoman* (Wallace, 1978), the author discusses how the representation of the strong Black woman can be detrimental to African American women's health and mental well-being, especially if the woman is faced with structural and systemic barriers that make it impossible to live up to the expectation of being resilient despite all obstacles. The cultural responsibility to show strength can contribute to lower rates of utilization of services among women of color (Neufeld et al., 2008); therefore, it is important for clinicians to inquire about these patterns and roles, as well as use innovative methods to reach women who have historically not engaged in or had access to self-care (i.e., individual practices of health and well-being) and help-seeking (C. Brown et al., 2010) practices. Although Black women are disproportionately affected by mental health disorders, there is a conflict between sharing feelings of being overwhelmed and needing help and the often-characterized strong Black woman (Abrams et al., 2014; Donovan & West, 2015). In counseling, it can be a difficult balance between recognizing the strengths of clients who subscribe to collectivistic ideas of caretaking, which emphasize the needs and goals of the group over the needs and desires of an individual, while also recognizing the potential negative mental health outcomes of an over-extended caretaker (Neufeld et al., 2008). According to Bryant-Davis and Comas-Díaz (2016), counselors should collaborate with clients to identify psychosocial needs, and then conduct self-care planning to promote healthy coping strategies such as reliance on social support systems. Additionally, integrating a womanist theoretical perspective and recognizing strength as both an asset and a liability, has the potential to increase the number of Black women who receive needed mental health support (Abrams et al., 2019).

Walker (1983) developed the term *Womanism* as a framework to address the intersections of identity for women of color. Womanism acknowledges and emphasizes the survival strategies of Black women, while also striving to encourage healing and balance (Lindsay-Dennis, 2015). Phillips (2007) contributed to the tenets of Womanism, which can be used as a theoretical framework to guide counselors in supporting women of color. At its core, Womanism focuses on wellness for women of color, allowing for optimal self-expression (Bryant-Davis & Comas-Díaz, 2016). Womanism also emphasizes empowerment, resistance, and embracing multiple identities (Bowman & King, 2003). Using a Womanist perspective, counselors can promote adaptive coping mechanisms, as well as challenge maladaptive coping in culturally responsive ways. For example, by processing societal messages and stereotypes in counseling, the counselor can help the client deconstruct externalized self-perceptions and differentiate her self-image from societally imposed perspectives. Additionally, counselors can collaboratively redefine personal characteristics in ways that support culturally congruent coping strategies and self-identity (Sanchez-Hucles, 2016).

Few (2007) also offered a general, applied Black Feminist methodological approach that consists of (a) deconstruct social constructions; (b) place the voices of Black females at the center of analysis; (c) identify the intersections to examine institutional inequalities and the resiliencies of Black women; and (d) integrate revisionist scholarship. Culturally tailored interventions increase client retention and are up to four times more effective than non-tailored interventions (Ward & Brown, 2015). Providing culturally responsive counseling to women involves examining the social and political structures that contribute to women's distress, while focusing on the goal of individual and group empowerment and social and political change. For example, a woman's experience of racism and harassment in the workplace is not seen as a personal problem, but is conceptualized as an outcome of workplace policies that do not protect women against such harassment.

COUNSELING INTERVENTIONS INFORMED BY CENTERING GENDER AND INTERSECTING IDENTITIES

Culturally responsive counseling with women emphasizes empowerment and strengths-based interventions. This idea can be facilitated in developing a positive therapeutic relationship, working toward a broader understanding of how their current circumstances are affected by sociopolitical factors, and building stronger relationships and communities, often by engaging in personal and/or social action. Interventions focus on how clients demonstrate strength in their lives and are resilient despite the detrimental effects of oppression.

Establishing an egalitarian relationship. The primary intervention as a culturally responsive, feminist counselor is establishing an egalitarian therapeutic relationship, which includes creating trust and safety, demystifying the process of counseling, discussing the counselor's approach to using assessment and diagnosis, and collaborative goal setting. Early counseling sessions are focused on creating safety, establishing an egalitarian relationship, and assessing sources of client distress and client strengths (Rader & Gilbert, 2005). The counselor will pay special attention to the process of informed consent, which in part consists of educating the client and clarifying the process of counseling. The counselor creates an atmosphere in which the client feels they have an active voice in determining the goals and process of counseling, rather than a prescriptive approach in which the client is a passive participant in counselor interventions. The time it takes to establish such safety and trust often varies depending on the client's life circumstances and experiences with others. For example, clients who have encountered trauma may take longer to trust the counselor and the therapeutic process (L. Brown, 2010). Establishing an egalitarian relationship includes educating clients on the theory and process of feminist counseling. This includes the goals and values of feminist counseling, as well as focusing on understanding each client's culture and treating clients as unique individuals. The approach does not assume that all clients have the same feelings, thoughts, or experiences based on their gender, race, social class, or other identities. Further, demystification of the counseling process is a way to develop a more egalitarian relationship by educating clients as to the expectations in counseling and their rights as a client, and jointly creating the rules for the therapeutic relationship. In line with the egalitarian, nonhierarchical ethos, culturally responsive feminist counselors work collaboratively to develop therapeutic expectations (Evans et al., 2011) and revisit those expectations intermittently throughout the counseling process.

Utilizing collaborative goal setting. Culturally responsive feminist counselors work collaboratively with clients to set goals for the therapeutic work. Goal setting can be a strengths-based intervention, as it empowers clients to define their own goals and take ownership of the counseling process. The counselor may ask questions such as, "What changes do you expect by the end of counseling?" or "How will we know when our therapeutic work is done?" In this regard, the client determines the counseling outcome. If a client is unsure of how to establish therapeutic goals, the counselor can assist the client in exploring presenting issues that may lead to developing goals for counseling.

Identifying external sources of distress. Gaining a deeper understanding of external sources of client distress is an important aspect of the counseling process. Using gender role and power analyses, counseling helps to separate the personal sources of distress from sociopolitical and/or environmental or external factors (Tzou et al., 2012). Counselors attend to how the status of clients' intersecting identities, such as race, ethnicity, gender, social class, religion, and ability, are contributing to their current level of functioning. For example, a counselor is working with Rosie, a 16-year-old Mexican young woman who has lived in the United States since coming from Mexico with her undocumented parents at age 5. Rosie was referred to counseling by her pediatrician with symptoms of depression and anxiety, which increasingly affected her academic and social functioning. She disclosed fear and hopelessness related to the uncertainty of her future after high school. She described the anti-immigrant sentiment at school and increasing hostility toward Mexican and Latinx students who were high academic achievers. Rosie was unsure about her ability to go to college and receive financial assistance due to her family's undocumented status. She stated that she did not talk to her parents about how she was feeling because she did not want to worry them and because she thought there was something wrong with her for feeling depressed and anxious. The counselor worked with Rosie to externalize the symptoms of anxiety and depression she experienced, validate her feelings and concerns, and attribute them to the systemic challenges she was facing rather than as an internal deficit or pathology.

By identifying external sources of distress during sessions, the counselor assists the client in understanding the difference between personal and sociopolitical/external sources of distress (L. Brown, 2010).

Gender role analysis. Gender role analysis is used to increase clients' awareness of how various role expectations affect their thoughts, feelings, and behaviors (Evans et al., 2005; Rosewater & Walker, 1985; Worell & Remer, 1992). The counselor asks the client to reflect on messages related to role appropriateness for men and women. For example, a woman client who struggles with juggling the multiple responsibilities of being a full-time worker and mother to young children may identify the message that "women can have it all and do it all." This belief illustrates the societal value that imposes unrealistic expectations on women to maintain the primary responsibility for household and caretaking duties, in addition to full-time work outside the home. Another example is a Latina corporate executive who is struggling with emotional expression in collegial relationships and is trying to resist company cultural notions that "executives should be emotionally detached" when she has a more demonstrative leadership style. To assist the client in identifying expectations based on identities, the counselor might ask, "What has been your experience of social, work, and/or family expectations for men and women?" and "Have you received any conflicting messages about gender roles?"

The counselor then helps the client examine the positive and negative consequences of living with those messages, challenges the role expectations, and redefines their thoughts, feelings, and behaviors based on the increased understanding. A positive meaning from the message that women are supposed to be caretakers might be that women are very good at building deep connections; however, this can be balanced with understanding that the negative side is that women may ignore self-care by focusing on others. However, the burden of not asking for help and wanting to be seen as strong has caused mental and physical distress. The primary purpose of gender role analysis is to examine messages and expectations related to gender; however, counselors can and should also ask clients to recall verbal, nonverbal, and modeled messages about their other identities (e.g., race, class, sexual orientation), as well as their intersecting identities (e.g., lesbian mother living in poverty).

The goal is to have clients identify the identity role messages that they have internalized. These messages, which they have automatically assumed to be correct, typically manifest in the form of both positive and negative self-talk. For example, a woman may tell herself "I look better when I am thinner" because of internalized messages about female beauty norms. This could result in hesitance to engage in activities due to body dissatisfaction, despite goals to be more social and try new activities. In this case, the counselor might point out the incongruences that exist between the client's chosen goals and her self-talk. Once identification of internalized messages has occurred, the client is encouraged to identify which internalized messages she would like to keep and those that she would like to challenge. Throughout the process of gender role analysis, the counselor aims to empower the client by validating the client's lived experience and encouraging her to examine how external forces have influenced her current struggles.

Power analysis. Culturally responsive feminist counselors understand and acknowledge that power matters in relationships and in the larger culture. When power and status differentials contribute to clients' life challenges, power analysis can be a helpful strengths-based intervention. It is like gender role analysis in that it helps clients increase awareness of external sources of their thoughts, feelings, and behaviors. Power analysis helps clients recognize the power differentials that exist among different societal groups, and the types of power they hold and use in their lives. It helps clients increase the use of their personal power in a manner that fits with their personal beliefs

(Evans et al., 2011). The goal is to increase authenticity by changing behaviors that do not fit with a client's values.

The process of power analysis focuses on helping clients identify the differences between the internal and the external contributions of stress, learn to distinguish between the two, and establish congruence between their personal beliefs and behaviors (Worell, 2001). *Power* refers to an individual's access to personal and environmental resources that can be used to produce both personal and societal change (Worell & Remer, 2003). The beginning phases of the intervention are informational in nature, and thus require the counselor to provide education about power on the part of the counselor. Following the informational phase of the intervention, the counselor and client identify ways in which the client already accesses power and possible alternatives. The counselor might ask, "How would you describe your use of power in your professional life? In your personal life? In your family growing up?" Through this discussion, the counselor and client can begin to explore patterns in the client's life. For example, a client may feel a great deal of power at work but very little power in their home. Finally, after expectations and power are explored, clients will then uncover how various cultural and societal expectations affect their use of power. The client will then identify messages that they have internalized, and then assess which messages and expectations they would like to keep and which ones they would like to change. The counselor and client will then consider how to increase existing methods of power and incorporate new ones into the client's daily life. An example of such change may be getting involved in community organizing through helping people register to vote or working for a political campaign.

Fostering empowerment. The process of empowerment highlights a client's strengths, knowledge, and capabilities as they relate to the achievement of the client's identified goals. The counselor helps the client identify sources of strength, resilience, and areas where the client feels empowered by asking the client questions such as, "In what ways are you already using your strengths?" or "How has your knowledge of relationships helped you thus far?" The counselor then reflects the strengths heard in the client's report. For example, the client may be discussing career development issues, and the counselor may ask, "It seems that you have made a lot of progress by using your resources and interviewing skills" or "I see that as a strength given that you already knew much more than you gave yourself credit for."

Empowerment can also be fostered using reframing and modeling. Reframing is needed because clients often view their challenges through an individual deficit lens rather than through problematic sociopolitical perspectives. Reframing emphasizes the importance of language, and challenges societal categorizations about mental health. Thoughts and behaviors that may have previously been evaluated as deficits or have been pathologized are reframed using the client's language. For example, a family member may describe an adolescent girl who gets into fights at school and refuses to complete her schoolwork as "resistant," "oppositional," or "attention-seeking." Rather than using these words to conceptualize the client, the counselor asks the client to describe her personality and behaviors using her own language. Additionally, the counselor can ask this client to identify real or fictitious people whom she admires and the qualities she wants to emulate, and then reflect on the shared qualities between the client and her role models. Through this discussion, the client may realize that she shares many positive qualities with these role models while the counselor works to help the client change problematic behaviors at school, reframing how she sees herself and examining models of strength and positive qualities works to give the client more options when thinking about herself and making choices about her behavior.

When working with clients who have experienced oppression and marginalization, the process of empowerment through fostering a sense of agency is critical. Culturally responsive counseling approaches place emphasis on trusting the therapeutic alliance and using it to increase a sense of competency and agency for change. Although a sense of agency does not effect change in and of itself, it may be a necessary condition for clients to create positive change. When clients feel a sense of agency about the future or a specific outcome, they engage in behaviors that increase the likelihood of that outcome occurring. The counselor can encourage agency by fostering empowerment, assisting clients in reframing their presenting concern, and eliciting client strengths and resources. At times, fostering agency also includes affirming anger. Women are often reluctant to express anger; however, it is often an appropriate and normal response to situations in which one feels invalidated, dismissed, oppressed, or victimized. When clients recognize anger as a signal that something is not right, they can explore the sources of anger, whether it be specific events or an underlying emotion such as sadness. To affirm anger, a counselor helps to increase the client's awareness of feelings, thoughts, and situations that lead to anger. For example, the counselor can ask the client, "What was occurring before you experienced anger? What thoughts did you notice? Feelings? After the anger was expressed, what did you notice?" This can increase understanding of where the anger is coming from, and how it may be better understood in the context of the situation. For example, for a Black client who is anxious about her teenage son driving on his own due to concerns about her son's safety or getting unjustly pulled over by the police, it would be normal to feel anger regarding the injustice of racism. The counselor can encourage the client not only to pay attention to the words she uses, but also to notice the tone of voice, body language, facial expressions, and other body cues. Incongruities in body language and tone of voice or facial expressions can undermine clients' expressions of negative feelings. Affirming anger can help the client understand that anger does not have to be used to hurt other people, but it can assist in taking action or asserting oneself.

Group work. Group work has been an important part of both multicultural and feminist counseling. Groups have been used to clarify and co-create goals for personal and social change. Empowerment groups help increase connectedness among members of marginalized groups who might otherwise experience isolation in their daily lives. Group work gives clients space to try out new behaviors and receive feedback from others. Consciousness-raising groups are focused on increasing awareness of oppression and developing strategies for resistance and change. They help clients realize that their distress is informed by external factors, and that the solutions lie in social change. Assertiveness training groups help clients become more authentic and forthright about their thoughts and feelings by teaching members to respond to situations in which they have been invalidated, provide a sense of strength from one another, and create a space in which new behaviors can be practiced and promoted.

BUILDING RESILIENCE AND ACTIVISM

The overt integration of activism and advocacy in the counseling process makes culturally responsive practices unique from other counseling approaches. Counselors must be prepared to work within multiple systems, draw on community resources, and advocate with clients for social change. Integrating activism and advocacy may include effecting change at the client level, within specific systems or communities, or at the broader societal level. Culturally responsive counselors could engage at the individual or client level by writing a letter to support accommodations for a client at work and may also engage with systems by working within school systems to provide gender-neutral bathrooms for TGNC students. Also at the individual level, counselors can overtly identify client strengths, connect client problems with systemic issues, explore the client's understanding of oppression and whether it plays a role in their presenting issues, and teach self-advocacy skills.

At the community level, counselors can provide activism and advocacy through outreach, such as providing a free workshop on disparities in mental health, or how to advocate for mental health parity. Encouraging clients to engage in activism and advocacy for themselves at the community level may include providing resources for them to stay informed about local workplace issues, how local organizations approach social responsibility, and empowering them to reach out to build relationships with organization leaders and local politicians, and/or join community committees. At the social/political level, culturally responsive counselors may engage through voting, community organizing, or using their position to educate law enforcement about de-escalation techniques for people with mental health issues. The way a counselor engages in activism and advocacy is often dependent upon the specific needs and goals of the client or community. Teaching clients to use social media to support organizations that focus on anti-racist or anti-sexist issues or teaching clients how to find their local, state, and federal representatives to email about their concerns can be also incorporated into the goals of counseling. Regardless of how counselors integrate activism and advocacy in their work, they intend to understand the lived experiences of the client and work with the client to effect change.

COUNSELING UTILIZATION AND HELP-SEEKING

In 2019, 19.2% of adults received mental health treatment in the past 12 months, including 15.8% who had taken medication for their mental health, and 9.5% received counseling from a mental health professional (Terlizzi & Zablotsky, 2020). Nearly one in four women received mental health treatment (24.7%) in the past 12 months, compared with 13.4% of men, and women were more likely than men to have taken medication for their mental health (20.6% and 10.7%, respectively) and to have received counseling (11.7% and 7.2%; Terlizzi & Zablotsky, 2020). Women are more likely than men to seek treatment for their mental health (Mackenzie et al., 2006; Moore & Mattison, 2017) and have a higher prevalence of common mental health conditions, such as anxiety and depression (Eaton et al., 2012).

Women are also more likely to be prescribed psychotropic medications and be diagnosed with depression than men when they seek help from a primary care physician, even when women and men present with identical symptoms (American Psychiatric Association, 2017). Further, women are less likely to disclose problems with alcohol use or disclose any history of victimization unless the provider directly asks (American Psychiatric Association, 2017). Often-cited barriers to accessing mental health care among women include cost, stigma, difficulty accessing care, and lack of time/support to access care. It is important to note that women shouldn't be lumped into one monolithic group, and that intersecting identities play a crucial role in access to mental health care, participation in mental health care, and mental health outcomes.

CULTURALLY RESPONSIVE PRACTICES: DRAWING FROM THE MULTICULTURAL AND SOCIAL JUSTICE COUNSELING COMPETENCIES AND CULTURAL HUMILITY

Moving beyond cultural proficiency to cultural humility and responsiveness with clients can be facilitated by incorporating feminist counseling tenets along with multicultural and social justice counseling competencies. Feminist approaches and culturally responsive practices include a commitment to ending forms of oppression and involve counselor humility and self-awareness. Additionally, the approaches value an egalitarian therapeutic relationship and recognition of the impact of culture and values in the counseling relationship. Both focus on client's strengths rather than deficits, wellness versus illness, as symptoms are viewed as survival strategies in the face of oppression and adversity. Culturally responsive counselors work with their clients to develop strategies to bring about change and increased power, not only at the individual level, but also at the social level. This effort will also include the counselor engaging in advocacy efforts with the client. For example, the counselor and client may work together on strategies to increase outreach to schools on social media literacy or engage in community activism on issues such as discriminatory practices against people with disabilities. Counseling goals will be as unique as the women themselves, their environments, values, attitudes, and behaviors. Therefore, to respond to diverse female clients, feminist counseling strategies alone are not enough and should be combined with a focus on cultural and other salient identities.

Culturally responsive counseling empowers clients to examine the social and political forces that contribute to their distress. Moreover, the approach offers a socially critical philosophy, while emphasizing egalitarian principles within relationships and including the therapeutic relationship. Growth-fostering relationships are seen as critical to human development across the life span. Empowerment and affirmation of a client's need for connection are critical as counselors work to expand the concept of mental wellness from the individual to the larger society. In other words, there is a reciprocal relationship between an increase in social justice and personal health. When the status quo is challenged and there are positive gains toward social justice, personal health is affected, and when personal health and well-being are improved, society improves.

Counselors practicing with a culturally responsive feminist lens believe that the personal is political (L. Brown, 2010). Feminist counseling has a focus on addressing how social and cultural factors contribute to clients' current difficulties. In other words, personal issues happen in the context of political and social environments. Understanding clients' social and cultural contexts helps to bring awareness to how societal problems can influence personal distress rather than attributing problems solely to the individual. For example, the counselor may suggest that gender differences in diagnoses of depression are due to stereotypes, patriarchy, and diagnostic bias women experience, rather than solely on biological differences between men and women (L. Brown, 2010; Worell & Remer, 1992). Additionally, the counselor may inquire about ways that a client's depression might be the result of maintaining the status quo of traditional gender roles by silencing herself in relationships or not setting healthy boundaries. Interventions from this perspective aim to externalize the distress, understand it from a social context, and encourage individual and social action to challenge traditional gender roles that may be contributing to distress.

An intake or assessment may include a formal clinical diagnosis using the *Diagnostic and Statistical Manual of Mental Disorders* (5th ed.; *DSM-5*; American Psychiatric Association, 2013) but does not rely exclusively on the manual without analysis of its impacts on the client. Feminist counselors have typically rejected the medical or illness model and viewed diagnostic categories as an incomplete conceptualization of their clients' distress (L. Brown, 2010). However, a rejection of the use of diagnosis may limit access to and benefits from counseling services. If a third party such as an insurance company is paying for part of or the full counseling fee, the counselor is normally required to give a diagnosis from the *DSM-5*. If that is the case, the counselor may include an explanation of how diagnosis is used in their professional disclosure statement (a document that informs clients about your professional background and the limitations of your professional relationship) and discuss this with the client before the counseling process begins and when a diagnosis is made. Culturally responsive feminist counselors reframe presenting issues as contextual, rather than pathologizing the individual, by framing the symptoms in strengths-based language and working with the client to learn healthier survival or coping strategies. For example, symptoms such as binge eating and self-injury may be reframed as survival strategies of a client who experienced childhood sexual abuse and strengths-based language such as "resourceful" or "resilient" may be used to describe a client who found a way to manage her traumatic experiences. The symptoms are seen as survival strategies because they have kept the client going and functioned as coping strategies. A strengths-based approach focuses on a client or group's positive attributes rather than negative attributes.

Culturally responsive feminist counselors base the therapeutic work on the client's understanding and meanings of their life rather than making treatment decisions based on the counselor's interpretation of the client's presenting issues. In other words, the client's perspective is at the center of counseling work, and counselors encourage and assist clients in reframing their perceived weaknesses into strengths (L. Brown, 2010; Worell & Remer, 1992). By honoring marginalized peoples' experiences, culturally responsive feminist counselors recognize their clients' inherent strengths and empower their clients to do so too. An example of this may be working with clients to identify intergenerational familial resilience, writing themselves as the hero in their life story, or journaling about their growth while overcoming obstacles.

These interventions promote the belief that clients are the experts in their lives, and power is shared within the therapeutic relationship. In a culturally responsive feminist approach, the therapeutic relationship is egalitarian and respectful. There is a sense that each person is an expert that brings a particular set of experiences, skills, and knowledge to the relationship. Shared power and appropriate use of counselor self-disclosure are encouraged (L. Brown, 2010; Worell & Remer, 1992).

CRAFTING AN ADVOCACY AGENDA

Since its inception, social justice and advocacy have been a part of the counseling profession's framework. Promoting social justice is cited in the American Counseling Association (ACA) *Code of Ethics* Preamble (ACA, 2014). Likewise, the ACA (2014) *Code of Ethics* standard states that "When appropriate, counselors advocate at individual, group, institutional and societal levels to examine potential barriers and obstacles that inhibit access and/or growth and development of clients" (A.7.a). Additionally, the *Code of Ethics* states: "Counselors obtain client consent prior to engaging in advocacy efforts on behalf of an identifiable client to improve the provision of services and to work toward removal of systemic barriers or obstacles that inhibit client access, growth, and development" (ACA, 2014, A.7.b). These ideas are further elucidated in the ACA's Multicultural and Social Justice Counseling Competencies (MSJCC; Ratts et al., 2016), which emphasizes awareness of counselor assumptions, values, and biases regarding gender, as well as learning about the client's understandings of gender. The MSJCC describes how issues of privilege and oppression may influence both the client and counselor in counseling interactions. While the MSJCC is a helpful reference to inform culturally responsive counseling practice with women, to date there has not been a specific set of cultural competencies in the counseling field that addresses specific competencies for working with women and girls. Jodry and Trotman (2008) wrote a "Call to the Profession: Incorporating Feminist Competencies Into Professional Counseling," which justified a specific set of competencies and encouraged professional counselors to view feminist competency synonymously with multicultural competency. Existing professional competencies specifically addressing practice with girls and women include the American Psychological Association's (2018) "Guidelines for Psychological Practice with Girls and Women" and the SAMHSA's (2011) "Addressing the Needs of Women and Girls: Developing Core Competencies for Mental Health and Substance Abuse Service Professionals." Similarly, the "Guidelines for Ethical Psychological Practice with Women" emphasize how important it is for practitioners to be knowledgeable about the issues and conditions that affect the lives of women (Canadian Psychological Association, 2007).

The American Psychological Association "Guidelines for Psychological Practice with Girls and Women" outline ways in which practitioners can provide gender-sensitive, culturally competent, and developmentally appropriate practices across the life span, with girls and women from all social classes, ethnic and racial groups, sexual orientations, and ability/disability statuses (American Psychological Association, 2018). The guidelines discuss stressors that have a unique impact on women, including social network-related stress and unemployment, sex-role orientation, racial discrimination, role strain, and unrealistic media images. They address the strengths of girls and women, life span considerations, the importance of intersectional identities, and include relevant research for each guideline. There are 10 guidelines in the document, and each includes a rationale and application. Counseling recommendations for working with girls and women include recognizing and cultivating their strengths and resilience, being aware of their identities within the context of socialized messages about gender and structural discrimination, using interventions and approaches that are affirmative and gender/culturally relevant, fostering practices that promote agency and expanded choice, mindfully and responsibly using diagnosis and assessment, and working to challenge and change hostile environments that interfere with the well-being of girls and women (American Psychological Association, 2018).

The SAMHSA guidelines provide a three-pronged approach that integrates public health, trauma-informed care, and a recovery-oriented system of care model (SAMHSA, 2011). The integration creates a comprehensive model for services that recognize that sex, gender, and cultural factors lead to differences in socialization, expectations, and lifestyle, as well as differences in the way women and girls experience risk and resiliency factors, stress, and access to resources. The inclusion of trauma-informed care acknowledges the high prevalence of traumatic experiences in girls and women who receive counseling services and highlights the need to recognize and respond to the significance of trauma when providing care to women and girls. Recovery-oriented systems of care are included to reflect gender differences in levels of formal and informal support, and the different pathways and risk factors for substance use. Women and girls often endure different consequences of substance use, barriers to treatment, and recovery-support needs than men. SAMHSA's guidelines direct counselors to studies of gender-responsive programs that help engage women, treat them, and support their recovery. They note that although significant gains have been made in research on the impact of sex and gender differences on mental health, most service delivery systems and professional training are created and implemented without considering gender responsiveness. They emphasize that gender-responsive core competencies and services are necessary to help ensure women's positive health outcomes.

Within the counseling literature, specific guidelines and models have been developed for work with different groups of girls and young women. Lee (2004) proposed recommendations for work with biracial girls, which suggested that in order to provide ethically and culturally appropriate counseling to this unique population, a sociopolitical perspective must be adopted and shared within the therapeutic setting. Lee urged counselors to focus on identity development and affirmation with their clients, along with increased community connections and communication among the family (2004). Likewise, Kassan and Sinacore (2016) reported that counselor awareness, knowledge, skills, and the multicultural counseling relationship are important competencies when working with female adolescents, along with cultural sensitivity, family interventions, and help beyond counseling.

Many of the models and guidelines that have been developed with specific female populations in mind place a great deal of emphasis on the role of one's worldview and identity development. In working from these conceptualizations, counselors are urged to develop an adequate cultural understanding of their female clients—a notion that touches the core of the concept of culturally responsive counseling. Knowledge, skills, and awareness, in addition to cultural humility, are necessary for providing culturally responsive counseling and working with issues of gender and sexism.

COUNSELING CHILDREN, ADOLESCENTS, AND YOUNG ADULTS

According to the U.S. Census Bureau (2020), there were nearly 42 million youth ages 10 to 19 in the United States, and about half identify as female. Most of what is researched and discussed related to girls and young women focuses on the problems they face. Adolescent girls are often seen through a problem-saturated or deficit-based perspective, rather than for their strengths and resiliency (Choate, 2014). Affirming the strength and resilience of girls and young women should be a primary focus in understanding what helps them to navigate their development. In other words, focus on resilience, coping, and wellness must be explicit in counseling to facilitate positive mental health.

Given that gender identity and socialization develop across time and context, it is important to go back to the importance of gender affirmation when discussing counseling with children, adolescents, and young adults (Reisner et al., 2016). Gender affirmative practice should be developmentally appropriate and include an understanding that gender variations are not disorders; gender expressions are diverse and vary based on culture, gender is not binary, mental health issues often stem from cultural reactions (e.g., transphobia, homophobia, sexism) rather than from individual psychological factors, and gender is interconnected with biology, development and socialization, and culture and context (Hidalgo et al., 2013). Working with children, adolescents, and young adults on issues related to gender identity development often means working with parents or caregivers, school personnel, or medical providers to affirm what the client is communicating about their ability to express gender without restriction or rejection. Research shows that individuals not allowed this freedom are at risk for developing negative mental health outcomes (Choate, 2014).

Culturally responsive counseling to address issues related to gender and sexism focuses on building a positive, growth-fostering therapeutic relationship, and implementing collaborative, strengths-based interventions that value relational development and social support. Interventions focus on client strengths and resiliencies, while also recognizing the detrimental effects of oppression and marginalization.

COUNSELING ADULTS, COUPLES, AND FAMILIES

Family and couple dynamics typically exist "behind closed doors." Historically, this private realm was not scrutinized for gender imbalance and, in some cases, gender violence that happened inside the home. As women's economic and social power has increased through participation in work and home life, and as policies regarding interpersonal violence, divorce, and reproductive rights have provided protections for women, there has been a shift in focus on the gendered dynamics within family and couple's relationships. By making gender visible, feminists have changed the way that counselors address power and privilege as played out in this private environment. A gender focus reveals social relations in the family and uncovers reticence related to imbalance in power within relationships. Counselors must recognize that gendered family dynamics do not occur in a vacuum. In other words, policies and cultural norms that occur outside the family also shape what happens inside the family.

Although family counselors recognize the importance of the systemic context as a driver of behavior, traditional family system theories did not overtly examine the consequences of gender socialization practices and sexism (Seponski et al., 2013). This often resulted in stereotyped gender roles going unexamined in family and couples counseling. Further, models of couples and family therapy typically reflect Western values and norms, and although cultural adaptations are made, many approaches continue to be inappropriate or inadequate for use with non-Western cultures. Counselors are examining ways of using systemic counseling approaches in a culturally sensitive manner. For example, a feminist, culturally responsive approach considers and challenges the consequences of gender roles in couple and family dynamics, while working to affirm couple and families' strengths, cultures, and beliefs (Seponski et al., 2013). It is critical to use a strengths-based, nonpathologizing stance, emphasize an egalitarian therapeutic relationship, and offer interventions that consider families within their sociopolitical and sociocultural contexts while paying special attention to neighborhoods, communities, and support systems (Waites et al., 2004). Recognition of intersectionality, as discussed previously in this chapter, adds to this examination of roles and statuses within relationships. For example, women of color who are single parents face marginalization by race and marital status in addition to gender while working to raise and support their families. Processing how these identities affect the family would be a part of a culturally responsive approach to working with couples and families. Most are uncomfortable with sexism and patterns of gender inequity that harm both women and men. Women and men are denied opportunities to expand roles beyond what is culturally gendered. Therefore, couples and family counseling can encourage women, partners, and family members not only to become aware of the oppressiveness of traditional roles, but also to gain experiences that enhance their self-esteem as they try new behaviors.

IMPLICATIONS FOR CLINICAL PRACTICE

Culturally responsive counseling with women is a collaborative, empowering approach that aims to identify client strengths, increase awareness and understanding of clients' gendered and intersecting identities, and work toward social justice, improved well-being, and equity. Counselors do this by using strengths-based interventions that promote a wellness model of mental health; collaborating with clients to examine personal, cultural, and institutional influences affecting their well-being; centering the client's experiences related to gender, sexism, and sociopolitical factors; and working to critically analyze cultural influences on thoughts, feelings, and behaviors. In providing culturally responsive counseling for women, counselors must practice with cultural humility and be aware of their attitudes and beliefs about women and men who are cisgender, transgender, and gender nonconforming. This gender-affirming approach is guided by the notion that individuals have the personal power and expertise to effect both individual and social change.

CLINICAL CASE SCENARIO 13.1

Jada is a 36-year-old multiracial woman who was recently divorced from her husband of 9 years. She works full-time as a paralegal. She currently lives with her mother while saving money to purchase her own home. She identified her presenting concerns as "relationship issues and problems at work." She reported a history of depression, anxiety, and anger, and said she needed help to "calm down" and "not take everything so seriously."

Jada is an only child and her parents divorced when she was 6 years old. Her mother was born in Columbia and came to the United States for college where she met Jada's father, an African American man from the southeast. After Jada's parents' divorce, she split time equally between them, which was difficult for her and created a sense of guilt and confusion. Jada described her mother as volatile—someone who could be loving one minute and dismissive in another. Her mother's unpredictable mood was a source of anxiety for Jada. However, she learned ways to avoid her mother's attention by maintaining good grades and being involved in several clubs and sports. Jada's relationship with her father was positive and loving, but due to the conflict between her parents, she did not see him as often as she would have liked. When Jada was 13, her father remarried and had two more children with his new wife. During adolescence, Jada and her father grew apart and their relationship has ebbed and flowed ever since. Jada does not maintain a connection with her half-siblings.

At work, Jada has been working on a case involving the sexual abuse of a 12-year-old girl by a neighbor, the father of the girl's friend. The case has been extremely stressful, so much so that Jada stopped eating and sleeping. Her alcohol consumption increased significantly, and she was unable to function well at work. Her co-worker, Joe, has been somewhat supportive, but his comments to her are insensitive and minimize her feelings. Some comments are sexist, such "you are a typical, overemotional woman" and "you are just going to have to get over it and move on." When she confronted Joe, he dismissed her by telling her to "calm down and not take herself so seriously." The experiences she has had with Joe mimic the invalidation she often felt from her ex-husband. He had often told her that she needed to "calm down," and when she felt passionate about an issue, he called her "overly sensitive." When she was married to her ex-husband she noticed that she tried to detach emotionally; however, this led to feelings of depression, anxiety, and resentment. She urged her ex-husband several times to go to couples counseling with her. After 9 years of marriage and months of couples counseling, they decided to divorce.

When Jada started counseling, her counselor worked to establish rapport, safety, and trust, as well as create an egalitarian (i.e., philosophy of equality in relationships) therapeutic relationship. Her counselor shared her approach to counseling, assessment, and diagnosis with Jada. She worked to gain an understanding of Jada's salient identities. Jada's identities included college-educated, cisgender,

(continued)

CLINICAL CASE SCENARIO 13.1 (CONTINUED)

multiracial, and Christian. The counselor also helped Jada identify her strengths; conceptualize her presenting issues in the context of her sociopolitical and professional world; externalize feelings of anxiety, depression, and anger; and empower Jada to increase assertiveness with her coworker and ex-husband. Over time, Jada understood her symptoms of anxiety and depression as survival strategies she has used since childhood and periodically through times of stress in adulthood. Jada learned new coping strategies to manage her symptoms and increased her sense of power in her life. Once the legal case she worked on had been resolved, she began volunteering for a sexual assault advocacy center in her city, providing legal assistance and outreach.

CLINICAL CASE SCENARIO DISCUSSION QUESTIONS

1. What are the gender and cultural factors that you might consider while working with Jada?
2. Why is it important to conceptualize Jada's presenting issues in the context of her sociopolitical and work worlds, as well as to externalize her experiences of anxiety and depression?
3. What strengths-based counseling interventions might you use with Jada?
4. If Jada was your client, what parts of her story would you identify with and what parts would be more difficult to understand?
5. Are there any gender-related biases or assumptions you would address as you worked with Jada?

END-OF-CHAPTER RESOURCES

A robust set of instructor resources designed to supplement this text is located at http://connect.springerpub.com/content/book/978-0-8261-3953-5. Qualifying instructors may request access by emailing **textbook@springerpub.com**.

SUMMARY

Culturally responsive counseling with women is a collaborative, empowering approach that aims to identify client strengths, increase awareness and understanding of clients' gendered and intersecting identities, and work toward social justice, improved well-being, and equity. Counselors do this by using strengths-based interventions that promote a wellness model of mental health; collaborating with clients to examine personal, cultural, and institutional influences affecting their well-being; centering the client's experiences related to gender, sexism, and sociopolitical factors; and working to critically analyze cultural influences on thoughts, feelings, and behaviors. In providing culturally responsive counseling for women, counselors must practice with cultural humility and be aware of their own attitudes and beliefs about women and men who are cisgender, transgender, and gender nonconforming. This gender-affirming approach is guided by the notion that individuals have the personal power and expertise to effect both individual and social change.

DISCUSSION QUESTIONS

1. When you think of women's strengths and vulnerabilities, what comes to mind?
2. How does sexism affect relationships among men, women, and people who are TGNC?
3. Give an example of gender disparities related to mental and physical health that may appear socially as well as clinically. How would you address them in counseling?
4. How would you introduce a conversation about gender role expectations with a client?
5. What are the important areas of consideration in counseling clients who are TGNC?
6. Describe how gender identity, gender expression, and biological sex are different, but overlapping, constructs.
7. Describe intersectionality as it relates to culturally responsive counseling for women.

▶ CULTURALLY RESPONSIVE COUNSELING FOR WOMEN CLIENTS

Guest: Dr. Natalie Arce Indelicato

https://connect.springerpub.com/content/book/978-0-8261-3953-5/part/part02/chapter/ch13

KEY REFERENCES

Only key references appear in the print edition. The full reference list appears in the digital product on Springer Publishing Connect: https://connect.springerpub.com/content/book/978-0-8261-3953-5/part/part02/chapter/ch13

American Counseling Association. (2014). *2014 ACA Code of Ethics*. Author. https://doi.org/10.1002/9781119221548

American Psychiatric Association. (2017). *Mental health disparities: Women's mental health*. https://www.psychiatry.org/psychiatrists/cultural-competency/education/mental-health-facts

American Psychological Association. (2018). *APA guidelines for psychological practice with girls and women*. http://www.apa.org/about/policy/psychological-practice-girls-women.pdf

Brown, L. (2010). *Feminist therapy*. American Psychological Association.

Crenshaw, K. W. (1989). Demarginalizing the intersection of race and sex: A Black feminist critique of antidiscrimination doctrine, feminist theory, and antiracist politics. *University of Chicago Legal Forum, 139*, 139–167.

Ratts, M. J., Singh, A. A., Nassar-McMillan, S., Butler, S. K., & McCullough, J. R. (2016). Multicultural and social justice counseling competencies: Guidelines for the counseling profession. *Journal of Multicultural Counseling and Development, 44*(1), 28–48. https://doi.org/10.1002/jmcd.12035

Worell, J., & Remer, P. (2003). *Feminist perspective in therapy: Empowering diverse women* (2nd ed.). John Wiley & Sons.

CHAPTER 14

Culturally Responsive Counseling for Men Clients

MICHAEL D. HANNON, DAE'QUAWN LANDRUM, GUY J. BEAUDUY, JR., AND FATHIYYAH F. SALAAM

LEARNING OBJECTIVES

After reading this chapter, students will be able to:

- Recognize the constructions of masculinity and how they influence the mental health of diverse men.
- Explain stigmatization associated with diverse men seeking mental health counseling.
- Assess the influence of culture, socioeconomic status, gender preference, and sexual identity on men's desire to seek mental health counseling.
- Identify risk factors associated with men seeking mental health assistance.
- Define masculinity and how it affects men's ability to seek mental health counseling.
- Recognize counselors as social justice advocates for marginalized populations.
- Demonstrate self-reflection to offer responsive forms of help to men clients.
- Explain the need for culturally competent and responsive counselors to meet the needs of diverse men clients.

SELF-REFLECTION QUESTIONS

1. Think about biases, prejudices, and assumptions you might have about men clients. How do these help and hinder your ability to provide culturally sensitive counseling?
2. What hesitancies, if any, do you have about working with men clients?
3. What attributes do you have that will enable you to work with men clients?

The need for culturally responsive counseling support for people underserved by counselors is arguably more critical now than ever before. Men, in particular, have historically been underserved by counselors and allied mental health professionals for a variety of reasons that include, but are not limited to, being socialized to believe in prescribed forms of masculinity; the stigmatization of seeking mental health care; disparities in access to and quality of mental health care by race, gender expression, sexual orientation, and other salient identities; and a dearth of research about culturally informed clinical interventions found to be effective in treating men (Englar-Carlson & Kiselica, 2013; Hannon, 2013; Hankerson et al., 2015; Kiselica & Englar-Carlson, 2010; Mays et al., 2017; Perkins et al., 2014). To begin to remedy this lack, this chapter provides an overview of contemporary research about diverse men's experiences with counseling services, with recommendations for culturally responsive clinical support for them in two broad sections.

The first section of this chapter illustrates the importance of, and offers suggestions on ways counselors treating men clients can engage in, personal exploration, introspection, and reflection to position themselves to offer responsive support. This is followed by a presentation of contemporary issues and trends that influence men's mental health, which includes a discussion of healthy masculinity and the negotiations of men's intersectional identities within their socialization processes. Relatedly, it also includes a presentation of the ongoing stigmatization of mental health care for men. This section concludes with an examination of identified disparate trends in access to mental health care and disparities in the quality of mental health care for men with varying identities (e.g., racial, sexual orientation, gender identity, socioeconomic status, etc.).

The second section of this chapter focuses on culturally responsive interventions for working with men clients. Drawing from the Multicultural and Social Justice Counseling Competencies (MSJCC; Ratts et al., 2015), we offer recommendations to assess counselors' readiness and fit to provide counseling services to men that speak directly to counselors' self-awareness and its influence on the counseling relationship with men clients. We offer ways counselors can develop and execute an advocacy agenda and then draw on the current research knowledge base to identify evidence-based clinical interventions found to be effective for men clients. This section closes with recommendations for additional research about counseling men to help inform counseling practice.

THE COUNSELOR: EXPLORATION, INTROSPECTION, AND REFLECTION

Mental health luminary Frantz Fanon (1967) encouraged mental health professionals to ask themselves three critical questions in pursuit of congruence and meaningful existence: (a) Who am I?; (b) Am I who I say I am?; and (c) Am I all that I ought to be? Given how the counseling profession prioritizes wellness (American Counseling Association [ACA], 2014) in counselors so that they can appropriately support clients, it behooves counselors to take intentional steps to engage in exploration, introspection, and critical reflection. What follows are recommendations to support counselors who elect to engage in the aforementioned activities as they ready themselves to provide culturally responsive counseling support to men clients, specifically using the RESPECTFUL model of counseling and development developed by D'Andrea and Daniels (2001).

The RESPECTFUL model (D'Andrea & Daniels, 2001) is a tool used by counselors to assist clients in identifying salient dimensions of their multiple, and often converging and intersecting, identities. The RESPECTFUL acronym stands for: **R**eligious/spiritual identity; **E**conomic class background; **S**exual identity; **P**sychological maturity; **E**thnic/racial identity; **C**hronological/developmental challenges; **T**rauma and threats to well-being; **F**amily background and history; **U**nique physical characteristics; **L**ocation of residence and language difference. We contend that counselors' exploration, introspection, and reflection on these identities foster readiness to high-quality counseling care and treatment.

The willingness for counselors to explore and be introspective about various influences on their identities requires courage. An activity counselors often use with clients can be aptly applied in this context. The first step is to share the RESPECTFUL model (D'Andrea & Daniels, 2001) acronym and explain to clients what the model represents. After confirming clients' understanding of the model and acronym, we suggest that the client identify up to three salient identities in the model and use those (up to three) responses as a springboard for further discussion.

In this spirit, we encourage counselors to consider their own three most salient identities reflected in the RESPECTFUL model (D'Andrea & Daniels, 2001). Counselors should reflect on and document the reasons why those three identities are most salient for them and specifically be willing to reflect on and share the ways those identities inform their counseling practice. This exploration, introspection, and reflection provides counselors with indicators of potential blind spots in their practice and reference points for supervision and consultation support. To provide counseling treatment to all clients, and men clients in particular, requires counselors to increase their awareness about the ways they have been socialized to think about men and expressions of masculinity in the various roles men are assigned and assume. Counselors' learning about themselves more deeply and learning about how they conceptualize men will aid them in their effectiveness with men clients.

CONTEMPORARY ISSUES AND TRENDS

The ability to effectively and responsibly serve men clients requires an appreciation and understanding about issues and phenomena that influence their mental health. Several factors influence men's health which include, but are not limited to, biological factors (e.g., medical history, physical health, predispositions to specific conditions), psychological factors (e.g., mental health conditions), and social factors (e.g., housing, employment), all of which contribute to men's experience and ability to maintain mental and emotional wellness (Pattyn et al., 2015). Several researchers have documented the differences in mental health treatment seeking between men and women, indicating important trends, which include that men seek mental health treatment less frequently than women (Addis & Mahalik, 2003), that men are more likely to report symptoms externalizing disorders (Judd et al., 2009), and that seeking mental health support has been socially constructed as a feminine behavior (Courtenay, 2000). In this section, we present insights informed by prior research about constructions of masculinity and how they can function as an influence and possible predictor of men's overall mental health (Pattyn et al., 2015).

Male Socialization and Concepts of Masculinity

Masculinity can be generally defined as a set of attributes, behaviors, and/or roles associated with being a man (Edwards, 2006). The social constructions of American masculinity, or the ways individuals, groups, communities, and institutions prescribe or endorse a specific demonstration of masculinity, certainly influence how boys and men make meaning of their masculinity, both individually and in the community. Acknowledging that, in many ways, constructions of masculinity are geographically informed, this discussion contextualizes the research about the meaning of being masculine in Western/American contexts.

Scholars have identified specific domains where Western/American masculinity is performed and assessed. For example, Edwards (2006) articulated at least seven domains where masculinity is performed: men's work, education, families, sexuality, health, crime, and representation. Additionally, there are unique considerations for how Black,

Indigenous, Asian, Latinx, and multiracial and multiethnic men, within their respective communities, assess and determine acceptable forms of masculinity. Men in the racial and ethnic minority may also be forced to conform to acceptable definitions of masculinity in the White culture because of their underrepresented status and/or because they generally possess less social, cultural, or economic capital (Bourdieu, 1986).

Counseling researchers have presented the ways that boys and male adolescents are socialized (i.e., ideas and behaviors taught and reinforced through social interactions) into manhood and masculinity through the use of persistent external narratives that become internal scripts (Mahalik et al., 2003). Their ideas subscribe very much to the work of scholars such as Edwards (2006) and Cooper (2006). Mahalik et al. (2003) introduced the construction of four pervasive scripts that men are socialized to adopt and actualize in their behavior. These scripts include the *strong and silent* script, the *tough guy* script, the *give 'em hell* script, and the *playboy* script. The *strong and silent* script suggests that appropriate masculinity is evidenced by restricted emotionality. In this scenario, strength is associated with silence, or the inability to emote unless it is an expression of anger or other forms of socially acceptable masculine emotion (e.g., heterosexual lust).

The *tough guy* script includes internalized and accepted messages by men and externally communicated messages from men that acceptable masculine performance is the ability to project fearlessness and invulnerability in a range of contexts. In other words, if men do not exhibit this particular form of masculinity, they run the risk of being, or their behaviors being, coded as feminine (i.e., the opposite of masculine). Being tough and behaving in tough ways present to others a sometimes false and dangerous willingness to withstand painful, abusive, and/or traumatic experiences without the need for external help or support.

The *give 'em hell* script reinforces that aggression is the best strategy for boys and men to manage uncomfortable feelings. This is one step beyond the *tough guy* script in that it is driven by performance. For example, when boys and men become scared, fearful, nervous, or embarrassed, the *give 'em hell* script prompts them to demonstrate some form of aggression to compensate for those uncomfortable feelings. Adhering to this particular message and its related behaviors can have a range of consequences for boys and men. For example, boys who adopt this script risk being coded as disruptive, destructive, and/or unable to engage with others in ways that are prosocial. This is relevant for all boys, but has particular relevance for boys of color, who continue to be diagnosed with mental illnesses that fall within the category of Disruptive, Impulse-Control, and Conduct Disorders (American Psychiatric Association, 2013).

Finally, the *playboy* script is a form of socially constructed and acceptable masculine performance evidenced by hetero-, hypersexual behavior. Boys and men are encouraged to demonstrate their masculinity in another performative way by engaging in frequent and sometimes risky sexual behaviors with girls and women to be considered real men. For example, boys and men may be pressured to initiate sexual relationships with multiple girls and women at one time, while those girls and women are unaware that the boys and men have multiple sexual partners. This might also be demonstrated by men having children with multiple women over the life span. This *playboy* script can undermine how much boys and men are willing to be honest about their authentic feelings about girls and women, prompt them to hide their vulnerabilities, and/or stand in the way of their being honest with themselves.

Men's ability to align their behavior to these socially acceptable—and narrow—expressions of masculinity (e.g., cisgendered, straight) have important implications for men's mental health (American Psychological Association, Boys and Men Guidelines Group, 2018). The American Psychological Association recently published the *APA Guidelines for Psychological Practices With Boys and Men* (American Psychological Association, Boys and Men Guidelines Group, 2018) reminding readers that, as Watkins (2019, p. 917) summarized, "(a) the lives of boys and men are heavily influenced by social determinants and (b) research on social determinants should shape how practitioners counsel boys and men." The consequences of boys and men being socialized with limited constructions of masculinity, particularly when boys and men do not or cannot authentically align themselves with said constructions, can yield significant distress and lead to depressive and anxiety disorders, among others (Clark, 2010; Rogers et al., 2017).

Coping With Stress

The preceding section highlighted how constructions of masculinity can influence how men seek help. The reconciliation of if, when, or how men seek help can be a source of significant stress. In this section we provide insights on how men have been found to cope with stress, as documented by researchers, with a particular emphasis on the relationship between stress and work.

Considering the sociopolitical climate in the United States today (e.g., anti-Black, anti-Asian, antigay, anti-trans violence, voter restriction efforts, lethal police violence), it is imperative to consider how men cope with the stress of maintaining society's status of masculinity. Because demonstrations of anger (e.g., when anger is physically destructive) can be coded as unacceptable in some contexts, some men tend to switch their responses rooted in a range of feelings to expressions of anger. These feelings range from feeling in a slump, feeling sad, feeling weak, and feeling helpless/hopeless (Perkins et al., 2014). For example, Black men might be considered weak or feminine if they show signs of depression (e.g., lack of motivation, melancholia; Perkins et al., 2014). It is important to note that some men may have difficulty expressing feelings associated with depressive symptoms which, potentially, impede their ability to seek help and/or engage in meaningful relationships (Perkins et al., 2014).

Researchers have reported that men tend to cope with stress in three ways: *isolated coping*, *engaged coping*, and *disengaged coping* (Goodwill et al., 2018). *Isolated coping* occurs when people choose to cope inwardly with their stress and manage it independently (Goodwill et al., 2018). In American/Western contexts, isolated coping means depending on oneself and avoiding discussing challenges and stressors (Goodwill et al., 2018). The *engaged coping* style occurs when individuals cope through outward behaviors such as putting more energy into social interactions, relationships, hobbies, physical activities, substance use, and/or fighting and violence (Goodwill et al., 2018). Instead of seeking therapeutic assistance, men who use engaged coping mechanisms tend to seek advice from others. Lastly, *disengaged coping* is the conscious or unconscious decision to do nothing (Goodwill et al., 2018). Disengaged coping can include ignoring the source(s) of stress as a consequence of feeling unable to address it without seeking assistance. Disengaged behaviors include accepting their issues without seeking assistance after they have attempted to find a solution on their own. Some men opt to wait for the stress to go away, do not take the stress seriously, or try to stay distracted to avoid dealing with the stress. Men who use disengaged coping mechanisms choose to either not deal with emotions, cut off their feelings, and/or hide their feelings. They do not want to burden others with their problems for fear of being labeled as weak and having their masculinity challenged (Goodwill et al., 2018).

Men and Work

Across the globe, one significant demonstration of manhood and masculinity is in the context of work. Historically, boys and men are socialized to be workers and financial providers in their families of orientation and for their families of procreation (Berdahl et al., 2018). Collectively, men in a study by Snipes et al. (2015) reported that masculinity is defined by their physical fitness and mental toughness (e.g., the ability to endure stress) and their ability to protect and provide for their families. When those expectations are not met, it can be a significant source of stress for men and can be a predictor of impaired mental health. These masculine norms force men to prioritize external responsibilities over mental health, which, at times, works counterintuitively. That is, the prioritizing of external responsibilities can become a source of stress and, in turn, contribute to a higher (i.e., doubled) level of stress. Work addiction may also emerge as a result of wanting external recognition of work accomplishments along with career advancements and/or having low self-esteem, self-worth, negative affect, or perfectionism (Reiner et al., 2019). Prioritizing those external responsibilities comes at the cost of deprioritizing one's mental health. Men must find the balance between work, providing for their families, and tending to personal and mental health.

A potential consequence of work/career success is financial reward, which can lead to work addiction (Clark et al., 2016). That is, the more men are financially rewarded in their job roles, the more money they earn, which grants more financial resources but offers little work–life balance (Reiner et al., 2019). Workaholism is related to achievement-oriented personality traits (e.g., perfectionism, Type A personality), but is generally unrelated to many other dispositional (e.g., conscientiousness, self-esteem, positive affect) and demographic (e.g., gender, parental status, marital status) variables. Workaholism is related to negative outcomes such as burnout, job stress, work–life conflict, and decreased physical and mental health (Clark et al., 2016).

CLIENT WORLDVIEWS AND PERSPECTIVES

There are at least two influences that men's help-seeking behavior is determined by: the safety to seek help, and the urgency of the need that requires help. Unfortunately, constructions of manhood and masculinity, as described earlier, function as a barrier to men seeking help overall, and particularly help for their mental health. Thus, we offer a presentation of historical and contemporary research about how stigma associated with mental health care continues to be a barrier to men seeking counseling support. Help-seeking behavior among men from various cultures has been found to be interpreted as feminine—by both men and women (Courtenay, 2000; Hannon, 2013). Stigmas associated with help-seeking behaviors include being seen as needy, being subject to belittling, and/or the idea that men are only allowed to seek help from a divine or godly source (Hannon, 2013).

The research of Farrimond (2012) and Griffith et al. (2011) indicate that the mere act of going to the doctor for preventative care can be challenging for men because of its propensity to be interpreted as a sign of weakness. Farrimond (2012) reported that men from the United Kingdom had to actively reframe their thoughts about going to the doctor to remind themselves that seeking medical care was responsible behavior. This is important because it reminds us that the internalized messages from external sources about help-seeking are a pervasive influence on if and when men seek preventative medical care. Griffith et al. (2011) discussed some unique considerations for safety among older Black American men and their willingness to seek medical care. The authors reported that participants relied more heavily on partner support (wives, girlfriends, etc.) than the advice or recommendation of expert medical professionals because of their experiences with being belittled by physicians.

Chang and Subramaniam (2008) wrote about this phenomenon among Asian and Pacific-Islander American men and their reservations about seeking mental health care. Similarly, Cabassa (2007) reported that Latino immigrants were more willing to rely on family members or their faith than seeking counseling services for depressive symptoms.

Black men reported challenges such as being misdiagnosed (Hankerson et al., 2015) when seeking mental health treatment (Harper et al., 2009), and consequently did not return for subsequent sessions (Zeber et al., 2017). Neighbors et al.'s (2003) article highlights that even with the use of the *Diagnostic and Statistical Manual of Mental Disorders* (3rd ed.; *DSM-III*; American Psychiatric Association, 1980) and a semi-structured instrument, Black people are more likely to be diagnosed with an acute mental health disorder, in contrast to their White counterparts being diagnosed with a mood disorder. The disparities that Black people experience increase the likelihood of not returning to or seeking treatment; furthermore, it contributes to the cultural mistrust (Terrell et al., 2009) that many Black people have for the healthcare system. The reluctance to participate in treatment or continue treatment also stems from a fear of being labeled, negative stigmatization, being perceived as weak, being referred to hospitalization (Harper et al., 2009), and lack of consideration of intersecting identities.

It is critical to note unique and important considerations for gay, bisexual, transgender, and gender-conforming men as they seek physical and mental health support. In 1995, Iian Meyer, a public health scholar, introduced the term *Minority Stress Theory* to explain how stigma and prejudice ultimately affect the mental and physical health of gay men (Meyer, 1995; Meyer et al., 2021). Meyer (1995) argued that gay men experience increased stress because of the stigmatization of their affectional orientation; however, Meyer et al. (2021) acknowledged that the theory can also apply to transgender men. Although the LGBTQ+ community has successfully advocated for more humane treatment (e.g., removal of homosexuality from the *DSM*, Fifth Edition [*DSM-5*; American Psychiatric Association, 2013]; legalization of gay marriage) since the introduction of *Minority Stress Theory*, gay and transgender men continue to be subjected to stigma and prejudice. Hubach et al. (2019) interviewed 40 men who sleep with men (MSM) in rural communities to understand the influence of social and cultural environments on mental health. The results of Hubach et al.'s (2019) study highlighted the impact of stigmatized environments on mental health. Moreover, the participants shared common structural challenges for MSM in a rural community, such as policies that do not address discrimination for sexual minorities and scarce resources. There is a gap in the literature that focuses on sexual minorities in rural communities, which contributes to the invisibility of the issues gay and transmen experience. Additionally, other research has noted the correlation between stigmatization and suicide attempts for gay men (Salway et al., 2018).

Consideration must be given to the impact of men with intersecting identities (e.g., Black and gay; transgender and Asian). Gay men of color are particularly at risk for mental health challenges given their marginalized status (Balsam et al., 2011). They are likely to be stigmatized by institutions, agencies, and people because of racism or heterosexism (Balsam et al., 2011). Counselors must consider their clients' intersectional identities, or the potential for those with multiple marginalized identities (e.g., ethnicity, race, class, gender, sexual orientation) to be victimized through various forms of bias (Crenshaw, 1991; Gillborn, 2015). For example, gay men of color experience discrimination at a disproportionate rate compared to White gay men (Balsam et al., 2011). English et al. (2018) discussed the impact of sexual and racial minority stigma for Black, Latinx, and multiracial men, such as difficulties regulating emotions.

Due to the stigmas associated with gender nonconformity, transmen have an increased need for mental health support (Bockting et al., 2013). Transmen who engage in sexual acts with men experience stigmatization for their sexual orientation and gender (Reisner et al., 2020). When transmen are visible to the public and unable to pass (i.e., be perceived as cisgender), they are potentially subjected to social stigma, such as people referring to them by the wrong pronouns or referring to their sex assigned at birth in a way that does not affirm their gender identities (Reisner et al., 2020). And, although some transmen may experience less stress from wanting to pass as cisgender, others might take their identity to be an act of deception, which could result in physical violence against them (Billard, 2019). All the cited research and examples underscore the risk with which diverse men live because of their identities: they must balance the need for mental health support with the risk of stigmatization for seeking mental health support or receiving assistance from individuals, communities, and professionals.

COUNSELING CONSIDERATIONS, STRESSORS, STEREOTYPES, AND DISCRIMINATION

Given men's risk for being stigmatized for seeking mental health care, it is predictable that they underutilize counseling services (Sagar-Ouriaghli et al., 2019). It is also important to note that overall disparities exist between men and women receiving mental health care, and disparities exist between different racial groups among men seeking care (Anderson, 2018; Pattyn et al., 2015). The following are considerations about what factors contribute to the persistent barriers that impede men's ability to seek help. The research base informs us of several reasons, which we assess to be predominantly related to inequitable access to and biased treatment in mental health care for men. Despite men seeking mental health treatment at a lower rate than women, men can experience a myriad of barriers when seeking treatment. Common barriers for some men, particularly men of color, are working with counselors who are not culturally responsive or knowledgeable, lack of healthcare access, and fear of mistreatment. For these reasons and many others, this can result in the likelihood of not returning for care (Zeber et al., 2017).

Men from different racial and ethnic groups have disparate access to mental health care, and when they do seek care, there are disparities in the quality of care. Primm et al. (2010) documented how White men clients receive higher quality mental health care than men of color clients, for a variety of reasons stemming primarily from racist bias and stereotypes, including lack of cultural competence and insensitivities to the unique needs that men of color have as racial and ethnic minorities. The authors also reported that male clients of color are overrepresented in inpatient treatment settings, and underrepresented in outpatient treatment settings, compared to White men clients, and male clients of color are more likely to use emergency services for the diagnosis or treatment of mental health disorders.

Biased mental health treatment against men can lead to a range of issues, including but not limited to misdiagnoses and discriminatory treatment (Hankerson et al., 2015; Starks, n.d.; Whaley, 2001). For example, schizophrenia and depression are two conditions commonly misdiagnosed among Black men (Hankerson et al., 2015; Starks, n.d.). Contributing to potential symptoms of these conditions is cultural mistrust (Terrell et al., 2009): the dispositions Black people have toward White people and institutions in response to historical and ongoing marginalization (e.g., lethal police violence against Black citizens). Latino men have also had experiences of racialized treatment when seeking mental health and substance abuse services (Guerrero et al., 2013). For example, Mays et al. (2017) aimed to study two phenomena: (a) prevalence of discrimination in mental health and substance abuse, and (b) association of perceived discrimination in mental health and substance abuse visits. The authors reported that Latino men experienced discrimination in mental health and substance abuse settings three times more frequently than White men. Furthermore, the results indicated that being uninsured or having public insurance (i.e., Medicaid) increased the likelihood of discrimination. This is particularly important, given that people of color constitute a large percentage of Medicaid and public healthcare consumers, and/or account for people who are uninsured or underinsured (Buchmueller et al., 2016). For men, being uninsured or underinsured can lead to living with untreated mental health diagnoses. Several scholars have highlighted the need for mental health services among men. Coleman et al. (2016) contend that Asian American men are less likely to be diagnosed with depression than White men, and Indigenous men are at higher risk for mental health diagnoses such as posttraumatic stress disorder (PTSD), depression, substance use disorder, and suicide (Ka'apu & Burnette, 2019). Call and Shafer (2018) reported that men are more likely to die by suicide than women.

COUNSELING RELATIONSHIP AND SELF-AWARENESS

Professional counseling continues to issue a clarion call for culturally relevant and responsive services in its preparation of counselors (Council for the Accreditation of Counseling and Related Educational Programs, 2016) and counseling practice (ACA, 2014; Ratts et al., 2015). This has become especially important as counselors respond to and intervene with mental health support for those affected by the COVID-19 pandemic and increasing documented evidence of ongoing systemic racism against marginalized people. As of the writing of this text, the COVID-19 pandemic has resulted in over 1 million deaths in the United States (Centers for Disease Control and Prevention, n.d.-a), of which over 580,000 are reported as males are reported as males (Centers for Disease Control and Prevention, n.d.-b). The following section includes recommendations for counselors to utilize the MSJCC (Ratts et al., 2015) to gauge their readiness for culturally responsive counseling support, followed by a summary of clinical interventions for men in treatment.

CULTURALLY RESPONSIVE PRACTICES: DRAWING FROM THE MULTICULTURAL AND SOCIAL JUSTICE COUNSELING COMPETENCIES AND CULTURAL HUMILITY

The MSJCC (Ratts et al., 2015) is a revised version of the Multicultural Counseling Competencies (MCC) developed by Sue et al. (1992). This framework is frequently cited in professional counseling, as it addresses how counselors work toward acknowledging the complexity of their cultural selves and influences how they work with clients who are culturally different from themselves. The competencies include developmental domains that "reflect the different layers that lead to multicultural and social justice competence: (a) counselor self-awareness, (b) client worldview, (c) counseling relationship, and (d) counseling and advocacy interventions" (Ratts et al., 2015, p. 3). Among the most important steps in developing the capacity to serve men clients humbly and responsively are to be critically reflective and to develop one's insight and awareness about oneself. We draw from the MSJCC development domains to offer suggestions for professional counselors.

Ratts et al. (2015) admonish counselors to "develop self-awareness, so that they may explore their attitudes and beliefs, develop knowledge, skills, and action relative to their self-awareness and worldview" (p. 5). One actionable step toward this is assessing the source of the counselor's beliefs about men and what it means to be a man. Counselors need to critically reflect upon their ideas about manhood and masculinity, and their associated presentations and behaviors necessary to illuminate preconceived or sustained notions of manhood. This is particularly important for two reasons. First, the reflection increases the counselor's awareness and helps identify the potentially complex history and sources of their conceptualization of manhood. Second, the awareness positions the counselor to take action to deconstruct, avail themself of, and potentially relearn and redefine manhood in healthier and more affirming ways.

Embedded in the MSJCC's first developmental domain, and throughout the competencies, is the need for appropriate clinical supervision. The Association for Counselor Education and Supervision (Association of Counselor Education and Supervision, 2011) indicated that clinical supervision for professional counselors involves activities in which counseling supervisors support counselors to improve the application of theory and techniques with clients. Effective clinical supervision can assist professional counselors to align their awareness work with the MSJCC by helping them progress from acknowledging attitudes, beliefs, and worldviews to developing knowledge about the sources of those attitudes, and taking action to challenge and modify them when necessary. Counselors with extensive experience, counselors early in their careers, and counselors-in-training have an ethical obligation (ACA, 2014) to seek and leverage clinical supervision in order to help meet the needs of their clients, especially when their clients are culturally different from them and/or the clients represent a population with whom the counselor hase not served.

The content provided in this chapter is helpful, but limited. It underscores the need for more research about men, their mental health needs, and how professional counselors can support them. It also acknowledges how social structures and care systems in the United States have been constructed to discount and minimize the importance of men's emotional wellness. The experiences of men as clients continues to be underrepresented, and as a consequence, those needs might be misunderstood. The range and possibilities of more research are endless; however, we offer the following recommendations to contribute to and hopefully enhance our knowledge base.

CRAFTING AN ADVOCACY AGENDA

Creating systemic change that amplifies the importance of men's mental health needs and its relationship to community wellness is a large undertaking. Counselors can start by enacting these recommendations to assist in this endeavor. Our first recommendation is for counselors to assess what counseling services are provided for male children, male adolescents, and adult males in their local communities. Counselors at all levels (e.g., counselors-in-training, counseling practitioners, and counselor educators/supervisors) can constructively assess the agencies, organizations, and institutions with which they have relationships to determine what range of services they specifically provide for men clients. For example, do agencies offer counseling groups for men for a variety of normative experiences (e.g., career challenges, fatherhood, pro-social relationships, etc.)? Furthermore, counselors at all levels can assess their partner organizations to determine what services they have specifically for male children and adolescents, given counselors' understanding of the importance and influence of boys' and adolescents' socialization experiences on their ideas about manhood and masculinity.

Our second recommendation is for counselor educators and supervisors to advocate for more specialized coursework and professional development in preparation programs on counseling men. This ultimately requires counselor educators to deepen their knowledge of and familiarity with men's mental health needs and how addressing them proactively and preventatively can be protective factors for optional functioning and higher quality of life for men clients. Our final recommendation is for political advocacy. Counselors can use their collective influence and platforms to illustrate the need for mental health support for men in a variety of ways with their locally, regionally, and nationally elected representatives. Issues affecting men's mental health in unique ways potentially include support for job readiness for adolescents and adult males and/or reentry programs for formerly incarcerated males. Ongoing political and legislative advocacy for these kinds of specialized programs will support men's mental health at a systemic level.

IMPLICATIONS FOR CLINICAL PRACTICE

Counseling literature highlights the mental health disparities that exist between men and women (Rosenfield & Mouzon, 2013). Included in the process of effectively serving men clients is for counselors to consider their clinical orientation and its influence on how they conceptualize the needs of their men clients. Singh et al. (2020) offered four key multicultural and social justice theories as considerations for professional counselors' use with diverse clients, including men. The scholars recommended relational-cultural theory (Miller, 1976), critical race theory (Bell, 1995), intersectionality theory (Crenshaw, 1989), and liberation psychology (Martín-Baró, 1994). Additionally, the use of queer theory (Sullivan, 2003) as a tool to assist counselors in their broader theoretical or clinical orientation is recommended. Issues including, but not limited to, gender role conflict, sexuality, masculinity, and race help influence men's attitudes and willingness to seek counseling services (Evans et al., 2016; Good et al., 1989; Hayes & Mahalik, 2000; Heath et al., 2017). Having the appropriate clinical approach to counseling men is just as important as men seeking and accessing counseling support. Counselors should be equipped with the information and tools needed to support the needs of all men, particularly men who underutilize or have barriers to counseling services.

Case Conceptualization Using Aforementioned Theories

Critical to appropriate counseling care is the clinician's conceptualization of the client's story and their presenting issues. The ACA (2014) and Ratts et al. (2015) recognize the importance of counselors' understanding and honoring clients' cultural identities as integral to providing appropriate clinical care. As previously articulated, men underutilize counseling services compared to women. Consequently, it is recommended that counselors be diligent in helping men clients understand the scope and sequence of counseling services as frequently as necessary. This may require action like a phone consultation before the intake session to discuss the counseling process and, as Mahalik et al. (2003) suggested, to clarify expectations and correct assumptions men may have about counseling.

CLINICAL CASE SCENARIO 14.1

Jaden is a 25-year-old heterosexual, cisgender Black man who is a full-time engineering student at a university in the southern region of the United States. He grew up in the deep South and is the oldest of five brothers, and his father passed away when he was 3 years old. Although Jaden's family is supportive of his educational and career endeavors, his mother depends on him to provide financial assistance with household bills and guidance for his younger siblings. In an effort to provide what he felt necessary for the rearing of his younger siblings, Jaden started working overtime at his overnight warehouse job during the summer before his final academic semester.

(continued)

CLINICAL CASE SCENARIO 14.1 (CONTINUED)

During the fall semester, Jaden failed a core course needed to meet his graduation requirements and was subsequently referred to the school's counseling and psychological services clinic by his academic advisor. After having missed three appointments with his therapist, Jaden finally made the decision to engage in services. On his intake form, Jaden noted that he was "just here" because his academic advisor suggested it. Gaining a clue to the possible reasons his client had rescheduled his intake several times, the therapist inquired about Jayden's home life. Jayden told his counselor that he grappled with attending therapy because he had been through many trials and tribulations in his life and never needed counseling to help him deal with his issues. He further stated that although he has been under immense pressure during his final academic year, he articulated that "what happens in the home, stays in the home" and that he's skeptical of doctors and feels that talking to a therapist is something only White people do.

CLINICAL CASE SCENARIO 14.1 DISCUSSION QUESTIONS

1. What was the client's dilemma in this scenario?
2. How is this dilemma creating problems for the client and getting in the way of him receiving services?
3. What could be the reasons this client held certain beliefs about who should and should not attend therapy?
4. What culturally responsive interventions might you use with this client?

CLINICAL CASE SCENARIO 14.2

Ricky is a 32-year-old Cuban-American man who grew up in a working-class neighborhood in Miami. With the help of his aunt, he and his two older sisters were able to legally migrate to Florida from Cuba when he was 7 years old. His mother currently resides in Cuba and his father passed away in 1991 in an attempt to migrate to the United States in a wooden fishing boat. Ricky is a devout Catholic and attends church religiously. Although Ricky identifies as heterosexual, he has never had a girlfriend. He currently lives with his aunt and works as a receptionist at a local immigration law office.

Ricky sought counseling due to "feeling that no one notices me" and expressing that he's "not worthy of a woman's time." His presenting concern was most recently triggered by not being called back after going on an expensive date with a woman companion from church. His low self-esteem was accompanied by existential guilt. Throughout adulthood, Ricky has consistently questioned what

(continued)

> **CLINICAL CASE SCENARIO 14.2 (CONTINUED)**
>
> it means to be "Cuban enough." In session, he complains of not living up to the role that men play in Cuban culture. Ricky is brown skinned, a virgin and, when feeling down, he eats large meals—and hence has gained 100 pounds within the past two years. He has been criticized by his male peers for lack of sex appeal. Not meeting everyone's expectations has left Ricky feeling hopeless and inadequate.

> **CLINICAL CASE SCENARIO 14.2 DISCUSSION QUESTIONS**
>
> 1. What social determinants help to dictate how this client feels about himself?
> 2. In what way is this client coping with his stress?
> 3. What culturally responsive interventions might you use with this client?

Strengths-Based and Culturally Relevant Clinical Interventions

Research about diverse men's experiences in counseling informs counselors of some interventions that could be useful in clinical practice (Addis & Mahalik, 2003; Englar-Carlson & Kiselica, 2013; Harper et al., 2009; Kimmel, 2013; Washington, 2018). It has been found that the most consistent messages about clinical care for men clients are that the interventions are strengths-based and culturally relevant. Acknowledging diverse presentations of manhood and masculinity, researchers such as Englar-Carlson and Kiselica (2013) and Kimmel (2013) have suggested that those counseling men should always affirm those diverse presentations and leverage them as a source of strength and resilience. Further, researchers have documented how diverse men have responded to more variety in the provision of counseling services. For example, Addis and Mahalik (2003) suggested that counselors should be open to changing the context of where counseling occurs, when possible. The authors encouraged counselors to consider outdoor spaces or workspaces to assist men with comfort and familiarity, particularly if they are first-time clients. The authors have found that these simple actions enhance feelings of safety, build trust, and communicate a more client-centered approach to therapeutic work.

Harper et al. (2009) recommended several interventions for counseling Black men that are believed to have potential utility in other men client groups, when appropriate. The following treatment approaches are suggested to have merit in the effectiveness of counseling: African-centered group counseling (or other culturally centered interventions, depending on the group composition), integrating hip-hop culture and rap music in individual or group counseling (Washington, 2018), systemic counseling (Gunnings & Lipscomb, 1986), transcendent counseling (Harper & Stone, 2003), poetry therapy (Au, 2005; Elligan, 2000), and/or the use of culturally appropriate humor and narrative storytelling (Solórzano & Yosso, 2001; Vereen et al., 2013). Based on the severity of presenting issues or symptoms, some authors have suggested the value of Posttraumatic Growth (PTG) approaches (i.e., experiences when traumatized people experience a sense of personal growth; Calhoun & Tedeschi, 2013) when working with male victims of race-related trauma (Evans et al., 2016).

Researchers have documented the ways economic hardships and racial discrimination influence the lived experiences and mental health of marginalized men, particularly

Latino men (Guzmán & Carrasco, 2011; Page, 2013). Additionally, some Latino men have been found to experience challenges with gender role conflict and restrictive emotionality, which can lead to increased levels of stress and depression (Fragoso & Kashubeck, 2000). Counseling interventions with Latino men—and potentially other men clients whose lived experiences contribute to restricted emotionality and unhealthy demonstrations of masculinity—can include the promotion of positive masculinity, which was found to show an association with enhanced perception of psychological functioning (Estrada & Arciniega, 2015), greater openness toward others, and stronger ties to ethnic identity (Arciniega et al., 2008).

Recommendations for Additional Research

Additional studies and subsequent books about strategies for the development of positive masculinity will be critical in creating a more robust and representative illumination of factors that support men's well-being. Studies that document the narratives of men whose masculinity has been supported to be healthy, balanced, and accepting are needed and timely. Studies that can help identify the relationship between variables that might predict such positive masculinity outcomes will be important.

Studies that highlight the experiences of men who are neurodiverse are also necessary for counseling literature. Considerations for neurodiverse men and their socio-emotional wellness needs, career needs, and interpersonal needs are all but absent in counseling peer-reviewed journals with the widest readership. We look forward to scholars and clinicians becoming willing to address this need. Finally, ongoing research about men who are consistently and systemically marginalized will continue to be needed. These include but are not limited to men of color, men who are queer or trans, men with varying abilities, and/or men of limited financial means. Scholarship that unapologetically amplifies the mental health needs of these diverse men will undoubtedly enhance our professional literature and assist us in providing culturally responsive support to men clients.

END-OF-CHAPTER RESOURCES

A robust set of instructor resources designed to supplement this text is located at http://connect.springerpub.com/content/book/978-0-8261-3953-5. Qualifying instructors may request access by emailing textbook@springerpub.com.

SUMMARY

Men have been socialized to not seek help, and often mental health professionals are not equipped to effectively counsel them when they do. These and other issues related to the constructs of masculinity, stigmatization, and risk factors, and their impact on men's mental well-being, were discussed in this chapter. Counselors who provide culturally responsive interventions to men offer nonsexist, gender-affirmative care that eradicates barriers men clients face to being mentally well.

DISCUSSION QUESTIONS

1. How do you assist men in understanding the idea of toxic masculinity?
2. What factors does culture have on how minority men perceive masculinity?

3. Do you feel competent to work with sexual minorities, specifically gay and transgender men? If not what support do you need?
4. What are ways you can advocate for inclusive policies for the LGBTQ+ community?
5. What organization can you join to further your knowledge about gay, bisexual, and transgender men?
6. What other theories outside of the ones mentioned in this chapter might be used when working with diverse populations?

▶ **CULTURALLY RESPONSIVE COUNSELING FOR MEN CLIENTS**

Guest: Dr. Michael D. Hannon

https://connect.springerpub.com/content/book/978-0-8261-3953-5/part/part02/chapter/ch14

KEY REFERENCES

Only key references appear in the print edition. The full reference list appears in the digital product on Springer Publishing Connect: https://connect.springerpub.com/content/book/978-0-8261-3953-5/part/part02/chapter/ch14

American Counseling Association. (2014). *ACA Code of Ethics*. Author.

Call, J. B., & Shafer, K. (2018). Gendered manifestations of depression and help seeking among men. *American Journal of Men's Health*, 12(1), 41–51. https://doi.org/10.1177/1557988315623993

Council for the Accreditation of Counseling and Related Educational Programs. (2016). *CACREP annual report 2015*. http://www.cacrep.org/about-cacrep/publications/cacrep-annualreports

Edwards, T. (2006). *Cultures of masculinity*. Routledge.

Estrada, F., & Arciniega, G. M. (2015). Positive masculinity among Latino men and the direct and indirect effects on well-being. *Journal of Multicultural Counseling and Development*, 43(3), 191–205. https://doi.org/10.1002/jmcd.12014

Gunnings, T. S., & Lipscomb, W. D. (1986). Psychotherapy for Black men: A systemic approach. *Journal of Multicultural Counseling and Development*, 14(1), 17–24. https://doi.org/10.1002/j.2161-1912.1986.tb00162.x

Harper, F. D., & Stone, W. O. (2003). Transcendent counseling: An existential, cognitive-behavioral theory. In F. D. Harper & J. McFadden (Eds.), *Culture and counseling: New approaches* (pp. 233–251). Allyn & Bacon.

Meyer, I. H. (1995). Minority stress and mental health in gay men. *Journal of Health and Social Behavior*, 36(1), 38–56. https://doi.org/10.2307/2137286

Ratts, M. J., Singh, A. A., Nassar-McMillan, S., Butler, S. K., McCullough, J. R., & Hipolito-Delgado, C. (2015). *Multicultural and social justice counseling competencies*. https://www.counseling.org/docs/default-source/competencies/multicultural-and-social-justice-counseling-competencies.pdf

Vereen, L. G., Hill, N. R., & Butler, S. K. (2013). The use of humor and storytelling with African American men: Innovative therapeutic strategies for success in counseling. *International Journal for the Advancement of Counselling*, 35(1), 57–63. https://doi.org/10.1007/s10447-012-9165-5

CHAPTER 15

Culturally Responsive Counseling Related to Religion, Spirituality, and Other Faiths

JANEÉ AVENT HARRIS AND CHRISTINE D. GONZALES-WONG

> ### LEARNING OBJECTIVES
>
> After reading this chapter, students will be able to:
> - Apply key concepts of spirituality, religion, and other faiths.
> - Apply Association for Spiritual, Ethical, and Religious Values in Counseling (ASERVIC) competencies from assessment to treatment planning and intervention.
> - Evaluate personal reflections and reactions related to religion and spirituality and identify how these insights may affect the integration of religion and spirituality in counseling contexts.
> - Identify religious and spiritual trends and how they affect the counseling relationship.
> - Critique discriminative and oppressive aspects of religion and spirituality.
> - Employ culturally responsive practices related to religion and spirituality based on the Multicultural Counseling and Social Justice competencies.
> - Create an advocacy agenda related to religion and spirituality.
> - Construct holistic client conceptualization based on spiritual development models.
> - Apply spiritual and religious constructs and interventions to counseling of individuals, couples, and families.

> ### SELF-REFLECTION QUESTIONS
>
> 1. When did you first become aware of your spirituality, religion, and other faith systems?
> 2. How do your religious and spiritual values appear in your day-to-day functions?
> 3. Consider how your spirituality, religion, and faith systems influence your counseling relationships with your clients.
> 4. How might you integrate spirituality, religion, and other faith systems in your clinical interventions?

THE COUNSELOR: EXPLORATION, INTROSPECTION, AND REFLECTION

When traveling on the road, traffic signs are used to guide, warn, or depict what your experience may be on your journey (e.g., stop, go, yield, curvy road, two-way traffic, road closed, construction zone, minimum speed, deer crossing, etc.). When you think about integrating the client's religious and spiritual beliefs and values, what traffic sign would you choose to represent your feelings about this? Are there multiple signs that match your thoughts on discussing religious and spiritual issues with clients? We use traffic signs as a metaphor and reminder that our growth as counselors is an ongoing journey. As counselors, we find ourselves in a unique position in our clients' lives. We are gifted with the opportunity to hold a sacred space for individuals, couples, and families, often at their most vulnerable moments. Thus, we must be able to appropriately integrate the client's spirituality and religious set of values into the counseling space. To do so, we must first examine our own beliefs, values, and experiences—and this is an ongoing journey. In this chapter, we invite you to take a moment to breathe, acknowledge any feelings you may be having as we begin this topic, and journal as you read and process the information we share. These reflective processes are an important aspect of understanding your beliefs and values, which is vital to be ethical and culturally competent.

What comes to mind when you hear the word *religion*? What comes to mind when you hear the word *spirituality*? These words can mean something different to each person and can evoke strong emotions. Because religion and spirituality can be how one derives meaning from life, these concepts can be sensitive and vulnerable topics to discuss with individuals outside of one's circle of trust. It can also be difficult to explore how and where these beliefs come from and how others may be affected by your religion and/or spirituality.

Counseling's History of Religion and Spirituality

Sigmund Freud, "the father of psychoanalysis," wrote that religion was "an illusion" and a symptom of neurosis (Freud, 1927). Freud argued that a personified God satisfied the need for a father and provided a sense of security for individuals (1927). While not everyone agreed with Freud, it is important to understand the impact that Freud's position about religion had on the profession. Even the dissenting theories were in reaction to Freudian concepts.

Almost a century after Freud's original writings on religion, researchers have found that counselors are reluctant to integrate religion and spirituality into counseling, even when they agree that it's necessary to meet clients' needs (Cashwell et al., 2013). This may be due to the historical lack of training in this area (Magaldi-Dopman, 2014; Saunders et al., 2014; D. F. Walker et al., 2004). Some counselor training programs may offer training on spirituality and training as an elective, whereas others are not able to offer it all. Spirituality and religion are often covered in a multicultural course and are limited to one class period because of the amount of material to be covered. Historically, researchers have found that most mental health professionals are not religious or are less religious than the general population (Delaney et al., 2007; Marx & Spray, 1969; Rosmarin et al., 2013; Sheridan et al., 1992). Updated research is needed to see if the religiosity of mental health professionals has changed over the decade and how these findings may affect counselors' feelings about integrating these concepts in the clinician's work. Many counseling diversity textbooks cover specific religions, such as Judaism and Islam, but do not address overarching guidelines and procedures for ethically incorporating religion and spirituality into the counseling process. This chapter aims to help you understand how religion and spirituality may affect your clients across belief systems and provide practical ways you can competently integrate your clients' values into the counseling session.

Your Personal History of Religion and Spirituality

We invite you to take a moment to explore how your views of religion and spirituality may inform your counselor identity and affect your approach to the therapeutic process. Find a peaceful place, take some mindful breaths to clear your mind, and reflect on the following questions. It is important to note that these questions are not limited to individuals who identify themselves as religious or spiritual beings. If you do not identify as religious or spiritual, you still have views and experiences related to religion and spirituality that have played a role in your journey and will inform your counseling process.

1. How did your family of origin view religion and spirituality?
2. How did your family of origin view individuals who had different beliefs about religion and spirituality?
3. How did your beliefs about religion and spirituality as a child and adolescent affect your life?
4. How have your beliefs about religion and spirituality changed over time?

We recognize that thoughts about religion and spirituality may evolve due to one's experiences. Like clients, moments of crises often force counselors to reckon with what they believe and how they apply those beliefs to their work (Avent Harris et al., 2017). Now, we move to questions that aim to understand your current relationship with religion and spirituality.

5. What thoughts do you have about people who have different beliefs about religion and spirituality than you?
6. In what settings do you feel safe sharing your thoughts about religion and spirituality? Why might that be?
7. In what settings do you feel reluctant to share your thoughts about religion and spirituality? Why might that be?

Clients may bring up their religion or spirituality in the counseling session.

8. What emotions do you feel when you think about a client wanting to integrate their religion or spirituality into their counseling treatment?
9. How prepared do you feel to address a client's religious or spiritual issues?
10. What might set you at ease in terms of integrating religion and spirituality into the counseling practice?

Reflection

This chapter explores diversity in beliefs and practices, religious and spiritual discrimination, religion and spirituality as strengths, and how we can become culturally competent in addressing these matters with our clients. As you read the rest of this chapter, pause after each section and be mindful of what you are thinking and feeling. We are not asking you to abandon or change your personal beliefs. Does anything stand out to you? Light a fire in you? Irritate you? Take note and approach those emotions with curiosity. Where might those feelings come from? What beliefs are being affirmed? What beliefs are being challenged? How might your values affect the counseling room?

RELIGION AND SPIRITUAL DIVERSITY: BELIEFS AND PRACTICES

Arguably, religion and spirituality are some of the most nuanced and complex concepts that we consider in counseling. We begin this section by tackling one of the most difficult tasks in the religion and spirituality discourse. How do we operationalize religion and spirituality to present a definition that you would be able to use to guide your learning experiences and application to your work? How do we define these concepts in the context of being culturally responsive, with an understanding that there are both between and within-group differences? That is, although there may be commonalities between those who practice Hinduism, for example, it does not mean this group is monolithic and that everyone would express their beliefs in the same way. Individuals, geographic regions, and certain subpopulations may have cultural nuances in their religious expressions.

Spirituality is often defined as an individual expression of one's connection to themself and divinity (Association for Spiritual, Ethical, and Religious Values in Counseling [ASERVIC], n.d.). This idea of divinity in spirituality is not limited to a Higher Power. For instance, for many people, spirituality can be cultivated through outlets such as nature and practices such as meditation and yoga. Gall et al. (2011) conducted a qualitative content analysis to understand how individuals define spirituality and religion. The themes that emerged in the participants' definition of spirituality were ideas about spirituality being connected to one's "core self," providing perspective for life, having a relationship with God or a Higher Power, tapping into the mysterious, being in tune with the world around them, and religion. These findings speak to the diversity and range of how people define spirituality. While there seem to be common elements, such as community and structure, there remains a thread of individuality and creativity in each person's expressions. Counselors often gravitate toward the use of the word *spirituality* over *religion*, to be more inclusive and culturally responsive rather than assuming a connection to a particular religion. Given the individual nature and vastness of spirituality, counselors may find it to be a more encompassing term (Koenig, 2017).

Although we appreciate the fluidity of spirituality, we also understand the need to define these constructs. And we know that counseling students will likely have to take some sort of standardized exam during your program. Here we present some of the most compelling definitions of spirituality we have found to guide a counselor's work.

> "Spirituality is the aspect of humanity that refers to the way individuals seek and express meaning and purpose and the way they experience their connectedness to the moment, to self, to others, to nature, and to the significant or sacred." (Puchaski et al., 2014, p. 643).
>
> "Spirituality is the universal human capacity to experience self-transcendence and awareness of sacred immanence, with resulting increases in self-other compassion and young" (Cashwell & Young, 2020, p. 12).
>
> "Spirituality is the drawing out and infusion of spirit in one's life" (ASERVIC, n.d., p. 1).

After reading these definitions, consider the following reflection prompts:

- *What resonates with me in each definition?*
- *How might the ideas in each definition show up in a counseling session?*
- *How do I define spirituality?*

Before we proceed with defining religion, we invite you to take a moment to reflect on this question: *How are spirituality and religion similar and/or different for you?*

Religion is often described as a set of organized beliefs and practices (Cashwell & Young, 2020). Religion, as opposed to spirituality, offers more rules and structured guidance on values and practices than spirituality (Cashwell & Young, 2020). We often find religion within communities, as opposed to being more individualistic like spirituality (Cashwell & Young, 2020). The participants in the Gall et al. (2011) study articulated a definition of religion and found hat the themes that emerged from the participants' definitions included tradition, belief in God and/or Higher Power, a means to engage in spirituality, life perspective, and extrinsic values. Moreover, the participants spoke about the negative connotations that are associated with the term *religion*. Because of this, a clinician's counseling office may be the first, and in some cases, the only place where clients feel safe expressing some of their negative views related to religion. The clients may fear feeling shame and guilt when expressing themselves among family and friends. In the spirit of diversity, we would also like to offer you the following definitions of religion:

> Religion is the "organization of belief which is common to a culture or subculture" (ASERVIC, n.d., p. 2).
>
> "Religion provides a structure for human spirituality, including narratives, symbols, beliefs, and practices that are embedded in ancestral traditions, cultural traditions, or both" (Cashwell & Young, 2020, p. 13).

For many clients, some of their most closely held beliefs and values may be hard to articulate to others given the philosophical nature of these concepts. Although religion and spirituality are uniquely defined for clinical and research purposes, clients may or may not choose to differentiate between these two ideas (Cashwell & Young, 2020). Although we are discussing the nuanced differences between spirituality and religion, we do not want to project that they have to operate in opposition to each other. In fact, for many people, they are one and the same or complementary. Cashwell and Young (2020) offer the following ways individuals may identify: *(a) spiritual and religious, (b) spiritual but not religious, (c) religiously tolerant and indifferent, (d) religiously antagonistic,* and *(e) religious but not spiritual*.

A client who identifies as both spiritual and religious may view these constructs synonymously or may be able to articulate how they differentiate the two in their own lives. Clients who are spiritual but not religious may have their own individual interpretation of their spirituality but do not associate with organized religion. Clients who are religiously tolerant and indifferent are more neutral in their attitudes and beliefs toward religion. Clients who are religiously antagonistic have strong negative feelings toward religion. Often, clients who carry these sentiments have experienced some hurt or oppression from an organized religious group. The last descriptor, religious but not spiritual, may be more difficult to identify. These clients may be dedicated to their religious practices and have strong group affiliations, but they do not have a personal connectedness to spirituality. Clients may not overtly declare these affiliations during the counseling process. However, the counselor may be able to ascertain the client's leanings through their language and stories. The counselor will want to be attentive to the labels clients use, their nonverbals, and their voice tone when discussing religious and spiritual matters.

One construct that may capture the sentiments of both spirituality and religion is faith. Parker (2011) defines faith "as a universal human activity of meaning-making, [that] is grounded in certain structures (inherent in human interactions) that shape how human beings construe and interact with self and world" (pp. 89–90). We suggest that while we, as counselors, have heavily relied on the concepts of religion and spirituality, using *faith* in our language may broaden and deepen our understanding of our clients, their worldview, and presenting concerns. For this reason, we encourage you to be creative when thinking about how to assess religion and spirituality in intake sessions. Faith-centered language may be helpful in these forms to learn as much as possible about your client and their connectedness to transcendental ideas. For example, one of the questions on an intake form could be: *What helps you make meaning in life?* Further, open-ended questions such as this one can make space for cultural nuances that may be missed by simply asking a yes-or-no question about religion and spirituality.

Religion and Spirituality in the United States

Most of our clients come to us in some sort of distress, and their values, beliefs, practices, and ideas for meaning making will come "into the room" with them. To that end, we want to spend some time in this chapter unpacking the religious and spiritual landscape of our country. This section will provide some insight into *what* people believe, but also *how* they live out those beliefs in their everyday lives. Counselors should be able to recognize not only differences in belief systems, but similarities and commonalities as well (Shaw et al., 2012).

According to the Pew Research Center, 70% of individuals in the United States identify as Christian (2014). However, Christianity itself is not monolithic, and there is a myriad of denominations represented. Twenty-five percent of Christians are considered Evangelical Protestant, 15% identify as Mainline Protestant, 6.5% are members of Historically Black Protestant churches, and 20% are Catholic (Pew Research Center, 2014). The next largest religious groups are Jewish Americans, who account for 2% of the country's population (Pew Research Center, 2014). Islam, Hinduism, and Buddhism account for approximately 3% of the population (Pew Research Center, 2014). Approximately 22% say that they believe in "nothing in particular" (Pew Research Center, 2014). We will explore this a bit later in the chapter. Remember, although individuals may be religiously indifferent, or even intolerant, you can still ask about their journey and beliefs, as this often provides incredible insight (Cashwell & Young, 2020).

It is important to understand the ways in which this religious landscape is evolving, and that we amplify the voices of those religion and spirituality traditions that are underrepresented and marginalized. Although Christianity is the largest religion in the United States, the number of individuals who identify as Christian continues to decline (Pew Research Center, 2019). The number of people who do not identify as a particular religion continues to grow (Pew Research Center, 2019).

Conversations with clients about religion and spirituality have to be open enough to allow for the nuances and complexities that occur when assessing personal beliefs. It is not enough to simply ask a client if they identify as a particular religion and, if so, what that religion may be. Intake questions and assessments should extend beyond simply asking clients to "check a box." Questions such as "Tell me how you make meaning in life" and "Tell me what you value" may provide the counselor with much more information than asking clients to align themselves with a particular identity. Thus, our clients may not identify as a particular religion, but they may still align with certain aspects of a religious tradition.

The Pew Research Center states that 4% of Americans identify as atheists (Lipka, 2019). Individuals who identify as atheists are most likely to be White, young, male, and college-educated (Lipka, 2019). While most atheists do not believe in a Higher Power, per se, researchers have noted spiritual beliefs that would be important for counselors' considerations (Lipka, 2019). Many atheists acknowledge a curiosity about the world, and a desire to understand meaning and purpose, and feel spiritual peace (Pew Research Center, 2019).

The integration of religion and spirituality is not so that we can judge our clients' beliefs and practices; rather, it is so that we can understand their identities and experiences on a deeper level. This insight helps counselors understand a person's image of their Higher Power, learn more about their faith communities, gain information on spiritual practices already present and possible treatment interventions, learn about places they go to feel connected to the sacred, and how they relate spiritually to creative arts (Oakes & Raphel, 2008).

DISCRIMINATION AND OPPRESSION IN RELIGION AND SPIRITUALITY

Christianity is the predominant religion in the United States (Pew Research Center, 2019). As Europeans invaded and colonized North America, they spread Christianity across the nation. The English Puritans came to North America for religious freedom (Blumenfeld et al., 2009). However, this religious freedom was restricted to the Puritans and was not granted to individuals practicing other religions (Blumenfeld et al., 2009). As the United States was founded and formed its government, Christianity permeated through positions of power in social institutions, including politics, education, and healthcare (Blumenfeld et al., 2009). History is taught from the White Christian perspective, with other perspectives sidelined or minimally discussed. Scholars point out that the holidays celebrated in our work and school calendars generally only include Christian holidays (Blumenfeld et al., 2009). Individuals wishing to celebrate or honor other religious holidays must request those days off or miss those days of school (Blumenfeld et al., 2009). Therefore, Christian individuals have privileges that are not afforded to individuals of other faiths. It is important to note that the number of individuals who identify as Christian in the United States is declining and the number of nonreligious and non-Christian religious individuals is increasing (Pew Research Center, 2019). However, a change in the demographics of the general population does not necessarily indicate a change in the demographics of who is in power and who holds privileges. We should be mindful of what voices and viewpoints have shaped our perspectives, even when the topic seems to be unrelated to religion.

In the 1800s, anti-Catholic sentiments grew alongside anti-Irish sentiments (Library of Congress, n.d.). These sentiments increased as many Irish Catholic immigrants came to the United States during the Great Famine. Protestant followers experienced fear that the religious freedom they had sought would be overcome by an increased Catholic presence and political groups blamed immigrants for economic issues (Library of Congress, n.d.). In the 1910s, anti-Semitism grew, and Jewish individuals experienced discrimination as the "native" middle class viewed Jewish immigrants as encroaching as they advanced in economic status (McWilliams, 1948). In the 1930s, Jews were blamed for the economic woes of the Great Depression (McWilliams, 1948). In 2001, anti-Muslim sentiments grew after 9/11, and Islamic communities experienced discrimination as individuals feared and blamed Muslims for the terrorist attack (Cainkar, 2009). Anti-Muslim and anti-Semitic discrimination and hate crimes increased again during and after the 2016 presidential election (Anti-Defamation League, 2017; South Asian Americans Leading Together, 2018). The events discussed in this section are by no means an exhaustive list of religious discrimination and oppression that have occurred in the United States. While each rise in religious oppression is nuanced and complex, there are political agendas associated with every rise. The underlying political threads woven throughout our history highlight how those with power and privilege can marginalize and oppress others when that privilege is abused.

Since 2016, hate crimes have steadily risen, including religious hate crimes. The Federal Bureau of Investigation (Federal Bureau of Investigation, 2020) reported that 20% of hate crimes in 2019 were due to religious discrimination. For example, in April 2020, a man was arrested and charged in Missouri after setting fire to an Islamic Center.

In May 2021, a man was arrested and charged in New York after setting fire to a yeshiva and synagogue (U.S. Department of Justice, n.d.). Most religious hate crimes are anti-Jewish in nature, followed by anti-Islamic hate crimes (Federal Bureau of Investigation, 2020). These statistics are based on crimes that were reported to officials, so actual numbers may be higher, as not all crimes are reported. In some cases, religious discrimination also intersects with other forms of discrimination based on gender, nationality, ethnicity, or race. For example, a Muslim woman may be the target of harassment due to her choice to wear a hijab. The recent increase in hate crimes is pertinent to counselors, as researchers have found that victims of hate crimes are more likely to experience psychological trauma than victims of non-biased crimes (Fetzer & Pezzella, 2019).

Spiritual and Religious Abuse

Spiritual or religious abuse is any kind of abuse that occurs within a spiritual or religious context, perpetrated by a spiritual or religious leader, by a spiritual or religious group, or by an individual using spirituality or religion as a part of abuse with the goal of conformity (Swindle, 2017; Ward, 2011). Examples of such spiritual or religious abuse include physical and sexual abuse; discrimination based on race, gender, or sexual orientation; and the use of sacred texts (e.g., such as the Bible or Koran) to justify abuse or discrimination (Cashwell & Swindle, 2018). When a spiritual leader is viewed as representing God or being appointed by God, disagreement or disobedience can be viewed as defiance against God (Ward, 2011). Individuals may comply with authority, even when they do not want to. Individuals may come to counseling with complex thoughts and feelings about their religion and/or higher power after experiencing abuse. Untangling perpetrators of abuse from their concept of religion and spirituality may be difficult or impossible. Religious and spiritual practices may evoke trauma responses such as anxiety, hypervigilance, and flashbacks (Cashwell & Swindle, 2018).

Religious Rejection

Rejection from a religious community may occur as a part of noncompliance or discrimination. Members of the lesbian, gay, bisexual, transgender, and queer (LGBTQ) community may experience tension if their religious community is not accepting of their sexual orientation or gender identity (Wood & Conley, 2014; Robertson & Avent, 2016). Due to negative messages regarding sexuality, individuals may experience dissonance in their religious identity and seek to resolve it in various ways (Gibbs & Goldbach, 2020; Rodriguez & Ouellette, 2002; Wood & Conley, 2014). Individuals may reject their LGBTQ identity, reject their religious identity, compartmentalize their identities based on context, or they may be able to fully integrate both identities (Rodriguez & Ouellette, 2002). Individuals who experience conflict between their LGBTQ and religious identities have a higher risk of suicidal thoughts and attempts (Gibbs & Goldbach, 2015). It should be noted that individuals can also develop strengths when they can integrate their LGBTQ and religious identities (Rosenkrantz et al., 2016). LGBTQ individuals have expressed feeling more secure in their LGBTQ identity because of their religious foundation and discovering deeper meaning in their religion/spirituality because of the challenges they have experienced being LGBTQ (Rosenkrantz et al., 2016). Because of the potential for both great inner struggle and strengths that can arise when managing both identities, clients may benefit from exploring the intersection of religion with LGBTQ identity, if it is salient to the client. Religion may be a very important identity or context for a client. However, as with all multicultural and intersectional identities, some identities may not be relevant for a client at a certain point in time. Because of this, it is important that counselors constantly assess and have conversations about what factors may be influencing the client's presenting concerns.

Individuals may also experience religious rejection from their counselor. There was a legal case in which a counseling student refused to counsel a gay client because of her religious values (*Ward v. Wilbanks*, 2009). In response, the American Counseling Association (ACA) clarified in the *2014 ACA Code of Ethics* that counselors cannot make referrals solely based on their beliefs (ACA, 2014, Section A.11.b.). Despite the ethical codes stipulating that one cannot refuse to see a client because of their values, the Tennessee state legislature passed a law that allows counselors to do so, if they provide a referral to another provider (Tennessee Code, 2016). The ACA opposed this law, as it allows counselors to discriminate against protected groups (Yep, 2016). There was much controversy around this law, as some counselors viewed it as protecting their rights and belief systems. On the other hand, some counselors said that the ACA was discriminating against religious counselors by not allowing them to practice their beliefs as counselors.

RELIGION AND SPIRITUALITY AS THE SOURCE OF STRENGTHS

In the previous section, we discussed some of the ways in which spirituality and religion can manifest as harmful and psychologically damaging. Whether one describes themselves as religious and/or spiritual, we would argue that, at the core, religion and spirituality can potentially offer similar psychological benefits as well. Although it is important that we engage in reflection on some of the negative consequences of religion and spirituality, it is equally necessary that we, as counselors, acknowledge religion and spirituality as sources of strength. While clients may be aware of ways in which religion and spirituality can be sources of strength, it may be up to counselors to help increase their awareness and facilitate their access to these resources. For example, counselors can integrate these aspects into treatment plans by identifying supports and resources in faith communities, incorporating spiritual practice as clinical interventions, and seeking ethically appropriate collaboration with spiritual leaders (Avent Harris et al., 2021; Pargament et al., 2011; Van Hook, 2016).

One of the greatest assets an individual can have is hope. Certainly, in times such as these when there are so many sources of stress, individuals can harness hope through their religion and spirituality. In fact, Witmer and Sweeney (1992) state that "at the center of wholeness is spirituality" (p. 140). Spirituality offers individuals optimism and hopefulness, which is an essential tool for coping with and responding to life's challenges (Witmer & Sweeney, 1992). As such, counselors may help clients understand that without some sort of spiritual connection they may be compromised in seeking health and wellness. Now, this does not mean that clients must subscribe to a *certain* type of religion and spirituality; however, this theory does suggest that humans are wired for connection to something larger than themselves (Witmer & Sweeney, 1992).

Therefore, it is important to consider how religion and spirituality and communities formed through these shared values and belief systems can be integrated into a client's treatment plan and therapeutic processes. People are invaluable resources that can be accessed through spiritual connections. Much of the therapeutic work is done outside of the counseling session. Counselors can help clients identify safe spaces within their spiritual networks. Also, leaders can serve in tandem with counselors to offer corrective experiences and spiritual support (Van Hook, 2016).

Religion and spirituality are also ways of making meaning and responding to pain (Pargament et al., 2000). Often, people will come to see a counselor in their most distressing times. Clients who have access to religion and spirituality supports, beliefs, and practices can apply these principles to their lives and use their belief systems to process events (Avent Harris et al., 2021). Counselors who omit religion and spirituality from their treatment planning are essentially eliminating an important resource. Religion and spirituality rituals are also an asset that counselors can integrate into their work. Spiritual rituals offer a pathway to peace and tranquility. When people engage in their spiritual rituals, they often feel calm and get answers to questions that are causing uncertainty and turmoil. Spiritual communities are often a source of strength for clients. In particular, communities of color have found emotional, economic, educational, and social support through their faith networks (Park et al., 2020). As individuals who identify with identities that have been marginalized and oppressed are often viewed from a deficit perspective, it is important for counselors to highlight aspects of cultural wealth (Park et al., 2020).

Religious Coping Assessment

Religious coping is the way in which many individuals enact their beliefs and values when trying to manage a life event or crisis (Pargament et al., 2000). Counselors may choose to assess clients' religious coping strategies so that they are able to get an understanding of their current behaviors as well as provide feedback to encourage adaptive strategies that promote healing and are not counterproductive to their emotional wellness. Assessments can be used at the onset of the counseling relationship, but we ask that counselors also consider how these ideas can be fused throughout the therapeutic journey (ASERVIC, 2009). Counselors can integrate both structured and more open-ended forms of religious coping assessments in the therapeutic journey. Some examples of structured survey assessments are the *Ways of Religious Coping Scale* (Boudreaux et al., 1995), *RCOPE* (Religious Coping, a 14-item measure of religious coping with major life stressors; Pargament et al., 2000), *Hindu Religious Coping Scale* (Tarakeshwar et al., 2003), and *Jewish Religious Coping Scale* (Rosmarin et al., 2009). Some examples of more open-ended assessments could include discussion questions, asking clients to share a song that articulates their coping (Avent, 2016), and artwork.

One of the most widely used religious coping assessments is the Brief RCOPE (Pargament et al., 1998). This assessment is unique and particularly useful because it measures both positive and negative religious coping strategies. Positive religious copings are those patterns and approaches that clients may use to seek closeness with their deity or community or find meaning in their suffering (e.g., collaborative efforts with God to seek resolution or find healing; Pargament et al., 2011). Negative religious coping is practices that are rooted in religious beliefs but that are psychologically counterproductive (e.g., feeling that a life event is God's punishment; Pargament et al., 2011). When working with clients, we have found that using the terms *maladaptive* or *unhelpful* has worked well to describe religiously grounded coping strategies that are not emotionally beneficial for individuals. Clients may have a strong reaction if the counselor uses the word "negative," so instead it may be more helpful to explain to clients that these coping strategies are not serving them well, and while they may be strategies that are easily accessible and familiar, they may not be the most appropriate in their healing processes. We acknowledge that these types of conversations with clients require a strong rapport and sense of trust between client and counselor. Further, counselors should still maintain cultural humility and avoid projecting blame and judgment which could elicit defensiveness from the client. Instead, the counselor may choose to share some of the possible consequences that arise from engaging in more maladaptive coping practices (Pargement et al., 2011).

Spiritual Bypass

When individuals use religion and spirituality to repress negative thoughts and emotions or avoid taking personal responsibility, they may be experiencing *spiritual bypass* (Cashwell et al., 2010). For example, a person may refrain from expressing their anger or sadness after a loss and report that they need to "focus on their blessings" and in this way invalidate their grief process (Avent, 2016). Assessing for spiritual bypass is important, as we want to make sure that we aren't perpetuating the client's spiritual bypass by encouraging further avoidance through religion and spirituality behavior (Cashwell et al., 2010; Fox et al., 2017). The Spiritual Bypass Scale-13 (SBS-13; Fox et al., 2017) is a quantitative measure that can be applied in clinical and research settings. For clients who may be experiencing spiritual bypass, counselors may integrate interventions such as mindfulness to help the client be present with their emotions, rather than repressing them (Cashwell et al., 2010; Fox et al., 2017). Because clients may have difficulty viewing their religion and spirituality as a hindrance to their growth, motivational interviewing techniques may be appropriate to help clients consider discrepancies between their presenting concerns and their desired goals (Clarke et al., 2013). For example, a counselor could use a scaling question to determine the client's motivation to address a bypass concern or discuss the client's values to determine where inconsistencies between the client's behaviors and values may lie (Clarke et al., 2013).

CULTURALLY RESPONSIVE PRACTICES: DRAWING FROM THE MULTICULTURAL AND SOCIAL JUSTICE COUNSELING COMPETENCIES AND CULTURAL HUMILITY

A multicultural orientation to counseling involves cultural humility, cultural opportunities, and cultural comfort (Owen, 2013). Cultural humility is an ongoing commitment to learn about clients' experiences and cultural identities with an other-oriented spirit (Owen, 2013). Cultural opportunities are moments in the counseling session to explore how the client's cultural identities may affect their presenting concerns (Owen, 2013). Cultural comfort is the counselor's ability to have discussions about cultural identities with ease and authenticity (Owen, 2013). When it comes to religion and spirituality identities and issues, it can be difficult to maintain cultural humility and comfort, as our beliefs and values shape how we view the world. Even if you don't identify as religious and/or spiritual, and perhaps are agnostic or atheist, your beliefs about religion and spirituality issues can have an impact on how you view yourself, the client, and their presenting concern (Davis et al., 2020). When this occurs, it may be helpful to reflect upon the Multicultural and Social Justice Counseling Competencies (MSJCC; Ratts et al., 2015). The MSJCC (Ratts et al., 2015) has been endorsed by the ACA and the Association for Multicultural Counseling and Development. These competencies provide a framework for counselors to understand how privilege and systems of oppression may affect the counseling relationship. The competencies consider the possible relationships between client and counselor such as privileged counselor/marginalized client, privileged counselor/privileged client, marginalized counselor/privileged client, and marginalized counselor/marginalized client (Ratts et al., 2016). These relationship statuses are fluid and can depend on the topic of conversation or relevant identity at the moment (Ratts et al., 2016). No matter the relationship status of the counselor and client, counselors are to develop and practice self-awareness, gain an understanding of the client's worldview by inviting honest and open discussions about the ways in which their cultural identities affect their life experiences and relationships, consider the impact of the counselor's and client's culture on the counseling relationship by understanding and identifying ways in which privilege and oppression intersect based on their individual identities, and engage in advocacy efforts (e.g., championing policies that promote and support equity in religious considerations) when appropriate (Ratts et al., 2015).

According to the MSJCC, counselors are to actively work toward continued self-awareness (Ratts et al., 2015). Religion and spirituality privileged counselors reflect on how their religion and spirituality gives them power and advantages that religion and spirituality marginalized clients may not have (e.g., values reflected in education, work and school holidays, etc.). Religion and spirituality marginalized counselors may reflect on the disadvantages they've experienced because of their religion and spirituality and how this has affected them. Culturally responsive counselors reflect on how their religion and spirituality values inform and shape their assumptions and worldview (e.g., possible moral absolution) and remain open to learning more about potential religion and spirituality privileges. Culturally responsive counselors develop and expand their knowledge of how history and events have contributed to religion and spirituality privilege (e.g., imperialism and colonization). Culturally responsive counselors research resources and then take action to promote self-awareness (e.g., continuing education, community learning, etc.). Culturally responsive counselors make it a point to learn about other religion and spirituality organizations and points of view (e.g., attend the service of a different religion, have conversations with different religion and spirituality leaders about how their community is affected by religion and spirituality privilege and other intersections of identity).

Culturally responsive counselors seek to understand their clients' worldviews, including their beliefs and values (Ratts et al., 2015). This may include learning how religion and spirituality privileged and marginalized clients have been affected, applying faith development models, and working through any discomfort that may arise when working through religion and spirituality issues. Additionally, culturally responsive counselors recognize any potential limitations they may have when working with clients. When working with someone with the same religion and spirituality status, privileged or marginalized, counselors should be careful not to overidentify with the client (Thomas & Schwarzbaum, 2011). Overidentification occurs when a counselor incorrectly assumes similar experiences, experiences countertransference, or overlooks symptoms of concern (Thomas & Schwarzbaum, 2011). Culturally responsive counselors also recognize the strengths they hold when working with religion and spirituality privileged and marginalized clients. Counselors with the same religion and spirituality beliefs may be able to offer specific empathy with the client by having a deeper understanding of their experiences. Counselors with different religion and spirituality beliefs can offer a unique perspective and may be able to help the client develop potential solutions that they otherwise may not have considered.

Culturally responsive counselors seek to understand how their and their clients' religion and spirituality privileged or marginalized status affects the counseling relationship (Ratts et al., 2016). This means that the counselor takes the initiative to introduce religion and spirituality issues in intake paperwork, assessments, and the counseling session. Culturally responsive counselors collaborate with clients to explore how religion and spirituality plays a role in the client's life and the presenting concern. This may lead counselors to advocate on the client's behalf, which is explored in the next session.

In addition to the MSJCC, we would like to introduce the ASERVIC *Spiritual Competencies* (ASERVIC, 2009). ASERVIC is an ACA division that provides resources and leads advocacy efforts to promote the ethical and culturally responsible integration of spirituality in counseling. The ASERVIC *Spiritual Competencies* were created to support counselors to ensure that this integration is ethical and culturally responsive. These competencies are not intended to be used in isolation. They should be applied in addition to the *ACA Code of Ethics* (2014), the MSJCC, other relevant competencies, and state ethical codes.

Counselors who practice the ASERVIC *Spiritual Competencies* (ASERVIC, 2009) have basic knowledge of major world religions and acknowledge that religion and spirituality inform an individual's worldview. Counselors practice self-awareness and explore how their religion and spirituality may affect the counseling session. Counselors can apply faith development models such as Fowler's States of Faith (Fowler, 1981) or Genia's Psychodynamic Spiritual Development (Genia, 1995) and empathically address religion and spirituality issues with clients when appropriate. Counselors use appropriate assessment strategies to learn about the client's religion and spirituality history and make diagnoses, treatment plans, and interventions with religion and spirituality in mind when relevant. Overall, counselors consider the impact of religion and spirituality from intake to termination, while managing countertransference.

CRAFTING AN ADVOCACY AGENDA

Advocacy has been mentioned throughout this textbook as counselors' professional responsibility. You may be wondering, "What does advocacy look like as it relates to religion and spirituality?" Some things that may come to mind for counselors may include advocating against oppression and injustices targeted toward someone because of their spiritual and/or religious identity. As counselors, we are being called to balance a focus on providing services for our clients, while at the same time considering our role in the larger society. As a profession, we have been moving toward a more intentional focus on advocacy and social justice. We must always keep our client's needs and experiences at the core of what we do. We understand the sensitive nature of religion and spirituality and how individualistic it can be, but we must not lose perspective of our call to affect the world around us (Ratts et al., 2016).

Counselors can begin their advocacy efforts by ensuring that religion and spirituality are included in counseling processes and are a recognized aspect of diversity and inclusion efforts in the mental health profession and the clinician's more immediate spheres of influence. Counselor educators need to ensure that religion and spirituality is sufficiently covered in the curriculum and infused in all courses so that counselors-in-training are equipped with the skill set needed to serve clients. Likewise, counselors-in-training are obligated to seek out additional educational opportunities to build upon their religion and spirituality knowledge base.

The ratification and implementation of the MSJCC have provided counselors with a framework for creating an advocacy agenda. As we think about creating an advocacy agenda for religion and spirituality with clients and communities, we propose integrating the MSJCC and the ACA Advocacy Competencies (Ratts et al., 2010). It is important to remember that counselors need to be informed and appropriately equipped to effectively engage in advocacy work. Advocacy is not only a reflection of passion; it is also a skill, as counselors want to avoid adding further harm to clients and communities who are already experiencing marginalization and oppression. Thus, good intentions matter, but they are not sufficient when developing advocacy initiatives. Counselors must take this self-assessment before engaging in advocacy efforts so that they are aware of the potential impact of their own biases and experiences (Ratts et al., 2016).

Advocating on a Systemic Level

There will be instances where you will have to advocate for clients and communities. The goal in these cases is never to advance the counselor's agenda; rather, it is to use power and privilege to access spaces to leverage on behalf of our clients. Counselors, in these instances, act in a consultation capacity to negotiate on behalf of those who are experiencing oppression. Counselors can also seek out co-conspirators (Love, 2019) who can serve as collaborators in these advocacy efforts.

Counselors may need to go beyond individual-level (client advocacy) intervention. Examples of advocacy may include the counselor reaching out to the provost to ask them to disseminate a memorandum that would require instructors to be flexible in observance of religious holidays. These advocacy efforts seek to implement lasting change that can help the individual the client is serving and others. Further, the counselor may engage in collaboration with the client community (Toporek et al., 2009), such as the Buddhist campus group, in advocacy initiatives. In this instance, the counselor can use their leverage as a university employee to get access to key stakeholders that would be able to respond to the client's concerns.

Historically marginalized communities have historically leaned on their faith communities for advocacy support. For example, Black Churches have often served as the cornerstone of political action and social justice efforts in Black communities (Avent et al., 2015; Avent Harris, 2021; Lincoln & Mamiya, 1990). Counselors can be open to learning from other community stakeholders, such as Black pastors (e.g., Rev. Otis Moss, III), who have been leaders in social justice efforts. Religious theologies such as Black Liberation Theology may provide counselors with a framework for supporting clients and communities as they work toward a release from oppressions experienced either in interpersonal relationships or within larger systems (Cone, 2010).

COUNSELING CHILDREN, ADOLESCENTS, AND YOUNG ADULTS

Faith Development Models: Spiritual Development Across the Life Span

Human development is an integral component of our understanding of the human experience. As counselors, we are exposed to this content to help us learn how our clients may develop over time as they progress through childhood, adolescence, young adulthood, and adulthood. You are probably familiar with theorists such as Freud, Erikson, Piaget, Bowlby, and Vygotsky. These theorists focus on individuals' cognitive, behavioral, and social development, and have long been discussed in counseling training programs. While these theories help us understand the human experience and provide insight into case conceptualization and treatment planning (Corey, 2016), it is noteworthy that truly culturally responsive understanding would include spiritual development (Avent Harris et al., 2021).

We understand that it is beyond the scope of this book chapter to review all of the religion and spirituality development theories. The brevity of our review does not reflect the value we believe exists in counselors' being knowledgeable of faith development models and able to apply them when working with clients. Like many of the aforementioned human development theories, faith development models are organized in ways that correspond with individuals' chronological age. However, it is important to remember that one's age does not necessarily indicate that a client will be in that particular faith development stage. These developmental models provide counselors with language to identify a client's current understanding of their religion and spirituality, how it informs their presenting concerns, and offer an outline for growth. We will not provide an exhaustive list of models, but we will discuss some of the most popular.

Fowler's Stages of Faith

One of the most well-known and widely used spiritual development models is Fowler's Stages of Faith (Fowler, 1981). This model, grounded in cognitive development principles, outlines six stages that narrate one's progression through their spiritual journey. The emphasis on the cognitive aspects of spiritual development is interesting, given that the very nature of religion and spirituality often transcends logic. Fowler (1981) begins with stage 0, primal-undifferentiated faith. Caregivers establish trust and security by tending to the needs of an infant. This trust, or lack thereof when an infant experiences neglect or abuse, can set the stage for how the infant will later feel about the divine. Stage 1, intuitive-projective faith, begins with children mimicking the actions of the adults in their lives as it relates to religion and spirituality. During this stage, you may see a child lift their hands while listening to worship music. This is not necessarily because they understand the spiritual practice, but because they have seen influential adults in their lives participate in this activity. In these beginning stages, counselors may utilize play therapy activities (e.g., role-playing, sand tray, storytelling) to get a sense of the child's religion and spirituality practices. Not only might this reveal pertinent information about the child, but it may also give counselors a glimpse into who is influential in the child's life and what religion and spirituality practices are important. In stage 2, mythic-literal faith, beliefs tend to be more literal and usually align with elementary school-aged children. This is where children begin considering others' truths. This is a good point of intervention for counselors to harness the ability to be considerate of others' truths. Most individuals will move through this stage. However, just because a person ages does not mean that they will move past this stage. Clients who are not able to hold multiple truths and who maintain a literal understanding can remain at this stage regardless of their age. Stage 3, synthetic-conventional faith, usually occurs during the formative adolescent years. Fowler (1981) suggests that individuals in this stage begin looking for a community in their religion and spirituality lives. People form identity at this stage through the commonalities they find within spiritual communities. Perhaps one of the most well-known examples of this stage is the popularity of youth groups in religious communities.

Stage 4, individuative-reflective faith, typically occurs during the mid-twenties to the late thirties and is characterized by the transition of religion and spirituality authority moving from external to internal. It is important to consider the roles that parental figures and spiritual leaders may play in either promoting or inhibiting this transition. Counselors can play an integral role in supporting individuals through this transition, as individuals at this stage may notice conflicts in their beliefs. College counselors, for example, will need to be aware of this, as clients may not explicitly state conflicts. Stage 5 typically occurs when an individual is in their mid-thirties. This stage is characterized by an individual's move from a dichotomy of beliefs to holding multiple truths at the same time. Individuals in this stage may no longer be as committed to categorize beliefs and behaviors as "right or wrong." One of the ways this stage may show up is for an individual who is in a relationship with someone who holds different religion and spirituality beliefs. Stage 6, universalizing faith, occurs when an individual is completely congruent in their ideals and behavior, transcends beyond doctrine, and treats every human with compassion, love, and justice. Most individuals do not reach this altruistic stage. Fowler organized the stages to correspond with chronological age. As culturally responsive counselors, we understand that the stages may not be literal in their progression. Different life events can advance or regress our development process. Counselors must be also open to clients revisiting stages when they are triggered by a life event.

Genia's Psychodynamic Spiritual Development

Genia's (1990, 1995) approach to spiritual growth and development is theoretical, as opposed to other models which are founded in research. In this model, Genia creates space to account for individuals' adaptive and maladaptive spiritual traits along their journey. The five stages are *egocentric faith, dogmatic faith, transitional faith, reconstructed faith,* and *transcendent faith.* Genia's model differs from those of other scholars in that it aligns with psychodynamic tenets and unpacks the role of Freudian constructs in the client's spiritual journey. Ideally, individuals will grow from a more dichotomized, self-centered understanding and presentation of religion and spirituality to reach a place where their actions are in full alignment with their spiritual beliefs. While this theory is designed such that the stages correspond to chronological age, it is more focused on an individual's development. Therefore, a person could be well advanced in age and remain at the infancy stage of spiritual growth development.

COUNSELING ADULTS, COUPLES, AND FAMILIES

We have spent a significant amount of time in this chapter discussing how religion and spirituality iaffects individuals. It is equally important to consider how our relationships with religion and spirituality influence our relationships with others. Religion and spirituality can be the lens guiding how we interact with others, how we interpret our roles in these relationships, inform our expectations of ourselves and others, and guide the values we hold dear. Therefore, counselors must be prepared and equipped to address religion and spirituality in couples and families counseling.

IMPLICATIONS FOR CLINICAL PRACTICE

We are aware that conversations about culture and diversity can be motivating but can also feel overwhelming. A lot of the information we have shared is considered theoretical, and imagining what these concepts will look like in use with clients can feel intimidating. We want to end this chapter with ideas for practical application. While these interventions are focused on clinical practice, we encourage you to imagine how you may also integrate these initiatives in education and supervision settings.

Help-Seeking Behavior

Many reasons prevent individuals from seeking mental health treatment, including gender, cultural norms, and self-stigma, which is a negative evaluation of oneself if one were to seek treatment (Brenner et al., 2018). Researchers have found that men with high religious commitment combined with self-stigma may be less likely to seek mental health treatment (Brenner et al., 2018). Additionally, religion and spirituality minority populations may be more likely to seek help from religion and spirituality leaders rather than mental health professionals. For example, religious African Americans may first seek help through the church (Andrews et al., 2011). Latino Americans and immigrants may seek help at *botánicas*, spiritual stores and centers, and through *curanderismo*, traditional healing practices that address mind, body, and soul (Ransford et al., 2010). Asian Americans and immigrants and others believing in karma may avoid mental health treatment, as they may believe that mental health problems are deserved, resulting in shame (Yamashiro & Matsuoka, 1997). Individuals practicing or influenced by Buddhist principles may not seek treatment due to the belief that suffering is a part of the human experience and may decide to endure their concerns (Yamashiro & Matsuoka, 1997). It's important to remember that the intersections of identities can play a crucial role in help-seeking behaviors. Religion and spirituality beliefs may play a role in how individuals decide to address their mental health concerns. However, other factors can affect a person's decision to seek or not seek treatment, such as accessibility of care, mistrust of health providers, financial concerns, language barriers, immigration status, and stigma of mental health treatment (Callister et al., 2011; Duncan & Johnson, 2007; Yamashiro & Matsuoka, 1997).

World Religion Calendar

It is important to be mindful of major world religious holidays. However, we also understand that we are all human and may not be able to remember every holiday. We encourage you to create a calendar with these dates. We also encourage you to invite clients to add to the calendar, as they may have knowledge of holidays that you did not include. In your first session with the client, you may invite them to review the calendar and begin to identify days or dates that may conflict with their religion and spirituality practices. The counselor initiating this conversation, rather than the client, indicates interest in the client's religious life and may decrease any fear of judgment the client may have about disclosing their religious activities. Even if the client still wants to attend a counseling session on a holiday, inclusion can make an impact.

Musical Chronology and Emerging Life Song

For many, music is a means of connecting to the divine and a form of expression for deeply held religion and spirituality beliefs. Music is interwoven in the fabrics of rituals and worship services, which lends itself to being integrated into therapeutic processes as well (Avent, 2016; Duffey, 2005a, 2005b).

The Musical Chronology and Emerging Life Song (MCELFS) is an activity that infuses music into the therapeutic process (Duffey, 2005a, 2005b). Creative interventions, such as music and art, can help facilitate difficult discussions and provide opportunities for clients to reach greater awareness. In this activity, clients are invited to choose a song that represents their past, present, and future selves. Avent (2016) gives the example of Luther, a recent widower who was having difficulty processing his grief. He had immersed himself in his duties at church, to the point where he was neglecting his emotional and mental health. In the case illustration, the counselor invited Luther to select three songs that would represent the past, present, and future. Through these songs, the counselor was able to aid Luther in processing his grief and lean into an adaptive spirituality that could be used as a strength and coping resource rather than as a hindrance to his full healing (Avent, 2016; Duffey, 2005a, 2005b).

Spiritual Genogram

Counselors have used genograms to help clients understand familial and relational patterns. Genograms can focus on biological traits and patterns that exist. We do acknowledge some of the cultural limitations of genograms, as families are not necessarily limited to those in biological relation with us. We encourage counselors to invite clients to create their genogram key rather than prescribing descriptors. Counselors can then ask clients to identify religion and spirituality beliefs among their family and friends on the genogram, illustrating patterns and points of reflection. Counselors can encourage reflection through questions such as the following:

What stands out to you in your genogram?
What patterns do you notice as it relates to religion and spirituality in your relationships?
Who would you identify as major influences in your spiritual journey?

Traffic Signs for the Spiritual Journey

Here we come back to where we started with the traffic sign exercise. At the beginning of the chapter, we asked you to choose a traffic sign that reflected your feelings about integrating religion and spirituality into your counseling practice. Similarly, this exercise can be used with a client. Ask clients to choose a sign that reflects how they feel about their spiritual journey at this point. Once the client has chosen the sign, you can process these reflections with questions such as "What resonated with you about this sign?", "How has your sign changed or remained the same over time?", "What sign would you like to see in 1 year? 5 years? 10 years?" These are sample questions and can be tailored more specifically for the client's presenting concern.

Theory and Theology

Like the traditional developmental models that most of you will become familiar with in your counseling training journey, there are also staple counseling theories that can be applied to the therapeutic process. One of the ways that counselors can integrate religion and spirituality in counseling is to expand counseling theories to include religion and spirituality theologies in case conceptualization and treatment planning. First, we imagine that counselor educators would need to reimagine counseling theories courses to include religion and spirituality frameworks and theology. *Theology* is defined as one's thoughts about their divine and/or higher power (Badham, 1996). Theology, in its traditional sense, is usually associated with Christianity (Badham, 1996). However, as we consider culture and diversity in this textbook and our application to the therapeutic process, we encourage you to expand this traditional knowledge of the word to apply the idea of theology to other world religions, as well as more individualized interpretations of spirituality. Although we encourage you to increase your knowledge of theology and consider integrating these ideas into your counseling practice, we also would remind you to resist the urge to feel like you need to be an expert in this area. Often, an honest curiosity in these subject matters can carry you a long way.

Theologies are different from traditional counseling theories in that they center the religion and spirituality identities and practices rather than religion and spirituality being an unnamed "add-on" and diversity consideration. For instance, Avent et al. (2015) suggested integrating Black Church theology for increasing culturally responsive counseling practices for Black communities. Black Church theologies explore individuals' understanding of the divine, specifically as it relates to Black communities. These theologies often fuse race and religion and illuminate the rich histories and injustice experiences of Black people. Some of the most well-known Black Church theologies include Black Liberation Theology (BLT; Cone, 2010) and Womanist Theology (Cannon, 1985; A. Walker, 1983). Black Liberation Theology wrestles with the oppression and liberation of Black Americans. These theological tenets may give voice to Black clients' experiences and present concerns in ways that traditional, White male-created theories cannot. This theology focuses on Jesus as more than a spiritual being, but as an activist for the liberation of the oppressed. BLT leans toward a more philosophical approach and may be difficult for counselors searching for practical applications. To that end, Haskins et al. (in progress) suggest integrating this theological approach with Narrative Therapy. These two frameworks, when used in conjunction with each other, empower individuals to work toward liberation and to tell their stories. Womanist Theology focuses on the nuanced experiences of Black women from a holistic, systemic perspective, including religion, economics, politics, education, and more. Womanist scholars challenge us to consider the scriptures through the lens of Black women, centering their experiences and acknowledging their pain and discrimination. This theology goes beyond BLT in that it considers the intersection of race and gender, and the specific barriers that exist for Black women. Avent Harris et al. (2021) suggest coupling Womanist Theology with Relational Cultural Theory (Jordan, 2009) for a culturally responsive approach when counseling Black women. The integration of Womanist Theology and RCT emphasizes relationships, empowers and centers Black women, and honors spiritual and religious foundations (Avent Harris et al., 2021).

Counselors can integrate Brown Church theology (Romero, 2020) when working with Latinx clients. Brown Church theology acknowledges the unique discrimination and oppression that Hispanic and Latinx communities have experienced through colonization and religion. It also addresses how the Christian faith can be used to promote social justice and advocacy efforts for the Latinx community, with an emphasis on community and belonging. Latinx Christian clients may find acceptance and identity affirmation when counselors integrate Brown Church theology into counseling treatment.

Consultation

When working with clients, religion and spirituality issues may arise in a variety of ways. Your client may want you to integrate religion and spirituality into treatment, you may have conflicting views with your client, or you may be experiencing your internal tension regarding religion and spirituality. You may feel uncomfortable sharing your thoughts and feelings about these issues, as it may require you to disclose to your counseling supervisor about your own religion and spirituality (Gonzales-Wong & Harris, 2021). This can be scary, but it's important to address any religion and spirituality issues that come up so that we can respond ethically and competently to our clients' needs. If your supervisor expresses apprehension or uncertainty about integrating religion and spirituality into counseling, we encourage you to seek further consultation and remember the competencies and ethical codes that you must consider. Even after supervision ends, it is wise to have a trusted group of professional counselors you can consult with when you need to. It can also be helpful to consult with religion and spirituality leaders in the community to help you on your quest to become more knowledgeable and aware of your clients' worldviews. Remember that if you are discussing any client information, you must have a signed release of information from the client to protect the client's right to privacy.

CLINICAL CASE SCENARIO 15.1

Esperanza is 16 years old and has been referred to counseling after her father was arrested for assault after a family violence incident. She and her 10-year-old brother are now living at her grandmother's house while their mother completes a service plan as required by Child Protective Services. Esperanza's mother tested positive for cocaine during a home visit. Esperanza knew her mother was using substances and was partly relieved that she would be getting treatment. However, Esperanza has mainly been feeling guilty, because she is the one who called the police after her father hit her mother. Her parents had always had a volatile relationship, but it had never escalated this far in her presence. She believes she is to blame for her father's incarceration, her mother's substance use being made public, and her grandmother having to take care of her and her brother. Esperanza has been in a depressed mood for the past month and has

(continued)

CLINICAL CASE SCENARIO 15.1 (CONTINUED)

lost interest in the things she once enjoyed, such as baking and watching YouTube videos with her friends. She hasn't been able to eat, and her grades have started slipping because she is unable to pay attention during class. Her grandmother has picked her and her little brother up from Esperanza's mom's house to take them to church every Sunday since she was a toddler; now her grandmother asks the pastor to speak with her. The pastor tells Esperanza that she needs to pray and have enough faith and she will feel better and see that everything happens for a reason. Esperanza listens but feels abandoned by God because she prays, and nothing changes about her family situation or her emotional state. When she thinks about God abandoning her or punishing her, she feels hopeless and worthless. Esperanza doesn't share these thoughts with the pastor because she feels ashamed that she isn't good enough for God to answer her prayers.

CLINICAL CASE SCENARIO DISCUSSION QUESTIONS

1. When you read this story, what thoughts and emotions come up for you?
2. What role do Esperanza's religion and spirituality beliefs play in her presenting concerns?
3. How might the pastor's advice affect how Esperanza thinks and feels about the situation?
4. What faith development stage might Esperanza be in and how does this affect her coping?
5. How might a mental health diagnosis affect how she is viewed from her religion and spirituality beliefs?

END-OF-CHAPTER RESOURCES

A robust set of instructor resources designed to supplement this text is located at http://connect.springerpub.com/content/book/978-0-8261-3953-5. Qualifying instructors may request access by emailing **textbook@springerpub.com**.

SUMMARY

In this chapter, we asked you to do the hard work of reflecting on your own experiences and beliefs about religion and spirituality. We acknowledge that religion and spirituality can be taboo topics to discuss and can evoke fear of judgment. We are often taught to intentionally avoid discussing spirituality and religion. As counselors, we do ourselves and our clients a disservice when we take this approach. Moreover, it is in direct contradiction to our ethical guidelines and our professional best practices. We can help clients feel comfortable with discussing religious and spiritual issues by initiating conversation, assessing the importance of religion and spirituality to the client's treatment, and using relevant religion and spirituality interventions in session. When discussing religion and spirituality, it's important to be aware of our reactions, as our values shape our worldview.

DISCUSSION QUESTIONS

1. How can you maintain your personal beliefs while counseling a client who has different beliefs and values than you?
2. How do you find strength in your religion/spirituality?
3. How does my client experience power and/or oppression in their religion and spirituality identity?
4. What resources do I have at my disposal to create a significant change with my client?

KEY REFERENCES

Only key references appear in the print edition. The full reference list appears in the digital product on Springer Publishing Connect: https://connect.springerpub.com/content/book/978-0-8261-3953-5/part/part02/chapter/ch15

American Counseling Association. (2014). *2014 ACA Code of Ethics*. Author. https://www.counseling.org/resources/aca-code-of-ethics.pdf

Avent, J. R. (2016). This is my story, this is my song: Using a musical chronology and the emerging life song with African American clients in spiritual bypass. *Journal of Creativity in Mental Health*, 11(1), 39–51. https://doi.org/10.1080/15401383.2015.1056926

Avent, J. R., Cashwell, C. S., & Brown-Jeffy, S. (2015). African American pastors on mental health, coping, and help seeking. *Counseling and Values*, 60(1), 32–47. https://doi.org/10.1002/j.2161-007X.2015.00059.x

Avent Harris, J. R., Haskins, N., Parker, J., & Lee, A. (2021). Womanist theology and Relational Cultural Theory: Counseling religious Black women. *Journal of Creativity in Mental Health*. https://doi.org/10.1080/15401383.2021.1999359

Cashwell, C. S., Glosoff, H. L., & Hammond, C. (2010). Spiritual bypass: A preliminary investigation. *Counseling and Values*, 54(2), 162–174. https://doi.org/10.1002/j.2161-007X.2010.tb00014.x

Ratts, M. J., Singh, A. A., Nassar-McMillan, S., Butler, S. K., & McCullough, J. R. (2015). *Multicultural and social justice counseling competencies*. https://www.counseling.org/docs/default-source/competencies/multicultural-and-social-justice-counseling-competencies.pdf?sfvrsn=8573422c_22

Ratts, M. J., Singh, A. A., Nassar-McMillan, S., Butler, S. K., & McCullough, J. R. (2016). Multicultural and social justice counseling competencies: Guidelines for the profession. *Journal of Multicultural Counseling and Development*, 44(1), 28–48. https://doi.org/10.1002/jmcd.12035

Ratts, M. J., Toporek, R. L., & Lewis, J. A. (2010). *ACA advocacy competencies: A social justice framework for counselors*. American Counseling Association.

CHAPTER 16

Culturally Responsive Counseling for Clients of Jewish Descent

KENNETH D. ROACH AND TZACHI FRIED

LEARNING OBJECTIVES

After reading this chapter, students will be able to:
- Identify characteristics and cultural factors related to Jewish individuals.
- Identify various Jewish subcultures and groups.
- Describe common stressors and challenges facing Jewish individuals.
- Recognize implications for clinical practice with Jewish individuals.
- Apply the information learned from the chapter to clinical case scenarios.

SELF-REFLECTION QUESTIONS

1. Think about biases, prejudices, and assumptions you might have about Jewish people. How do these help and hinder your ability to provide culturally sensitive counseling?
2. What hesitancies, if any, do you have about working with Jewish clients? What attributes do you have that will enable you to work with Jewish clients?

THE COUNSELOR: EXPLORATION, INTROSPECTION, AND REFLECTION

What would be your first thoughts if you learned that your next client was a Jew? What stereotypes about Jews do you believe? Is it your view, for example, that Jews can be identified by their appearance, their mannerisms, or their speech? What expectations would you have about your client's level of education and socioeconomic status? Would you presume that your client dresses in distinctive Jewish garments, wears a *kippah* (male-identified) or headscarf (female-identified), and adheres to the teachings and practices of Judaism? This chapter explores the religious beliefs, practices, languages, history, heritage, and culture of American Jews, including the rich diversity of these people and their experiences.

INDIVIDUAL IDENTITIES

Jews in a Multicultural Framework

It was not until the 1990s that Jews were first considered a culturally distinct group in the field of multicultural counseling (Langman, 1995; Weinrach, 2002). Before then, Jews were overlooked as a topic of interest, perhaps because—according to the prevailing viewpoint at the time—Jews had completely and successfully assimilated into dominant American (i.e., White) society (Fein, 1988; Friedman et al., 2005; Gilman, 1994; Hartman & Hartman, 2011; Rubin, 2017). Jews enjoyed above-average levels of education and wealth in America (Fein, 1988; Langman, 1995; Pew Research Center, 2014). As a result, there was no reason to attend to the unique needs of Jews because they were regarded as quintessential, successful Americans (Kakhnovets & Wolf, 2011).

Placing Jews in a multicultural framework has not always been easy (Langman, 1995). After all, Jews are not an underrepresented minority, nor are (most) Jews people of color, nor are (most) Jews economically disadvantaged, nor are (most) Jews recognizable by their appearance. Indeed, many Jews have seamlessly assimilated into mainstream American culture. At the same time, "many assimilated, non-observant Jews still carry a strong sense of being outside mainstream American culture" (Langman, 1995, p. 4).

The reality of being Jewish in the United States has always been complicated. Being Jewish is not a race (Kakhnovets & Wolf, 2011; Langman, 1999); there are Jews of all races. It is nevertheless true that most American Jews are White (Pew Research Center, 2014). Some Jews consider themselves to be conventional Americans; others do not. For many Jews, however, irrespective of the degree to which they embrace the religion of Judaism, there is an awareness that one is never completely safe as a Jew. "What is the first lesson a Jew learns? That people want to kill Jews … . To be a Jew in America … is to carry with you the consciousness of limitless savagery" (Fein, 1988, pp. 59–60).

Judaism in the United States

Since the 1650s, there has been a consistent Jewish presence in the land that would one day become the United States of America (Karesh & Hurvitz, 2008). Approximately half of the world's 14 million Jews now reside in the United States (Jewish Virtual Library, n.d.). Approximately 2% to 3% of Americans identify as Jewish (Langman, 1995). Apart from a shared identity, there are significant differences among Jews. Indeed, there are virtually no assumptions that a counselor can safely make about the client who identifies as Jewish.

A Jew could be an Ashkenazi or Sephardi Jew. A Jew might identify as Orthodox, Conservative, Reform, Reconstructionist, or none of these branches of Judaism. Some Jews affiliate with a synagogue; some do not. Not all Jews identify as Jews, even though they would be considered Jews according to Jewish law. Jews may or may not believe and adhere to the teachings and practices of their religion. Some Jews believe in God; some do not. Most Jews are Jews from birth, but some are converts to Judaism. A Jew might or might not select as a spouse someone who is also Jewish; the two could then raise their children according to Jewish teachings and practices. Some Jews are strong supporters of the nation of Israel; some are not. Some Jews speak Hebrew, Yiddish, or both. Any combination of these dimensions, to any degree, could be consistent with a Jewish identity. A brief overview of the various dimensions of being Jewish is provided in this chapter.

Judaism as a Religion

According to the Jewish, or Hebrew calendar, the earth was created in the year 3761 BCE (i.e., "before the common era"). Jews generally prefer *BCE* to *BC,* and *CE* (i.e., "common era") to *AD* (Anno Domini), because the birth of Christ holds no special meaning for Jews. The Hebrew calendar is lunisolar, meaning that it is synchronous with both the sun and moon.

Devout Jews believe that God's name is YHVH (or YHWH). According to Jews, the name of Deity is written without vowels because it would be considered sacrilege to write God's name. Judaism does not consider God to be gendered, although the male pronoun is often used when referring to Deity. In Jewish prayer, God is typically referred to by the title *Adonai* (i.e., "Lord"). Some more observant English-speaking Jews, to demonstrate respect when referring to Deity, use the term *G-d* in written communication. In speech, God is referred to as "Hashem," Hebrew for "The Name." Historically, not all Jews were monotheistic, but Judaism has been a monotheistic religion for millennia.

Jewish religious services involve prayer and reading from the *Torah*, a scroll containing the first five books of the Hebrew Bible, or Pentateuch. The word *Torah* may also be used to refer to the Pentateuch and the entire compendium of Jewish law and biblical interpretation and exegesis over the centuries. Because Jews do not embrace the Christian "New Testament," they use the terms *Bible, Hebrew Bible,* or *Hebrew Scripture* instead. Most Jews accept that Jesus of Nazareth was a Galilean Jew who preached and taught, but Judaism teaches that the Messiah has yet to arrive to liberate and redeem the Jewish people. Historically, a small number of Jews have accepted Jesus as the Messiah.

The Jewish Sabbath begins at sundown on Friday and ends at sundown on Saturday. For Orthodox Jews, the Sabbath (also known as *Shabbat* or *Shabbos*) is spent at home with family and friends. This is largely because going to work or school is forbidden on the Sabbath, as is transportation, the use of electricity, and cooking. Appliances, lights, and air conditioners are either left on from before sunset on Friday or operated by timers set up before sunset. Food for the sabbath meals is either left to cook in a slow cooker from before sunset or prepared beforehand and heated up on hotplates. Given the numerous religious requirements of *Shabbos*, Orthodox Jews leave work or school early on Friday to prepare. Most Jewish holidays, with some exceptions, include the same requirements.

Jewish worship services take place in a *synagogue* (sometimes called a *temple* in Reform and Reconstructionist Judaism), and services are conducted by a *rabbi*. Rabbis receive their training at any number of rabbinical seminaries (*yeshivahs*) throughout the world. Judaism is not a hierarchical religion, and disagreeing with one's rabbi would not, by itself, be considered disrespectful. In Judaism, the rabbi is not considered an intermediary between the congregant and God, and Jewish law demands the same of the observant Jew that it does of the rabbi. Nevertheless, rabbis are often regarded with great respect, and Judaism includes a rich heritage of rabbinical writings and teachings. Orthodox Jews observe three daily prayer services, which are supposed to be conducted in the presence of a group of 10 males above the age of 13 (called a *minyan,* or quorum). Seating in Orthodox synagogues is segregated by sex. This is not the practice in most non-Orthodox synagogues.

Observant Jews adhere to a set of dietary laws which govern what foods may and may not be eaten. This is referred to as *keeping kosher*. The laws of *kosher* are quite extensive and include instructions for the preparation and storage of food as well. For example, only meat from certain animals may be eaten, and only if the animal is slaughtered in a specific manner. Meat and dairy foods cannot be consumed together. Fish with fins and scales may be eaten, but no other seafood is permitted. Though most food in restaurants and supermarkets is not kosher, the average supermarket in the United States contains a wide variety of kosher products, identifiable by certain symbols on the packaging.

In Judaism, religious practices are often considered to be more important than religious beliefs (Jewish Religion). As a result, there are wide differences among American Jews in the degree to which they accept the teachings of Jewish Orthodoxy. Some of the religious practices considered most important to Jews are male circumcision, observing the Sabbath, learning Hebrew, respecting *kosher* dietary laws, honoring the passage into adulthood for male Jews (the *bar mitzvah*), observing Jewish holidays (especially *Yom Kippur, Rosh Hashanah, Passover, Sukkot,* and *Shavuot*), the Jewish wedding, the Jewish funeral, and ritual mourning after the death of a loved one. Jews are expected to bury their loved ones within 24 hours after death. Among Orthodox Jews, regular Torah study and ritual purity laws are also emphasized. It is beyond the scope of this chapter to discuss these practices in detail. Due to the communal nature of these practices, more observant Jews typically reside in clustered communities where amenities such as kosher food, Jewish educational institutions, and synagogues are more readily accessible.

There are broad differences among American Jews in the degree to which they embrace the teachings of Orthodox Judaism, some of which follow:

- Judaism does not teach that life begins at conception, but abortion is only acceptable only in specific circumstances.
- Judaism has adopted a favorable view of human sexuality, yet sexual activity between members of the same sex is considered unacceptable, as is sexual activity in general before marriage.
- Divorce is permissible, but only the husband can grant a divorce. Husbands who refuse their wives a divorce are subject to communal pressure to grant it.
- Judaism teaches that burial, rather than cremation, is appropriate.
- Judaism teaches that there is an afterlife, although the nature of this existence is not agreed upon.

The Denominations of Judaism

There are four major denominations of Judaism: Orthodox, Conservative, Reform, and Reconstructionist. In 2018, 29% of American Jews identified as Reform, 11% identified as Orthodox, and 3% identified as Reconstructionist (Jewish Virtual Library, n.d.). Fully 41% of Jews identified as "secular" or "other." Some (e.g., Langman, 1995) have argued that Judaism ought to be divided conceptually between Orthodox and non-Orthodox Judaism because the heterodox Jewish denominations are far more similar to each other than they are to Orthodox Judaism. To non-Jews, these differences can be difficult to comprehend. Many Orthodox Jews do not consider non-Orthodox Jews to be Jewish, and some non-Orthodox Jews regard Orthodox Judaism as a cult. There are also important differences between the so-called modern Orthodox and the more conservative Haredi Jews, among whom the Hasidic Jews are most numerous (Jewish Virtual Library, n.d.; Langman, 1995). Some refer to the Haredi as ultra-Orthodox, although Haredi Jews believe that theirs is the correct interpretation of Judaism.

So-called modern Orthodox Jews tend to be the most integrated into mainstream society of all Orthodox groups. This can be discerned with regard to their choice of clothing, music, and cultural activities, among other things. This being said, modern Orthodox Jewish children and adolescents are still more likely to attend exclusively Jewish schools, summer camps, and other extracurricular activities.

Ultra-Orthodox Jews are more likely to self-segregate to a greater extent and tend to be more identifiable by their dress (white shirts, dark slacks, and black fedora hats for men; long-sleeved shirts and long skirts for women; married women also wear a hair covering or wig). Hasidic Jews often speak Yiddish as a first language, even in the

United States. Most reside in communities in the New York area. Hasidic men are even more distinctive in their dress and appearance, which can include beards and long sidelocks of hair.

Among Orthodox Jews in America, the Hasidic Jews have the highest birth rate, although Orthodox Jews overall have a higher birth rate than heterodox Jews. Orthodox Jews tend to be more isolated from mainstream American society. Heterodox Jews have children at rates that fall well below replacement (Joffe, 2011).

Judaism as an Ethnicity and Culture

According to the Pew Research Center (2014), only 35% of American Jews reported that religion was "very important" to them. Only Buddhists, Hindus, and religious "Nones" reported lower rates of religious importance. In a Pew study (2021), just 21% of Jews said that religion was "very important" to them.

In the Pew Study (Pew Research Center, 2014), just 19% of Jews said they attended religious services weekly, and 62% of Jews said they "seldom or never" participated in prayer, scripture study, or religious education. Only 17% of Jews reported that religion provided guidance on what was right and wrong, and fewer than one in five Jews believed in absolute standards of right and wrong. Just 40% of Jews believed in Heaven, and 37% reported they were "certain" that God existed.

It would seem reasonable to infer from the Pew Study that many Jews did not feel a strong connection to their religion. Despite this, there are strong disagreements about the degree to which the religion of Judaism can be separated from a Jewish ethnicity and culture. To more observant Jews, the very suggestion that one can be a cultural Jew—without a strong mooring to the teachings and practices of Judaism—is incomprehensible. Rosenthal Kwall (2015) asserted that "Cultural Judaism absent any connection to Jewish law is an impossibility" (p. xiii). According to this perspective, Jewish culture and law are inseparable: Both are part of Jewish tradition. "Jewish law ... produces Jewish culture, and Jewish culture produces Jewish law" (Rosenthal Kwall, 2015, p. xiii).

Counselors will find considerable variation in how Jews relate to their religion and culture. In their study of post-baby boom American Jews, Kelman et al. (2017) found that a large number of Jews considered themselves Jewish and not religious. Cultural Jews tended to regard Jewish religious teachings as obsolete and no longer relevant to modern life. Their relationship with Judaism involved a shared heritage, tradition, community, and culture. Kelman et al. (2017) considered these to be ethnic, cultural, or secular Jews. One study participant stated, "I'm proud that that's my culture, but truthfully, Judaism does not play a very large role currently in my life" (Kelman et al., 2017, p. 149). Another said, "Being Jewish is very important to me and I'm very proud of my heritage and where I've come from" (Kelman et al., 2017, p. 142).

Kelman et al. (2017) found that many of these cultural Jews continued to engage in certain religious practices, even though they did so simply because it was their tradition and heritage. They did so because they still felt a connection to the Jewish culture. For these Jews, rejecting their religion did not automatically mean rejecting the practices of Judaism. One study participant said, "I still very much enjoy songs and prayer, the experience, and I still connect to the community, and I still feel connected to friends and family, especially [those] who are Jewish" (Kelman et al., 2017, p. 142). Another reported, "The religion itself means very little to me ... . I practice certain observances ... not out of belief in God ... [but] more out of being part of a community" (Kelman et al., 2017, p. 143).

Not all Jews, of course, reject their religious identity (Kelman et al., 2017). These more observant Jews could be characterized as having both religious and ethnic identities.

Characteristic of this Jewish identity was the participant who stated, "I don't consider myself a cultural Jew ... I consider myself a religious, if not always observant Jew. I consider myself a cultural Jew, too .... [C]ulture is included .... [T]o think of [Judaism] primarily as a culture seems to be missing the essence. It would be like the sandwich without the stuff in the middle" (Kelman et al., 2017, p. 146).

Ashkenazi (or Ashkenazic) and Sephardi (or Sephardic) Jews

After the expulsion from Judea in 73 AD, the Jewish nation was scattered throughout the Roman Empire. Over time, disparate Jewish communities evolved differing religious customs and cultural mannerisms. Those who settled in the Iberian Peninsula became known as Sephardi Jews. Jews who settled in Central and Eastern Europe became known as Ashkenazi Jews. After the Spanish Inquisition in the Middle Ages, Sephardi Jews resettled in North Africa and the Middle East. Though smaller communities of Jews settled in other areas of the world, most Jews today categorize themselves into one of these two larger groups. Before World War II, 90% of the world's Jews were Ashkenazi. Because of the Holocaust and low birth rates among Ashkenazi Jews, they now make up just 80% of the world's Jews. The majority of American Jews are Ashkenazi Jews (Berlin, 2011; Karesh & Hurvitz, 2008; Wigoder et al., 2002).

Judaism as a Civilization

Kaplan (2010) claimed that the Jewish people constituted a civilization, because of their land (Judea), society, religion, history, and culture. Kaplan argued that the Jewish people had the essential elements of civilization: a native land; a language (Hebrew) and literature; customs and laws (e.g., Sabbath observance, circumcision, and diet); folk sanctions (i.e., taboos and notions of sanctity); folk arts (e.g., literary, musical, visual); and social structures (i.e., society's ability to coerce behavior by physical force or social expectation). The implication of this was that the Jewish identity was more than a religion, more than an ethnicity, more than a nationality. Indeed, there are Jewish communities around the world (Langman, 1995), although most Jews reside in Israel and the Western Hemisphere.

Modern Jewish thinkers such as Ravid have followed Kaplan's tradition with the idea of Jewish "peoplehood" (Ravid, 2007). According to Ravid, "being part of the Jewish People transcends time .... We are connected whether we know each other or not, regardless of our knowledge of Judaism or degree of faith, and even without the consciousness of being part of the collective" (2007, p. 1). This definition of peoplehood describes the sense of belonging that many Jews report, even those who do not identify as religious (Friedman et al., 2005; Kakhnovets & Wolf, 2011). Irrespective of the degree to which Jews regard themselves as a civilization or peoplehood, it is reasonable to infer that most Jews are extremely proud of their heritage, their resilience as a people, and their significant contributions to the sciences, the humanities, and the arts. As of 2020, Jews accounted for more than 20% of all Nobel Prize recipients (Jewish Virtual Library, n.d.).

Jews as the Chosen People

Jews believe that they are God's "chosen people"; this is based on several statements in the Hebrew Bible. Interpretations of what it means to be the "chosen people" vary considerably, but definitely can include the notion of superiority. Indeed, some Jews embrace the belief that they are favored above the *Goyim*—non-Jewish Gentiles who do not follow God's laws (Stein, 1984).

Other Jews view the mantle of being chosen as a moral obligation. According to Stein (1984), being the chosen people involves "a call to service, not entitlement or overbearingness" (p. 18). Other Jews believe that being chosen involves the duty to disseminate Jewish insights into the relationship between the human and the divine.

Reconstructionist Judaism has disavowed completely the notion that Jews are somehow a chosen people. Irrespective of these beliefs about the blessings, or obligations, of being the chosen people, being a Jew is not considered a guarantee of eternal salvation.

The irony of being God's chosen people—all while suffering hatred, persecution, and genocide—is not lost on Jews. Fein (1988) stated that "what comes with being Jewish is not just pride but pain, not only a celebration but also sorrow, not only blessing but also burden" (p. 5). Stein (1984) observed that the suffering is the price of being the chosen people; Jews experience martyrdom as "timeless, dreaded, and expected" (p. 5).

Who Is a Jew?

According to Orthodox Jewish law, "If the biological mother is a Jew, then regardless of the biological father, all her children are Jewish. If she is not a Jew, all her children are not Jews as well" (Brackman, 1999, p. 806). Pressure from non-Orthodox Jewry, both within Israel and the United States, ultimately resulted in a modification of this dictate, at least for the purposes of Israeli citizenship.

Israel now accepts as citizens any applicant whose parent or grandparent was Jewish (Berlin, 2011; Brackman, 1999; Karesh & Hurvitz, 2008; Wigoder et al., 2002). Although these individuals are citizens under Israeli law, they are not recognized as Jews by the state, which enforces the Orthodox definition of being Jewish. These citizens are not permitted to marry under Israeli law, which does not recognize civil marriage. A Jew who converted to another religion would be considered to have betrayed the faith and would not be accepted as a citizen by Israel.

Since the early 1980s, Reform Judaism in America has recognized as Jews the children of a Jewish father in an interfaith marriage (Berlin, 2011; Karesh & Hurvitz, 2008; Sasson et al., 2017; Wigoder et al., 2002). These Jews, however, would be required to undergo an Orthodox conversion ceremony before being allowed to participate in Orthodox religious ceremonies such as marriage. These disagreements have created tension in different religious and secular settings about who is recognized as Jewish.

According to Jewish teachings and practice, Jewish identity is considered an "integral and permanent characteristic of the Jew—analogous to a racial or ethnic identity" (Brackman, 1999, p. 805). "Regardless of the level of observance of a born or ... converted Jew, their identity as Jews is not called into question" (Brackman, 1999, p. 805). As a result, one's Jewish identity cannot be taken away. Nevertheless, Judaism does recognize excommunication, although the practice is extremely uncommon.

According to Klaff (2006), about a quarter of all Jews identify as Jewish even though they do not embrace Jewish teachings or practices, are not affiliated with any Jewish religious denomination, and are not members of a Jewish synagogue. This is consistent with a more recent Pew Research Center Study (Pew Research Center, 2021) which found that 27% of American Jews—40% of Jews under the age of 30—described themselves as "atheist, agnostic, or 'nothing in particular'" instead of Jewish. In the Pew Study, one-third of Jews reported that they were not affiliated with any branch of Judaism.

Perhaps it seems difficult to comprehend for those who are not Jewish, but it would be a mistake to minimize or dismiss the likelihood that many of these Jews still have a strong sense of being Jewish. Indeed, these Jews might continue to engage in various Jewish religious practices and customs, and they might maintain a cultural connection with Israel and various Jewish organizations. The culturally competent counselor would explore with each Jewish client how they define and experience being Jewish.

Gender Roles in Judaism

Judaism is a patriarchal religion in which traditional gender roles and family life are emphasized (Berlin, 2011). Only men are counted toward the *minyan* (quorum), the requisite number of people required for prayer. Traditionally, only men were ordained as rabbis, cantors, and community leaders. However, women have begun to fill these roles in non-Orthodox congregations over previous decades, and a trend toward women playing a larger role in religious life and leadership is currently in motion in more liberal Orthodox communities.

Although most major religious obligations apply equally to men and women, Orthodox practice differentiates certain requirements that are unique to each gender. For example, women are exempt from prayer times and certain fasts, as it is assumed that they are taking care of children. Men are required to set aside time from work to pray and study the Torah. Women are required to dress in a modest fashion and to cover their hair after marriage (though adherence to these requirements varies by community), whereas men are required to wear a special fringed garment (*tsitsis*) under their clothes and wear phylacteries (*tefillin*) during morning prayers.

According to Orthodox law, Jewish identity was conferred by a Jewish mother. Nevertheless, children were historically considered to be the offspring of the father, and the father was routinely awarded custody following a divorce (Kaplan, 2008). This practice has fallen out of favor in modern times, and the welfare of the child is now more likely to be the primary consideration in custody disputes.

As with other dimensions of Jewish law and practice, one would expect to find more defined gender roles among Orthodox Jews (Berlin, 2011). In non-Orthodox Judaism, the liberalization of gender roles is seen not only in the family but also in the ordination of female and LGBTQ+ rabbis. In non-Orthodox religious services, men and women are generally treated more equally, in some cases with full equality.

The Languages of Judaism (Hebrew, Yiddish)

Nearly all Orthodox, and many non-Orthodox, Jews learn to read and speak Hebrew. For non-Orthodox Jews, Hebrew is often learned by taking classes at their synagogue (or temple). For Orthodox Jews, Hebrew is taught as part of a broader religious education at a private school. The language of the Bible is a simplified version of spoken Hebrew (Berlin, 2011; Karesh & Hurvitz, 2008; Wigoder et al., 2002). Jewish prayers are uttered in Hebrew, and the Torah is read in Hebrew. Hebrew is spoken during Jewish religious services, although non-Orthodox services typically include more English. Modern Hebrew is used for both religious and non-religious purposes and is the language spoken in Israel.

Yiddish is approximately 1,000 years old; it is primarily a blend of German, Hebrew, and Aramaic (Berlin, 2011). Most European Jews spoke Yiddish, so the language was nearly lost during the Holocaust. Its use was further diminished by the assimilation in America of the Jewish people. Yiddish is a rich language that was used in daily communication as well as in literature. There are still some Jewish communities, primarily Hasidic, that speak the language. Most non-Jewish Americans are familiar with at least a few Yiddish words, such as *chutzpah*, *klutz*, and *schmooze*.

The *Shoah* (Holocaust)

The annihilation of approximately 6 million Jews during World War II was by no means the only genocide or holocaust in world history, and Jews were certainly not the only group to suffer the horrors perpetrated by the Nazis. In addition to Jews, political prisoners, Roma (Gypsies), Jehovah's Witnesses, individuals with disabilities, and "homosexuals" were also murdered in Nazi concentration camps (Jewish Virtual Library, n.d.).

Jews readily acknowledge, and remember, that there have been other holocausts (Karesh & Hurvitz, 2008). "Jews do not see or feel the Holocaust of WWII to be unprecedented in human history. They assimilate it into the mainstream of human history" (Stein, 1984, p. 6). Jewish persecution and tragedy in the diaspora are recurring themes in Jewish folklore and history; the Holocaust is merely the most recent and relatable iteration of this theme. One can debate the many possible meanings of the Holocaust, but it has become the Jewish identity (Stein, 1984).

The World War II Holocaust stands out in history for the systematic and efficient way in which the Nazis murdered Jews. The sheer number of deaths, and intent to annihilate an entire population, make the Jewish Holocaust especially atrocious. The Holocaust was an act so fundamentally evil that it defied comprehension, although many have since tried to explain the inexplicable. Some Jews have found a small degree of comfort in knowing that the nation of Israel was founded, in 1948, as a result of the Holocaust.

Jews and Israel

Jewish prayer and traditional liturgy are replete with references to Zion, the land of Israel, and God's eventual return of the Jewish people to the land of Israel. A small Jewish community had always existed in the land of Israel, but aside from scattered groups over the centuries who made their way back to the land of Israel, the majority of the world's Jews remained in the diaspora. The Zionist movement arose in the late 1800s to advance the Jews' right to national self-determination as a response to centuries of persecution. The movement was secular and nationalistic, arising in the worldwide context of waning colonialism and emerging nationalism and emancipation. As such, many Orthodox Jews did not support the Zionist movement, and some religious opposition to the secular nature of the state of Israel continues to this day. Some in the reform movement also opposed Zionism for its highlighting of the Jews' outsider status in their countries of residence.

Following the establishment of the state of Israel, the question of Zionism became moot and most Jewish groups placed their support behind it. Today, Orthodox Jews are more likely to support and identify with Israel and are also more likely to have visited Israel. Many Orthodox high school graduates spend a year or more studying at a religious institution in Israel before beginning college in their home countries. Many Orthodox Jews look favorably on *aliyah*, or immigration to Israel.

According to the Pew Research Center, two-thirds of American Jews over the age of 65 stated that they were "very or somewhat" emotionally attached to Israel (Pew Research Center, 2021), compared to just under half of Jews under the age of 30. Among Jews over the age of 50, half reported that caring about Israel was an "essential" part of their Jewish identity. This compared with only a third of Jews under the age of 30.

Although there is considerable support among Jews for the nation of Israel, there are significant differences of opinion about the Israeli government, its policies, and its commitment to finding peace with the Palestinians. Most Jews would not react negatively to another Jew who criticized Israel. If a non-Jew were to level the same criticism, however, these same Jews might be suspicious of the underlying sentiment. The presumption would be that a Jew who criticized Israel also recognized the nation's absolute right to exist; the non-Jew might not. Criticism of Israel is not necessarily rooted in antisemitism, but criticism of Israel by a non-Jew might not be received well.

Jewish Culture

Some would argue that Jewish culture and Jewish law are inseparable, that Jews are Jews only to the extent that they adhere to Jewish law (*halakhah*). Other Jews strongly defend the concept of the cultural or secular Jew; these Jews are likely to select the beliefs, commandments, practices, holidays, and traditions that they find meaningful. It is a safe generalization that the majority of Jews still embrace their Jewish identity.

Although ultra-Orthodox (or Haredi) Jews and, to a lesser extent, modern Orthodox Jews, have characteristic ways of dressing, non-Orthodox Jews are not usually identifiable by their dress. Among non-Orthodox Jews, one would expect to find a wide range of dietary practices, including some who maintain kosher dietary laws. Even Jews who do not adhere completely to kosher law might refrain from eating pork (and certain cuts of meat) and might refrain from eating meat and dairy products at the same meal.

Jews generally employ a communication style that is direct and highly verbal. Judaism is not a hierarchical religion, so conflict and debate—within marriages, families, synagogues, and communities—are valued. Those who are unfamiliar with this style of communication might find it brash.

Jewish humor covers a broad range of topics, including God, family, rabbis, guilt, and antisemitism (Karesh & Hurvitz, 2008). Jewish humor often involves wordplay, sarcasm, and interpretation skills. To those who are unfamiliar with Jewish culture, Jewish humor may seem unusually harsh and self-deprecating. Some have argued that Jewish humor is a response to centuries of oppression. Indeed, it serves multiple purposes: relieving fear and depression, expressing covert anger and resentment, and acknowledging Jewish shortcomings.

Although most American Jews are White, they have not always been accepted as such (Langman, 1995). For hundreds of years in Europe, Jews were not regarded as White. The Nazis retained this classification, of course, and attempted to annihilate Jews because they were not Aryan. Many White supremacist groups in the United States continue to look upon Jews as something other than White. Some Jews consider it ironic that they are now grouped with the same racial group that oppressed them for centuries, and many Caucasian Jews consider their primary identity to be Jewish rather than White.

Client Worldviews and Perspectives

Jewish worldviews vary considerably as a function of geography, family history (including psychological distance from the *Shoah*), degree of identification with being Jewish, adherence to Jewish law, affiliation with a Jewish congregation, and experiences with antisemitism. A young, secular Jew in San Francisco might be affiliated with a Reconstructionist synagogue; attend services only sporadically; consider themself agnostic; marry outside of their religion; observe only a handful of Jewish laws, traditions, and holidays; identify as a political liberal; and be quite critical of Israel. A modern Orthodox Jew in New York might believe in God, identify strongly with their religion, attend religious services regularly, faithfully adhere to Jewish law (*halakhah*), be a staunch supporter of Israel, marry another Jew, raise children according to Jewish law, and identify as a political conservative.

Notwithstanding these differences, there are some values and perspectives shared by the majority of Jews, including the importance of family and education (Kadushin & Tighe, 2008). Many Jews embrace a strong commitment to social justice (Dollinger, 2019). With respect to education, a Pew Research Center study found that more than 60% of American Jewish adults have earned a college degree, and more than 30% have earned a graduate degree, although educational achievement is slightly lower among Orthodox

Jews (Hartman & Hartman, 2011; Pew Research Center, 2021). No other American religious group achieves the same levels of education (Hartman & Hartman, 2011). Perhaps this is a reflection of the fact that Jews are also the most secular of all American religious groups.

Jewish teachings, culture, and values also include charity, community and social welfare, civil rights, education, and achievement in one's career (Langman, 1999). Jews are justifiably proud of their contributions to the sciences, the arts, literature, religious thought, the labor movement, the women's movement, and the civil rights movement, as well as international and American politics. Although Jews might not refer to *tikkun olam* as the reason for serving one's community, the value is frequently embraced by Jews.

According to the Pew Research Center (2021), nearly two-thirds of American Jews report that they are Democrats or lean Democratic. Only 21% of Jews identify as conservative; 43% report that they are liberal, compared to 33% who identify as moderate. Orthodox Jews, however, are more politically conservative, and most Republican Jews are Orthodox (Jewish Virtual Library, n.d.).

Counselors would be unwise to make assumptions about the religious beliefs and practices of Jewish clients. Although it is safe to assume that Orthodox Jews are more likely to believe in God and adhere to Jewish law (*halakhah*), the counselor can expect a broad range of beliefs among non-Orthodox Jews about God, spirituality, life after death, prayer, and morality. With respect to sexuality, for example, non-Orthodox Jews have a broad range of attitudes. Orthodox Jews, however, are likely to have more conservative beliefs about morality and sexuality, including sexual orientation and gender identity.

DISCRIMINATION AND STEREOTYPES

Antisemitism and Antisemitic Violence in America

There is no doubt that America has been the land of opportunity for Jews. The fact that nearly half of the world's Jews reside in America is evidence that the Jewish people feel welcome here. At the same time, America has always been the land of antisemitism and antisemitic violence. Consider hate crimes, for example, as just one measure of antisemitic violence (the Federal Bureau of Investigation [FBI; n.d.-b] defines a *hate crime* as a "criminal offense which is motivated, in whole or in part, by the offender's bias" [para. 5]). According to the FBI, only about 20% of single-bias hate crimes are motivated by religious bias, yet Jews are the targets of these hate crimes about 60% of the time—more than all other religious groups combined (FBI, n.d.-a). It is impossible to overstate the significance of this statistic, given that Jews comprise only about 2.5% of the U.S. population.

According to a survey by the Anti-Defamation League (2020), nearly two-thirds of American adults agree with one or more antisemitic tropes. Examples include beliefs that Jews are responsible for killing Christ, that Jews stick together more than other Americans, and that Jews are more loyal to Israel than they are to the United States. In surveys about antisemitism during the past 25 years, about 11% to 14% of American adults (as many as 36 million people) have consistently admitted to biases that are intensely antisemitic.

Many Americans are unaware of the history of discrimination against Jews in the United States (Langman, 1999). In colonial times, Jews were forbidden to live in Massachusetts, Connecticut, and New Hampshire. Some states denied Jews the right to vote or hold public office. This pattern continued during the 19th century. Early in the 20th century, some hotels posted signs that read "No Jews or dogs allowed," or "No Hebrews or tubercular guests received" (Langman, 1999, p. 8).

Epstein and Forster (1962) carefully documented discrimination experienced by Jews in America. Although the examples are now more than 60 years old, they included pervasive discrimination in housing, education, employment, and even leisure. In the case of employment opportunities, many jobs required that the applicant be Christian. With respect to housing, Jews were often denied the opportunity to purchase homes that were for sale. Many colleges and universities asked applicants about their religion and imposed a quota on—or outright denied entry to—Jewish students. Representative of these practices was a 1959 rejection letter from a South Carolina school for girls to a Jewish family that included the following: "It is a wise policy not to accept students of religious faiths different from the majority of the girls here. ... Our resident girls are all members of Christian churches" (Epstein & Forster, 1962, p. 144).

Langman (1999) argued that there are multiple manifestations of antisemitism, including religious (e.g., holding the view that Jews are "Christ-killers," espousing the lie that Jews murder children to use their blood in religious rituals), social (e.g., restricting access to various housing, education, or career options), political (e.g., blaming Jews for a variety of world events and problems), economic (e.g., believing that Jews control the U.S. economy; suggesting that Jews are unusually shrewd and cheap, as captured in the expression that someone "Jewed me down"), sexual (e.g., denigrating Jewish women as sexually withholding, seeing Jewish men as impotent or "defilers of Christian women" [Langman, 1999, p. 95]), and racial (e.g., regarding Jews as impure, unclean, dirty, or smelly).

Many holidays (Easter, Good Friday, Christmas) can serve as reminders to Jews that they do not have a place in America. Even sports teams, with names like "the Crusaders," celebrate individuals and events in world history that resulted in the slaughter of thousands of Jews. Langman (1999) points out how preposterous it would be to name a team "the Gestapo" (p. 96).

Many Jews remember that the Holocaust might not have happened had the German people opposed Hitler. Furthermore, the Holocaust might not have happened had the Pope denounced the killing of Jews. Finally, the Holocaust might have been less deadly had the United States granted entry to Jewish refugees attempting to flee Europe (Langman, 1999). More Nazis might have been held accountable had the Catholic Church not facilitated their escape to South American countries. More Nazis might have been held accountable had the United States not granted asylum to some Nazi scientists, including war criminals.

Yet another manifestation of antisemitism, in the eyes of many Jews, is the attempt to convert Jews to Christianity. In 1989, a small group of evangelical scholars met in Bermuda and drafted a manifesto about the urgency of converting Jews to Christianity (World Evangelical Fellowship, 1989). The document called upon Christians to "encourage the Jewish people ... to accept God's gift of life through Jesus the Messiah" (World Evangelical Fellowship, 1989, p. 161). Evangelicals asserted that proselytizing was the "supreme way of demonstrating love" (World Evangelical Fellowship, 1989, p. 161). The American Jewish Committee condemned the manifesto, arguing that it was a "blueprint for [the] spiritual genocide" of the Jewish people (Myers, 1990, p. 41). After all, a Jewish Christian is considered an apostate (no longer a Jew) in all branches of Judaism and the nation of Israel. Converting all Jews to Christianity is tantamount to eliminating Judaism—hardly an expression of love.

Some Christian denominations, including the Catholic Church, have since renounced attempts to convert Jews (Wilkins, 2008). The rationale for this change is summed up in this excerpt: "While the Catholic Church regards the saving act of Christ as central to the process of human salvation ..., it also acknowledges that Jews already dwell in a saving covenant with God" (U.S. Conference of Catholic Bishops, 2002, p. 7). Unfortunately, the adoption of institutional policies such as this does not always mean that church members will adhere to these guidelines.

Rubin (2017) shared a poignant account of the discrimination he encountered when he applied for a teaching position at "a national university in the United States" (p. 131). He reflected on checking the "White" box on applications that asked his race. He observed, "How can I possibly be White in American society if, as a Jew, my people are still being victimized and persecuted by those who are labeled as White? How can I be White if many White people in this country still dislike and distrust me due to my religious and cultural traditions?" (Rubin, 2017, p. 131). Even for Jews who appear to be White, the intersection of race and Jewish identity dramatically changes one's experience in the United States.

Internalized Antisemitism

It is widely accepted that those in the United States who suffer prejudice and discrimination (e.g., individuals who are Black, Indigenous, and People of Color [BIPOC], LGBTQ+, differently abled, or female-identified) often internalize the negative attitudes they regularly encounter. "Where some measure of integration is a desideratum, and there is also bigotry in the 'majority culture,' minority self-loathing will occur" (Reitter, 2009, p. 360). It is therefore unsurprising that internalized antisemitism is widely observed among Jews. "Jews, like other minorities with persecution in their histories, must struggle to integrate and digest the persecuted victim as part of one's history and ultimately one's self-concept" (Klein, 1989, p. 5). Some Jews cope by disaffiliating from their identity: "If being Jewish [means] wearing a yellow star, they [want] no part of it" (Klein, 1989, p. 5).

For Jews who retain their identity, "the conflict between assimilation and identification for Jews exacts a price in discontent, alienation, and various forms of self-hate" (Klein, 1989, p. 7). Schlosser et al. (2009) define internalized antisemitism as "the passive and/or active concealment of one's Jewish identity and feelings of self-hatred" (p. 56). In a phenomenological study involving 10 Jews in a community in the northeastern United States, Friedman et al. (2005) found considerable ambivalence among Jews about their identity: "Most Jews expressed pride but also a sense of being 'less than' from Gentiles" (p. 82). Both secular and Orthodox Jews feared the judgment of other Jews for their respective lifestyles.

Many Jews try to hide their Jewish identity (Rubin, 2017) by adjusting their appearance to not look Jewish. Some Jews undergo rhinoplasty to try to hide their identity (Gilman, 1994). Fear is the natural response to four thousand years of persecution (Altman et al., 2010). Many Jews try to keep a low profile and avoid calling attention to themselves (Langman, 1995). "Historically, being Jewish has been dangerous, and that legacy is deeply imbedded in the consciousness of Jews" (Langman, 1995, p. 6).

Langman (1995) argued that assimilation actually contributed to internalized antisemitism. When Jews were forced to live in ghettos, assimilation was not an option, and Jews had no option but to embrace their culture and their community. In the 1960s, society became more accepting of Jews: "Once assimilation became an option, Jewishness became a stigma" (Langman, 1995, p. 229). Some Jews responded with shame and embarrassment about their identity and attempted to hide their identity. Some even repudiated Judaism, Yiddish, and Jewish culture.

CHALLENGES THAT JEWISH AMERICANS EXPERIENCE

Stressors, Stereotypes, and Discrimination

The most common stressors Jewish clients are likely to experience are antisemitic violence, attitudes, and behaviors. As summarized elsewhere in this chapter, there is a long history of antisemitism in the United States (Langman, 1995). As previously mentioned, Jews comprise only 2.5% of the U.S. population, yet they are the targets of roughly 60% of all religiously motivated hate crimes (FBI, n.d.-a). According to Weinrach (1990), Jews may dread being asked whether they are Jewish. "This question is feared because Jews never know what will happen if they answer it truthfully" (Langman, 1995, p. 225).

Many Jews experience the prevalence of Christian prayer in public spaces, with the common implication being that morality is defined by Christianity, the belief by some Christians that Jews were responsible for the death of Jesus, and attempts by Christians to convert Jewish people to Christianity, as assaults on the Jewish religion (Weinrach, 2002). "To be a Jew in a predominantly Christian population is not always comfortable" (Langman, 1995, p. 222). Jews may hesitate to draw attention to antisemitism and antisemitic violence (Langman, 1995). This hesitation can reflect several influences, including the fear of being identified publicly as Jewish, a belief that antisemitism will not be taken seriously by others, and an acknowledgment that some marginalized groups in America do in fact experience more frequent and more severe discrimination. The result of this silence can be feelings of isolation and alienation.

In addition to encounters with a range of antisemitic attitudes and behaviors, many Jews harbor negative internalized attitudes about their identity (internalized antisemitism). The various manifestations of antisemitism represent significant sources of stress for many Jews. Many Jews experience distress at the public misbehavior of other Jews, concerned that it will affect others' perception of them. Similarly, individuals who appear Jewish in dress or manner often feel as if their actions are under scrutiny, and that their actions as an individual might be taken to be representative of Jews as a whole.

In addition to stressors related to antisemitism, Jews often experience pressures related to their religion and culture. These include standards of conduct (e.g., Jewish law) and expectations to achieve. Weinrach (1990) described the need to achieve as "a theme that connects one generation of Jews to the next" (p. 548). He added, "If I were to win a Nobel Prize, my mother would probably know someone ... whose son had won two" (p. 548). Many Orthodox Jews experience the pervasive challenge of reconciling religious practice with their public life. For example, most workplaces and schools do not offer kosher food. It can be stressful to be seen leaving early on Friday to prepare for *shabbos* while coworkers are still busy trying to meet deadlines. Numerous vacation days must be used to account for religious holidays on which work is forbidden, and it is distressing for Orthodox college students to be disbelieved when asking for extensions on papers or exams due to yet another Jewish holiday. In particular, Orthodox nurses have been known to encounter discriminatory hiring practices due to their inability to work Friday afternoons or Saturdays (Leichman, 2016).

Finally, Jews may experience concern about the nation of Israel. This can be true even for Jews with no family members in Israel. Many Jews regard the nation of Israel as the emblem of Judaism in the world. Jews may feel anxious when there is turmoil in Israel and might feel peaceful when Israel is at peace.

COUNSELING CONSIDERATIONS FOR CLIENTS OF JEWISH AMERICAN DESCENT

As indicated previously in this chapter, there are many Jewish identities, from those who are religiously Orthodox to those who are secular. Orthodox Jews are more likely to experience their religion as central to their identity. Non-Orthodox Jews may identify with their religion and culture more peripherally. As a result, Jews may experience very differently the issues identified in this section.

In a recent Pew Research Center survey, more than 90% of all Jews reported that there was at least some antisemitism in the United States (Pew Research Center, 2021). Nearly 40% of respondents reported that they had observed anti-Jewish graffiti or vandalism. Fear of antisemitism and antisemitic violence is common among Jewish clients.

The majority of American Jews reside in larger population centers (New York, Los Angeles, Miami). In smaller cities, the number of Jewish synagogues could be small, so a failure to feel an attachment—to one's rabbi, one's congregation, or to the degree to which the congregation adheres to Orthodoxy—can result in isolation. Jewish clients in smaller cities may have difficulty building relationships with other Jews (Alper & Olson, 2013). It remains to be seen whether Jews will continue to make their homes in larger cities or move in greater numbers to smaller cities and towns.

The majority of Jews marry outside of their religion (Sasson et al., 2017). A number of religious and cultural changes have contributed to this trend, including increased secularism, lower levels of religiosity, greater acceptance by non-Orthodox Judaism of interfaith marriage, recognition by non-Orthodox Judaism of children of Jewish fathers as also being considered Jewish, and the difficulty that some Jews have in finding Jewish mates (Sasson et al., 2017; Wertheimer, 2018). Jews in interfaith marriages may experience challenges in navigating religious differences, and in deciding the extent to which their children will be raised in the beliefs and practices of Judaism (Phillips, 1998). Another question is the effects on Judaism of mixed-faith families (Sasson et al., 2017; Wertheimer, 2018). How will American Judaism evolve? Will the rift between Orthodox and non-Orthodox Jews become even more important? These trends and influences may also affect the Jewish client.

Finally, the nation of Israel will continue to be an issue for Jewish clients, if only because non-Jewish Americans tend to associate Jews with Israel. When Israel receives negative attention for something it has done, Jews may fear that they will be the target of anti-Israel anger, even when Jews disagree themselves with what Israel has done. As stated elsewhere, Jews are generally supportive of Israel, but it is a mistake to equate Jews with Israel.

IDENTITY DEVELOPMENT FOR CLIENTS OF JEWISH AMERICAN DESCENT

Although Jewish identity has been written about in the research literature, no comprehensive model of Jewish identity development has yet been developed (Langman, 1999). A willingness to explore the meaning of Jewish identity to the client may, of course, be a helpful intervention (Alper & Olson, 2013; Flasch & Fulton, 2019; Kelman, 1998). The counselor who wishes to adopt an identity development perspective might wish to draw from concepts advanced in other identity models. For example, the counselor might notice parallels to the Cass (1984) Homosexual Identity Formation stages of identity confusion (e.g., perceptions that one's behaviors may be seen by others as "Jewish"), identity comparison (e.g., feelings of alienation as one recognizes differences between one's Jewish identity and the identities of others), identity tolerance (e.g., seeking the company of other Jews), identity acceptance (e.g., more positive view of one's Jewish identity), identity pride (e.g., pride in one's Jewish identity), and identity synthesis (e.g., acceptance of both self and those who are not Jewish).

COUNSELING UTILIZATION AND HELP-SEEKING

Many famous therapists have been Jews (e.g., Beck, Ellis, Frankl, Freud, Glasser, Gottman, Meichenbaum, Minuchin, Perls, Yalom), and non-Orthodox Jews are frequent consumers of psychotherapy (Schlosser, 2006). Whereas majority White culture tends to value stoicism, Jews generally embrace the expression of emotion (Langman, 1999). To people who are unfamiliar with Jewish culture, Jews might seem dramatic or theatrical. Jews may also appear unusually comfortable in speaking about personal matters. Perhaps because they place great value on education, Jews tend to have confidence in and rely upon those who are experts.

Consistent with the importance and prevalence of education in Jewish culture, Jewish clients may want to fully understand the interventions and therapeutic modalities that the therapist will use. Though they may turn to the counselor as the expert, Jewish culture does not encourage blind obedience and it is not uncommon for the client to try to get a "second opinion" if a therapeutic alliance is not formed early. As a result, counselors may find that Jewish clients respond well to transparency about therapeutic processes.

Large Orthodox Jewish communities have wide social networks and communal organizations dedicated to referring individuals to appropriate medical and mental healthcare. When choosing medical as well as mental healthcare, care is taken to find the "best" resource. Hence, Orthodox Jews are more likely to choose a therapist based on reported expertise or specialty in a specific area or therapy modality rather than based on location or cost. Rabbis and community leaders can often be involved in the referral process.

CULTURALLY RESPONSIVE PRACTICES: DRAWING FROM THE MULTICULTURAL AND SOCIAL JUSTICE COUNSELING COMPETENCIES AND CULTURAL HUMILITY

No matter how familiar counselors are with Jewish people, Jewish culture, and the religion of Judaism, counselors are wise to examine their stereotypes, biases, and prejudices. Antisemitism has thrived in America for centuries; there is little reason to believe that a counselor could escape these pervasive negative attitudes about Jews. Counselors who are aware of pervasive antisemitic attitudes may be better prepared to challenge internalized antisemitism in their clients.

When working with Jewish clients, the counselor might find it helpful to explore clients' experiences as Jews, as well as their relationship to their religion and culture. Topics might include the client's relationship to the Holocaust, religion, and culture, other Jews, family, and Israel, for example. It is important to remember that clients are free to identify as Jewish even if their branch of Judaism does not consider them Jewish.

The counselor's faith would not typically be an issue for the Jewish client unless there is any indication of trying to convert the Jewish client or evidence of antisemitism. Some ultra-Orthodox Jews maintain a view of mental health professionals as being godless and anti-religious and may be relieved upon learning that the counselor indeed believes in God and/or is religious. Some communities of ultra-Orthodox Jews may harbor stigmas related to mental health problems and may seek out a non-Jewish or secular therapist in order to keep knowledge of such problems out of the community. One common fear may be that communal knowledge of their psychological problems may prevent them or their family members from finding a suitable marriage partner (*shidduch*).

Sometimes the Jewish client may be suspicious about how a non-Jewish counselor might view Jewish people, even in the absence of any evidence of antisemitism. Orthodox Jews are likely to seek out a Jewish (and often specifically Orthodox) counselor, mainly out of the belief that only another Jew or Orthodox Jew can understand them and the many nuances of their culture and identity. This belief is not without merit. It should be noted that beyond the practices of Orthodox Judaism discussed earlier, Orthodox Judaism is a lifestyle and culture that encompasses the moment-to-moment existence of daily life and the life span as a whole. There is a great deal of variability between Orthodox subcultures and the broader American culture.

Given the recent proliferation of portrayals of Orthodox Jews in mass media (e.g., Netflix shows such as *Unorthodox*, *My Orthodox Life*, and *Shtisel*), counselors should pay attention to beliefs or feelings regarding Orthodox Jews that arise from watching such shows. It goes without saying that the portrayal of any character or culture on mass media is designed for its entertainment value. Critical thinking can minimize the harm from oversimplifications, stereotypes, and caricatures.

In a phenomenological study of 10 Jewish adults in the Northeast, Friedman et al. (2005) found that most Jews considered themselves to be bicultural (i.e., Jewish and American). These identities were fluid and depended on the circumstance, including age and geography. Secular Jews reported more shame and embarrassment about their Jewish identity and experienced their American identity as more salient. Orthodox Jews, in contrast, were more likely to experience their Jewish identity as more salient. The counselor should be aware that some Jews might identify as American, some as Jewish, and some as Jewish American.

In a nationwide study of 300 Jewish adults, Kakhnovets and Wolf (2011) found that a stronger Jewish identity (defined by concepts such as belonging and ethnic behaviors) was associated with lower levels of depression. Jewish ethnic identity was also positively correlated with self-esteem, satisfaction with life, and general well-being. It follows from these findings that supporting and strengthening the connection between Jewish clients and their identity is likely to have a range of positive effects.

Some Jews are outspoken critics of various Israeli policies; others might seem blindly loyal. Regardless, when the nation of Israel is under attack, most Jews are likely to feel loyalty to Israel. For some Jews, an attack on Israel can trigger historical trauma; these Jews might have unusually strong negative reactions to any perceived assault on Israel.

Culturally Responsive Therapeutic Interventions and Approaches

Although Jews often appreciate insight-oriented approaches to counseling (Langman, 1999), any therapeutic intervention and approach may be effective for Jewish clients. In recent years, clinical research has been done in the Jewish population to better understand the unique mental health needs of the population and to develop measures suited to this population. We refer the reader to JPsych, a nonprofit organization dedicated to conducting and disseminating psychological research related to the Jewish population. A list of publications is available at www.jpsych.com/peer-reviewed-publications.

Jewish clients may experience strong connections to their community and to Jewish communities around the world (Langman, 1995). This sometimes reflects the fact that family members may live in other countries; sometimes it is simply that Jews feel concerned for the welfare of other Jews. Remaining sensitive to this connection to a community can be important for the Jewish client.

As noted elsewhere in this chapter, Orthodox Jews may be concerned that they are seen as too extreme by non-Orthodox Jews. Non-Orthodox Jews, in turn, may wonder whether they are "Jewish enough." Helping Jewish clients explore the meaning of their Jewish identity may be helpful for clients with these concerns. Note the previous discussion about possible applications of the Cass (1984) Homosexual Identity Formation model to Jewish identity development.

Competencies for Counseling the Jewish Client

An important competency for counselors is the ability to listen carefully to their clients' experiences of themselves with an open mind. It is critical for counselors to keep in mind that the information in this chapter is not exhaustive, and no Jewish client will fit exactly in the categories described here. The counselor can do much to create a safe environment by acknowledging that they understand that Jewish culture and practices are varied and nuanced, and by indicating a desire to learn about it. A counselor's curiosity and genuineness in asking questions are unlikely to lead to a Jewish client being offended. It is also important for counselors to be aware of any previously held beliefs or expectations regarding Jews and Jewish culture.

The ability of the counselor to separate themselves from their own cultural values is critical when treating the Orthodox or ultra-Orthodox Jewish client, as there may be occasions where the client's and therapist's differing cultural values may lead to mismatched agendas. A client who experiences attraction to someone of the same sex, for example, may not want to identify as gay or act on those romantic or sexual feelings. Their religious-cultural values and identity may be more important to them than their sexual orientation.

In such situations, the best practice would be for the counselor to engage the client in an examination of real challenges involved when an Orthodox or ultra-Orthodox Jew experiences this conflict between sexuality and religion. The counselor should refrain from adopting the stance that one value system and behavioral course is correct and healthy whereas others are incorrect. Counselors should not view the patient as subject to a repressive culture, as the client's experience may be quite different. The counselor should remain aware of the personal, family, and social costs in these client decisions.

CRAFTING AN ADVOCACY AGENDA

No advocacy agenda has been advanced for working with Jewish clients. One obvious interpretation of this concept is for the counselor to remain mindful of the effects of historical trauma (e.g., the Holocaust) and antisemitism on the Jewish client. Another, less obvious, interpretation is for the counselor to remain mindful of the challenges of observant Jews in reconciling their religious values and observance with the values and pressures of the surrounding culture.

Advocating for Social Justice

Because social justice is important to so many Jews, the counselor may find it helpful to reinforce their clients' desire to make the world better for others. At the same time, acknowledging challenges that Jews experience because of antisemitism may be important for the Jewish client. The Jewish client might benefit from recognizing that internalized antisemitism is internalized oppression. Challenging the client's internalized negativity also represents social justice work.

COUNSELING CHILDREN, ADOLESCENTS, AND YOUNG ADULTS

Counseling Children

Among some ultra-Orthodox Jews, the stereotype of mental health professionals professing antireligious views may take on particular importance when seeking a counselor to treat their children. The counselor should be aware of the potential that the parent fears the influence a secular or non-Jewish counselor might have on their children. This may manifest in the parents' desire to be involved with the therapy and treatment plan, or inquiries about the counselor's professional credentials.

In some ultra-Orthodox communities, as in other insular, closed communities, behavioral conformity is socially reinforced, and nonconformity socially punished. Sometimes, it is the behavioral nonconformity that provides the impetus for parents to bring their children to therapy rather than what the counselor perceives as the underlying problem. To maintain the therapeutic alliance, it would be important for the counselor to provide the parents with validation and reassurance rather than engage in a debate regarding the nature of the problem.

Orthodox Jewish families, and especially ultra-Orthodox families, tend to be relatively large, which can limit the time and attention parents devote to each child. It is not uncommon for the oldest daughter to take on some childcare responsibilities. Saturdays (*shabbat*) are generally spent together at home as a family.

Orthodox children attend private religious schools which, in ultra-Orthodox communities, meet most days, including Sundays. Tuition at these schools is high and represents a significant expenditure for large families. As a result, it is difficult to determine a family's socioeconomic status based only on the family's income.

Due to the Jewish people's long history of persecution and discrimination, many ultra-Orthodox Jews are mistrustful of governmental authorities. This is particularly true of child welfare services. When it is necessary to involve such authorities, counselors are encouraged to relate to families with an extra measure of sensitivity, validation, and reassurance.

Children raised in an insular ultra-Orthodox environment may be unfamiliar with non-Jews and may be confused when the counselor is uninformed about certain elements of their culture. Conversely, they may feel frightened or curious upon finding out that the counselor is not Jewish. They may be confused upon finding that the counselor is Jewish but secular or non-Orthodox. This is not to say that the counselor should hide their identity, but rather that these issues should be addressed in an open and developmentally appropriate manner.

Counseling Adolescents and Young Adults

A major task of adolescence is identity exploration and definition. For Jewish adolescents, exploring the meaning of their Jewishness and the integration of their Jewishness with other cultural or identity affiliations is an integral part of this process. This may take the form of questioning religious and community practices. It is important for the counselor to be respectful of value systems that differ from their own, even when they do not agree. It is similarly important for the counselor to keep in mind the social significance of conformity, and the risks of nonconformity, in closed communities—even if the adolescent seems to be indifferent about these expectations. This is important especially when the adolescent does not respect the values of their community. The counselor need not compromise the relationship to accomplish this, only maintain the importance of these expectations on the client.

Exploration of sexuality is complicated for Orthodox adolescents. First, sexual behavior before marriage is discouraged. In ultra-Orthodox communities, males and females are segregated in schools and all extracurricular activities, and interactions between the sexes are strongly discouraged. Second, formal sexual education is less prevalent in Orthodox Jewish society. Third, Orthodox Jewish culture has a strong heteronormative bias. For Jewish adolescents, exploration of sexuality can therefore involve levels of shame, isolation, and exclusion that might not be witnessed in more open communities. Because of Biblical prohibitions against the behavior, male masturbation is considered a grave sin in many Orthodox communities. Adolescents may experience a great deal of shame and fear surrounding this behavior and may see it as wrong. It is important for counselors to normalize sexual behaviors, thoughts, and feelings while staying morally neutral regarding them.

As Orthodox Jewish culture is oriented around family, sexual relationships are reserved exclusively for marriage. Recreational dating is therefore frowned upon. Dating is reserved for seeking a marriage partner only and typically begins in the early 20s. Nevertheless, this process begins earlier in some Hasidic communities, where seeking a suitable marriage partner can begin at 18. In these communities, dates sometimes take place in the family home, with parents watching from a distance.

In many cases, a potential match (called a *shidduch*) is suggested by a professional matchmaker, friend, relative, or neighbor, and a blind date is arranged between the parties. In many instances, this is the first-ever prolonged contact with a member of the other sex. Parents (usually the mother) are often involved with the initial vetting process. Dating generally lasts no more than a few months before a decision is made regarding marriage, at which point the couple becomes engaged. Engagements are also typically brief, usually lasting no more than a few months.

Social convention in many communities is that young women marry at younger ages than young men, and those past their mid-20s become less desirable as a *shidduch*. A common fear among young women is that they will be left single. Therefore, beginning in mid-late adolescence, young Orthodox, and especially ultra-Orthodox, girls are increasingly concerned with obtaining a good *shidduch*, and go to great lengths to ensure that they look and act in accordance with community standards.

COUNSELING ADULTS, COUPLES, AND FAMILIES

As with clients of other faiths, Jews may seek counseling to treat one or more *Diagnostic and Statistical Manual of Mental Disorders* (5th ed.; *DSM-5*; American Psychiatric Association, 2013) disorders, for personal growth and development, and for matters more specific to their identity (Schlosser, 2006). Some of these issues include the client's identity as a Jew, converting to/from Judaism, religious practice and spirituality, relationship with one's religious community, interfaith marriage, child-rearing, sexual orientation, gender identity, antisemitism, and historical trauma.

There are specific challenges involved in working with Orthodox Jewish couples, most of whom experience their first sexual interaction only after marriage. In ultra-Orthodox communities, this means that after being brought up segregated from one another, males and females are meant to establish relationships that lead to marriage and sex within months. The adjustment can often be complicated and awkward, but most couples navigate the rite of passage successfully. Often a mentor or rabbi is involved to give the couples guidance, but sometimes this is not enough for young Orthodox or ultra-Orthodox couples, who experience high levels of anxiety or shame surrounding sexual activity, in addition to learning how to deepen their relationship.

There are also several religious laws and requirements relating to sexual activity. It is not uncommon for there to be disagreements between the couple regarding how to navigate challenges that arise. Other challenges may include the role of parents in the young couple's life and family or communal pressure to have children as soon as possible.

Counseling Families

It ought to be evident that Jewish families experience the same challenges and conflicts that non-Jewish families encounter. In addition to these, Jewish families may encounter difficulties that are more closely related to their religion. For example, Jewish parents may struggle if their child resisted going to Hebrew school, became affiliated with a different branch of Judaism, stopped identifying as a Jew, identified as queer, no longer obeyed Jewish law, or converted to another faith. Some Jewish families would find it equally challenging if their child became a more observant Jew. When Jewish families experience religious conflicts, the counselor might find it beneficial to explore with individual family members how each experiences their relationship with Judaism.

When working with any of the issues identified in this chapter, the counselor must, of course, remain neutral. Failing to do so would almost certainly jeopardize one's working relationship with family members. At the same time, the counselor should remain sensitive to the possibility that some more conservative Jewish communities, especially Orthodox communities, might reject those who stray too far from Jewish law. It is important to acknowledge the potential consequences of one's behaviors, even when the clinician does not understand community values, rules, beliefs, and practices.

IMPLICATIONS FOR CLINICAL PRACTICE

It is important for counselors to gain an understanding of the Jewish religious, cultural, and ethnic identities. Counselors must also investigate their Jewish clients' intersectional identities. Doing so will allow the clinician to take a culturally responsive approach. Counselors must hold knowledge of the cultural practices and their value in helping the client with their clinical presenting concerns. As noted in the chapter, Jewish folks can hold varied sets of beliefs related to their Jewish religion and/or their cultural identities. Counselors must also pay close attention to understanding where the client is related to their Jewish faith system and their ethnic identities.

Equally important is to be mindful of the Jewish holidays. Upon scheduling the client's counseling sessions, counselors should already notate the holidays and either avoid and/or hold the conversation regarding the client's availability on the holiday date. A best practice is to include the Jewish holidays on the counselor's scheduling calendar in order to avoid any scheduling mishaps that can be construed as insensitive to the Jewish client's practice.

Jewish American people are said to be more educated than most other American ethnic groups (Hartman & Hartman, 1996); therefore, it is advantageous for counselors to leverage the client's strengths in the treatment process. Clinicians can empower their Jewish clients to create their own coping approaches. Collaborative work will be valuable in the therapeutic alliance.

CLINICAL CASE SCENARIO 16.1

Josh is a 27-year-old Jewish man who lives with his wife, Amy, in a mid-sized city in North Dakota. Josh recently graduated with a bachelor's degree in engineering, and he recently began working for a petroleum company. Josh and his wife have been married for 2 years, and she is pregnant with their first child.

(continued)

CLINICAL CASE SCENARIO 16.1 (CONTINUED)

Josh's parents were raised in the teachings and traditions of Conservative Judaism in a larger East Coast city with a sizeable Jewish community. After they married, they moved to a Midwest city with a relatively small Jewish community. Although Josh's family never affiliated with a synagogue, they always identified strongly as Jews and continued to adhere to many Jewish practices and traditions (e.g., Sabbath observance in the home, holding a Passover Seder, and attending Yom Kippur services). Josh's father attended Hebrew school as a child, and he completed the bar mitzvah ceremony.

In part because Josh did not know many Jewish children in his schools, Josh rarely attended Jewish religious services, never learned Hebrew, and did not complete the bar mitzvah ceremony. None of the girls he dated were Jewish, and he eventually fell in love with a woman who was a nonpracticing Christian. As Josh and Amy anticipate the birth of their first child, they have begun discussing how they are going to raise their daughter. Amy was raised in a home that celebrated Christmas with traditional Christmas decorations (e.g., trees, lights). On Christmas Eve, it was customary to read from the book of Luke, in the New Testament, to commemorate the birth of Jesus. Although Amy is supportive of including Jewish traditions, such as Hanukkah, she knows almost nothing about them.

Josh has begun to realize how uncomfortable he is at the prospect of teaching his daughter about Christianity. It is not enough for him that his daughter learns about her Jewish religion and heritage; he is struggling to accept the likelihood that his daughter will believe in Christian teachings about Jesus. He understands that his wife identifies as Christian, so it is unfair for him to ask her to deny her own religious identity. At the same time, he is beginning to realize that his Jewish identity is more important to him than he thought. Josh seeks the services of a counselor in the community.

CLINICAL CASE SCENARIO DISCUSSION QUESTIONS

1. What are your thoughts and feelings with respect to this case?
2. What religious and cultural biases might you have when approaching your work with Josh?
3. What kinds of questions would you ask to better understand this client's beliefs and culture?
4. How might the counselor best support and help this client?
5. How might the counselor choose appropriate clinical interventions?
6. Is being Jewish a religious, cultural, or ethnic identity?
7. Who decides whether one is Jewish?
8. In what ways is being White and Jewish different from being White in America?
9. How do the experiences of American Jews vary by religious identity, geography, and history?

10. To what extent might this client be negatively affected by antisemitism and antisemitic violence in America? How could antisemitism affect them even if they have never been directly affected by antisemitic violence?

END-OF-CHAPTER RESOURCES

 A robust set of instructor resources designed to supplement this text is located at **http://connect.springerpub.com/content/book/978-0-8261-3953-5**. Qualifying instructors may request access by emailing **textbook@springerpub.com**.

SUMMARY

The Jewish people have a documented history that spans nearly 6 millennia. Defining Jewishness is no easy task. Some consider Jews to be a civilization; others define Jews by the nation of Israel. Still others focus on the Jewish diaspora. American Jews trace their ancestry to various nationalities. American Jews generally present as White, but not all do. Even those who present as White are well aware that two generations ago, they were victims of genocide for not being White enough.

Judaism is a religion, yet how that religion should be practiced (if it is practiced at all) is not agreed upon. The contrasts between the various branches of Judaism are significant, to the extent that Orthodox and non-Orthodox Jews may appear to have little in common. The State of Israel is the world's only majority-Jewish country, but not all Jews support its policies or even its existence. Though Jewish people are generally successful and safe in America, antisemitism and antisemitic violence are still strongly present.

Jewish culture and identity, therefore, are varied and complex. Counselors should avoid making assumptions based on their personal knowledge of Jewish individuals, and instead listen carefully to their clients' lived experiences, beliefs, challenges, and sense of identity. At the same time, knowing what questions to ask and what information to hold in mind is critical to understanding and counseling the Jewish client.

DISCUSSION QUESTIONS

1. What factors, beliefs, or experiences might influence a White-presenting Jewish individual to identify as White? What factors, beliefs, or experiences might influence them not to identify as White?
2. Are there elements in your own lived experience that might have an influence on your perspective of potential Jewish clients? Previous exposure to Jewish stereotypes? Political events or beliefs? Religious beliefs or attitudes toward religion?
3. Do you know any Jewish individuals on a personal or professional level? After reading this chapter, are you thinking differently in some way about their identity? How so? Is there anything that you might be curious to ask them?
4. How has the information in this chapter shaped your thinking about Jewish individuals? In what ways can you apply this information to your future work with Jewish clients?
5. What could it mean for the future of Judaism that most American Jews marry outside of their religion and do not raise their children to be practicing Jews?

> **CULTURALLY RESPONSIVE COUNSELING FOR CLIENTS OF JEWISH DESCENT**
>
> Guests: Dr. Kenneth D. Roach and Dr. Tzachi Fried
>
> https://connect.springerpub.com/content/book/978-0-8261-3953-5/part/part02/chapter/ch16

KEY REFERENCES

Only key references appear in the print edition. The full reference list appears in the digital product on Springer Publishing Connect: https://connect.springerpub.com/content/book/978-0-8261-3953-5/part/part02/chapter/ch16

Altman, A. N., Inman, A. G., Fine, S. G., Ritter, H. A., & Howard, E. E. (2010). Exploration of Jewish ethnic identity. *Journal of Counseling & Development, 88*(2), 163–173. https://doi.org/10.1002/j.1556-6678.2010.tb00005.x

Berlin, A. (2011). *The Oxford dictionary of the Jewish religion* (2nd ed.). Oxford University Press.

Dollinger, M. (2019). Judaism, Jewish history and social justice: How defining "Who is a Jew?" tells us how to fix the world. *Practical Matters Journal, 12*, 53–66.

Friedman, M. L., Friedlander, M. L., & Blustein, D. L. (2005). Toward an understanding of Jewish identity: A phenomenological study. *Journal of Counseling Psychology, 52*(1), 77–83. https://doi.org/10.1037/0022-0167.52.1.77

Kelman, H. C. (1998). The place of ethnic identity in the development of personal identity: A challenge for the Jewish family. In P. Y. Medding (Ed.), *Coping with life and death: Jewish families in the twentieth century* (Vol. XIV, pp. 3–26). Oxford University Press.

Langman, P. F. (1999). *Jewish issues in multiculturalism: A handbook for educators and clinicians.* Jason Aronson.

Pew Research Center. (2021, May 11). *Jewish Americans in 2020.* https://www.pewforum.org/2021/05/11/jewish-americans-in-2020

Schlosser, L. Z. (2006). Affirmative psychotherapy for American Jews. *Psychotherapy, 43*(4), 424–435. https://doi.org/10.1037/0033-3204.43.4.424

CHAPTER 17

Culturally Responsive Counseling for Clients of Muslim and Middle Eastern/North African Descent

DANA T. ISAWI

> **LEARNING OBJECTIVES**
>
> After reading this chapter, students will be able to:
> - Identify characteristics and cultural factors related to individuals of Muslim and Middle Eastern/North African (MENA) descent (Arab and Muslim Americans).
> - Describe the common stressors and challenges facing individuals of Muslim and MENA descent (Arab and Muslim Americans).
> - Recognize the implications for clinical practice with individuals of Muslim and MENA descent (Arab and Muslim Americans).
> - Apply the information learned from the chapter to a case study.

> **SELF-REFLECTION QUESTIONS**
>
> 1. Think about biases, prejudices, and assumptions you might have about MENA, Arab, and/or Muslim clients. How do these help and hinder your ability to provide culturally sensitive counseling?
> 2. What hesitancies, if any, do you have about working with MENA, Arab, and/or Muslim clients?
> 3. What attributes do you have that will enable you to work with MENA, Arab, and/or Muslim clients?

THE COUNSELOR: EXPLORATION, INTROSPECTION, AND REFLECTION

The counselor is the tool for change and the counselor–client relationship is the conduit for growth. It is particularly important that counselors working with Black, Indigenous, and People of Color (BIPOC) clients venture on a journey of self-exploration, introspection, and reflection to examine their beliefs, gain awareness of their biases, and reflect on their commitment to providing culturally responsive services to their clients. Given the prevalence of the current anti-Arab and anti-Muslim rhetoric in the American society, counselors have the responsibility of being anti-racist and advocating alongside the communities toward liberation. Additionally, counselors must not only possess multicultural competence, but also enact cultural humility to best serve these marginalized and oppressed communities. Finally, counselors have the ethical obligation to avoid unintentionally inflicting harm to their clients due to lack of knowledge and experience. Thus, this chapter provides necessary knowledge that will contribute to the work of counselors serving Middle Eastern/North African (MENA) and Muslim American clients.

The terms *MENA Americans* and *Arab Americans* are used throughout this chapter to acknowledge both the population's ancestry and their integration into the American culture. The more inclusive term "MENA" will be used when referring to both Arab and non-Arab individuals descending from the MENA region, an area in the Middle East that includes the Arab League countries in addition to Iran and Turkey. These terms refer to ethnically, culturally, racially, and religiously diverse communities. The term *Muslim Americans* is used to refer to all individuals in the United States who follow the religion of Islam. Many conflate Arab and Muslim Americans, and the terms are often used interchangeably, suggesting that all Arab individuals are Muslim (Awad et al., 2017). It is important to make a distinction between the two populations, while also recognizing the considerable overlap between them. Contrary to common misconceptions, most Muslims in the United States are not Arab (DeSilver & Masci, 2017) and the majority of Arab Americans identify as Christian (63%) as opposed to Muslim (26%; Arab American Institute Foundation, 2002).

Middle Eastern/North African Descent Americans

The MENA identifier is considered the most inclusive because it encompasses individuals of Arab descent, as well as those of non-Arab descent within the MENA region. The MENA region includes the 22 Arab League countries (Algeria, Bahrain, Comoros, Djibouti, Egypt, Iraq, Jordan, Kuwait, Lebanon, Libya, Mauritania, Morocco, Oman, Palestine, Qatar, Saudi Arabia, Somalia, Sudan, Syria, Tunisia, United Arab Emirates, and Yemen) as well as Iran and Turkey. Arab Americans have ancestral, cultural, ethnic, linguistic, familial, or heritage connections to one of the 22 Arab League countries from the Middle East and North Africa (Abuelezam, 2020; Awad et al., 2021). The Arab identity comprises adhering to the Arab culture, having Arab ancestry, and speaking the Arabic language. Although other languages exist in the Arab region (e.g., original Aramaic, Berber, and Kurdish), the Arabic language is a core part of the Arab identity and culture (Awad et al., 2021). There are also colloquial dialects that vary from the standard official version of the language (Al Khateeb et al., 2014). It's important to understand how individuals in this population self-identify their ethnic and racial identity (Awad et al., 2021). It's also critical that counselors recognize that MENA and Arab Americans are culturally, linguistically, and religiously diverse groups (Goforth et al., 2017). Despite this diversity, Arab Americans share much in common in terms of history, religion, cultural heritage, and language.

Foad (2013) suggest that Arab Americans immigrated to the United States in three waves from the Middle East and North Africa. The first wave began in the 1800s, which brought mostly Christian immigrants from Lebanon, Palestine, and Syria, who immigrated for financial reasons and assimilated into the American society. The second wave occurred between the 1940s and 1960s due to political instability in the Middle East, such as the 1948 Arab–Israeli War that resulted in the displacement of large numbers of Palestinians. This wave brought individuals with higher education and socioeconomic status who immigrated primarily for political reasons, and preserved their Arab identity. The third wave, which continues to the present, occurred due to the passage of the 1965 Immigration and Nationality Act, which lifted the restrictive quota system that limited immigration from the Middle East. Recent immigrants are a more heterogeneous group based on race, ethnicity, socioeconomic status, and religion, and include refugees fleeing persecution. These immigrants primarily immigrated for political and economic reasons and identify more closely with their Arab culture than do immigrants from previous waves (Foad, 2013).

Currently, the U.S. Census includes individuals of Arab or MENA descent under the "White" category, which is an inaccurate identifier due to the racial and ethnic diversity among the population, thus making them an invisible minority group (Abuelezam, 2020). Despite the advocacy of Arab American organizations and community members to include a MENA identifier in the U.S. Census, the request was overlooked during the 2020 Census (Awad et al., 2021). Arab Americans consider themselves an ethnic minority due to being a numerical minority, experiencing discrimination, and being underrepresented in leadership (Awad et al., 2021). The lack of an accurate mechanism for identifying MENA and Arab Americans results in limited health and mental health data, as well as inadequate preparation for serving this population (Ahmed, 2018). Thus, this population is relatively understudied and underrepresented in mental health research.

The Arab American Institute Foundation (2018) estimated that there are approximately 3.7 million Arab Americans in the United States. Nonetheless, due to the lack of a MENA category and lack of recognition of the group as a minority, it is difficult to get an accurate count. Twenty-five percent of the Arab American population is under 18 years of age (Brittingham & de la Cruz, 2005), and the majority are U.S. citizens who were born in the United States (Sue & Sue, 2019). Most Arab Americans have ancestry from Lebanon, Egypt, Iraq, Morocco, and Somalia (Arab American Institute Foundation, 2018).

MENA and Arab Americans are considered one of the most diverse ethnic groups in the United States in terms of ethnicity, ancestry, and religious affiliation, customs and traditions, family structure, generational status, and acculturation (Abdel-Salam et al., 2019; Awad et al., 2021; Cho, 2018), and counselors must recognize this wealth of diversity (Fisher-Borne et al., 2014). Furthermore, Arab Americans have been described in literature as "one of the most misunderstood ethnic groups in the United States" (Erickson & Al-Timimi, 2001, p. 308). To help counselors better understand the unique behaviors, perceptions, and needs of Arab American clients, a general overview of salient aspects of Arab culture is provided, while also cautioning readers against treating these cultural attributes as stereotypes to be generalized to all clients.

Family

The family is the single most important social and economic institution for most Arabs (Al Khateeb et al., 2014). Emphasis on family is a core value that is shared among MENA Americans (Erickson & Al-Timimi, 2001; Haboush, 2007). As such, Arab American individuals might give familial and societal expectations more importance than their individual needs (Haboush, 2007; Nassar-McMillan & Hakim-Larson, 2003). Family is typically a source of support in decisions related to social, financial, and emotional issues. Traditional Arab families may be characterized as patriarchal, and may be "hierarchical and interconnected family relationships" (Ajami et al., 2016, p. 109), with men being the authority and head of the family. Women are responsible for child-rearing and instilling cultural values in the children (Sue & Sue, 2019). Nevertheless, the degree to which an Arab American family adheres to the traditional structure may vary depending on the family's acculturation, socioeconomic status, generational status, and country of origin, among other factors (Ajami et al., 2016). Collectivism, hierarchical family structure, and patriarchy are important cultural values in Arab American and Muslim American populations. Consequently, family issues can be a central presenting problem in therapy due to the strong influence of the family on the Arab individual's feelings, thoughts, and behaviors. However, family connectedness has been established in the literature as a protective factor against negative psychological outcomes (Abu-Rayya & Abu-Rayya, 2009).

Religion

Religion is central in the lives of MENA Americans (Erickson & Al-Timimi, 2001). Both Muslim and Christian Arabs hold similar levels of religious centrality (H. Hashem et al., 2020). It may influence many domains of life, including family life, social practices, marriage, child-rearing, and education (Haboush, 2007). Although several religions have their roots in the Middle East, such as Islam, Christianity, and Judaism (Amri & Bemak, 2013), there are two main religions within the Arab American population, Christianity and Islam (Nassar-McMillan & Hakim-Larson, 2003). A survey estimated that approximately 63% identified as Christian and 26% identified as Muslim (Arab American Institute Foundation, 2002). Arab Americans hold highly interconnected religious and ethnic identities (Amer & Kayyali, 2016; Awad et al., 2019). Because religious affiliation is a crucial aspect of Arab identity, some Arab Americans live in cultural enclaves with others who have similar religious beliefs, to preserve their cultural values, beliefs, and traditions (Soheilian & Shantoyia, 2019). Arab Americans often use religion as a means of coping with discrimination and acculturative stress (Ahmed et al., 2011; H. Hashem et al., 2020). Muslim Arabs reported higher levels of discrimination compared to Christian Arabs, and both Muslim and Christian Arabs report psychological distress. However, H. M. Hashem and Awad (2021) found that Muslims in their study were more likely to report that their religion was disrespected by the broader American society. This is not surprising, given that Islam is a minority religion within the United States and the current sociopolitical context perpetuates anti-Muslim rhetoric (Awad et al., 2019). Specifically, individuals with higher religious centrality are more likely to report psychological distress compared to those for whom religion was not an important part of their identity (H. M. Hashem & Awad, 2021).

Gender

Generally, Arab American culture is patriarchal: males hold more power than females and cultural and religious customs reinforce traditional gender roles (Meleis, 1991). Arab women are viewed as submissive and oppressed. It is noteworthy that variations exist in attitudes about gender roles depending on factors such as country of origin, education, religious affiliation, geographic location, socioeconomic class, and acculturation (Soheilian & Shantoyia, 2019). For example, new immigrant, less educated, and nonworking women are more likely to abide by the traditional gender roles. Despite common stereotypes, family provides support to women and women learned to advocate for themselves within Arab cultural norms (Stephan & Aprahamian, 2016). In traditional Arab households, interactions between men and women are primarily limited to close family members, meaning that women do not have close interactions with men who are not family members (Hammad et al., 1999). Arab American women often struggle with inequality and are at higher risk of distress due to the conflict between cultural expectations and American culture (Meleis, 1991).

Education

In Arab culture, education is highly valued and encouraged. Arab American adults tend to be highly educated compared to other ethnic groups (Arab American Institute Foundation, 2012). The high education rate is due to the immigration trend where the more recent waves of MENA migrants included highly educated individuals or students who came to the United States for quality education. For instance, 41% of Arab Americans aged 25 and older hold a bachelor's degree or higher, compared to 24% of the American population as a whole (U.S. Census Bureau, 2000). This emphasis on education in Arab culture has an impact on career choices (Haboush & Barakat, 2014). Additionally, education serves as a protective factor that enhances individual identity and community resilience (Stephan & Aprahamian, 2016).

Muslim Americans

Muslim Americans are a diverse group with individuals who originate from at least 60 different nations (Hodge, 2005). Muslim Americans are one of the fastest-growing minority groups in the United States; there are nearly 3.45 million Muslims in the United States. This number is growing rapidly due to the high rates of immigration and religious conversions (Lipka, 2017). By 2040, Muslims are estimated to become the nation's second-largest religious group (Pew Research Center, 2017). Out of the total Muslim population living in the United States, 82% are American citizens, which includes 42% American-born and 40% who were born abroad (Lipka, 2017). Most people in the United States who have converted to Islam are African Americans, constituting 40% of all American-born Muslims. Other Muslim Americans are Hispanic, Asian, and a large proportion are from Arab countries (25%; Pew Research Center, 2007; Pew Research Center, 2017). Arab American Muslims are the fastest growing group within the Muslim population (Amer & Kayyali, 2016). The diversity in the national origin of Muslim Americans reflects differences in language and culture among this population. Muslim Americans come from diverse cultures and traditions, which contribute to the richness of U.S. society (Amri & Bemak, 2013). While the religious philosophies of Muslims are connected by common themes, today Muslims are one of the most ethnically and culturally heterogeneous groups, with followers from all continents, belonging to most major racial groups, and speaking myriad languages (Pew Research Center, 2016). Muslims have been part of North American society since many immigrated early on or were brought on slave ships from Africa (Abu-Bader et al., 2011). Some Muslims may express their faith visibly through wearing *hijab* (headscarf), *kufiya* (traditional Arab headdress worn by men), or *niqab* (head and face covering worn by women; Ashraf & Nassar, 2018).

Family

Like Arab Americans, family and community are key to Muslims. They value the role of immediate and extended family members, as well as members of the mosque and their religious leaders (Springer et al., 2009). One of the most important aspects of Muslim identity is belonging to a family (Jisrawi & Arnold, 2018). Muslim individuals are viewed first and foremost as members of a family or community, thus instilling a sense of obligation toward others early on (Chang et al., 2012). For immigrant families, power shifts after immigration are common. For example, typically children learn English and acculturate faster than their parents and start taking on adult responsibilities (Akram-Pall & Moodley, 2016). Furthermore, many are accustomed to strong extended family support in their home countries, with everyone sharing responsibilities and providing help during hard times; losing that support can be devastating.

Religion

Religion is central in the lives of many Muslim Americans. Islam is a religion that is 1,400 years old (Jisrawi & Arnold, 2018). Muslims believe in the divine will of Allah, God. The Qur'an, the words of Allah, guides Muslims in all aspects of their lives (Springer et al., 2009). Additionally, the five pillars of Islam are basic principles that are recognized by all Muslims (S. R. Ali et al., 2004): (a) *Shahaada*, a verbal declaration of Islam; (b) *Salat*, prayer five times a day; (c) *Zakat*, charity; (d) *Sawm*, fasting during the month of Ramadan; and (e) *Hajj*, pilgrimage to Mecca if health and finances permit (Cho, 2018). For Muslims, Islam is not only a belief system but also a way of life. Although this information is generally applicable to Muslims, counselors must be aware of the great diversity among Muslims and their practice of the Islamic faith, which may be influenced by assimilation to American culture and secular values and generational status, among other individual factors (S. R. Ali et al., 2004). Often, religious identity serves as a source of strength, but it can also be a target of hate (Ashraf & Nassar, 2018). Identifying as Muslim predicts discrimination (Ikizler & Szymanski, 2018). Nevertheless, a higher level of religiosity is linked to fewer depressive symptoms for Arab Muslims and not Arab Christians (Amer & Hovey, 2007). In general, Muslim American participation in mosques and other religious centers tends to prevent social isolation and can buffer against loss of heritage and religious self-identity for immigrants (Akram-Pall & Moodley, 2016). These trends suggest that encouraging Muslim clients to participate in religious activities, should they wish to do so, can lead to positive therapeutic outcomes (Jisrawi & Arnold, 2018). Though spirituality can moderate the impact of acculturation, religious affiliation can be a cause for underutilization of mental health services due to stigma (Amri & Bemak, 2013) or to the general belief that illness is the result of one's destiny (Ciftci et al., 2013).

Gender

The complexity of gender within Muslim American populations is an area that is also subject to misinformation. Even within the same country, gender expectations may differ between regions. This discrepancy may be attributed to the fact that for many Muslims, gender roles are defined by both Islamic and ethnic or national cultural norms, which sometimes differ (Abbott et al., 2012). Moreover, gender perceptions can sometimes restrict help-seeking behavior. For example, Muslim males may feel embarrassed to seek help due to dominant cultural expectations for men to be strong (Saleem, 2015). It is noteworthy that Islamic teachings regard women with respect and advocate for women to be educated and pursue careers (Husain & Ross-Sheriff, 2011). For example, in Western countries, the hijab is seen as a symbol of gender oppression (Esposito & Mogahed, 2008), whereas most Muslim women have some say about whether to wear it or not. Practicing Muslim families may encourage gender segregation in social situations (Dhami & Sheikh, 2000). Likewise, Muslim clients may seek out a counselor of the same gender to feel more comfortable discussing personal issues. Many Muslim women avoid physical contact with non-related males, such as shaking hands or hugging (Tummala-Narra & Claudius, 2013).

COUNSELING UTILIZATION AND HELP-SEEKING

Both Arab and Muslim cultures hold negative cultural attitudes toward seeking mental health services and are reluctant to seek help from outside of the family (Martin, 2014; Nassar-McMillan & Hakim-Larson, 2003). For instance, some Arab families may hide mental health problems and would only seek treatment as a last resort (Nassar-McMillan & Hakim-Larson, 2003; Nobles & Sciarra, 2000). Mental illness is stigmatized in Arab culture because it may be thought of as a sign of weakness and inability to cope. Having a family member with a mental illness may confer a risk of shame and dishonor to the family (Al-Krenawi & Graham, 2000; Hammoud et al., 2005; Sayed, 2003). Similarly, Muslim Americans underutilize services due to stigmatization of mental illness, mistrust of the mental health system in the United States, experiences of discrimination, and the lack of culturally responsive services (Amri & Bemak, 2013; Vogel et al., 2007). When compared to men, women Muslim Americans are more open to seeking professional mental health assistance (Vogel et al., 2007). This stigma has led Arab and Muslim Americans to turn to family, friends, community, mosques, and culturally specific agencies for help (S. R. Ali et al., 2004; Weng et al., 2019). The manifestation of psychopathology in Arab Americans may be different from Western conceptualizations of psychopathology. Individuals from Arab cultures may report more somatic symptoms, whereby psychological concerns are expressed in physical symptoms (e.g., clients who are anxious may report having a stomachache) and fewer affective symptoms (e.g., headaches) than individuals from Western cultures, and thus differ from Western conceptualizations of psychopathology (Al-Krenawi & Graham, 2000). For example, it is common for a MENA client, when asked "How are you feeling today?", to answer, "I have really bad body aches and stomach pain" instead of saying "I'm anxious." Muslim Americans may seek therapy for a wide range of issues, including issues specific to their religious identity such as concerns over committing sins within Islam, like drug and alcohol use, and engaging in premarital sexual activity (Rassool, 2015). Nevertheless, because many indigenous Muslims were born and raised Muslim, such Muslims may not present to therapy with mental health concerns related to their religious identity or conversion to Islam (Al'Uqdah et al., 2019).

CULTURALLY RESPONSIVE PRACTICES: DRAWING FROM THE MULTICULTURAL AND SOCIAL JUSTICE COUNSELING COMPETENCIES AND CULTURAL HUMILITY

The Council for the Accreditation of Counseling and Related Educational Programs (CACREP) considers multicultural and social justice counseling competence as one of the defining aspects of counselor identity (i.e., Standard 2.F.2. Social and Cultural Diversity), and thus this is a core component of counselor training. Additionally, cultural competence in counseling is emphasized in the American Counseling Association (ACA) *Code of Ethics* (e.g., A.2.c; E.8; ACA, 2014). *Multicultural competency* refers to a range of theoretical perspectives and practical guidelines on providing interventions that respect the multiple identities of individuals, such as their race, gender, sexual orientation, socioeconomic status (SES), and religion (Ratts et al., 2015). The counseling field has endorsed multicultural competencies that have three main components: skills, knowledge, and awareness of beliefs and attitudes (Sue et al., 1992; Ratts et al., 2015). Consequently, mental health providers have traditionally used cultural competence frameworks as sufficient for working with minority groups, including immigrants, refugees, and other ethnic and religious groups (Fisher-Borne et al., 2014).

Recent research indicates that mental health professionals lack competence in working with Arab Americans, as indicated by reports on their own perceptions of competence (Basma et al., 2020; Khoury, 2019; Sabbah et al., 2009). Several studies (Basma et al., 2020; Sabbah et al., 2009) reveal that counselors reported the least level of comfort and competency in counseling Arab Americans, compared with counseling other minorities. Counselors' lack of cultural competence is a contributing factor to the disparities in mental health services among racial and ethnic minorities. Regarding providers' knowledge, reports vary significantly. In a sample of mental health providers, a majority (66.7%) reported moderate or high previous knowledge of Arabs. The source of information was from television (15.4%), the internet (14.7%), and books (39.2%; Khoury, 2019). In contrast, Basma et al. (2020) found that more than half of the participants indicated they know very little about the beliefs, norms, and values of Arab Americans, due to limited to no interaction with the population. Additionally, participants reported receiving little training in their programs focusing on Arab Americans. Consequently, approximately one-quarter of the participants agreed that they felt uncomfortable with Arabs, suggesting that there may still be some implicit biases when working with this population since they are less knowledgeable about the cultural experiences of their clients. Clinicians who were directly associated with Arabs (through family, professional or community relations), possessed higher levels of knowledge of Arabs, and exhibited significantly higher levels of cultural competence toward the group. Nevertheless, clinicians receiving their knowledge from television exhibited lower levels of cultural competence. Contributors to the levels of cultural competence toward Arabs included previous knowledge of Arabs and clinical readiness for change. Therefore, for counselors to improve their cultural competence, they must learn about the culture and use books as a source of their knowledge as opposed to the media, interact with the population, and demonstrate readiness for change. In addition to the traditional cultural competence model (awareness, knowledge, and skills), there are indications that the addition of cultural encounters and cultural desire enhance cultural competence (Khoury, 2019). *Cultural encounters* refers to the clinician's engagement in cross-cultural exchanges with cultural diversity. In working with ethnic and religious diverse clients, counselors who are culturally humble seek to accommodate aspects of culture that are most salient to the client, and this may mean including family in the clinical care (Jisrawi & Arnold, 2018).

Multicultural Awareness

Self-awareness is an integral part of multicultural training (Constantine & Ladany, 2000). Multicultural awareness requires clinicians to critically analyze their own biases, prejudices, assumptions, and preconceptions, and to explore how their upbringing and socialization can be reflected in their work (Ratts et al., 2015). Studies found that counselors tend to perceive themselves as having higher levels of multicultural awareness than of multicultural knowledge (Holcomb-McCoy, 2005; Basma et al., 2020). Typical activities that training programs have implemented to enhance self-awareness include requiring multicultural courses that can reduce implicit bias, decrease racist behaviors, and positively influence racial identity (S. P. Brown et al., 2006; Castillo et al., 2007; Constantine & Gushue, 2003).

Multicultural Knowledge

Multicultural knowledge refers to factual knowledge about "the political, economic, historical, social, and psychological development specific to a particular cultural group" (Arthur & Stewart, 2001, p. 8). It is believed that multicultural knowledge will reduce a clinician's discriminatory behaviors and biases (Arthur & Stewart, 2001), and specific knowledge about a group could reduce racial biases (Sue et al., 1992). Conversely, one of the dangers of this approach is assuming a superior understanding of culture and influencing the therapeutic alliance (Rosenblatt, 2016). There is limited inclusion of Arab Americans in multicultural training. Pieterse et al. (2008) inspected 54 multicultural counseling syllabi from accredited counseling and counseling psychology programs, and found that only 11% of the courses mentioned Arab or Middle Eastern Americans. With limited knowledge of empirical research and little exposure to Arab American culture, clinicians may be influenced by these negative stereotypes, which may lead to internalized negative attitudes, stereotypes, and prejudice, and thus discrimination (Haboush, 2007).

Multicultural Skills

The limited focus on the Arab American population in multicultural training may inevitably affect the multicultural skills of counselors working with this population. Perhaps training programs can consider increasing the time allotted to multicultural counseling courses, in order to target the higher levels of knowledge that will inevitably affect overall competence. Programs can also increase student exposure to diverse populations by including practicums and internship sites that serve diverse populations; diversifying course materials to include Arab American authors, theorists, researchers, and clinicians; and offering workshops and seminars that address and attend to expanding understanding around marginalized populations. Finally, exposure to the population can occur through diversifying faculty to include members of the Arab American population (Basma et al., 2020). Although gaining knowledge about Arab culture is crucial, it is equally important for counselors to refrain from assuming that all Arab American clients and families endorse and practice the same values and customs. Counselors must assess their client's unique worldview, beliefs, values, and expectations, and tailor their interventions to the specific client instead of generalizing knowledge about the group as a whole to their client (Cardemil & Battle, 2003).

In terms of modalities of treatment with Arab Americans, it has been suggested that insight-oriented individual therapy is not as effective and can be highly anxiety-provoking because of the cultural emphasis on individuation. Systems-based approaches tend to yield better results (Erickson & Al-Timimi, 2001). Furthermore, experts have suggested that the directive and structured approach in cognitive behavioral therapy (CBT) may be particularly suitable with Arab Americans, since they may value the psychoeducational aspect (El-Jamil & Ahmed, 2016). Although there are no specific guidelines for how to implement CBT with Arab Americans, there are indeed guidelines and recommendations for how to implement CBT with Muslim clients that may be useful (e.g., Beshai et al., 2013; Hodge & Nadir, 2008). Additionally, in one of a few randomized clinical trials reviewed, brief narrative exposure therapy was used with Iraqi refugees who had experienced posttraumatic stress. Investigators found that those who received brief narrative exposure therapy had greater posttraumatic growth and increased well-being, alongside reduced symptomology for depression. Brief narrative exposure therapy helps clients in confronting their painful memories, which results in enhancing one's self-efficacy and supporting cognitive processing of the trauma and the development of new meaning that in turn can enhance well-being and reduce depression symptoms. Additionally, narrating traumatic stories can foster validation and connectedness, which facilitates posttraumatic growth (Hijazi et al., 2014).

Recommendations for multicultural responsive counselors who are working with Arab American clients include:

- Assess their own cultural counseling competence related to Arab Americans. Khoury and Manuel (2016) developed the Multicultural Counseling Competence toward Arabs and Arab Americans scale. The scale is a culture-specific measure of cultural competence that consists of five constructs, including cultural awareness, cultural knowledge, cultural skill, cultural encounters, and cultural desire.
- Address negative attitudes or biases against Arab Americans that may interfere with effective treatment through continued training and education from reliable and credible sources if they identify any bias against Arab Americans (Cho, 2018).
- Recognize the need to gain multicultural competence specific to Arab culture and undertake efforts to obtain competence, including seeking training, clinical experience, consultations, or supervision to enhance their competence (Cho, 2018). Ensure that they are reading narratives written by the Arab American community itself. It is valuable to understand the narrative from their perspective.
- Expand their knowledge through reviewing empirical research on Arab Americans, reading published guidelines for providing services to this group, taking a course or attending professional development opportunities focusing on Arab American culture or mental health, and learning about Arab culture from Arab American organizations or cultural centers (Cho, 2018).
- Seek consultation from supervisors or other providers who have experience treating Arab Americans (Basma et al., 2020), as well as community and religious leaders in the community.
- Be aware of cultural and religious celebrations that may affect client's attendance or involvement in sessions.

Mental health service providers appear to lack knowledge about Islam (Sabbah et al., 2009), further warranting the need for expanding the competence of practitioners to better serve this population. In working particularly with Muslim Americans, it's helpful to refer to the competencies developed by the Association for Spiritual, Ethical, and Religious Values in Counseling (ASERVIC; 2009) for guidance. Similar to the Multicultural Counseling Competencies framework, these competencies focus on the three dimensions (awareness, knowledge, and skills). Awareness requires a counselor's self-exploration and self-understanding related to personal beliefs, values, attitudes, fears, biases, doubts, and prejudices when working with clients' spiritual and religious beliefs (Cashwell & Young, 2011). Once counselors explore how their identity affects others, they may increase the therapeutic alliance and improve the effectiveness of therapy (Al'Uqdah et al., 2019).

To enhance their knowledge about Muslim Americans, counselors are encouraged to familiarize themselves with religious resources, leaders, and diverse colleagues (ASERVIC, 2009). Possible sources of information include local mosques, religious leaders or *Imams*, Muslim community service organizations, and national Muslim organizations (Cashwell & Young, 2011). Another way of learning about Islam is by increasing interactions, exposure, and relationships with members of the Muslim community (Al'Uqdah et al., 2019). Furthermore, exploring the client's religious and spiritual values may help in creating an accepting therapeutic environment and aid in diagnosis, treatment, and interventions (Cashwell & Young, 2011). Counselors may also explore their Muslim clients' beliefs, daily religious habits, rituals, and history of trauma and discrimination, to develop a thorough multicultural conceptualization (Al'Uqdah et al., 2019).

Cultural Humility

In recent years, there has been a shift in the multicultural literature, away from focusing on mere competence (Ratts et al., 2015) toward utilizing cultural humility (Hook et al., 2013; Owen et al., 2016; Rosenblatt, 2016) as an emerging framework that is more responsive to the needs of diverse clients, and better equips culturally responsive clinicians (Jisrawi & Arnold, 2018). Cultural humility involves having an interpersonal stance that is other-oriented, evidenced by respect for and lack of superiority toward another individual's cultural background and experience. Counselors who possess cultural humility recognize the influence of their own socialization and cultural backgrounds and accept that there is a limit to understanding a culture other than their own (Hook et al., 2016). Furthermore, they are mental health clinicians who are self-critical and aware of the cultural contexts of diverse clients (Jisrawi & Arnold, 2018). This framework focuses less on the clinician's knowledge and more on the clinician's "way of being" with diverse clients (Jisrawi & Arnold, 2018). Cultural humility can facilitate the working alliance and perceived improvement in therapy (Hook et al., 2013).

To provide culturally responsive services to Arab and Muslim Americans, clinicians must develop cultural competence using a cultural humility approach (Goforth et al., 2016). First, clinicians must develop cultural humility, which is a way of being that is the opposite of prejudice, discrimination, judgment, hostility, cultural imposition, intolerance, and oppression. Cultural humility can facilitate trust, self-disclosure, and mutual learning (Owen et al., 2014). Through cultural humility, clinicians can develop an awareness of their own prejudices and stereotypes they might hold around Arab American culture and values (Goforth et al., 2017). This awareness and critical self-reflection can then lead to increased openness about working with Arab Americans (Goforth et al., 2016). Second, clinicians should gain knowledge about Arab American culture, values, and religious beliefs. Furthermore, clinicians may also want to consider connecting with a cultural consultant who would be able to provide guidance about cultural norms, while keeping in mind the heterogeneity of this group. Finally, clinicians should develop multicultural skills that will enable them to provide culturally responsive services to this population. Through professional development and consultation, clinicians can learn to conduct culturally sensitive assessments and utilize evidence-based treatments that have been found to be effective with this population (Goforth et al., 2017). Culturally sensitive assessments utilize methods that recognize cultural characteristics and the stigma associated with mental health in many Arab American communities (Goforth, 2011). In addition to focusing on building self-awareness, knowledge, and skill, it may be important to address developing an interpersonal stance of humility when engaging with a client about their cultural background (Hook et al., 2013). This involves heightened self-awareness of values and biases and active listening to enhance understanding. Cultural humility is a lifelong process of self-awareness, reflection, and mutuality that acknowledges oppression and power inequities between practitioners and clients, by enhancing understanding of the worldviews of others (Chang et al., 2012). Specifically, cultural humility begins with heightened self-awareness of values and biases, active listening to enhance understanding and mutuality, as well as engaging in an ongoing process of cultural exploration (Chang et al., 2012). Through cultural humility, differences are viewed as an asset and an opportunity for learning rather than as a threat to one's own identity or worldview (Captari et al., 2018).

Similarly, research has demonstrated that cultural humility can decrease negative attitudes and increase religious tolerance (Van Tongeren et al., 2016). Not surprisingly, cultural humility is positively correlated with openness to immigration and inversely related to prejudicial attitudes—meaning that counselors who demonstrate cultural humility are more open toward their clients and do not possess prejudicial mindsets. Moreover, cultural humility was found to be uniquely associated with more positive attitudes toward refugees (Captari et al., 2018). Culturally humble counselors working with Muslim clients are urged to engage in introspection, to examine their own views and assumptions about Muslims and how that may affect the therapeutic alliance. Some questions that could help counselors include: "What assumptions about Islam and Muslims do you hold that could hinder progress in a therapeutic relationship? How familiar is the practitioner with Islamic principles and traditions? What are sources of your information? How much exposure do you have to Muslim people on a daily basis? How aware are you of the media's role in shaping perceptions of Islam and Muslims, and how these perceptions impact the lives of Muslims and their participation in society?" (Jisrawi & Arnold, 2018, p. 46).

Liberation Counseling

Serving marginalized communities calls for counselors to move beyond a focus on individual development and address the larger systemic structures that have perpetuated issues of oppression and marginalization (Sue & Sue, 2013). As such, discussion of liberation psychology is imperative in addressing the unique needs of marginalized populations because mental health issues often stem from structural and sociopolitical oppression (Martín-Baró, 1994). Liberation psychology not only recognizes the virtues and resources of marginalized communities (Martín-Baró, 1994), but also addresses the sociopolitical context of clients (Chávez et al., 2016). Counselors can use the tenets of liberation psychology (Martín-Baró, 1996) to analyze the sociopolitical etiology of mental health issues and engage social change principles in working with MENA and Muslim clients. Those include *recovering historical memory*, *deideologizing daily experiences*, *conscientization*, and *problematization*.

According to Martín-Baró (1994), *recovering historical memory* involves reauthoring counternarratives of experiences of oppression. This urges counselors to examine societal systems of oppression and educate others through sharing accurate counternarratives by authors who are MENA individuals themselves. Because anti-Arab and anti-Muslim rhetoric is prevalent, *deideologizing* refers to counselors deconstructing any oppressive messages about MENA and Muslim individuals that are embedded in counseling theories and then developing theories that are responsive to the unique needs of this population (Tate et al., 2013). This could entail counselors critically examining their own beliefs and biases, as well as explicitly identifying the oppressive history within the mental health field over the years and intentionally exploring client issues of distrust (Singh, 2016). *Problematization* refers to the act of deconstructing and disrupting oppression by recovering historical memories to identify potential solutions to mental health concerns related to justice (Martín-Baró, 1994). Counselors working with MENA and Muslim clients ought to challenge social injustice and emphasize *conscientization* or consciousness-raising, which includes examining structures of oppression with marginalized groups to reach liberation (Martín-Baró, 1994). Counselors engage in consciousness-raising within and outside of sessions (Singh, 2016). They assert that cultural values and beliefs create power differentials while validating client experiences of the world with regard to culture (Sue et al., 1992). Counselors working with MENA and Muslim populations are not only aware of their own beliefs and values, but also facilitate exploration of client ethnic and religious identities and challenge notions of oppression and discrimination. This journey begins with naming oppressive systems (e.g., policy, media, etc.) and revisioning what these systems might look like from an affirmative lens (Martín-Baró, 1994). Within the Liberation Model, counselors not only examine structures of oppression that prevent MENA and Muslim clients from seeking mental health services, but also work alongside clients to advocate for the changes in such oppressive systems that will eventually lead to liberation.

Empathy

Empathy is another counselor variable that is important to consider when working with diverse clients, such as MENA and Muslim Americans. Counselor empathy and acceptance of clients' experiences, beliefs, and cultures are essential for cultural humility. Acceptance can be achieved by practicing through empathy (Jisrawi & Arnold, 2018). B. C. Brown (2007) defined *empathy* as "the skill or ability to connect with an experience someone is relating" (p. 33). Reflective counselors use empathy and acceptance as tools to connect with clients. Counselors can strengthen their alliance with Arab and Muslim clients by empathizing with them, and accepting that they have the right to their beliefs and practices (Jisrawi & Arnold, 2018). For example, the perception of Muslim women as oppressed is still prevalent in some counseling literature (Qasqas & Jerry, 2014); nevertheless, culturally humble counselors must reflect on their own biases and enter the therapeutic relationship without any assumptions about their Muslim clients, recognizing that Muslim women do have agency.

IDENTITY DEVELOPMENT FOR CLIENTS OF MUSLIM AND MIDDLE EASTERN/NORTH AFRICAN DESCENT

A brief discussion of identity development is necessary as it relates to the acculturation process of Arab and Muslim Americans. *Ethnic identity* refers to the internal process that determines the cultural identity of individuals (Yoon et al., 2013). Strong ethnic identity may moderate psychological distress by enhancing collective self-esteem, providing a sense of pride and belonging to one's ethnic group by focusing on the strengths and resources of their ethnic group, and increasing the chances of seeking community support (Ikizler & Szymanski, 2018; Yoon et al., 2013). In a sample of Middle Eastern Arab Americans, Ikizler and Szymanski (2018) found that ethnic identity served as a protective factor against psychological distress in the face of discrimination. Muslim Americans may grapple with the multiple identities they hold, including religious, ethnic, and national identities. At times, they may even struggle to reconcile conflicting views from each of these groups (Amri & Bemak, 2013). This may influence the development of individual identity and group affiliation (Jisrawi & Arnold, 2018).

The ethnic and cultural identity of MENA Americans is multifaceted and complex (Awad, 2010). There are contextual factors that must to be taken into consideration. For instance, the lack of recognition of MENA as an ethnic or racial category on the U.S. Census (Abdel-Salam et al., 2019) may affect the identity development process of Arab Americans who self-identify as such, because this term accurately captures their identity of being Arab while also acknowledging their acculturation to the American culture. Similarly, discrimination and the negative portrayal of Arab and Muslim Americans in the media create conflict in their identity development process. Furthermore, acculturation patterns are closely tied to identity development (Berry, 2005).

Psychosocial factors that influence Arab Americans' acculturation and identity development include country of origin, religion, age at immigration, reason for immigration, gender, length of time in the United States, generational status, education, and English language skills (Hakim-Larson & Menna, 2016). For example, Ajrouch and Jamal (2007) found that Lebanese and Syrian Christian Arab Americans with a long history of immigration to the United States reported higher levels of acculturation and were more likely to identify themselves as White, compared to more recent Muslim immigrants from Iraq. Those who are older and more religious tend to separate from mainstream American culture (Abu-Bader et al., 2011; Goforth et al., 2016) because they remain closely connected to their cultural heritage and may fear losing the core aspects of religion due to external pressures (Jisrawi & Arnold, 2018). There is also evidence that gender may affect acculturation patterns. Ellis et al. (2010) found that Somali Muslim refugee girls in the United States are less likely to assimilate and remain closely connected to their heritage culture than their male counterparts, because they are typically held to stricter rules and are not granted much freedom. Arab Americans express ethnic pride in their Arab heritage (Awad et al., 2021). Language is particularly important to Arab Americans' identity and culture. Several scholars highlighted the importance of language as part of retaining culture (Awad et al., 2021; Sehlaoui, 2008). It provides a sense of pride for parents that their children retain their cultural heritage and language. It is common for Arab American parents to invest time and resources in teaching their children the Arabic language in formal or informal ways through community centers, churches, and mosques that offer Arabic language classes to foster Arab ethnic identity.

Arab American racial identity development seems to move through stages, from ambivalence to embracing their ethnic identity, which is consistent with minority racial identity development. In a study, the participants explained that in childhood they did not clearly understand their ethnic identity, yet they recognized that they were different. As one participant elaborated, "You just knew that you were different, or that you were being othered" (Abdel-Salam et al., 2019, p. 261). In adolescence, they rejected their Arab identity; finally, in college, they had heightened awareness and began to embrace their Arab identity, while recognizing that some are fearful about identifying as Arab in light of the increasingly negative rhetoric around Arabs and Muslims. When Arab Americans do not fit the stereotypes that many Americans seem to have about Arab American women, others find it difficult to place them within their worldviews (Abdel-Salam et al., 2019). Furthermore, family is an important factor that influences the identity development of Arab American individuals, and typically serves as a protective factor. Differentiation, the development of an individual identity independent of one's family, is typically discouraged in Arab culture (Abudabbeh, 1996).

CRAFTING AN ADVOCACY AGENDA

The revised Multicultural and Social Justice Counseling Competencies (Ratts et al., 2015) expand the role of counselors to include advocacy for their clients. Counselors are responsible for providing their clients with the tools to stand up against racial and social injustices, advocating for clients who may not be able to advocate for themselves, challenging barriers their clients face, connecting clients to resources and services they otherwise could not access, and joining community groups that advocate for social justice issues (Ratts & Hutchins, 2009; Toporek et al., 2009). On the systemic level, counselors can support the Arab American population by advocating for the recognition of the group as an ethnic minority through the inclusion of a MENA category in the U.S. Census. The racial ambiguity of Arab Americans and lack of census recognition affect their emotional well-being and create opportunities for mental health providers to advocate for these clients. Additionally, on the individual level, clinicians can add an Arab American or MENA category to intake forms to recognize this invisible population and reaffirm cultural sensitivity (Abdel-Salam et al., 2019). Furthermore, clinicians are encouraged to be involved in advocacy efforts to eliminate discrimination and eradicate barriers that the MENA American population face outside of the therapy session (Ahmed, 2018), including advocacy and policy efforts aimed at contesting unjust and psychologically harmful policies (Awad et al., 2019). Because the extant mental health literature on MENA is primarily reliant on theoretical inquiries and exploratory studies with small samples, mental health clinicians can advocate for dedicated funding for the conduct of empirical research to inform the clinical treatment of Arab Americans (Ahmed, 2018; Cho, 2018).

The role of counselors has extended beyond the counseling room and counselors are responsible to advocate for their clients. According to the *ACA Code of Ethics*, "When appropriate, counselors [should] advocate at individual, group, institutional, and societal levels to address potential barriers and obstacles that inhibit access and/or the growth and development of clients" (ACA, 2014, A.7.a). Thus, counselors working with Muslim Americans must advocate for their clients by considering the following recommended advocacy activities related to Muslim Americans.

Media

Given the harmful effects of the media, counselors should advocate for ceasing the dissemination of anti-Muslim statements to promote safety and affirm healthy attitudes toward Muslim Americans and all minority groups. Service providers can partner with the Muslim American community to target local media entities that contribute to sensationalized and vilified depictions of Muslim Americans. The media can also play a positive role in disseminating accurate public education about Islam and the Muslim population (Weng et al., 2019). Moreover, policy about training within the media would also be vital. Journalists would benefit from cultural competence training (Ashraf & Nassar, 2018). Lastly, service providers and leaders of the Muslim American community can make themselves available as resources for media portrayals of Muslim American diversity, concerns, and everyday life (Weng et al., 2019). Finally, policies encouraging more Muslim involvement and presence in the media would help to reduce the levels of bias when reporting on Muslims or Islam (Ashraf & Nassar, 2018).

Clinical Service Provision

As allies, clinicians are able to emphasize the strength and courage of Muslim Americans, and address stereotypes, discrimination, and oppression with the community at large. Additionally, they could advocate for the provision of culturally responsive mental health services (Weng et al., 2019) through their places of practice and professional organization, and advocate for existing discrimination policies to be implemented and enforced (Weng et al., 2019). For instance, counselors can contribute to developing training on serving this unique population, as well as ensuring that the policies in place do not further marginalize underserved populations.

Policies

When working with policy makers related to laws that affect Muslim Americans, advocates can encourage policy makers to think about the unintended consequences of those laws (Weng et al., 2019). Additionally, advocates can help policy makers "learn about what is important to Muslims, what inspires them, and then make the policies that would truly help them get whatever they need" (Weng et al., 2019, p. 12). Recommended policy strategies include the connection of personal stories of individual mistreatment to highlight the human impact of policies and public opinion, particularly among those who are constituents of policy makers (Weng et al., 2019). In addition, policies that support the rights, liberty, and safety of Muslims should be reinforced (Abu-Ras et al., 2018).

Advocates can provide statistics on hate crimes and discrimination related to the mistreatment of Muslim Americans (Weng et al., 2019).

Psychoeducation/Awareness Raising

Given the current sociopolitical atmosphere of the anti-Arab and anti-Muslim rhetoric in the United States, American adults and children would benefit from education on Muslim and Islamic contributions to American society. Mental health professionals can conduct or advocate for mandatory training with key professionals such as law enforcement, education, and healthcare to address potential biases (Ashraf & Nassar, 2018). Mental health professionals can deliver training to religious and community leaders on mental health issues. Finally, through workshops and information sessions that seek to reduce stigma about mental health services, professionals and religious leaders can educate Muslim communities about the reality of mental health, and the benefits of seeking counseling when necessary (Saleem, 2015).

COUNSELING CHILDREN, ADOLESCENTS, AND YOUNG ADULTS

Challenges

There is a dearth of data on the academic performance of Arab youth compared to other BIPOC groups (Goforth et al., 2017), due to the lack of an Arab American ethnic category. Arab and Muslim American youth face several challenges in school, such as discrimination (Tabbah et al., 2016), problematic peer relationships (Ahmed et al., 2011), and acculturative stress (Ahmed et al., 2011), that affect their mental health and academic performance (Goforth et al., 2017). Young Arab Muslim immigrants who lived through the events of September 11, 2001, reported experiencing more acculturative stress and discrimination compared to Christian Arab immigrants (Awad, 2010). Furthermore, Muslim Arab refugee adolescents report having more challenges with academic performance (Aroian et al., 2014). Nevertheless, cultural resources such as strong ethnic identity, religious coping, and religious and family support may provide protective factors for Arab American adolescents (Ahmed et al., 2011; Aroian, 2012; Trentacosta et al., 2016). Maintaining their Arab cultural heritage is associated with fewer psychological concerns (Goforth et al., 2016). Furthermore, living in ethnic enclaves with high numbers of Arab Americans may also be a protective factor (Kumar et al., 2014), because living in a community with others of similar ethnic or religious backgrounds can provide adolescents with social support (Goforth et al., 2017). Nevertheless, these coping resources do not completely mitigate the negative impact of discrimination. Thus, it is important to encourage the utilization of protective factors for clients. Counselors may not be able to eliminate the negative impact of discrimination, due to the pervasiveness and reality of the existence of discrimination in the lives of Arab Americans (Ahmed et al., 2011).

Stressors related to discrimination and acculturation, and the stress of wanting to adhere to cultural traditions and meeting the mainstream cultural expectations to belong, are linked to poor mental health (specifically depression and anxiety) in Arab American adolescents (Ahmed et al., 2011; Goforth et al., 2017). There are gender differences in the expression of psychological symptoms. For Muslim Arab American girls, higher levels of acculturative stress were associated with higher internalizing symptoms (Goforth et al., 2017). Additionally, immigrant youth need to adjust to schools where expectations and social norms may differ from those in their native country while also learning a new language. These changes may lead to lower self-esteem, stress, and social adjustment problems (Abu-Ras et al., 2018). Furthermore, Arab American adolescents report significant involvement in cyberbullying, as perpetrators (26.7%) and as victims (34%), which are higher than the national average. Arab and Muslim American adolescents are at a higher risk of cyberbullying because of their perceived immigrant status, ethnic/racial background, religious beliefs, and the negative portrayal of Arabs and Muslims in the media, in addition to other factors that are similar to those affecting the general adolescent population, such as low socioeconomic status and health problems (Albdour et al., 2019).

Counseling Considerations

Counselors and educators often have a limited understanding of both Arab and Muslim children, which leads to misconceptions, pernicious beliefs, negative stereotypes, and ultimately discrimination (Aburumuh et al., 2009). Thus, clinicians need to examine their beliefs and stereotypes because they cannot provide effective services and promote systemic change while they hold stereotypes against different cultures (Aburumuh et al., 2009). They also need to understand the cultures that they are working with (Artiles & Ortiz, 2012). Given that positive relationships with classmates and teachers predict positive self-concept in children, counselors can focus on helping children strengthen these supports. Furthermore, counselors should engage children in meaningful activities that validate their culture, language, and perspectives (Aburumuh et al., 2009). Counselors must serve as catalysts for change in their communities. Mental health providers may help clients develop a sense of control over perceived discrimination by sharing their experiences or by joining organizations geared toward their ethnic group. Specifically, school counselors may help schools develop anti-bullying policies and programs to address discrimination (Tabbah et al., 2016). Moreover, the responsibilities of culturally humble mental health practitioners extend beyond the therapy room: practitioners must attempt to address existing inequalities and power imbalances that can hinder self-actualization, exacerbate acculturative stresses and identity crises, and perpetuate underutilization of services among Arab and Muslim youth (Owen et al., 2016; Rosenblatt, 2016).

Goforth et al. (2017) provided specific recommendations for school-based mental health providers to use within multitiered systems of support (MTSS) in providing culturally competent services to Arab American youth in schools (Goforth et al., 2017). Some of these guidelines included developing skills in culturally responsive assessment, working with English language learners, and entering into home-school collaborations with Arab American families. Additionally, counselors are encouraged to seek specific training opportunities through universities or their professional associations to ensure that they develop skills to work with Arab American adolescents and families. These skills may include developing a biopsychosocial approach to assessment that recognizes sociocultural factors, as well as biological factors, that might be contributing to a client's mental health issue (Hakim-Larson & Menna, 2016).

COUNSELING ADULTS, COUPLES, AND FAMILIES

MENA and Muslim Americans may seek counseling for a variety of reasons, including fear, anxiety, depression, and stressors evoked by the experience of discrimination. Counselors working with adults, couples, and families of MENA and Muslim descent must avoid the many stereotypes and misconceptions about the Arab culture and Islamic faith that may result in biases (S. R. Ali et al., 2004). Consequently, culturally competent mental health providers need to be familiar with the religious beliefs, customs, and traditions of MENA and Muslim clients, if clients are to receive sound counseling services. Furthermore, culturally humble counselors adopt a stance of "not-knowing" (Anderson

& Goolishian, 1992) and an other-oriented stance (Hook et al., 2013). These approaches help in suspending the counselor's cultural assumptions that can reinforce discrimination and favor a curious stance of genuine not-knowing (Springer et al., 2009).

Counseling Women

Generally, there are many misconceptions related to women in the Arab and Muslim cultures. They possess at least two marginalized identities, which may potentially lead to increased experiences of discrimination, and in turn, vulnerability to poorer mental health outcomes (Abdel-Salam et al., 2019). While the family is typically a great source of economic, emotional, and social support for Arab American women, it can also function as a source of stress. Arab and Muslim American women have the additional pressure of maintaining family honor (Stephan & Aprahamian, 2015). In some families, a girl's chastity is a prime determinant of the reputation of the family (Awad et al., 2013). Thus, Arab American women often face higher relationship-related stress concerning the maintenance of their family's honor and reputation, as sexual activity before marriage is deemed shameful within Arab culture (Mourad & Carolan, 2010). Furthermore, in many families, maintaining family honor also includes getting a good education and following assigned traditional gender role expectations (Abdel-Salam et al., 2019). Therefore, counselors working with Arab American women must be cognizant that navigating gender roles may be a source of additional stress for women (Stephan & Aprahamian, 2015). Patterns of violence among Muslim immigrants are similar to those in the U.S. culture generally, where women often struggle to leave the abusive environment (Amri & Bemak, 2013). Reasons include the belief that they must preserve the family because it is their duty, or due to financial reasons, and/or the risk of isolation from their community (Gharaibeh & Oweis, 2009; Amri & Bemak, 2013). Family violence is rarely discussed due to cultural stigmas and beliefs that domestic violence is an appropriate form of discipline (Douki et al., 2003). Nevertheless, acculturation can positively affect Arab American women's help-seeking tendencies in the cases of intimate partner violence and depression (Kulwicki et al., 2015).

Counseling Families

Given the prominence of the family in Arab culture, family issues may be common topics in treatment, and the family may need to be involved in the treatment. Within families with multiple generations, differences in acculturation may lead to conflict, even in expectations about treatment (Haboush, 2007). The youth and parents might also bring up issues related to intergenerational differences, such as attitudes toward dating or decision-making. Given the potential for such issues to arise, clinicians should consider how these issues can be addressed during the informed consent procedure. It is customary for clinicians to involve the family in the treatment of individuals or couples—after seeking the client's permission, of course (Haboush, 2007; Nassar-McMillan & Hakim-Larson, 2003)—thus clinicians providing services to Arab Americans should be competent in family therapy, specifically related to their culture (Cho, 2018). For example, suicide is forbidden in Islam; there is religious scripture that denounces taking one's own life and considers it a sin. Thus, Arab and Muslim Americans may deny suicidal ideation if mental health professionals ask directly about suicidal thoughts, intentions, or plans (S. R. Ali et al., 2004). Instead, mental health professionals should assess for suicide risk by asking indirect questions, such as, "Do you ever wish that Allah would take you away from all your problems?" or "Do you wish that God would let you die?" (S. R. Ali et al., 2004).

IMPLICATIONS FOR CLINICAL PRACTICE

The information presented in this chapter has implications for the clinical practice of mental health professionals. The literature further indicates that there is a lack of specialized and culturally responsive mental health services for Arab and Muslim Americans (Abu-Ras et al., 2018). Furthermore, mental health professionals are not immune to taking part in discrimination and oppression due to misunderstandings of and misconceptions about these populations. Therefore, counselors should be aware of the ethnic, racial, and religious diversity of MENA and Muslim Americans, and avoid making any assumptions about the structure of the family or gender roles, keeping in mind that traditional Arab families tend to be hierarchical and patriarchal. New generations of Arab Americans might struggle between adhering to traditional familial expectations and seeking individuation. Due to the profound discrimination facing MENA and Muslim Americans, counselors must begin by examining their own biases and assumptions about these groups, recognizing the effect of discrimination on clients. Paying attention to the potential effects of discrimination on the client's well-being is crucial. Additionally, counselors must assess clients' dimensions of ethnic identity development and assist them in further developing their ethnic identity (Atari & Han, 2018). Relatedly, counselors must discern the level of acculturation of each client, as some might adhere closely to traditional cultural and religious values. Counselors can assess level of acculturation by asking questions and learning about the client's adherence to traditional cultural values. Due to the heterogeneity of these populations, it is also essential to be mindful of clients' intersectional identities (Abdel-Salam et al., 2019). Because many MENA and Muslim Americans have immigrant or refugee backgrounds, counselors need to ask about trauma history and spend time addressing those traumatic experiences. Finally, clinicians have the moral and professional responsibility to advocate for these marginalized groups. Clinicians can support clients in advocating for themselves, and provide them with information about resources for discrimination (e.g., reporting hate crimes to the police or reporting discrimination in the workplace).

The following are recommendations for working with Arab American and Muslim American clients:

- First and foremost, establishing a relationship in which clients feel safe to discuss their intersecting identities and the impact of discrimination on them is crucial. To establish such a relationship, clinicians must engage in self-reflection regarding their own biases and perceptions of Arab culture, including Islam and other religions in light of the plethora of negative misinformation available (Ahmed, 2018).
- Mental health professionals should be aware of their attitudes toward and biases against Muslims. Acquiring additional knowledge about this population, and seeking supervision and consultation, are some ways to achieve that goal. Mental health professionals should also seek opportunities for learning about and engaging with the communities in which their clients belong (Ratts et al., 2015; Weng et al., 2019).
- Next, counselors working with Arab Americans should develop an understanding of cultural characteristics and practices, while avoiding making generalizations and assumptions about a client's identity (Al Khateeb et al., 2014). Clinicians can also inquire about clients' belief system, ascertain the importance of that belief system, and identify how it shapes the client's everyday life (Weng et al., 2019).

- Of utmost importance, mental health professionals should not assume that the source of the challenges that Muslim clients may experience is solely a function of their Muslim identity (Ashraf & Nassar, 2018).
- Given the close-knit nature of the community and great emphasis on family honor, some clients may be hesitant to work with an Arab clinician due to the fear of judgment (Abdel-Salam et al., 2019). Thus, upon beginning treatment, confidentiality should be emphasized during the informed consent process (Abdel-Salam et al., 2019; Cho, 2018).
- Given that religion is central to the lives of many Arab and Muslim Americans, collaboration with trusted religious and community leaders may enhance treatment (O. M. Ali et al., 2005; Nassar-McMillan & Hakim-Larson, 2003). Moreover, integrating spirituality into treatment plans may be beneficial, depending on the client's needs (O. M. Ali, 2016; D'Souza, 2002; Lemkuil, 2007).
- Due to the collective nature of Arab and Muslim communities, recognizing the significance of family and utilizing holistic approaches that incorporate family members and the religious or social community is important, especially with clients who hold traditional values (Abdel-Salam et al., 2019).
- It is important to recognize that discussing intimate relationships and sexuality is considered taboo in the Arab American culture, especially for women, because it is connected to maintaining the family honor (Abdel-Salam et al., 2019). Therefore, avoiding asking questions about these topics unless the client brings them up is an appropriate course of action.
- Cross-gender counseling relationships may be problematic for Arab or Muslim clients, especially those who are more traditional. Clinicians must inquire if the gender of the therapist is a factor to be considered.
- Cultural heritage and religion may influence the expressions of psychological distress and their explanations; hence, clinicians should accept those without the imposition of a Western worldview. For example, mental illness may be attributed to fate within the Arab culture, and counselors must demonstrate respect for these explanations without passing judgment.
- Arab and Muslim American communities possess many strengths (e.g., connectedness, religiosity, resilience) that counselors can build upon to enhance resilience and improve psychological well-being (Awad et al., 2019). Empowerment and agency, faith, and community serve as the most powerful tools for healing among Muslim Americans (Ashraf & Nassar, 2018).
- Because religion is important to Christian and Muslim Arab Americans, consideration should be given to religious views, without stereotyping or assumptions (Al Khateeb et al., 2014). Furthermore, exploring faith and spirituality as coping mechanisms may be appropriate and helpful in counseling sessions (Ashraf & Nassar, 2018).
- When working with immigrant and refugee populations, assessing the client's English language fluency and communication pattern, as well as using an interpreter, may be necessary (Cho, 2018). In Arab culture, verbal expression of feelings may be discouraged, and thus some Arab Americans' communication may appear relatively impersonal and restricted (Haboush, 2007).
- Many Arab Americans have unique verbal and nonverbal communication styles, and some of them may face language barriers. Accordingly, counselors and other service providers will be better equipped to help Arab Americans with disabilities and their families if they attend to issues related to communication styles (Al Khateeb et al., 2014).

- The role of clinicians should extend to assisting clients in finding adequate community resources for social, economic, or advocacy support.
- The use of proper terminology in regard to referring to the Muslim population is essential. Clinicians should understand the difference between the terms Islam and Muslim, because they are frequently misused and connected to negative connotations. Islam defines the religion, and the followers of this religion are identified as being Muslim (Hodge, 2005).
- When addressing mental health concerns in marginalized groups, it is necessary to link health with social justice, and examine how discrimination may affect clients' well-being (Abu-Ras et al., 2018).
- One way to combat the stigmatization of seeking mental health services is to collaborate with systems that Muslims already trust: Imams (spiritual leaders) and families, since Imams often have considerable influence on Muslim families and understanding of community attitudes (O. M. Ali, 2016). Furthermore, to provide authenticity to mental health care and foster trust between mental health practitioners and Muslim clients, sessions may be cofacilitated in familiar settings such as a local mosque (Amri & Bemak, 2013).
- Using discretion is important when working with cases that may involve cultural taboos or religiously prohibited matters, such as alcohol or drug use, which are prohibited in Islam (O. M. Ali, 2016).
- Mental health professionals should be prepared to address power and privilege within the counseling relationship (Ratts et al., 2015).

CLINICAL CASE SCENARIO 17.1

Leila is a 35-year-old Arab woman who was referred to a community agency by the county community services board because she was struggling with adhering to substance abuse treatment. Leila does not speak English well. At the time of referral, Leila was 7 months pregnant and addicted to cocaine. She was living with her father, who was emotionally abusive and took whatever money she made. Her mother died when Leila was 7 years old. Leila immigrated to the United States 9 years ago, and when she arrived, she was forced into an arranged marriage by her father. This is common for women who immigrate from Arab countries when they do not find a partner or do not marry early enough to suit their families; they are set up through the mosque or friends. Often those arranged marriages end up in violence and abusive relationships. Leila's husband was also an Arab American with similar cultural and religious backgrounds. Leila was married for nearly 2 years before they divorced. She was not able to conceive during her marriage, although she wanted to have children. To cope with the disappointment, and feelings of hopelessness, she began experimenting with drugs. Thereafter, she began using heavier drugs, like cocaine. Leila also did whatever she needed to do to get drugs; although she didn't explicitly say that she was selling her body for drugs, she could often be found roaming the streets in search of drugs. That is how she met her most recent partner who was already out of her life by the time of referral. They had communication issues because Leila's English is not very good, and she felt very isolated.

(continued)

CLINICAL CASE SCENARIO 17.1 (CONTINUED)

When Leila began counseling, the counselor's main dilemma was that Leila was pregnant and actively using drugs, endangering her life and that of her unborn child. Leila constantly minimized her drug use, reporting that it conflicted with her moral and religious values. She also expressed feelings of guilt because she was finally pregnant and was jeopardizing her ability to become a mother. The counselor also noted feelings of hopelessness, helplessness, denial, and avoidance. The counselor was able to admit Leila into an inpatient substance use program where she was in and out of treatment until she went into early labor. The baby girl was born with cocaine in her blood system and was taken into custody by Child Protective Services (CPS), and eventually placed into foster home care.

Following the baby's birth, the counselor worked intensively with Leila and the CPS social worker to regain custody of her baby. Fortunately, the baby was assigned to a great couple who lived within walking distance of Leila, so she was able to go frequently for supervised visits. When the COVID-19 global pandemic led to social distancing, it was difficult for Leila to see her baby. The foster parents were kind and called Leila using Zoom (a video platform for communication) as frequently as they could so she could see her baby. Social isolation exacerbated Leila's sense of loss and abandonment, an issue she'd been dealing with since her mother's death and her unhealthy attachment to her father and others. This time, Leila was more determined and went back into inpatient substance use treatment. She continued to work with the community agency counselor. One of the things Leila worked on with the counselor was to expand her distress tolerance (since it was minimal), so her ability to care for her daughter would not be compromised. She also worked on self-regulation. Additionally, through therapy, Leila worked to develop basic life skills, executive functioning, and critical thinking skills. She was able to have in-person visits with her baby. When she completed substance use counseling, she moved to affordable housing and left her abusive father's home. With the support of her counselor, Leila gained employment and health insurance, saw an outpatient psychiatrist and counselor, and was able to address a history of trauma and capitalize on her survival skills. Slowly, spirituality was incorporated into her treatment. Leila was able to navigate the complicated legal system and navigate for herself. Eventually, she was able to be reunified with her daughter.

CLINICAL CASE SCENARIO DISCUSSION QUESTIONS

1. What do you think the agency did to overcome language barriers so they could help Leila?
2. In what ways did the helping professionals respond with cultural humility, empathy, and advocacy toward Leila?
3. Are there any things you would have done differently?

END-OF-CHAPTER RESOURCES

 A robust set of instructor resources designed to supplement this text is located at http://connect.springerpub.com/content/book/978-0-8261-3953-5. Qualifying instructors may request access by emailing **textbook@springerpub.com**.

SUMMARY

MENA/Arab and Muslim Americans are culturally, linguistically, and religiously diverse groups, so mental health professionals must develop cultural competence and cultural humility to provide culturally responsive counseling services. It is important to make a distinction between the two populations, while also recognizing the considerable overlap between them. Contrary to common misconceptions, most Muslims in the United States are not Arab, and the majority of Arab Americans identify as Christian. Despite the many challenges that these populations face, they possess many strengths. Family, community, and religious identities are a few of the protective factors that these populations utilize to cope with ethnic- and religious-based discrimination.

DISCUSSION QUESTIONS

1. What can counselors do to demonstrate cultural humility in working with MENA and Muslim clients?
2. What things can counselors do to advocate for MENA and Muslim clients?
3. Have you been influenced by the negative stereotypes about MENA and Muslim clients? What biases do you have about these groups?
4. What do you know about MENA and Muslim Americans? What are your sources for such information? Are your sources credible or biased?
5. How familiar are you with Islamic principles and traditions? What are your sources for such information? Are your sources credible or biased?
6. How much exposure do you have to MENA and Muslim people on a daily basis?

KEY REFERENCES

Only key references appear in the print edition. The full reference list appears in the digital product on Springer Publishing Connect: https://connect.springerpub.com/content/book/978-0-8261-3953-5/part/part02/chapter/ch17

Goforth, A. N., Nichols, L. M., Stanick, C. F., Shindorf, Z. R., & Holter, O. (2017). School-based considerations for supporting Arab American youths' mental health. *Contemporary School Psychology*, 21(3), 191–200. https://doi.org/10.1007/s40688-016-0117-7

Hodge, D. R., & Nadir, A. (2008). Moving toward culturally competent practice with Muslims: Modifying cognitive therapy with Islamic tenets. *Social Work*, 53(1), 31–41. https://doi.org/10.1093/sw/53.1.31

Hook, J. N., Davis, D. E., Owen, J., Worthington, E. L., & Utsey, S. O. (2013). Cultural humility: Measuring openness to culturally diverse clients. *Journal of Counseling Psychology*, 60(3), 353–366. https://doi.org/10.1037/a0032595

Khoury, D. Y. (2019). Mental health provider cultural competence in the provision of services to Arabs. *Journal of Ethnic & Cultural Diversity in Social Work: Innovation in Theory, Research & Practice*, 28(4), 370–388. https://doi-org.mutex.gmu.edu/10.1080/15313204.2017.1409677

Khoury, D. Y., & Manuel, J. I. (2016). The development and validation of a measurement of multicultural competence towards Arab Americans. *Best Practices in Mental Health*, 12(1), 43–60.

CHAPTER 18

Culturally Responsive Counseling for Older Adults and Addressing Ageism

WHITNEY GEORGE

LEARNING OBJECTIVES

After reading this chapter, students will be able to:
- Recognize the impact of ageism on clients at various points in the life span.
- Discuss specific topics related to ageism and culturally specific topics associated with aging.
- Apply cultural competencies and ethical principles to work with older adults.
- Summarize ways in which students, counselor educators, and clinicians can advocate for older adults in their communities.

SELF-REFLECTION QUESTIONS

1. Think about biases, prejudices, and assumptions you might have about older adult clients. How do these help and hinder your ability to provide culturally sensitive counseling?
2. What hesitancies, if any, do you have about working with older adult clients?
3. What attributes do you have that will enable you to work with older adult clients?

The older adult population—those aged 65 and older—is the fastest growing age group in the United States, with 20% of the population expected to be over the age of 65 by 2030 (Federal Interagency Forum on Aging-Related Statistics, 2016). Mental health service utilization in the older adult population has traditionally been low (Myers & Harper, 2004). However, the Institute of Medicine (2012) indicated that there will be a need for increased service provision to older adults due to the population increase, decreased stigma associated with mental health, a greater understanding of mental health needs, and the fact that at least 25% of older adults have a diagnosable mental health disorder. Given this data, counselors need to be prepared to work with older adults, advocate for their mental health needs, and understand the impact that culture and ageism have on one's work with older adults (Wagner et al., 2019).

Working from a liberation counseling perspective requires counselors to view the client from a strengths-based perspective and identify ways in which clients thrive and become whole regardless of the multiple oppressions and inhumanity that they may have experienced (French et al., 2019). In order to apply this perspective to counseling with older adults, counselors, counselor trainees, and counselor educators must learn specific skills and gain cultural competence in the area of counseling older adults, namely gerocounseling (Myers, 1995). McBride and Hays (2012) reported that most counseling students have limited exposure to courses in gerontology; Foster et al. (2009) noted that counselors described limited interest in learning about aging or receiving education in gerocounseling, and did not feel prepared to work with older adults. Palmore (1999) reported that a construct relevant to counselors' interest in working with older adults is ageism. Ageism is the most prevalent form of prejudice, and it affects older adults and younger people similarly (Bratt et al., 2020). Ageism occurs when someone is discriminated against based on their age, and this can occur at both ends of the life span (Raymer et al., 2017). Could ageism be affecting counselor self-efficacy and interest in working with older adults? Through an exploration of, reflection into, and introspection of oneself as a counselor, we can broaden the lens of gerocounseling by incorporating liberation counseling with older adults and challenge existing stigmas and biases associated with ageism.

THE COUNSELOR: EXPLORATION, INTROSPECTION, AND REFLECTION

When working with any population, it is important for the helping professional to consider their attitudes, beliefs, biases, and values. However, this consideration is particularly important when counseling older adults. Attitudes and beliefs can affect a clinician's behavior toward older people and can influence how the counselor interacts with them (Hinrichsen, 2019). Unfortunately, our society has often devalued older adults. This devaluation can come in the form of holding negative stereotypes about older people, having a fear of aging, or not fully understanding the experience of being older (Kampfe, 2015). Because counselors are human, they may also hold negative views of older adults or have fears about working with this population. Counselors may unknowingly hold negative beliefs about aging and older people. They may hold varied beliefs about aging that are associated with cognitive decline, disability, end of life, dependence, indecision, inability to learn new things, and a lack of contribution to society (Kampfe, 2015). Conversely, holding overly positive beliefs about this population, such as that older adults possess inherent wisdom and demonstrate unwavering kindness, can be ageist as well, in that older adults are seen as all the same. These beliefs and thoughts may limit counselors' ability to accept older clients, and may hinder counselors' openness to working with them (Kampfe, 2015; Myers & Schwiebert, 1996). Therefore, counselors will need to explore and reflect on their beliefs and attitudes about aging, and challenge their misconceptions about older adults.

For a counselor working with the aging population, self-reflection is a critical place to start. As a counselor, it may be important to ask self-reflective questions, such as "Why or why don't I want to work with older adults?" "Does working with older people make me think about my aging process and mortality?" and "What transference or countertransference might I be faced with when working with an older population?" These types of questions can help the counselor to explore and think introspectively about their experiences and personal beliefs or fears about aging and working with an aging population.

For most of people's lives, the idea of aging is an "us-versus-them" phenomenon; however, eventually all of *us* will be in the older adult category (if we are lucky; Kampfe, 2015). This us-versus-them idea can lead to anxiety in the counselor and require the counselor to reflect on what is perpetuating the anxious feelings. In considering the history of psychotherapy, reflecting on one's thoughts, reactions, or feelings about a client is a useful strategy (Hinrichsen, 2019). If a client is bringing up a topic that has personal meaning to the therapist, then it is the therapist's responsibility to gain supervision on this topic so as to not interfere with the progress of the client. This holds especially true for topics for which the therapist may hold a blind spot. Counselors may not realize the social message that is constantly reinforced: You may not be old now, but you will be one day. Conversely, the message may be: I am also older, and I have carried messages of aging with me. Attitudes about aging, along with one's own aging, can complicate the counseling relationship and make it difficult to provide effective treatment (Hinrichsen, 2019).

A tool that might assist with gaining higher levels of self-awareness regarding our attitudes about aging is the Johari Window (Ryan, 2018). The Johari Window is a tool that was created to illuminate and detail interpersonal awareness. The actual window is made up of four quadrants (the open area, the blind area, the hidden area, and the unknown area) and conceptualizes how we see ourselves and how we are seen by others (Ryan, 2018). Using this tool could assist counselors to understand and improve their interpersonal communication and relationships. It can also assist by bringing awareness to conceptions and specific attitudes or beliefs that a counselor may hold about older adults and aging.

Research has indicated that attitudes toward older adults are most strongly related to personal or individual values, rather than the values that the overall culture tends to hold (Zhang et al., 2016). This research shows that processing attitudes about aging is best conducted at the individual counselor level, and that the work is best done through self-reflection, introspection, and personal exploration. Additional research has demonstrated that not only can negative stereotypes have detrimental effects on the mental and physical health of older persons or people who are aging, but also that positive stereotypes and positive views of aging can counteract those negative consequences (Levy, 2009). To work through this process of self-reflection and challenge the negative stereotypes associated with older adults, Nelson (2016) suggests confronting societal myths and promoting the educational training of healthcare and mental health care workers. Nelson suggests reframing for oneself the idea of aging to include the recognition that people enjoy continued activity, growth, and fulfillment in this period (2016). Nelson also noted that older people and those who work with them should be encouraged to think more positively about retirement and aging in general (2016). Counselors are also encouraged to attempt to work with older adults and let those experiences influence perceptions and attitudes. However, at the society level, if careers related to aging were more highly encouraged, then people would have less apprehension about entering this workspace (Nelson, 2016).

To further understand the counselor's attitudes about aging and challenging societal beliefs, Kampfe (2015) recommended a series of exercises, two of which are described here. The first is an exercise aimed at understanding the counselor's perceptions of aging: the counselor makes a list of descriptors of older people, being as honest as possible, and then reflects on the sources of those perceptions or attitudes. The counselor should think about how accurate the perceptions are, how they came to exist for the counselor, and how the counselor has personally contributed to those views (Kampfe, 2015). The second exercise Kampfe (2015) suggested is a group exercise that encourages counselors to consider how stereotypes can interfere with the counseling process. In this activity, the counselor and a role-played "older client" stand facing each other with some distance apart, and group members call out negative perceptions about older adults. As the words are called out, the group members physically place themselves between the counselor and client. The question is then asked, "Can the counselor see the client?" This exercise is followed by discussion and process (Kampfe, 2015).

Once therapists address their own attitudes and beliefs about aging, it is important to reflect on how to remain resilient. Therapist resilience is an important factor to consider when working with any population that challenges our attitudes and belief systems. Luthar et al. (2000) defined *resilience* as "a dynamic process encompassing positive adaptation within the context of significant adversity" (p. 543). In defining *adversity*, two conditions must be present: "(a) exposure to significant threat or severe adversity, and (b) the achievement of positive adaptation despite major assaults on the developmental process" (Luthar et al., 2000, p. 543). While addressing beliefs and attitudes is a process that inherently changes and challenges the mental health professional, there have been few studies on understanding how counselors who work with diverse client populations have overcome professional and personal adversities across their career life span and have sustained resilience (Hou & Skovholt, 2020). As we take time to personally reflect, note that resilience is an important part of working with multicultural populations, not only for the practicing counselor, but also for many clients who have been marginalized. The difficult task of changing the culture around working with older adults can challenge the counselor's resilience, but the helper should also be mindful of the resilience that older clients bring to the counseling relationship.

To effectively work with marginalized populations, the counselor should also be well versed and prepared to engage in liberation counseling, which argues in favor of engaging and understanding communities within the context of their social conditions (Domínguez et al., 2020). For example, it is important to understand our clients' preferences, virtues, value systems, strengths, and local resources to best provide counseling services to them (Domínguez et al., 2020). For older adults, this is particularly important, as they are not only a marginalized population, but also one that has varying levels of individual needs, strengths, and resources among and within their communities.

As a final thought for self-exploration, what can counselors learn from a population that has been seen as "other," has demonstrated resilience in many areas, and continues to forge ahead despite negative societal beliefs? Knowing that two of the four factors that increase counselor resilience are (a) a desire to learn and grow and (b) being able to actively engage with oneself (Hou & Skovholt, 2020) can help us to connect with the older adult population and maintain resilience through ongoing work to overcome the stigma associated with aging.

THE EFFECTS OF SOCIETAL AND CULTURAL FACTORS RELATING TO AGEISM

There is a lack of agreement about who comprises the older adult population, and how this group is defined within the context of aging in the United States (American Psychological Association, 2014; George & Dixon, 2018; Hinrichsen, 2019). The term *geriatrics* refers to the older adult population and the medical services related to old age and aging. The most widely accepted definition of the geriatric or aging population is those adults over the age of 65 years (Administration on Aging, 2020; Hinrichsen, 2019; George & Dixon, 2018). However, medical literature does not offer a precise age range that encompasses this group (Berman & Silverman, 2021). The basal ages of the geriatric population may include individuals at the ages of 50, 60, 65, or even 70 (AARP, n.d.; Medicare.gov, n.d.; Neugarten, 1974). For example, organizations such as the AARP, designed to enhance the quality of life for the aging in the United States, may have a minimum membership age of 50 (AARP, n.d.). Medicare, the U.S. government's healthcare program for the disabled or aging, provides coverage only to those 65 years of age or older (Medicare.gov, n.d.). Additionally, Neugarten (1974) makes the distinction between the young-old (55–74 years of age) and the old-old (75 years of age and older). Recently, further subdivisions of the old-old into other subcategories have evolved (National Institute on Aging, 1986). Namely, the category for those 75 to 84 years old is now known as the elderly, and those 85 years and over are known as the very-old or the oldest old (National Institute on Aging, 1986). Because each of these subcategories represents a broad range of the aging population and is based on definitions of chronological age, other factors for understanding geriatric clients can then become more useful. Among the many areas to be considered in addition to age is the impact of the U.S. psychosocial and societal factors on the aging process. By taking a broader look at the aging population in America, counselors can understand their developmental processes and how they relate to the mental health services offered to older adults.

Many older adults have multiple characteristics and intersecting identities that influence their worldview and life experiences (Potter et al., 2019). These identities can be in the form of race, age, gender, socioeconomic status (SES), ability, sexuality, and so on, and as these identities intersect, it can shape people's experiences, particularly disparities. The term *double jeopardy* (Ferraro, 1987) refers to the idea that individuals begin to experience beliefs, attitudes, and discriminatory practices based on multiple identities that may be perceived as negative. Understanding the multiple identities that older adults can experience will be useful to those approaching this work from a liberation counseling perspective. Having a counselor who can use a liberation counseling lens to focus on the uniqueness of the person, and the values held within their communities, can help to combat the marginalized experiences of older adults.

Everyone approaches aging in their own way based on gender, culture, and individual differences (Potter et al., 2019). Given the societal factors that affect each group, for example, an African American male might experience aging differently than a Hispanic woman. Although many aging persons are oppressed or have experienced oppression, their understanding of oppression might look different based on many factors. Calasanti and Slevin (2006) proposed that oppression occurs if the advantages of one group depend on the disadvantages of another, and if the disadvantages of the oppressed group depend on the exclusion of this group from their ability to gain resources, rewards, and privileges. For example, within the context of gender relations, it could be said that the advantages men hold in society depend on the disadvantages of women, or within aging, the advantages that younger people have depend on the disadvantages of the elders. A liberation counseling framework takes into consideration oppression and disadvantages experienced by marginalized groups (Chávez et al., 2016). Historically, psychology and other helping professions failed to examine the experiences of oppressed people and often pathologized those experiences. However, liberation counseling promotes the recognition of the group strengths of marginalized communities. By focusing on the strengths and resources that people have, liberation counseling advocates for the appreciation of community assets and works to help with collaboration within communities to ignite social change (Chávez et al., 2016). This framework can be particularly useful in working with marginalized older adults who bring vast experiences to counseling.

Cultural and Racial Factors Affecting Older Adults and Aging in the United States

The group that comprises older adults in the United States is very heterogeneous, and there is much diversity among their characteristics (Kampfe, 2015). Even though this group shares the same descriptor of *older*, there is much variation within the older adult population with regard to gender, race, ethnicity, culture, education, employment occupation, SES, religion, immigration and migration patterns, personality, life experiences, family constellation, health status, disability status, and functional abilities (Kampfe, 2015). As the current younger population ages, this diversity is only expected to increase (George & Dixon, 2018). The older adult population is also diverse because of the large age range of this group (65 to 105+ years), which represents at least four decades and multiple generations. Each segment of this population will have varying worldviews that shape their beliefs, attitudes, habits, sense of self, and other aspects of their lives (Kampfe et al., 2007). Counselors should not assume that older people are one unified group of individuals with similar histories, values, and behaviors. In fact, liberation psychology posits that counselors will understand their clients from the worldview with which that client enters the counseling relationship (Chávez et al., 2016).

Several tenets of liberation psychology guide counselors to consider the human experience associated with mental health. First, it is imperative to understand that psychological problems are often the result of structural and sociopolitical oppression and that counselors need to examine the current societal structures and work to recover the historical memory of the oppressed (Chávez et al., 2016). Additionally, because dominant social structures have historically been used to establish narratives of the poor and oppressed, it is important to create a new understanding that is free from the dominant set of beliefs that can distort true lived experiences (Chávez et al., 2016). Challenging assumptions and questioning power dynamics is another important tenet of liberation psychology. Many of us can take for granted our assumptions and how those came to be (Chávez et al., 2016). Liberation counseling also requires that we understand any issue faced by oppressed populations from the perspective of the oppressed (Chávez et al., 2016). Finally, it is vital that we as counselors, from a liberation counseling perspective, acknowledge the power and virtues of oppressed individuals in improving their own lived experiences (Chávez et al., 2016). In doing so, we can empower older adults to challenge the messages and societal structures in which they live.

Old age intersects with other systems of privilege and oppression, such as racial and cultural issues of power and inequality (Fang et al., 2019). As age increases, the poverty rate rises, especially for those who live alone. The poverty rate for those over 65 years old, in 2017, was 7% for Whites, 17% for Hispanics, and 19.3% for African Americans (Congressional Research Service, 2019). It is also noted that older adults of Hispanic origin are among the most educationally and economically disadvantaged (Tarraf et al., 2020). Along with adequate income, access to healthcare has been identified as one of the critical bases for a safe and secure old age. Both income and healthcare are among the inequalities faced by the Hispanic people living within the United States (Tarraf et al., 2020). Because much of the health insurance system is based on employer-sponsored programs or qualifying for Social Security, the low employment rates and immigration status of Hispanic people leave them at a disadvantage for a lifetime of health problems. These issues also directly relate to an unwanted dependence on social programs and community members, which can lead to stifled development in the process of positive aging (Tornstam, 2005).

In 2018, there were 52.4 million people 65 years or older in the United States, comprising one in seven of all Americans (Administration on Aging, 2020). The population of African American people is also increasing. In 2018, 12% of the total U.S. population was African American; however, African American elderly made up about 9% of the total elderly population. By the year 2040, the number of Black, Indigenous, and People of Color (BIPOC) elders is projected to increase to about 34% of the U.S. population (Administration on Aging, 2020).

Aging is an important part of the life span and is often accompanied by a reduction in social and economic status and a loss of roles. For African American people in particular, Jenkins (2019) notes that there are ethnocultural, historical, and contemporary reasons that affect caregiving in African American communities, and family roles play a part in turning to informal community resources for support. Thus, African American elderly play a prominent role in community and family relationships, an important contributor to the quality of their lives (Jenkins, 2019). However, these extended caregiving roles and tasks may disproportionately place African American older adults at great health risk (Cannon & Fawcett, 2018).

Women and Aging

In many Western cultures, aging has been viewed negatively, and people are often encouraged to refer to this group as "senior citizens" to avoid the negative connotations associated with old age (Kampfe, 2015). Additionally, Crawford and Unger (2004) noted that aging women in Western societies are viewed as unappealing, whereas older men are viewed with respect. Women are not only subject to ageism, but also to continued sexism (Crawford & Unger, 2004). Women are said to be placed in double jeopardy as they age and begin to experience beliefs, attitudes, and discriminatory practices based on age and gender (Crawford & Unger, 2004). The gender differences in the aging population also reveal themselves in power differentials, and give men an unearned advantage over women in areas such as domestic labor, retirement, education, and occupations (Calasanti & Slevin, 2006).

The development of positive aging seems to be impeded in cultures with a high incidence of poverty. However, despite the high rates of poverty in African American groups within the United States, African American women have consistently been found to have the lowest rates of suicide of all age and ethnic categories (Winterrowd et al., 2017). Winterrowd et al. (2017) also reported that despite a lifetime of racism and poverty, women of color are survivors who expect fewer societal privileges than their privileged counterparts and seem to view old age as a reward. Older African American people also seem to have a more positive view of losing independence, due to their relationships within the community and with family members. Older African American women are more likely to both give and take from the community, as well as support and receive support from family members than either White women or Latinas (Jenkins, 2019). Nevertheless, almost all ethnic minorities have been noted to place a larger importance on interdependence and the needs of the family over the needs of the individual despite age. Because of the lack of guilt and remorse associated with losing their independence (Tornstam, 2005), this acceptance of dependence on others helps BIPOC in the United States to reach a level of positive aging that the majority culture may never experience.

Non-Western cultural images of women can be positive and represent them as powerful, wise, and individuals to admire (Crawford & Unger, 2004). These cultures also usually emphasize tenets of gerotranscendence (a theory of positive aging) throughout the life span (Tornstam, 2006). For example, the old Hebrew tradition holds age and wisdom in high esteem (Tornstam, 2005). Traditional Japanese culture views the aging as wise, beautiful, and hardworking, and in certain Native American tribes older women are viewed as strong, with power and privilege that the other society members do not have (Crawford & Unger, 2004). In many of these mentioned cultures, positive aging strategies are seen in early age through end of life, and are often looked upon with great regard (Dehkordi et al., 2020; Tornstam, 1997).

Research on parental caregiving by adult women (Amankwaa, 2017) suggested that it is common for women to provide care for their parents at some point in their lifetimes. African American women received more support from their adult children than their counterparts (Cannon & Fawcett, 2018). Some of the factors that influence the frequency of contact between adult children and elderly parents were the number of children, proximity to the nearest child, and parental education. The study also found that older African American people with children manifested a positive appraisal of the family life dimension and tended to reside in closer proximity to relatives than elders who were childless. Results of the study indicated that adult children are frequent providers of assistance to parents.

Among African American people, the presence of such family ties determines the use of formal support among the elderly. Analysis of the life course of adult children reveals that separation from spouse, household responsibility, and increased stress may affect the provision of care for elder parents. Differences across gender suggest that daughters more frequently provide care to their elder parents (Cannon & Fawcett, 2018). An explanation for the care given by women may be attributed to differential expectations and socialization experiences for women versus those for men (Cannon & Fawcett, 2018). These factors may affect not only positive aging in this population, but also their need for and willingness to participate in formal counseling services.

AGEIST AGEISM AND REVERSE AGEISM

Ageism is prejudice directed against someone based on their age (Butler, 1969). Iversen et al. (2009, p. 15) defined *ageism* as "negative or positive stereotypes, prejudice, and/or discrimination against (or to the advantage of) elderly people based on their chronological age, or on the perception of them as being 'old' or 'elderly'." Negative attitudes, stereotypes, and discrimination against older adults (ageism) can be noted as a culturally ingrained practice in Western cultures (Raymer et al., 2017). Many negative concepts, signaled by terms such as *old-fashioned*, *slow*, and *forgetful*, can result in patronizing behaviors experienced by older adults and can result in workplace discrimination and other negative treatment. Even the word *ageism* by its origins conjures up an image of older people and the elderly, in that ageism is discrimination on the grounds of being older (Comfort, 1977).

However, in defining ageism in such a way, we find ourselves falling into an ageist viewpoint, as this definition does not allow for or acknowledge experiences of ageism on the younger end of the spectrum (Rodham, 2001). Rodham (2001) first described the concept of ageist ageism, noting that the emphasis on ageism had been given to beliefs concerning the ability of older workers or to the discrimination experienced by older workers. However, Rodham (2001) pointed out that regardless of a person's age, when discrimination occurs based on age, the experience is discrimination irrespective of age. With this in mind, *ageist ageism* can be defined as a "nearly exclusive focus on older adults as the subjects of ageism ... as little attention has been paid to stereotypes and discrimination that younger adults face in the workplace because of their (young) age" (Raymer et al., 2017, p. 149).

If ageism is not just experienced by older adults, then who else could be the recipient of such prejudices? Bratt et al. (2018) reported that in many countries, younger people reported age discrimination more often than older adults. However, the social sciences have paid little attention to youth as the main targets for discrimination, which has implications for reverse ageism on life span development. Raymer et al. (2017) noted that a growing body of research supports the phenomenon of reverse ageism, or ageism directed at younger people. For example, research has noted that millennials are discriminated against in the workforce based on stereotypes associated with their generational affiliation (Raymer et al., 2017). Regardless of the reason someone is discriminated against based on their age, ageism in any form can have negative implications for mental health. A survey conducted by Lyons et al. (2017) found that ageism was strongly related to poor mental health in the areas of depression, anxiety, general stress, and positive mental health. These findings suggest that experiences of ageism, regardless of age, are an important factor in the health and well-being of older adults and should be accounted for when providing support for healthier and happier aging. de la Fuente-Núñez et al. (2021) note that intergenerational contact is a useful tool to reduce ageism and reverse ageism. They also suggest that policies might be relevant in addressing reverse ageism. However, there is a notable gap in the literature surrounding interventions that would reduce or eliminate ageism against younger people (de la Fuente-Núñez et al., 2021).

ETHICAL AND COUNSELING CONSIDERATIONS FOR THOSE EXPERIENCING OR CONTRIBUTING TO AGEISM

Within the United States, many groups of adults are oppressed within the context of aging, and it remains that all older adults, regardless of gender, culture, or privilege, endure ageism and other forms of oppression (Calasanti & Kiecolt, 2012). Older adults within the United States lose authority and autonomy, experience workplace discrimination, and often see a decrease in wealth and income; the poverty threshold is higher for older people than the rest of the population (Calasanti & Kiecolt, 2012). The reality is that being older is a position of low status in a culture that values youth and vitality (Shannonhouse et al., 2018). Additionally, guiding theories and conceptualizations that emphasize productivity, effectiveness, and independence (mid-life values) are propounded by Euro-American Western, middle-class males, who comprise the majority of the geriatric researchers (Tornstam, 2005). It is assumed that older age implies the continuity of these values even though, according to some theorists, these values become less important to us as individuals age (Tornstam, 2005).

Hinrichsen (2019) noted that, through the media portrayal of the U.S. Social Security and Medicare programs, ageism is promoted in the thoughts of younger people who view the aging as dependent on society and as a burden. Because many of those in Western cultures believe that it is activity, productivity, efficiency, individuality, independence, wealth, health, sociability, and a realistic view of the world that matters most, societal views may be stifling the positive aging process (Tornstam, 2005). These societal views may make an aging individual feel guilty about their developmental changes, and doctors, nurses, and family members may inadvertently obstruct a natural process toward positive aging (Tornstam, 1994). The attitude that older adults are socially withdrawing is not understood from a cultural standpoint, and this is not part of "normal" mid-life activity, productiveness, and social commitments that count in our society. Therefore, older adults may feel guilty or apologize for having reached a different view of life and living (Tornstam, 2005). Coupled with life changes is the growing number of older adults in the United States. Thus, specifying an age range for this group is ever important as more adults in the United States live longer lives and come of age.

IMPLICATIONS FOR COUNSELING STUDENTS, COUNSELOR EDUCATORS, AND CLINICAL PRACTITIONERS

Counselors have the power to change the attitudes of the community, family members, other care providers, older adults, and the counselors themselves. Kampfe (2015) suggested that one of the most effective strategies for changing attitudes is for the counselor to model the appropriate behavior. The most evident implication is the creation and description of a means to assist in educating about the differences in needs of older adults seeking counseling services. The *Gerontological Competencies for Counselors and Human Development Specialists* (Myers & Sweeney, 1990) calls for all counselors to graduate with sufficient knowledge of the needs of older adults, as well as the skills to provide effective helping interventions to meet those needs. The use of multicultural counseling and therapy with older adults could provide a good foundation, and a wealth of information for counselor educators to draw from when examining the needs of older adults in educating their students. Counseling supervisors in particular should have culturally relevant information available to assist in the supervision of their students working with the aging population. This would ensure that the clients being served would have access to culturally sensitive therapy, and that the students' knowledge about one of the largest underserved populations in this country—aging adults—would increase.

While it is understood that social justice and advocacy are important concerns for counselors, research has noted that training for social justice and advocacy continues to be inadequate or lacking in most counselor education programs (Steele, 2008). The Liberation Model, based on the tenets of liberation counseling, is a model that can be employed for social justice training with master's-level counseling students (Steele, 2008). Instructors who use this model are asked to infuse social justice advocacy in their courses, and engage students in conversations on social justice and advocacy in counseling (Steele, 2008). There are four phases in integrating the Liberation Model into the curriculum. Steele (2008) suggests, "(a) examining the explicit and implicit cultural and political ideology in the United States today, (b) examining the explicit and implicit cultural and political ideology of counseling, (c) interdisciplinary study of relevant issues, and (d) applying the Liberation Model to the practice of counselor advocacy" (p. 77). By doing so, we can better educate counseling students with social justice training and assist in developing critical thinking skills determined by the profession to be necessary for social justice advocacy (Steele, 2008).

In addition to social justice training, many believe that providing counselor training in gerontology and multiculturalism is daunting (American Psychological Association, 2014; Sue et al., 2007). Recent evidence has illustrated that many counselor education and counseling psychology programs across the country are not training students to meet the needs of this growing population of aging adults (American Psychological Association, 2014). It should also be noted that there is a lack of current research about the type of training counseling students are receiving with respect to older adults (American Psychological Association, 2014). Researchers believe that working with older adults requires some kind of specialized training and preparation to assist in understanding the developmental changes experienced by the aging population (American Psychological Association, 2014; Shannonhouse et al., 2018). Therefore, training of counselor educators should focus on models specific to older adults, and students should be able to apply specific principles to their work (American Psychological Association, 2014). Through helping counselor education students to focus on the application of theory, we may also begin to train them to look for ways in which these various factors may be impeding the process of positive aging and techniques specific to working with diverse racial and ethnic older adults. This fact only solidifies the justification for understanding the developmental process of diverse aging adults through the use of a model that encompasses theory specific to older adults and the incorporation of liberation counseling techniques.

ADVOCACY AND FUTURE TRENDS IN AGING

The future of how we view older adults and aging is changing, with the anticipated life span of older adults having a life expectancy of at least 20 years beyond the age of 65 (Arnett et al., 2020). Of the most notable changes associated with adult development is the transition of entering adulthood with finishing education, obtaining stable work, marriage, and parenthood coming later than ever before (Arnett et al., 2020). Another striking change is that adulthood lasts longer than it previously did. Longer lives and declining fertility rates have resulted in a dramatic increase in the proportion of older adults in developed countries in the past several decades (Arnett et al., 2020). Future trends should be noted, not only with regard to the quantity of years (which is increasing), but also to the quality of life, which is improving with individuals living more healthy years. Additionally, the grandparent role is becoming more common than before and it is a trend that is likely to continue (Choi et al., 2016). As people live longer, more people than in the past stay healthy enough to be involved as grandparents and even great-grandparents (Arnett et al., 2020). A future trend is also growing in the area of custodial grandparents, who are taking on the primary role of raising their grandchildren (Choi et al., 2016). A final trend worth noting is in the area of retirement and continued work in the later years. Coile (2018) notes that the rise in workforce participation later in life is not just due to economic rewards, but also to improvements in health, increases in education, fewer jobs that involve physical demands, and more desirable benefits such as healthcare for workers. Advocacy efforts in this area are discussed later in this chapter.

COUNSELING UTILIZATION AND HELP-SEEKING

Many older adults in the United States have mental health needs. Of the older adult population in the United States, 20% have a diagnosed mental illness (American Psychological Association, 2018). The most common mental disorders affecting older adults are depression, dysthymia, and generalized anxiety disorder (American Psychological Association, 2018), although studies suggest that of older adults with common mental disorders, only 3% seek services (American Psychological Association, 2018).

Depression is perhaps the most frequent cause of emotional suffering in older adulthood and can significantly decrease quality of life and increase mortality rates (Karavatas et al., 2020). Depression refers to a person's mood and follows the criteria stated in the *Diagnostic and Statistical Manual of Mental Disorders* (5th ed.; *DSM-5*; American Psychiatric Association, 2013). These criteria include a person showing symptoms such as feelings of worthlessness or guilt, social withdrawal, agitation, and a generally low mood, among others (American Psychiatric Association, 2013). Psychosocial factors, as well as physical health status and behavioral factors, may be important in understanding older adults' experiences of depressive symptoms (Karavatas et al., 2020). People with low SES generally have fewer psychosocial resources than people with high SES (Roy & Walsh, 2020). Low SES is related to feelings of low self-control, negative coping styles, poor social support, and more stressful life events (Roy & Walsh, 2020). Several studies have found a favorable effect of social support on mental health, whereas stressful life events are noted to have a negative impact on depressive symptoms (Karavatas et al., 2020). Physical health status may also be important in the explanation of depressive symptoms. Depression in late life is frequently found in conjunction with other physical and psychiatric conditions, especially in the oldest old (Karavatas et al.,

2020). For example, depression is common in older patients experiencing renal failure, chronic obstructive pulmonary disease (COPD), and Parkinson's disease, which are in fact some of the most common physical conditions plaguing this age group (Karavatas et al., 2020). Additionally, people who have been diagnosed with dementia often suffer from depression, anxiety, and paranoia (American Psychological Association, 2018). Although depression is one of the most prevalent mental illnesses among older adults, help-seeking by older adults is often delayed. This can result in a longer duration of untreated symptoms, poorer health outcomes, and higher healthcare use (Polacsek et al., 2019). Polacsek et al. (2019) found that barriers to help-seeking were attributable to stigma around mental health issues, low self-motivation, difficulty in accessing formal support, ageism, and difficulty obtaining an initial diagnosis. They also noted that factors that increased help-seeking behaviors were accepting personal responsibility, mental health literacy, therapeutic alliances, and informal support (Polacsek et al., 2019). Mental health workers should seek to reduce help-seeking barriers and find ways to facilitate the identified factors that promote help-seeking, particularly with older adults experiencing depression (Polacsek et al., 2019).

Along with depression, anxiety is a leading mental health problem that older adults face. Recent studies have shown a higher rate of anxiety symptoms (18.1%) in older adults than those of depression (15.4%; Thapa et al., 2020). Risk factors for anxiety in older adults include being female, lower household wealth, poor health, smoking, chronic health conditions, and exposure to adverse life events (Thapa et al., 2020). However, depression and anxiety are often comorbid with one another. The *DSM-5* (American Psychiatric Association, 2013) notes that those who meet the criteria for generalized anxiety disorder are likely to meet the criteria for another anxiety or depressive disorder.

Anxiety causes distress, reduces life satisfaction, and increases the risk of disability and mortality in even high-functioning older adults (Thapa et al., 2020). In older adults, social disconnectedness and perceived isolation can increase the risk of mental health problems such as depression and anxiety (Santini et al., 2020). Women tend to have elevated symptoms of anxiety in late life, compared to men of similar demographic characteristics (Thapa et al., 2020). However, as women and men age, anxiety tends to be seen as more of a physical and cognitive impairment than a focus on somatic symptoms (shortness of breath, racing heart, etc.) as it is viewed in younger adults (American Psychological Association, 2018), leading to the idea that anxiety is an understandable part of aging. It is also understood that many cultures view the symptoms of anxiety and depression differently than do those in the Western and particularly U.S. cultures (Thapa et al., 2020). For example, research on Native Americans and Alaska Natives suggests that the role of family is a protective factor for anxiety in this population, and that low income and adverse childhood experiences are associated with higher levels of anxiety and depression (McKinley et al., 2021). Similarly, while close family relationships and caregiving responsibilities were correlated with lower levels of anxiety in both Asian and Hispanic/Latino populations, trauma and cognitive impairments were found to be related to higher levels of anxiety (Saadi et al., 2021).

It is necessary that counselors develop specific interventions and frameworks for particular cultural groups and the aging population within the United States. Interventions and techniques could help in the rapport-building process. Additionally, there is a noted reluctance of diverse racial and ethnic individuals to seek counseling services. It has been noted that many individuals lack trust, do not want to provide information that might be too revealing, and are reluctant to receive counseling services (George & Dixon, 2018). Previous research has also noted the increased levels of depression and anxiety as adults age (American Psychological Association, 2018); however, a discussion of counseling implications would not be complete without a reinforcement of the findings related to these two mental illnesses. To address this issue, it is important to note such increases in these symptoms when working with older clients. Older adults are also at a disadvantage in the United States with respect to healthcare, mental health, and social services (Calasanti & Kiecolt, 2012). Due to this fact, clinicians might use this knowledge to increase counselors' interventions and strategies to use with their older clients.

COMPETENCIES AND CULTURAL HUMILITY

"I love the term cultural humility: The world is so complex—and so are people—and we need to reflect on what we know and don't know" (Hinrichsen, 2019, p. 34). The world is complex, our clients are complex, the field of counseling is complex, and our ability to distinguish what we do and do not know is paramount to our clients' success and ours. As mental health workers, we should have an intense curiosity and open-heartedness about our clients and how we can best help them. In having these traits, we can help our clients understand themselves and the barriers in their lives that brought them to counseling. Our intense curiosity and open-heartedness can also help us to reflect on our own aging process and older adulthood (Hinrichsen, 2019).

Service provision is a fundamental aspect of mental health counseling, and understanding the breadth of services is paramount when serving the geriatric population or older adults in the United States. Previously developed competencies and guidelines have outlined the necessity for counselors to work with older adults. *The Gerontological Competencies for Counselors and Human Development Specialists* (Myers & Sweeney, 1990) indicated "all counselors [must] graduate with some knowledge of the needs of older persons and the skills to provide effective helping interventions to meet those needs" (Myers & Sweeney, 1990, p. 2). However, these dated guidelines have recently lost recognition as the counseling field has done away with many programs that focused on training counselors in the area of gerontology (Rollins, 2008b). More recently, the Council for the Accreditation of Counseling and Related Educational Programs (CACREP; 2001) established standards that gerontological counseling programs and counselors working with older clients should have. This 2001 set of standards suggested the need for skills, techniques, and practices beyond the scope of a "generalist" counselor (CACREP, 2001). However, CACREP Executive Director Carol L. Bobby and CACREP Director of Accreditation Robert I. Urofsky noted, "The 2009 Standards delete the program area for Gerontological Counseling because few counselor education departments have sought accreditation for this specialization" (Rollins, 2008b, p. 32). Neither the CACREP 2016 nor the proposed 2024 standards specifically address training specific to gerontological counseling. Additionally, Myers and Schwiebert (1996) recommended 16 specific "Minimal Essential Competencies" (skills) for all counselors (p. 13). One of the competencies outlined a counselor's need to demonstrate "skill in applying extensive knowledge of the intellectual, physical, social, emotional, vocational, and spiritual needs of older persons and strategies for helping to meet those needs" (Myers & Schwiebert, 1996, p. 13). However, these competencies have neither been updated nor reestablished since their development in 1996. Although Maples and Abney (2006) reaffirmed the 1996 standards and competencies for counselors working with geriatric populations and recognized the above-mentioned standards as current working competencies, no updates or changes have been made since the mid-1990s.

Due to the seeming lack of concern by the field of counseling for the growing number of older adults that may require counseling services, the Association of Adult Development and Aging (AADA), a division of the American Counseling Association (ACA), has developed brochures for counselors to reference when working with older clients as a replacement for the lost standards and competencies (Rollins, 2008b). This alarming lack of interest in gerontology has not gone unnoticed. Foley and Luz (2020) revisited a 2008 Institute of Medicine (IOM) report which predicted that as more adults enter into older adulthood, the United States will face a healthcare workforce that is too small and unprepared to meet their health needs (Institute of Medicine, 2008). Although the updated research does not focus on counseling, it urges initiatives to boost the recruitment and retention of geriatric specialists and emphasizes that more healthcare providers need to be trained in the basics of geriatric care (Foley & Luz, 2020). As of 2018, of all full-time doctoral students and practicing psychologists, only 0.4% and 2%, respectively, specialize in the field of aging (American Psychological Association, 2018). Additionally, with a growing number of older adults from diverse backgrounds (Administration on Aging, 2020), counselors need to be aware of the competencies and ethical standards of the ACA on multicultural counseling issues (American Counseling Association, 2014). Shannonhouse et al. (2018) also note the importance of multicultural counseling with older adults and confirm that all counseling relationships must consider cultural and ethnic concerns when working with older adults. To be effective, counselors must possess and demonstrate multicultural competencies and applications (Shannonhouse et al., 2018). Furthermore, they remind practitioners that all clients come from unique cultures, and an effective counselor must apply this knowledge and awareness in all counseling relationships (Shannonhouse et al., 2018).

For a counselor to be competent in working with geriatric clients, it is necessary for them to understand theories applicable to the geriatric population, understand the life experiences of the population, and have an in-depth understanding of developmental processes (American Psychological Association, 2014). Given the lack of formal counselor preparation and training in gerontology (Rollins, 2008a), it may be that counselors will need to seek out these experiences and prepare to educate themselves through continuing education, reading scholarly works, or engaging in discussions with other gerontological counselors. There are differences between members of the geriatric population, such as ethnic background, socioeconomic status, healthcare coverage, familial support, and many others (Shannonhouse et al., 2018). As the population of older adults in the United States increases, it is important for clinicians working with them to be able to provide competent counseling services and to understand the struggles and needs of older individuals. The implication of the vast diversity among the aging population is that counselors must continue to develop cultural competency and strive to grow in their knowledge and skills related to older adults through a liberation counseling framework (Kampfe, 2015).

CRAFTING AN ADVOCACY AGENDA

As mental health professionals, we are seen as natural advocates for older adults facing mental health challenges. There are also important opportunities to address how we view older adults, mental health, and aging, and become advocates to promote additional policy. For example, counselors can advocate for additional policies for older adults to have greater access to healthcare, create policy to better protect and support victims of elder abuse, or encourage older adults to self-advocate for their many needs. Of the areas where counselors can be the best advocates, addressing the stigma associated with aging and mental health is a good starting point. Counselors also need to advocate for themselves and the profession to increase our knowledge surrounding older adults and aging. Not only do we as counselors have the opportunity to advocate with our clients, but we also have the ability to influence change in the larger community (Falk & Taylor-Schiller, 2019).

According to the Substance Abuse and Mental Health Services Administration (SAMHSA; 2017), the stigma surrounding mental health and receiving a diagnosis is perceived as a barrier to seeking services. This stigma is present with older adults who may be reluctant to seek counseling services due to embarrassment or fear of this stigmatized process. Older adults may fear that if they receive a mental health diagnosis, they may be further stigmatized (Falk & Taylor-Schiller, 2019). Effective advocacy within counseling and other medical and health professions can help older adults to overcome their fears, decrease the stigma, and open a pathway for older adults to seek counseling or mental health treatment.

An additional area where advocacy is needed is within our profession: advocating for increased training in working with older adults and gerontological competencies related to counselor training. As counselor educators, students, and trainees, we should advocate for mental health professionals to develop an expertise in gerontology (Kampfe, 2015), much like some colleagues do with populations such as children, marriage and family, substance and addictions, and other subspecialties. As noted, CACREP (2009) removed the competencies related to gerontological counseling because few academic institutions sought specific accreditation in this area (Rollins, 2008a). With the growing number of older adults who will need counseling services, counselor educators should advocate for the reinstatement of formal training opportunities for counseling students to receive education beyond that of a generalist counselor who has no specific working knowledge of the unique issues older adults might bring to counseling.

It is also important for counselors to assist their older clients in learning how to advocate for themselves. Bui et al. (2021) note that creating ways for older adults to be civically engaged is an important dimension of an age-friendly community. They suggest that while volunteerism is typically the focus of research in this area, advocacy and political involvement are other areas that should be the focus of attention. It is noted that creating programs for self-advocacy and educating older adults about policy-making processes can assist them in incorporating their voices in local policy and planning (Bui et al., 2021).

By being advocates, counselors can raise awareness on mental health issues and ensure that mental health gets national governmental attention (Falk & Taylor-Schiller, 2019). Advocacy can lead to improvements in policy, legislation, and availability of services (World Health Organization [WHO], 2003). Falk and Taylor-Schiller (2019) provide a series of actions that health professionals can take to advocate for their older adult clients. They propose developing an advocacy pathway through using the internet, collaborating with other disciplines via coalitions, engaging nonprofit organizations, staying current on issues, pursuing opportunities to create change, and practicing to the fullest extent of education and training that one has as a professional. Overall, counselors should identify a way to advocate that suits their personal energy level, passion, time availability, financial resources, and commitment to older adult mental health (Falk & Taylor-Schiller, 2019).

COUNSELING ADULTS, COUPLES, AND FAMILIES

Counselors working with older adults should be mindful of working not only with the individual client, but also with the system in which the client is living. Often, counseling older adults also means establishing relationships with a partner, spouse, child, caregiver, or others who are active participants in the client's life. Working from a family systems approach (Bowen, 1978) can be very valuable for therapists who look at the client in the context of the life span. However, many types of therapies can be used with this population, and it is important that a genuine, nonjudgmental relationship be established, and that trust, unconditional positive regard, respect, and safety be at the forefront of the counseling relationship (Kampfe, 2015). In addition to individual counseling, several other therapies may be relevant when working with older adults and those who constitute their system. These therapies may include group work, creative problem-solving, bibliotherapy (the use of books as treatment), life review work (recollecting and sharing personal memories), pet therapy, relaxation therapy, dance/movement/music therapy, family therapy, and horticultural therapy (engaging in gardening or plant-based activities with the goal of reducing stress; Kampfe, 2015).

Additionally, geropsychologist Bob Knight created a therapy to inform assessment and treatment of older adults called the Contextual Adult Life Span Theory for Adapting Psychotherapy (CALTAP; Knight & Pachana, 2015). Knight proposed that therapy and counseling with older adults are similar to the work conducted with younger adults, and that when more comprehensive understanding of the later stages of adulthood is developed, the therapeutic relationship and counseling outcomes are enriched (Knight & Pachana, 2015). The CALTAP model includes five elements: (a) developmental forces (positive and negative developmental changes that come with aging), (b) specific challenges (unique problems associated with aging), (c) social context (the environment in which the older person lives), (d) cohort influences (age cohort experiences), and (e) cultural context (experiences nested in the larger culture; Hinrichsen, 2019).

There are also some common life problems that may become a focus of counseling when working with older adults. These can include life transitions, medical problems, caregiving, job loss or retirement, financial problems, grandparents parenting grandchildren, moving from a long-time home, marital and interpersonal disputes, social isolation, loneliness, and grief (Hinrichsen, 2019). There has been long-term skepticism about how psychotherapy can be successfully utilized with older adults. However, we now know that most empirically validated treatments that are effective for younger adults—when a foundational understanding of late life is considered—are effective for older people (Hinrichsen, 2019). These treatments can include psychopharmacological treatments for mental disorders (Hinrichsen, 2019). Scogin (2007) also discussed effective therapies with older adults who experience depression, anxiety, dementia-related problems, and insomnia. He found that the three most effective treatments for older adults are reminiscence therapy (a therapy involving the discussion of past activities, events, and experiences; Woods et al., 2018), behavioral treatments to manage problematic behavior related to dementia, and treatments to reduce distress in caregivers of older adults with health problems (Scogin, 2007). However, most research supports the contention that therapies used with younger adults are still effective when working with older adults (Hinrichsen, 2019).

IMPLICATIONS FOR CLINICAL PRACTICE

A discussion of implications for clinical practice would not be complete without including a conversation on ethical and legal issues relevant to working with older adults. Ethical issues apply to all aspects of our work as counselors, including counselor preparation for working with certain populations. However, Hinrichsen (2019) notes that a recurring ethical issue in working with older adults is balancing safety with autonomy. How do we as clinicians manage client safety with the psychological well-being that comes with a possibly overly restrictive daily life? Karel (2011) summarizes the key ethical and legal issues relevant to working with older adults. She notes that cognitive deficits may impair decision-making, so how do we ethically make decisions on the behalf of our client? Professional and familial collaboration is important when working with older adults, but how do we still protect confidentiality? How do we protect the rights to privacy and self-determination of clients in institutional settings, when that environment may be the safest for the client? How can end-of-life decision-making best be facilitated? Finally, how can cultural and diversity factors be incorporated into all of these issues in a way in which the older adult's wishes are honored? As with most ethical dilemmas, there are no clear answers to these questions, and the answers for any particular person will be client- and family-specific. However, it is important for counselors engaging in this work to know what ethical issues they may need to navigate. Counselors need to be aware of state laws and professional ethics, engage in self-reflection, and consult with supervisors to make sure they are properly managing these ethical issues (Hinrichsen, 2019).

CASE VIGNETTE

Claudio was born and raised in Santiago, Dominican Republic. He grew up with four siblings and a single mom who always inspired them to educate themselves in order to earn a better future. In his teen years, he got involved as a youth volunteer and later as a student staff member with his church. He and his wife met when she led a group of adolescents on a mission trip to Santiago. They soon got married and moved to the United States after he finished his bachelor's degree in theology. Through discussions with other professionals, he and his wife both decided to pursue degrees in social work to serve and help people in their community.

After working with AmeriCorps Health Care and completing a master's degree in social work, Claudio and his wife moved to Florida, where he worked with a local outpatient children's agency providing mental health services. In less than a year he changed jobs, to align more with his interest in working with older adults, and started working at an Area Agency on Aging, where he provided mental wellness services for adults and seniors. He started as a Mental Wellness Counselor, and was then promoted to Mental Wellness Director. After completing all requirements, he became a Licensed Clinical Social Worker.

AN INTERVIEW WITH CLAUDIO

What Does a Typical Day Look Like for You?

At my current agency, we provide mental wellness services to adults and seniors at their home and/or community settings. On a typical day when I was a mental wellness counselor, I would go to the office to review my schedule and plan to visit my clients at their homes from 9:30 a.m. to 3:00 p.m. I usually conducted three to five home visits per day. I would then go back to the office to finish my documentation, which would last until 5:00 p.m.

Now my typical day as a mental wellness director, I review everyone's schedules, census, emails, clients' requests, and new referrals. I also oversee the budget, and target productivity for the week, current month, and our overall trajectory for the year. As mental wellness director, I also oversee and monitor the compliance of two other programs: Daily Money Management and Self-Directed Care.

(continued)

CASE VIGNETTE (CONTINUED)

What Are Your Biggest Challenges in Your Work With Older Adults?

Some of the biggest challenges we face are related to clients who suffer from severe physical health problems or family relationship issues. Clients who struggle with health problems such as being morbidly obese, being bedbound, and having other physical limitations make it difficult to focus on improving their mental wellness due to their limitations. Some of them are not able to complete their daily needs or complete the activities outlined on their activities of daily living (ADLs) and instrumental activities of daily living (IADLs) checklists. Many times, clients want to physically feel better before working on their mental wellness. Therefore, we provide a lot of psychoeducation to help clients use effective coping skills to manage their depression and feelings of hopelessness.

Our clients also face complex family challenges. Many times these can be due to issues such as lack of effective communication skills, caregivers feeling overwhelmed, or even lack of close family relationships. In this case, we try to connect the client to other community resources who can provide additional support and comfort for the client and their caregiver. Additionally, many of our older adult clients expect that their family members will come to visit and bring them everything they need without asking for it. At times they may also feel too proud to ask for help or assistance. We help educate and empower our clients to be their own advocates, and to openly communicate and share their needs and feelings with their family and friends, in order to improve their well-being.

What Do You Enjoy Most About Your Work?

What I enjoy the most is having the opportunity to improve people's lives and their well-being. I have also learned a lot from our seniors when they share their life history and greatest moments. It can be very fulfilling to give older adults the opportunity to discuss and have closure to issues that have gone unresolved, or that they have been holding onto for so many years.

Do You Ever Encounter Ageism With Your Clients (Either Ageist or Reverse Ageism)? If So, What Does That Look Like?

There is an emphasis in my profession as a social worker and in my agency to treat every client with dignity and respect. This default attitude helps to build rapport and to always be aware of ways to improve a client's wellness. I never present myself as the expert or as the all-knowing; since I am way younger than all my clients, I want them to be able to teach me about their needs and lives. Nevertheless, from this standpoint as a learner, I present myself as one with knowledge and competency, which qualifies me as someone who can help the client to improve their emotional well-being.

(continued)

CASE VIGNETTE (CONTINUED)

When I first started, I had two clients who stated that I was too young to be their counselor. In order to respect their wishes, I was able to transfer one of these two clients to my supervisor at that time who was older than me. I was able to build a good rapport with the other client and help her to better manage her depressed mood and overwhelming feelings. These experiences have helped me be more aware of how I present myself and things I can do to improve connection. I noticed the question of my age comes up less the more comfortable and competent I become in my field.

CLINICAL CASE SCENARIO 18.1

Lois, a physically healthy 84-year-old White female, sought counseling on the encouragement of her three adult children. A few months earlier, Lois's children had noticed that she had begun to isolate herself, withdraw from social situations, and stay at home more frequently. For about a year, Lois had been the primary caregiver for Roger, her 86-year-old husband, who had been diagnosed with Parkinson's disease, and subsequently Lewy body dementia (a degenerative condition with many similarities to Alzheimer's disease). To Lois, caregiving for Roger was her duty as a spouse, and one she felt she owed to her husband of more than 50 years. However, lately Lois had been feeling overwhelmed. As Roger's health continued to deteriorate, so did Lois's spirit. Although Lois had full-time certified nursing assistants (CNAs) to help her with the chores of assisting Roger, such as toileting, transferring, changing, and feeding, she believed it was her responsibility to really "care" for him. After 50 years of marriage, she wasn't about to abandon him now. In the evenings, once Roger was put to bed, Lois would eat dinner alone and then retreat to her bedroom and read. This became her routine each evening. Her daily activities became so focused on Roger's care that she rarely left the house to eat lunch with friends, visit her grandchildren, or go shopping. When invited out, she used Roger's care as an excuse to decline outings, even though her children assured her that the nursing assistants could manage without her for a few hours.

About 2 years after Roger was first diagnosed, his health started to decline more rapidly. Hospice was eventually called to assist with his end-of-life respite care so that he could pass away at home with his family. Roger died peacefully a few weeks later, surrounded by Lois and their children.

After Roger's death, Lois initially found a sense of freedom. She no longer felt "tied" to the house to care for Roger, and she knew he was no longer suffering. However, Lois found that her time was still occupied with chores at home. She spent her days cleaning out the now unused medical equipment, discarding old medications, going through Roger's old clothes and other belongings. She found herself spending hours looking at old pictures and reminiscing over memories

(continued)

CLINICAL CASE SCENARIO 18.1 (CONTINUED)

of family vacations and all of the things that she and Roger had planned to do before he got sick.

Lois's children began visiting with her during the day and inviting her for family dinners at night, but Lois often cut these visits short. Lois insisted that she was "fine" but her children noticed that she seemed increasingly irritable, refused to have more than surface-level conversations with her children, and started declining invitations even from family members to spend time together. It seemed as though new and different concerns surfaced. Her family barely recognized the mother they had been so close to only a few short years earlier. One day Lois and her daughter were at the pharmacy together, and Lois became irate at the pharmacist over what her daughter saw as a minor misunderstanding. Her daughter couldn't get Lois to calm down, and when they left the pharmacy Lois was in tears.

Lois is a vibrant and capable woman who has so much life left to live. Her family decided that they needed to get help for Lois. They were certain, based on her age and history with Roger, that a gerocounselor would be the right fit. Now it was just a matter of convincing Lois that counseling would help and get her to understand the benefits of therapy.

DISCUSSION

Lois entered therapy a bit reluctantly. She did not see her current behavior as problematic or as an interference with her family or personal relationships. However, after a few sessions she began to warm up to the idea of having someone to talk to other than her children. Lois disclosed that life had been hard for her since Roger's diagnosis, and that she wasn't prepared for his death when it happened. Now, she felt like she would be the burden, which is why she did not want her children feeling like they needed to take care of her. She desperately wanted to maintain her independence. Lois also felt conflicted. On one hand she was very lonely living alone. She didn't even have the daily socialization that came with the presence of the nursing assistants. On the other hand, it had been so long since she had connected with her friends. She really didn't want to talk about Roger's end of life, and certainly didn't want anyone to feel sorry for her.

During her therapy sessions, Lois learned about Kubler-Ross's Stages of Grief (five common experiences of grief, which include Denial, Anger, Bargaining, Depression, and Acceptance), and felt like she could relate to that concept. In fact, it helped Lois to think about how she had moved back and forth through the stages even before Roger's death. She realized she had been grieving for a long time, and that loss didn't just come once Roger had died. Lois was beginning to make progress and find value in her personal reflection. Although she knew her life would never be the same without Roger, she did feel as though there was a new sense of hope to rebuild her future.

(continued)

CLINICAL CASE SCENARIO 18.1 (CONTINUED)

CONCLUSION

Although Lois still struggled to reengage socially, she began to venture out and explore new hobbies that would give her meaning. She did small projects that helped her feel a sense of pride, such as gardening, cooking, and updating some of the spaces around her house. Lois's therapist talked with her about the benefits of therapy and taught her how to recognize early warning signs and triggers that could indicate the need for seeking help. Lois realized that maybe she should have been getting counseling all along, even during Roger's illness while she was a caregiver. Even though she would be embarrassed if anyone found out that she was in counseling, she knew that this was the best option for her now.

CLINICAL CASE SCENARIO DISCUSSION QUESTIONS

1. Lois was new to counseling and doubted the relevance of treatment at first. How might you help her to understand the value of counseling while being empathetic to her hesitance?
2. What are some age-related or cultural factors that you might consider to effectively work with Lois?
3. How is grief different from depression? What would you do to assess Lois to differentiate the diagnoses and to make an appropriate treatment plan?
4. What treatment approaches might you use with Lois? What value might it offer to include her adult children in family therapy?
5. Why is it important to understand the unique aspects of Roger's diagnosis from a perspective that accounts for knowledge of psychopathology? What do you think it would mean to Lois to have a counselor who knew the impact that the cognitive decline of a loved one had on her as his caregiver?

END-OF-CHAPTER RESOURCES

A robust set of instructor resources designed to supplement this text is located at http://connect.springerpub.com/content/book/978-0-8261-3953-5. Qualifying instructors may request access by emailing textbook@springerpub.com.

SUMMARY

Understanding the unique needs of older adults requires counselors to gain knowledge specific to the population, but also to engage in exercises of reflection, introspection, and self-exploration. Many individuals, including counselors, have underlying attitudes and beliefs about the older adult population that may carry over into the counseling work that is being provided. As the older adult population grows globally, it is important for us to challenge the stereotypes and biases related to older adults and understand the growing needs and diversity considerations around this population. There are many factors to consider when working with diverse older adults, including SES, race, religion, gender, age within the context of aging, and familial support, which a liberation counseling approach could support. These cultural and life factors may contribute to a person's ability or willingness to seek formal counseling versus informal community support. Finally, we as counselors have the ability and responsibility to advocate for our older clients. Through increased counselor training, challenging our personal beliefs, and engaging in advocacy work, the older adult population can be better served as we see a growth in need from this group.

DISCUSSION QUESTIONS

1. What is ageism and how does it affect clients at various points in the life span?
2. What specific biases, attitudes, or beliefs do you have about the aging population that might affect your work as a counselor?
3. Are there specific ethical considerations that you think counselors working with older adults should be aware of?
4. How do you think the increased number of aging adults will affect the counseling profession over the next few years? What types of training can counselors do to be prepared to work with this growing population?
5. What types of counseling strategies might be helpful when working with older adults? Are there specific interventions or counseling techniques that would be best to use?
6. Assess your interest in working with older adults. Why or why wouldn't you want to work with this population, and what would you need to do to prepare yourself for this work?

KEY REFERENCES

Only key references appear in the print edition. The full reference list appears in the digital product on Springer Publishing Connect: https://connect.springerpub.com/content/book/978-0-8261-3953-5/part/part02/chapter/ch18

American Psychological Association. (2018, August). *Growing mental health and behavioral health concerns facing older Americans.* https://www.apa.org/advocacy/health/older-americans-mental-behavioral-health

Chávez, T. A., Fernandez, I. T., Hipolito-delgado, C. P., & Rivera, E. T. (2016). Unifying liberation psychology and humanistic values to promote social justice in counseling. *The Journal of Humanistic Counseling*, 55(3), 166–182. https://doi.org/10.1002/johc.12032

Hinrichsen, G. A. (2019). *Assessment and treatment of older adults: A guide for mental health professionals.* American Psychological Association. https://doi.org/10.1037/0000146-000

Kampfe, C. M. (2015). *Counseling older people: Opportunities and challenges.* American Counseling Association. https://doi.org/10.1002/9781119222767

Karavatas, S. G., Eugene, R., & Evans, B. S. (2020). The link between geriatric depression and functional mobility in older adults: A systematic review. *Journal of the National Society of Allied Health*, 17(1), 36–45.

Shannonhouse, L. R., Rumsey, A. D., & Mize, M. C. B. (2018). International perspectives on advocacy against ageism. In C. C. Lee (Ed.), *Counseling for social justice* (3rd ed., pp. 107–126). American Counseling Association Foundation.

Steele, J. M. (2008). Social justice: A liberation model. *Counselor Education & Supervision*, 48, 74–85.

CHAPTER 19

Culturally Responsive Counseling for Clients With Disabilities and Addressing Ableism

DAMION R. CUMMINS

LEARNING OBJECTIVES

After reading this chapter, students will be able to:

- Recognize the sociocultural, racial, and historical issues that influence clients with disabilities to increase counselor awareness and reduce cultural insensitivities.
- Develop a deeper awareness of identity development and competencies to address the needs of clients with disabilities.
- Identify ways to advocate for improved learning and address the ongoing needs of clients with disabilities.
- Apply culturally responsive strategies and techniques that will support people who live with disabilities (PWD).

SELF-REFLECTION QUESTIONS

1. Think about biases, prejudices, and assumptions you might have about PWD. How do these help and hinder your ability to provide culturally sensitive counseling?
2. What hesitancies, if any, do you have about working with PWD?
3. What attributes do you have that will enable you to work with PWD?

There is a significant increase in mental health issues among people who live with a disability (PWD). Due to historic ableism—the intentional or unintentional discrimination or oppression of individuals with disabilities—individuals with disabilities have to overcome many obstacles. This chapter explores the history of those with disabilities. It also focuses on misconceptions about individuals with disabilities, specific language of those with disabilities, and effective ways to provide counseling. The myriad of challenges that PWD bring to the counseling space is explored, as are culturally responsive interventions.

The negative aspects of having and living with a disability continue to be a primary focus and feature for people who do not understand disability and perpetuate the misconceptions about PWD (Smart, 2009), which can lead to ableism. *Ableism* refers to targeting physical, emotional, and mental differences from the social norm; defining people by their disability; and considering people with these differences to be a burden, object of pity, and/or problem to society, as well as incapable of independence (Mackelprang & Salsgiver, 2015). Ableism and the negative attitudes, beliefs, and misconceptions inherent in it extend beyond the general public and those without a disability. Even well-intentioned counselors are subject to the effect of societal and historical beliefs pertaining to disability and may inadvertently contribute to the perceptions of PWD as diseased, broken, and in need of fixing. These perceptions may negatively affect the counseling relationship and how counselors work with PWD (Hartley, 2012).

THE COUNSELOR: EXPLORATION, INTROSPECTION, AND REFLECTION

Due to the lack of appropriate training, lowered expectations, and ableist microaggressions, counselors may inadvertently contribute to pathologizing and stigmatizing PWD by viewing them as diseased, broken, and in need of fixing without an understanding of their perspective (Stuntzner & Hartley, 2014). Counselors with these beliefs may in turn negatively affect the counseling relationship with PWD and their families (Hartley, 2012; Öksüz & Brubaker, 2020). Despite their diverse counseling needs, counseling services for PWD have been exclusively shaped around rehabilitation practices (Olkin & Pledger, 2003; Smart & Smart, 2006). Thus, the counseling profession has overlooked PWD and their needs beyond rehabilitation (Emir Oksuz, 2019).

Counseling training is also insufficient (Deroche et al., 2020; Smart & Smart, 2006). In a study on disability-related content integrated into multicultural counseling courses, Feather and Carlson (2019) found that only 50% of counselor educators from Council of the Accreditation of Counseling and Related Educational Programs (CACREP)-accredited programs taught curriculum about PWD and other disability-related topics. Counselors in other specialty areas have felt weakly prepared to work with PWD (Feather & Carlson, 2019; Öksüz & Brubaker, 2020; Rivas & Hill, 2018). All these issues negatively influence the counseling practice, and are accompanied by other systemic barriers, all of which further hinder PWD from getting quality care. As a result, many counselors have either had to practice beyond their scope of competency due to lack of disability-related training and resources, or needlessly refer PWD to rehabilitation or medical specialists, who often lack the training from other specialty areas (Deroche et al., 2020).

Nario-Redmond et al. (2019) surveyed people who live with disabilities about their experiences of benevolent behaviors such as sympathetic pity, protection, and charitable praise, as well as hostile ableism, in their own words. Indeed, sympathy and lowered expectations from counselors without disabilities may be considered to be stigmatizing and prejudicial; sympathy and lowered expectations toward PWD often result in withholding helpful and honest feedback, reduce the range of opportunities open to the individual client, foster dependence, and subtly communicate the message to clients with a disability that standards will be lowered for them because they are not perceived (by the counselor) to be capable (Marini & Stebnicki, 2018).

Clinicians who hold attitudes of sympathy and lowered expectations for PWD can also inadvertently be less likely to attribute PWD's suicidality to treatable conditions, such as depression (Lund et al., 2016), or transient life stressors. Counselors may see suicidality in PWD as rational and logical given their disability (Lund et al., 2016). This could interfere with PWD access to proper treatment and assessment for suicidality. Lund et al. (2016) suggested that clinicians who work in suicide prevention should be aware of societal attitudes toward disability and suicide, and should work to confront those misconceptions, especially when working with individuals with disabilities. Dreer et al. (2018) recommended that counselors initiate suicide screening and prevention efforts at the time of intake and do regular follow-up, especially during periods of stress or transition.

Counselor Introspection

Before exploring the ways to improve counselor care for clients who are PWD, internalized biases about PWD must be confronted. Countertransference, and other emotional reactions to the client's disability, may prevent the counselor from fully understanding the client and therefore negatively affect the counseling relationship (Balva & Tapia-Fuselier, 2020; Chapin et al., 2018; Marini & Stebnicki, 2018). This could lead to discriminatory referrals based solely on the presence of a disability. Balva and Tapia-Fuselier (2020) encouraged counselors to consider the meaning placed on the word *disability* and to examine their thoughts and feelings associated with disabilities to help work through biases and misconceptions. This will better prepare counselors and equip them with more internal resources to inquire into and manage aspects of the client's life that may be difficult or uncomfortable to discuss (e.g., sex, relationships, barriers, life plan, etc.). Stuntzner and Hartley (2014) suggested that counselors identify and address counseling topics that make them uncomfortable (e.g., sexuality and disability). Deroche et al. (2020) emphasized the critical need for counselors and counselors-in-training to explore their attitudes, beliefs, and assumptions regarding individuals with different types of disabilities.

DIFFERENT TYPES OF DISABILITY

The WHO (2021) estimated that 15% of the world's population has a disability, and recent estimates suggest that one in four Americans (61 million) has a disability (Okoro et al., 2018). This makes PWD a sizable minority worldwide and the largest minority group in the United States (Erickson et al., 2020). The Americans with Disabilities Act of 1990 (ADA) characterizes a person as having a disability when they: (a) have a physical or mental impairment that substantially limits one or more major life activities; (b) have a record of such an impairment; or (c) are regarded as having such an impairment (ADA, 1990). According to the ADA definition, a PWD is someone who experiences a physical or mental condition that limits the ability to perform a major life activity, such as walking, breathing, seeing, hearing, thinking, or working. Disabilities come in many different forms and can be congenital (medical condition present at or before birth), acquired (illness or injury sustained after birth), and even invisible to others (mental and cognitive disability). Individuals with the same type of disability can be affected in different ways that can limit and impair their day-to-day activities (Disabled World, 2021).

The following are examples of disability types:

- *Mobility*: This type of disability includes people with upper and lower limb disability, and/or impaired manual dexterity, due to severe accidents or congenital conditions (e.g., spinal cord injuries, paralysis, amputation).
- *Psychiatric*: This disability category includes individuals whose mental health can be affected by mood disorders or feeling states that can be short or long term (e.g., depression, bipolar disorder, schizophrenia, posttraumatic stress).

- *Auditory*: The hearing disabilities category includes people who are completely or partially deaf; the disability may be evident at birth or can occur later in life from biologic causes (e.g., deafness, hearing impairment).
- *Visual*: These are minor to serious disabilities or impairments that decrease the ability to see to a degree that causes problems not fixable by means of glasses or medication.
- *Cognitive/Developmental/Intellectual*: Disabilities in this category are defined by diminished cognitive and adaptive development (e.g., autism spectrum, learning disabilities, dementia).
- *Medical*: Examples of disabling medical conditions include cancer, AIDS, epilepsy, asthma, diabetes, myalgic encephalomyelitis/chronic fatigue syndrome (ME/CFS), cystic fibrosis, and severe arthritis.

MISCONCEPTIONS ABOUT INDIVIDUALS WITH DISABILITIES

Societal attitudes toward disability, which have generally been negative, play a significant role as barriers and affect the psychosocial adjustment of PWD (Chan et al., 2009). Some stereotypical attitudes toward PWD include perceptions that they are perpetual children, objects of pity, a menace or threat to society, sick, asexual, incompetent, and/or a psychological and economic burden to society (Mackelprang & Salsgiver, 2015). The origins of these attitudes can be complex and often develop from attributional thinking such as blaming the victim, viewing disability as a punishment for sin, anxiety-provoking situations, childhood influences, sociocultural conditioning, existential angst, aesthetic aversion, minority status, prejudice-inviting behavior, disability-related factors, media portrayal of disability, and environmental factors (Marini & Stebnicki, 2018).

DIFFERENTLY ABLED IDENTITY DEVELOPMENT MODELS

Very few counseling programs provide adequate training on disability issues (Marini & Stebnicki, 2018; Olkin, 1999; Olkin & Pledger, 2003; Smart & Smart, 2006). This lack of training and the resulting failure to provide adequate services may be due to the powerful influence of models of disability. For example, counselors may view a PWD as pathological solely because of their disability or focus less on the individual and more on the person's ability to contribute to society. There are different models of disability that determine in which academic discipline the experience of disability is studied and taught. Bogart and Dunn (2019) suggested that disability models should describe the individual or social-level beliefs about disability and include four broad perspectives: biomedical model, functional model, environmental model, and sociopolitical Model.

Biomedical Model

The biomedical model is the dominant model in Western culture and presents disability as an individual pathology, abnormality, or difference from a standardized norm (Olkin & Pledger, 2003). This model presents disability as a problem of the individual or the individual's family that should be dealt with by specialized individuals (e.g., doctors, special educators), and perceives the "solution" to be a cure or normalization, or a form of assimilation (Dirth & Branscombe, 2018; Marini & Stebnicki, 2018). Olkin and Pledger (2003) suggested that individuals with a disability, regardless of personal qualities and assets, may believe they belong to a devalued group. Smart (2009) proposed that when viewed through the biomedical model, clients with an identified disability seeking counseling may believe that in the view of others, a life with a disability is worth less investment. Many PWD do not struggle with the difficulties of having a disability, but do struggle with the social isolation, prejudice, and discrimination from others who define disability through the biomedical model (Smart, 2007). A benefit of the biomedical model is that it centers around psychiatric disabilities and can assist with diagnosis and treatment. Counselors can use this model to provide education and support for the PWD with psychiatric disability.

Functional Model

The functional model, similar to the biomedical model, conceptualizes disability as an impairment or deficit (Smart, 2009). Proponents of this model define disability as a physical, medical, or cognitive deficit that limits a person's functioning and ability to perform daily activities and work. The functional model defines disability by the skills, abilities, and achievements of the individual. The main focus of this model is to provide accommodations for the PWD. This model reduces PWD to their economic value or ability to contribute to the economy and focuses much less on the individual (Smart & Smart, 2006). However, counselors incorporating this model into practice can use it to find suitable resources and referrals to improve functioning, skills, and job seeking/performance.

Environmental Model

The environmental model recognizes the importance of biology and the biomedical model, but places more emphasis on the environment and how it can cause and contribute to the barriers and issues for PWD (Smart & Smart, 2006). The environment and barriers that PWD encounter are viewed as the issue and less focus is placed on the individual with the disability. The thinking is that if the environment and location of the problem were to change, the problem would no longer exist or be relevant. Disadvantages or limitations such as poverty or a lack of education, though they are social ills, are not considered to be disabilities. Also, although everyone is at some point required to successfully negotiate difficult environments, to undertake demanding functions, and to experience disadvantages, not everyone has a disability. With the environmental and functional models, the disabling effects of prejudice and discrimination by individuals without a disability are not taken into consideration. Counselors incorporating this model into helping PWD can assist with interventions and ways of adapting the environment to the needs of the PWD (Smart & Smart, 2006). Counselors can also be advocates for PWD in lessening the impact of environmental barriers.

Sociopolitical Model

The sociopolitical model of disability holds that disability is created by a society that is inaccessible to and biased against PWD. This model centers around the PWD, rejecting the biomedical model of diagnosis and categories and the aspiration to achieve equality and civil rights. This model parallels other social constructivist movements of racial, gender, and sexual/gender minority groups, and places the onus of change on society, rather than the individual or specialists seeking to change the individual (Olkin & Pledger, 2003). For this reason, the sociopolitical model engenders action to reduce social barriers and establish/protect civil rights (Dirth & Branscombe, 2018). In other words, the meaning of *disability* cannot be reduced to objective medical terminology and function; instead, the meaning fluctuates depending on personal (e.g., growing up with a disability; acquiring a disability during one's lifetime), political (e.g., passage and continued enforcement of the ADA; ADA, 1990), institutional (e.g., establishing a disability studies program at one's university), and even global (e.g., United Nations Convention on the Rights of Persons with Disabilities; Dirth & Branscombe, 2018) contexts. Counselors using this model allow the PWD to define disability and the outcome of their lives (Smart, 2009).

STRESSORS AND DISCRIMINATION

History of Disability in America

For counselors to competently help PWD, it is important that they explore the history and treatment of this population (Marini & Stebnicki, 2018). Throughout American history, PWD, and their families, allies, and advocates, have had to fight and overcome many forms of ableism and oppression, rejection, and discrimination which have resulted in persecution, institutionalization, imprisonment, death, sterilization, and so on (Disability History, 2019; Stern, 2020). Despite these challenges and many other barriers, PWD and civil right activists fought to change the landscape and how PWD are treated (e.g., protesting institutionalization, making schools and hospitals disability inclusive) and to enact laws and policies (e.g., the ADA) guaranteeing equal treatment; this effort continues today.

Although it was not the first federal legislation to address disability, the ADA (1990) was the first comprehensive civil rights law designed to prevent discrimination against PWD in employment and increase access to public and private services. However, this law was passed only after many delays, protests, and an event known as the "Capitol Crawl." On March 13, 1990, more than 1,000 advocates, protesters, and PWD marched from the White House to the U.S. Capitol to demand that Congress pass the ADA. To demonstrate how inaccessible architecture and other barriers affect PWD, several of the protesters with wheelchairs and mobility aids crawled up the Capitol steps, leading the event to become known as the Capitol Crawl. The ADA was signed into law on July 26, 1990, by President George H. W. Bush (ADA, 1990).

Barriers for Persons With Disability

Despite overcoming many historical obstacles and adversities, PWD still face many barriers rooted in ableism. The Centers for Disease Control and Prevention (CDC, n.d.) described different types of ableism-based barriers for PWD, including attitudinal barriers such as ableism, stereotypes, stigma, and discrimination; communication barriers (e.g., printed materials that are not available in braille or for electronic readers; a lack of American Sign Language [ASL] interpreters); physical barriers (e.g., buildings that are physically inaccessible to those in wheelchairs); policy barriers, described as the lack of familiarity with or not adhering to enacted laws and regulations (ADA, 1990); programmatic barriers (e.g., difficulties with the provision of healthcare services and programming); social barriers, including unequal employment rates and a lessened likelihood of graduating high school; transportation barriers (e.g., inaccessible public transit); and even celebrating those with disabilities simply for being "brave" enough to function as members of society (Young, 2014).

Ableism and other barriers can run the gamut from well-intentioned and kindly sentiments down to hostile discrimination. Nario-Redmond et al. (2019) surveyed PWD about experiences of benevolent (sympathetic pity, protection, charitable praise) and hostile ableism and discovered that common experiences were unwanted help, being called "inspirational" for doing an everyday activity, invalidation, jealous ableism, dehumanization, and objectification. The researchers showed that paternalistic ableism (which consists of others making decisions for PWD) was the most frequent form of ableism. Infantilization (treating a PWD like a child) was more likely to be experienced by individuals with visible disabilities (Nario-Redmond et al., 2019).

The tendency to admire PWD who are perceived to have "overcome" their limitations or are "inspiring" by daring to appear in public (or become romantically involved) has transformed into a modern form of ableism and is known as "inspiration porn" (Grue, 2016; Nario-Redmond et al., 2019). Inspiration porn is the objectification and devaluation of PWD when they are portrayed as specimens of wonder and amazement which can be used to motivate those without disabilities to self-improve. For example, social media often depicts visibly disabled people engaged in sporting or recreational events with the caption, "So what is your excuse?" (Haller & Preston, 2016). This form of ableism can send the message that if one person with a disability can overcome their limitations, so should everyone else, and all it takes is a little hard work (Nario-Redmond et al., 2019).

Another form of ableism is delivered through microaggressions. "Microaggressions are the brief and commonplace daily verbal, behavioral and environmental indignities, whether intentional or unintentional, that communicate hostile, derogatory or negative slights and insults to a marginalized group" (Sue, 2010, p. 6). Ableist microaggressions perpetuate ableism and may not be obvious to other individuals, yet the accumulated impact is harmful (Kattari, 2017). Findings indicate that the visibility of disabilities is correlated with experiencing ableist microaggressions and increased mental health issues (Kattari, 2017).

These everyday interactions between individuals and groups work to maintain stereotypes and inequalities that harm PWD who already exist within marginalized communities (Sue, 2010). There are many ways that ableist microaggressions can occur; some examples include making jokes to wheelchair users about speeding in their wheelchairs (Storey, 2007), grabbing a blind person's arm to direct them without their consent, joking that someone is "lucky" because they have a disabled parking permit, praying over someone who is disabled without their consent, speaking to a disabled person's companion instead of the disabled person, or telling a PWD that their experiences of ableism are not actually that bad.

Regardless of the type of disability, high levels of ableist microaggressions have been reported by all PWD (Kattari, 2020). However, there are differences in mental health outcomes across types of disabilities. Those with physical disability reported the highest level of mental health issues, which was significantly higher than for those with psychiatric/socioemotional disabilities and multiple types of disabilities. This may provide evidence that even though some mental health diagnoses may result in someone identifying as disabled, ableist microaggressions may negatively affect an individual's mental health status and lead to a PWD hiding the disability for fear of being treated differently and discriminated against (Santuzzi et al., 2019).

Santuzzi et al. (2019) found that displaying one's disability risks negative treatment by others, especially in the workplace where a worker's ability to perform job duties is of primary importance. This treatment by people in the workplace can lead to negative beliefs that workers with disabilities are dependent, hypersensitive, unsociable, and less competitive (Stone & Colella, 1996), as well as less competent than others (Fiske et al., 2007). Part of this treatment of PWD could be related to perceptions about whether or not the disability is considered controllable or could be acquired by individuals who are not currently disabled (Bogart et al., 2018).

Olkin (1999) theorized that people with an acquired disability (e.g., paralysis resulting from medical error, illness, accident, loss of limb from an accident, or Alzheimer's or dementia), whose conditions could be perceived as more controllable and more personally threatening, would be more easily blamed for their disability and would consequently be more stigmatized than people with a congenital disability (i.e., an often-inherited medical condition that occurs at or before birth). Similarly, Bogart et al. (2018) and Stump et al. (2016) found that when nondisabled people believe a disability is controllable, that belief can lead to stigmatization and evoke feelings of anger toward and less empathy for the PWD, leading them to distance themselves from the PWD and be unlikely to help the PWD (Stump et al., 2016). Encountering someone with an acquired disability may remind people without disabilities that they too could acquire a disability, so they might engage in disability avoidance blame and blame those with acquired disabilities for their conditions, to avoid the threatening idea that they could acquire a similar disability (Dunn & Brody, 2008).

Having a positive disability identity—that is, possessing a positive sense of self and feelings of connection to, or solidarity with, the disability—has been shown to help PWD with finding value and meaning in the disability while helping to overcome barriers (Forber-Pratt & Zape, 2017; Nario-Redmond et al., 2013). However, PWD face many challenges while building a positive disability identity (Bogart & Dunn, 2019). When disability intersects with other social identities such as gender, race, sexual orientation, people who live with disabilities may experience multiple forms of discrimination. Disability is unique as one of the only marginalized group identities one could either be born into or acquire later in life (Bogart & Dunn, 2019).

Unlike racial and ethnic identities, PWD often have solo status (Bogart & Dunn, 2019), potentially being the only member of their family or community who shares that identity, which challenges the formation of in-group identity (Bogart & Dunn, 2019). Whereas other marginalized groups have been able to create subcultures of pride (e.g., Black Pride, Gay Pride), Bogart (2014) discussed how disability pride is still a foreign concept for many PWD due to barriers. PWD are often isolated in their communities (Olkin, 2012), and well-intentioned nondisabled family and community members often try to "normalize" PWD so they will fit in with their majority culture (Olkin, 2012), rather than fostering a sense of disability identity.

Lund et al. (2016) found that suicide was seen as significantly more acceptable when the person expressing suicidal ideation had a disability than when they did not have a disability. Surprisingly, this difference was true for participants both with and without disabilities. The lowest difference in acceptability was for mental illness, whereas the greatest difference was for spinal cord injury. If individuals with disabilities experience suicidal ideation and receive a social message that their disability makes suicide more acceptable or understandable, they may feel that they have implicit social permission to attempt suicide (Lund et al., 2016). The results of this study strongly suggest that the presence of disability makes suicidal ideation more understandable and acceptable to individuals without a disability. It is also postulated that the permanence of disability generates a greater sense of hopelessness. People who are less willing to consider that the PWD's situation may improve and believe that having a disability is undesirable tend to justify suicidal ideation (Fadem et al., 2003; Krahn, 2010).

COUNSELING UTILIZATION AND HELP-SEEKING

Disability is growing more common due to several factors and advancements (ADA, 1990; Okoro et al., 2018). The increasing number of PWD may be attributed to baby boomers' aging and more veterans returning home with mental illnesses and disabilities incurred during military conflicts (Shallcross, 2011). Moreover, improvements in medical care enable greater numbers of people to survive life-threatening incidents that often leave them with disabilities (Shallcross, 2011). Due to technology, wider availability of health insurance, and a generally higher standard of living that provides more services and support, people who would have died in the past now survive with a disability (Smart & Smart, 2006). Disability is especially common in older adults (e.g, cardiovascular disease, osteoporosis, dementia), women (e.g., breast cancer), and marginalized people (e.g., chronic medical conditions, anxiety, depression, etc.; Okoro et al., 2018).

This large and growing population of PWD faces challenges with employment, poverty and other health issues (U.S. Bureau of Labor Statistics, 2017). PWD are 3.5 times less likely to be employed (U.S. Bureau of Labor Statistics, 2017) and three times more likely to be at or below the poverty line (Erickson et al., 2020) than their nondisabled counterparts. In 2020, 17.9% of PWD were employed, down from 19.3% in 2019, compared to individuals without a disability, who were 61.8% employed in 2020 (U.S. Bureau of Labor Statistics, 2021). PWD also experience significant health disparities and are more likely to be obese; smoke; have heart disease, diabetes, and substance use disorders; and have experienced sexual assault (Chan et al., 2015; Okoro et al., 2018). These health disparities are higher among PWD than people without disabilities because PWD are less likely to receive preventative care; more likely to lack private insurance, so that their access to care is limited by public insurance (e.g., emotional/psychiatric disabilities); have lower employment rates; and have inadequate or no transportation (Krahn et al., 2015).These contributors exacerbate unhealthy lifestyle behaviors and poor mental health and can create a cycle of chronic conditions (Krahn et al., 2015).

Conducting a holistic assessment of PWD is important, but so is understanding the counseling services they need. This large and diverse group of people may require a variety of counseling services from all specialty areas (Marini & Stebnicki, 2018; Öksüz & Brubaker, 2020), including school, couple and family, mental health, substance use, career, aging and adult development, sexual issues, multicultural concerns, spiritual, ethical, and religious values, and group counseling (Chapin et al., 2018; Evans, 2017; Feather & Carlson, 2019; Olkin & Pledger, 2003; Smart, 2009). In order to practice effectively, counselors need awareness and knowledge about the multifaceted services available to and needed by PWD, and critical skills to work with them (Rivas & Hill, 2018).

Many PWD endure challenges associated with stigma and being pathologized while accessing mental health care, especially those who hold multiple marginalized identities (Kattari, 2020). Others have trauma, whether personal or historical, from our society's past (and sometimes current) treatment of PWD with coercive and, at times, nonconsensual interventions (Brown & Ciciurkaite, 2021). Moreover, these challenges rooted in stigma or past trauma might be exacerbated by providers who are unsure of how to adapt to working with disabled clients. Such providers perpetuate ableist microaggressions by not accommodating their clients' disability-related needs (Kattari, 2020).

Substance Use and Addiction

According to the Substance Abuse and Mental Health Services Administration (SAMHSA; 2019), people with physical and cognitive disabilities have a higher prevalence of serious mental illness and substance use disorder, as well as lower treatment rates for both conditions, than do people without disabilities. The rates of substance use disorders in persons with traumatic brain injuries (TBIs), spinal cord injuries (SCI), and mental illness in the United States approach or exceed 50%, as compared to 10% for the general population (SAMHSA, 2019). Individuals who live with deafness, arthritis, and multiple sclerosis have a risk for substance use disorders that is at least double the rate of the general population (Davis & van Wormer, 2016). PWD who live with chronic pain and other medical issues managed by addictive medication may be at high risk of misusing prescription medication and/or self-medicating with nonprescription substances. Moreover, identification of potential substance use problems is not timely. Therefore, a lack of accessible and appropriate prevention and treatment services contribute to an increased risk of substance addiction (Davis & van Wormer, 2016).

Programmatic and structural barriers often prevent PWD from accessing treatment (Chan et al., 2015). As shown by the high prevalence rates and minimal participation in treatment, substance use disorders are a very difficult problem, with consequences for both the individual and society (American Addiction Centers, 2021). This draws attention to the need for effective and accessible substance abuse interventions in rehabilitation settings (Chan et al., 2015).

Besides substance use, there can be other demographic and challenging factors that can significantly affect the mental health of PWD. Noh et al. (2016) researched this issue and found that individuals with physical disabilities had increased depressive symptoms and that females showed more symptoms than males. The depressive symptoms were strongly correlated with stereotypic social and personal attitudes from individuals who had no disabilities; abuse; loss of roles; and stressors related to poverty, environmental barriers, and/or lack of access to appropriate healthcare (Chevarley et al., 2006; Nosek & Hughes, 2003).

Due to these barriers, lack of access, and attitudes from individuals who are nondisabled, mental health can be a struggle: PWD are at least three times more likely to experience depression compared to the general population (Bu & Duan, 2021; U.S. Department of Health and Human Services, 2010). These barriers can operate in a cycle, with one reinforcing another (Bu & Duan, 2021). In economically disadvantaged areas, individuals with physical disabilities suffer the most from catastrophic consequences brought on by the poor conditions associated with poverty, such as lack of accessible transportation, rehabilitation services and professionals, and effective training programs (World Health Organization [WHO], 2021). These disparities and disabilities also affect military veterans.

Military Veterans

Recent veterans report high rates of service-connected disabilities (i.e., disabilities that were incurred in, or aggravated during, military service). An estimated 27.9% (2,451,100 out of 8,775,000) of veterans aged 21 to 64 years reported having a service-connected disability (Erickson et al., 2020). According to the U.S. Bureau of Labor Statistics (2021), about 41% of Gulf War–era II (post 9/11) veterans report having a service-connected disability. Common injuries incurred by these veterans include missing limbs, burns, spinal cord injuries, posttraumatic stress disorder (PTSD), hearing loss, traumatic brain injuries, and other impairments. According to the Department of Veterans Affairs (2019), approximately 17 U.S. veterans die by suicide every day, which is about 1.5 times that of nonveterans. The Department of Defense (DOD) announced that 325 active-duty soldiers, sailors, airmen, and Marines died by suicide in 2018. This number is up by 40 more than in 2017 and the highest number since the DOD began collecting suicide data in 2001.

Little attention has been paid to the unique needs of the culturally diverse veteran populations with PTSD (Norris & Alegria, 2005). Despite high rates of PTSD, African American, Latino, Asian, and Native American veterans are less likely to use mental health services. Reasons cited for the underutilization of services include lack of culturally competent providers and increased feelings of shame and guilt related to PTSD in African American veterans; Latino veterans are more likely to believe that asking for help will bring dishonor to their families. These responses are exacerbated when African American and Latino veterans feel that a health provider has judged them unfairly (Norris & Alegria, 2005). Linguistic access can be a challenge for service members and veterans who have family members with limited English proficiency because of the important role of families in encouraging veterans to seek services and in locating those services; thus, multilingual outreach and family support are necessary (U.S. Bureau of Labor Statistics, 2021).

CRAFTING AN ADVOCACY AGENDA

Before counselors begin advocating for equality, inclusion, and participation in society, development of skills and a commitment to social justice at the individual, group, institutional, and societal levels are necessary (Chapin et al., 2018). When working with PWD, it is essential to advocate for accessible spaces in the counseling setting. These include accessibility in the parking lot at the building entrance and in the waiting area, restrooms, offices, and meeting rooms. It is important to develop a safety and evacuation plan for wheelchair users and people with other disability-related needs (Chapin et al., 2018).

Counseling PWD also extends beyond the counseling office. Counselors need to establish professional relationships with outside agencies that PWD typically go to for assistance, such as state vocational rehabilitation offices (Geisinger & Stein, 2016). A counselor advocate learns and stays abreast of federal and state laws that support and protect PWD. They intervene at institutional and political levels when appropriate, and they advocate for changes in systems and policies, alert the public to prejudice and discrimination in the media, and advocate for environmental accessibility. Individual counselors, as well as those who engage in statewide, regional, or national professional organizations, can create change.

Counselors are encouraged to help foster a positive disability identity through connections with support groups, mentoring, and collective action that focuses on finding commonalities among PWD and improvements to impairment, personal, and environmental factors (Bogart et al., 2017; Olkin, 2012). This can increase psychosocial well-being, self-advocacy, and political engagement. Dunn and Burcaw (2013) formulated six main themes toward developing a disability identity: (a) communal attachment, (b) affirmation of disability, (c) self-worth, (d) pride (Bogart, 2014), (e) discrimination, and (f) personal meaning (Marini & Stebnicki, 2018; Rumrill Jr. et al., 2019). Counselors should also recognize that most individuals with disabilities do not accept the basic tenets of the biomedical model of disability (Olkin, 2012). Rather, they may view the disability as a valued part of their identity (Bogart, 2015). These PWD see positive aspects in having a disability, do not view the disability as tragic or limiting, do not consider themselves inferior, and would not choose to eliminate the disability if they could.

Nario-Redmond et al. (2013) researched disability identity and found that it was positively associated with the collective strategies of social change, community pride, and valuing disability, and negatively associated with the individualistic strategies of overcoming, minimizing, and concealing disability. PWD with more visible impairments were more willing to advocate for social change, but were less likely to value their disability experiences as a source of strength. However, the longer a PWD had been living with a disability, the more they valued their disability experience (Nario-Redmond et al., 2013).

Advocating for Military Veterans

According to the National Council on Disability (2021), the military environment must change its values and practices to help veterans with disabilities. Researchers found that among military service members who returned from Iraq and Afghanistan and reported mental health symptoms, only slightly more than half sought treatment (Tanielian & Jaycox, 2008). Barriers to seeking care (Hoge et al., 2006) include distance from services, availability of specified types of services, bureaucratic obstacles to accessing care, lack of user-friendliness, restricted clinic hours and policies, perceived stigma and concerns with the impact on job or reserve unit status, lack of information about what services are available, and public misperceptions of individuals with mental illnesses.

Some common concerns reported by service members include believing that their military careers will suffer if they seek mental health services and that seeking care will lower the confidence of others in their ability, and possibly cause them to be removed from their unit (Department of Defense Task Force on Mental Health, 2007). According to the Department of Veterans Affairs (2019), economic disparities, homelessness, unemployment, level of military service-connected disability status, community connection, and personal health and well-being are barriers and issues that contribute to the high rates of suicide among military veterans. Over the past 20 years, the number of service members and veterans who died by suicide have outnumbered those who were killed in combat, 30,177 and 7,057 respectively (DeSimone, 2021).

The counseling profession needs to go beyond accessibility expectations in its services and advocacy for PWDs (Öksüz & Brubaker, 2020), and be more multiculturally aware and competent. For example, in addition to advocating for the inclusion of disability culture-related content within the multicultural counseling course, a better representation of PWD in the counseling profession is needed, which would create a unique advocacy focus for counselors. However, there are still many barriers to overcome.

CULTURALLY RESPONSIVE PRACTICES: DRAWING FROM THE MULTICULTURAL AND SOCIAL JUSTICE COUNSELING COMPETENCIES AND CULTURAL HUMILITY

Due to the barriers and challenges PWD face in accessing appropriate counseling, an understanding of how to work with clients with disabilities and the systems they navigate is vital to addressing the concerns of this population while providing culturally and ethically responsive care (American Counseling Association [ACA], 2014; Balva & Tapia-Fuselier, 2020; Tapia-Fuselier & Ray, 2019). It is recommended that counselors and counselor training programs support recognition of disability as a part of personal identity and cultural diversity and commit to social justice (Chapin et al., 2018). When providing culturally responsive counseling to PWD, it is important for counselors to use the *ACA Code of Ethics* to guide and facilitate the counseling relationship and process. According to the ACA (2014), counselors are required not to condone or engage in discrimination against clients based on disability, to use caution with assessment techniques and recognize the effects of disability on test administration and interpretation, and to include websites that provide accessibility to PWD. Chapin et al. (2018) emphasized that when administering certain tests and assessments, counselors must demonstrate sensitivity, knowing that some of them are steeped in ableism and may reflect and/or reinforce stereotypes or disability-negative perspectives about the abilities and characteristics of PWD. When scoring and interpreting test results, counselors should remain cognizant of the potential ways disability, culture, or other considerations may cause misinterpretation of results (ACA, 2014).

Smart (2009) recommended that counselors ascertain the benefits that could be gained from incorporating the functional and environmental models in work with PWD, because an individual's cultural identification can be defined by their function, roles, and environment. Therefore, it is suggested to use the functional and environmental models to better understand the experience of PWD and counsel individuals who are not White, middle-class, heterosexual, male, or Euro-American (Smart, 2009). The sociopolitical model can also assist in understanding how society creates barriers that inhibit PWD (Dirth & Branscombe, 2018).

Disability-affirmative therapy (Olkin, 2012), a culturally affirmative approach to counseling, may be a useful example of how to support PWD in the adaptation process. Disability-affirmative therapy assumes that disability is not inherently pathological, and that it has value and meaning. It encourages clients to develop an affirmation of disability identity by finding mentors with disabilities, becoming involved with the disability community, and engaging in positive reframing of stigmatized traits. Engaging with others with disabilities will provide a PWD an opportunity to learn self-management skills and find resources from others. Additionally, value changes involved with disability identity may result in changing a PWD's goals to ones that can be accomplished with a disability, improving self-efficacy (Sharoff, 2004).

Adaptation to Disability

Despite the barriers and challenges faced by many, PWD have developed ways of adapting and learning resilience in a nondisabled environment and society. This can be seen in the way that some individuals with acquired physical disabilities acknowledge and adjust to the disability. Psarra and Kleftaras (2013) found that prevention of depression was strongly correlated to developing the meaning of life (Martz & Livneh, 2016) after a chronic illness or physical disability. To reach this pinnacle, the authors believe there are eight phases and a chain of psychological reactions that begin with the initial experience of becoming disabled that are needed to facilitate meaning of life and positive adaptation to a disability (Livneh & Antonak, 2005). The phases are shock, anxiety, denial, depression, internalized anger, externalized anger, acknowledgement, and adjustment.

Similarly, Martz and Livneh (2016) discovered themes that help those with chronic illness and disability to positively adapt. The researchers reviewed current trends of research that examined positive psychology constructs in the context of adapting to chronic illness and disability. The researchers found that acceptance of disability, psychological adaptation, quality of life, and well-being are strongly influenced by six positive psychology constructs: optimism, hope, resilience, benefit-finding, meaning-making, and posttraumatic growth. The six positive psychology constructs also showed lower negative outcomes (e.g., depression, distress, anxiety). These findings suggest that emphasizing positive aspects in the lives of PWD, despite the existence of stressful life events triggered by the chronic illness and/or disability, may be effective in facilitating adaptation. Developing a disability identity has also been researched and suggested as a way for PWD to adapt and accept their disability (Dunn & Burcaw, 2013).

Disability identity refers to possessing a positive sense of self and feelings of connection to, or solidarity with, the disability community. Strong disability identity is believed to help individuals adapt to a disability, navigate social stresses and daily hassles, and guide PWD toward what to do, what to value, and how to behave in situations where their disability stands out, as well as those where it is not salient (Dunn & Burcaw, 2013). Dunn and Burcaw (2013) reviewed the available literature and identified six main themes regarding the formation of a disability identity: communal attachment (participation in and identification with the disability community; Bogart, 2015; Nario-Redmond et al., 2013), affirmation of disability (feeling included in society, having the same rights and responsibilities as other citizens), self-worth (PWD see themselves as possessing the same worth as nondisabled), pride (being proud of one's identity, rather than denying it; acknowledging possessing a socially-devalued quality, such as a mental or a physical disability), discrimination (awareness and recognition that PWD are often the targets of biased, prejudiced, and unfair treatment within daily life), and personal meaning (finding benefits associated with disability; Martz & Livneh, 2016; Psarra & Kleftaras, 2013).

Counseling Individuals Who Are Deaf

When counseling individuals who are deaf, language and identity are important. The majority of people who are deaf prefer to be called "deaf" or "the deaf" because in the deaf community many do not identify as disabled, but rather as a linguistic minority. Doing so allows a person or a group of disabled people to claim disability as an important and prominent aspect of their identities (Bogart & Dunn, 2019; Dunn & Andrews, 2015). The term *hearing impaired* may seem politically correct, but according to Leigh (2010), most deaf people find it insulting because many of them do not see themselves as disabled, but rather as a cultural, linguistic minority. Living in a non-signing world can be disabling, not the experience of being deaf. Being deaf is considered a biological characteristic. It is not a condition; it is a way of being (Whyte et al., 2013).

Counseling Needs and Implications

The stressors and discrimination experienced by individuals who are deaf have a higher and more significant impact on psychological and physical health compared to their hearing counterparts (Mousley & Chaudoir, 2018). This has resulted in higher rates of depressive symptoms, impulse control disorders, developmental disorders, poor physical well-being, and decreased use of healthcare systems (Mousley & Chaudoir, 2018). Therefore, it is important to understand the many needs of the deaf population.

According to Whyte et al. (2013), ASL is the language of people who are deaf in North America. However, it is not universal. If a hearing counselor has minimal awareness of deaf culture and the deaf community and does not know ASL, this counselor can refer the client who does not hear to a signing counselor (Cabral et al., 2013). Or, the hearing counselor can counsel the individual who is deaf with the assistance of a sign language interpreter. It is important to discuss this issue with the client to ascertain their preferences (Cabral et al., 2013). Usually, deaf clients prefer to work with deaf counselors (Whyte et al., 2013). However, there is a lack of qualified mental health professionals who are proficient in ASL, and those providers with qualified language skills may have long wait lists to access services. Experiences with interpreters vary, with many feeling that interpreters do not always accurately communicate between the parties. The literature suggests that interpreters can add a filter that negatively affects the relationship between a therapist and a client (Pertz et al., 2018).

There are some key counseling approaches and considerations for working with people who live with deafness or are hard of hearing:

- People who live with deafness are visual beings. Visual, expressive, and tactile approaches may be beneficial, including the use of art and play therapy, particularly in school counseling settings (Cabral et al., 2013). Be mindful that assignments or handouts in the English language may not be culturally compatible with deaf clients. As a useful form of communication, Leigh (2010) suggested that nonverbal communication can include body language, facial expressions, pantomime, and gesture.
- Avoid asking clients who are deaf to teach you about people who are deaf or ASL. It is not their responsibility.
- Do not devalue ASL. Learning the basics of ASL does not make you fluent enough to work with deaf clients. However, learning some basic sign language and fingerspelling may aid in building rapport and demonstrate that you are interested in your client's language.

- Some deaf clients may have misconceptions about deaf people and being deaf. Some treatment goals and activities may include unpacking perspectives (realistic and unrealistic) of deaf people, meeting other deaf people, joining deaf organizations, finding deaf role models, and so on (Geisinger & Stein, 2016).
- Ensure that your agency or private practice is deaf-friendly. For example, list "deaf" under ethnicity in your forms and checklists. Include a question about communication preference or if an interpreter is needed in sessions. Become familiar with the relay phone services that deaf people use, including video relay service and text relay. Make efforts to ensure that client communication is available in alternative formats as needed (e.g., closed captioning and digital versions).
- Telepsychiatry can mitigate the deaf community's lack of access to care by allowing deaf individuals in remote communities to access care through facilities that cater to their needs (Crowe et al., 2016).
- Purse (2021) recommends that counselors be aware of and address the differences in how a deaf individual displays feelings and expressions from those who are hearing. Members of the deaf community count on the vivid expression of emotion to convey meaning, which can seem aggressive but is part of deaf culture.

Counseling Individuals Who Are Blind

There are specific recommendations and requirements for counselors working with clients who are visually impaired/blind. It is also important to keep in mind the challenges faced by individuals who acquire a visual impairment. Thurston (2010) researched individuals who had acquired visual impairments and their transition from sight to blindness. Research findings showed some common themes with diagnosis, such as coping with deterioration of sight, loss in different areas of life, changed perceptions of self in relation to society, experiencing others in a changed way, and social isolation (Thurston, 2010). These themes are expanded on in the following sections.

Blind Culture and Identity

According to Bogart and Dunn (2019), language and how individuals with sight loss/blindness identify is important. This population often prefers to be called blind people. Many individuals who are blind use Braille (Hopfe, 1999), a form of communication that uses abbreviations unique to the blind community. In order to navigate and be mobile in an inaccessible society, individuals who are blind may use a white cane that is generally recognized worldwide (Hopfe, 1999). The American Foundation for the Blind is a nonprofit organization that helps to expand possibilities for the nearly 25 million Americans living with vision loss. It strives for access and equality, new technology, and evidence-based advocacy.

Counseling Needs and Implications

For counselors, it is important to help clients make sense of the diagnosis of sight loss on three levels: intellectually, practically, and emotionally (Thurston, 2010). There is a particular need for emotional support at the time of diagnosis, as well as during rehabilitation and the transition to blindness. Counseling can help with problems concerning mood, social connectedness, identity, and feelings of loss. Thurston et al. (2013) acknowledged key factors in assisting individuals with acquired sight loss/blindness. Based on the particular client's experience, counselors may want to assist with

- telling the story of what happened (having time and space to reflect on events),
- feeling understood (feeling that someone understands the impact of sight loss),
- expressing difficult emotions (fear, despair, and loss of hope),
- exploring identity (old and new; who am I now that I can't see?),
- examining and challenging negative self-concepts (feelings of uselessness and hopelessness),
- exploring the possibility of a future without sight (finding a purpose in life), and
- identifying helpful cultural resources (local groups, carers, relationships, and religion).

It is also useful to explore with the client the language around sight loss, to assist in understanding its meaning and significance (Taylor, 2020). Logistically, it is important to consider practical considerations of working with a client who cannot see. For example, guiding a blind person to the counseling office, arranging the room in exactly the same way for every session, and checking for light sensitivity may be necessary. Also, Taylor (2020) suggested modifying the counseling approach, such as attending to the tone of voice used by the counselor; sometimes describing nonverbal reactions can help clients who are unable to see and read facial expressions. Bogart and Dunn (2019) encouraged counselors to print intake forms and other paperwork in a larger font size for clients who are visually impaired (using 14-point Verdana on yellow paper is highly recommended, unless the client specifies a different need or preference). For clients who are blind, Chapin et al. (2018) proposed that counselors ensure that client communication is available in alternative formats as needed (e.g., Braille).

COUNSELING CHILDREN, ADOLESCENTS, AND YOUNG ADULTS

Children

Children with disabilities may encounter a variety of issues at an early age, such as developmental disabilities, behavioral mental health disorders, chronic medical issues, below average birthweight, premature birth, and so on (Breiner et al., 2016). For some children with disabilities, there can also be a transitional period and adjustment that occurs from hospitalization to home, from home to school, and from home/school to the community (Labhard, 2010). When counseling children with disabilities, traditional models of counseling do not always work (Lorenz, 2008). Due to their lack of emotional, cognitive, and behavioral development, it can be challenging for all children to participate verbally in the therapeutic process. Therefore, play therapy is a recommended modality, as it allows children to utilize toys, art, sand trays, music, and other experiential means to display their emotions without having to verbalize what they are experiencing (Lorenz, 2008). This alternative to traditional models of therapy is especially useful with children who have disabilities.

Children with disabilities may require medical procedures that invoke feelings of inadequacy, low self-esteem, incompetence, fear, anxiety, and lack of control. Due to the non-directive and child-centered approach, play therapy can assist children with disabilities in building strength, self-esteem, autonomy, competence, and social skills. When using play therapy with children who have disabilities, it is important to be familiar with cultural constructs within the family. This may include how certain cultures express emotions, primary and other languages spoken by the child and family, and directive versus non-directive communication used (Lorenz, 2008).

Due to their special needs, many parents face challenges and need support and care for their children with disabilities (Breiner et al., 2016). Beyond the general knowledge, attitude, and practices that all parents need, parents of children with disabilities may require additional special skills. Intervention strategies recommended in working with children with disabilities also include family systems programs that focus on parents' stress, depression, and ways to cope; parent management training; and parent–child interaction therapy (Breiner et al., 2016).

Adolescents

The most common causes of disabilities during adolescence are emotional and behavioral disorders, learning disabilities, mild intellectual disability, speech and language impairments, and autism (Gage et al., 2012). Other disabilities can include blindness/low vision, deafness/hard-of-hearing, and mobility disabilities (Boyle et al., 2011). Adolescents with a disability can struggle more than adolescents without disabilities with identity development, self-esteem, sexuality, victimization, sense of belonging, social activities, coping with puberty, engaging in risky behavior, and communication challenges (Berg et al., 2015; Horner-Johnson & Sauvé, 2019; Lindsay, 2021).

Due to the many issues that adolescents with disabilities encounter, it is important for counselors to provide a multifaceted approach. When counseling, it is necessary to be aware of incidences of victimization and sexual trauma and provide trauma-informed care and services as needed (Berg et al., 2015). Sexual health education in schools can also be overlooked with adolescents who have a disability. Therefore, counselors may need to provide psychoeducation around sexual health education. Developing a positive sexual identity in adolescence is important because it is a critical stage of development, in which youth need guidance and education to understand the potential consequences of unprotected sexual activity, sexually transmitted infections, unplanned pregnancies, and so on (Lindsay, 2021). In the research, Lindsay (2021) found three main themes that health professionals struggle with regarding addressing sex and sexuality with adolescents: lack of training and education and feeling unprepared with clients disclosing their sexual identity, lack of attention to sex-related issues, and difficulty in navigating parental concerns around privacy and confidentiality. Horner-Johnson and Sauvé (2019) stressed the importance of connection with the disability community as key to development of a sense of belonging. This coincides with Bogart and Dunn's (2019) emphasis on the positive impact of positive disability identity on sense of self, feelings of connection, and solidarity with the disability community.

Young Adults

Young adults with spinal cord dysfunction (due to disease, spina bifida, or traumatic spinal cord injury) have specific challenges relating to personal independence. Transitioning from the hospital to home and life outside the hospital can be an overwhelming stressor for the young adult and family (Labhard, 2010).

COUNSELING ADULTS, COUPLES, AND FAMILIES

Adults

Counselors need to think more systematically about how the ongoing experiences of ableism affect clients who are disabled, and how they can support those clients in ways to be resilient in an ableist society. Treatment should include using disability-inclusive language (Geisinger & Stein, 2016), and not framing disability as either something problematic or idealized, which is common in a medical model of disability (Kattari, 2017). This also keeps one from attributing PWD's negative outcomes to the disability without considering the possible contribution of other external stressors and barriers involved in living with a disability, including inadequate access or accommodation in the community.

This concern is echoed by Marini and Stebnicki (2018), who point out that the sole focus and presenting problem are not always specific to the disability. Therefore, when counseling PWD, it is recommended to not under- or overestimate a client's disability. Regardless of the disability, it is vital for counselors to focus on a holistic assessment and to incorporate all major life domains. Typically, the disability is one of several important parts of the individual's self-identity. On the one hand, when counselors dismiss or ignore the disability, a critical part of the client's self-identity remains unexplored. On the other hand, counselors may tend to overemphasize the salience of the disability and automatically assume that the disability is the "presenting problem" or the cause and source of all the client's concerns (Chapin et al., 2018; Smart & Smart, 2006; Stuntzner & Hartley, 2014). Research has highlighted that most PWD do not live their lives focused on their disability and limitations. Counselors need to view the client with a disability as an individual with multiple identities, roles, functions, and different environments to competently facilitate the counseling process (Marini & Stebnicki, 2018).

Due to the high rates of ableist microaggressions experienced by PWD, counselors need to take this information into account when supporting clients (Kattari, 2020). Much time and energy are spent on empowering clients, but it is also important that counselors acknowledge how pervasive ableism is, and how much the experiences of ableist microaggressions may resonate with and harm their clients. (Marini & Stebnicki, 2018). Counselors should listen to their clients and be willing to hear about experiences of prejudice and discrimination experienced by their clients with disabilities. Learning the basic tenets of the sociopolitical model of disability (Bogart & Dunn, 2019) will provide counselors with some introductory understanding of this stigmatization and the discrimination created by a society that is inaccessible to and biased against PWD (Bogart et al., 2018).

For counselors to help PWD with acquired disabilities, Stuntzner and Hartley (2014) recommend fostering forgiveness, self-compassion, and resilience. Forgiveness and self-compassion have been shown to reduce negative emotions and improve overall functioning and well-being for PWD (Enright, 2001; Neff, 2011), while resiliency is an identified skill taught to enhance functioning. Marini and Stebnicki (2018) and Noh et al. (2016) found that perceived social support, sense of control, and self-esteem can mediate the effects of functional disability on depressive symptoms.

Telemental health has provided a much more open platform and accessibility for PWD (Chapin et al., 2018). Telemental health increases access to counseling for individuals with physical, medical, and/or mobility disabilities; provides access to disability specialists regardless of geographic area; enables services in areas with few mental health resources; and allows access to counselors with disability training and experience, counseling in native language (e.g., ASL), and counseling for individuals who may have difficulty attending sessions on-site (e.g., those with PTSD or agoraphobia).

Couples

Due to prejudice and discrimination pertaining to disability, many PWD struggle with romantic relationships and are less likely to marry compared to people without disabilities (Brown & Ciciurkaite, 2021). Also, prejudice and discrimination can contribute to mental health stressors for both the individual with a disability and the one without in a relationship (Brown & Ciciurkaite, 2021). There is a gap in literature specifically related to marital relationships and disability (Engblom-Deglmann & Hamilton, 2020; Munro, 2011).

Counselors working with couples who have intellectual disabilities can use a specific model developed by Munro (2011) called positive support couples therapy (PSCT). This model focuses on what is right with the couple and other significant people in their lives: couple resilience, resourcefulness, and the ability to rebound from past trauma, rejection, and ostracism are emphasized. The PSCT model also draws ideas from integrative couples therapy and narrative therapy with its emphasis on cognitive-behavioral strategies, support, empathy, no-violence contracts, social justice, and liberation through the development of alternative, empowering stories (Munro, 2011).

Older adults with disabilities are often overlooked and their needs ignored or discounted. Media messaging around intimacy and sex are that sex is acceptable for those who are young, attractive, and able-bodied. Counselors helping older adults with disabilities are encouraged to help them learn about their ability to have sex, consenting to sex, and negotiating accommodations for intimacy and sex with their spouses or partners; there should also be counseling for those who took on caregiver roles for their spouses (Linton & Williams, 2019).

Couples facing an acquired physical disability (e.g., a spinal cord injury) encounter significant marital stressors (Engblom-Deglmann & Hamilton, 2020). Results of recent studies show patterns in the adjustment processes in couples: challenges in intimacy, negotiating care needs, redefining masculinity, and social disconnection. Counselors need to focus on the systemic physical and emotional aspect of the trauma in the early stages of the disability. Counselors are encouraged to be aware of and process the potential for underlying shame in the individual with a disability (Johnson, 2019). Engblom-Deglmann and Hamilton (2020) encourage counselors to use emotionally focused therapy to access primary emotions such as fear, isolation, and shame. Specifically, having the couple verbally address emotions associated with disability, along with their fears, vulnerability, and needs for adaptation, can help a couple establish a more secure bond (Engblom-Deglmann & Hamilton, 2020; Johnson, 2019).

Lia and Abela (2020) highlighted the significance of counselors involving the romantic partner in the counseling process when there is an acquired disability within the relationship. This entails exploring the individual's and couple's experiences along with processing their loss, the societal barriers, and intimacy and sexuality concerns. For newly acquired disabilities, counselors are encouraged to provide psychoeducation on disabilities to both partners, fostering resilience and strength-focused frameworks to provide a sense of hope and ways to adapt.

Families

In order to best help PWD, counselors need to be prepared to provide supportive services and/or counseling to the entire family (Chapin et al., 2018; Evans, 2017). Disability can affect all of the family system and cause extra demands and challenges financially, emotionally, physically, and relationally (Marriage and Family Encyclopedia, n.d.). For example, a PWD may have a financial burden of obtaining health, education, and social services and in making accommodations to their home and transportation. Emotional issues can have an impact on the family; these may stem from uncertainty about the cause of the disability, future of the disability, and grieving over the loss of function, among other things. The physical challenges can be marked by the responsibilities of caretaking for the PWD (Marriage and Family Encyclopedia, n.d.). However, depending on multiple factors—such as who in the family has the disability, the nature of family relationships, socioeconomic status, education, and community attitudes toward disability—the impact on the family can vary (Marini & Stebnicki, 2018). Therefore, it is important for counselors to recognize the wide range of individual responses to disability, and collaborate with their clients who have disabilities and with those clients' families (Geisinger & Stein, 2016). Counselors also need to ensure that information about long-term planning (e.g., personal future planning, special needs trusts) is available to PWD and their families (Evans, 2017).

Family members can also have a strong influence on the identity of PWD. According to Balva and Tapia-Fuselier (2020), cultural beliefs and limitations of the PWD can negatively influence a family member's view of the PWD as being incapable. Depending on the family's understanding of disability and the various identities held by the PWD, those negative messages can be perpetuated and further suppress the PWD's abilities and strengths. Therefore, family support has been strongly linked with a sense of belonging and positive disability identity. Raver et al. (2018) found that PWD who perceived greater social support from family, friends, or a special person were more likely to report a stronger sense of belonging and positive disability identity. Along with social support, Bogart (2014) highlighted that self-esteem, disability identity, disability self-efficacy, and income were significant predictors of satisfaction with life, thus emphasizing the importance of disability self-concept.

Counselors can help families of a PWD foster family resilience and emphasize the adaptive capacity of families (Marriage and Family Encyclopedia, n.d.). The authors highlight that families have reported that the presence of disability has strengthened them as a family. Family resilience can contribute to families becoming closer, more accepting of others, having deeper faith, discovering new friends, developing greater respect for life, and improving their sense of mastery, among other things (Marriage and Family Encyclopedia, n.d.).

Counselors can also help families that include a loved one with a disability by focusing on their spirituality. If the families of PWD have spiritual beliefs and practices, this can be conducive to overall family resilience, good functioning, and well-being across the life span (Jenkins & Graf, 2020). Research reveals that spiritual beliefs and practices for PWD and their family can help with coping and adaptation to the disability (Marini & Stebnicki, 2018). The spiritual beliefs can help families interpret disability when other information is not available (Zhang & Bennett, 2001).

IMPLICATIONS FOR CLINICAL PRACTICE

For counselors to employ best practices with PWD, it is critical to be aware of the history of disability, cultural diversity, the different kinds of disabilities, barriers PWD have encountered, and ways they have endured discrimination, while also recognizing internal biases and assumptions that could affect the counseling relationship. The future of the counseling profession lies in improving to help with this.

The projected 2023 CACREP Standards will better prepare disability-competent counselors (Deroche et al., 2020). Instead of only one core area, the proposed future standards are expected to include disability-related content across the eight core areas (professional counseling orientation and ethical practice, social and cultural diversity, human growth and development, career development, counseling and helping relationship, group counseling, assessment and testing, and research and program evaluation; CACREP, 2022). Also, recognizing the power and influence of models of disability is important for counselors in understanding how PWD are defined in multiple ways (Smart, 2009).

Smart (2009) encourages counselors not to focus on one single model, but instead to get a thorough grounding in each of the models (i.e., biomedical, functional, environmental, sociopolitical). This will help emphasize the strengths of each model and will allow counselors to recognize the limitations of the models. Having a cross-model approach will allow counselors opportunities for interdisciplinary collaboration and interdependent professional services to help PWD (Solarz, 1990).

Deroche et al. (2020) suggest exposure to and contact with basic instructional strategies, such as reading books and blogs written by PWD, finding opportunities to interview PWD, and having counseling programs that require clinical experience with PWD during pre-practicum, practicum, and internship. This also draws attention to the need for effective and accessible substance abuse interventions in rehabilitation settings (Chan et al., 2015).

CLINICAL CASE SCENARIO 19.1

Rodrick is a 50-year-old African American man who is married and has three kids under the age of 25. Six months ago Rodrick was in a diving accident and broke his neck, sustaining a traumatic spinal cord injury. After 6 months of hospitalization and extensive rehabilitation, Rodrick requires a power wheelchair for mobility and has limited movement in his upper body. Upon discharge from rehab, Rodrick had to go into a nursing home because his house was not wheelchair accessible. After being out of work for so long, Rodrick—the sole provider for his family—lost his job and had to file for bankruptcy.

After 4 months in the nursing home, Rodrick returned home. Due to the severity of his spinal cord injury, Rodrick requires support from his children and wife for his activities of daily living, including feeding, dressing, and bathing. One night, Rodrick tried to be intimate with his wife, but feelings of low self-esteem stemming from his disability interfered with his ability to perform sexually. In frustration, he asked his wife to sleep on the couch. Rodrick continued to struggle, and soon he became overwhelmed with the reality of living with a disability, losing his independence and job, and having filed for bankruptcy. He began to feel like a burden to his family and found it difficult to ask for help. Rodrick began drinking heavily and sleeping throughout the day. Soon after, Rodrick's wife encouraged him to seek counseling.

CLINICAL CASE SCENARIO DISCUSSION QUESTIONS

1. Given what you know about Rodrick, what else would you need to know so that you can best help him heal and cope with his situation?
2. Based on the information provided, what would be the first area to address with Rodrick? What would you do about the other concerns?
3. What would be your potential struggles and barriers in helping Rodrick?
4. What multicultural considerations should be taken into account when working with Rodrick?
5. How would you support Rodrick's wife and kids using systemic counseling?

END-OF-CHAPTER RESOURCES

 A robust set of instructor resources designed to supplement this text is located at http://connect.springerpub.com/content/book/978-0-8261-3953-5. Qualifying instructors may request access by emailing **textbook@springerpub.com**.

SUMMARY

Disability is and can be a natural part of human development and is growing more common as a larger proportion of the U.S. population experiences some type of disability (ADA, 1990; Okoro et al., 2018). Despite the increase in the number of individuals with disabilities, it is often perceived by persons without disabilities and society as a negative experience, something undesired and needing to be "fixed." These attitudes are pervasive throughout history from individuals without disabilities; however, such perceptions and beliefs are not necessarily the same as those held by PWD and their families (Dunn & Brody, 2008). It is essential that counselors develop culturally responsive counseling skills to ensure that the techniques and strategies they use align with students' or clients' cultural and physiological backgrounds to further social justice in practice.

DISCUSSION QUESTIONS

1. In what ways might the worldview of a client with disability differ from those of able-bodied mental health providers?
2. What might it look like to address intersectionality within the therapeutic relationship between a client who lives with a disability and a mental health professional who does not, or vice versa?
3. Identify ways in which you, as a future professional counselor, can integrate elements of liberation counseling within your practice. Consider, specifically, liberation of self, the client, and the counseling profession.
4. Considering the models presented in this chapter (biomedical, functional, environmental, and sociopolitical) and your worldview about living with disability, what aspects do you anticipate being the most and least challenging? Why? How, exactly, will you work through the challenges you identified to ensure that you are effective in implementing the respective models in practice?
5. How will you ensure that your office or working space is culturally sensitive to people who live with disabilities?

CULTURALLY RESPONSIVE COUNSELING FOR CLIENTS WITH DISABILITIES, INCLUDING DEAFNESS AND BLINDNESS

Guest: Dr. Damion R. Cummins

https://connect.springerpub.com/content/book/978-0-8261-3953-5/part/part02/chapter/ch19

KEY REFERENCES

Only key references appear in the print edition. The full reference list appears in the digital product on Springer Publishing Connect: https://connect.springerpub.com/content/book/978-0-8261-3953-5/part/part02/chapter/ch19

Americans With Disabilities Act. (1990). *42 U.S.C. § 12101.*
Balva, D., & Tapia-Fuselier, J., Jr. (2020). Working with clients with disabilities: Implications for psychotherapists. *Psychotherapy Bulletin, 55*(1), 19–22. https://societyforpsychotherapy.org/working-with-clients-with-disabilities
Bogart, K. R. (2014). The role of disability self-concept in adaptation to congenital or acquired disability. *Rehabilitation Psychology, 59*(1), 107–115. https://doi.org/10.1037/a0035800
Bogart, K. R. (2015). Disability identity predicts lower anxiety and depression in multiple sclerosis. *Rehabilitation Psychology, 60*(1), 105–109. https://doi.org/10.1037/rep0000029
Bogart, K. R., & Dunn, D. S. (2019). Ableism special issue introduction. *Journal of Social Issues, 75*(3), 650–664. https://doi.org/10.1111/josi.12354
Bogart, K. R., Rosa, N. M., & Slepian, M. L. (2018). Born that way or became that way: Stigma toward congenital versus acquired disability. *Group Processes & Intergroup Relations, 22*(4), 594–612. https://doi.org/10.1177/1368430218757897
Bogart, K. R., Rottenstein, A., Lund, E. M., & Bouchard, L. (2017). Who self-identifies as disabled? An examination of impairment and contextual predictors. *Rehabilitation Psychology, 62*(4), 553–562. https://doi.org/10.1037/rep0000132
Chan, F., Berven, N. L., & Thomas, K. R. (Eds.). (2015). *Counseling theories and techniques for rehabilitation and mental health professionals* (2nd ed.). Springer Publishing Company.
Rivas, M., & Hill, N. R. (2018). Counselor trainees' experiences counseling disability: A phenomenological study. *Counselor Education and Supervision, 57*(2), 116–131. https://doi.org/10.1002/ceas.12097
Shallcross, L. (2011). Seeing potential, not disability. *Counseling Today.* https://ct.counseling.org/2011/08/seeing-potential-not-disability

CHAPTER 20

Culturally Responsive Counseling With Immigrant and Refugee Clients

CLAUDIA G. INTERIANO-SHIVERDECKER, ELVITA KONDILI, CODY MCKENZIE, AND RAVZA NUR AKSOY EREN

LEARNING OBJECTIVES

After reading this chapter, students will be able to:

- Outline the demographics and characteristics of foreign-born populations such as immigrants, refugees, and asylum-seekers.
- Discover counseling utilization and help-seeking behaviors of immigrants, refugees, and asylum-seekers.
- Identify culturally responsive practices when working with foreign-born populations.
- Recognize how the implications of clinical practice can guide assessment and counseling interventions with immigrants, refugees, and asylum-seekers.

SELF-REFLECTION QUESTIONS

1. What are some of your assumptions and beliefs about immigrants, refugees, and asylum-seekers?
2. What do you know about immigrants, refugees, and asylum-seekers?
3. What are some of your concerns about working with immigrants, refugees, and asylum-seekers?

The U.S. Census Bureau (2019a) uses the term *foreign-born* to refer to individuals who are not U.S. citizens at birth. This includes "naturalized U.S. citizens, lawful permanent residents (i.e., immigrants), temporary migrants (i.e., international students), humanitarian migrants (i.e., refugees and asylees), and undocumented migrants" (U.S. Census Bureau, 2019a, para. 2). In 2019, the foreign-born population in the United States was estimated at a record 45.8 million individuals, nearly 14.1% of the total U.S. population (U.S. Census Bureau, 2019b).

THE COUNSELOR: EXPLORATION, INTROSPECTION, AND REFLECTION

Counselor Self-Awareness and Cultural Humility

Cultural awareness should consistently focus on the role and impact of culture and diversity on the development and maintenance of the client's worldview. Besides building cultural awareness, cultural humility reminds the counselor to move toward developing a habit of reflexivity in counseling practice (Zhu et al., 2021). Hook et al. (2013) defined *cultural humility* as the ability to express openness, respect, and lack of superiority toward another person's cultural identity (e.g., race/ethnicity, gender, sexual orientation, and religion), especially in situations where cultural differences threaten to strain the relationship. Cultural humility is central to cultural competency and has been linked to a stronger therapeutic alliance, higher likelihood of continued treatment, and greater perceived benefit and improvement in therapy (Hook et al., 2013, 2017; Owen et al., 2016). Cultural humility requires awareness and acknowledgment of one's lack of cultural knowledge and limitations in understanding someone else's experience, which can only be accomplished by taking an other-focused, egoless stance in the therapeutic relationship. While cultural humility is an important part of cultural competency, there are some important distinctions between these two constructs. Yeager and Bauer-Wu (2013) suggested that cultural competency might promote stereotyping and thinking of culture in terms of majority and minority groups, whereas cultural humility promotes respect, flexibility, and ability to think of culture from an individual, contextual, and intersectional perspective. Cultural humility is not merely a set of knowledge and skills, but rather an attitude or dispositional orientation where the counselor assumes a stance of open-mindedness and curiosity about the client's cultural background. Thus, when working with foreign-born clients—a diverse group in race, ethnicity, culture, religion, and language—cultural humility becomes extremely important. In this chapter, we discuss factors that require open-mindedness from the counselor and offer suggestions to engage with the foreign-born population using a stance of cultural awareness and humility.

Counseling Relationship

Culturally responsive counselors acknowledge the importance of building a therapeutic relationship in the context of clients' sociocultural framework and within the client–counselor intrapersonal dynamics of power, privilege, and oppression that may affect the counseling relationship (Gangamma & Shipman, 2018). Moreover, counselors must identify their cultural assumptions and how these may affect the therapeutic engagement with clients, while also acknowledging the impact of their client's culture on both the therapeutic engagement and the notion of mental health (Ibrahim & Heuer, 2016). When counselors apply Euro-American and Western approaches across cultures without attention to the appropriateness of the approach for a specific client, this poses a threat of cultural oppression (Ibrahim & Heuer, 2016). Culturally responsive counselors assess and understand clients' cultural assumptions as they build the therapeutic relationship and invite clients to discuss any discomfort that may increase the risk of early termination or a rupture in the therapeutic relationship.

Counseling Intervention and Advocacy

Following the Multicultural and Social Justice Counseling Competencies (MSJCC) and liberation frameworks, counselors consider avenues that expand their professional roles beyond the individual to also include work at other levels, including communities, organizations, and political institutions (Freire, 1993; Ratts et al., 2016). Although individual counseling remains beneficial, it is limited in remediating mental health concerns that may arise from systemic issues in society, such as poverty, discrimination, and immigration procedures (Chung et al., 2011; Interiano-Shiverdecker et al., 2020, 2021). The following discussions therefore target interpersonal services, as well as social justice and advocacy efforts at the community and public policy levels.

IMMIGRANTS, REFUGEES, AND ASYLUM-SEEKERS IN THE UNITED STATES

As previously mentioned in this chapter, the term *foreign-born* encompasses several statuses regarding U.S. citizenship, including immigrants, refugees, and asylum-seekers. You may be wondering how these statuses differ from one another. There are different immigrant status types (U.S. Department of Homeland Security, n.d.), such as an *immigrant*, who is a person who came to live in the United States from another country, and *temporary migrants or visitors*, who have permission from the government to live (and sometimes work) in the United States for a limited time and a specific purpose (e.g., studying, working, tourism). A *lawful permanent resident*, typically known as a green card holder, is someone who has permission to live and work in the United States but is not eligible for certain benefits such as voting. *Naturalized citizens* have the right to live, work, and vote in the United States, and are eligible for many federal benefits such as educational loans and social services. An *undocumented immigrant* does not have permission to live or work in the United States and is at risk of deportation. Acquiring any of these immigration statuses typically requires considerable time and money, can be prolonged and arduous, and depends ultimately on the approval (or rejection) of the United States Citizenship and Immigration Services.

Refugees and *asylum-seekers* differ from immigrants in that the former are seeking residence in the United States "for reasons of feared persecution, conflict, generalized violence, or other circumstances that have seriously disturbed public order and, as a result, require international protection" (United Nations, n.d., para. 1). Although both groups pursue refuge in the United States, refugees apply from outside of the country, whereas asylum-seekers apply either from within the nation's border or while en route to an American port of entry (Baugh, 2020). Applicants do not qualify for refugee or asylum-seeker status unless they are outside of their country of nationality or are otherwise absent from their last country of residence (Baugh, 2020). Individuals who wish to submit principal applications for refugee or asylum-seeker status in the United States undergo a more rigorous admissions process than do those seeking immigrant visas.

Racial and Ethnic Diversity

In 2019, foreign-born individuals identified their race as White (45.2%), Asian (27.2%), Black or African American (9.7%), American Indian and Alaska Native (0.45), Native Hawaiian and Other Pacific Islander (0.4%), and some other race (14.7%). Regarding ethnicity, 44.2% identified as Hispanic or Latino origin, whereas 17.2% identified as White alone, not Hispanic or Latino (U.S. Census Bureau, 2019b). While it is tempting to view foreign-born individuals as a homogenous group based on a single definition, it is important to emphasize that racial and ethnic diversity make certain groups more vulnerable to acculturative stress and discrimination, further discussed later in this chapter. Arrival in the United States exposes refugees to the long history of tumultuous relations between different races and ethnicities. Individuals may respond to immigrants, refugees, and asylum-seekers based on phenotypic ranking systems that result from historical classifications of race and ethnicity. For example, Black immigrants, refugees, and asylum-seekers may experience heightened levels of discrimination, in comparison to their non-Black counterparts, as they are immediately assigned membership to a historically oppressed group in the United States. Culturally responsive counselors, therefore, consider the client's racial and ethnic makeup within the therapeutic relationship and process, while considering external factors (e.g., discrimination) that foster or hinder their mental well-being.

Educational Diversity

According to the U.S. Census Bureau (2019b), more than half of the foreign-born population has some college or associate degree (18.7%), a bachelor's degree (18.5%), or a graduate or professional degree (14.2%). The remaining (22.3%) population completed their high school graduate (or equivalent degree) or did not complete their high school degree (26.3%). However, educational attainment varies among foreign-born populations. For instance, 47% of Central American and 54% of Mexican immigrants did not achieve a high school diploma, compared to only 8% of native-born individuals; nevertheless, immigrants (excluding those from Central America and Mexico) were just as likely to achieve a bachelor's or advanced degree as every other nationality (Budiman, 2020). Immigrants from South Asia (71%) and Central Asia (57%) were the most likely to have achieved a bachelor's degree or higher, standing in stark contrast to the 33% of the U.S. native-born population with these degrees (Budiman, 2020). As further discussed in this chapter, many foreign-born populations experience significant barriers that could hamper educational attainment.

Language Diversity

By 2018, more than 65.9 million individuals over 5 years of age (21.6% of the total population) spoke a language other than English at home (U.S. Census Bureau, 2019b). Among this number, English proficiency was unsurprisingly highest for foreign-born individuals from English-speaking countries such as Canada (96%), Oceania (82%), and Europe (75%), while immigrants from Mexico (34%), Central America (35%), and Asia (50%) rated the lowest. Spanish was the second most spoken language at home, followed by Chinese, Hindi, Filipino/Tagalog, and French (Budiman, 2020). In the United States, speaking English is considered a positive social value, and speaking other languages (e.g., Spanish, Chinese) has at times been received with hostility and discriminatory behavior.

Economic Diversity

In 2019, approximately 56.5% of the foreign-born population over the age of 16 earned less than $50,000 per year, with more than 1 million under the poverty threshold (U.S. Census Bureau, 2019b). The remaining earned from $50,000 to $74,999 (17.8%) and over $75,000 (25.7%). These numbers, however, change for undocumented immigrants. Most (74%) undocumented immigrants are at 100% to 200% of the poverty level (Migration Policy Institute, 2018). Moreover, foreign-born workers constituted roughly 17% of the national labor force in 2017 (Budiman, 2020). Despite the common belief that undocumented immigrants steal American jobs, the numbers of both native-born workers and lawful immigrant workers increased from 2007 to 2017, while the number of unauthorized workers decreased during this same time period (Budiman, 2020). For example, only 7.6 million (4.6%) were unauthorized immigrants, compared to the 21.2 million

(12.9%) lawful immigrant workers (Budiman, 2020). However, undocumented immigrants account for nearly a tenth of all U.S. workers in industries that produce and distribute food, such as food production, food processing, food retail, and food distribution, all of which are considered essential jobs (Budiman, 2020).

Religious Diversity

Concerning religiosity, foreign-born individuals identify as Christian (66%), non-Christian (12%), unaffiliated (20%), and nothing in particular (15%; Pew Research Center, n.d.). Among Christian faiths, the most common was Catholicism (39%), while Islam (4%) and Hinduism (4%) tied as the most common non-Christian faiths. Other religious affiliations included Evangelical Protestant, Mainline Protestant, Historically Black Protestant, Mormon, Orthodox Christian, Jehovah's Witness, Jewish, and Buddhist (Pew Research Center, n.d.). Around 56% of all foreign-born individuals believe in God with absolute certainty, and 58% assess their religion as very important to their life (Pew Research Center, n.d.). Belief in heaven (70%) and hell (56%) was also most frequently observed. Many (33%) also seek guidance from their religion on determining what is right and wrong, with more than 75% of respondents attending religious services at least a few times a year if not more (Pew Research Center, n.d.).

CLIENT WORLDVIEWS AND PERSPECTIVES

Collectivism and Family-Oriented Culture

Hofstede (2001) defined *individualistic cultures* as those that foster and facilitate the needs of an autonomous and unique self over those of any group, organization, or other collective groups. Individualists value independence, pursuing personal rather than social goals, and resisting pressures to obey group norms (Cozma, 2011). Meanwhile, collectivistic societies value group membership, value interdependence, derive self-definition through relationships with others, and yield to the obligations expected by their friends, family, and their larger community (Ady, 1998). As evidenced by recent worldwide immigration patterns, foreign-born populations originate largely from Latin America, Asia, Africa, the Caribbean, and the Middle East—regions where collectivism is emphasized over individualism (Schwartz et al., 2010; Sue et al., 2019). In the United States, individualism represents a core value of the dominant culture (Hofstede, 2001). Therefore, Euro-American Western mental health systems that value independence over interdependence, separate mental functioning from physical functioning, and attribute causation as internally located can contrast sharply with the cultural belief systems of many foreign-born populations (Sue et al., 2019). Culturally responsive counselors recognize that individualistic cultural models may inhibit working from a framework that focuses on interpersonal relationships, social networks, interdependence, and a holistic approach to healing, which is frequently preferred by foreign-born clients (Bemak & Chung, 2021).

Acculturation and Identity

Acculturation theoretical frameworks offer insight into foreign-born populations' acculturation experiences and how they shape their identity in the United States. Redfield et al. (1936) were some of the first scholars to define *acculturation* as the "phenomena which result when groups of individuals having different cultures come into continuous first-hand contact, with subsequent sociocultural and psychological changes in the original cultural patterns of either or both groups" (p. 149). Sociocultural changes refer to foreign-born individuals' adaptation to the societal practices and norms of the host country, whereas psychological changes refer to the individual's mental receptiveness and willingness to identify with the new culture (Berry et al., 2006). Two underlying fundamental attitudes comprise acculturation change: (a) cultural maintenance (the importance of maintaining key aspects of the heritage culture) and (b) cultural participation (the importance of adapting to key aspects of the receiving culture; Berry et al., 2006; Schwartz et al., 2010).

Currently, the most popular and widely used bidimensional model is that of Berry (1997). Berry developed four possible acculturation strategies from this model. (a) assimilation (dismissal of heritage culture and acceptance of receiving culture), (b) separation (retention of heritage culture and rejection of receiving culture), (c) marginalization (rejection of both cultures), and (d) integration (successful balance of heritage-cultural maintenance and participation in the receiving culture; Berry, 1997). However, recent studies pointed out one important limitation with Berry's model (Schwartz et al., 2010, 2014): it considers four acculturation categories that provide only four acculturative strategies, suggesting that all foreign-born populations, regardless of their background, countries of origin, or experiences in the host country, fall into one of the four defined categories. Researchers (Schwartz et al., 2010, 2014) contend that even when individuals fall into the same acculturative strategy category, each person's acculturation process is unique.

Schwartz et al. (2010) reconceptualized the Berry (1997) acculturation model by creating a framework that independently measures cultural changes across three domains. The first domain refers to behavioral acculturation, the ability to engage in cultural practices such as language use, culinary preferences, choice of friends, and use of media (Schwartz et al., 2010). Within the United States, behavioral acculturation includes an overall tendency to speak English, eat American foods, associate with American friends and romantic partners, and read American newspapers, magazines, and websites (Schwartz et al., 2010). The second domain, value acculturation, particularly focused on the relative importance of collectivism and individualism (Schwartz et al., 2010). The third domain, identity acculturation, evaluated solidarity and commitment with one's ethnic group.

Unlike many models of acculturation that believe all domains (e.g., practices, values, and identity) change at the same rate, Schwartz et al. (2010) argued that acculturative changes at each domain do not occur at the same rate or in the same direction. This model elucidated how bicultural endorsement—commonly referred to as integration—can appear in multiple forms (Benet-Martínez & Haritatos, 2005; Rudmin, 2009). For example, an individual may assimilate receiving-cultural practices and integrate values from both cultures, while identifying solely with their ethnic identity (Schwartz et al., 2014). Previous studies have proven that these dimensions do in fact operate independently among immigrant populations (Benet-Martínez & Haritatos, 2005; Schwartz et al., 2010, 2012, 2014; Interiano-Shiverdecker et al., 2019). A study conducted with foreign-born counseling students found that individualistic values and a strong ethnic identity had a positive correlation with counselor self-efficacy, while behavioral acculturation had no relationship to counselor self-efficacy (Interiano-Shiverdecker et al., 2019). Interestingly, a positive relationship between individualistic values and counselor self-efficacy did not indicate a similar pattern with the behavioral or identity acculturation domains. Each acculturation domain operated independently from the others and had different interactions with counselor self-efficacy. Therefore, their integration was multidimensional, as illustrated with Schwartz and colleagues' model. Therefore, defining acculturation, with any foreign-born group, as a singular process that identifies an individual as simply integrated, assimilated, separated, or marginalized oversimplifies a very complex phenomenon (Schwartz et al., 2010).

STRESSORS AND DISCRIMINATION

Foreign-born individuals may experience trauma, psychological distress, and discrimination through three distinct, yet summative, phases of migration: pre-migration, migration, and post-migration. Pre-migration stressors (e.g., trauma, loss of family) and trying to cope with post-migration resettlement (e.g., culture shock, discrimination, language barrier) display a direct relationship with a decline in mental health. Therefore, culturally responsive counselors working with foreign-born clients supplement their knowledge and awareness of their client's experiences to the best of their ability.

Pre-Migration and Migration Stressors

Given the implicit increased potential for traumatic experiences provided by the definition of refugees and asylum-seekers when compared to immigrants, literature has broadly focused on the pre-migration experiences of those leaving their countries of origin due to fear, persecution, and oppression. However, Goodman et al. (2015) found that immigrants were just as likely to experience trauma and stressors before resettlement as refugees and asylum-seekers. Among the most common pre-migration stressors experienced by the foreign-born population are the loss of and separation from home and social support and exposure to traumatic experiences.

Loss of and Separation From Home and Social Support

From the moment displacement begins, foreign-born individuals are faced with the reality of no longer living in the home country they knew, regardless of whether or not their migration was chosen. They also experience a loss of loved ones, either through death or separation, and loss of social support systems, familiar physical environment, and language. Refugees and asylum-seekers who experience persecution, war, and oppression in their country of origin often report overwhelming remorse or survivor's guilt in having left their family, friends, and home environment amid danger and distress, while they instead experience peace and a sense of safety in their host country (Bemak & Chung, 2015). Many refugees and asylum-seekers must also abruptly leave their homes without much notice or time to pack. Forced displacement causes them to leave important documents (e.g., passports, birth certificates), objects of sentimental value (e.g., family jewelry, pictures, videos, pets), and acquired furniture, clothes, and vehicles. Even immigrants who chose and planned their immigration often pack only a limited amount (e.g., two to three bags), leaving most of their belongings in their country of origin due to expensive exportation fees. Additionally, foreign-born individuals often lose the professional status and social prestige they had obtained in their country of origin (Interiano-Shiverdecker et al., 2021). Therefore, foreign-born individuals frequently start from the ground up in the United States. Although their journey can inspire pride, joy, and resilience for many, others also report that numerous losses, incurred as a result of their migration, affect their self-esteem and prompt distress, grief, depression, and anxiety (Ibrahim & Heuer, 2016).

Exposure to Traumatic Experiences

Pre-migration war experiences are highly variable. While not all foreign-born individuals have traumatic experiences, others witness war atrocities, are victims of torture or intimidation, and/or experience food deprivation, separation from family, and disruption of schooling (Pacione et al., 2013). These violations can occur in their home country, during the escape, in refugee camps, and during post-migration, making this population susceptible to mental health problems. Unaccompanied minors are particularly at risk because their migration experiences may include separation from caregivers, exposure to violence and harsh living conditions, poor nutrition, and uncertainty about the future (Brannan et al., 2016; Tello et al., 2017). Recent policies in the United States have, for example, led to the fairly routine separation of children from parents. Moreover, unaccompanied children and adolescents are highly vulnerable to human trafficking (Brannan et al., 2016). In addition, refugee or asylum-seeker claimants may have to undertake lengthy negotiations with the legal system to avoid rejection of their claim and forced repatriation (Ibrahim & Heuer, 2016).

Post-Migration Stressors

As this section will elucidate, foreign-born individuals in America rarely find themselves adjusted to their host country without experiencing a myriad of discriminatory and traumatizing circumstances (Goodman et al., 2015; Sangalang et al., 2018). Immigrants, refugees, and asylum-seekers encounter numerous stressors once resettled in the United States in the form of language barriers, lack of access to services, decreased physical health, deficient social support, family concerns, acculturation, shifts in cultural identity, gender role conflicts, intergenerational conflict within the family, and experiences of discrimination, social ostracization, isolation, and social exclusion (Pacione et al., 2013). Lindencrona et al. (2008) identified pre-migration torture as the strongest predictor of posttraumatic stress disorder (PTSD). However, several scholars (Kim et al., 2018; Cowling et al., 2019; Interiano-Shiverdecker et al., 2021) also found resettlement stressors (i.e., social/economic barriers, discrimination, language barriers) to be predictive of PTSD and depression. The first and second authors of this chapter conducted a four-year, three-state study exploring refugees' resettlement experiences based on individual interviews with 22 refugees and 23 staff members working with this population. In Texas, we found that refugees' experiences of discrimination affected their economic stability, educational attainment, sense of community in the neighborhood and built environments, social and community context, and health and healthcare access (Interiano-Shiverdecker et al., 2021). Most refugees reported high levels of stress attributed to experiences of discrimination in work, educational, and social settings rather than war trauma. Bemak et al. (2003) noted higher post-migration stress among older refugees with more internalized culture norms, unaccompanied children immigrants, widowed women refugees, men 21 years or younger without family support, and female refugees who became the victims of sexual assault and rape during migration. We discuss in detail the most common post-migration stressors in the following sections.

Discrimination and Political Countertransference

Discrimination in the host country can exacerbate feelings of personal rejection and perceived hostility, which, in turn, increases opportunities for retraumatization (Aydin et al., 2014). Discrimination takes covert and overt forms, and while overt discrimination (e.g., "Go back to your own country!") is potentially more threatening and frightening, covert discrimination encounters (e.g., inability to obtain a job due to lack of English proficiency) can often be more arduous to process and move past due to their hidden, elusive, and even systemic natures (Noh et al., 2007). Individuals who experience a potential covert discriminatory action against them often feel confused as to whether it was in fact an act of discrimination, or if, instead, they are the ones to blame (Noh et al., 2007). Regardless, overt and covert instances of racial discrimination, nationality-based discrimination, and religious discrimination have a negative impact on foreign-born individuals' mental well-being (Kim et al., 2018).

Xenophobic perceptions reside on a level broader than individual discrimination and, consequently, have also been linked to negative impacts on mental health (Aydin et al., 2014). Foreign-born individuals who already experience diminished access to resources and limited social connectivity are frequently not only ignored or unaided by systemic factors and legislation but also harmed by them. For example, research by Interiano-Shiverdecker et al. (2021) with refugees and staff members working with this population occurred from 2016 to 2020. Both groups reported direct and indirect negative community and political messages toward refugees (Interiano-Shiverdecker et al., 2021). Participants reported an increase in government rhetoric that demonized or belittled immigrants and refugees and therefore increased fear and anxiety among these groups. Eurocentric and ethnocentric perspectives fostered harmful and untrue beliefs about foreign-born groups, such as all Latinx being "illegal" and all Muslims being "terrorists" (Interiano-Shiverdecker et al., 2021). These collective perspectives and widespread beliefs about immigrant groups seem to instill in native-born Americans a desire to support and voice anti-immigrant policies (Interiano-Shiverdecker et al., 2021). Moreover, a reduction in the refugee annual cap observed during the Trump administration minimized resources for refugees within the country (Interiano-Shiverdecker et al., 2021). Chung et al. (2011) coined the term *political countertransference* to describe a counselor's negative reaction or perception toward foreign-born population clients. Without their choice, counselors in America are surrounded by the same host attitudes that promote falsehoods and myths about migrant populations. Therefore, awareness of political views and beliefs concerning immigration laws and other charged issues is fundamentally essential.

Language, Employment, Educational, and Social Barriers to Integration

As previously discussed, many foreign-born individuals, particularly refugees and asylum-seekers, experience trauma as part of their journey. They see their resettlement in the United States as a long-awaited rest and refuge. Yet, along with pre-migration experiences, discrimination, lack of host language proficiency, unemployment, and barriers to educational attainment all contribute to stressors and risk of (re)traumatization (Interiano-Shiverdecker et al., 2021). The discriminatory experiences faced by foreign-born individuals outlined earlier are added to their social interactions, educational pursuits, professional attainment, and employment endeavors in the United States (Interiano-Shiverdecker et al., 2021).

Scholars have found that language difficulty was at the top of the list as the greatest challenge for many non-English–speaking foreign-born populations (Bemak & Chung, 2015; Interiano-Shiverdecker et al., 2020, 2021). In a national study with refugees, the researchers found that refugees encountered a disadvantage in the job market due to limited language proficiency despite previous education, skills, or experience (Interiano-Shiverdecker et al., 2020, 2021). Moreover, the language barrier negatively affected their ability to thrive in their new environment and interact with community members (Interiano-Shiverdecker et al., 2020, 2021). Some foreign-born individuals understood English in a casual conversational style, yet found it challenging to understand slang terminologies or English in a formal context. Lower levels of English proficiency appeared as predictors of acculturative stress, depression, increased feelings of helplessness and culture shock, and decreased self-worth and social status. Although refugees expressed a desire to improve their English fluency, many, especially refugees with younger children, had to prioritize work above language acquisition (Interiano-Shiverdecker et al., 2020, 2021). Therefore, culturally responsive counselors not only recognize the diversity of language among the foreign-born population, but also acknowledge discrimination based on language, including the oppressive nature of demanding that foreign-born individuals be proficient in the English language.

Many foreign-born individuals, particularly refugees and asylum-seekers, face poor conditions during their first years of resettlement. Many refugees in Texas required donations to meet basic needs (e.g., clothing, diapers, food, hygiene products, school supplies) during their first years of resettlement (Interiano-Shiverdecker et al., 2021). Yet, foreign-born individuals also face several specific barriers to education and employment. Current exploration of refugee resettlement experiences (Interiano-Shiverdecker et al., 2020, 2021) identified the following barriers to employment: (a) language barriers, (b) decreased educational attainment, (c) lack of awareness and access to U.S. resources of support and information, (d) acculturative and adjustment stress, (e) lack of reliable or efficient transportation, and (f) incompatible cultural values. Moreover, a cyclical relationship occurred among English proficiency, education, and work stability. Many refugees required education and English proficiency for employment and upward mobility. However, the full-time work required to afford their life in the United States used up the time and energy they needed to seek educational and language-learning opportunities. Few, if any, degrees, educational accolades, training, specializations, titles, or certifications acquired by foreign-born individuals in their countries of origin are transferrable to the United States. This leaves many individuals with the difficult decision of either returning to school to complete a degree or certification already obtained or going straight into working in jobs for which they are vastly overqualified (Bemak & Chung, 2015). This decision is even harder for refugees who are required to repay the federal assistance provided for their travel and resettlement in the United States. The nontransferability of accreditation, combined with the urgency of financial stability, forces many foreign-born individuals into a downward vocational trajectory as soon as they get established in America. Culturally responsive counselors, therefore, resist generalizations of foreign-born clients as "uneducated" and consider institutional barriers that impede educational attainment or recognition in the United States.

COUNSELING UTILIZATION AND HELP-SEEKING

Culturally responsive counselors understand how culture affects foreign-born individuals' manifestation and conceptualization of mental health, help-seeking behaviors, and treatment expectations (Sue et al., 2019). Multiple barriers exist for foreign-born populations in their utilization of social and mental health services. Foreign-born populations use less than half of the available healthcare resources and are significantly less likely to take prescription drugs than the average U.S. citizen (Lee & Matejkowski, 2012). For instance, one study of Asian and Latino immigrants found that only 6% of immigrants had ever received mental health care, making them 40% less likely than U.S.-born participants to access services (Lee & Matejkowski, 2012). The following section discusses the most common barriers that foreign-born populations experience when seeking treatment.

Conceptualizations of Mental Health and Treatment

It is important to recognize that the Euro-American and Western conceptualization of mental health is not universal and can limit our understanding of mental health across cultures/subcultures. The *Diagnostic and Statistical Manual of Mental Disorders* (5th ed.; *DSM-5*; American Psychiatric Association, 2013) favors Euro-American and Western conceptualizations of mental illness and does not typically include other cultural explanations of illness and health. For example, African refugees who believe that deceased ancestors provide wisdom and guidance may present with symptoms of head pain or insomnia, which they believe are caused by upset ancestral spirits (Bemak & Chung, 2015).

Moreover, several factors may lead foreign-born populations to view counseling as the best means of dealing with mental health problems or to reject a Euro-American perspective to mental health treatment. Some may prefer alternate sources of help rooted in their heritage culture (e.g., priests or imams). Religion and spirituality and religious coping tend to play a central role in help-seeking behaviors among many foreign-born populations (Silva et al., 2017). Some researchers have suggested that foreign-born clients who identify themselves as more religious and who attribute mental illness to religious or supernatural reasons are more likely to engage in religious/spiritual coping and seek help from religious leaders than from counselors (Moreno & Cardemil, 2013). Second, the cultural importance of privacy and protecting the family causes many foreign-born clients to hesitate when speaking about personal or family issues (Sue et al., 2019). For example, many East Asian communities embrace a collective emphasis and place great value on maintaining harmonious relationships among in-group members and protecting the integrity of the group. Face-saving behaviors (i.e., efforts to keep others from losing respect for oneself or to avoid embarrassment) enhance smooth relations among group members (Zane & Yeh, 2002) and may therefore reduce the utilization of services. At the same time, higher satisfaction with one's social support can predict less willingness to seek counseling for mental health problems among foreign-born clients (Bemak & Chung, 2021). Third, greater adherence to heritage-cultural values seems to interfere with psychological help-seeking among foreign-born populations (Masuda et al., 2012). Therefore, utilization of mainstream services is often a last resort and pursued only after exhausting all other cultural treatment modalities.

Fear of Deportation or Impact of Immigration Procedures

Fear of deportation or the impact of immigration procedures further decreases the utilization of medical or government services by foreign-born populations. In particular, undocumented individuals, or citizens with undocumented family members, are even more hesitant to seek help because of concerns that this process might result in the deportation of their spouses, siblings, or other relatives (Derr, 2016). Other immigrants, even those who are permanent legal residents, are afraid that seeking assistance might suggest an inability to live independently or impede their ability to acquire citizenship. Research has shown that fear of deportation also increases the risk for victimization among foreign-born populations. Women who experience abuse by their husbands or who have been sexually assaulted may not seek services (e.g., counseling, medical, legal) about these issues due to fear of deportation (Reina et al., 2014). Undocumented immigrants may be less likely to report abusive labor practices and exploitation by their employers and face increased sexual harassment from supervisors (Fussell, 2011).

In 2020, these concerns became acute for unaccompanied minors. *The Washington Post* (Dreier, 2020) published the story of an unaccompanied minor whose counseling notes were used against him in an immigration court. Whereas the American Counseling Association (ACA; 2014) *Code of Ethics* binds counselors to ethical standards and promotes confidentiality between client and counselor, the Department of Homeland Security implemented limits on privacy rights of undocumented individuals, giving government entities discretion over the collection, use, and dissemination of individually identifiable information (Pierce, 2019). For example, if a counselor reported that a minor struggled with feelings of abandonment from their mother who traveled to the United States undocumented, the court may deem the mother unfit and may choose to detain her (Marzouk, 2016). As a response, the ACA denounced the federal Office of

Refugee Resettlement's sharing of mental health professionals' notes from immigrant youths' counseling sessions as violating the clients' confidentiality.

Communication Difficulties Due to Language Differences

The *ACA Code of Ethics* (2014) clearly states the need for counselors to accommodate clients' language preferences to maintain cultural sensitivity, ensure comprehension, and account for client diversity in areas such as assessment and informed consent. With Spanish being the second most spoken language in the United States, mental health programs are supporting the need to create additional training to provide counseling services in Spanish. A search in 2020 indicated 17 bilingual certificates or concentrations for counselors, of which 10 existed within Council for the Accreditation of Counseling and Related Educational Programs (CACREP)-accredited counseling programs.

While the *ACA Code of Ethics* (2014) mentions the importance of counselors attending to the language preferences of clients, the use of interpreters may be necessary. In general, counselors are appreciative of interpreters and do not perceive any long-term negative effects on the therapeutic progress (Paone & Malott, 2008). Interpreters can connect counselors with clients they otherwise would not be able to effectively communicate with, bridge existing cultural gaps, and educate counselors regarding the client's culture and culturally informed behaviors (Paone & Malott, 2008). Interpreters' cultural knowledge and language can also ensure culturally sensitive care, increase client satisfaction, decrease inappropriate diagnosis and treatment, mediate and advocate for clients, improve clinical outcomes, help clients find resources, and comfort clients by simply having someone who speaks the same language available (Acquah & Beck, 2013; Tribe & Lane, 2009).

Although interpreters can assist counselors in reducing language barriers, there are possible challenges when using an interpreter in counseling that we encourage you to consider. Further miscommunications can occur due to cultural misunderstandings and social class differences (Lipton et al., 2002). When emotions are translated, affect can get "flattened" and the counselor may not recognize or understand the depth of emotion connected to the situation (Lipton et al., 2002). Many counselors and interpreters are not aware of the dynamics involved when another individual is assisting in the therapeutic relationship. Initially, clients may develop a stronger attachment to the interpreter, leaving the counselor feeling "left out." Most interpreters receive little or no training in working with distressed or traumatized individuals, and they may experience emotional distress when hearing traumatic stories (Miller et al., 2005). Without proper training to work in mental health settings, interpreters can also interject their own opinions, intervene directly with clients, or question interventions based on their limited understanding of the counseling process (Miller et al., 2005).

CULTURALLY RESPONSIVE PRACTICES: DRAWING FROM THE MULTICULTURAL AND SOCIAL JUSTICE COUNSELING COMPETENCIES AND CULTURAL HUMILITY

To be effective when working with foreign-born populations, culturally responsive counselors must understand pre-migration factors (e.g., loss, displacement, trauma), post-migration factors (e.g., acculturative stress, discrimination, policy changes), and the client's historical, sociopolitical, cultural, and psychological context. This section delineates a multidimensional model for providing culturally responsive treatment to foreign-born populations. This model incorporates constructs of other models, such as

Bemak and Chung's (2021) Multiphase Model of Psychotherapy, Counseling, Social Justice, and Human Rights (2021); the MSJCC of Ratts et al. (2016); and the Liberation Model (Freire, 1993). This model begins with guidelines that can assist culturally responsive counselors to engage in the client–counselor relationship with cultural humility and develop culturally responsive practices informed by non-Western perspectives of mental well-being. However, this framework also calls on culturally responsive counselors to advocate for the systemic and societal changes required to improve mental well-being among foreign-born populations.

Engaging in the Client–Counselor Relationship With Cultural Humility

From a cultural humility point of view, it is more important to be humble and respectful than to know a lot about a particular culture or group. Competence means rejecting the position of expert to build an equal collaborative partnership with each client. This may present an interesting challenge for the counselor trained for and expected to possess a certain level of cultural knowledge. For example, after reading the large body of literature on refugees and trauma, a counselor might erroneously conclude that all refugees experience trauma and approach treatment from this reference standpoint. Moreover, counselors might assume that all trauma necessarily involves war or death. However, refugees experience trauma on a continuum from war and prosecution to being separated from family, experiencing overall uncertainty, encountering racism and xenophobia, and facing the culture shock of resettlement in a different country. Thus, by assuming a stance of curiosity the counselor can create an opportunity for clients to explore their complex experiences from different (and unexpected) points of view.

Furthermore, a culturally humble counselor should consider the possibility that, for the foreign-born client, trauma may not be as salient as the literature makes it out to be. Not all foreign-born clients experience resettlement as traumatic because for many of them it also means a newfound sense of safety and freedom (Interiano-Shiverdecker et al., 2019). For example, Interiano-Shiverdecker et al. (2019) found discrepancies between refugees and staff members working with them on what was most important for successful resettlement. Staff members emphasized individual factors such as motivation, education level, previous work experience, and English language capacity. Refugees, in contrast, focused more on community and systemic factors such as feeling welcomed by Americans; having American friends to exchange food, customs, and culture with; and having opportunities to learn English, further their education, and make a decent living. Counseling refugees and immigrants with cultural humility means allowing them to discover their path to healing and mental well-being. Instead of assuming what mental health means and what treatment outcomes the client should strive for, a culturally humble counselor would elicit each client's meaning of mental well-being to help that client discover a unique path to happiness and success.

Culturally Responsive Practices and Non-Western Perspectives of Mental Well-Being

Western counseling is largely dominated by a diagnose-and-treat model of mental health disorders. This model requires, first and foremost, the presence of a diagnosis, thus excluding individuals who need psychosocial support but do not meet full diagnostic criteria. This model also relies heavily on funding sources that determine the type, length, and setting of mental health services (Bedi, 2018). Such tight boundaries restrict utilization of services by foreign-born individuals, apply undue pressure, and limit counselors' creativity in designing culturally responsive practices and services (Hayes et al., 2015; Owen et al., 2012). Furthermore, foreign-born individuals from non-Western societies may verbalize and express psychological and emotional suffering by using a somatic language rather than a psychological one (Bemak & Chung, 2015). Using solely Euro-American and Western assessments may not accurately capture and interpret this set of somatic symptoms (Ibrahim & Heuer, 2016; Sue et al., 2019). To close the gap in counseling service utilization, scholars proposed the Culturally Adaptive Counseling Practice (CACP) model, which modifies existing counseling and psychotherapy practices to include indigenous healing practices, cultural values, beliefs, and worldviews. CACP is widely utilized in working with culturally diverse clients and appears to be the most effective in increasing utilization and improving treatment outcomes (Bedi, 2018). More specifically for foreign-born individuals, the Multi-Phase Model (MPM), a form of CACP, emphasizes integrating indigenous healing practices into counseling of refugees who have experienced trauma (Bemak & Chung, 2021). It is a psychological model that includes affective, cognitive, and behavioral interventions, resilience, and prevention. It also considers cultural background, community, and social processes. MPM is comprised of five phases: mental health education, psychotherapy, cultural empowerment, indigenous healing, and social justice and human rights (Bemak & Chung, 2021). This model is based on the idea that counselors should be aware of basic concepts within the refugee's contexts, and it covers other trauma-based models' constructs (Bemak & Chung, 2021). Even so, the MPM promotes the idea that not all indigenous healing practices or indigenous healers are "effective" and that counselors should assess the credibility of indigenous healers before including them in the therapy process (Bemak & Chung, 2021). It is unclear how counselors should evaluate for effectiveness, but the underlying assumption appears to be that Western values and beliefs would serve as the benchmark. Many foreign-born populations come from collectivistic cultures and may perceive and experience Euro-American counseling paradigms that value individualist cultural norms as threatening and inappropriate (Ibrahim & Heuer, 2016; Interiano & Lim, 2018; Sue et al., 2019).

CRAFTING AN ADVOCACY AGENDA

Social justice advocacy for foreign-born individuals begins with an understanding that the very services meant to help them are often culturally insensitive and deeply embedded in biased Euro-American ideals of mental health. Often counseling services do not include careful consideration of oppression and discrimination nor a critical examination of the systemic factors that perpetuate injustice and inequity for foreign-born individuals. Furthermore, mental health professionals are poorly trained in and often resistant to social justice advocacy (Sue et al., 2019). Counselors often lack an understanding and knowledge of how their ethnic values represent a society that is racist and ethnocentric. For example, counselors often fail to recognize that being born in an English-speaking society gives them a significant privilege. Moreover, service providers working with foreign-born individuals are usually operating under the assumption that clients need to learn to speak English and are much less focused on building bilingual programs and expanding translation services (Interiano-Shiverdecker et al., 2019). Furthermore, inequities in social determinants of health such as education, housing, employment, healthcare resources, and power contribute to increased disparities for foreign-born individuals (Interiano-Shiverdecker et al., 2021). For example, refugees have higher rates of distress, limited material resources and social support, poverty discrimination, and devaluation of their cultural practices (Commission on Social

Determinants of Health [CSDH], 2008). Thus, providing counseling services to foreign-born clients is inseparable from engaging in social justice advocacy efforts to eliminate inequities and ensure justice and equity for this population. As explained in a World Health Organization report, levels of mental distress among communities need to be understood less in terms of individual pathology and more as a response to relative deprivation and social injustice, which erode the emotional, spiritual, and intellectual resources essential to psychological well-being (CSDH, 2008). Nevertheless, even the most prominent models of social justice advocacy with foreign-born populations focus heavily on intervening at the individual and family level from a Eurocentric perspective. For example, while the MPM (Bemak & Chung, 2021) promotes the inclusion of indigenous healing practices, it assumes that said practices will be integrated into the existing model of Western psychotherapy, which is inherently individual-bound and limited by systems of diagnosis.

We rely on the MSJCC (Ratts et al., 2016) and Liberation Model (Freire, 1993) to provide practical suggestions for social justice and human rights advocacy with foreign-born populations. The MSJCC suggests that culturally competent counselors strike a balance between intervening at four levels: individual, professional, organizational, and societal. Interventions at the individual level include helping clients gain new insights and learn adaptive behaviors. Most traditional forms of counseling fall within this category. At this level, social justice advocacy efforts can include helping clients understand and label their experiences of discrimination and oppression and dismantle forms of internalized oppression and internalized loci of responsibility and control. For example, counselors could help clients understand their anxiety and depression as a normal reaction to post-migration stress and adverse events involving bullying, exclusion, or microaggressions, rather than as psychiatric disorders. Interventions at the professional level recognize that the counseling profession standards, codes, and ethics are culture-bound.

COUNSELING CHILDREN, ADOLESCENTS, AND YOUNG ADULTS

Considering that more than 2.5 million of the total foreign-born population is under the age of 18 (U.S. Census Bureau, 2019b), it is important to acknowledge specific considerations when working with children, adolescents, and young adults. There are significant stress factors that affect foreign-born youth. Pre-migration and migration problems include witnessing horrific events (e.g., death of family members, war) and difficulties experienced before and throughout their resettlement in the United States (e.g., leaving their home, language barriers, discrimination, adjusting to a new society). The risk factors for poor developmental outcomes among young children are substantial because the effects of immigration trauma can have a particularly damaging impact when the trauma is severe and persistent during the first years of a child's life and when there is no supportive buffer to ameliorate the trauma risk (Bemak & Chung, 2021). Studies show that foreign-born youth experience internalizing behavior problems (e.g., anxiety, depression) and externalizing behavior problems (e.g., aggression) that have long-term negative consequences for psychological, social, and academic success (Hoffman et al., 2018; Mancini, 2019).

Counseling at Schools

Because schools are one of the most important places for children and adolescents, school-based mental health services are ideal to provide easy access for children who have emotional disturbances, enhance psychosocial and academic functioning, and decrease stigma toward mental health treatment (Mancini, 2019; Sullivan & Simonson, 2016). Studies done with refugee and immigrant adolescents showed that trauma and distress have an impact on students' attitudes toward school and discrimination perceptions (Hoffman et al., 2018), while school participation correlated with youth's resilience (Sullivan & Simonson, 2016). Therefore, positive peer relationships in schools enrich students' social-emotional functioning (Sullivan & Simonson, 2016). School-based programs are also beneficial to develop local programs that consider specific cultural and environmental factors (Sullivan & Simonson, 2016). Schools are also important for foreign-born youth because they serve as a stable source for social support while youth adjust to the host culture (Sullivan & Simonson, 2016).

Counseling Approaches Used With Foreign-Born Youth

Culturally responsive counselors consider the following approaches when working with foreign-born youth.

Trauma-Focused Cognitive Behavioral Therapy

Cognitive behavioral approaches focus on thoughts, behaviors, and feelings, and they are mostly goal-oriented. Trauma-focused cognitive behavioral therapy (TF-CBT) is commonly used with children who have had traumatic experiences, and it includes stress management skills, psychoeducation, training for parents, relaxation methods, affective modulation, cognitive processing, and addressing of safety concerns (Sullivan & Simonson, 2016). Lawton and Spencer's (2021) systematic review illustrated that TF-CBT had positive effects on alleviating PTSD, depression, and anxiety symptoms among refugee youth.

Creative Expression Interventions

Creative expression interventions generally incorporate creative elements designed to provide individuals with outlets to express feelings and process emotions by using art, music, drama, or play. This therapeutic approach also makes room for students' trauma processing, establishment of social-emotional skills, and enhancement of academic performance (Sullivan & Simonson, 2016).

Sandplay and Play Therapy

Sandplay and play therapy are client-centered approaches, geared toward children, that integrate play into the therapeutic process. Because sandplay and play therapy are practices that do not rely on language as a primary means of expression, they have direct application as a cross-cultural methodology with foreign-born youth.

Child–Parent Psychotherapy

Child–parent psychotherapy is an evidence-based treatment that integrates multiple approaches (e.g., developmental, psychoanalysis, attachment theories) for children aged birth to 5 years who have been exposed to traumatic events and who are experiencing mental health, attachment, or behavioral problems. Counselors work with the parent or primary caregiver in joint dyadic sessions to facilitate increased emotional and behavioral regulation.

COUNSELING ADULTS, COUPLES, AND FAMILIES

Exposure to different values, attitudes, and behavioral expectations can result in acculturation-based problems among families with different degrees of acculturation (Bemak & Chung, 2015). Common themes when working with foreign-born families include changes in family roles, changes in power dynamics, fear of loss of culture, and the intergenerational impact of trauma (Bemak & Chung, 2021). Due to language barriers, many parents often rely on their children for resource access and communication (Deng & Marlowe, 2013). Traditional ways of parenting, child-rearing, discipline, and punishment may contradict legal practices in the resettlement country, creating additional frustration and stress (Bemak & Chung, 2015; Deng & Marlowe, 2013). As a result, children may lose confidence, trust, and respect for their parents as they witness them transform from autonomous and culturally competent caretakers to individuals who are overwhelmed with trying to learn a new language and customs (Bemak & Chung, 2021; Deng & Marlowe, 2013). Moreover, parent–child acculturation discrepancies can result in strained relationships, a sense of alienation between family members, and changes in family dynamics (Bemak & Chung, 2015; Deng & Marlowe, 2013). Trauma-exposed families may experience emotional and relational difficulties because of experiences in their home country and the changes in adapting to a different environment (Montgomery, 2011). Additionally, parents' own traumatic experiences (and the resultant mental and physical health implications) may also affect their ability to adequately attend to the needs of their children (Montgomery, 2011). Therefore, many foreign-born families seek counseling services when parent–child acculturation discrepancies lead to intergenerational conflicts or produce psychological symptoms among members of the family.

IMPLICATIONS FOR CLINICAL PRACTICE

This section provides implications for counselors to consider based on the information presented in this chapter:

- Examine your own biases and expectations that can detrimentally influence your perceptions of and interactions with individuals who are ethnically and racially different from yourself throughout the assessment and the therapeutic process.
- Be aware of factors that can affect the therapeutic relationship such as the counselor's and client's intersecting identities of privilege and oppression, stigma, location, language barriers, and documentation status.
- Recognize the cultural limitations encountered when applying Euro-American models of counseling with foreign-born populations. These may include (a) lack of standardized translations of instruments, (b) lack of assessments standardized with foreign-born populations, (c) threats of cultural oppression, (d) emphasis on diagnosis, (e) focus on individualistic values, and (f) lack of inclusion of indigenous forms of healing.
- Cultivate alternative approaches to mental health treatment rather than imposing a single Euro-American cultural perspective.
- Consider enlisting the help of individuals who respect and honor their clients' cultural belief systems, such as traditional healers.

CLINICAL CASE SCENARIO 20.1

Farid, an 18-year-old Muslim male from Syria, arrived in Charlotte, North Carolina, in 2014 with his parents, older brother, and younger sister. Due to the conflicts and bombings in Syria, he and his family were forced to flee their home and resettle in Turkey. During this time, he and his family registered with the United Nations Refugee Agency and received refugee status. After many interviews and 3 years of waiting, their application to resettle in the United States was granted. Farid explains that they experienced discrimination in Turkey, where Syrians were often called "beggars" and "criminals" and rejected due to their cultural differences. After 8 months of having resettled in the United States, Farid is happy. He finally feels that his life is stable and can begin to build his life and career. He just started community college and has a part-time job. Although he has accomplished a sense of relief, he also expressed certain challenges during his adjustment. His family finally bought a car after 8 months of not owning one, yet his father must use it to travel to work. Farid and his brother must use public transportation, which is not easily organized in the city, to travel to school and work. Farid has also become aware of negative perceptions of Syrians and Muslims in the United States. He is concerned that people will think he is a "terrorist." He also feels that once again Syrians who enter the United States as refugees are perceived as "beggars." He wishes that people could see how hard he and his family are working to rebuild their lives in the United States. He states, "We came here with nothing. It's not that easy to rebuild your life in a completely different country."

CLINICAL CASE SCENARIO DISCUSSION QUESTIONS

1. What is Farid's immigrant status?
2. How would your intervention and advocacy efforts look in helping Farid?

END-OF-CHAPTER RESOURCES

A robust set of instructor resources designed to supplement this text is located at http://connect.springerpub.com/content/book/978-0-8261-3953-5. Qualifying instructors may request access by emailing textbook@springerpub.com.

SUMMARY

This chapter provided an overview of the foreign-born population in the United States, comprised of documented and undocumented immigrants, refugees, and asylum-seekers. Foreign-born individuals migrate to the United States for several reasons. Yet, the rise of political, socioeconomic, and natural crises occurring around the world has led to the forced displacement of a concerning number of individuals and families, many of which seek refuge in the United States. Foreign-born clients are exposed to multiple stressors before, during, and after their migration. Although many are significantly affected by the horrific events that led to their displacement, immigrants, refugees, and asylum-seekers are subject to individual, institutional, and societal prejudice and discrimination. In particular, individuals with visible cultural differences (i.e., race, ethnicity, religion) experience more instances of racism and discrimination than do those who resemble the majority culture. Recent increases in anti-immigrant rhetoric and policies provoke fear and unease within all immigrant communities. Social and institutional barriers create social inequities in access to healthcare, education, economic opportunities, and community connection and acceptance. Culturally responsive counselors must recognize their own biases toward this group, enter the therapeutic relationship with cultural humility, and consider linguistic issues, pre-migration loss and trauma, post-migration stress and discrimination, barriers and factors affecting access to mental health, culturally responsive interventions, and social justice and advocacy when working with immigrants, refugees, and asylum-seekers.

DISCUSSION QUESTIONS

1. What did you learn about the foreign-born population in this chapter that surprised you?
2. As a culturally responsive counselor, how did this chapter better prepare you to work with foreign-born clients?
3. What individual, community, and sociopolitical factors are important to consider when working with immigrants, refugees, or asylum-seekers?
4. After reading this chapter, what do social justice and advocacy mean for immigrants, refugees, and asylum-seekers?

KEY REFERENCES

Only key references appear in the print edition. The full reference list appears in the digital product on Springer Publishing Connect: https://connect.springerpub.com/content/book/978-0-8261-3953-5/part/part02/chapter/ch20

American Counseling Association. (2014). *2014 ACA Code of Ethics.* Author. https://www.counseling.org/resources/aca-code-of-ethics.pdf

Bemak, F., & Chung, R. C.-Y. (2015). Counseling refugees and migrants. In P. B. Pedersen, W. J. Lonner, J. G. Draguns, J. E. Trimble, & M. R. S. Rio (Eds.), *Counseling across cultures* (pp. 323–346). Sage.

Bemak, F., & Chung, R. C.-Y. (2021). Contemporary refugees: Issues, challenges, and a culturally responsive intervention model for effective practice. *The Counseling Psychologist, 49*(2), 305–324. https://doi.org/10.1177/0011000020972182

Bemak, F., Chung, R. C.-Y., & Pedersen, P. B. (2003). *Counseling refugees: A psychological approach to innovative multicultural interventions.* Greenwood Press.

Berry, J. W. (1997). Immigration, acculturation, and adaptation. *Applied Psychology: An International Review, 46*(1), 5–34. https://doi.org/10.1111/j.1464-0597.1997.tb01087.x

Chung, R. C.-Y., Bemak, F., & Grabosky, T. K. (2011). Multicultural-social justice leadership strategies: Counseling and advocacy with immigrants. *Journal for Social Action in Counseling & Psychology, 3*(1), 86–102. https://doi.org/10.33043/JSACP.3.1.86-102

Interiano, C. G., & Lim, J. H. (2018). A "chameleonic" identity: Foreign-born doctoral students in U.S. counselor education. *International Journal for the Advancement of Counselling, 40*(3), 310–325. https://doi.org/10.1007/s10447-018-9328-0

Interiano-Shiverdecker, C. G., Foxx, S. P., & Flowers, C. (2019). Acculturation domains and counselor self-efficacy. *Journal of Professional Counseling, 46*(1–2), 48–63. https://doi.org/10.1080/15566382.2019.1669373

Interiano-Shiverdecker, C. G., Hahn, C. D., McKenzie, C. A., & Kondili, E. (2021). Refugees, Discrimination, and Barriers to Health. *Journal of Professional Counseling, 48*(2), 91–105. https://doi.org/10.1080/15566382.2021.1947106

Interiano-Shiverdecker, C. G., Kondili, E., & Parikh-Foxx, S. (2020). Refugees and the system: Social and cultural capital during U.S. Resettlement. *International Journal for the Advancement of Counselling, 42*(1), 48–64. https://doi.org/10.1007/s10447-019-09383-9

Ratts, M. J., Singh, A. A., Nassar-McMillan, S., Butler, S. K., & McCullough, J. R. (2016). Multicultural and social justice counseling competencies: Guidelines for the counseling profession. *Journal of Multicultural Counseling and Development, 44*(1), 28–48. https://doi.org/10.1002/jmcd.12035

Sue, D. W., Sue, D., Neville, H. A., & Smith, L. (2019). *Counseling the culturally diverse: Theory & practice* (8th ed.). John Wiley & Sons.

CHAPTER 21

Culturally Responsive Counseling for Military Clients and Families

GIGI HAMILTON AND CORI MARIE COSTELLO

> **LEARNING OBJECTIVES**
>
> After reading this chapter, students will be able to:
> - Recognize the uniquely impactful aspects of military culture on the service member, veterans, and their families.
> - Identify the intersectionality of the service member's individual culture, developmental, emotional, and familial lenses.
> - Assess the impact of military stressors and discrimination on the service member, veterans, and their families, and apply social justice and advocacy.
> - Demonstrate applications of cultural competencies and cultural humility.
> - Create an advocacy agenda that serves military service members, veterans, and families through a multicultural, social justice, and sociopolitical perspective.

> **SELF-REFLECTION QUESTIONS**
>
> 1. Think about biases, prejudices, and assumptions you might have about military clients and families. How do these help and hinder your ability to provide culturally sensitive counseling?
> 2. What hesitancies, if any, do you have about working with military clients and families?
> 3. What attributes do you have that will enable you to work with military clients and families?
> 4. Are you familiar with military rankings and how they might help you assess your military client's presenting problem?

This chapter explores how counselors can address the duality of culture for military service members, veterans, and families, as it relates to their personal, relational, and collective experiences. The clinical goal is to provide support from a multicultural, social justice, and sociopolitical perspective. Through comprehension of the unique mental health needs of military personnel and their families, counselors can integrate cultural responsiveness and competence into the therapeutic relationship and the counseling process. By exploring the intersectionality of the military service member's cultural lens with the distinctive cultural experiences present in military life, this examination seeks to strengthen and support clinical approaches that honor and value the power of the diverse viewpoints. The counselor may strengthen social justice and advocacy outlooks by utilizing culturally responsive interventions and therapeutic approaches with service members, veterans, and families.

The exploration begins by discussing the clinical role of the counselor through investigation, introspection, and reflection of the ethical and professional considerations necessary for counseling military service members, veterans, and families. As we better understand service members' worldviews and perspectives, we recognize the dichotomies of culture that exist for military service members and their families. By understanding the stressors and discrimination present within military culture, the authors utilize strengths-based approaches to support military service members, veterans, and families. Likewise, the liberation counseling framework and life-course theory approaches are discussed to educate counselors how to work from a clinical perspective with this population.

Next, the writers offer their review of culturally responsive approaches that enhance multicultural and social justice practices through counseling competencies and cultural humility. A review of the processes through which members of the military might seek counseling or ask for help is included. By understanding current systems available for mental health support, effective advocacy agendas may be crafted. Finally, this chapter explores counseling approaches for family members such as children, adolescents, and young adults and examines approaches for clinical support of the military service member and the considerations of family dynamics in clinical treatment.

One author is a mental health counselor with three years of military service, who identifies as a woman and veteran with extensive mental health counseling training. The other author identifies as a woman who is a civilian with some knowledge of and training in the military world, and has extensive mental health counseling training. This variety of experience allows the authors to review the military counseling experience with some depth; however, we acknowledge that there are other perspectives not represented in this discussion. There may be other counselors who have not had any military experience. We have chosen to utilize our various lenses of experiences with the military to better inform the broad range of counselors who may work with this unique population.

THE COUNSELOR: EXPLORATION, INTROSPECTION, AND REFLECTION

What would you do if a 25-year-old African American woman Sergeant First Class E7 entered your counselor's office dressed in her military uniform? Note that she chose you because your office is located off base, to avoid anyone identifying her seeking mental health services. Although her uniform might be unnerving, the battle dress uniform (BDU) is her daily standardized uniform. The soldier is wearing camouflage trousers and a jacket (known as "fatigues") and beige "coyote brown" combat boots (matching the uniform) that made little sound on your linoleum floor. You notice that her last name and rank insignia are listed on the jacket, and you recognize the U.S. flag emblem on the right shoulder patch flap of the jacket, and her unit patch is worn on the left shoulder. Where would you start—putting yourself at ease, or the military client facing you?

Believe it or not, your work began without you knowing it. The head-to-toe observation of your client is the beginning of the mental status examination. You noticed that the service member's stature is poised, her affect is flat, and her demeanor is detached. Her facial expression is stoic, teeth are clenched, and her body posture is stern. There was no sound when the service member entered the room. You took a few deep breaths to overcome the trepidation and awe you felt. When a counselor has no military training, the military client is imposing, powerful, and commanding. Simply direct the client to the couch where you notice the service member sit down with gentle authority. It will not be uncommon for the military client to scan the room with apprehension and limited trust in the clinical space.

There is an unspoken contradiction in the military about mental health (Vogt, 2011). The military speaks of the need for mental health support, but the stigma of receiving mental health treatment is viewed as "weakness," which deters the pursuit of seeking mental health support (Sanchez-Bustamante, 2021). The service member is cognizant that coming to see a counselor does not look good for them and might consider many questions such as, *"If I have a mental health issue, will I be kicked out of the military?" "How will this impact my military occupational specialty (MOS)?" "Will my chain of command be notified that I am here?" "What if I cannot be fixed?" "Does Duty to Warn work in this case?" "What if the counselor reports the information I share to my commanding officer (CO)?"*

A counselor who uses culturally responsive interventions knows that the best way to begin a session is by introducing themselves and giving enough information to invite the military client to do the same. When the two are acquainted, the counselor might review the professional disclosure statement, being sure to acknowledge the limits of confidentiality in counseling. This is where the counselor speaks about their therapeutic philosophy and informs the client of their level of awareness of military life. Whether the counselor has limited experience or vast, they work to practice cultural humility where they are always open to learning about and from the client. The counselor continues to build trust in the relationship by listening to what and how the service member communicates. The service member slowly exhales, and her shoulders relax. The clinical mental health relationship, between the counselor and the service member, has begun.

Exploration

Exploring the diversity in the military is essential to supporting the military client. As such, to be most effective counselors must understand the experiences of clients' military life and their service to the country. According to Cole (2014), recognizing the military's overt and covert cultural norms aids in providing support and unconditional positive regard. This military experience includes unique practices, traditions, and beliefs, as well as understanding the unifying language and guiding philosophies that support the military branch served.

There is a duality in the soldier's culture as it resides within the military life culture. According to Sue et al. (1992), the diversification of America makes it essential for counselors to be intentional about cultural diversity. There is a critical need to support military personnel from their unique cultural lens. To be most effective in this supporter role, mental health professionals must honor the conflicts between service to the country and personal cultural experiences that may occur as they reside within the confines of mental health.

Cultural proficiency within the mental health setting requires providers to be aware of their attitudes about diverse cultural groups, maintain knowledge about the diverse cultural groups they serve, and engage, promote, and advocate for the well-being of people from diverse cultural groups (Betancourt, 2003). Military culture is governed by dichotomous norms with a military–civilian divide. This formally structured cultural group is governed by norms that rest in a collective of *we* but is different from *us*. The collective goals of the government exist, but we are individuals as well.

As culturally responsive clinicians, we must take steps to understand the military experience from which our clients may come. To be culturally knowledgeable, clinicians must be aware of three approaches of concern. The first is an attitudinal approach that involves the provider's belief about a particular cultural group. The next approach is cognitive competence, which pertains to the provider's knowledge about military culture and the structural system of military life. Finally, behavioral competence refers to the provider's skill set in assessing and treating military members and veterans (Atuel & Castro, 2018). Culturally competent clinicians are aware of their own racial biases and the existence of institutional racism at various levels (Sue, 2001). Within different systems of care, clinicians are knowledgeable of the culture of their client, and are equipped with culturally appropriate treatments. Clinicians are also engaged in both therapeutic and advocacy work for their clients.

The White House has been working with both the Department of Defense (DOD) and the Department of Veterans Affairs (VA) to ensure that mental health professionals and programs are dispersed within veteran communities to address mental health needs. However, the capacity for support is far exceeded by the demands for service. As part of ongoing efforts to improve all facets of military mental health, President Obama enacted an executive order that directs the Secretaries of Defense, Health and Human Services, Education, Veterans Affairs, and Homeland Security to expand suicide prevention strategies and take steps to meet the current and future demand for mental health and substance abuse treatment services for veterans, service members, and their families (Obama, 2012).

Currently, the DOD provides a variety of counseling options for all active-duty, National Guard, and reserve service members, survivors, designated DOD expeditionary civilians, and their families. The military services include *Installation's Chaplains* who are chaplains in military units that are trained counselors and offer spiritual guidance. The next option is the *Combat Stress Control Teams*, which are available as a field resource support during deployment. *Nonmedical Counseling Resources* provide confidential, short-term counseling with service providers, who provide therapeutic interventions seeking to address life adjustment issues and concerns. The system is set so that mental health information may be reported to other social services and the soldier's military unit if needed.

The two primary resources for nonmedical counseling services are *Military OneSource* (www.militaryonesource.mil) and the *Military and Family Life Counseling Program* (www.militaryonesource.mil/confidential-help/non-medical-counseling/military-and-family-life-counseling/the-military-and-family-life-counseling-program). Nonmedical counseling services are available face-to-face, by telephone, online, and in video. The *Family Advocacy Program* is a supportive resource for service members and their families (www.militaryonesource.mil/family-relationships/family-life/preventing-abuse-neglect/the-family-advocacy-program). The program provides support and resources to help families develop and sustain healthy, strong relationships.

Mental health treatment for veterans whose service is completed is run by the U. S. VA, providing counseling at Veterans Centers. The military also currently maintains *Tricare*, which is charged with providing lifelong healthcare services to military veterans at VA medical centers and clinics. The VA provides counselors that are embedded within the system to provide mental health support for veterans. Due to a very high demand for services, the VA is outsourcing mental health support of veterans to civilian mental health clinicians.

CLIENT WORLDVIEW AND PERSPECTIVES

The military maintains its own identity, belief systems, resources, and command structure through which it is defined as a culture. According to Hajjar (2013), *culture* is "a contested toolkit or repertoire filled with tools schemas [cognitive structures], frames, codes, narratives, habits, styles, language, symbols, values, beliefs, and assumptions that provide a group, organization, institution, or society with shared meaning, collective identities and orientations, and strategies of action" (p. 119). Other considerations related to cultural constructs are having a common set of beliefs, norms, functions, and shared values, and largely learned attributes of a group of people, according to the Substance Abuse and Mental Health Services Administration (SAMHSA; 2014a).

Anthropologists often describe culture as a system of shared meanings, and individuals who may be placed into a group, either by census categories or through self-identification, are often assumed to share the same culture (Kleinman & Benson, 2006). The military is defined as a culture because it has its own missions, values, language, and organizational and sociopolitical structure, according to the SAMHSA (2010).

The military service culture's scope is widespread throughout various communities around the United States. According to the United States DOD (2017), there are 1.3 million military active-duty personnel and 800,000 reserve forces. In his Fiscal Year 2020 posture statement on March 26, 2019, General Milley noted how busy the Army is by "providing Combatant Commanders over 179,000 Soldiers in more than 140 countries, including 110,000 Soldiers deployed on a rotational basis" (Cancian, 2019, p. 4). Of these troops, Milley highlighted that 30,000 were in the Middle East and Afghanistan, 17,000 were forward-deployed in South Korea, and 8,000 were in Europe supporting the European Deterrence Initiative. In 2001, the U.S. Armed Forces participated in three operations in the Middle East: Operation Iraqi Freedom (OIF), Operation Enduring Freedom (OEF), and Operation New Dawn (OND; Institute of Medicine, 2010). More than 2.2 million service members were deployed during these operations (Institute of Medicine, 2013).

The various branches of the military are discussed here so that readers can better understand the scope of the U.S. Armed Services. The U.S. Armed Forces include five branches: The Army is the largest and oldest service in the U.S. military, and provides the ground forces that protect the United States. The Navy serves the United States on, above, and below the water, and serves as a deterrent around the world. The Air Force serves as flexible and lethal air and space capacity to deliver forces anywhere in the world. The Marines are a component of the Department of the Navy and maintain amphibious and ground units for combat operations. The Coast Guard provides law and maritime safety enforcement, marine and environmental protection, and military naval support (Bushatz, 2021).

The U.S. Space Force is the newest military branch, created in December 2019 under the guidance of the Secretary of the Air Force. The Space Force organizes, trains, and equips space forces to protect the United States and allied interests in space and space capabilities to the joint forces. The Army National Guard and the Air National Guard are reserve components of the military services and operate under state authority (Bushatz, 2021).

Individuals who serve in the military do so for a variety of reasons. According to Kilburn and Klerman (2001), service members join the armed forces for many purposes, including socioeconomic concerns; a family history of service, honor, and respect that is earned through patriotic service; to learn discipline; to avail themselves of job training that is offered or benefits that are provided; to have adventures or opportunities gained through military travel or experiences; or to escape a negative environment.

Members of this military culture understand and experience combat training, disaster response drills, and executing war tactics as a standard way of life. With the mindset and spirit of a warrior, service members in the military remain committed to a common mission which may be a matter of life or death (Dalessandro, 2009). Because of this embedded viewpoint regarding the mission, service members carry a variety of unique, diverse experiences that may also affect safety and wellness. According to Pflanz and Ogle (2006), there is a growing amount of data to suggest that "work stress may be a significant occupational health hazard in the military, affecting both the emotional and physical health of our troops as well as mission performance" (p. 864). Military service members learn early on in their careers the importance of balancing their daily job duties with their emotional well-being (SAMHSA, 2010).

Military service members may be hesitant to seek out mental health support. There is stigmatization connected with receiving mental health services, which lead to service members having a higher degree of discomfort in discussing potential psychological problems (Ahmedani, 2011).

Other reasons for the apprehension about receiving mental health services may include a belief that psychological issues are a sign of weakness, fear of the negative impact on career, or concern that a higher-ranking superior may judge or label the service member upon gaining access to mental health records (Army Behavioral Health, U.S. Army Medical Department, 2013). Duty and camaraderie equate to macro-level peer pressure and create powerful motivators that encourage service members to avoid seeking professional mental health care. Many service members carry the fear of their superiors potentially losing confidence in their ability to effectively perform their duties. There is concern that the superior may worry about a service member being unable to fulfill their duties.

It is also believed that the culture of the military motivates people to avoid seeking help from medical professionals for mental health concerns (Kulesza et al., 2015). Service members may also face negative consequences with their chain of command if they are *unfit for duty*, as being labeled as unfit for duty can result in the loss of security clearances or can lead to a medical discharge from the military (Weiss et al., 2011). Having a negative label of a mental illness could be considered an occupational hazard, which can be severe, have a seriously negative impact on the service member, and create a variety of concerns requiring even more mental health support and guidance. In preparing for physical and psychological battle or mortal combat readiness, service members are trained to weather any difficulties to be combat-ready. Military-specific mental health concerns include anxiety and mood disorders, posttraumatic stress disorder (PTSD), addiction, sexual assault, and suicide (Reisman, 2016).

Deployments and any transitions of the service member and their families, as well as the processes of reintegration and environmental stressors related to deployment (Reed-Fitzke & Lucier-Greer, 2020) are all impactful events that may lead to mental health struggles or concerns of service members. *Deployment* is the act of moving military service members to a place or a position to conduct military action. Sometimes the military action can lead to traumatic events both directly and indirectly. When service members return home, this transitional act is called *reintegration*. Reintegration includes coming back home to the local community and family. There is a physical transition that occurs by returning home for the military service member. Additionally, there is an emotional transition that occurs for both the military service member and the service member's family.

With the high number of service members active in the military, the need for mental health support is overwhelming the current military system. According to the U.S. VA (n.d.-b), the Veterans Health Administration operates the nation's largest integrated healthcare delivery system, providing care to nearly 9 million enrolled veteran patients. The VA health services can be viewed as a fully functioning integrated healthcare system which provides primary medical care, medical specialty, and mental health services. The services are designed to provide inclusive and expansive medical and mental services within one area of service.

Because of the extreme need for additional support, community mental health professionals are answering the call to assist in working with the military population. According to Tanielian, Farris, Batka, Farmer, Robinson, Engel, Robbins, and Jaycox, "this raises a new concern about the capacity of the civilian mental health service sector to meet the needs of veterans and their families" (Tanielian et al., 2014, p. 1). It is critical to have properly trained and culturally aware counselors serving the needs of the military and its veterans. There have been nationwide endeavors to increase understanding of military- and veteran-related issues among community-based mental health counselors.

As a result of these ventures, mental health counselors understand that the military population has its own unique cultural system, which is multifaceted and intersects with other cultural populations (Ratts et al., 2016). Working with the military's diverse populations requires proper cultural understanding for clinical effectiveness. Understanding that military service members operate from a military cultural construct is one facet of this cultural awareness. It is also important to learn more about the service member's, veteran's, or family member's unique cultural background regarding their beliefs, values, and interests.

THE DUALITY OF CULTURES

One of the most notable changes in the military culture of the 21st century is that there is no homogeneous cultural group identified as the "military culture" (Dunivin, 1994). There are various racial and ethnic groups, including Hispanic Latinx, African American, Native American, Asian American, and other cultural groups serving in the military. More recently identified within the military culture is the lesbian, gay, bisexual, and transgender community (Barroso, 2019). This is in sharp contrast to previous generations of military personnel and their demographic identities.

In the United States, the racial and ethnic minority demographics have grown steadily in recent years. According to Noe-Bustamante et al. (2020), there are 60 million Hispanics in the United States. Reviewing the racial and ethnic profile of active-duty service members shows that while most of the military is non-Hispanic White, Black and Hispanic adults represent sizable and growing shares of the armed forces (Noe-Bustamante et al., 2020). Individuals are increasingly identifying their cultures in more recent years, and Hispanics/Latinx have increased their participation in the U.S. military two times as much as other cultures (Noe-Bustamante et al., 2020).

As we explore the ever-changing demographics of the activity duty military, we are cognizant of the subgroup changes as well. The military culture maintains various within-group differences based on military specialty: occupation, geographic location, combat versus noncombat units, deployment for humanitarian missions, hostile geographic locations, within or outside the continental United States, and allied nations, as well as cultural differences in ranking officers versus enlisted and noncommissioned officer ranks. These subgroups add more diversity to a highly diverse cultural experience.

When a person joins the military, the new service member becomes acclimated to cultural norms that are quite different from what they experienced growing up. The culture in which an individual grows up has rules, customs, and values. In joining the military, the service member must learn a completely new culture and adapt to, live, and enact the new cultural norms. Adaptation occurs when the service member learns and adapts through integration of the presented values. However, difficulty occurs when the learned values are contradictory to the service member's original norms or values and the service member cannot integrate those values. In order to work effectively with military service members, veterans, and their families, it is paramount to have an understanding of the duality of cultures.

Bouchard (2011) purports that multiculturalism and interculturalism reside within two different cultural constructs. Bouchard believes that multiculturalism lives within the structure of diversity, in that individuals and groups have equal status and there is no recognition of majority culture. Interculturalism is believed to operate from a duality paradigm where diversity is embedded by virtue of relationships between minorities and a cultural majority that could be described as foundational (Bouchard, 2011).

The duality of cultures is "a global model for social integration[;] interculturalism takes shape principally within the duality paradigm. One of the inherent traits of this philosophy is having a keen awareness of the majority/minority relationship and the tensions associated with it" (Bouchard, 2011, p. 445). The blending of military culture with one's intercultural experiences must be understood in order to be effective in providing culturally relevant clinical care. The blending of culture can place an individual in difficult and uncomfortable situations, and lead to contradictions of the person's belief system. This leads to the construct of a moral injury.

Moral Injury

A *moral injury* may be defined in various ways, including as what occurs when someone does something that goes against that individual's beliefs (Griffin et al., 2019). In traumatic or stressful situations, individuals may witness, perpetuate, or fail to prevent events that contradict their deeply held moral beliefs and expectations. When someone does something that goes against their beliefs, it may be referred to as an act of commission; when they fail to do something in line with their beliefs, that is often considered an act of omission (Shay, 2014).

This type of injury may be seen in the context of feeling betrayed by leadership or others with power in a way that resulted in adverse outcomes. As a result, moral injury may occur. A moral injury occurs in response to acting or witnessing behaviors, or even after the event when the individual is in the process of making sense and integrating a situation that is not in alignment with their values and moral beliefs (Litz et al., 2009).

The term *moral injury* originated in the writings of Camillo Bica, a Vietnam War veteran, according to Brock and Lettini (2012). The construct of moral injury applies when an individual is faced with confusing lessons that challenge their identity, leading to a personal identity crisis, according to Norman and Maguen (2021). In the military, the nature of war and combat creates experiences for military personnel that contradict the values of civilian life. Within the military, a moral injury may manifest as a distressing psychological, behavioral, social, and sometimes spiritual aftermath of exposure to such events. A moral injury may also occur upon transitioning out of the military and returning to civilian life. In traumatic or unusually stressful circumstances, people may perpetrate, fail to prevent, or witness events that contradict deeply held moral beliefs and expectations (Griffin et al., 2019).

LIBERATION COUNSELING FRAMEWORK FOR MILITARY SERVICE MEMBERS AND VETERANS

Clinical treatment of the moral injury that arises from the duality of culture should include a focus on and understanding of oppression leading to growth, development, and resilience.

Liberation psychology/counseling was first articulated by Ignacio Martín-Baró (Aron & Corne, 1994) and has been further developed in significant ways by others such as Martiza Montero from Venezuela (Montero, 2009). Liberation counseling was created for and on behalf of those who are oppressed. Throughout these therapeutic counseling frameworks, the central theme focuses on the professional intention and the practice on the lived experience of the poor and oppressed from the perspective of a social justice approach (Tate et al., 2013).

Clinicians who utilize the framework of liberation counseling engage in clinical practice to heal individuals and groups. They honor clients' inner strength and promote resilience. This framework acknowledges the confluence of clients' internal world with the systemic sociopolitical forces affecting health and well-being. As practitioners deal with the duality of cultures and create the best approaches to assist military service members, their families, and veterans, liberation counseling will be one of the foundational constructs utilized to assist with personal and emotional growth and development for this population. Liberation psychology takes the view that many negative patterns have their origins in oppressive social conditions, and emphasizes the importance of changing these social conditions.

Changing social conditions within the context of military service experiences or addressing issues that occurred while serving in the military involves changing the structural patterns, mechanisms, or thoughts of control that create oppressive social conditions. How such change can happen, what role individuals and groups can play in that change, and how to be effective and prevent frustration and despair are some of the questions that require further attention (Moane, 2003).

Liberation practitioners work in a collaborative and participatory manner with oppressed people and populations. They place individuals in multiple contexts, including cultural, historical, gender, sexual orientation, sociopolitical, geopolitical, and other intersecting factors. In this way, liberation psychologists recognize the impact of the confluence of context, history, social location, and power–powerlessness on health and well-being (Comas-Díaz & Torres Rivera, 2020).

The principles of liberation counseling are reorientation of psychology, recovering historical memory, deideologizing everyday experience, virtues of the people, problematization, conscientization, praxis, and transformation of the social scientist (Tate et al., 2013). Martín-Baró (Aron & Corne, 1994) argued that Eastern psychology had very little to offer in terms of addressing the oppressive circumstances of marginalized populations. Therefore, he posited that for psychology to be relevant to the mental health concerns that individuals deal with, psychology must be reoriented toward the lived experience of those who contend with the most severe and intense conditions. For many populations, history is typically written by the oppressors (Mohatt et al., 2014). Recovering historical memory is based on the notion that marginalized populations need to be rediscovered by discussing their shared history. Having an understanding of combined historical content can allow one to discover challenges and opportunities that have been collectively created over time.

According to Tate et al. (2013), without an understanding of the actual etiology of the oppression and subsequent conditions, true understanding from the perspective of the oppressed cannot be attained. Deideologizing everyday experience speaks to the created spoken and unspoken realities that have been developed about oppressed populations. As such, Martín-Baró (Aron & Corne, 1994) posited that a key step in achieving a socially just and mentally healthy context for these populations was to investigate these dominant messages while considering the lived experiences of those living on the margins. Within the role of liberation counseling, the counselor acknowledges the past sociocultural conditions that led to these current stressors.

Virtues of the people as a practice stem from utilizing the current virtues the oppressed currently possess to ameliorate their current experiences. This strengths-based approach allows the social scientist to depend on those who are oppressed to produce the tools and energy that may lead to liberation (Tate et al., 2013). Utilizing the virtues already applied and showing how they can continue to be used as coping tools for continued emotional growth is a form of liberation.

Problematization is the construct derived from understanding the issues the oppressed may face from their perspective. In short, problematization focuses on the content of recovered historical memory, a deideologized understanding of current circumstances, and knowledge of a people's virtues, and the application of those understandings to a particular issue that a group of oppressed individuals is experiencing in a specific context. The professionals utilizing liberation psychology seek to present "problems" in terms of conflicts between the lived experience of the affected individuals and their beliefs about what should be (Aron & Corne, 1994).

Conscientization, the Spanish word for critical consciousness, is the main principle of liberation counseling. In other words, to become conscious of reality in this sense is to become aware of, and involved in, a process of continual discovery and action related to "truth." Through rediscovering historical memory, deideologizing understandings of cultural truths, discovering the virtues of the people, and applying this knowledge to specific contexts and lived experiences through problematization, the process of critical consciousness emerges and is maintained (Tate et al., 2013).

Praxis is another foundational construct of liberation counseling. It is the convergence of theory and action. The critical consciousness that arises from reclaiming one's history, deideologizing understandings of cultural truths, discovering the virtues of the people, and using that as a method for making sense of current oppressive circumstances (i.e., problematization) is only made "real" when it is applied in action to current lived experiences in the effort to liberate self and others from these circumstances (Tate et al., 2013).

Transformation of the social scientist occurs when utilizing all these principles. The liberation counselor must be invested, not only for the client, but also with buy-in on a personal level as well. For psychology to be "true," it must come from the engaged, praxis-based perspective of those it purports to describe and help. This requires that the social scientist's role "becomes that of a convener, a witness, a co-participant, a mirror, and a holder of faith for process through which those who have been silenced may discover their capacities for historical memory, critical analysis, utopian imagination, and transformative social action" (Watkins & Shulman, 2008, p. 26).

Another important element of liberation psychology is the understanding of how individuals become oppressed. Liberation psychology also addresses the intersection of social ramifications of oppression and the psychological behaviors associated with oppressive implications (Comas-Díaz & Torres Rivera, 2020). According to Moane (2003), "psychological patterns such as a sense of inferiority or helplessness ... clearly have their origins in social conditions of powerlessness and degradation ... . Thus, liberation must involve the transformation of the psychological patterns" (p. 92).

It is believed that regardless of the theoretical and professional orientation, one can incorporate liberation psychology into one's work. The cornerstone of liberation psychology is that it is about action (Comas-Díaz & Torres Rivera, 2020). As liberation practitioners, we can engage in microaggressions during therapy when we define oppression for clients, instead of listening to our clients' definitions of oppression. If we engage in radical humility and practice authentic collaboration, this practice reduces the experiences of clinical microaggressions. In other words, we need to become aware of how we can harm when we fail to accompany clients on their journey by not developing collaborative and/or participatory relationships (Comas-Díaz & Torres Rivera, 2020).

Liberation psychology in clinical work with service members, veterans, and their families supports their inner strength and resilience. This framework acknowledges the strength, courage, and bravery relevant within the individual's internal world while recognizing the systemic sociopolitical forces affecting health and well-being related to military life.

LIFE-COURSE THEORY FOR MILITARY SERVICE MEMBERS AND VETERANS

While working with the military population, one blanket counseling or theoretical model cannot and should not be utilized to try and help everyone. The many unique factors a service member deals with, which include their inter- and intracultural underpinnings, and war-time experiences, as well as past familial and developmental experiences on a basic continuum, and the service member's age should all be considered as important aspects in the decision of how best to assist a client during the counseling process. To assist military personnel, their families, and veterans to the best of one's ability, it is important to understand how the life-course theory can play a significant role in revealing the developmental, psychological, structural, and emotional context of their lives. A life-course perspective acknowledges that the trajectory from birth to death is highly personal and unique to each person, and yet also contains experiences and events common to most members of a social group (Davey, 2001). The life structure is an ecological construct: a composite of the person; their physical, social, and cultural context; and the relationship between the person and the immediate world of which that person is a part. For counselors, this is a useful framework for military personnel and families because it allows attention to be focused, as appropriate, on the individual, on external factors, or on relationships (Sugarman, 2004).

Before delving into the life-course process, it is imperative to examine Erik Erikson's stages of psychosocial development, which he created in the 1950s. Erikson, trained as a psychologist, expanded upon Freud's psychosexual development ideas (Erikson, 1964). He posited that each stage of life development can embody either a positive or negative psychological propensity. In his psychosocial theory of human development, Erikson (1964, 1985) introduced a conception of ego virtues or ego strengths. The terms "virtue" and "strength" appear to be used interchangeably by Erikson, and seem to imply instinctual, inherent, and internal strengths gained only by healthy individuals.

Knowing where a service member is in their developmental and emotional phase aids the therapist in working with the service member or veteran and their families. The therapist recognizes that the positive experiences can create growth and development, and the negative experiences can create maladaptive behaviors and/or pathology (SAMHSA, 2014b). It is important to note that within the context of seeing the experiences on a continuum of positive and negative, the goal is to strike a healthy balance for optimal functioning (Carrey, 2010).

In clinical work with the service member, who must be 18 years of age or older, developmental phases include young adulthood through later adulthood. The service member is learning about themself and navigating the military culture, all while experiencing life within the context of preparation for wartime or conflict situations. Understanding the developmental phases will be important for clinical work with all members of the service member's family. The psychological conflict of trust versus mistrust in infancy creates a sense of trust if dependency needs are met during this part of the life course. The virtue within this phase that can occur is hope, and the maladaptive behavior that can be created is withdrawal. The next phase, the autonomy versus shame period, creates autonomy for the toddler. If autonomy is not allowed, independent abilities are questioned. The virtue within this phase that can occur is will, and the maladaptive behavior that can be created is a compulsion.

In the next phase, preschoolers learn to take initiative, and if their ability to do so becomes stifled, guilt arises. The virtue within this phase that can occur is the purpose, and the maladaptive behavior that can be created is inhibition. After this phase, the industry versus inferiority experience is based on children learning to independently apply themselves to specific assignments. The inability to be able to work independently during this phase causes inferiority. The virtue within this phase that can occur is competency, and the maladaptive behavior that can be created is inertia (passivity).

Teenagers deal with solidifying their own identities, and failure to do so confuses who they are. The virtue within this phase that can occur is identity, and the maladaptive behavior that can be created is repudiation. Then, in the young adulthood phase, searching for connection and intimacy with others is paramount. The inability to create intimate connections can lead to isolation. The virtue within this phase that can occur is love, and the maladaptive behavior that can be created is exclusivity.

During adulthood, creating a sense of purpose and contributing to society in the form of family and/or work is necessary. If one is unable to achieve meaningful contributions, isolation can be the outcome. The virtue within this phase that can occur is care, and the maladaptive behavior that can be created is rejectivity. Finally, for older adults, having a sense of accomplishment throughout their life span is critical. The inability to feel valued as a contributing member of society can cause overall despair. The virtue within this phase that can occur is wisdom, and the maladaptive behavior that can be created is disdain.

Erikson emphasized that the ego makes positive contributions to development by mastering attitudes, ideas, and skills at each stage of development. This mastery of virtues helps children grow into successful, contributing members of society. During each of Erikson's eight stages, there is a psychological conflict that must be successfully overcome for a child to develop into a healthy, well-adjusted adult. The absence of completing the psychosocial conflict may lead to maladaptive experiences, according to Erikson (1964, 1985). Virtues may be effectively created during each psychosocial stage if the conflict is effectively completed and resolved.

As we move into adulthood, many opportunities can occur such as increased family relational experiences, attending college, or employment options. In contrast, difficult life-course situations could arise because of growing up within an oppressed/marginalized situation. As a result of being in disadvantaged situations, "some of us will experience spells as inmates in the criminal justice system, while others of us will serve on active duty in the U.S. military" (Wilmoth & London, 2013, p. 23).

Glen H. Elder, Jr., is responsible for the most influential early theorizing about the role of military service in the life course (Elder, 1986, 1987). He is well known for his empirically-based research about understanding military service within the confines of life-course studies. The extensive research purports that the U.S. military is a critical social institution that can (re)shape educational, occupational, income, marital/family, health, and other lifecourse trajectories and outcomes (London & Wilmoth, 2006).

When thinking about the life-course trajectory, there are five tenets that guide a person's journey throughout their lives where clinical intervention can be beneficial. Lifelong development, human agency, location in time and place, timing, and linked lives are the foundational components of the life course that shape the lives of military service members, veterans, and families (Elder & Shanahan, 2006).

First, the principle of lifelong development asserts that aging and the human development process occur over time (Riffin & Löckenhoff, 2017). The growth and development of each phase are dependent upon the preceding life phases and experiences in treatment. One can miss important aspects of a person's historical context that shape who they are, what they believe, and how they show up in life, and more specifically, in the context of service in the military.

Second, the principle of human agency is a compilation of roles that individuals have within their own lives. The ability to choose opportunities is based on the limitations and experiences one obtains over the life course. Both prospects and disappointments are created by historical, social, political, and economic circumstances (North, 1991). Conversely, assumptions must not be made that if two people came from similar socio-economic backgrounds or social arenas, their lived experiences would be the same. The service members will engage in their military work as a unit and all unit members will affect the success of the mission. A service member's human agency is dependent upon all of the life roles that member plays.

Third, the principle of location in time and place considers geographic (to include online) locations where certain cultural dynamics are or are not experienced. Many interactions or events do or do not happen based on locale. Moving through the life course from childhood through adulthood, the influences of historical events shape our daily lives and create a commonality among families, friends, networks, communities, and online networks. There are many cultural facets connected to the military including the United States governmental structure, the military community, the military base, the military unit, and the individual service member. Any of these components can have a life-altering impact on a service member's view of the world and how that person engages, interacts, and functions.

Fourth, the principle of timing focuses on periods of change and life events concerning age. Both the life stages and the individual create resources and context about lived experiences based on any given historical event. The goal is to teach service members how to adapt to new situations and learn how to use skills previously learned to assist in managing future experiences.

The fifth principle concentrates on both social connections and the interdependence of one's life. Old connections can wane as new connections are created. Through the interconnectedness of different social relationships, events within those relationships (whether positive or negative) can have a dramatic impact on the individual. Social connections support the military service member while they are performing their military duties and/or while they are away on a mission.

The life-course perspective includes an examination of how military service acts as a mechanism affecting individuals' life-course trajectories, before, during, and after military service. The life-course perspective "looks at how chronological age, relationships, common life transitions, and social change shape people's lives from birth to death" (Hutchison, 2007, p. 8). The life-course trajectory provides a sound theoretical framework for a culturally aware and sensitive practice.

INDIVIDUAL IDENTITIES

The life-course theory discusses an individual's life trajectory throughout their life span, which consists of a set of finite age groups and phases. It is equally important to consider how a person's individual identity, in conjunction with their life course, plays a major role in how the individual would receive counseling (Jacob et al., 2017). According to Critical Media Project (2021), identity can be seen as a historically constructed concept. The features of identity include but are not limited to gender, social class, age, sexual orientation, race and ethnicity, religion, and ability. More often than not, social identity can be tied to the accumulation or absence of power within these structures. Individual identity is intertwined with so many different facets of life that a counselor must be aware of how the intersection of many of these social constructs can create a complex web of understanding as it relates to one's individual identity (Ratts et al., 2016). How one feels about oneself matters as it relates to how one behaves (Leary & Tangney, 2012). Counselors will need to consider individual identity as it relates to the many facets a military service member, a veteran, and family members present.

CULTURALLY RESPONSIVE PRACTICES: DRAWING FROM THE MULTICULTURAL AND SOCIAL JUSTICE COUNSELING COMPETENCIES AND CULTURAL HUMILITY

Being culturally responsive as a counselor is layered with an understanding of being aware of the construct of worldviews from a multicultural perspective along with understanding cultural identity. Ibrahim (1984, 1985) defines *worldview* as the core of cultural identity pertaining to beliefs, values and assumptions that are derived from the socialization process, in a specific cultural, familial, social, and historical context. Understanding the client's worldview and identity can help counselors become culturally sensitive and responsive while understanding diverse societies (Ibrahim & Heuer, 2016). A culturally responsive counselor should have a mastery of awareness, knowledge, and skills regarding specific aspects of culture (Hook et al., 2016).

In addition to working within a framework of being culturally responsive, it is equally important for counselors to operate from a mindset of being culturally humble. *Cultural humility* has been defined as "the ability to maintain an interpersonal stance that is other-oriented or (open to the other) in relation to the aspects of cultural identity that are most important to the client" (Hook et al., 2013, p. 354). By practicing cultural humility counselors can assist military service members, veterans, and their families from the multicultural orientation perspective. The counselor's intentional value of working with diverse backgrounds can improve the therapeutic relationship between counselor and client.

STRESSORS AND DISCRIMINATION

The U.S. military provides a large population of healthy adults with access to comprehensive and universal healthcare. As a result, there is much data available for researchers to examine psychiatric issues and concerns related to military culture. Military service members, veterans, and their families are at high risk of exposure to traumatic events as well as psychological distress related to mental health problems including depression and anxiety, violence within the family, substance abuse, PTSD, deployment adjustments, stress management, moving preparations and getting settled, relationship building, and the grieving process following the death of a loved one or colleague.

Longer-term occupational functioning concerns are also raised by mental health problems and trauma experiences. The military experience also often includes issues related to sexuality, transgender, sexual assaults, trauma, and racial discrimination. For example, thousands of lesbian, gay, bisexual, transgender, and queer or questioning veterans were discharged from the military under the "don't ask, don't tell" policy that went into effect in 1994 (Glantz, 2011).

COUNSELING UTILIZATION AND HELP-SEEKING

The American Public Health Association (APHA) supports the health of all people and communities and combines a 150-year perspective, a broad-based member community, and the ability to influence policy to improve the public's health. The APHA has issued a few policy statements on mental health, which as of 2014 were outdated, and there has been a call for new policy proposals to fill this gap. There are no existing APHA policies that specifically address mental health services for veterans. More advocacy work must be done as we recognize the high level of mental health challenges with veterans, including family instability, homelessness, and joblessness. Counselors can be proactive with community engagement efforts that can affect social policy and reform for this population (Reynolds & Osterlund, 2011).

Military veterans face several problems as they try to access mental health care, including the requirement to have been honorably or generally discharged to receive VA benefits. Another major problem is the long wait list for care due to a shortage of healthcare providers, poor scheduling practices, and problems related to transitioning from active-duty military care systems to the veterans' care system (APHA, n.d.). Finally, there are social barriers to care-seeking behavior related to military culture. Counselors within the community can specialize in working with this population to expand service delivery options (SAMHSA, 2014a). The U.S. VA creating a portal where clinicians can be located and can identify that they are specifically trained to work with military service members, veterans, and families to increase access to care (U.S. VA, n.d.-a).

CRAFTING AN ADVOCACY AGENDA

The military offers The Family Advocacy Program (FAP), and services are available at every military installation where families are assigned. Trained FAP victim advocates and clinicians provide a wide range of services and programs (including workshops to build skills for healthy relationships), help in planning for safety in a crisis, and offer support to new and expecting parents. They respond to reports of domestic and child abuse, as well as problematic behaviors in children.

The Veterans of Foreign Wars (VFW) of the United States is a nonprofit veteran's service organization composed of eligible veterans and military service members from the active, guard, and reserve forces. They established the Veterans Administration, developed the national cemetery system, and worked to pass the 21st Century GI Bill of Rights Act of 2007, which gives expanded educational benefits to America's active-duty service members and members of the National Guard and reserves. The VFW assisted in helping to pass the Veterans Access and Accountability Act of 2014 and worked toward improved VA medical centers services for women veterans.

The military offers confidential counselors available for service members and their families through Military One Source. Another resource for service members is the National Alliance on Mental Illness (www.loc.gov/item/lcwaN0000280), the nation's largest grassroots mental health organization dedicated to building better lives for the millions of Americans affected by mental illness.

Real Warriors is a site for all soldiers, whether they be active duty, National Guard, Reserve, or veterans and their families (www.realwarriors.net). The information and tools there can help with everything from budgeting and work to insomnia, PTSD, and depression. Other services support the body and mind in veteran-friendly health services in the soldier's area, and this information is available through *My HealtheVet* (www.myhealth.va.gov/index.html), the VA's online personal health record. This site for veterans, active-duty service members, and their families provides access to health records, a personal health journal, online VA prescription refill information, and details regarding federal and VA benefits and resources.

Other resources from the DOD sponsor coaching and support at *In Transition* (www.health.mil/Military-Health-Topics/Centers-of-Excellence/Psychological-Health-Center-of-Excellence/inTransition; 1-800-424-7877). Medical professionals can help you come out of this transition stronger than before. There is the *Veterans Crisis Line* (www.veteranscrisisline.net) which is available 24/7 by dialing 1-800-273-8255 and pressing 1. The *Mental Health America* organization respects and appreciates current and former members of the military; provides information to help to break down the stigma of mental health issues among soldiers, veterans, and their families; and makes medical staff available to ensure that a greater number of military families receive the prompt, high-quality care they deserve.

Reynolds and Osterlund (2011) posit that comprehensive cultures of advocacy for military families could be created within counseling programs by having an in-depth understanding of the concerns, dynamics, and cultural experiences this population deals with. Counselors would be more prepared to advocate for this population proactively. Additionally, Bronfenbrenner's (2005) ecological systems theory supports creating services and programs as an advocacy effort to help military service members, veterans, and their families by creating multisystemic levels of support and programming.

COUNSELING CHILDREN, ADOLESCENTS, AND YOUNG ADULTS

The military offers the Military and Family Life Counseling Program which assists service members, their families, and survivors with mental health counseling when and where it is needed. Military and family life counselors are highly qualified professionals trained to understand the unique challenges of military culture and offer counseling services, as well as briefings and presentations to the military community both on and off the installation.

Children, adolescents, and young adults may face a variety of issues that affect their abilities to manage the difficulties of the military culture. These include changes at home from deployment, reunion, divorce, grief, self-esteem issues, communication and relationships at home and school, and life skills that involve problem-solving and adjustment, including bullying and anger management. There are various warning signs to be aware of when dealing with children and adolescents who might have some struggles with coping due to military life. These may include sleep trouble (too much or too little); physical issues of headaches, backaches, stomachaches, or muscle tension; dietary issues such as not eating or overeating; and smoking, drinking, or using drugs. Behavioral concerns might include irritability, anxiety, frequent crying, and withdrawing from friends or family. Finally, failing or falling grades in school may be an indicator of children or adolescents struggling to cope.

COUNSELING ADULTS, COUPLES, AND FAMILIES

We consider the various and diverse dynamics that occur with military service people and their families. This interpersonal and challenging issue may be related to spouses, children, blended families, deployment, employment, or being wounded in the line of duty. As military families must shift and alter their physical locations based on the needs of the U.S. government, the process of pre-deployment, deployment, and integration becomes challenging for the whole family unit. The military family is often asked to make sacrifices well beyond any expected of their civilian counterparts (SAMHSA, 2010). For active component family members, the military is a daily part of who they are, and the family is as much a part of the military as is the actively serving military member.

Active component family members are expected to move, or permanent change of station (PCS), every 3 to 5 years. Although the military is attempting to lengthen the time for which service members and their families remain at one duty location, the reality is that the needs of the services come first, and personnel change duty locations as necessary.

Aside from concerns related to the military, many families deal with issues common to all families, including childcare, elder care, education, parenting concerns, and career choices. However, military families also are subjected to unique stressors, such as repeated relocations that often include international sites, frequent separations of service members from families, and subsequent reorganizations of family life during reunions. Furthermore, military families cope with these stressors in a structured environment that pressures families to behave a certain way. Also included in these stressors are extended and lengthy deployments, increased anxiety, and mental health struggles of children due to frequent moves. The soldiers and their families have a lot to deal with connected to the soldier's military service.

IMPLICATIONS FOR CLINICAL PRACTICE

As mentioned earlier within this chapter, there are more than 1,400,000 military service members who have taken part in OIF and OEF (Baiocchi, 2013), which together have lasted more than 10 years (OIF: 2003–2011; OEF: 2001–present; Torreon, 2012).

The men and women who serve within the military have a myriad of different ranks, time in service, different experiences while serving (where some have experienced multiple deployments), different duration of service, and unique familial dynamics because of the demands of the military service itself. When reintegrating back into their home environment, issues surrounding family, finances, substance abuse, posttraumatic stress, and medical concerns are some of the struggles military service members contend with (Carrola & Corbin-Burdick, 2015).

For many years, the medical model has been used by helping professions and has been both praised and criticized (Beecher, 2009). The mental health model has also been used by mental health professionals to assist clients in obtaining both diagnosis and treatment. Beecher (2009) shares that the medical model was instrumental within the mental health systems, and asserts that this model has had a tremendous influence on the mental health community. The medical model also created a considerable number of important policies and solidified mental health practices over the years. However, Lovell and Ehrlich (2000) discovered that the medical model approach within the mental health arena is harming psychotherapists, as it has resulted in constricting treatment options, minimizing independence, and creating decreased self-efficacy.

The U.S. VA APHA has numerous hospitals, centers, and facilities throughout the United States that offer veterans a variety of services, ranging from medical and mental health treatment to financial assistance. Mental health services include outpatient treatment, awareness/information sessions, call centers, peer support services, parenting support and classes, and residential/inpatient treatment (U.S. VA, n.d.-a). Treatments within these services may be evidence-based psychotherapies, such as cognitive behavioral therapy, Acceptance and Commitment Therapy, illness management and recovery, psychotropic medications, psychosocial interventions, and social skills training. Substance use disorders, military sexual trauma, depression, PTSD, anxiety disorders, bipolar disorder, schizophrenia, and family-related issues are the main concerns that such services are directed to address (U.S. VA, n.d.-a).

Utilizing a wellness model shifts the focus from a pathology-based assessment and treatment regime like that of the medical model of treatment. The wellness model was characterized as a way of life, creating the best possible health and well-being where body, mind, and spirit are unified by the individual to live a more complete, healthy life within their natural environment (Myers et al., 2000). The wellness model focuses on assisting the individual with achieving the most ideal type of overall health and wellness.

Myers and Sweeney (2008) also noted that in 1989, the American Association of Counseling and Development (now known as the ACA) passed a resolution, "The Counseling Profession as Advocates for Optimum Health and Wellness," that reaffirmed the profession's commitment to its foundations in a developmental guidance approach. The wellness model has been found to create an understanding of cultural groups and may benefit other minority groups, including those with disabilities or certain faith traditions, who continue to receive less service from professional counselors (Myers & Sweeney, 2008). Studies assessing outcomes have shown that wellness interventions are effective, and that they were helpful for people who had job-related stress that put them at risk for decreased wellness (Myers & Sweeney, 2008). The wellness model can also be used to help clients to strengthen their military experiences as part of their identity rather than being the sole defining aspect of who they are.

One of the best-known wellness models specifically related to the military service member and veteran treatment is that of Posttraumatic Growth (PTG). PTG creates positive changes in how people view themselves. The models assist in ameliorating one's life philosophy, and spirituality can be obtained after experiencing trauma (Tedeschi & Calhoun, 1996). PTG is a rational alternative approach to the pathological view of how to treat PTSD. Its proponents posit that positive psychological gain can result from trauma (Tedeschi & Calhoun, 2004). This approach examines the positive growth that may occur out of the experience of trauma. In the world of the military, many of the experiences deal with high-stakes decision-making strategies, life-and-death safety and security, and existential approaches to traumatic situations. The PTG approach allows for intentionality in making the paradigm shift from utilizing the medical model, which is based on creating pathology, and instead incorporating wellness interventions as a form of total wellness for military service members, their families, and veterans.

When working with military service members, their families, and veterans, counselors will fine that there is a higher propensity for depression in those who have been diagnosed with a traumatic brain injury (TBI) and/or PTSD (Bryant, 2011). Military sexual trauma (MST) is a specific type of sexual assault that can only occur during one's time serving in the military; it includes any severe or threatening harassment that is sexual (Kimerling et al., 2007). Moreover, death by suicide numbers remain high in the military, with rates exceeding that of the general/civilian population at times (Department of Defense Task Force on the Prevention of Suicide by Members of the Armed Forces, 2010). Addiction is commonly seen in the military context, likely a comorbid condition with another psychological disorder (e.g., depression, PTSD, anxiety, etc.; Seal et al., 2011). Service members and veterans may present with all types of substance use disorders, from alcohol use disorder to illicit drug use (including prescription drug misuse; Barlas et al., 2013).

For counselors to provide the best quality therapeutic services, it is paramount that they understand the foundations of military culture and have a cultural understanding of the military service member, family member, or veteran within their cultural context before applying any therapeutic practice. According to RAND Corporation (2019), effective treatments are those that have been shown to work, based on scientific research and clinical experience. Evidence-based practice (EBP) refers to specific forms of care that meet specific criteria, such as client/patient values, clinical expertise, and current best evidence. EBPs have been peer-reviewed by scientists and clinicians, and there is empirical evidence for their effectiveness. In some cases, EBPs have been proven to produce significant reductions in symptoms in controlled experimental research studies, which represent the gold standard of scientific evidence for medical treatments.

Current EBPs to assist with the treatment of PTSD include prolonged exposure therapy, cognitive processing therapy, eye movement desensitization and reprocessing therapy, and specific cognitive behavioral therapies. Acceptance and Commitment Therapy, behavior activation/behavioral therapy, mindfulness-based techniques, and the use of problem-solving therapy have been shown to be clinically effective in treating major depression. As related to treating alcohol use and substance abuse disorders, cognitive behavioral therapy, motivational enhancement therapy, 12-step facilitation, and behavioral couples therapy for have also been proven to be successful as treatment modalities (Hepner et al., 2017).

As a counselor working with military service members, their families, and veterans, one should recognize that advocacy efforts are required to move the profession toward continued wellness for this population. According to RAND Corporation (2019), increasing the number of highly trained mental health professionals, reducing barriers to care, adopting and enforcing consistent quality-of-care standards, improving monitoring and performance measures, continuing to develop and test new models of care, and continuing to strengthen the evidence base are crucial aspects of leading the fight to provide the best treatment for this population. In addition to advocating for these methods to increase quality of care, creating policy around these approaches will continue to guide the profession in the direction of wellness for all.

CLINICAL CASE SCENARIO 21.1

Marion, your new 72-year-old wheelchair-bound client, was brought to your office by his adult son. Marion's hospice nurse recommended counseling because "he is lonely and could use someone to talk to." Marion is terminally ill, uses oxygen and tubing to manage severe chronic obstructive pulmonary disease (COPD), and is a Vietnam-era army veteran with Agent Orange status. Hospice reports that Marion has six months to live. He recently relocated to your state to live with his adult son and daughter-in-law. His son reported that his father moved in with him two months ago so he would not die alone in their hometown. He told you that Marion was doing well until the VA denied the recent application they made for benefits. Marion believes that his Agent Orange status should have qualified him for these benefits, and the denial revived negative emotions he had felt while serving in the military. As a Black man, in the military, he was harassed, discriminated against, and spoken to abusively. "Vietnam messed me up," he told you. Then he disclosed that his best friend died by suicide when they returned home. Marion asserted that he would never have applied for any support from the service for himself, but he wanted to be able to leave something to his adult children after his death. Marion does not believe he needs counseling, but he does hope that your notes will help his appeal with the VA. His son reported that Marion does need counseling because he does not want to do anything at home; he gets anxious and has panic attacks and cries a lot.

CLINICAL CASE SCENARIO DISCUSSION QUESTIONS

1. How would you prioritize Marion's counseling needs?
2. What is your response to Marion's request for your assistance with his appeal?
3. How does his terminal illness affect your work?
4. As a military client, what things do you need to consider while working with Marion?
5. What goals and interventions will you add to his treatment plan?

END-OF-CHAPTER RESOURCES

 A robust set of instructor resources designed to supplement this text is located at http://connect.springerpub.com/content/book/978-0-8261-3953-5. Qualifying instructors may request access by emailing textbook@springerpub.com.

SUMMARY

This chapter has explored the duality of cultures for military service members and veterans, and examined the experience through the individual, relational, and collective experiences of military service. In supporting service members through multicultural, social justice, and sociopolitical perspectives, counselors can better understand the unique mental health needs of military personnel and their families. Adding cultural responsiveness and competence integration into the therapeutic relationship and the counseling process can strengthen and support the service member and honor the power of the service member's diverse experience. The military experience is in and of itself a culture built upon the patchwork and intersectionality of other cultures, and mental health counselors must be prepared for this work. The counselor may strengthen their social justice and advocacy outlooks by utilizing culturally responsive interventions and therapeutic approaches with service members, veterans, and their families.

DISCUSSION QUESTIONS

1. What are the unique and impactful aspects of military culture that service members, veterans, and their families face?
2. Discuss the impact of military stressors and discrimination on the service member, veterans, and their families. How do counselors advocate for them?
3. What would an advocacy agenda look like for a military service member, a veteran, and/or their family?

CULTURALLY RESPONSIVE COUNSELING RELATED TO MILITARY PERSONNEL AND VETERANS

Guests: Dr. Gigi Hamilton and Dr. Cori Marie Costello

https://connect.springerpub.com/content/book/978-0-8261-3953-5/part/part02/chapter/ch21

KEY REFERENCES

Only key references appear in the print edition. The full reference list appears in the digital product on Springer Publishing Connect: https://connect.springerpub.com/content/book/978-0-8261-3953-5/part/part02/chapter/ch21

Carrola, P., & Corbin-Burdick, M. (2015). Counseling military veterans: Advocating for culturally competent and holistic interventions. *Journal of Mental Health Counseling*, 37(1), 1–14. https://doi.org/10.17744/mehc.37.1.v74514163rv73274

Cole, R. F. (2014). Understanding military culture: A guide for professional school counselors. *The Professional Counselor*, 4(5), 497–504. https://doi.org/10.15241/rfc.4.5.497

Department of Defense. (2017). *2017 demographic: Profile of the military community*. Author. https://download.militaryonesource.mil/12038/MOS/Reports/2017-demographics-report.pdf

Kulesza, M., Pedersen, E., Corrigan, P., & Marshall, G. (2015). Help-seeking stigma and mental health treatment seeking among young adult veterans. *Military Behavioral Health*, 3(4), 230–239. https://doi.org/10.1080/21635781.2015.1055866

Substance Abuse and Mental Health Services Administration. (2010). *Understanding the military: The institution, the culture and the people*. https://www.samhsa.gov/sites/default/files/military_white_paper_final.pdf

Vogt, D. (2011). Mental health–related beliefs as a barrier to service use for military. *Psychiatric Services*, 62(2), 132–142. https://doi.org/10.1176/ps.62.2.pss6202_0135

CHAPTER 22

Culturally Responsive Counseling Related to Poverty, Middle Class, and Affluence

AMI CAMP AND MERRY LEIGH DAMERON

LEARNING OBJECTIVES

After reading this chapter, students will be able to:

- Define social class, classism, and socioeconomic status and understand their relationship to counseling and the counseling relationship.
- Recognize intersectionality within the context of working with students and clients from various socioeconomic backgrounds.
- Discuss specific frameworks for conceptualizing class and classism.
- Identify culturally responsive practices, rooted in social justice and advocacy, for working with clients from various socioeconomic backgrounds.

SELF-REFLECTION QUESTIONS

1. Think about biases, prejudices, and assumptions you might have about people who live in poverty and those who are affluent. How do these help and hinder your ability to provide culturally sensitive counseling?
2. What hesitancies, if any, do you have about working with people who live in poverty or those who are affluent?
3. What attributes do you have that will enable you to work with poor and affluent clients?

The purpose of this chapter is to define social class, classism, and socioeconomic status and address intersectionality in the context of counseling. Furthermore, this chapter examines the dynamics of socioeconomic privilege and marginalization that may be present when working with clients from low-income, middle-income, and upper-income backgrounds. There are specific frameworks for conceptualizing class and classism that further promote counselor self-awareness and the provision of services that are culturally responsive. The following frameworks are addressed and applied to counseling sessions: the I-CARE Model, Poverty Counseling Best Practices, the Social Class Worldview Model (SCWM)–Revised, and the Social Class and Classism Consciousness Model (SCCC). Lastly, culturally responsive counseling, social justice, and advocacy practices are discussed.

THE CLASS OF THE COUNSELOR: EXPLORATION, INTROSPECTION, AND REFLECTION

The term *social class*, though commonly used in our society, is not well-defined or well-understood (Bird & Newport, 2017); however, Liu (2011) defines social class as an individual's status within the social and economic hierarchy, commonly assessed through one's educational attainment, occupation, and income. Moreover, social class can be considered "a worldview or lens by which individuals experience, interpret, and make sense of the more objective economic world around them" (Liu, 2011, p. 79). Identities of social class are significantly influenced by social stratification, class mobility, and classism (Cook & Lawson, 2016). Given the myriad constructs that influence one's worldview and cultivate social class identity, it is essential that counselors consider the potential implications that social class can have on how clients perceive themselves, particularly when comparing themselves to others in different social classes (Cook & Lawson, 2016; Kudrna et al., 2010). Within the context of counseling, many are reluctant to broach the topic of social class and its impact on one's life. This reluctance not only affects counselors' and clients' understanding and awareness of social class and socioeconomic status but also limits counselors' ability to validate their clients' lived experiences (Cook & Lawson, 2016). Moreover, "entitlement and self-confidence, as aspects of class, are themes that repeatedly surface ... [They] may surface in therapy and counseling relationships, if and when class becomes an explicit topic" (Ryan, 2019, p. 50).

Social class is often conceptualized as an aspect of social stratification that legitimizes "the ranking of people and the unequal distribution of valued goods, services, and prestige" (Kerbo, 2017, p. 1). From this perspective, social class in the United States is comprised of upper-income, middle-income, and lower-income (Kochhar, 2018), and generally based on (a) economic resources; (b) education and occupation status; or (c) attitudes, self-perception, and mindset (Bird & Newport, 2017). For many individuals, class is a state of mind or means of self-identification (Pew Research Center, 2012). In 2018, approximately half of U.S. adults (52%) lived in middle-income households, three-in-ten (29%) were in lower-income households, and 19% were in upper-income households (Bennett et al., 2020). There remains a decades-long trend of a "widening income gap between upper-income households and middle- and lower-income households" (Kochhar, 2018, para. 6). This trend further illuminates the overall rise in income inequality in our society (Kochhar, 2018). A national analysis conducted by Pew Research Center in 2018 classified middle-income as "those with an income that is two-thirds to double the U.S. median household income" (Bennett et al., 2020, para. 6). Regarding the income range, middle-income households accounted for $48,500 to $145,500 annually, lower-income households reflected incomes less than $48,500, and upper-income households reflected incomes greater than $145,500 (Bennett et al., 2020). In 2019, the poverty rate was 10.5% (34 million), with 7.3% having identified as White, non-Hispanic, 18.8% as Black, 7.3% as Asian, and 15.7% as Latinx (Semega et al., 2020).

The resources (e.g., income) of upper- and lower-income individuals vary and affect their day-to-day priorities and concerns (Kraus et al., 2012). Generally, upper-income individuals experience greater autonomy and diminished social and environmental threat due to access to vast resources, cultivating "an internal, self-oriented focus—greater attention to one's internal states and goals and increased independence from others" (Kraus et al., 2012, p. 903). Inversely, while low-income individuals are likely to experience or be exposed to adverse experiences (e.g., increased violence and crime, inadequately funded schools, food insecurity) that threaten their overall well-being, they are less likely to have adequate resources to aid in mitigating such threats (Kraus et al., 2012). As a result, low-income individuals "develop an external, other-oriented focus—greater vigilance to the social context and interdependence with others" (Kraus et al., 2012, p. 903). According to a national survey, 36% of lower-income adults and 28% of middle-income adults reportedly lost a job or were impacted by a pay reduction due to the coronavirus disease 2019 (COVID-19) pandemic, compared with 22% of upper-income adults (Igielnik, 2020). For many lower-income adults, the global pandemic only exacerbated financial stress, with only 23% of lower-income adults reportedly having 3 months' worth of an emergency fund saved, compared with 48% of middle-income adults and 75% of upper-income adults (Parker et al., 2020).

Classism

Bourdieu (1986) contends that the "social world" is a "multidimensional space" that is significantly influenced by different forms of capital (p. 4), namely *economic capital*, *cultural capital*, and *social capital*. Accordingly, *economic capital* is adaptable to money and may be established in property rights; *cultural capital* can be presented in three forms: (a) embodied state, or "the form of long-lasting dispositions of the mind and body" (Bourdieu, 1986, p. 79); (b) objectified state, or cultural goods; and (c) institutionalized state, which is "a form of objectification which must be set apart because, as will be seen in the case of educational qualifications, it confers entirely original properties on the cultural capital which it is presumed to guarantee" (Bourdieu, 1986, p. 79).

When considering social class, one can classify from an objective or subjective perspective. An objective perspective on social class determines an individual's status or position based on measurable variables such as income, wealth, education, and occupation. In contrast, a subjective perspective on social class is based on how an individual perceives their status or position and, subsequently, the category in which they place themself (Bird & Newport, 2017). Awareness of one's subjective social class is valuable, as an individual's perspective informs their worldview.

Liu (2011) contends that classism is "employed to maintain psychological equilibrium, to feel normal within one's social class group, and to determine out-group members" (p. 86) and identifies four forms of classism: (a) *downward classism*; (b) *upward classism*; (c) *lateral classism*, and (d) *internalized classism*. The first form of classism, *downward classism*, is oppression of and discrimination against individuals in lower social classes by individuals who are either in or perceived to be in positions of power or higher social classes. In contrast, *upward classism* is prejudice and discrimination directed toward those individuals perceived to be in a higher social class. The third form of classism, *lateral classism*, occurs via a horizontal comparison: individuals self-evaluate and are simultaneously evaluated by others within the same social class according to what they have and do. It is because people are "continuously reminded of personal deficiencies that are not congruent with being in a certain social class" that lateral classism occurs (Liu, 2011, p. 200). Lastly, *internalized classism* engenders an emotional state of disequilibrium, especially as challenges with maintaining one's social class persist.

A few of the questions that Pedrotti (2013) presents for counselors to consider when reflecting on one's economic background and the impact of internalized classism include: "What did my caregivers teach me about people in poverty? Was I excluded or rejected by social groups because of my social status? When have I engaged in classist behavior?" (p. 140).

These forms of classism are particularly helpful for counselors to recognize as clients seek to identify, and perhaps negotiate, their respective social class statuses (Colbow et al., 2016; Liu, 2011). These types of questions were critical for me (MLD) to examine as I worked as a school counselor with students from various socioeconomic backgrounds. As someone from a middle-class background, I realized that attaining at least an undergraduate degree was one of the pressures related to my family's income level and view of success. As a school counselor, I fostered an awareness of my bias that students needed to attain a certain level of education in order to be successful. When discussing postsecondary options with students, it was important to balance raising awareness of postsecondary opportunities and helping remove barriers students might face with an understanding that students may (and have every right to) explore options outside of traditional postsecondary education.

In addition to the aforementioned forms of classism, Liu et al. (2007) identify yet another type of classism: social class bias. Central to social class bias is upward mobility and the notion that upward mobility is typical; this presumes that individuals should aspire to improve their respective social class status, and those who are unable to do so are an anomaly. According to Ryan (2019), "class is increasingly seen as about difference—who you are not—as much as or more than belonging to, or identifying with, a specific defined group" (p. 49). It is imperative that counselors acknowledge the intricacies of class and consider the intersectionality of class not only with other aspects of their identity (e.g., race/ethnicity, gender, sexual identity, religion/spirituality, developmental challenges) but also that of their clients.

According to Choi and Miller (2018), "additional factors that contribute to potential classism include the fact that traditional counseling methods draw from middle-class and upper-middle class White social norms" (p. 767). In addition, media significantly influences how people conceptualize and perceive images of social class groups and socioeconomic status, often engendering stereotypes and biases (Cook & Lawson, 2016). It is important to note that while some people may ascribe to the notion that everyone is equal, or minimize the existence and effects of social class in the United States, others may acknowledge the systemic oppression that exists and intentionally refuse to endorse classist beliefs (Colbow et al., 2016).

Privilege and Power

Liu (2013) defines *privilege* as "invisible benefits given to people based solely on identity aspects that the individual had no part in developing, creating, or nurturing" (p. 5). Identity within a particular social group can lead to either privilege or marginalization within society (Adams et al., 2016). Within the United States examples of privilege include, but are not limited to, being White (racial privilege), being Christian (religious privilege), being male (gender privilege), and being a young adult or middle-aged individual (age privilege; Adams et al., 2016). In the context of identity within a social group, upper-classed individuals may be considered economically privileged in the United States (Adams et al., 2016), and thus enjoy certain benefits associated with that privilege. These privileges may be obvious or less apparent. For example, while many consider greater access to material resources as an advantage of economic privilege, research also indicates that children of more highly educated parents display fewer mental health problems during a stressful life situation (e.g., stress related to divorce or separation within the home; Reiss et al., 2019)—an unseen but nevertheless material advantage.

Examining the relationship between privilege and power reveals that members of privileged groups (e.g., Whites, males, or upper-classed individuals) possess power and privilege within society (Adams et al., 2016; McIntosh, 1986). Contrarily, "marginalized group members are those who are oppressed in society and lack the systemic advantages bestowed on privileged groups" (Ratts et al., 2016, p. 36). The power afforded by privilege extends beyond the personal level, connecting also to systems of marginalization, oppression, and power (Liu, 2013). "Pure privilege works invisibly, is unconscious and automatic, and is considered 'normative' by society" (Liu, 2013, p. 5).

Insulation from consequences is a principal benefit of economic privilege, providing protection in several ways (Liu, 2013). These include protection from (a) "environmental and contextual consequences such as living in toxic or violent environments" (Liu, 2013, p. 5); (b) "the consequences of their behaviors and attitudes" (Liu, 2013, p. 5); and (c) "assaults on their cultural identity" (Liu, 2013, p. 5). In addition to protection from consequences, Ballinger (2020) describes both external and internal benefits of economic privilege. Economic privilege allows both access to "valued resources" as well as benefits related to "how we are valued by others and, by extension, our self-esteem" (Ballinger, 2020, p. 68).

While those who have economic privilege may experience certain tangible and internal benefits (Ballinger, 2020; Liu, 2013), it is important to acknowledge the interplay between identity, marginalization, and privilege (Ratts, 2017). While economic privilege is unquestionably connected to an individual's level of education, income, and profession, other elements of a person's identity are also impactful (Liu, 2013; Ratts, 2017). "This complication and tension between identities provides some impetus for our understanding of social class and classism as intrapsychic, subjective, and phenomenological experiences within an economic structure and system" (Liu, 2013, p. 6). We thus urge practitioners to take an intersectional approach to work with students and clients (see Ratts, 2017), understanding that economic privilege does not insulate individuals from experiencing the benefits and obstacles of their other privileged and marginalized identities, respectively.

Intersectionality

In the academic world, intersectional thought originated in the 1970s when the concept was utilized to contest the void of sociological inquiry explicitly examining the phenomenological experiences of those subject to several forms of oppression (Shin et al., 2017). Crenshaw (1989/1993) coined the term and promoted the approach, which is now widely utilized among various disciplines (e.g., psychology, sociology, counseling) and in examining numerous points of difference (e.g., religion, race/ethnicity, social class, ability status; Shin et al., 2017). As it applies to research, Shin et al. (2017) define *strong intersectionality* as "scholarship which foregrounds relationships and outcomes among multiple intersecting social categories *and* critiques interlocking forms of power and privilege" (p. 460). Shin et al. (2017) go on to provide an example of strong intersectional research in which scholars "investigating the relationship between racial microaggressions and masculinity threat among a sample of high achieving, LGB identified Black high school students" could provide "a critique of how historical factors like Jim Crow intersect with contemporary racism, whiteness, and heteronormativity to produce unique experiences for Black men" (p. 460).

While this chapter is focused on counselors' practice working with clients from various socioeconomic backgrounds, rather than on research related to social class, classism, and privilege, Shin et al.'s (2017) description of "strong intersectional research" (p. 460) provides a clear example of what it might look like to approach a client from an intersectional approach. We cannot isolate a client's social class and their experiences with privilege and classism as the only impactful factors in their phenomenological experience. Rather, we need to understand and counsel our clients as individuals experiencing the world as likely privileged in some ways, marginalized in others, and vacillating in terms of the impact of these elements of their identities. Scholars acknowledge the difficulties associated with functionally (rather than rhetorically) applying an intersectional perspective (Moradi & Grzanka, 2017). Recognizing this challenge, Brinkman and Donohue (2020) purport "doing intersectionality" describing it as "a dynamic, relational, contextualized practice rather than a generalized theoretical framework that can be learned abstractly and then applied to any situation" (p. 110). The scholars further explain:

> As we understand it, intersectionality is a way of being in relation to clients that encompasses affect and action as well as thought. It is an awareness of both the particularities of identities (who I am as a particular clinician in relation to a particular client) and the generalities of social locations, institutional structures, and practices of power. This "doing" means learning to think, feel, and respond both critically and dynamically within the specific, concrete, contextualized relationships that comprise clinical practice. (Brinkman & Donohue, 2020, p. 110)

Doing intersectionality, then, is an active effort on the part of the clinician, and necessitates continual personal growth and intentionality within the therapeutic relationship.

In their mixed-methods examination of 32 counseling psychology graduate students' conceptualization of intersectionality within clinical work, Brinkman and Donohue (2020) utilized an intersectionality questionnaire to examine (a) "students' knowledge of intersectionality," (b) "the importance they assigned to understanding clients according to multiple social identities," and (c) "their perceived confidence in their abilities to conceptualize clients according to multiple social identities" (p. 112). Additionally, the scholars explored whether or not students, who were enrolled in one of two sections of a course entitled "Psychology of Culture and Identity," increased in multicultural competence over the course of the semester. Among other findings, results revealed that 78% of participants self-reported they did not know what intersectionality was, yet the majority ($n = 25$) "indicated intersectionality is important because it facilitates effective therapy" (Brinkman & Donohue, 2020, p. 113).

In discussing these results, Brinkman and Donohue (2020) made several recommendations that we would like to highlight and apply in the context of working with clients through an intersectional lens. The first recommendation is that students be introduced "to the concept that subjectivity is unfixed and that clients' experiences of their own social identities are influenced by the systems they navigate through as well as social and political events" (Brinkman & Donohue, 2020, p. 113). For example, a person experiencing poverty may feel more aware of their social class when at an event attended primarily by people situated within the middle class. "Further," the scholars note, "the meanings given to our identities as well as the aspects of privilege or oppression associated with those meanings can shift based on sociopolitical and historical context" (Brinkman & Donohue, 2020, p. 113). Clients may bring into the clinical space, for example, feelings of anxiety or guilt associated with their ability to access resources during the recent COVID-19 pandemic. Brinkman and Donohue also "suggest that doing intersectionality with social justice oriented clinical training includes encouraging clinicians to examine their own social identities to facilitate genuine relationship building with their clients" (2020, p. 113). Understanding that counselors may hold negative stereotypes about people from lower socioeconomic classes (Smith et al.,

2013) *and* that perceived differences in social class between client and counselor may negatively affect the counseling relationship (Balmforth, 2009; Ryan, 2019), counselors should actively self-reflect on their own social class, and the ways it affects their work with clients. I (MLD) needed to continuously self-reflect upon my own social class and the impact it had on my work with students. As a school counselor within a nontraditional high school, I would frequently meet with students to discuss their post-graduation plans. One student expressed an interest in going to community college, and I asked if they were interested in applying to the one within our county or a neighboring county. The student responded that they had never traveled to the neighboring county (which was less than seven miles from our current location). I realized that I was making assumptions about my students' access to transportation and that I needed to be much more intentional about having discussions with students on barriers they might be facing.

The last suggestion is "instructors integrating intersectionality into social justice oriented clinical training help their students explore the idea of centering/decentering as an intentional practice" (Brinkman & Donohue, 2020, p. 114). The scholars conceptualize decentering and centering as both addressing power imbalances and shifting perspectives. For example, Moussawi and Vidal-Ortiz (2020) apply the concept of decentering by arguing for "a queer sociology" (p. 1272) that simultaneously names and decenters Whiteness while centering race and processes of racialization. A counselor committed to decentering and centering within this context, then, might be committed to addressing any imbalances of power related to social class and classism within the counseling relationship, and creating space to center perspectives of those historically marginalized (e.g., people whose incomes are below the federal poverty threshold).

ETHICAL MANDATES AND MULTICULTURAL COUNSELING COMPETENCIES

Counselors are mandated to not discriminate against clients from diverse backgrounds, and this includes people of various socioeconomic statuses. For example, Standard C.5: Nondiscrimination of the American Counseling Association (ACA; 2014) *Code of Ethics* states, "Counselors do not condone or engage in discrimination against prospective or current clients . . . based on age, culture, disability, ethnicity, race, religion/spirituality, gender, gender identity, sexual orientation, marital/partnership status, socioeconomic status, immigration status, or any basis proscribed by law" (p. 9). In addition to the ethical standards outlined in the *ACA Code of Ethics*, the profession endorses the Multicultural and Social Justice Counseling Competencies (MSJCC; Ratts et al., 2016) and the ACA Advocacy Competencies (Clark et al., 2020; Lewis et al., 2003; Toporek & Daniels, 2018).

The MSJCC are beneficial in challenging counselors to consider how personal experiences of power, privilege, and oppression, coupled with the experiences of their client(s), influence the counseling dynamic, social justice, and advocacy (Ratts et al., 2016). Moreover, the MSJCC can be especially helpful in further navigating the intricacies of social class and socioeconomic status in counseling, as both are salient facets of one's lived experiences and identity. The ACA Advocacy Competencies provide a framework for social justice and advocacy with and on behalf of clients at various levels: (a) *micro*, or individual; (b) *meso*, or community; and (c) *macro*, or sociopolitical. These ethical mandates and multicultural competencies are essential for counselors to provide culturally responsive services to all clients.

FRAMEWORKS FOR CLASS AND CLASSISM

I-CARE Model–Revised

The I-CARE Model, a revision of the original CARE Model (Foss et al., 2011), is a strengths-based framework that counselors can utilize when working with and empowering clients currently experiencing poverty (Foss-Kelly et al., 2017). The stages of the I-CARE Model include: (a) Internally reflect; (b) Cultivating relationship; (c) Acknowledge realities; (d) Remove barriers; and (e) Expanding on strengths.

Internally Reflect

A counselor's self-awareness is central to culturally responsive counseling (Liu & Ali, 2008; Ratts et al., 2016; Sue et al., 1992). As such, it is most appropriate that this is the first stage of the model. The attitudes, beliefs, expectations, and values that accompany counselors in session could present challenges depending on the extent of their cultural encapsulation, or "way of interacting on the basis of a limited understanding of others' cultures, resulting in a failure to incorporate new knowledge into preexisting conceptualizations that would help one understand the lived experiences of others" (Foss-Kelly et al., 2017; West-Olatunji & Gibson, 2012, p. 204). Essential factors in this stage include introspection and awareness of preconceived bias toward people currently experiencing poverty and its potential impact on the counseling process, as well as knowledge of diverse economic backgrounds of clients and the impact on one's overall well-being (Goodman et al., 2013; Wadsworth, 2012).

Cultivating Relationship

Counseling should be a safe space for all clients, including those currently experiencing poverty. In this stage of the model counselors should demonstrate cultural humility and "deep respect for the humanness of the client and faith in their ability to more effectively cope with challenging life circumstances" (Foss-Kelly et al., 2017, p. 205). Acknowledging and working alongside the client in processing any internalized stigmas and defense mechanisms associated with poverty can aid in fostering a positive therapeutic relationship (Liu, 2013). Furthermore, maintaining awareness of the power differential that may be amplified during the counseling process could further cultivate a strong therapeutic relationship (Foss-Kelly et al., 2017).

Acknowledge Realities

In this stage it is essential that counselors acknowledge the realities of clients currently experiencing poverty (e.g., limited transportation; disparities in healthcare, education, and the workforce; poor neighborhoods; etc.) and not shy away from critical conversations related to institutional racism and injustices impeding a client's access to resources (Overholser, 2016). Moreover, it is beneficial for counselors to remain open to financial-related discussions during sessions rather than avoid or determine them to be less relevant to counseling (Foss-Kelly et al., 2017). It is especially helpful for counselors to acknowledge early in the process the myriad effects of low socioeconomic status, particularly related to mental health, and foster increased "critical consciousness" among clients to recognize potential social structures affecting their presenting issue(s), thus mitigating internalized shame and self-blame (Foss-Kelly et al., 2017, p. 206).

Remove Barriers

Barriers for clients currently experiencing poverty can be vast, ranging from inconsistent work hours and transportation to limited childcare. Consequently, the barriers that clients face directly impact access to and progression in counseling. Counselors' knowledge of the realities of clients currently experiencing poverty can cultivate a positive therapeutic alliance and influence the collaboration of goals (Foss-Kelly et al., 2017). Given the high rate of premature termination among racially and ethnically diverse clients and clients currently experiencing poverty (Foss-Kelly et al., 2017), it is imperative that counselors establish a trusting, positive therapeutic alliance early in the therapeutic process. Furthermore, counselors can engage in advocacy to eradicate existing barriers, integrate case management practices to address external stressors and urgent needs of the client, and be more flexible in scheduling and service options (e.g., counseling locations in client's community; Foss-Kelly et al., 2017).

Expanding on Strengths

The skillset of clients currently experiencing poverty is exceptional compared to those with more financial security and privilege (Foss-Kelly et al., 2017; Harper et al., 2015). Accordingly, "[a] careful evaluation of clients' strengths and the ways in which they have managed to survive poverty is the foundation for building strategies to successfully tackle other challenges" (Foss-Kelly et al., 2017, p. 208). In this stage counselors should empower clients to identify and uphold personal values and life meaning, integrate financial literacy strategies, and utilize collaborative partnerships within the community to expand clients' accessibility to resources (Foss-Kelly et al., 2017; Overholser, 2016; Wadsworth, 2012).

Poverty Counseling Best Practices: A Grounded Theory Model

Researchers have determined that "training, awareness, knowledge, skills, and advocacy combine to establish a level of poverty counseling best practices above and beyond existing competencies" and developed a best-practices model for counselors working with clients currently experiencing poverty (Clark et al., 2020, p. 292). Central to this model is the framework of the MSJCC (Ratts et al., 2016). The themes of this model are (a) training; (b) awareness; (c) knowledge; (d) skills; and (e) advocacy.

Training

A counselor's competence and self-efficacy in working with clients experiencing poverty are affected by their level of training. This model highlights both formal and informal training experiences as significant contributors in counselors' abilities to work with clients currently experiencing poverty. Whereas formal training includes graduate programs, in-service training, or professional development, informal training is comprised of either informal exposure to poverty or personal experiences of poverty (Clark et al., 2020).

Awareness

The three sub-themes of awareness include: (a) self-awareness of social class identity; (b) client worldview of social class identity; and (c) counselor boundaries and wellness. First, counselors' awareness of power, privilege, and personal social class identities is crucial so as to not "inadvertently oppress or marginalize clients with their social class expectations" (Clark et al., 2020, p. 289). Second, awareness of the client's worldview regarding social class and their respective identity plays an integral role in demonstrating empathic understanding of their values. Third, counselors' awareness of personal boundaries (e.g., emotional) and maintenance of routine self-care practices are critical.

Knowledge

The five sub-themes of knowledge include: (a) complexities and barriers of poverty experiences; (b) privilege, oppression, and intersectionality; (c) systems theory; (d) severe and persistent mental illness (SPMI); and (e) crisis and trauma. It is essential that counselors be knowledgeable of and further explore with their client the complexities of poverty and the impact of related barriers in the client's life (Clark et al., 2020). In addition, counselors should acknowledge personal social justice issues and those of their clients, to include privilege, oppression, and intersectionality and their impact. Engaging in systemic and collaborative work within the systems with which clients associate (e.g., communities, extended family members, etc.) can engender better client outcomes (Clark et al., 2020). Lastly, given the prevalence of SPMI in high-poverty communities (Foss-Kelly et al., 2017; Wadsworth, 2012), counselors' knowledge of effective interventions for addressing crisis and trauma is critical.

Skills

When working with clients currently experiencing poverty, there are four skills counselors should employ: (a) poverty-sensitive assessment, (b) person-centered and relational skills, (c) cultural broaching, and (d) recognition of client strengths and empowerment (Clark et al., 2020). Counselors should be intentional in obtaining a holistic assessment of clients' needs. For example, counselors can include inquiries on intake forms about housing and food security, financial security, healthcare access, and transportation to capture a more holistic picture of clients' presenting needs. Second, a counselor who demonstrates "a strong, collaborative, person-centered counseling relationship is particularly effective when counseling clients experiencing poverty" (Clark et al., 2020, p. 290). Third, broaching, or openly addressing differences (e.g., social class) with clients can evoke deeper dialogue and therapeutic experiences for clients. Lastly, utilizing a strengths-based approach and acknowledging the successes, intrinsic motivation, and resilience of clients currently experiencing poverty can be empowering and serve as even greater motivation.

Advocacy

Counselors' advocacy efforts are contingent upon their awareness, knowledge, and skills (Clark et al., 2020). Counselors can engage in advocacy either on behalf of or collaboratively with their clients in three specific ways: (a) assist clients with problem-solving and finding resources, (b) increase client access, and (c) challenge poverty stereotypes (Clark et al., 2020). Utilizing a more directive approach during counseling sessions (e.g., budgeting, identifying and connecting with community resources, etc.) is most effective in working with clients currently experiencing poverty.

As a school counselor at a traditional high school, I (AC) recall facilitating a senior meeting during the beginning of the school year with a student and their mother to discuss postsecondary endeavors and identify "next steps" in the planning and preparation process. During the meeting the student expressed an interest in further exploring options to attend either a traditional, four-year college or a community college in-state. The student had maintained an average grade point average (GPA), which would have been advantageous for their application, in addition to their involvement in various extracurricular activities. The student's mother, however, envisioned and expressed a different postsecondary plan for the student; she shared that, because it was just the student and their younger sibling (4 years old) in the home, she wanted the student to stay home, gain employment, and help contribute financially. The student, visibly discouraged by their mother's statement, immediately shifted their postsecondary plan and stated that in a year or so they would consider attending college. Being from a middle-class environment in which education was valued, I was presented only two (acceptable) postsecondary options by my parents, namely college or military. I understood, however, the importance of me not imposing my personal values on the family or trying to talk them into a specific plan; rather, my role was to be attuned, supportive, and present for all options and resources while respecting the decision they ultimately considered to be best. While I was aware that the student was from a low-socioeconomic background and would have been a first-generation college student, I was also increasingly aware of the need to engage in advocacy on behalf of the student to ensure they had equitable access to resources that would further support their development during and after high school.

The Social Class Worldview Model–Revised

Liu (2001, 2002) originally conceptualized the SCWM as "a theoretical framework that shifts the psychological discourse around social class away from the stratification and sociological paradigms that have permeated much of the theoretical and empirical literature" (Liu, 2002, p. 9). Liu (2012) notes that the original SCWM (Liu, 2001, 2002; Liu & Ali, 2008; Liu, Ali, et al., 2004; Liu, Soleck, et al., 2004) inherently presumed that individuals both comprehended and were able to engage in discourse surrounding social class and their lives. Acknowledging that individuals are at different levels of awareness related to social class and classism consciousness, in 2012 Liu introduced the SCCC as a parallel framework that is both complementary to and embedded within the SCWM–Revised (SCWM-R; Liu, 2012). The three primary components of the SCWM-R are (a) economic cultures, (b) worldview, and (c) classism.

Economic Cultures

Liu (2012) describes economic cultures (ECs) as the localities (e.g., communities, neighborhoods) in which individuals seek social class status and position. Liu posits that there is not a unitary definition of lower-, middle-, or upper-class. Rather, the demands and expectations placed on an individual within an EC vary, so what is expected of a middle-class person in one EC may be entirely different in another EC. For example, I (MLD) live in a community in which engagement in adventurous outdoor activities is prized among middle- and upper-middle-class individuals. This is different from previous communities in which I have lived, where different things (e.g., living in particular neighborhoods) were expected of the middle class. An important element of maintaining one's social status, then, is an understanding of the ECs related to one's perceived or desired social status, and the types of capital needed to maintain that status. The three types of capital within the SCWM-R are (a) cultural (developed aesthetics reflective of the social group), (b) social (important relationships and connections), and (c) human (intellectual or physical characteristics and capabilities; Liu, 2012, 2013). This connects with an important assumption of the SCWM-R: that people strive to preserve a sense of normalcy and similarity with those they perceive as their peers, and successfully acting and relating to the world in this manner creates a sense of homeostasis within the individual. Conversely, when new expectations for the individual arise, homeostasis is disrupted, and the disequilibrium will continue until the individual is able to adjust to meet the new demands related to their attitudes, behaviors, or resources (Liu, 2012).

Worldview

Worldview is the second component of the SCWM-R. Liu (2012) defines *worldview* as "the lens through which the individual attempts to understand ... different capital demands and how these resources are to be used" (p. 10). Elements of the worldview include: (a) socialization messages (provided by family, peers, and one's aspirational social group), (b) an individual's materialistic attitudes, (c) perceived social class-congruent behaviors (e.g., language, etiquette), and (d) considerations related to lifestyle (e.g., where one lives, how one spends their time). Liu acknowledges that different elements of the worldview carry different levels of weight and prominence for individuals, depending upon the EC in which one is situated.

Classism

The third component of the SCWM-R is classism. Liu (2013) describes individuals as both "aggressors and targets" of classism (p. 9). As aggressors, individuals both interpret and utilize classism as a means of maintaining social class. As targets, individuals are on the receiving end of classism when interacting with others from different perceived social classes. As previously mentioned in this chapter, the four types of classism are (a) downward, (b) upward, (c) lateral, and (d) internalized. To briefly review, downward and upward are classism against those perceived to be in lower or higher social classes, respectively. Lateral is against those perceived to be in one's perceived same social class, and internalized is against oneself (Liu, 2012). Internalized classism, as conceptualized within the SCWM-R, refers to "the feelings of anxiety, depression, or inadequacy resulting from one's inability to maintain one's social status" (Liu, 2012, p. 11).

The Social Class and Classism Consciousness Model

Noting that individuals are at different levels of cognizance of their own status as classed individuals, Liu (2012) developed the SCCC as a means to explore both an individual's social class self- and others-awareness and how this consciousness develops. Within the framework, there are three levels and 10 statuses. Within the first level (no social class consciousness) are three statuses: (a) unawareness, (b) status position saliency, and (c) questioning. Within the second level (social class self-consciousness) are four statuses: (a) exploration and justification, (b) despair, (c) the world is just, and (d) intellectualized anger and frustration. Within the third level (social class consciousness) are three statuses: (a) reinvestment, (b) engagement, and (c) equilibrium. Additionally, within each level there are four relational components (i.e., self, peers, others, society), which relate to how individuals in the different statuses potentially perceive and interact with others. It is beyond the scope of this chapter to go into detailed explanations regarding each level, status, and relational component; the reader is encouraged to see Liu (2012) for more details regarding the SCCC.

Of important note for clinicians seeking to work with clients through the SCCC framework, it can be broadly stated that the SCCC mirrors a developmental model in that the statuses progress from less to more complex and aware (Liu, 2012). Liu suggests that an individual needs to experience progressing through the statuses in some hierarchical order, while also noting the possibility that the levels may also exist in every individual, but to varying levels of relevance and significance. Thus, the process of gaining awareness of social class and one's status as a socially classed individual is an iterative process, rather than a one-time event (Liu, 2012).

APPLICATION AND RELATED CLINICAL CASE SCENARIOS

Counselor Self-Exploration: I-CARE Model

The I-CARE Model is a framework that guides counselors in their approach to providing adequate services to clients experiencing poverty (Foss-Kelly et al., 2017). The stages (i.e., internally reflect, cultivate relationship, acknowledge realities, remove barriers, and expand on strengths) help ensure that the counselor "treats the client as an active participant in the counseling process, instilling hope that the client is truly capable of success" (Foss-Kelly et al., 2017, p. 205). Use of this model enhances and increases counselor self-awareness regarding personal social class identity, attitudes and beliefs about poverty, and knowledge of both the impacts of poverty on one's overall well-being and also culturally appropriate interventions (Goodman et al., 2013).

While social class can be a cultural "blind spot" for many individuals (Liu et al., 2007, p. 194), others may subjectively connect one's wealth to one's worth as a person, resulting in perpetual maladaptive thoughts and biases (Foss-Kelly et al., 2017). Counselors may either be unaware of the impact of poverty on mental health and daily functioning or overlook ways in which poverty might adversely affect the therapeutic process. Thus, the absence of a counselor's internal reflection significantly limits their ability to optimally conceptualize potential factors exacerbating the presenting issues of clients experiencing poverty (Foss-Kelly et al., 2017).

CLINICAL CASE SCENARIO 22.1

The following case scenario applies the I-CARE Model to a counseling session with Esadowa, a 26-year-old, biracial (Indigenous and African American), gender nonconforming client who is unmarried and lives in a rural area of the Southwestern region of the United States with their 4-year-old. Esadowa was reared in a high-poverty environment and aspired to break the cycle of intergenerational poverty, yet to no avail. Esadowa was referred to counseling by their workforce development program as a result of increased fluctuations in mood, inappropriate and aggressive outbursts, apathy, and diminished ability to concentrate. Because Esadowa was among one of the most creative and advanced trainees in the program, their supervisor sought to first pursue an intervention rather than dismiss them from the program and disrupt their pending job placement (Esadowa is currently unemployed).

Prior to meeting with Esadowa for the first session, the counselor, who identified as upper-middle-class, internally reflected (Stage 1; Foss-Kelly et al., 2017) on personal attitudes, biases, and perceptions related to poverty, recognizing the impact of biases on the counseling relationship and process (Wadsworth, 2012). The counselor acknowledged that although they had had few professional and personal interactions with individuals living in poverty, they were committed to empowering and supporting the client in working through their presenting needs. During the first session Esadowa was transparent and disclosed that they most recently experienced depressed mood, decreased appetite, fatigue, feelings of worthlessness and guilt, and decreased concentration and productivity. At one

(continued)

CLINICAL CASE SCENARIO 22.1 (CONTINUED)

point during the session Esadowa stated, "I am extremely overwhelmed and losing all hope of getting out of this deep hole (poverty). The little bit of hope I have left is because of my child. I don't want this cycle to continue with them but nothing I've tried seems to be enough to get us out." The counselor reflected and validated Esadowa's feelings and further explored with them specific ways in which poverty has affected their overall well-being, demonstrating understanding of self and the client's socioeconomic experiences (Wadsworth, 2012). Esadowa also questioned, "I wonder if this is continuing to happen to me because I have drifted in my spirituality and neglected spiritual practices?"

Immediately upon sharing, Esadowa became embarrassed to have displayed such vulnerability and emotion to someone whom they had just met and appeared to have it "all together." Having internalized the stigma of poverty, Esadowa began to think that they would be rejected, judged, and viewed as "less than" by the counselor. Ruminating over those thoughts, Esadowa became withdrawn and sank down in their chair, no longer making as much eye contact with the counselor as they did previously. A silence filled the room for approximately 30 seconds. For the duration of that time Esadowa looked down and fidgeted with their hands before slowly looking up at the counselor. Being fully attuned, the counselor made note of Esadowa's sudden change in disposition and stated, "I have noticed that after sharing some of your experiences with me, there was a shift; you retreated further back in your seat and are not as engaged. Describe to me what you're thinking and feeling right now." Esadowa took a deep breath and stated, "I feel embarrassed and stupid for getting all emotional and sharing things with you that you clearly don't understand; I'm sure you know nothing about this struggle. I'm sure you're judging me as you sit back, dressed in your fancy clothes." The counselor, having reflected Esadowa's feelings and paraphrased what had been shared, remained focused on cultivating the relationship (Stage 2; Foss-Kelly et al., 2017). The counselor "demonstrated deep respect for the humanness of the client" (Foss-Kelly et al., 2017, p. 205), treated Esadowa as an active participant in the process, and sought to "understand and process painful emotional defense mechanisms" with them (Foss-Kelly et al., 2017, p. 205). The counselor's attunement and attentiveness to Esadowa's feelings engendered yet another shift; Esadowa's posture and disposition became more engaged and, for the first time in their life, they felt seen, heard, cared for, and understood.

As the session continued, Esadowa shared experiences of discrimination and challenges maintaining adequate work due to transportation-related issues and inconsistent childcare, relying on family and close friends to watch their child due to having no money for childcare services. The counselor's previous and continued acknowledgement of Esadowa's realities (Stage 3; Foss-Kelly et al., 2017) fostered even more of an open discussion and authentic relationship. The counselor further addressed Esadowa's poverty-related stressors that were exacerbating the physical and mental health issues. Collaboratively, Esadowa and the counselor began discussing goals for their time together. In addition, the counselor informally assessed whether Esadowa's basic needs were met.

(continued)

CLINICAL CASE SCENARIO 22.1 (CONTINUED)

Esadowa disclosed several barriers impeding their ability to maintain work and adequately provide for their family of two. The counselor was aware that in order to eradicate the barriers mentioned (Stage 4; Foss-Kelly et al., 2017), advocacy efforts on behalf of the client would need to be primarily focused on transportation. The counselor challenged Esadowa not only to create a list of barriers they faced in order of significance but also to identify community resources to which they were connected. This assignment was yet another way for the counselor to determine Esadowa's most pressing needs and appropriate community resources to connect them with.

As the session was nearing the end, the counselor summarized the session and expanded on strengths (Stage 5; Foss-Kelly et al., 2017) Esadowa had displayed and disclosed during the session, the first being the fortitude to follow through with the referral and attend counseling. A respectful evaluation of a client's strengths, skillset, and navigation amid circumstances of poverty not only improves the therapeutic relationship but also promotes the foundation for identifying strategies to endure other challenges (Foss-Kelly et al., 2017). Recognizing the need to utilize a multidisciplinary approach, the counselor emphasized to Esadowa the collaborative nature of the process (Overholser, 2016), not only with them (counselor) but also community resources. The counselor asked, "Is there anything else you would like to share with me before we end our session?" Esadowa smiled and said, "My hope is coming back."

CLINICAL CASE SCENARIO 22.1 DISCUSSION QUESTIONS

1. What evidence of the I-CARE Model did the counselor use?
2. What, if any, opportunities did the counselor miss (i.e., blind spots) to provide anti-oppressive care to Esadowa?
3. Is there anything you would have done differently?

Counselor Self-Exploration: Social Class Worldview Model–Revised

Ballinger (2020) describes the historical inattention to the significance of class within the profession by stating, "any attempt to build a therapeutic system that can best meet the needs of all its potential users needs to bring class in from the borderlands" (p. 65). Through the SCWM-R and the SCCC, Liu (2012) provides frameworks that may be helpful in bringing social class, classism, and their impact on clients in from the frontiers of clinical consciousness. In order to do so effectively, Liu (2012) emphasizes the importance of the clinician being at a more complex or advanced level of social class consciousness than the client. This, Liu (2012) notes, aids clients in developing their own consciousness and awareness related to social class.

Liu (2012) encourages clinicians to explore the interconnected elements of the SCWM-R (e.g., economic cultures, classism, and worldview) as a way of aiding clients in developing insight about their experiences as a classed individual and "develop healthy coping and skills to navigate his or her economic culture and environment" (p. 14). Liu (2012) provides specific social class interventions utilizing the SCWM. These interventions are described in greater detail through a case scenario with a middle-class client (Lila).

CLINICAL CASE SCENARIO 22.2

Liu (2012) describes a process of employing social class interventions utilizing the SCWM. This process could be utilized over the course of the therapeutic relationship (see Liu & Arguello, 2006). In the following case scenario, however, the counselor employed the four steps (and two sub-steps) with a 42-year-old client, Lila, who identified as a bisexual, cisgender, Asian American female who lived with a male partner and their two children in an urban area of the Northeast United States. Lila initially sought counseling for symptoms related to anxiety and depression. During the first session with Lila, the counselor noted the potential salience of social class and classism.

While outwardly presenting as well-groomed and fashionably dressed, Lila described feeling stressed about finding clothes for her children that she felt were "suitable" for the school they attended. The counselor decided to help the client identify and understand her economic culture (Step 1; Liu, 2012) by asking Lila to describe any pressure she felt to keep up with other families at her children's school (Liu, 2012). "I feel enormous pressure," she replied. She then went on to describe a series of incidents throughout her childhood and adolescence when she felt excluded by other children because of what she described as her "raggy" clothing.

Utilizing Step 2, the counselor sought to help Lila identify the social class messages she received (Liu, 2012). The counselor asked Lila about how her parents might help resolve this situation in which she felt such a great amount of pressure to dress her children a certain way. In answering this question, Lila noted that her parents "weren't concerned about outward experiences." While she voiced an appreciation for this, she also said that her parents' lack of emphasis on material possessions, and accompanying lack of desire to put money toward material possessions (including clothes), left her feeling powerless on several levels.

In addition to feeling insecure about her clothing, she was unable to participate in many of the activities her friends enjoyed (e.g., going to the movies) that her parents saw as "frivolous." In order to further assist Lila with identifying social class behaviors, lifestyles, and possessions of salience in her current situation (Step 2a; Liu, 2012), the counselor asked her to describe how she imagined her life (Liu, 2012). She described a life in which she, her children, and her partner were happy and well-accepted among their peers. The counselor noted that, in this description, Lila did not describe having any particular material possessions, but rather connected happiness to being well-accepted by others. Probing further in this area, the counselor asked Lila what others had that she wanted (Liu, 2012). "It's not anyone thing that they have, in particular," she replied. "It's more that I want to look, and I want my children to look, like we fit in."

In Step 3, the counselor sought to identify Lila's experiences with classism and move toward developing an adaptive, realistic, and healthy expectation about herself (Liu, 2012). The counselor asked Lila what it felt like when she couldn't

(continued)

CLINICAL CASE SCENARIO 22.2 (CONTINUED)

keep up with her peers (Liu, 2012). "It feels terrible," she replied. "Like I'm back in second grade and I'm being made fun of for wearing my sister's hand-me-down clothing." She described avoiding those feelings at all costs, and living with a sense of fear and dread that her children would be rejected or made to feel "less than" if they didn't look a certain way.

After asking Lila a few more questions related to her experiences with classism, the counselor moved to Step 4: helping the client integrate her experiences of classism (Liu, 2012). "We've talked a lot today about elements of your social class experience," the counselor stated, "and now I'm curious what it means to you?" (Liu, 2012). Lila went on to describe the conversation as "eye-opening," noting that she had not previously realized the impact of her experiences with classism on her current thoughts, attitudes, and behaviors.

Finally, the counselor desired to help Lila take action and make changes in her life (Step 4a; Liu, 2012). After allowing her some time to process meaning, the counselor asked Lila to identify one thing she could do to change her awareness, situation, or perception (Liu, 2012). Lila noted that she wanted to heighten her awareness of when she was doing things only for the sake of gaining acceptance or avoiding rejection. She set a goal with the counselor to write down times during the week when she felt compelled to buy something for herself, her children, or her partner for the sole purpose of gaining acceptance or maintaining her middle-class status, and then discuss the list with her counselor during their next session.

CLINICAL CASE SCENARIO 22.2 DISCUSSION QUESTIONS

1. What evidence appears of the counselor's use of the SCWM?
2. Did the counselor adequately assess the client's social, cultural, and human capital? How so?
3. What, if any opportunities did the counselor miss (i.e., blind spots) to provide anti-oppressive care to Lila?

Self-Exploration: Poverty Counseling Best Practices and Counselor

Considering the prevalence of poverty (Clark et al., 2020; Semega et al., 2020) and various barriers individuals experiencing poverty face, they are less likely to access mental health services than individuals in middle-income or upper-income populations (Borges & Goodman, 2019). To increase access and promote engagement and more positive outcomes among this population, modifications to counseling (e.g., addressing power dynamics, negotiating boundaries, and navigating intrapsychic and contextual poverty-related stressors) may be necessary (Borges & Goodman, 2019). Counselors should acquire and demonstrate the following skills when supporting clients experiencing poverty: training, awareness, knowledge, skills, and advocacy as they "build on and reinforce each other" (Clark et al., 2020, p. 292).

CLINICAL CASE SCENARIO 22.3

The following case scenario applies the Poverty Counseling Best Practices Model to a counseling session with Perry, a 35-year-old Hispanic, cisgender male who lived in the Southern region of the United States with his spouse and three children. Perry and his wife, Eva, were initially furloughed from their jobs at the beginning of the COVID-19 outbreak; however, both had since been terminated. Although Perry was able to secure a job working from home, his salary was less than half of what he was making pre-pandemic; however, he was grateful to have some income. While Eva remained unemployed and focused primarily on assisting their children, ages 4, 6, and 10, with virtual learning, she had been fortunate to receive unemployment funds. Having previously been classified, objectively and subjectively, as middle-income and the sole financial provider of his family, Perry found it increasingly challenging to endure the financial stressors, pressure, and uncertainties of his family's current situation.

Although resistant to the idea of counseling, Perry surrendered to Eva's pleas as she grew concerned that he was "spiraling" emotionally and "becoming more and more depressed." Perry and his family were not experiencing poverty prior to COVID-19, but the counselor he was working with had been formally trained (Theme 1; Clark et al., 2020) to adequately support the needs of clients with low income. The primary focus of this session was relationship building and establishing a positive, trusting rapport, especially considering that Perry had never received counseling before. The counselor presented follow-up questions to the intake assessment related to family unit, passions and interests, and presenting issues. As Perry pressed through his resistance in disclosing his current situation due to embarrassment, guilt, and internalized stigma, the counselor demonstrated awareness (Theme 2; Clark et al., 2020) not only of personal social class but also the interplay of power, privilege, and respective class (to include Perry's) and its influence on the counseling relationship. Moreover, having had close family members affected by COVID-19 and experiencing circumstances similar to Perry's presented challenges for the counselor. To minimize countertransference and maintain personal boundaries, the counselor actively listened, remained attuned to, and removed "self" from Perry's narrative. Furthermore, the counselor was aware of the influences of intrapsychic problems and poverty-related stressors that, combined, often amplify one's presenting issues (Borges & Goodman, 2019).

As Perry continued to speak about his situation, he admitted, "I'm scared to become a failure and I fear that I will never get me and my family back to where we were before this pandemic. Life was so good for us." He continued to say, "I have never faced so many barriers before in my life at once. I feel invisible, helpless, and like nobody cares to help get me and my family back on our feet. It's like every man for himself out there." Being knowledgeable (Theme 3) of the (a) complexities and barriers of poverty experiences; (b) privilege, oppression, and intersectionality; (c) systems theory; (d) SPMI; and (e) crisis and trauma, the counselor discussed with Perry the complexities of his current

(continued)

CLINICAL CASE SCENARIO 22.3 (CONTINUED)

experiences and the poverty-related impact (Clark et al., 2020). After validating Perry's feelings and concerns through reflection and highlighting some of his strengths (e.g., fortitude and dedication to provide for his family, strong work ethic, ambition, intrinsic motivation, etc.), the counselor further explored with him systemic and collaborative partnerships which he had maintained, recognizing the impact of multidimensional approach in this process. Throughout the session, the counselor (Theme 4; Clark et al., 2020) demonstrated the skills of cultural sensitivity and humility, person-centered and relational approach, cultural broaching, and recognition of the client's strengths. Toward the end of the session, the counselor considered efforts of advocacy (Theme 5; Clark et al., 2020) they could employ on behalf of Perry and his family, while recognizing that those efforts would take time. First, however, the counselor presented Perry with a list of community resources available to him and his family under their current circumstances, many of which Perry was unaware of due to having had a plethora of resources and minimal need pre-COVID. Despite feeling reluctant upon entering the session, Perry began to feel more empowered and encouraged that his present circumstances were only temporary.

CLINICAL CASE SCENARIO 22.3 DISCUSSION QUESTIONS

1. What evidence of the Poverty Counseling Best Practices Model did the counselor use?
2. What, if any, opportunities did the counselor miss (i.e., blind spots) to provide anti-oppressive care to Perry?
3. Is there anything you would have done differently?

CULTURALLY RESPONSIVE COUNSELING, SOCIAL JUSTICE, ADVOCACY, AND LIBERATION COUNSELING

Ballinger (2020) elucidates a culturally responsive approach to working with clients across socioeconomic backgrounds. The scholar describes a "class-sensitive approach to therapy" (Ballinger, 2020, p. 70), noting that this method includes lowering barriers to access for "working-class" clients and "drawing in" counselors from a wide range of social class backgrounds (Ballinger, 2020). Additionally, training that incorporates sociological understandings, promotes class awareness, and embraces critical thinking, while simultaneously highlighting the way language and value systems are based in class, would be included in this approach. Ballinger further emphasizes that classism should be addressed as an area rife with potential prejudice and discrimination, and recommends extending critical thinking "to the questioning of the goals of counseling alongside its impacts" (2020, p. 74). "Has the striving to become more embedded and accepted as a profession," Ballinger asks, "led to our involvement in the 'medicalization of misery' and indeed to the drive to become accepted as the treatment of choice for a range of mental health issues?" (2020, p. 74).

Ballinger (2020) illustrates personal application of these principles, explaining a personal decision to work within agencies where long-term counseling is available free of charge, and also personally providing free or low-cost therapy and counseling supervision. Ballinger also describes feminist theory and existential theory as impactful underpinnings, noting that feminist theory understands the relationship between external circumstances and internal distress, and existential theory draws on the notion of situated freedom (i.e., the conditioning and constraining of choices by life circumstances). In articulating the importance of continual critical thinking, Ballinger (2020) notes:

> I have incorporated ongoing critical thinking into my way of being as a counsellor. I have learnt that I can burden clients with an agenda for change when their focus is on survival. I have also learnt that effective help for some clients involves practical help and a willingness to have flexible boundaries. I came to understand my job as listening to the unlistened to—be it people in their entirety or their secrets and pains. I have concluded that counselling means different things to different people and that is okay. (p. 75)

Social Justice

Social justice has been identified as the fifth force in the field (Ratts et al., 2004) and is reflected in the revised counseling competencies (MSJCC; Ratts et al., 2016). This shift in paradigm has engendered greater intentionality among counselors to consider sociopolitical implications and integrate more culturally responsive interventions into practice. Advocacy, according to Fickling (2016), is "the active component of a social justice paradigm" (p. 174). Counselors are better equipped to support the needs of their clients when culturally responsive counseling and social justice advocacy are integrated (Ratts et al., 2016). There are several factors that may affect counselors' abilities to engage in advocacy. Some of those factors include lack of time, minimal competence in self-efficacy, and negative perceptions of advocacy (e.g., "flag waving," "yelling and screaming" about injustices; Fickling, 2016, p. 183).

Ratts (2017) identifies social justice praxis as at the center of the MSJCC (Ratts et al., 2016). Counselors, the scholar notes, should both utilize techniques and strategies in alignment with the client's cultural background and further social justice through their practice. To promote the practical application of the MSJCC, Ratts introduced the MSJCC-AF (assessment form), which can be used both to outline client and counselor identities and privileged and marginalized statuses, and to scaffold interventions around the socioecological model (SEM). It is beyond the scope of this chapter to go into detail regarding the MSJCC-AF (see Ratts, 2017). What we would like to highlight here is the manner in which a counselor can utilize the SEM to "explore spheres of influence and . . . identify potential counseling and advocacy interventions" (Ratts, 2017, p. 95). Ratts identifies the following spheres of influence on the client's life: intrapersonal, interpersonal, institutional, community, public policy, and global/international. An examination of these spheres of influence not only provides the counselor and client with a framework for conceptualizing the client's problem(s), but also helps establish the extent to which interventions need to occur on the various levels.

A counselor utilizing the SEM to work with a client might explore the *public policy* realm by identifying "policies (e.g., rules and laws) that support and/or do not support the client" (Ratts, 2017, p. 95). For example, a client may approach the counselor with issues related to experiences with their child's school, noting that their child is often counted tardy, which may soon result in the school taking legal action against the parent. Further exploration of the issue reveals that the student rides a bus that often only arrives at school five minutes before the bell rings, and is left with the difficult choice of getting breakfast in the cafeteria and arriving to class late, or missing the meal. It is often students within the lower income brackets who ride the school bus and rely on the cafeteria for meals, resulting in a disproportionate amount of tardies for bus-riders. The counselor, then, can either work collaboratively with the student to self-advocate for a change in the tardy policy, or advocate on the student's behalf.

Advocacy

Clark et al. (2020) present three specific ways in which counselors can engage in advocacy on behalf of their clients: (a) assist clients with problem-solving and finding resources; (b) increase client access; and (c) challenge poverty stereotypes. Services that can further aid in this initiative include offering occasional sliding-scale or pro-bono sessions, flexibility in service delivery methods (e.g., community-based location), and advocacy at the sociopolitical level. When working with clients currently experiencing poverty, it may be necessary for counselors to assume a quasi-case management role to help the client secure their most basic needs (e.g., food, shelter, financial planning, etc.) in addition to connecting them with other resources in the community (Clark et al., 2020). While the continued engagement in social justice and advocacy on behalf of and with clients is essential, it is equally important to recognize that the journey toward cultivating multicultural and social justice competence is lifelong (Ratts et al., 2016).

Liberation Counseling

We encourage readers to consider additional social justice and advocacy efforts that can be made to provide more equitable, culturally responsive services to clients and students. To this end, we would like to discuss liberation within the context of social justice advocacy. In this portion of the chapter, we have discussed the concepts of social justice and advocacy as separate, but related, concepts. Within the literature, these terms are often used interchangeably (Steele, 2008). Integrating these terms, Steele defines *social justice advocacy* as "professional practice, research, or scholarship intended to identify and intervene in social policies and practices that have a negative impact on the mental health of clients who are marginalized on the basis of their social status" (2008, pp. 75–76). Examples within counselor education of utilization of core concepts and tenets from liberation psychology include, but are not limited to, a method of training counseling students to advocate for social justice (Steele, 2008) and increasing critical consciousness (Domínguez et al., 2020).

According to Chávez et al. (2016), the psychological theory and practice of liberation psychology can be traced to the work of Ignacio Martín-Baró (1991, 1996). Chávez and colleagues explain:

> In traditional psychology, the subjective experiences of oppressed people are seldom examined and are often pathologized; liberation psychology, however, promotes the recognition of the within-group strengths and virtues of marginalized communities. Furthermore, by focusing on local strengths and resources, Martín-Baró advocated for the appreciation of community virtues and collaboration with local communities in working toward social change. (p. 167)

Noting the need for pedagogical approaches to prepare burgeoning counselors to advocate for social justice, Steele (2008) described the Liberation Model as "a constructivist approach to social justice advocacy training of master's-level counseling students" (p. 74). Based on and grounded in the work of Freire (1993), the four phases of the model are:

1. Investigating, examining, and deconstructing U.S. society (primarily through instructor lecture and discourse analysis).

2. Examining, investigating, and deconstructing the implicit and explicit political and cultural ideology of counseling (through research and discourse analysis).
3. Interdisciplinary study and synthesis of findings from Phases 1 and 2 (including analysis, integration, and explanation of findings in a written report).
4. Application through the development of plans of action to address problems identified in Phase 3 (including an oral presentation on findings; Steele, 2008).

In defining a counseling psychology of liberation, Singh (2020) notes that liberation must be enacted to have meaning. "Liberation," the scholar notes, "moves us beyond the debates of whether or not we should engage in advocacy and social justice, and moves us to envision the world we want to leave behind as counseling psychologists and actively build towards that world" (Singh, 2020, p. 1114). While outlining 10 steps toward collective liberation within the profession of counseling psychology (e.g., "Learn our migrant stories as counseling psychologists to heal from historical trauma"; Singh, 2020, p. 1122), Singh notes that the values and practices associated with social justice and advocacy are important, but if "not grounded in the larger project and work of liberation, we are lost" (Singh, 2020, p. 1117). We encourage counselors-in-training as well as counselor educators, then, to move beyond an understanding of social justice and advocacy as concepts, and to actively engage in practices that will promote liberation of self, the client, and the counseling profession.

END-OF-CHAPTER RESOURCES

A robust set of instructor resources designed to supplement this text is located at http://connect.springerpub.com/content/book/978-0-8261-3953-5. Qualifying instructors may request access by emailing textbook@springerpub.com.

SUMMARY

Social class, an individual's status within the social and economic hierarchy, plays an integral role in shaping one's worldview and the specific ways in which one experiences, interprets, and makes sense of the objective economic world. Limited awareness and understanding of social class and intersectionality may adversely affect counselors' abilities to validate their students' or clients' lived experiences, thus negatively affecting the therapeutic relationship. There are several frameworks counselors can use to better understand class and classism (the I-CARE Model, Poverty Counseling Best Practices, the SCWM-R, the SCCC). It is essential that counselors develop culturally responsive counseling skills to ensure that the techniques and strategies they use align with students' or clients' cultural and socioeconomic background and further social justice in practice.

DISCUSSION QUESTIONS

1. What is the relationship between social class and classism? Between privilege and power?
2. What might it look like to "do intersectionality" within the therapeutic relationship?
3. Identify ways in which you, as a future professional counselor, can integrate elements of liberation counseling within your practice. Consider, specifically, liberation of self, the client, and the counseling profession.

4. Considering the models presented in the chapter (the I-CARE Model, Poverty Counseling Best Practices, SCWM-R, and SCCC) and your social class identity, what aspects do you anticipate being the most and least challenging? Why? How, exactly, will you work through the challenges you identified to ensure that you are effective in implementing the respective model in practice?

KEY REFERENCES

Only key references appear in the print edition. The full reference list appears in the digital product on Springer Publishing Connect: https://connect.springerpub.com/content/book/978-0-8261-3953-5/part/part02/chapter/ch22

Ballinger, L. (2020). Context, social class and counselling: It's not all just psychology. In G. Nolan & W. West (Eds.), *Extending horizons in therapy: The healing encounter in the helping and caring professions* (pp. 65–77). Routledge.

Brinkman, B. G., & Donohue, P. (2020). Doing intersectionality in social justice oriented clinical training. *Training and Education in Professional Psychology, 14*(2), 109–115. https://doi.org/10.1037/tep0000274

Clark, M., Ausloos, C., Delaney, C., Waters, L., Salpietro, L., & Tippett, H. (2020). Best practices for counseling clients experiencing poverty: A grounded theory. *Journal of Counseling & Development, 98*(3), 283–294. https://doi.org/10.1002/jcad.12323

Foss-Kelly, L. L., Generali, M. M., & Kress, V. E. (2017). Counseling strategies for empowering people living in poverty: The I-CARE model. *Journal of Multicultural Counseling and Development, 45*(3), 201–213. https://doi.org/10.1002/jmcd.12074

Liu, W. M. (2012). Developing a social class and classism consciousness. In E. M. Altmaier & J.-I. C. Hansen (Eds.), *The Oxford handbook of counseling psychology (Oxford Library of Psychology)*. Oxford University Press. https://doi.org/10.1093/oxfordhb/9780195342314.013.0012

Liu, W. M. (2013). Introduction to social class and classism in counseling psychology. In W. Ming Liu (Ed.), *The Oxford handbook of social class in counseling (Oxford Library of Psychology)* (pp. 3–20). Oxford University Press. https://doi.org/10.1093/oxfordhb/9780195398250.013.0001

Overholser, J. C. (2016). When words are not enough: Psychotherapy with clients who are living below the poverty level. *Journal of Contemporary Psychotherapy, 46*(2), 89–96. https://doi.org/10.1007/s10879-015-9313-4

Ratts, M. J. (2017). Charting the center and the margins: Addressing identity, marginalization, and privilege in counseling. *Journal of Mental Health Counseling, 39*(2), 87–103. https://doi.org/10.17744/mehc.39.2.01

Ratts, M. J., Singh, A. A., Nassar-McMillan, S., Butler, S. K., & McCullough, J. R. (2016). Multicultural and social justice counseling competencies: Guidelines for the counseling profession. *Journal of Multicultural Counseling and Development, 44*(1), 28–48. https://doi.org/ doi:10.1002/jmcd.12035.

CHAPTER 23

Culturally Responsive Counseling Related to Polyamory, Kink, and Taboo Culture

ERIC JETT

LEARNING OBJECTIVES

After reading this chapter, students will be able to:

- Outline the historical context of polyamory, kink, and taboo communities to increase counselor awareness and reduce cultural insensitivities.
- Analyze the sociopolitical and modern societal influences of polyamory, kink, and taboo to address the needs of diverse relationship styles.
- Identify ways to advocate for improved clinical approaches to address the needs of clients who identify as being in the polyamory, kink, and taboo communities.
- Review culturally aware strategies and techniques aligned with theoretical frameworks to support clients in the polyamory, kink, and taboo communities.

SELF-REFLECTION QUESTIONS

1. Think about biases, prejudices, and assumptions you might have about people who are polyamorous, kink, or taboo. How do these help and hinder your ability to provide culturally sensitive counseling?
2. What hesitancies, if any, do you have about working with polyamorous, kink, or taboo clients?
3. What attributes do you have that will enable you to work with polyamorous, kink, or taboo clients?

The interaction between individuals in complex and diverse ways is what forms the bond of relationships (Brunning, 2018). The intricacy of interaction in relationships ranges from emotional engagement to physical intimacy, which creates an endless potential of what it means to be with others. Individuals have found themselves engaging in various dynamics to make that connection with others because people are social creatures.

Historically, many of those actions have been met with resistance in society from a lack of knowledge and labeled as taboo (Boyer, 1999; Brunning, 2018). While none of the topics presented here are new, cultural shifts have created innovative ways to perceive and understand the needs of others. This chapter uses the lens of the liberation counseling framework to explore how sociopolitical, historical, and cultural contexts created resistance and the persecution that led to subcultures of like-minded individuals in the polyamory, kink, and taboo communities. Each community has its specific defining aspects, but they share many commonalities that intertwine the three communities as they expand their social support network of acceptance (Scott, 2015). Throughout this chapter, a discussion of the historical development, oppression, and current standing of each of these communities is presented. Looking at each concept through different theoretical frameworks of liberation, feminism, and affirmative counseling models will provide a deeper understanding of acceptance and core perceptional needs.

THE COUNSELOR: EXPLORATION, INTROSPECTION, AND REFLECTION

The polyamory, kink, and taboo communities are not new in society. Although the communities have existed for a while now, a counselor may find it is their first experience working with someone who identifies as a member of one or more of these communities. It is important for the counselor to be able to step into the exploration, introspection, and reflection of not only these communities but also their own cultural perspectives, including values and morals that could affect the counseling experience (Abe, 2020). Counselors do not have to identify as polyamorous, kink, or taboo to work with clients who do carry one or more of those identities. Building allyship is important in creating a safe space that allows clients to talk openly about their experiences. Brunning (2018) identified that professionals who are not part of the polyamory community can find themselves in conflict with accepting their clients' experiences based on the counselor's perceptions of monogamy. This can be true of any sexual practices, such as kink or other actions in the taboo community, that do not align with the counselor's own lived experiences (Brunning, 2018; Downing, 2015). For example, a counselor who is unfamiliar with polyamory might assume that conflict in a polyamorous relationship is occurring *because* it is polyamorous with multiple adults. This assumption could lead to other distortions, such as that there would be less conflict if it were a monogamous relationship.

Hutchins (2001) emphasized the importance of education and understanding of what was current and relevant in the events of polyamory, kink, and taboo communities. Hutchins (2001) defined *events* as current issues and changes in the communities, such as laws that affect the community; growth in models of counseling approaches; and the needs of the community regarding social support. Additionally, Obadia (2020) identified the importance and role of supervision and collaboration. The counselor working with clients in the polyamory, kink, or taboo communities is not expected to have answers to every situation. Counselors who are unsure of community needs may find themselves doubting their own professional abilities and thus could shy away from working with individuals who are part of this community. Supervision and collaboration with other mental health professionals can provide support in gaining knowledge and comfort in working with diversity in counseling (Obadia, 2020). Scott (2015) identified that it is important for counselors to reflect on their role in supporting social injustices by refusing to work with individuals based on their own lack of knowledge. Counselors hold an ethical responsibility to continue professional growth through trainings, supervision, and having open conversations with clients when topics are unfamiliar to them (Hutchins, 2001; Obadia, 2020).

CLIENT WORLDVIEWS AND PERSPECTIVES

Clients who are members of the polyamory, kink, or taboo communities may present with a wide range of worldviews and perspectives when seeking counseling. Clients may be hesitant to seek out counseling in the first place, and may be reluctant to fully open up in counseling due to negative lived experiences (Fershtman et al., 2011). For example, a polyamorous family who is concerned that calls about suspected child abuse or neglect will be made because the parents are in a polyamorous relationship might be hesitant to identify their relationship status. The National Coalition for Sexual Freedom (NCSF) identified that few protections exist to protect individuals in the kink or taboo communities professionally. Individuals in these communities may be concerned about being scrutinized by society or fear losing their jobs because of practices they engage in.

The worldviews and perspectives of the clients may not always be against or opposite to the polyamory, kink, or taboo communities. Cultural worldviews might encourage an individual to have multiple spouses as an expectation based on spiritual or family beliefs. In this instance the client's worldview is rooted in acceptance of the communities discussed in this chapter, but they may struggle with cultural integration into expectations of societal norms outside of their own (Kant, 2015).

Heteronormative

When working with those in the polyamorous, kink, or taboo communities, it is vital to understand what the concept of heteronormative means and the interplay that exists among the communities. The term *heteronormative* was popularized in the 1990s, defined as a belief that heterosexuality is the norm or preferred sexual orientation in society (Downing, 2015). Over time, the definition or construct of heteronormativity has expanded beyond sexual orientation to also define gender roles and expectations. Subcategories of heteronormativity have created sex hierarchies, identifying what are morally acceptable sexual acts and what are immoral sexual acts (Downing, 2015). Polyamory, kink, and taboo communities are often compared to being non-heteronormative to demonstrate their existence outside of the societal norm. While this comparison helps deepen the understanding of the communities by showing the oppression the communities might experience, it can also build additional stigma, supporting the concept that those who do not adhere to a heterosexual, monogamous, moral identification are not normal. It is important for the counselor to understand that while the construct of heteronormativity defines heterosexuality as the preferred or majority in society, that is not necessarily true when looking at other cultural acceptance of communities (Downing, 2015).

POLYAMORY VERSUS POLYGAMY

The etymology of the word *polyamory* can be found rooted in Greek and Latin: *poly* having the root meaning of "many" from the Greek language, and *amor* is the Latin root for "love." *Polyamory* means "many loves" (Brunning, 2018; Sheff, 2020). The engagement in polyamory is the action of having more than one intimate relationship. In the polyamory community, relationships may or may not be sexual, leading to relationships which also include those that entail emotional intimacy with more than one person (Obadia, 2020).

Historical Context

The concept of having multiple spouses or intimate relationships is not a modern-day view. Nonmonogamous relationships date back to the earliest known written accounts of humankind. Throughout history, humans often have had more than one spouse (Hutchins, 2001). Looking at the cultural changes in the United States, we see the first wave of non-monogamy during the 19th century. The word *polyamory* did not exist yet, but the tenets of living a nonmonogamous life did. In the mid- to late 1800s in the United States, there was heavy influence from the transcendental movement (Hutchins, 2001). The transcendental movement began in New England and was made up of those who considered themselves liberated from society's expectations, focusing on careers as writers, poets, and artists (Ferrer, 2019). The group was held together by a common thought based on the innate goodness of humanity, equality for those involved, and—above all else—community. The transcendental movement pushed back against the sweeping religious beliefs at the time, with its encouragement of engaging in a more "Bohemian lifestyle" (Hutchins, 2001). This style of living included communal living, shared responsibilities for the greater community, raising children together in communal homes, and of course openness in relationships to sexually express oneself and one's needs, and to help others fulfill their needs (Ferrer, 2019; Hutchins, 2001).

The second wave of non-monogamy emerged during the 1960s and 1970s. The United States experienced a sexual revolution in which individuals began to demonstrate the evolution of identities not only with sexuality, but also in gender roles (Hutchins, 2001). There was the birth of the feminist movement, which established a new framework for looking at experiences that did not use a patriarchal lens. *Polygamy* is a relationship structure focused on the role of a male having multiple wives. At this time in history, the status of monogamous relationships focused on those who identify as male providing for their family financially while those who identify as female took care of the home. The feminist movement created an opportunity to address gender hierarchy in relationships. The understanding of gender roles being a social construct began to form, and there was no longer a hidden community of nonheterosexual individuals. A new sexual orientation, bisexuality, was identified, which destabilized the construct of sexual orientation (Ferrer, 2019; Hutchins, 2001). It was also recognized that an individual could be attracted to a partner without emphasis on the gender expectation. Social and economic conditions shifted as well. This allowed women and nonheterosexual sexual orientations the opportunity to be seen in the community and make choices regarding their relationship styles and needs; this established the "free love" movement of the 70s. There was a need for escapism from the perils of wars that were happening. Nonmonogamous communities in the late 70s also provided new protection for those within established pods.

By the late 1970s a new illness had been identified, a virus that was labeled the human immunodeficiency virus (HIV). The virus was soon linked to being sexually transmitted, and that changed how society saw the free love movement. The more sexual partners you had, the greater risk you put yourself and your partners at of potentially contracting HIV. The virus was new, and because of the unknown variability of the virus, it was not known whether medical professionals could find a treatment for the virus, nor whether one would be able to live (and for how long) once diagnosed. Those factors led those practicing non-monogamy to reconsider how to maintain their relationships in a way that provided protection from contracting the virus. Groups of individuals in relationships created pods. Pods constituted a way to trust a select few with whom the pod members could have sexual relationships, without the fear of contracting this lethal illness from someone they didn't know (Butler, 1990; Hutchins, 2001; Sheff, 2020).

By the late 1980s and into the early 1990s, the third wave of non-monogamy in the United States arose. In the early 1990s, *polyamory* was introduced as a term. The word was introduced to replace the phrase "responsible non-monogamy" and to act as a more comprehensive term that would represent various relationship styles that were outside the defining boundaries of monogamy (Sheff, 2020). The growth in technology also influenced polyamory. With the advent of the internet, there was an ability to create convenient networks of community to give each other advice, find partners, and find direction (Bargh & McKenna, 2004). Polyamory conferences held in larger cities created opportunities for people to gather and discuss the topic. The image of diversity within polyamory was also evident, making the community open to all individuals regardless of sexual orientation or gender identification (Ferrer, 2019; Sheff, 2020).

Polyamorists may have one legal marriage, with their spouse being referred to as a *primary spouse*. What we do not see is legal marriage to more than one spouse. *Bigamy* is the illegal act of being legally married to more than one person and is punishable under existing laws (Ferrer, 2019). Polyamorists may refer to others as spouses, and even as being husbands or wives, but it is important to note that there is never more than one legal marriage. Today, that is beginning to shift in society, bringing in the newest wave of polyamory. Some states are beginning to grant spousal rights to multipartner relationships that formerly were reserved only for legal marriages. These rights are not nationally recognized yet, and are often established state by state, and in some instances county to county within a state.

CURRENT PERCEPTIONS OF OPPRESSION AND CHALLENGES

When one learns that someone is in a multipartner relationship, there may be an assumption that someone is a polygamist. Several factors separate polyamory and polygamy. Polygamy does include the act of having more than one spouse, like polyamory. However, polygamy is patriarchal, allowing only males to have more than one wife. Women, in contrast, are only allowed to have one husband and are not allowed to have intimate relationships with their husband's other wives. Additionally, polygamy is often driven from a religious perspective, creating a narrative of why the relationship dynamics exist the way they do (Brunning, 2018; Ferrer, 2019; Obadia, 2020; Strassberg, 2003). Polyamory is neither patriarchal nor matriarchal by nature; rather, it allows acceptance for anyone to have more than one spouse. Regardless of gender or sexuality, individuals are free to express themselves in various relationship styles. Polyamory, though it may be supported by individuals' spiritual or religious views, is not rooted in a religious ideology as is polygamy (Brunning, 2018; Strassberg, 2003).

Polyamory is often identified as an excuse to "cheat" or have "affairs" (Brunning, 2018). The polyamory community engaged in a sociopolitical movement to address separating a multipartner relationship from the identification of cheating by mainstream society. Today, polyamory is often associated with the phrase *ethical non-monogamy* (Easton & Hardy, 2013). The emphasis of ethical non-monogamy is on open communication so that all members within the relationship are aware of the relationship dynamics, there are no secrets, and individuals can make an informed decision about the relationship (Easton & Hardy, 2013). Several words are used to describe the subcommunities of polyamory today. Phrases such as *swingers, open marriage, triad, pod, polyfidelity, intimate network*, and *multilateral marriage* are a few, each having their own focus and influence. While not all of these phrases are defined here, understanding a few of them can shed light on the sociopolitical influences that guide some of the polyamory community. Swingers, or those in open marriages, may not be looking for an emotional relationship with others, but do want a physical relationship. Those relationships may be either long-term or short-term, but usually do not entail living together (Brunning, 2018). Those in the polyfidelity community might include those in triads or pods, but the emphasis of polyfidelity is an emotional relationship that stays within the relationship (triad or pod), with no one seeking an emotional or sexual relationship outside of that group (Brunning, 2018). A *triad* is a relationship among three individuals, which may or may not hold a polyfidelity perspective. A *pod* is four or more individuals intertwined in a relationship that may or may not have polyfidelity, depending on the relationship expectations (Brunning, 2018; Easton & Hardy, 2013).

As we saw in the 1970s and into the 1980s, one of the sociopolitical influences in engaging in polyamorous relationships was the then-current health climate and risk of HIV (Brunning, 2018; Easton & Hardy, 2013). Having a pod or polyfidelity community that you knew was being sexually active only within the agreed-upon group reduced the risk of potentially contracting a sexually transmitted disease such as HIV. Today, we see additional sociopolitical implications for polyamorous relationships beyond sexual and emotional intimacy, such as financial security, emotional support, and safety of self-expression (Brunning, 2018).

KINK AND TABOO

Kink is a word that was not always synonymous with sexual acts as it is today. The root meaning of *kink* is a bend or knot in a linear path (Scott, 2015). This is reflective of how perceptions based in the heteronormative perspective may view those who engage in sexual acts that are for more than procreation (Butler, 1990; Scott, 2015). Nowadays, there is an entire kink community, a network of individuals who are like-minded about sexual experiences, relationship styles, and open to allowing others to consensually explore their interests. The historical context of the kink community and the influences that the community is often faced with will be explored later in this chapter. The kink community has many subcategories. When considering the subcategories of kink communities, you may find words such as *swingers*, *bondage*, *dominance*, *submissive*, and even *furry play* (Butler, 1990) This is an extremely small sample of what falls within the kink community, because today any sexual interaction that is not with the intent to reproduce could be considered kink because it is outside of the heteronormative linear path.

Sociopolitical and Modern Cultural Influences Related to Kink

We can see throughout history how sociopolitical influences determined what was considered kink practice, even before the word was applied to sexual acts. Throughout the Middle Ages and the Renaissance period, acts such as masturbation and sodomy (anal or oral sex) were punished because neither of these sexual acts would result in pregnancy (Downing, 2015). Dr. Krafft-Ebing began the cultural influences of the medical and mental health professions on identifying what would eventually be called kink. Dr. Krafft-Ebing identified many of these acts as being caused by "hereditary taintedness," implying that sexual acts or sexual turn-ons could be genetic and degenerate behavior was a core cellular aspect. John Binet debated this account and brought in a different perspective that fetishism was a learned behavior (Scott, 2015). *Fetishism* is defined as an attraction or behavior where gratification is found to an abnormal degree. Abnormal degree is a subjective phrase but is defined as a sexual act that is not considered a generalized sexual act by the larger society. This creates a shift in understanding that what is considered fetishism in one culture, because it is not generally accepted, may not be considered fetishism in another culture due to cultural acceptance. Sociopolitical influences began to shift with regard to kink when it was reported in research that sexual interest outside of procreation followed a statistical norm (Scott, 2015). Other changes also occurred: for example, that masturbation was an expected act and was not a precursor to medical disease or mental health concerns. Additionally, there was a push to decriminalize homosexuality as shifts in mental health perceptions took place, no longer viewing homosexuality as mental health disease (Downing, 2015; Scott, 2015).

But who defines kink today? Many sociopolitical and modern cultural influences create the influences of what is or is not considered kink. One of the first influences that those in the field of mental health should consider is the *Diagnostic and Statistical Manual of Mental Disorders* (*DSM*). The first *DSM* was published in 1952 (Pillai-Friedman et al., 2015). In this early version of the *DSM*, sexual preferences that fell outside of the heteronormative monogamous ambit were considered deviant behavior and thought to be indicative of psychological issues (Downing, 2015). An example of this period in mental health is homosexuality. Homosexuality was considered a mental illness and listed in the first *DSM* as a "sociopathic personality disturbance," along with other sexual acts such as masturbation and oral sex (American Psychiatric Association, 1952). In 1973, the *DSM* was revised and there were shifts in the field of mental health that created some changes. Homosexuality was removed from the *DSM* and was no longer considered a mental illness. The *DSM-5*, the fifth edition and current version, now includes a broader descriptor of "paraphilias" (American Psychiatric Association, 2013). This is a blanket term used to identify sexual deviations from mainstream society and was an attempt to identify sexual preferences that were considered harmful to self or others. While homosexuality was removed, there remained a greater challenge with the new term "paraphilias." It was an umbrella term that had no boundaries, leaving it up to the professional generating the diagnosis to determine whether or not a person's interests fell into category. This umbrella term included individuals who participated in bondage/discipline/sadism/masochism (BDSM), oral or anal sex, or gender-bending, as a few examples. The focus of the *DSM* change was to identify acts that were potentially harmful to self or others, but that was subjective as there wasn't much known about many of the kink subcommunities (Pillai-Friedman et al., 2015). In the next revision of the *DSM*, "paraphilias" was broken down into different categories because subcommunities began to be formed, showing that there was no possible way to group all people of interest into one area. There was also community influence that began to shift some kink communities away from the focus that this was only about sexual acts. The BDSM subcommunity of kink is a great example, as more individuals began to speak out and explain that BDSM was not always about sexual gratification, but also about relationship dynamics. It was a lifestyle approach for many that may not always include sexual interactions. This was also true for other kink subcommunities, such as the leather communities and the transvestic communities. By 2010, the *DSM* had specific diagnostic codes for subcommunities such as BDSM, fetishism, and transvestic fetishism (finding sexual pleasure dressing in opposite-birth-gender clothing). However, the *DSM* underwent another revision in 2013. The NCSF played an influential role in revisions regarding kink and the communities represented. In the *DSM* 2013 revisions, a new definition marked the distinction between behavior and actual pathology (American Psychiatric Association, 2013). Sexual acts or lifestyles that were among consenting adults were no longer deemed to be mental illnesses (Downing, 2015; Scott, 2015). This shows the influence that the mental health and medical field have had in the determination of what is or is not acceptable.

Another influence on the kink community appeared during the 1970s and continues to the present. That influence is the impact and support kink communities have from the lesbian, gay, bisexual, transgender, queer (LGBTQ+) community. From the time that the LGBTQ+ community began to push for equal rights to be themselves in mainstream society, there was support for the kink communities. One example of this support became apparent when the LGBTQ+ community began to vocalize about their subcommunities that overlapped into what society considered kink, such as the leather community, bear communities (gay males who display body hair and are often older adults), and even age-focused communities such as younger members of the LGBTQ+ community who prefer to date those older or younger than them. Historically, the LGBTQ+ community has been faced with societal perceptions that have considered members of the community to be outside of the "norm," particularly when judged by the heteronormative expectations of society. Because of this, LGBTQ+ communities have acknowledged the importance of recognition to advance the civil rights of those around them. Examples of this were the events of the Stonewall riots in 1969 (Speciale & Khambatta, 2020). This event in the history of the LGBTQ+ community is the birth of what we now know as "Pride" recognition, which happens annually across the country in the form of parades, gatherings, and presentations to educate others on the LGBTQ+ community (Speciale & Khambatta, 2020). Today the LGBTQ+ community continues to influence the kink community through support and recognition. Many within the LGBTQ+ community believe that a "K" should be added to the existing acronym to recognize the kink community. This push is related to the question of whether kink should be considered an orientation like other sexualities (Speciale & Khambatta, 2020). While there is debate on whether kink is a sexual orientation, a lifestyle, or a choice, what we do know is that kink may look different from one individual to the next. Whereas one individual may engage in BDSM, that does not mean every person who identifies as part of the kink community will engage in BDSM.

New defining boundaries are also developing around the kink community. *Kink* today is considered a broad term, whereas *fetishism* has a narrower definition. There are also defining boundaries between kink sexuality and kink lifestyles. *Kink* today is a broad term that emphasizes consensual, nontraditional sexual, sensual, and intimate behaviors (Speciale & Khambatta, 2020). Kink includes fetishism, but not all kink is considered a fetish today. The term *fetish* inow describes a subcommunity of kink for individuals who have an interest in other erotic engagement such as costumes, nonhuman objects, smells, and sights, to name a few. There is also a greater understanding of the developmental stages of kink, which include early encounters, exploration of self, evaluation, finding others, and finally exploration with others. These stages are the ways the individual overcomes stigmas associated with kink. These developmental stages of kink are critical to addressing internalized feelings of anxiety, depression, and even suicidality, which can often be present when dealing with external and internal stigmatizations (Pillai-Friedman et al., 2015; Speciale & Khambatta, 2020).

One of the greatest influences today on the kink community is technology. The growth of technology has expanded the kink community considerably. Today individuals have the ability to connect with others who have similar interests and focuses in kink practices. The expansion of subcommunities in the kink world is becoming more predominant, because if a person's interest is in a specific area, they can find others who share those specific interests online, instead of being compelled to join communities of noninterest. Beyond the influence of the internet, there are other social media means whereby individuals can connect with online groups. Many of these communities have annual gatherings and offer support groups for those interested in or exploring kink practices. Additionally, the expansion of applications on cellular phones has also created a new way for individuals to connect with kink communities. A scroll through an online app store will show that there are apps for everything from BDSM to tickle fetishes. The advances of technology have allowed individuals to have greater access to communities, knowledge about the subject, and freedom to explore areas of interest anonymously if they need that added protection (Pillai-Friedman et al., 2015; Speciale & Khambatta, 2020). Technology also allows individuals to gain access to this information at a younger age, raising new challenges in the kink society to place a greater emphasis on ethical practices, a move that continues to be supported by associations such as the NCSF.

Taboo Culture

Thus far, we have discussed the polyamory community and the kink community. Each community has its identification and various subcommunities that make up the greater whole. Now we are going to bring all these communities together into one larger understanding of taboo culture. Today the word *taboo* signifies an implicit prohibition of topics that are based on cultural expectations and are often driven by morals or values that are set by cultural standards, familial culture, and spiritual beliefs. It has been reported that anything that is not within the construct of mainstream society can be classified as taboo (Fershtman et al., 2011). Taboo today is taking on a different context due to the advocacy of organizations such as the NCSF to represent a community of like-minded individuals who are okay with not meeting the mainstream societal expectations. This is true of communities such as polyamory and kink. Both communities and their subcommunities are considered taboo, and many individuals within those communities now see the word *taboo* as a point of change, something to be proud of because it shows individuality and acceptance of self (Fershtman et al., 2011).

Sociopolitical and Modern Cultural Influences Related to Taboo

Societies hold shared values and standards of acceptable behaviors. The acceptable behaviors create defining constructs for how members of the community act. The culture within that society guides the behaviors and thoughts of those within it, setting an agreed-upon social norm of expectations and rules to follow. What falls outside of those social norms is taboo (Fershtman et al., 2011). These standards have a large impact on people's lives, and affect the way individuals dress, eat, drive, interact with others, and even express their sexual preferences and practices.

Taboos are not limited to sexual acts. The constructs of taboo change over time based on societal expectations (Fershtman et al., 2011). Fershtman et al. (2011) identified that some taboo practices may even disappear over time, while new taboo rituals develop. For example, a hundred years ago the idea of a 15-year-old being married and becoming a parent was acceptable and expected. Today, someone under the age of 18 getting married is taboo because of expectations about what it means to be a youth compared to what it means to be an adult. Another example is that in many cultures, the discussion of mental health issues—even as straightforward as feeling sad—can be completely taboo (Fershtman et al., 2011). The United States has pushed to reduce the stigma of engaging in mental health discussions and thus make this topic not taboo (Fershtman et al., 2011).

Taboo practices are identified and condemned by society, often through punishment and stigma surrounding acts; this social punishment is the reaction others in society have to someone not meeting the social norms. One might assume that the punishment must be applied because of observable actions; however, individuals who have thoughts about engaging in a taboo action often experience internalized punishment. Social punishment can be self-inflicted, which diminishes the value one may place on oneself. Consider an individual who identifies as polyamorous, acknowledging that they do not fit the expectations of a monogamous lifestyle. Internalized social punishment might take the form of emotionally beating themself up for not being able to be faithful to one person, maybe forcing themself to stay in an unhappy relationship, or experiencing shame about having more than one spouse and hiding those relationships from others important in their life. An individual within the kink community may encounter social punishment in having to sneak around to explore their interests, thoughts, and feelings; be ashamed of their thoughts; or risk other social punishments such as expulsion from families, spiritual places of worship, or support systems (Agonito, 2014; Fershtman et al., 2011).

Currently, taboo is a community encompassing anything that is outside of the societal norm. It is not always involved with sexuality or sexual exploration; it can be as simple as using hair color to express yourself as an individual compared to those around you. Taboo is a statement of wanting to separate oneself from social punishment and accept the individualistic nature of people in a consensual and ethical way.

STRESSORS AND DISCRIMINATION

Individuals practicing as part of the polyamory, kink, or taboo communities may experience negative physical and mental health outcomes, such as increased depression and anxiety. As marginalized groups, there are minimal protections for individuals within these groups in the workplace, housing, or family law (Bigner & Wetchler, 2012; Fershtman et al., 2011).

Currently, individuals practicing polyamorous relationships do not have the legal ability to marry more than one spouse. Current laws established to prevent polygamy in the United States identify anyone who attempts to marry more than one individual legally as a bigamist. *Bigamy* is the act of being married to more than one individual in a culture where monogamy is mandated or considered the legal norm (Brunning, 2018; Conley & Piemonte, 2020). Legal marriage provides legal protections to monogamous relationships that polyamorous relationships do not have because of the inability to legally marry more than one person. Examples of legal complications that polyamorous communities face include not being able to make decisions for spouses in medical emergencies and fear of having children taken away from non-biological parents (Brunning, 2018). Polyamorous families may also face stigma in the medical, mental health, and other professions due to a lack of understanding of what polyamory is. This can manifest as discrimination that affects the polyamorous family in various ways. For instance, child abuse and neglect reports might be made due to the family being polyamorous, even though no abuse or neglect is present. In mental health providers, this discrimination could take the form of presuming that mental health struggles are related to the individual being polyamorous and overlooking the actual root cause of the disturbance.

Stressors and discrimination are just as prevalent in the kink and taboo communities as they are in the polyamory community. The kink community is focused on acts that are considered sexual or lead toward sexual interaction. Individuals may find themselves faced with the potential of being terminated from their job if their sexual practices go against the morality of the workplace (Pillai-Friedman et al., 2015). Individuals in the kink community may also be hesitant to discuss their community involvement, particularly if they have children, out of fear that they might lose their children or be seen as unworthy parents. Individuals in the kink communities may struggle with intimacy with others due to fear of discrimination and being seen as different after expressing their kink practices or desires (Scott, 2015).

The taboo community may face different discriminations that are not specifically legal. For example, Agonito (2014) identified that women who choose not to give birth may be discriminated against as less than those who do bear children. Fershtman et al. (2011) stated that discrimination based in the taboo communities may differ from region to region based on the dominant culture and how other communities are perceived. Lesnik-Oberstein (2006) provided a strong example of this when discussing discrimination around body hair. In the United States, a woman who chooses to keep body hair in areas such as the legs and armpits might be faced with discriminatory views of being dirty. In other countries where the dominant culture is different, body hair may not be subject to discriminatory views. Taboo is anything that is outside of the dominant culture's acceptance (Fershtman et al., 2011), which means that taboo communities are not always or necessarily tied to polyamory or kink. An individual in their 20s or 30s who chooses to live at home with their parents might be considered taboo and faced with the discriminatory stigma of being lazy by persons who have no knowledge or understanding of their cultural or familial circumstances. Individuals labeled as gamers may face similar taboo stigma, especially as they age (Rickel, 1999).

MODERN THEORETICAL FRAMEWORKS

Understanding the history of these various communities is important. It shows both the external and internal challenges that individuals might face when going through the stages of self-discovery. Counselors must consider what would be ethical and effective approaches when working with individuals who do not fall within the societal norm. The question that often comes to the surface is how clinicians can address the needs of their clients in a way that is supportive and efficient. Training programs on relationship-style counseling can be complicit in perpetuating a focus on monogamously styled dynamics, rather than bringing in specific skills, interventions, theories, and contexts to support those in polyamorous relationships. This is similarly true regarding the lack of specific skills, interventions, theories, and context to support individuals in the kink and taboo communities. Several theoretical frameworks provide appropriate support for those in the polyamory, kink, and taboo communities, addressing the sociopolitical pressures that might be felt to conform to the heteronormative monogamous expectations of others. Following are four theoretical frameworks that could help support those in the polyamory, kink, and taboo communities.

Affirmative Therapy

Affirmative therapy is a form of psychotherapy that was initially developed to support members of the LGBTQ+ community (Bigner & Wetchler, 2012). In 1982, a new approach to LGBTQ+ psychotherapy was coined "gay affirmative therapy" (Bigner & Wetchler, 2012). The focus of this new approach was to challenge the pathological perspective of homosexuality, and to meet the needs of clients who were part of the LGBTQ+ community. Gradually, as continued research was conducted and this approach to counseling was refined, the focus expanded, no longer aimed only for the LGBTQ+ community; it is now known as affirmative therapy (Bigner & Wetchler, 2012). Affirmative therapy is about validation and advocacy for minority identities (Bigner & Wetchler, 2012). While there is still an emphasis in affirmative therapy on sexuality, gender identity, and gender expression, it is aligned well for working with the polyamory, kink, and taboo communities (Bigner & Wetchler, 2012).

McGeorge et al. (2018) identified that families and couples can also benefit from affirmative therapy, for example, when an individual within the family comes out as being part of the polyamory, kink, or taboo community. Affirmative therapy helps families work through biases and issues in communication with the goal of greater acceptance. Additionally, couples might benefit by learning about and understanding the different relationship dynamics, gender identification, and sexualities that can occur across the spectrum of relationships. Affirmative therapy is about integrating an understanding of diverse identities into the practice of marriage and family therapy and examining identities that do not align with the societal norm. This is particularly important in families that have children, parents, spouses, or others who identify as part of the polyamory, kink, or taboo communities.

Affirmative Therapy Principles

Affirmative therapy explores the mechanisms through which underrepresented populations experience compromised mental health stress and fear of being their genuine selves. These principles are intended to provide the affirmative counselor with the means needed to understand the impact of the societal expectations that clients are unable to live up to.

1) Normalize the Impact of Minority Stress and How It Influences Mental Health

Counselors need to understand that sexual minority stigma can manifest in various ways, such as feelings of guilt, shame, fears of negative evaluation, or exhaustion from hiding one's personal life. Becoming comfortable talking with clients about the impact of stresses and the distress of holding stigma due to identifying as a member of these communities creates space to process deeper feelings. It is important for the counselor to bridge the discussion of stressors and its connection to sexual orientation, gender identification, and relationship dynamics. Clients might struggle to see the association, particularly if they do not identify as a minority based on their cultural background. Counselors will want to specifically reflect feelings of vulnerabilities, anxiety, or depression that are tied to activities involved in the polyamory, kink, or taboo communities, as ways to demonstrate and help the client understand minority stressors (Proujansky & Pachankis, 2014).

2) Increase Emotional Awareness, Regulation, and Acceptance

When we consider the impact of minority stress on individuals related to relationship dynamics or sexual actions, there can be a hindering impact on emotional awareness, tolerance, and regulation. There is the propensity for increased anxiety and depression. An individual who feels that they must hide their involvement in any of the above-named communities due to being viewed negatively may experience higher levels of anxiety (Proujansky & Pachankis, 2014). When an individual who is not able to openly be themselves or have those they care about in the communities be a regular part of their life, the person may face a potential struggle with moments of depression. This can lead clients to attempt to regulate their emotions through unhealthy actions. As counselors, we want to provide clients a path to healthier means of emotional regulation. This is facilitated by the counselor through active listening, hearing the client's experience, and decreasing avoidance (Proujansky & Pachankis, 2014).

3) Decrease Avoidance

Affirmative therapy holds a core concept that avoidance behaviors lead to emotional disturbances. Clients who feel less than or judged by others may choose to engage in the act of avoidance. Avoidance can look different based on the client but could take the form of an individual refusing to talk with their support system, avoiding activities that might highlight their lived experiences, or refusing to engage in communities they identify with. One cannot avoid one's feelings, thoughts, or needs and maintain a robust mental health state. Decreasing avoidance is an opportunity for the counselor and the client to identify the treatment target: the thoughts, feelings, or behaviors the client is trying to avoid out of fear of judgment (Proujansky & Pachankis, 2014).

4) Restructure Cognitions Related to Minority Stress

Bigner and Wetchler (2012) identified that while much of affirmative therapy is rooted in a psychotherapeutic approach, there is a moment where cognitive techniques are important in helping clients during their mental health journey. Individuals might internalize negative schemas about themselves or others in communities such as polyamory, kink, and taboo, even though they are pulled toward those communities due to interest. This can lead them to anticipate rejection and discrimination from others and cause social withdrawal. Counselors working with clients during this stage need to address the internalized stigmas their clients may have constructed, to help them see the cognitive distortions (irrational thoughts based on lived experiences) and begin to change the narrative. Techniques such as free association, where clients are given words or images associated with the community they are struggling with and asked to respond with first thoughts, can provide the counselor and client opportunities to explore those thoughts and the root of where they developed (Proujansky & Pachankis, 2014).

5) Empowerment With Assertive Communication

A client coming out as a member of the polyamory, kink, or taboo community is demonstrating an act of self-assertion. The individual is stating, "This is who I am." One of the important aspects of affirmative therapy is empowering the client to assert their wants, needs, and rights to be who they are. Often this is explored through role-playing in the counseling session, allowing the client to practice and gain comfort in making empowerment statements. Counselors practicing affirmative theory should assess for client safety when moving a client into this area of treatment. Encouraging a client to be empowered and own their identity is important, but should not be done at the cost of safety.

6) Validate Unique Strengths

Affirmative therapy is about facilitating resilience. It is valuable to identify the resilience of those who have experienced stress, stigma, and oppression. Proujansky and Pachankis (2014) stated that forms of resilience to promote are social activism, social and sexual creativity, and a sense of shamelessness and pride for individuality. Social activism for the client means becoming active within the identified community, through gatherings, conferences, or other events. Proujansky and Pachankis (2014) identified that encouraging social and sexual creativity allows the individual to take pride in who they are while reducing the feelings of shame. Keep in mind that coming out as a sexual minority means the individual may be leaving the prescribed traditions of a heteronormative path (Proujansky & Pachankis, 2014).

7) Facilitate Supportive Relationships

Many individuals who have sexual minority experiences may report having fewer social supports, fewer feelings of comfort in social settings due to feelings of being different, and more socially-related vulnerability. While including those important in the client's life in the counseling process can be valuable in increasing social support for the client, there are additional actions the counselor and client can discuss. Guiding the client toward supportive relationships in a diverse way can be important. This may include encouraging the client to attend support groups for the client's area of interest. The counselor will need to search for or work with clients to identify what groups are available in the area. These support groups provide the client an opportunity to feel more supported, accepted, and connected to the community by hearing the experiences of others (Proujansky & Pachankis, 2014).

8) Affirm Healthy, Rewarding Expressions of Community

The affirmative counselor is sex-positive and able to express views of communities that involve sex and relationship dynamics as normal, natural, and healthy. Clients who struggle with shame at being part of these communities may find that they try to escape the shame by trying to be what they are not, which creates mental health stress. The affirmative counselor asserts that identifying as polyamorous, kink, or taboo is normal, natural, and healthy if it is consensual (Proujansky & Pachankis, 2014). Helping the client bridge the movement from feeling shame to being able to say statements such as "I am in a polyamorous relationship" or "my sexuality is my own to determine" creates empowerment in identity.

Feminist Theory

Feminist counseling holds the tenets that individuals are in disadvantaged positions when their sex, gender, sexuality, race, ethnicity, religion, and age are used against them (Trier-Bieniek, 2015). The feminist counselor engages the client to work on ways to disempower social forces that place expectations on the client to conform in ways they may not be able or want to. This counseling approach focuses on societal, cultural, and political causes in the client's life, and works to recognize the client's empowerment to overcome those expectations. In comparison to other theoretical orientations, the counselor and the client need to work as equals in the counseling session and recognize that both counselor and client have their own lived experiences that will be present in the session. The feminist counselor acknowledges different experiences that they and their client have, while drawing from similarities of empowerment, survival, and goal setting. Although feminist therapy grew out of the need to provide women with an established and valid approach to counseling, feminist therapy has grown to include help for any individual who may be dealing with gender bias, stigmas, stereotyping, trauma, and stress of meeting the heteronormative traditional family perspective (Benstead, 2021; Trier-Bieniek, 2015). These factors make feminist theory beneficial for working with individuals in the polyamory, kink, and taboo communities (Evans, 1995; Trier-Bieniek, 2015).

Feminist Therapy Principles

Feminist therapy explores the mechanisms through which individuals experience disparities based on gender, sexuality, and social expectations. These principles help to provide the feminist counselor the steps needed to understand the impact clients are living with from societal expectations that they are unable to live up to. A feminist therapy framework recognizes that many clients will have experienced a form of suppression or oppression in society due to heteronormative expectations. To support clients in moving through feelings of suppression or oppression, the feminist therapy counselor bases the work on principles of egalitarian relationship, revision of the theory, accountability, non-victim blaming, and client well-being (Trier-Bieniek, 2015).

1) Egalitarian Relationship

One of the important principles of the feminist counseling approach is the egalitarian relationship. In the feminist counseling session, the counselor and the client need to be considered equal, and the inherent power differential between counselor and client must be addressed. This demonstrates to the client that the counselor is not giving the client the power to create change: that power comes from within the client. This creates a focus on the client's strengths, provides validation, and accepts that the client's weaknesses do not need to be fixed but instead accepted (Trier-Bieniek, 2015).

2) Allow for Revision of the Theory

The feminist counselor understands that feminism is not static and must adapt to the current social contexts the client is dealing with. Discourse in society causes the feminist counselor to develop and work with their client to adapt skills as needed to address the current situation the client may be dealing with (Evans, 1995). For example, the feminist counselor takes into consideration that discord can be tied to many aspects of a client's life. In this instance, discord could arise from the stress of trying to fulfill family expectations to have a monogamous relationship when the individual identifies as polyamorous. An individual who identifies as being part of the kink or taboo communities may find discord in their life by trying to deny their interest or the communities they relate to. The feminist counselor may adapt skills as needed to address these situations through challenging the client to address cognitive distortions (irrational thoughts) that might be causing anxiety and stress (Evans, 1995).

3) Retain Accountability

Feminist counseling is a process of acknowledging that power is often given away by the client as a means to meet societal expectations. For instance, a client may choose to stay in a monogamous relationship due to societal expectations, even though the client identifies as polyamorous. Individuals who identify as part of the kink community may manifest giving power away by showing signs of guilt or anxiety over their interest. That power may also be taken away when an individual does not meet expectations. This may be seen in fear that an individual has about losing their job, children, or loved ones due to their affiliation with one or more taboo communities. The feminist counselor helps the client address the accountability of power that they can retain. Acknowledging the individual's experience of having that power reduced, minimized, or taken away has its emotional impact (Evans, 1995).

4) Non-Victim Blaming

Feminist counseling maintains the role of not blaming the victim. The tenet of feminist counseling is that individuals are discriminated against due to factors that are outside of their control. The feminist counselor will focus on the individual's strengths and how they can be empowered to overcome challenging situations. The feminist counselor is not going to tell the client that they could be different, but instead will empower the client. For example, instead of saying "you could stay in a monogamous relationship," the feminist counselor may ask, "How can we educate others about what polyamory is?" The inclusion of "we" statements is important for the feminist counselor, as it demonstrates that the counselor is part of the therapeutic process and empowers the client to become their own advocate.

5) Client's Well-Being

The feminist counselor is focused on the client's well-being at all stages of the counseling process. This is the process of helping the client find acceptance of self and the empowerment to own their identity. These are aspects that individuals who are part of the polyamory, kink, or taboo communities often struggle with (Benstead, 2021; Trier-Bieniek, 2015). These factors make feminist theory beneficial for working with individuals in the polyamory, kink, and taboo communities. Feelings of shame or guilt that individuals in the polyamory, kink, and taboo communities may feel are gradually replaced during the counseling process by self-acceptance and empowerment.

Liberation Framework

A liberation framework is an approach to counseling that gives support in understanding the experiences of oppressed and impoverished communities. Concisely, the liberation framework is an approach that understands the sociopolitical structure that communities exist in and how those structures create oppression (Chamsanit et al., 2021). The liberation framework was born in social psychology, but the construct of this framework is valuable as an approach in mental health counseling, particularly when working with individuals in the polyamory, kink, and taboo communities. The core principles of the liberation framework include concientizacion, realism-critico, de-ideologization, a social orientation, preferential option for oppressed majorities, and methodological eclecticism (Abe, 2020; Chamsanit et al., 2021).

Liberation Framework Principles

A liberation framework explores the mechanisms through which communities are oppressed and impoverished through the sociopolitical structure. These principles are meant to help provide the counselor working from a liberation standpoint with the steps needed to understand the impact of the oppressions clients are living with, because of the oppressive sociopolitical structure that exists around them.

1) Raising Politico-Social Consciousness

Understanding the individual's experience and the construct of sociopolitical experiences are important to the liberation framework. Initially introduced by Paulo Freire as *Concientizacion*, the initial principle of the liberation framework is to raise politico-social consciousness. The process helps the individual become more conscious of self and how their life is structured by social reality. Within that social reality is the discussion of oppression and understood expectations, and as a result the individual becomes what Paulo Freire called a social actor, trying to fit into the dominant social norms. It is important in the liberation framework for counselors and clients alike to understand the importance of interconnectedness, which often leads individuals to comply with oppression, to be subjugated, and to perform other complicit behaviors to belong (Chamsanit et al., 2021). This is important to consider when working with individuals in the polyamory, kink, and taboo communities, who want that sense of connection but were raised in an oppressive environment, with the expectation to conform to the heteronormative values of the world around them.

2) Social Orientation

Many mental health theories were criticized for attempting to provide a framework that explained human behavior without taking into consideration the sociopolitical, historical, and cultural context of people (Abe, 2020). The argument was that individual characteristics, thoughts, and actions were related to social relations and conditions, and that not considering that fact meant counseling was missing a valuable factor in understanding an individual's experience. Taking into consideration the sociopolitical, historical, and cultural context of alienating environments helps conceptualize the impact on a client's mental health, both externally and internally (Kant, 2015; Singh et al., 2020).

The social orientation principle is based on understanding the role of society in shaping the current conditions the individual is experiencing. This includes understanding the history of oppression connected to communities. The counselor will need to evaluate the social power and structures around the individual (Chamsanit et al., 2021). In working with those in the polyamory, kink, and taboo communities, it is important to consider the history of monogamy and the traditional focus of intimate relationships on procreation. This historical context helps reveal the framework of how individuals within these communities may experience oppression to not be themselves and could develop internalized stigmas related to not wanting a monogamous lifestyle or even wanting children.

3) Preferential Option

Liberation psychology is constructed as a form of mental health perspective that was developed from "oppressed people" rather than for "oppressed people" (Kant, 2015). This statement is powerful for the client in realizing that the liberation framework is adaptable to their experiences and is about understanding the impact in their life. Under this principle, it is expected for the counselor and client to acknowledge that there are societal oppressions the client is dealing with, but they may be unaware of at that moment (Chamsanit et al., 2021).

4) Realismo-Critico

Theories should not define the problems that are explored in the counseling session. The liberation framework allows the situations the client is living with to generate the theories that should be used based on need. In "traditional" mental health counseling, the theory may create a preconceived notion of how to address an issue with a client, and the counselor then works to fit the client into the theoretical model (Kant, 2015). With realismo-critico there is empowerment in understanding the client's theory based on the experiences they have lived (Kant, 2015; Singh et al., 2020). For the polyamory, kink, and taboo communities, this can be valuable because the liberation framework allows ample opportunities to integrate other theoretical orientations based on the clients' needs. This can also be seen in an additional subset of the liberation framework that has shown how the framework fits with other theories, such as the feminist liberation framework (Chamsanit et al., 2021). What needs to be understood in this construct is that the client's experiences are explored before the counselor implements a theory, and only then is the client matched to a theory.

5) Deideologized Reality

Kant (2015) identified that it is important when using the liberation framework to understand the role of ideology. Ideology is the overarching idea that solidifies majority groups and leads to unjust sociopolitical environments. In the liberation framework, the counselor and client will work to deideologize reality. This means both counselor and client gain an understanding of social reality transparently instead of it being obscured by the majority or dominant ideology. The process encourages individuals in marginalized communities to create and endorse ideologies that promote their interests (Chamsanit et al., 2021). When considering application to the polyamory, kink, and taboo communities, we can link deideologizing actions to building advocacy within the community. Encouraging individuals to create their ideologies is a core tenet of polyamory, creating relationships that are agreeable to the consenting adults involved (Brunning, 2018). This also is mirrored in the kink community by overcoming social expectations to be comfortable in self-expression that is consensual (Pillai-Friedman et al., 2015).

6) Methodological Eclecticism

The liberation framework is about using what is necessary to help the client. This means not feeling confined to one methodological approach but instead incorporating methodologies from diverse domains. This applies not only to the research around the liberation framework, but also to the clinical application. Counselors are encouraged to step away from the "traditional" approach of methodological styles to counseling, and to consider how diverse methodologies translate to multicultural clients to meet their needs.

Attachment Theory

Attachment theory is an orientation that can be useful when working with clients in the polyamory, kink, or taboo communities when the tenets of the theory are considered. Katz and Katz (2021) defined *attachment* as the communication of safety through proximity and protection that is provided by another. This could be a parent or caregiver in the case of children, but for adults can be romantic partners. When attachment-related issues are present, there can be an increase in anxiety and avoidance within the individual (Katz & Katz, 2021). In traditional counseling approaches, the goal of attachment theory is to help individuals develop healthy or secure attachments. In application of attachment theory in polyamory, kink, or taboo communities, research has found that these communities create an opportunity for a variety of attachment styles to find balance with each other. For example, an individual who is anxiously attached to others is often sensitive to threats of being alone. An individual with this style of attachment who is in the polyamory community may find it easier to deal with their anxious attachment style by having more than one partner. Although polyamorous relationships are considered inherently insecure with more risk of potential breakups, if one partner leaves the relationship there are other partners who may still be present to provide support. Another example would be an individual who has an avoidant attachment style, who might find mental health support from the kink community by connecting with others who have similar interests and styles.

Attachment Styles

The tenets of attachment theory are the three styles of attachment that can be seen. Attachment theory is built on the foundation that people are hardwired from birth to connect with others. Disruptive events can cause challenges in attachment development leading to various styles of attachment (Moors et al., 2017). A counselor may approach the polyamory, kink, or taboo community differently in providing support depending on the style of attachment seen or that the individual wishes to build. While there are many styles of attachment, with the goal of any attachment being movement into secure attachment, for the purposes of this section two types of attachment will be discussed.

Anxious Attachment

Anxious attachment is seen in individuals as sensitivity. Individuals with anxious attachment are sensitive to criticism and arguments. To seek attention from others, the individual may choose flight or fight (Katz & Katz, 2021). In counseling, this style of attachment can feel challenging to the counselor. Katz and Katz (2021) noted that in the polyamory community this style of attachment may become easier for both counselor and client, as the counselor can bridge support with others in the polyamorous relationship who hold differing attachment styles. For example, someone with anxious attachment may find it easier to connect with others who have different attachment styles.

Avoidant Attachment

Avoidant attachment styles manifest as distancing oneself from others. This attachment style is about minimizing frustrations and fears that others will abandon or leave (Katz & Katz, 2021). In counseling a client in the kink community, this style of attachment could be worked with by understanding the subcommunity the individual is part of.

With an individual who is taking part in the submissive and dominance community, this could mean taking on the role of either the submissive or the dominant one in the relationship. The counselor can work with the individual to understand how this relationship helps balance the attachment style. For example, someone with an avoidant attachment style may choose a dominant role in the kink community because it gives them empowerment to choose when a relationship will end (Scott, 2015).

COUNSELING UTILIZATION AND HELP-SEEKING

Due to the marginalization of the polyamory, kink, and taboo communities, counseling is underutilized. Individuals in each of the communities may hold fears of being judged or being stigmatized (Abe, 2020; Brunning, 2018). The number of individuals identifying as polyamorous and/or part of the kink or taboo communities is increasing yearly (Ferrer, 2019). With the growth of organizations such as the NCSF and the research and growth in theories that understand these communities' needs, such as affirmative theory (McGeorge et al., 2018), the mental health profession is prepared to support the needs of individuals in the polyamory, kink, and taboo communities. It is important for counselors to be able to identify themselves as being polyamory, kink, and taboo aware to help persons in those communities identify professionals they can seek help from.

IMPLICATIONS FOR CLINICAL PRACTICE

There are several implications for clinical practice in working with diverse communities and communities that are outside of the counselor's own identity (Bigner & Wetchler, 2012). These implications are important for client consideration as well as the counselor's growth in working with others.

Combatting Stigma/Assumptions

Polyamory, kink, and taboo communities often carry implied stigmas due to assumptions made about each (Agonito, 2014; Ferrer, 2019; Pillai-Friedman et al., 2015). One implication for clinical practice is helping reduce stigma and overcome assumptions through advocating and empowering clients to advocate. An example of reducing stigma and assumptions for the counselor is to further their knowledge and assist others in the profession to understand these various communities. This can be done through professional conferences and trainings. Additionally, the counselor needs to stay current on current sociopolitical factors affecting each of the communities. Being aware of current laws, societal perceptions, and cultural influences is important when combating stigma and assumptions (Evans, 1995; Kant, 2015).

Contesting Counselor Bias

Counselors should be aware of and be willing to do their own reflective work on potential biases. Downing (2015) noted that individuals are a product of their surrounding environment, cultural background, and lived experiences. The counselor should be aware of their own perceptions of topics such as monogamy, heteronormativity, and taboo to understand their own biases (Conley & Piemonte, 2020; Downing, 2015). A counselor who is aware of how they view polyamory, kink, and taboo practices can shift their views through supervision, consultation, and additional trainings. It is important for a counselor to understand that biases may hinder the therapeutic process, if not addressed, by increasing negative assumptions and clouding the counselor's judgment.

Psychoeducation

The counselor will find that psychoeducation is an important part of working with the polyamory, kink, and taboo communities, for both the counselor and the client. Each of the three communities is complex and has numerous subcommunities. Counselors who are able to identify resources and provide psychoeducation can help clients better understand the communities and practices they identify with. For example, clients who are in the kink community may not be aware of sexual safety plans between consenting participants. The sexual safety plan is a document that those involved in the kink activity would create together, identifying what is sexually acceptable, what is not, and key phrases such as safe words that indicate one or more of the individuals wants to stop. In the polyamory community, this may be a communication plan where those involved in the relationship identify what they need for communication, including time to reflect, listen, and talk. Psychoeducational resources may vary depending on the community; however, the NCSF is one of many examples of psychoeducational resources for counselors and clients.

Not Pathologizing

The stigmas and assumptions discussed in this chapter can lead to pathologizing the actions of individuals in the polyamory, kink, and taboo community. Historically, there has been over-pathologizing of these three communities (Speciale & Khambatta, 2020). It is important for the counselor to understand what the client's perceptions are of attending counseling and their root concern before aligning their involvement in the polyamory, kink, or taboo communities with diagnosis. A client may come to counseling with support being part of the communities: for example, addressing relationship challenges that might be occurring in a polyamorous relationship or family. It is critical for the counselor to understand the communication barriers that might be occurring rather than assuming that the challenge is because it is a polyamorous relationship.

CLINICAL CASE SCENARIO 23.1

Jared, Tonya, Corey, and Shy'Neisha are in a polyamorous relationship, and are seeking counseling services due to changes that have occurred at their central home. Tonya, Corey, and Shy'Neisha live together in what they call their primary residence, while Jared has an apartment that is across town. Jared spends most of his time with his "pod" at the primary residence. Tonya, Corey, and Shy'Neisha have been together in a polyamorous relationship for 7 years. Three years ago, Tonya met Jared through their work, and they got closer as they spent time together. Tonya reports that when she told Jared she had two spouses, Corey and Shy'Neisha, and was in a polyamorous relationship, he jokingly referred to her as "kinky." At first, she was offended, but the more they talked and got to be around each other, Tonya developed feelings for Jared and asked if he wanted to meet her other spouses. Corey states that when they all met and had dinner, Jared almost instantly felt like a brother, and it didn't take long for everyone

(continued)

CLINICAL CASE SCENARIO 23.1 (CONTINUED)

to become comfortable with Jared being around. Other personal factors to be aware of for each of the four individuals include:

- Jared is a 34-year-old Latino American male who identifies as bisexual.
- Tonya is a 32-year-old Caucasian female who identifies as bisexual.
- Corey is a 31-year-old Caucasian and identifies as nonbinary and pansexual.
- Shy'Neisha is a 28-year-old African American female who identifies as bisexual.

Recently the group has been discussing the potential of Jared permanently moving into the primary home. There are financial factors that the group is taking into consideration. Shy'Neisha states that Jared spends most of the time at the primary house, and she believes it is "silly" to spend almost $1,000 a month on an apartment that isn't really being used when that money could go toward the family expenses. Jared appears to agree and is excited about "feeling like a more permanent part of the family."

Along with the discussions of moving in, there are additional circumstances that have prompted the decision to seek counseling. Shy'Neisha recently discovered that she is pregnant, and Jared is the biological father. Tonya states that one of the family rules is to always use precautions when being sexually intimate. According to Tonya, the family never wanted to have children, but now that Shy'Neisha is pregnant, she believes that changes the dynamics of the family. No one appears to be upset that Shy'Neisha is pregnant, and both she and Jared state they thought they had been cautious sexually and are unsure about what happened. Corey expressed that while there was never a push to have children, there is an excitement about this being a new adventure for the family. Shy'Neisha, however, expresses concern because her family knows that she is in a relationship, but they do not know it is polyamorous. She is not sure how they will react knowing that she is pregnant, not legally married, and has three spouses. All four agree that they want grandparents to be part of the child's life, but do not want to change their relationship dynamics to fit family-of-origin values because they are happy and in love.

CLINICAL CASE SCENARIO DISCUSSION QUESTIONS

1. What are the cultural issues that are presented in this case?
2. What cultural and relationship components are missing that you would need to know more about?
3. What types of strategies or techniques would be relevant and appropriate in supporting those in a polyamorous relationship?
4. How would you address the needs of the relationship as a group, while also addressing the needs of the individuals, such as Shy'Neisha?
5. What are the implications for you as their counselor to address the heteronormative norms that these clients might be facing?

END-OF-CHAPTER RESOURCES

 A robust set of instructor resources designed to supplement this text is located at http://connect.springerpub.com/content/book/978-0-8261-3953-5. Qualifying instructors may request access by emailing **textbook@springerpub.com**.

SUMMARY

Supporting clients who are part of the polyamory, kink, or taboo communities begins with the counselor being open to learning about the cultures and subcultures of each of these communities and learning what it means to be part of these communities. It is important for the counselor to understand that they do not have to belong to any of these communities to demonstrate allyship with those who identify as polyamorous, kink, or taboo and to support clients through inclusion, social justice, and advocacy. Counselors must understand how the ideology of heteronormative and monogamous perceptions create a state of oppression for those within the polyamory, kink, and taboo communities.

It is important to be able to deconstruct predominant ideologies through the process of learning and unlearning the dominant cultural norms, such as heteronormativity, which create oppression. A culturally responsive approach is a process of growth for the counselor which affects how they look at the diagnosis of clients, the creation of treatment plans, and the language used with clients, such as being aware of referring to spouses as spouses instead of husband or wife. Consider this perspective of learning and unlearning how society impacts every essence of a client's life and influences every ethos of the counselor's work.

Many individuals in the kink and taboo communities found themselves at one point in history being told that their actions were diagnosable. The *DSM* was written from a perspective of societal expectation and may not always use descriptors that do not create stigma or oppression (Agonito, 2014; Pillai-Friedman et al., 2015). The creation of diagnoses related to kink or taboo communities is based on the concept of heteronormative expectations. Though this construct is slowly being changed, advocacy work is still needed to normalize the role of kink and taboo communities, and to create an understanding that not everyone falls into a heteronormative monogamous ideology (Downing, 2015).

The terms *polyamory*, *kink*, and *taboo* are larger umbrella terms. Each community and subcommunity has its own vision and valid social identity. Polyamory may be categorized into polyfidelity, triads, pods, and open marriages (Brunning, 2018). Kink may be compartmentalized into the BDSM community, leather community, furry play, or other communities of like interest (Pillai-Friedman et al., 2015). The taboo community or culture is what represents all communities that are outside of the societal norm of heteronormative monogamous expectations (Agonito, 2014). Every counselor needs to remember the role of multiple identities and work with the client to validate and honor each identity that makes the client who they are.

The liberation framework was developed to change the fact that as counselors we are conditioned to put into use theoretical orientations and models of counseling that address the individual and what they need to change based on a narrow scope of techniques (Kant, 2015). These theories and techniques apply a singular view of the oppression clients in the polyamory, kink, and taboo communities might experience. A broader eclectic approach allows exploration of stigma that is both internal and external, empowering the client to identify and determine their needs in the counseling setting so that treatment can be individualized to the client. It requires advocacy and acceptance that "politics are personal" and create a heavy presence in the lives of our clients.

Many counselor training programs do not explore ways of working with and healing those who are in communities outside of the heteronormative expectations. Additional ways to work with clients who are outside of the societal majority expectations include affirmative acknowledgement that individuals are faced with discrimination for being outside of the heteronormative norm (Downing, 2015) and feminist approaches that focus on naming the oppression and empowering clients to resist the societal norm through advocacy (Benstead, 2021). The liberation framework helps bring clarity to the impact those societal expectations have in creating oppression that manifests in internalized stigma and fear (Abe, 2020). It is important to discover the identities of our clients, discern how they may differ from or align with cultural identities, and consider what type of discord is being created in the client's life by any mismatch. If the client is willing, engage them in finding resources to help build connectedness and support.

Counselors also need to be aware of microaggressions that may occur unconsciously because of our placement in heteronormative societies. Assumptions about gender identification and relationship perceptions can create discomfort for clients. The counselor should be willing and comfortable using phrases that defer to and reflect the client's preferences regarding gender, sexual orientation, and relationship status (Downing, 2015).

Counselors need to be wary of making assumptions when working with individuals who are in the polyamory, kink, and taboo communities. Counselors should ask what polyamory or kink or taboo means to the client. This shows awareness of subcommunities and the diversity within them. Counselors may assume that various levels of oppression may affect a member of any of these three communities, but should explore the topic with the client to gain a larger understanding of the impact of the oppressive experiences (Abe, 2020; Brunning, 2018; Pillai-Friedman et al., 2015).

DISCUSSION QUESTIONS

1. How can you work to decenter heteronormative expectations so that you honor all clients, especially those who are polyamorous, kink, or taboo?
2. What knowledge might you need to gain to better understand the experiences of communities outside of your norm?
3. How can you adequately prepare yourself to hold space for clients who discuss sexual experiences that are outside of your knowledge or comfort?
4. How can you continue to honor and hold space for clients who carry multiple identities, such as polyamorous and kink?
5. How will you explore and incorporate methods of counseling that address social injustices and include advocacy?

CULTURALLY RESPONSIVE COUNSELING RELATED TO POLYAMORY, KINK, AND TABOO CULTURE

Guest: Dr. Eric Jett

https://connect.springerpub.com/content/book/978-0-8261-3953-5/part/part02/chapter/ch23

KEY REFERENCES

Only key references appear in the print edition. The full reference list appears in the digital product on Springer Publishing Connect: https://connect.springerpub.com/content/book/978-0-8261-3953-5/part/part02/chapter/ch23

Downing, L. (2015). Heteronormativity and repronormativity in sexological "Perversion Theory" and the *DSM-5*'s "Paraphilic Disorder" diagnoses. *Archives of Sexual Behavior*, *44*(5), 1139–1145. https://doi.org/10.1007/s10508-015-0536-y

Ferrer, J. N. (2019). From romantic jealousy to sympathetic joy: Monogamy, polyamory, and beyond. *International Journal of Transpersonal Studies*, *38*(1), 185–202. https://doi.org/10.24972/ijts.2019.38.1.185

Fershtman, C., Gneezy, U., & Hoffman, M. (2011). Taboos and identity: Considering the unthinkable. *American Economic Journal*, *3*(2), 139–164. https://doi.org/10.1257/mic.3.2.139

Pillai-Friedman, S., Pollitt, J. L., & Castaldo, A. (2015). Becoming kink-aware—A necessity for sexuality professionals. *Sexual and Relationship Therapy*, *30*(2), 196–210. https://doi.org/10.1080/14681994.2014.975681

Scott, C. (2015). *Thinking kink: The collision of BDSM, feminism, and popular culture*. McFarland.

CHAPTER 24

Culturally Responsive Counseling for Clients of the Gamer Culture, Fandoms, and Related Subcultures

ERIC J. PERRY

LEARNING OBJECTIVES

After reading this chapter, students will be able to:

- Define areas of culture/subcultures related to popular culture, specifically gaming, fandoms, and other related subcultures.
- Identify how each cultural consideration related to popular culture, specifically gaming, fandoms, and other related subcultures, plays a part in client conceptualization and consideration.
- Describe how to conceptualize elements of client identity related to culture/subcultures based on popular culture, specifically gaming, fandoms, and other related subcultures, as part of client conceptualization.
- Identify problems and challenges specific to each cultural group and subculture discussed in this chapter.
- Describe counseling approaches and strategies specific to each of the cultural groups and subcultures addressed in this chapter.

SELF-REFLECTION QUESTIONS

1. Think about biases, prejudices, and assumptions you might have about gamers, furries, or those who engage in anime or cosplay. How do these help and hinder your ability to provide culturally sensitive counseling?
2. What hesitancies, if any, do you have about working with gamers, furries, or those who engage in anime or cosplay?
3. What attributes do you have that will enable you to work with gamers, furries, or those who engage in anime or cosplay?

THE COUNSELOR: EXPLORATION, INTROSPECTION, AND REFLECTION

This chapter focuses on gamer culture, fandoms, and related subcultures as elements counselors will need to consider as something that may be an integral part of their clients' identities. The counselor will need to consider potential biases and the societal influences that can shape how the counselor interprets these parts of the client's identity, as well as the impact their perceptions may have on their clients. Finally, we address how the incorporation of knowledge of gamer culture, fandoms, and related subcultures can positively influence the development and maintenance of a strong therapeutic alliance, built on a base of understanding, empathy, and acceptance.

As we consider culture, we often think of elements of one's customs, traditions, values, goals, and practices that reflect how the individual identifies with a group. Under this broad definition, we can see the need to conceptualize culture in counseling in a manner that considers elements that may be outside even the most inclusive definitions of *culture*. In this chapter, we review elements of an individual's cultural identity that have roots in the person's interests, hobbies, leisure, and desires, as well as elements of popular culture. This chapter will challenge you to think outside of even some of the most inclusive models of multicultural conceptualization and consider factors that individuals actively choose as a part of their identity, as part of their definition of self. As a counselor, having knowledge related to these areas of client identity can assist you in a better understanding of the client's worldview, their potential challenges, and their strengths, as well as special considerations related to these elements of their identity.

Our first task may very well be to tackle common discourse. Throughout the course of our lives, we are exposed to the words *normal* or *normative*. Within the definition of these words is the assumption that something is universally accepted and—perhaps more concerning—that anything not within this universal standard is a deviation that could be considered nonnormative, problematic, unacceptable, or abnormal. But who decides normal?

What defines normal is thought to be both socially and individually constructed, thus leaving the word to become a term prone to the assignment of stigma, harm, and exclusion. Instead, the discourse this chapter uses has been moved to adopt person-centered language in conceptualization, thinking, diagnosis, and treatment, removing the need for "normality" as a descriptor. It is no longer necessary to refer to something as "outside the norm," abnormal, or any other deviation from normality. As an example, mental health professionals can refer to symptoms as "clinical" or "nonclinical," or in terms of severity, rather than as "normal" or "abnormal." When considering cultural aspects of an individual's identity, we should endeavor to do the same, allowing the client to determine what is and is not "normal" by their own definition. Instead of striving to define what is normative, we can endeavor to determine what is held true by the client. After all, clients are the experts on themselves and should be encouraged to define their own "normal," their own culture, and their own definition of who they are and the problems they face.

The topics discussed in this chapter are new and novel elements of identity, some of which hinge upon technology and others that grow slowly and subtly over time. Thus, available research is limited and emergent. Theoretical considerations, clinical applications, and other considerations related to providing mental health services are still being approached as new research and understandings become more prevalent. The recommendations provided later in this chapter, specifically related to clinical approaches and working with clients, are made based on their relevance to theory, the limited amount of available research, and accepted best practices in the counseling profession.

CLIENT WORLDVIEWS AND PERSPECTIVES

In this chapter, we review the culture surrounding those who identify themselves as gamers, members of fandoms, furries, LARPers (live-action role-players), and other related subcultures. Each of these elements, considered as part of an individual's culture, has unique traits associated with membership and identification with that particular group. Still, there are some elements all of these groups have in common.

At its core, we could define *culture* as an individual's values, behaviors, beliefs, and ways of understanding the world around them. A common misconception about culture is that it is always or usually linked to tradition, history, or background. Although these elements surely have a role in influencing one's culture, we should also consider the experiences we have apart from our families of origin, our genetic history, and geography, such as the elements we *choose*.

One element that binds these groups together is that they may include something that someone chooses to identify with that may not link or hark back to the physical, familial, and environmental factors we attribute to other areas of culture. Instead, these groups are bound by activities, ideologies, interests, and desires, with most of them being a relatively new phenomenon. Even though these groups appear to apply choice, being based on elements like interests, some are so strongly drawn that they do not view membership as a choice; this is the case for group membership that crosses from interests to desires and forms of self-expression that link very strongly to identity (Plante et al., 2014). As a result of their novelty, most of these groups also suffer from some very powerful stigmatization and challenges.

As we explore each of these groups, we will provide a brief history for each group, identify the characteristics that make them unique, relate membership in these groups to a person's cultural identity, identify associated challenges and strengths, and offer strategies to assist counselors in conceptualizing and providing treatment.

GAMER CULTURE AND GAMER IDENTITY

A Brief History

As a form of entertainment, games have been around for thousands of years. Every culture, through every period of recorded history, has left evidence of games they played for entertainment. The oldest game in the world, based on archeological evidence, is the game of Mancala, which is believed to have originated in Jordan in 6000 BCE. Ancient Mesopotamian dice and stick games have been found and dated back to the year 5000 BCE (Bikić & Vuković, 2010). Evidence of more formalized board games dates back as early as 2620 BCE in Egypt. One game, referred to as Senet, involved position, strategy, and a bit of luck to win (Aarseth & Grabarczyk, 2018).

Over the next few thousand years, games became more common and available to the masses. The rules for each game became more standardized and competitive play became something more than just playing at home with friends and family. Card games, having originated sometime in the ninth century CE, started to approach more common and contemporary styles of play sometime in the 15th century CE. From the 15th century to the late 1800s, board games, card games, and role-playing games were beginning their transitions from elements of individual and regional culture into representations of modern and broader popular culture. Board games draw on a wide variety of concepts, history, and elements of popular culture. These games leverage spiritual themes, humor, strategy, morality, vocabulary, and even the concept of life itself, to take players around a board, on an imaginary journey, or simply to obtain the highest score

(Bikić & Vuković, 2010). The first trademarked board game was an adaptation of the ancient Indian game of Pachisi, which would later become known as Parcheesi, in 1863 (Whitehill, 2015).

As gaming started to extend beyond an individual's own culture and into the broader world, competitive play on a global scale was born. In 1851, the first international chess tournament was held in London. In 1924, the International Chess Federation (FIDE), an organization created and established to govern the rules of international chess competition, was founded in Paris.

The development of video games began as early as 1947, with the first publicly demonstrated video game, Bertie the Brain, released in 1950. Bertie the Brain was an arcade game of tic-tac-toe played for a few days at the Canadian National Exhibition by participants and then torn down afterward. In 1951 the Nimrod computer was created and enabled participants to play the game of Nim using buttons that corresponded with lights.

Interactive visual games, those more related to modern video games, start to appear around 1958 and persisted through the 1970s, though the public had very little access to games due to their cost and lack of availability of computers to play them on. The earliest gaming system cost the equivalent of $1,000,000 and only 55 were ever produced. Commercial gaming started in earnest with arcade machines in the early 1970s with games such as Computer Space, Galaxy Game, and, of course, Pong. Later, in the mid-1970s, the Odyssey was released, becoming the first in-home gaming device that connected to a screen.

From the 1970s to the present, video gaming moved at breakneck speed. In the past 50 years, gaming has moved from light bulbs that match players' moves in tic-tac-toe to immersive experiences that span a wide gamut that incorporates nearly any concept or genre. As technology has advanced, so has the study of gaming. In recent years, the idea of gaming as a cultural consideration has taken hold and can be seen in books such as *Gaming as Culture* (Skelton, 2008), in academic journals such as *Games and Culture* (SAGE), and within the realm of scholarly research related to cultural studies, anthropology, philosophy, psychology, and more (De Grove et al., 2015; Shaw, 2013).

According to the Entertainment Software Association (ESA), "[m]ore than 214 million people in the United States today play video games one hour or more per week [and] 75% of all U.S. households have at least one person who plays" (ESA, n.d., para. 3). Still, it is often acknowledged that gaming and gamer culture represent opportunities for additional research, specifically as they relate to implications for cultural consideration and conceptualization, often leaving many more questions than answers.

Defining Gamer Culture

As mentioned in the preceding section, the study of gaming as a cultural consideration is relatively new, simply because the phenomenon of playing video games began so recently, in the late 1970s. As with any early study, the terminology is often the cornerstone of early debate. The term *gamer* has seen drastic shifts in meaning over a relatively short period of time, and thus is a point of fierce academic debate, especially among researchers (Shaw, 2010, 2012, 2013). As a socially constructed label, the term *gamer* is one that can be adopted or not based on how the individual perceives the factors associated with that label—and these factors can change over time. This makes the label of "gamer" different from some other cultural considerations that are linked to more stable or concrete factors with criteria that are more tangible, such as region, socioeconomic status, or genetic background.

Several factors are generally considered when attempting to define the term *gamer* and how to describe or categorize "gamer" as a characteristic of cultural identity. These factors include frequency of play, game modes played, gaming platform or device of preference, the genre of interest, the inclusion of competitive play, socialization, and game type, to name just a few. Shaw (2010) suggested a means of helping determine who might identify as a gamer, and the particular factors that make up this socially constructed category.

To begin to break this down, Shaw (2010) described those who engage in gamer culture by first defining three categories: "(a) who plays video games, (b) how they play, and (c) what they play" (p. 2). The question of who plays video games is answered in the earlier section by the ESA. The next category, how they play, can help us further define the variation in behaviors and cultural elements related to gamers. Within the category of "how," we should consider the method by which someone plays. Games can often be designed as individual experiences, local multiple-player experiences (or LAN party experiences) which involve players in the same geographic locations, and/or online multiplayer experiences that can involve engaging with others in gameplay, partying, or even single, quick game teams that are formed at the start of each match. The latter is associated with gamers who connect solely at a distance, geographically apart from one another. This aspect is important because "video games provide a means to connect individuals over geographical boundaries and create a shared meaning; this [is a] unique ability of video games" (Howe et al., 2019, p. 2). Gamers may be drawn to one or multiple methods of play depending on their genre(s) of interest and desire to engage in socialization through the game.

In addition, considering the "how" means to consider the frequency of play. The term *casual gamer* has been used to describe those who engage in gaming on a variety of platforms with some form of regularity, but without the dedication seen in other gamers. Those who are more frequently engaged in gameplay often take the title of "gamer" without the "casual" modifier. These individuals engage in gaming activity regularly, are often engaged in competitive ways beyond the standard functions of the game, and make this a regular part of their routine or even daily life.

The question of "how they play" also refers to their choice of medium to play games. This can include, but is not limited to, card games, video games, mobile games, board games, live-action games, and virtual reality. Video games create another layer of consideration in that there are several platforms on which video games can be played. The most common examples of platforms are console players (those who use console systems such as the PlayStation, Xbox, or Nintendo Switch), PC/computer players, and mobile players who use a mobile device like a cell phone or tablet.

At first, talking about what gamers play might seem daunting. Video games in particular can range from the mundane to those that include extreme gore, violence, and sexual content. Earlier it was mentioned that gaming has evolved from light bulbs that matched players' moves in simplistic games like tic-tac-toe to immersive experiences that span the gamut of types to encapsulate or incorporate nearly any concept or genre. So, how do we begin to think about "what they play"? Some recognized genres can help organize games. Keep in mind that a game may fit within several genres and have multiple types of game play (such as action, adventure, idle, role-playing, and simulation, to name just a few). In addition to being classified by genre, the type of gameplay can also be used to classify games. As with genres, games can encompass multiple gameplay types; examples are massively multiple online games such as the World of Warcraft series and third-person shooter or over-the-shoulder game view players such as *Fortnite*.

FANDOMS AND FANDOM IDENTITY

Fandoms: A Brief History

Fandoms have existed, in one form or another, for as long as media has existed. The first organized and modern fandom group is often credited to the Sherlock Holmes novels after public events were held to mourn the characters' deaths in the book series in 1893. The public's reaction was so strong that more than 20,000 readers of *The Strand* magazine canceled their subscriptions in protest. The earliest fandoms were often related to science fiction, railroad and railway enthusiasts, and Westerns. The first World Science Fiction Convention was held in 1939. The genesis of media fan communities—those that centered entirely around television or other media—were attributed to the fan base for the original *Star Trek* series in the mid-1960s (Bury, 2017).

Defining Fandoms

Fandoms are often described as collective groups bonded with something in popular culture. Those engaged in fandoms exceed casual consumption of entertainment. Members of fandoms have emotional investment and often assume some parts of the content as part of their lifestyle. Fandoms provide the opportunity for individuals to engage with a group that identifies with the object of attention in similar ways, creating a sense of support, community, and identity (Mock et al., 2013; Peeples et al., 2018; Svegaard, 2015).

These groups can range from formal organized collectives to simply named collective identities that individuals take on or ascribe to themselves. Members can choose to have little or no association with one another. One important consideration to keep in mind is the difference between a fan and membership in a fandom. An individual can be a fan (for example, of a sports team) without being a member of a fandom. One individual described the difference between being a "Steelers fan" and part of the "Steelers Nation" as being either casual or fanatical about the success of the team. Given that the definition of *fanatical* is to be filled with excessive and single-minded zeal, the rationale behind this distinction certainly makes sense. Generally, what separates a fan from a member of a fandom is a connection to a social network or group of people with similar interests in some way that goes beyond casual, individual engagement in that interest (Billings & Ruihley, 2013).

Fandoms can emerge from all sorts of media, including, but not limited to, literature, television shows, graphic novels, comics, movies, theater, music, and more. More organized fandoms will take on names that are representative of the media they attach to, such as the "Potterheads," who are members of the Harry Potter fandom, and Tolkiendils, members of the J. R. R. Tolkien fandom, both of which are cross-platform. *Cross-platform* refers to those who are fans of multiple types of media related to a specific interest. In this case, both subjects of these fandoms include books and movies. A few examples of the fandoms in music include Beatlemaniacs (fans of the Beatles), Juggalos (fans of the Insane Clown Posse [ICP]), and KPOPers (fans of the genre of South Korean pop music; Peyron, 2018).

Related Subcultures

Related to gamer culture and fandoms are other subcultures that stem from popular culture and other media. Much like gamer culture and fandoms, these subcultures can include individuals who engage at different levels, and identify at varying levels with the customs, traditions, values, goals, and practices that are central tenets of that group. Often, these subcultures require the development or invention of identities that include a creative element, are uniquely expressive, hold their own unique cultural elements, and go beyond what might be considered a hobby or interest, much like the fandoms discussed previously.

Furries

Furries are "individuals who are especially interested in anthropomorphic or cartoon animals" (Hsu & Bailey, 2019, para. 1). The Furry community, thought to have originated in the early 2000s, is comprised of individuals who engage in fursuiting, the act of wearing full costumes that represent a character, usually of their own design. While in costume, furries portray their unique persona, or fursona as it is often called. A fursona, however, is not just about the look. When in costume, furries also act out the specific characteristics of their fursona's personality. These characteristics can be close to their own or vastly different from those exhibited in the furry's everyday life.

This fursona's design can be made to resemble a character from popular culture, art, comics, and other media, or may be developed and crafted entirely by the individual. Although their fursona can largely be something that exists online within social media, websites, and other spaces dedicated to furry culture, furries sometimes engage in acting out their fursona in public as well in gatherings or even large conferences. In addition to fursuiting, those engaged within the community often share art, stories, comics, and other representations of their fursona as part of their engagement with the furry community. As with other fandoms and related subcultures discussed here, there is reason to believe that engagement in this community provides a sense of community, social support, and belonging (Mock et al., 2013; Roberts et al., 2016; Satinsky & Green, 2016).

Although furries have been portrayed in popular media as having a dedicated sexual element, there is an ongoing debate about its prevalence among researchers. The media often portrays the furry community as a sexually motivated group, but criticism exists for this assumption, especially within the furry community. There are groups within the furry community that cater specifically to furries who include sexual desires as a part of their fursona, which can include erotic artwork, media, stories, and pornography (Hsu & Bailey, 2019). In a study conducted by Hsu and Bailey (2019), the researchers indicated that of the 334 furries included in the study, 99.4% indicated "some degree of sexual interest in being furries and thus some sexual motivation" (p. 17). Still, the research is new, emerging, and limited in scope. Reysen et al. (2016) asserted that attention should be placed on the needs that drive furry identification rather than focusing on "inaccurate mischaracterization of the fandom as a fetish or being motivated by sexual deviancy" (p. 639). Although sexuality can be an element within furry culture, the assumption should not be made that it is primary to all members or that it is a central tenet of the community (Heinz, 2020; Plante et al., 2014).

Live-Action Role-Play, Cosplay, and Reenactors

LARPing, or live-action role-playing, is a role-playing game in which individuals act out their characters and play games in a physical manner, rather than using media, boards, gaming systems, computers, or other devices (Kamm & Becker, 2016). *Cosplay* refers to those who wear costumes designed as likenesses of characters or as original works, but generally engage in less organized role-play rather than game play. LARPers (the name for those engaged in these games) may engage in role-playing of several genres which include, but are not limited to, fantasy, medieval or historical, horror, Western, and completely player-generated games. LARPs can include highly organized structures or just basic rules for enjoying the game, allowing the story to play out organically based on the characters' interactions. The more structured games often include roles such as organizers, player characters (PCs), and non-player characters (NPCs). Organizers are responsible for setting up the games, setting and enforcing game rules, and ensuring that the "plot" of the game moves forward in a scripted direction. The PCs hold roles that are central to the plot and generally are asked to react to the story with only a basic knowledge of the script. The NPCs know the entire plot and may play several parts within the story but are more like extras in a movie.

The LARP community is so vast and variable that getting involved with LARPing might seem arduous at first glance. However, some resources exist to help interested persons join LARPing. LARPing.org is one of those resources. The site provides a search tool for prospective LARPers that permits them to search by location for games and meetings within their area, and use tags to filter for a specific genre, type of play, rule preferences, and more. LARP events can include food, after-parties, and camping, and can vary widely in length from a few hours to a few days or even a week. Additionally, LARPers can find child-appropriate events, adult-themed role-plays, and LGBTQI+ events, and even search based on accessibility for LARP events.

Combat role-play within LARPs can vary from no contact to light or full contact, but always with "weaponry" that is modified to ensure that the wielder and those on whom it is wielded on are safe from major injury. This weaponry can include foam or plastic swords, shields, lightsabers, wands, or other equipment used to facilitate the battle. Although simulated combat is a part of the experience, LARPing becomes as much about the acting, especially when wounded or struck down, as it is about the action and skill. LARPers will take on their character personas, dress in costume, and maintain their character part throughout the game, and sometimes even after.

Fan-Fiction Writers, Vidders, and Artists

Within fandoms, some individuals engage in writing fan fiction, create and share videos or "vids" (these individuals are often referred to as "vidders"), and create artistic content related specifically to their fandom. Vids can be expressive, original content that includes music, compilations of fandom content, or spliced from various forms of artistic depictions of content that tie into the individual's favorite areas of popular culture (Svegaard, 2015). Fan-fiction writers, or commemorative writers, craft stories that are inspired by elements of their fandom. These may take the form of short stories, novels, graphic novels, comics, and other means of storytelling. Most often, those who create such content are engaged in their fandom's activities and create their original material without the promise or intent of financial gain; rather, they do so to contribute socially to their fandom, group, or the public at large (Svegaard, 2015, 2019; Wilson, 2016).

Fan-fiction writers, vidders, and artists are considered here separately as they tend to engage in fandoms uniquely. Rather than just being passive observers and engaged with others in communities related to the fandom, those engaged in this subculture actively engage with the content. Through this engagement, individuals create transformative works that challenge their fandoms and the creators of the original content. They express what they feel might be missing from the stories they have seen through the creation of their own literature and media. "Transformative fanworks often focus on supplying the kind of narratives that are under-represented in the mainstream" (Svegaard, 2015, p. 106). Through this expression, individuals can show more of who they are, how they define themselves, and how they engage with society and its media landscape.

APPLICATIONS TO CONCEPTUALIZATION OF CLIENT IDENTITY

Gamers

Gamers, as discussed earlier, have frequently fallen victim to stereotyping. One common stereotype asserts that gamers are teenage males, or adult males having not outgrown their teenage years, who are socially outcast and largely White (Grooten et al., 2014; Paaßen et al., 2017). Yet surveys show that women and men are almost equally represented in their use of video games, despite popular culture and marketing still being largely aimed at male audiences (Paaßen et al., 2017).

Another stereotype gamers face is having few or poor social skills, and lacking or desiring connections (Cade & Gates, 2017). As seen in Clinical Case Scenario 24.1, the social relationships built through gaming can be positive. Discouraging those relationships could lead to feelings of isolation. At the same time, the social connections created can be negative as well. A phenomenon often referred to as "toxic gamer culture" is evidenced in YouTube videos, streamers, and other content produced by some gamers that include hate speech, threats of violence, hypermasculinity, and other forms of harassment (Paaßen et al., 2017). According to the Anti-Defamation League and studies conducted there, more than 65% of gamers experience some form of severe harassment, and 53% feel they were targeted related to gender, race or ethnicity, sexual orientation, religion, or ability (Rouse & Corron, 2020).

Video game content has long been a subject of debate, with many positing that video game violence may lead to an increase in violent crime, aggressive behavior, and other issues among those who play. Recent studies seem to push back at this idea, citing that correlational studies and laboratory results may not apply to real-world effects of exposure to violence through video games (Markey et al., 2015). Still, it cannot be discounted that exposure to violence, highly sexual content, and other mature themes may have an impact on clients' perceptions and beliefs, as well as their definition of their own gamer culture.

Additionally, there are very real challenges associated with gaming that have been well documented within the literature (Belfort & Miller, 2018). The *Diagnostic and Statistical Manual of Mental Disorders* (5th ed.; *DSM-5*; American Psychiatric Association, 2013) now includes "Internet Gaming Disorder" as a condition requiring further study. Proposed criteria in the *DSM-5* are:

> A preoccupation with gaming, withdrawal symptoms when gaming is discontinued, tolerance for increasing amounts of time spent gaming, unsuccessful attempts to control participation in gaming, loss of interest in other hobbies or activities as a result of gaming, continued excessive use of gaming despite knowledge of psychosocial problems, deceiving others regarding the amount of gaming, and the use of gaming to escape or relieve negative moods, and jeopardizing or loss of a significant relationship, job, or educational or career opportunity because of gaming (American Psychiatric Association, 2013, p. 795).

Because games are a significant part of the lives of so many, a client's relationship to gaming will have to be considered as a cultural factor in the conceptualization of a client's cultural identity. As discussed in earlier sections, gaming preferences (and thus influence on the client's self-defined culture) can vary. Care should be taken to separate problematic elements of the gamer's experience from those that contribute positively to a sense of self and identity.

Fandoms

Fandoms can be important elements of an individual's culture. As people identify and seek out connections through their interests, they can gain both positive and negative elements of personal and communal meaning. Also, there is the added benefit or harm of the accrual of additional social capital (Seregina & Schouten, 2017). Although it will likely be helpful for the counselor to know details of the fandom the client belongs to, it may be more important to the counselor's conceptualization to ask what particular facets of the fandom the client "takes away" as a part of that identity. For example, some clients may identify with a heroic character, whereas others might identify with a musician who prizes philanthropy, or an evil princess who finds a way to redemption. There are some who might identify with darker or more worrisome traits that could be both abstract and direct reflections of the client's self-perception and developed identity.

It is important to note that fandoms can be based around any media form, including those that may have an appreciation for the more macabre elements of the available media. These fandoms can extend both to fictional and nonfictional events. Elements of horror, violence, and death have long been an element of popular culture and are found within a great many fandoms. Researchers have used the term *dark fandoms* to describe the act of engaging in a fandom that includes the idolization of mass and serial murders, acts of violence, and other heinous acts and to distinguish such fandoms from those related to a cultural interest in the macabre (Broll, 2020).

Dark fandoms would include fandoms that describe themselves as groups or communities that include a reverence for violence, torture, death, and despair, with particular attention paid to nonfictional events and appreciation or even celebration of these acts. Those who engage in these fandoms are often engaged in "dark tourism": travel to visit sites of significance where these acts occurred. Some examples of dark tourist sites are homes where atrocities occurred, decommissioned prisons, sites of famous assassinations, or sites of famous mass murders. Rather than doing so out of historical curiosity or a desire to learn, dark tourists are drawn in by a fascination with the acts of violence and celebration of those acts (Broll, 2020).

Related Subcultures

Furries have an additional layer of consideration for case conceptualization unique to their group. In addition to engaging in the fandom, generating fursonas, and contributing through artistic endeavors, some furries also describe themselves as therians. *Therians* are individuals who also feel a special or spiritual kinship to the animals their fursonas are based on. Still others, who are referred to as *Otherkin*, feel that this spiritual connection also extends to mystical or fictional species (dragons, for example). Additionally, sexual motivation may be part of an individual's furry identity, although this should not be assumed. This possible sexual motivation and attraction to anthropomorphic animals or other furries in fursuits must be considered as part of the client's identity if revealed; also, caution must be taken, as clients may worry about negative consequences and stigma.

LARPers are engaged in immersive experiences that go beyond just performance art. Kamm and Becker described LARPing as an act in which LARPers "become cultural mediators" (2016, para. 1) in how they engage with their art, performance, and implicit acting-out of fictional cultures. Those who engage in LARPing and ascribe some given part of their identity to the activity may find group membership particularly powerful, both through their representation of characters in each LARP event and their moments of "dropping out" of character, a practice that is largely frowned upon within the LARP community. Even though generally discouraged, connections and relationships are formed in this action, giving players the opportunity to connect and develop "off-game identities" within the group (Vorobyeva, 2015).

Those who are dedicated to creating media, such as fan-fiction writers and vidders, may seem like a less connected group at first glance. After all, with so many engaging in social media, some scholars have made the argument that all who create content in spaces like Instagram, Facebook, and other related platforms are vidders in their own right, reacting in a "fannish" way to the content they have experienced (Meneghelli, 2017). By definition and for the sake of conceptualization, we should consider vidders and fan-fiction writers to be those who are engaged in media creation who are also fans or even members of the fandom, creating with a similar sense of connection and belonging as those who engage in a typical fandom. By the same token, we would then have similar considerations for both positive and negative elements of personal and communal meaning taken from this experience that apply to the client's sense of self.

COUNSELING UTILIZATION AND HELP-SEEKING

Very little can be found on how often individuals who identify as gamers seek out mental health services, but it can be surmised that with the prevalence of gaming, as discussed earlier in this chapter, those who identify as gamers may be more common than we realize. Those who identify as "gamers" hold this element of their cultural identity as more central than those who simply play games for enjoyment or as a hobby. Most studies have centered on exploring what it means to be a gamer, how to define the identity of a gamer, and the role of gamer identity rather than attempting to determine the size of the gamer community (De Grove et al., 2015).

Much of the same is true when considering fandoms, furries, and other related subcultures. The International Anthropomorphic Research Project (IARP) is a group of researchers dedicated to the study of furries. IARP defines *furries* as "people with a self-proclaimed interest in anthropomorphism and zoomorphism" (Roberts et al., 2015, p. 42). IARP estimated that there may be as many as 1.4 to 2.8 million furries worldwide, and that this population is growing (Plante et al., 2016). Currently, there are no statistics related to participants in fandoms, fan-fiction writers, content creators, and LARPers and other subcultures in large peer-reviewed studies. This makes it difficult to surmise how participation in fandoms may affect the utilization of mental health services (McInroy, 2020).

CURRENT RESEARCH AND CULTURALLY RESPONSIVE THERAPEUTIC INTERVENTIONS AND APPROACHES

Gamers

Clients should be encouraged to share details about gaming, its impact on their identity, and their level of engagement in the gaming community. Additionally, counselors are encouraged to be curious, maintain unconditional positive regard, and show interest, with an understanding that their client's identity as a gamer may be representative of a large part of their individual experience. These details not only allow the counselor to know the client and their story better but can also give clues as to how the client chooses to engage with others, cope, and communicate. At the same time, counselors should make efforts to learn about what their clients share (Cade & Gates, 2017).

As mentioned previously, those who define part of their cultural identity as "gamer" encounter plenty of assumptions, stereotypes, and other challenges counselors should be prepared to engage with and consider. First, as is wise with any population being considered, counselors should be prepared to examine their own biases and assumptions about gamers and those who play games. Something that may be helpful is to study the difference between healthy gaming and unhealthy gaming. Cade and Gates (2017) argue that "video games can be used as a virtual playground for players to experience the cognitive, motivational, emotional, and social benefits of gaming" (p. 72), creating a space for healthy gaming.

In addition to the proposed *DSM-5* (American Psychiatric Association, 2013) definition for "Internet Gaming Disorder," unhealthy gaming represents the other side of the spectrum. When gaming interferes with cognitive, motivational, emotional, and social processes, it can be unhealthy. In addition to proper diagnostic interviewing, reviewing symptoms, pathology, and other potential problems related to gaming when doing an assessment may be considered to enhance case conceptualization. Ensure that the assessment is properly screened for validity, reliability, proper norming, and available and recent research, as well as other psychometric properties. Two potential assessment tools are the Internet Gaming Disorder Scale (IGDS9) and the Internet Gaming Disorder Scale Short Form (IGDS9-SF). Both assessments are based on the proposed criteria from the *DSM-5* (Lemmens et al., 2015; Lortie & Guitton, 2013). Additional options may include the Gaming Addiction Scale, Gaming Addiction Scale for Adolescents, the Shorter PROMIS Questionnaire (SPQ), the Digital Addiction Scale for Children (DASC), and the WASTE-Time Structured Interview. Assessments that screen for addictive or problematic behaviors, socialization issues, and other outcomes associated with problematic gaming (Bruni et al., 2015; Hawi et al., 2019) can be considered, too.

Counselors are encouraged to learn more about gaming by reviewing the available research, becoming familiar with the standards and content ratings that govern the gaming industry, and examining the vernacular or language used by gamers. As it relates to terminology, clients who describe themselves as gamers may use specific words, phrases, or abbreviated forms of text that would be helpful for counselors to understand. These terms are often used in chat or text format but sometimes are also voiced, often in the abbreviated format. For example, a gamer may refer to someone as "AFK" in conversation, indicating that this person is inactive.

Fandoms

It should be noted that very little exists in the recent literature and research related to the impact of fandoms regarding the counseling process, counseling relationship, or its role in conceptualizing the client. A few studies describe the impact of fandoms on individuals and their engagement in fandoms within social media, but few make specific reference to the implications of fandom membership for the counseling relationship.

One recent study conducted by McInroy (2020) provides some ideas on how counselors might work with those engaged in fandoms through her research with sexual and gender minority youth (SGMY) and online fandom communities. McInroy (2020) asserts that fandoms can be an important source of social support, mentoring and role-modeling, resilience, and positive adjustment. Mental health professionals are encouraged to explore these factors as part of their work with clients. Additionally, fandoms provide an escape for some who are victims of negative experiences offline. Escapism is sometimes described as a negative or dysfunctional coping mechanism, but it can also be viewed as a positive route for those engaged in fandoms to seek out support where other options may be limited (McInroy, 2020).

Fandoms offer a sense of belonging, elements of collective identity, and an opportunity for individual expression. Those engaged in fandoms can have a positive emotional relationship with the content they follow, and the individuals associated with that content. Members of fandoms engage not just with the content, but also with the other members within the community. Thus, they can learn from one another, engage in meaningful relationships, and use fandom as a means to further engage in self-exploration.

Related Subcultures

With a positive therapeutic alliance, it is possible that clients will reveal these elements of their culture to clinicians, but there is an acknowledged fear of judgment or disapproval based on the portrayal of these subcultures in media and within certain groups. Individuals who ascribe these subcultures to their identity often face real challenges of fear of discrimination, being ostracized, or even violence (Roberts et al., 2015).

The idea of being "someone else," as is the case for furries, is not unique in the therapeutic relationship. Several examples of this type of creativity exist in the counseling literature. Consider Dr. Mark Savickas's career construction theory of counseling. This narrative approach not only emphasizes the use of the client's "story," but asks the client to develop the next chapter in their career journey using metaphors of real and imagined heroes and characters to identify the client's construction and concept of self. One question for clients from Savickas's text *Life-Design Counseling Manual* reads "Who were your heroes/heroines?" (2015, p. 28) and asks clients to describe make-believe people, characters, or cartoon characters in the media that fit this definition. Savickas explains that he does this as "clients' favorite stories lay open their lives" (Savickas, 2015, p. 32).

A study conducted by Roberts et al. (2015) indicated that there are several ways in which counselors and other health professionals can positively engage with clients who identify with one of the related subcultures noted in this section. First, having knowledge and awareness about a client's specific subculture, such as LARPers and specific fandoms a client may belong to, would help address their concerns. Additionally, the authors note that unconditional positive regard helps to develop the relationship, trust, and therapeutic alliance.

Clients who are members of the furry community assert that the client's fursona should be accepted as an equal part of the individual's personality, culture, and sexual identity. Roberts and associates (2015) further assert that about 20% identify as "therians, [showing] an interest in anthropomorphism or spiritual identification with a particular species, not unlike the spirituality experienced in some indigenous cultures, and a desire to be not human" (p. 7). This additional component would require clinicians to include this cultural element in their conceptualization, not just as an area of personality or expression of the individual's personality, but as a spiritual component as well.

COUNSELING CHILDREN, ADOLESCENTS, AND YOUNG ADULTS

In this section, emphasis will be placed on examining practices that may assist in counseling children, adolescents, and young adults who belong to one of the groups mentioned in this chapter. As mentioned previously, a critical first step is to examine our own conscious and unconscious thoughts, attitudes, and beliefs about a client's cultural background. Keep in mind that these tools and reflective exercises may be appropriate for children, adolescents, and young adults, as well as individuals, couples, and families.

Another potential option for self-reflection may be using a culturally focused genogram to consider your own thoughts, attitudes, and beliefs about a client's cultural background. Cultural genograms can take many forms and are often focused on depicting an individual's culture of origin as a means of exploring implications of cultural identity (Hardy & Laszloffy, 1995). As a counselor, you could complete a cultural genogram that relates to the areas studied in this chapter. The instructions for completing a cultural genogram were developed by Hardy and Laszloffy (1995) with a specific focus on considering media as an element of significance. In this context, *media* should be broady interpreted rather than limited in scope. When considering media, be sure to include reflection around writing and literature, painting and drawing, movies and film, theater, music and dance, recreation and games, and other forms of self-expression including creativity and art. You might define your culture of origin related to media. For example, what were the media influences your family passed down? Here is a sample response: "My mother always liked soap operas and so we watch them together, and my grandmother was a classical pianist and hearing it makes me feel comfortable and calm."

You might also examine the pride and shame related to your culture of origin and media. For example, what are the media influences you share with others and which do you not share? Here are a few sample responses: "My father was a fan of *Star Trek* but I would never tell my friends" (shame); "My mother and I listened to Irish folk music since I was young and I played in a folk band for years" (guilt). You can create symbols and select colors to denote elements of pride and shame and use these to denote which influences are positive or negative. A yellow star may represent pride whereas a red "X" could represent shame. After reflecting, creating your symbols, and deciding on a color scheme, complete your cultural genogram by adding as many generations of influence as you can. In examining the results of your genogram, consider how these influences may have affected your perceptions, biases, and assumptions related to specific groups, particularly the gamer and fandom cultures.

After taking time to critically reflect on your biases, assumptions, and perceptions of these groups, we can consider implications for children, adolescents, and young adults. During the intake or initial session, it can be helpful to gauge digital media habits, internet use, and gaming habits (Carson et al., 2018). This knowledge can help conceptualize client issues, inform the counselor of potential areas of identity to be considered, and highlight possible strategies for media use as a form of intervention (Good & Mishna, 2021).

Related to gamers, specifically in dealing with problematic gaming, Young (2009) stated that "adolescent gaming addicts may experience symptoms of withdrawal, which include anxiety, depression, irritability, trembling hands, restlessness, and obsessive thinking or fantasizing about the Internet" (p. 360). In working with parents, it is important that parents know and understand the warning signs of problematic gaming and potential addictive behavior. These can include a preoccupation with gaming, loss of interest in other activities, social withdrawal, defensiveness, anger, lying about playing, and irritability. Parents should be encouraged to set limits on the amount of time their child can play, establish clear expectations, find alternatives to gaming that provide the same types of engagement (such as imaginary play or outdoor activities), and enforce rest breaks for eyes to avoid eyestrain and posture issues, as well as considering family therapy (Bruni et al., 2015; Hale et al., 2018; Mayhew & Weigle, 2018).

Those who assert membership in fandoms and those who engage in fan fiction, vidding, and other content creation may benefit from reduced isolation, increased connectedness, guidance, and mentorship to assist with the navigation of challenges and allow for positive adjustment. Although engagement in fandoms does come with risks, it may be that these risks are less impactful than the advantages gained (McInroy, 2020). Counselors should take the time to thoroughly examine engagement in the fandom and the activities the client chooses as a means to engage with the fandom to determine the youth's benefits, risks, and experiences within the group.

Members of the IARP indicated that "furries tend to be teens and young adults, though there are also plenty of adults in their late 20s and 30s in the fandom, too" (FurScience, n.d., para. 5). On the IARP website, the researchers provide some suggestions and even YouTube videos related to parental involvement, commonly asked questions, and risks. IARP maintains that the furry fandom is like any other fandom, with adult content and sexual elements that would present in other fandoms such as comics, sports, and video games. Counselors should take the time to review the available resources and research in peer-reviewed journals to assist youth who are members of a fandom as well as aid in proper conceptualization of client identity.

COUNSELING ADULTS, COUPLES, AND FAMILIES

In this section, we explore practices that may assist in counseling adults, couples, and families who belong to one of the groups mentioned in this chapter. As noted previously, a critical first step is to examine our own conscious and unconscious thoughts, attitudes, and beliefs about a client's cultural background (see the previous section for useful reflective tools). Keep in mind that these approaches and exercises may also be appropriate for children, adolescents, and young adults.

From a Rogerian perspective, considering gamer identity, fandom, or other subcultures may be as simple as following the theoretical framework of the counselor as a partner in the client's journey. After all, this theory calls not just for unconditional positive regard, but also for accurate empathetic understanding. When facing problems like gaming addiction, it may be beneficial to consider strategies that include elements of creativity, action, and even art. Expressive arts theory, created by Carl Rogers's daughter, Natalie Rogers, integrates the use of any form of art as a means to explore how clients define themselves and meaning, and even as a way to promote positive change (Ono, 2018). Using this perspective, clients would be encouraged to share and create art in a way that would be in line with their individual interests and potentially with their group membership as well.

As another example, practitioners using the social constructionist approach could ask clients to explore their reality relative to their cultural values and worldview, and in relation to social forces around them.

Metaphors can be another way to better understand clients and their internal dialogue, and have meaning that can be impactful in understanding the client's worldview. The use of metaphors is noted in several approaches to counseling, including narrative therapy, gestalt therapy, and others. Metaphors connect one's inner thoughts to the outer world. These metaphors may be related to and require an understanding of the client's gamer identity, fandom, or other subculture. Counselors can listen for these metaphors and are encouraged to ask questions to better understand the context. For example, a client might indicate they "ran like Naruto" from their addiction. A "Naruto Run" refers to a style of running performed by the anime title character of the same name. Unless you were familiar with this particular anime, you would not understand the expression. Thus, as a counselor, it will be helpful to familiarize yourself with the metaphors the client uses by asking questions, conducting your own research, and maintaining a stance of curiosity and positivity in engaging your client's metaphors. This could be an especially powerful tool if you were to come across metaphors that link to positive characteristics, coping, or problem-solving.

Adlerian therapy has several focuses, one being on social interest and community feeling (referred to in German as *Gemeinschaftsgefühl*; Watts & Ergüner-Tekinalp, 2017). The concept of community feeling can be defined as an individual's connection to humanity over the course of the past, present, and future. From an Adlerian perspective, identification with gamer culture, fandom, or other subculture may provide or create barriers to that community feeling (Turner, 2015). Because many of these groups engage with each other over time, their individual histories are preserved in media, and they often form close bonds with one another.

IMPLICATIONS FOR CLINICAL PRACTICE

This chapter has reviewed several areas of consideration related to cultural identity that may seem outside of what counselors may hold as standard or what is included in popular models of cultural conceptualization. As counselors, our goal and aim to understand our clients require us to understand our client's worldview, to view our clients in a holistic fashion, and approach our relationship with our clients with unconditional positive regard. To do so, we must be able to consider elements of a client's identity that may fall outside of these models or simply be too novel to fully understand through the lenses of traditional models.

CLINICAL CASE SCENARIO 24.1

Anthony, a second-generation Italian American, has always felt a deep-rooted connection to his family. When he thinks of family, he remembers big dinners, full plates, and large gatherings. This makes it strange that he feels so connected to a community of people he has never met, seen, or entertained at his home. During the day, he works for a local food production company and handles everything from inventory to maintenance to some light bookkeeping. In the evening, he logs on to serve as the magic-wielding mage in a gaming group that conducts nightly raids of villages in a fictional world, storming dark castles and having various great adventures, and quite a few laughs, along the way.

Anthony's nightly escape from reality is much more than a hobby or even a mere coping skill. The members of his raiding party know as much about him as any of his friends at home and, when he sits down to think about it, he isn't entirely sure where "home" is for most of them. Still, he often shares with them the details about his problems at work and with family, and even his struggle with depression, especially on evenings when the mood seems serious. Although they joke and banter, the other members are always great about offering advice or simply making him laugh enough to forget about his problems, at least for a while. When his father heard about Anthony's hobby from his fiancée at dinner a few nights ago, Anthony was surprised at how readily he defended his time with the gamers and the friendships he had made. His father laughed, calling them "fake friends," and asked, "Why do you have to be into these strange things?"

For Anthony, counseling has been a long road. He often finds it hard to maintain relationships and social supports over the long term, but has started improving with the development of his online connections. For a while, it seemed as if he felt accepted and prepared to meet each day, despite his struggle with depression. He looks forward to meeting with his friends each night, but now he wonders if there is something wrong with him. He can't help but think that maybe his father was right, and he has begun considering cutting ties with the game and his virtual party. After all, this is not what friends really are, right?

CLINICAL CASE SCENARIO DISCUSSION QUESTIONS

1. Where would you begin to help Anthony process his values versus his father's?
2. As a counselor, you might be inclined to help Anthony build a "real" social support by recommending that he get out and meet people, or attend support groups. How might this recommendation help and hinder Anthony's well-being?
3. In what ways does your office show that you are gamer friendly?
4. What things might you do to show Anthony that you are culturally sensitive to gaming?

END-OF-CHAPTER RESOURCES

A robust set of instructor resources designed to supplement this text is located at http://connect.springerpub.com/content/book/978-0-8261-3953-5. Qualifying instructors may request access by emailing **textbook@springerpub.com**.

SUMMARY

In this chapter, we reviewed elements of cultural identity related to gaming, fandoms, and other subcultures, in order to gain knowledge and awareness of cultural values individuals who identify with these groups may hold, to help you as counselors-in-training better identify your own potential biases and values, and to help you consider appropriate strategies for engaging with clients who identify with one of these groups. It is important to note that most of the cultural elements discussed within this chapter are novel and recent, meaning that more research is needed to fully explore and understand the specific needs of clients who share them as part of their identity.

DISCUSSION QUESTIONS

1. What problems and challenges are there for each cultural group and subculture discussed in this chapter?
2. Are there any approaches or strategies discussed in this chapter that you foresee challenges implementing? Explain your answer.

CULTURALLY RESPONSIVE COUNSELING FOR CLIENTS OF THE GAMER CULTURE, FANDOMS, AND RELATED SUBCULTURES

Guest: Dr. Eric J. Perry

https://connect.springerpub.com/content/book/978-0-8261-3953-5/part/part02/chapter/ch24

KEY REFERENCES

Only key references appear in the print edition. The full reference list appears in the digital product on Springer Publishing Connect: https://connect.springerpub.com/content/book/978-0-8261-3953-5/part/part02/chapter/ch24

Billings, A. C., & Ruihley, B. J. (2013). Why we watch, why we play: The relationship between fantasy sport and fanship motivations. *Mass Communication and Society*, 16(1), 5–25. https://doi.org/10.1080/15205436.2011.635260

Cade, R., & Gates, J. (2017). Gamers and video game culture: An introduction for counselors. *Family Journal*, 25(1), 70–75. https://doi.org/10.1177/1066480716679809

Heinz, M. (2020). "There's a little bit of that magic where I'm becoming something else": LGBT+ furry identity formation and belonging online. *Journal for Undergraduate Ethnography*, 10(2), 21–37. https://doi.org/10.15273/jue.v10i2.10351

Howe, W. T., Livingston, D. J., & Lee, S. K. (2019). Concerning gamer identity: An examination of individual factors associated with accepting the label of gamer. *First Monday*, 24(3). https://doi.org/10.5210/fm.v24i3.9443

Peeples, D., Yen, J., & Weigle, P. (2018). Geeks, fandoms, and social engagement. *Child and Adolescent Psychiatric Clinics of North America*, 27(2), 247–267. https://doi.org/10.1016/j.chc.2017.11.008

Roberts, S. E., Plante, C. N., Reysen, S., & Gerbasi, K. C. (2016). Not all fantasies are created equal: Fantasy sport fans' perceptions of furry, brony, and anime fans. *The Phoenix Papers*, 2(1), 40–60.

Skelton, S. B. (2008). Gaming as culture: Essays on reality, identity and experience in fantasy games. *The Journal of Popular Culture*, 41(1), 178–180. https://doi.org/10.1111/j.1540-5931.2008.00497_12.x

SECTION III: PRACTICAL APPLICATION OF MULTICULTURAL COUNSELING

CHAPTER 25

Broaching Race and Other Cultural Identities

NORMA L. DAY-VINES AND ANITA YOUNG

LEARNING OBJECTIVES

After reading this chapter, students will be able to:

- Apply the Continuum of Broaching Behavior.
- Explain the Multidimensional Model of Broaching Behavior (MMBB).
- Describe the Organizational Development Model of Broaching Behavior.
- Identify specific strategies for broaching racial, ethnic, and cultural factors with clients using the broaching framework.
- Use the broaching framework with clients and organizations.

SELF-REFLECTION QUESTIONS

1. How comfortable do you feel talking about race and culture?
2. Are you comfortable talking with others about your race and culture?
3. Whose responsibility is it to initiate conversations about race and culture—yours or your client's? Please explain your rationale.
4. What challenges do you think you might encounter talking about race and culture with your clients in session?

Many scholars have asserted that talking about race and culture is a difficult proposition because it engenders feelings of dread, anxiety, personal angst, guilt, shame, and resentment. To date, we live in a society in which we have not had a meaningful or substantive national dialogue on the topic of race and representation. As a consequence, such conversations have remained taboo (Day-Vines et al., 2007; DuBois, 1903/1996; hooks, 1992; Livingston, 2021). Throughout the annals of time, many people have been conditioned to avoid racialized discussions. Yet, even in the wake of George Floyd's murder, a global pandemic, and political upheaval, conversations have become even more polarized, not less polarized.

THE COUNSELOR: EXPLORATION, INTROSPECTION, AND REFLECTION

One might assume that, because counseling relies heavily on communication about difficult topics, the counseling profession would be in the vanguard of broaching discussions around race. Ironically, the counseling dyad is a microcosm of society, and counselors often struggle to discuss issues of race with their clients. Experts in counseling maintain that helping professionals may minimize racial, ethnic, and cultural issues with clients because of concerns about saying something offensive, limited skill sets, lack of racial self-awareness, and concern that they may not be able to control the direction of the dialogue once such a conversation unfolds (Sue et al., 2019; Utsey et al., 2005). This chapter is unique in that it provides a framework for discussing issues related to race, ethnicity, and culture (REC) on both an individual and organizational level.

Previous research has demonstrated that the counselor's inability to help Black, Indigenous, and People of Color (BIPOC) clients alleviate distress contributes to: (a) dissatisfaction with the counseling process, (b) suppression of personal disclosures, (c) premature departure from treatment, and (d) clients seeking to meet their culture-specific needs outside of the counseling relationship (Drinane et al., 2018; Kearney et al., 2005; Pope-Davis et al., 2002; Thompson & Jenal, 1994). Hook et al. (2016) found that more than 80% of respondents who had previously received counseling services reported at least one microaggression (e.g., slight or indignity perpetrated against people on the basis of their presumed inferiority such as race, gender, social class, sexual orientation, etc.) during treatment. Counselors' avoidance of racial, ethnic, and cultural concerns emerged as the predominant microaggressive event, followed by clients' presumption that counselors (a) harbored stereotypes about clients, (b) denied having cultural biases or stereotypes, or (c) minimized the importance of cultural issues during treatment. Microaggressive faux pas can damage the therapeutic alliance and are commonly classified as cultural ruptures (Constantine, 2007; Hook et al., 2017). Although the client's perception of microaggressions contributes to premature termination, a strong therapeutic alliance mediates the relationship between microaggressions and therapeutic outcomes (Owen et al., 2011). In light of the foregoing discussion, researchers have advocated for the discussion of racial, ethnic, and cultural concerns during treatment (Hook et al., 2017).

This chapter provides an overview of the broaching construct by introducing the Continuum of Broaching Behavior, a conceptual model that identifies orientations counselors may adopt as they determine whether or not to explore the contextual dimensions of REC with clients (Day-Vines et al., 2013). Next, the chapter examines the Multidimensional Model of Broaching Behavior (MMBB), a framework that identifies the specific contexts in which counselors can explore clients' racial, ethnic, and cultural concerns. The chapter continues with a discussion of four specific strategies that counselors can use to implement the broaching framework, and closes by introducing a framework for broaching within an organizational development context. First, though, a review of the profession's shift from multicultural counseling competence to multicultural orientation is appropriate (Day-Vines et al., 2021).

Historically, scholars and practitioners have focused on training models that emphasize multicultural competence, or the notion that a finite set of cultural competence skills epitomizes clinical care and equips counselors to work effectively with BIPOC clients (Metzl & Hansen, 2014). More recently, scholars have begun to eschew the idea of "cultural competence" and now define optimal care using a multicultural orientation framework (MCO; Hook et al., 2016; Owen et al., 2011). This tripartite framework involves three specific components: (a) cultural humility, (b) cultural opportunities, and (c) cultural comfort. *Cultural humility* refers to the counselor's ability to demonstrate a sense of openness and curiosity toward the client's values and viewpoints. Additionally, humility involves the recognition that counselors may have personal limitations in understanding clients' cultural values and viewpoints. *Cultural opportunities* refer to the counselor's willingness to explore the client's cultural concerns. *Cultural comfort* refers to the counselor's ease of manner in forging a connection with clients and demonstrating appropriate levels of multicultural communication.

INTRODUCTION TO BROACHING AND THE CONTINUUM OF BROACHING STYLES AND BEHAVIORS

The counselor's broaching behavior functions as a specific application of the MCO framework. The Continuum of Broaching Behavior is an empirically supported conceptual framework that guides the counselor's effort to discuss those REC issues that are germane to the client's presenting concerns (Day-Vines et al., 2007, Day-Vines et al., 2013, Day-Vines et al., 2018, 2020). Counselors can assume one of four broaching orientations: avoidant, continuing/incongruent, integrated/congruent, and infusing. Counselors often exhibit the lowest level of broaching effectiveness, based on their refusal to discuss concerns related to REC (Avoidant). Counselors who harbor less trepidation about broaching REC issues with clients may do so awkwardly and mechanically (Continuing/Incongruent), and in ways that belie their ease of manner with clients. At higher levels of broaching behavior, counselors engage in meaningful and substantive discussions about how issues of REC shape the client's presenting concerns (Integrated/Congruent). At the highest level of the broaching continuum, counselors implement social justice and advocacy interventions that eliminate barriers for clients (Infusing). Ideally, counselors will broach at the Integrated/Congruent and Infusing categories. Elsewhere, Day-Vines et al. (2007) have provided a more detailed and fully elaborated discussion of the broaching construct.

The broaching framework is an innovative therapeutic model that provides counselors with guideposts for exploring REC with clients. A growing body of literature has documented the benefits that accrue when counselors broach or discuss the contextual dimensions of REC during the treatment process, such as engagement and persistence in counseling (Burkard et al., 2006; Drinane et al., 2018; Thompson & Jenal, 1994; Zhang & Burkard, 2008). Some preliminary evidence related to the broaching construct demonstrates that BIPOC counselors and experienced counselors are more inclined to broach REC with clients (Day-Vines et al., 2013); school counselors and White counselors reported a greater likelihood of avoiding conversations involving REC (Day-Vines, Bryan, et al., in press), and higher levels of racial identity functioning were associated with greater investment in broaching REC with ethnic minority clients (Day-Vines, Brodar, et al., in press).

Multidimensional Model of Broaching Behavior

A secondary component of the broaching framework is the MMBB (Day-Vines et al., 2020). This framework identifies four specific contexts in which clinicians can explore clients' racial, ethnic, and cultural concerns: (a) Intra-Counseling; (b) Intra-Individual; (c) Intra-REC; and (d) Inter-REC. These contexts are not mutually exclusive, and clinicians can move fluidly between broaching contexts depending on clients' counseling needs. The MMBB dimensions allow counselors to explore more than sociocultural differences between the counselor and client or the client's encounters with racism and discrimination. This framework is a robust conceptual tool that broadens counselors' ability to explore the complex nature of REC, without essentializing clients, or reducing them to only their race.

For instance, Intra-Counseling broaching dimensions include consideration of the counselor–client relationship, wherein counselors engage in cultural immediacy by exploring the quality of the counseling relationship, exhibit cultural humility by divesting themselves of their expert status, and reduce the power imbalance by inviting the client to talk authentically about their REC concerns in an effort to strengthen the therapeutic alliance. To illustrate, Alex is a gay Latinx male with a chronic illness. He sought counseling to explore his transition to working in person as a result of the pandemic given his compromised immune system. The counselor enlisted Intra-Counseling broaching dimensions to establish a healthy therapeutic alliance, by communicating that discussions of REC were appropriate within the counseling dyad. This disclosure put Alex at ease and served as an indicator that he didn't have to conceal aspects of his identity. The counselor encouraged Alex to talk openly about his illness and his sexual orientation without having to conceal salient aspects of his identity. The counselor's disclosure that Alex could be authentic within the safety of the counseling dyad was reassuring to Alex and strengthened the therapeutic alliance. Alex appreciated the fact that his counselor explored their working relationship. In particular, the counselor inquired about whether Alex had reservations about working with a heterosexual therapist. Alex noted that although he would have preferred a gay therapist, he felt very comfortable with the progress he was making in treatment. This earnestness set the stage for a very productive counseling relationship.

Intra-Individual broaching dimensions refer to the counselor's exploration of the client's intersectional identities, and permit the client to explore the manner in which they may experience multiple oppressions within the safety of the counseling dyad. That is, although race may be a salient identity dimension, race is not the client's only identity marker. The client may possess other identity dimensions that warrant consideration within the counseling dyad. More specifically, a client may want to discuss not only issues of race, but also the confluence of their racial, ethnic, gendered, and social class identity dimensions. To illustrate, Tim is a White corporate executive who struggles with imposter syndrome. He grew up in the remote mountains of West Virginia in substandard housing. At times, his family experienced homelessness, living in the family car, moving between shelters in the winter, and lodging with relatives in the summer. As a child, he knew all too well what it was like to not get new clothes or school supplies for the start of school. And although he eventually benefited from an elite private education, he felt like he was straddling two social worlds, the impoverished one in which he was born, and the elite milieu he currently occupied where he worked tirelessly to conceal his humble beginnings. Tim confided to his counselor that he found it ironic that his coworkers automatically assumed he had been born into privilege, yet presumed that many of his colleagues of color had been born into poverty. Tim's counselor provided a safe therapeutic environment that allowed him to engage in catharsis, and explore why he was less than forthcoming about his humble origins.

Intra-REC broaching dimensions consider within-group cultural dynamics. Sahil is an Asian Indian male who is experiencing depression because he struggles to fit in with his family of origin. He feels a sense of isolation and alienation because when he attends family gatherings, he is the only one of his cousins who cannot speak Hindi. This puts him at a distinct social disadvantage that prohibits him from more intimate engagement with his family members. Sahil's parents immigrated to the United States and raised him in a predominantly White community, away from other members of the Indian community. Although Sahil appreciates Indian culture, he feels somewhat estranged from his culture of origin because he was socialized within a White world. He feels similarly estranged from many of his Caucasian peers because they do not accept him as a true equal. Although his colleagues socialize with him at work, he senses their cool distance and seldom receives invitations to gatherings outside of work. As part of his goal for counseling, Sahil is working to reconcile his bifurcated sense of identity.

Inter-REC broaching dimensions refer to encounters with racism and discrimination. To illustrate, Eun is a second-generation Korean emergency room physician who is having second thoughts about practicing medicine. During the COVID-19 pandemic, she experienced numerous microaggressions in which patients accused her of being responsible for the virus, refused to accept medical care from her, and ridiculed her accent. The barrage of racialized stressors left her questioning whether she wanted to continue to pursue her medical interests and career. Eun's counselor allowed her to express her ambivalence regarding the tension between her desire to practice medicine and her feelings that the racial hostility was too much to bear. Instead of redirecting her attention to more optimistic topics of discussion, the counselor permitted Eun to process her feelings of grief, resentment, and personal violation about the fact that many of her encounters occurred within the direct view of her colleagues who said absolutely nothing. In essence, Eun feels victimized by both her patients and her colleagues and supervisors. The section that follows provides some useful guidelines for facilitating broaching dialogues with clients.

Strategies for Broaching Race, Ethnicity, and Culture

The MMBB is a heuristic device for considering specific broaching contexts that counselors may pursue. Most scholars have stated the importance of exploring REC with clients, but very little scholarship reflects on the specific metacognitive processes that guide counseling discussions. Many clinicians avoid REC conversations altogether because they harbor concerns about saying something biased, fear that REC discussions may spiral out of control, or lack sufficient efficacy levels (Knox et al., 2003). The next component of the broaching framework involves the implementation of four specific stages for cultivating discussions about the client's REC concerns: (a) joining, (b) assessment, (c) preparation, and (d) delivery (Day-Vines et al., 2021). These stages require the clinician to be able to establish a productive working relationship with the client, conceptualize the client's sociopolitical realities and needs, formulate relevant questions, process client responses, and center the client's racial, ethnic and cultural concerns as appropriate.

The joining stage involves the counselor's effort to connect with the client, validate and affirm the client's strengths and resources, and build rapport. Rapport building serves as the foundation for a productive working relationship (Davis et al., 2018; Owen et al., 2011). The counselor's ability to demonstrate an interest in the client builds the foundation of a trusting therapeutic relationship, which in turn sets the stage for the client's more personal disclosures around REC. Day-Vines et al. (2021) have identified four steps associated with the joining stage. First, the counselor uses the client's language to facilitate communication. During the second step, the counselor helps the client feel heard and understood by acknowledging client feelings and viewpoints using paraphrases, reflective statements, and minimal encouragers. In the third step, the counselor affirms the meanings the client attaches to their experience, and in step four the counselor acknowledges the client's strengths and resources. The experience of feeling deeply understood enhances the depth of client self-disclosures. As an example, the counselor's ability to acknowledge that Eun felt attacked by her patients and abandoned by her coworkers who witnessed the slights and indignities she endured but chose to remain silent, convinced Eun that the counselor exuded empathy. This understanding provided catharsis for Eun and allowed her to talk more openly about her concerns.

During stage 2, the assessment stage, the counselor engages in thoughtful consideration of the client's culturally oriented concerns, the therapeutic alliance, and the counselor's own self-efficacy around exploring the client's racial, ethnic, and cultural concerns. In particular, the counselor engages in the following metacognitive processes: (a) multicultural case conceptualization; (b) racial identity functioning; (c) other relevant intersectional identities; (d) client readiness to explore REC concerns; (e) the strength of the therapeutic alliance; and (f) counselor self-efficacy. That is, the counselor pays selective attention to the client's varying identity dimensions and counseling-related concerns. The assessment process is a cerebral process in which the counselor weighs the client's sociocultural and sociopolitical realities, as well as therapeutic realities, before launching into a broaching statement.

During treatment, the counselor engages in multicultural case conceptualization by hypothesizing about the client's cultural concerns. For instance, in the case of Tim, the White corporate executive, the counselor works to gauge Tim's values and beliefs and how his status as a poor White man shaped his sense of marginalization and the great lengths he has gone to in order to conceal his humble origins. The counselor determines that this may be an appropriate area of exploration. The counselor also assesses Tim's sense of racial identity functioning. Day-Vines et al. (2007) hypothesized that the counselor's racial identity development would likely influence their openness to explore the contextual dimensions of REC with clients. More recent research suggests that counselors operating at higher levels of racial identity functioning reported greater openness to facilitate broaching dialogues with clients (Day-Vines, Brodar, et al., in press). Given the importance of considering the client's intersectional identities described within the Intra-Individual dimensions of the MMBB, counselors must also examine the client's other identities related to race, gender, sexual orientation, religion, immigration status, beauty privilege, and so forth. That is, the counselor may not explore every possible identity domain, but should discuss the multiple identities that serve as a source of subordination and privilege for the client. The counselor hypothesized that Tim's social class status functions as a source of ambivalence that contributes to his psychological distress. The counselor believes that Tim remains mired in a state of subordination despite his accomplishments, even as he experiences other sources of privilege. Given this conjecture, the counselor may want to explore Tim's inner thoughts and experiences in more depth.

Before introducing a broaching event, the counselor must assess the extent to which the client is prepared to discuss their REC concerns. In instances where the counselor presumes that the client is prepared to discuss REC concerns, the client will proceed with the aforementioned preparation stage. In instances where the counselor perceives that the client is hesitant to talk about REC, the counselor may table REC discussions until the client experiences greater levels of readiness. Readiness may be developed by working to strengthen the therapeutic alliance. Stronger alliances between counselor and client may be indicative of greater readiness to broach. The final assessment consideration involves the counselor's self-efficacy or confidence in their ability to broach. Counselors with lower self-efficacy levels may need more training and supervision. Counselors who feel ill-prepared to broach may refrain from broaching until they develop a greater skill set, as broaching prematurely and ineffectively may create cultural ruptures that undermine the counseling process.

The preparation stage involves the clinician's effort to set an intention by determining the purpose of the broaching efforts, selecting an MMBB dimension to explore, and labeling the client's sociopolitical concerns. During the preparation stage, the counselor organizes their thoughts and determines why broaching is a relevant counseling skill to implement. If the counselor determines that broaching is not a relevant skill that will facilitate client self-understanding and self-exploration, the counselor should refrain from broaching. Once the counselor ascertains that broaching is appropriate, they should broach along the higher end of the broaching continuum (*integrated/congruent* or *infusing* categories) and select at least one dimension of the MMBB.

For instance, as the counseling process got underway, Joaquin's counselor thought it was appropriate to explore intra-counseling dimensions. The counselor worked to establish a sense of mutuality by inviting Joaquin to explore all of their salient identities (e.g., race, gender, sexual orientation, health status), such that the counseling session would move beyond superficial discussions of Joaquin's counseling concerns. The counselor also processed the counselor–client relationship to explore how Joaquin felt about working with the counselor given their shared and different identity dimensions. An important component of the intra-counseling broaching dimensions is cultural humility, wherein the counselor acknowledges limitations in understanding some aspects of the client's experience. The counselor's investment in building a viable counseling relationship, sense of curiosity about Joaquin, and emphasis on the appropriateness of REC discussions within the counseling dyad helped strengthen the therapeutic alliance and contributed to more productive counseling sessions.

If—and only if—the counselor has carefully and methodically considered the specific broaching stages, the counselor should proceed with delivery, the fourth stage as mentioned earlier. During the delivery stage, the counselor communicates the broaching statement, uses silence, labels the client's sociopolitical concerns, and integrates and synthesizes broaching statements with foundational counseling skills (e.g., a reflection of content, reflection of feeling, silence, interpretation). For instance, when Eun, an emergency room physician of Korean descent, explained to her counselor that she had endured enormous amounts of abuse at the hands of both her patients and her coworkers, the counselor validated Eun's experience by noting that Eun had encountered numerous microaggressions that left Eun reeling and psychologically exhausted—and Eun wept. Eun experienced her counselor's compassion and concern at a deep emotional level. The counselor's words served as a bull's-eye statement. Afterward, the counselor was able to integrate and synthesize foundational counseling skills with broaching statements. Additionally, the counselor labeled Eun's sentiments accurately and concisely, achieving what Metzl and Hansen (2014) refer to as structural competence by giving voice to the client's struggles with racism and discrimination. Naming the client's concerns provided catharsis and set the stage for eventual problem resolution.

BROACHING RACE AND CULTURE IDENTITIES IN CULTURALLY MATCHED THERAPEUTIC ALLIANCES

We recommend that counselors implement the broaching strategies discussed herein, whether or not the counseling dyad is racially matched. It has been our experience as counselor educators that some counselor trainees presume sameness between themselves and their clients. As a consequence, they may contend that broaching the client's REC concerns is unnecessary when they share the same identity dimensions as their clients. Nevertheless, we require counselor trainees to broach with all clients. In most instances, counselor trainees come to learn that although they may share a particular identity dimension (e.g., race, age, or gender), with their clients, there are other dimensions (e.g., sexual orientation, religion, social class status) that render their identities with clients dissimilar. In one instance, a counselor trainee insisted that she did not need to broach the shared and different identity dimensions between herself and her client. When the counselor did eventually broach, she learned that although she and her client shared the same racial, age, and gender status, the client was a gay female who wanted to discuss her coming-out experience. Had the counselor trainee operated on the supposition that the two of them were identical, she may have squelched an important concern that the client needed to explore during the counseling process.

We contend that in instances where the counselor trainee and client share the same racial and ethnic designation, they may still experience those dimensions differently. For instance, Carmelita (counselor trainee) and Maria (client) are both Puerto Rican females; however, Carmelita's family has been living on the mainland for three generations and she does not speak Spanish. In marked contrast, Maria's family has recently moved to the U.S. mainland and she is bilingual. It is possible that Carmelita may be more acculturated than Maria, by virtue of the fact that her family has resided in the U.S. mainland for multiple generations. It may be necessary for Carmelita to use cultural immediacy with her client and acknowledge that although they share the same racial and ethnic designations, those designations may not manifest themselves identically. *Cultural immediacy* refers to the counselor's consideration of relational dynamics that may affect the counseling process in an effort to enhance the sense of connectedness between counselor and client and to promote effective cultural communication (Day-Vines et al., 2020).

In the final section of this chapter, attention is shifted away from the individual counseling interventions that counselors enlist to process the client's REC concerns and directed toward addressing the importance of broaching REC within organizational settings.

Organizational Continuum of Broaching Behavior

While the Continuum of Broaching Behavior operates as a conceptual tool for addressing counselors' ability to explore REC with clients in individual counseling contexts, the broaching model has limited utility outside the counseling dyad. The organizational culture in which people work determines how REC concerns are managed broadly (Livingston, 2021). More recently, Wise and Day-Vines (2020) adapted the Continuum of Broaching Behavior to demonstrate that although counselors may explore issues related to REC with clients, those conversations are limited outside an organizational context that supports diversity, equity, and inclusion (DEI; see Table 25.1). The Organizational Continuum of Broaching Behavior provides an institutional approach to addressing REC. There are four categories along this continuum: Avoidant, Continuing/Incongruent, Integrated/Congruent, and Infusing. We use Clinical Case Scenario 25.1 to describe orientations that organizations may assume as they determine how to navigate the continuum.

The Organizational Continuum of Broaching Behavior parallels the Continuum of Broaching Behavior. For instance, Avoidant organizations do little in the way of addressing issues related to REC because they regard the examination of REC concerns as unnecessary and inconsistent with the organizational mission. By minimizing employees' concerns, the organization perpetuates and reinforces racism and discrimination because the organization does not engage in substantive action. Table 25.1 delineates the Avoidant company's response. The emblem for the Avoidant school is an ostrich whose head is in the sand, ignoring pertinent issues. The predominant theme for Avoidant organizations is "silence." Rather than take a courageous stance, such organizations prefer instead to say nothing, the consequence is that problems fester.

Continuing/Incongruent organizations are aware that the organizational culture is awry and that dissatisfaction abounds among many counselors, yet they lack the tools to facilitate systemic change. When counselors come forward with concerns, Continuing/Incongruent organizations make things worse by mismanaging those concerns. This could involve accusing complainants of exaggerating their claims, or it could involve leaders who want to effect change but lack the tools to facilitate dialogue and usher in change. The graphic representation for Continuing/Incongruent organizations is a caution sign, which reflects the fallout that can occur from mismanaging grievances.

TABLE 25.1 ORGANIZATIONAL CONTINUUM OF BROACHING BEHAVIOR

	AVOIDANT	CONTINUING/ INCONGRUENT	INTEGRATED/ CONGRUENT	INFUSING
Organizational Stance	Refusal to address controversial issues	Address controversial issues in awkward, mechanical, superficial manner	Certain individuals within the organization have a deep structural understanding of diversity, equity, and inclusion	Social justice and systemic change are part of the organizational culture
What Is Said/Done	Nothing	Poorly thought out statements are issued; response is considered performative	Thoughtful and heartfelt responses by individual members of the organization	Engage racial, ethnic, and cultural issues directly and effectively
Rationale	Fear of making the problem worse	Lack tools to manage controversial issues	Organization leaves management of problems to handful of members within the organization	Addressing issues related to diversity, equity, and inclusion is the right thing to do; it is part of the organization vision and mission
Systematic DEI Initiatives	None	None	What gets done is done by a handful of members within the organization	Collection, analysis of data; use of data to drive decision-making; emphasis on racial justice and equity
Theme	Silence	Limited Engagement	Some of Us	All of Us

DEI, diversity, equity, and inclusion.

Integrated/Congruent organizations engage in what Morris (2020) referred to as performative allyship. Performative allyship is superficial support that lacks depth to effect change. Effectual allyship involves the use of one's privilege to transfer benefits of privilege to those without it. Phillips (2020) addressed the limitations of what she referred to as public allyship, in which people enlist social media to express outrage at social injustice. In particular, she suggested that public allyship can spur positive change, although it is a necessary but insufficient criterion for engaging in systemic change. That is, expressing outrage distinguishes one from those who are engaged in wrongdoing and can assuage feelings of guilt, but it does not address the root causes of systemic racism. Love (2020) asserted that people from marginalized groups need coconspirators, not allies. Unlike allies, coconspirators (in the spirit of abolitionists) exercise a sense of personal agency and accountability for transforming unjust systems.

Integrated/Congruent organizations are performative in the sense that only a select few members of the organization have committed to systemic change. The few individuals who are invested in systemic change give the false impression that the entire organization is invested and committed to change, when in reality efforts toward change are superficial and short-lived, and championed by a very small nucleus. Performative allyship in organizations involves shallow commitments and minimal efforts to address structural problems. On the surface, Integrated/Congruent organizations appear to manage challenges effectively. In reality, however, a handful of socially conscious organization members shoulder responsibility for managing problem situations and standing in solidarity with those in the organization who feel marginalized. The Integrated/Congruent organizational response does not reflect the entire company culture. It more accurately reflects the efforts of individuals who have a heightened sense of social consciousness. The thumbs-up sign characterizes the Integrated/Congruent organizations and the predominant theme is "some of us."

Infusing organizations address REC concerns that emerge by addressing issues head-on. They commit to social justice and advocacy. Rather than ignore or respond inappropriately, infusing organizations work to address concerns that emerge. For instance, they may want to learn more about the issues that surface within the organization. They adopt more action-oriented strategies, such as using data to drive decision-making to obtain a clear understanding of problem situations that may undermine organizational effectiveness. An example of this can be seen in Clinical Case Scenario 25.1, when Rising Son used a data-driven method that involved the collection and analysis of client records to capture baseline statistics about how clients are assigned to counselors. Infusing organizations cultivate open dialogue and facilitate professional development initiatives for employees. The graphic representation for the Infusing category is a recycling symbol, which reflects the fact that organizations work continuously to develop systematic changes that lead toward cultural responsiveness and systemic change. The theme for the Infusing category is "all of us," which reflects the fact that the entire organization is committed to the eradication of organizational bias.

Livingston (2021) developed a P-R-E-S-S framework that guides the work of antiracism within organizations. The model contains five specific stages (a) Problem awareness, (b) Root causes, (c) Empathy, (d) Strategies for rectifying the problem, and (e) Sacrifice, which refers to the organization's willingness to prioritize the concern. Infusing organizations recognize the utility of moving systematically through each of these five stages, and are more inclined to draw on and adopt the P-R-E-S-S model. As can be seen in the Clinical Case Scenario 25.1, Rising Son was willing to address these issues corporately. They hired a consultant to help them navigate the impasse they had reached so that tensions would not undermine the success of the company. As Rising Son worked through the Problem awareness stage, they recognized that BIPOC and White counselors had vastly different beliefs about the nature of the problem. Many of the White counselors did not recognize the grievances reported by BIPOC counselors. They believed that Rising Son was a great place to work, and that issues of diversity, equity, and inclusion were addressed effectively, as evidenced by Rising Son's recent hire of three new therapists of color. The counselors of color saw this argument as a *non sequitur*. It was through dialogue that White therapists began to better understand the specific and unique concerns of their BIPOC colleagues.

With the help of the consultant, Rising Son counselors worked to understand the Root causes of the perceived inequality within the organization. Counselors came together weekly to explore the dynamics that may have contributed to some of Rising Son's problems. For instance, the counselors of color were able to explain how they enjoyed working with clients of color, but felt that ethically all counselors should be able to work effectively with all manner of clients. Several of the White counselors confided that they had had very little training in working cross-culturally. It was through the process of dialogue that counselors were able to engage in perspective-taking, and see values and viewpoints that did not coincide with their own personal values and viewpoints, which Livingston (2021) refers to as *empathy*. The earnest discussions helped White counselors recognize that by not working with clients of color, counselors of color perceived their actions as culturally insensitive. Through dialogue, BIPOC counselors recognized that several of the White therapists were not necessarily being biased, but lacked core training around MCO and the broaching framework.

The Strategy stage required Rising Son to determine how it would address equity-oriented problem situations. Together, a diverse group of counselors identified strategies that included professional development training which would allow counselors to examine their attitudes, biases, and assumptions. A secondary strategy involved efforts to help all counselors work more effectively with culturally and linguistically diverse clients. A tertiary strategy involved the implementation of formal institutional policies. More specifically, counselors developed more equitable protocols that determined how clients would be assigned to therapists. The new protocols took into account areas of expertise and the number of clients on a caseload before assigning a counselor a new client. The final component of Livingston's (2021) is Sacrifice. This is where an organization must determine how they will remain committed over time to their antiracism goals. Although counselors within the organization felt like they had limited time to take on new initiatives, they sacrificed to work on systemic strategies that would improve workplace culture and the delivery of culturally responsive counseling services that all counselors were equipped to provide.

CLINICAL CASE SCENARIO 25.1

The Rising Son Counseling Center is a moderate-sized counseling center with 20 counselors, located in a suburban community just 30 minutes from an urban metropolis. More recently, Rising Son has shifted its core mission to be more inclusive and has hired three new counselors of color. Although the new counselors enjoy their new place of employment, they are acutely aware that they are only assigned clients of color. The three counselors met to share their concerns, and agreed that the practice of only being allowed to see BIPOC clients perpetuated racial bias and did not position White therapists to work effectively with all clients. The organization's response is dictated by its level of functioning along the Organizational Continuum of Broaching Behavior.

CLINICAL CASE SCENARIO DISCUSSION QUESTIONS

1. Is the concern of the counselors of color a valid one? Why or why not?
2. If you were one of the counselors of color, what words would you use to present your concern?
3. If you were head of the Rising Son agency, how would you address the concern?
4. Use the Organizational Continuum of Broaching Behavior to respond to the concern at each level.

END-OF-CHAPTER RESOURCES

A robust set of instructor resources designed to supplement this text is located at http://connect.springerpub.com/content/book/978-0-8261-3953-5. Qualifying instructors may request access by emailing **textbook@springerpub.com**.

SUMMARY

This chapter addressed the broaching construct, and explicated a broaching framework that counselors can use to guide their exploration of REC with clients. The Continuum of Broaching Behavior is a conceptual framework that identifies orientations counselors can assume as they determine whether or not to discuss REC concerns with clients. The MMBB identifies specific contexts in which counselors can broach and robustly explore REC. Counselors can use the guidelines enumerated in this chapter to conceptualize and deliver broaching statements. As counselors think about broaching in much broader contexts, they can enlist the Organizational Continuum of Broaching Behavior. This model parallels the original Continuum of Broaching Behavior, but also identifies systemic strategies that are warranted in organizations.

DISCUSSION QUESTIONS

1. Where are you along the Continuum of Broaching Behavior? Explain your answer.
2. Where do you believe your university is along the Continuum of Broaching Behavior?
3. How could your university department use the Organizational Development Model of Broaching Behavior?

KEY REFERENCES

Only key references appear in the print edition. The full reference list appears in the digital product on Springer Publishing Connect: https://connect.springerpub.com/content/book/978-0-8261-3953-5/part/part03/chapter/ch25

Day-Vines, N. L., Booker Ammah, B., Steen, S., & Arnold, K. M. (2018). Getting comfortable with discomfort: Preparing counselor trainees to broach racial, ethnic, and cultural factors with clients during counseling. *Journal for the Advancement of Counselling*, 40(2), 89–104. https://doi.org/10.1007/s10447-017-9308-9

Day-Vines, N. L., Brodar, J. R., Hicks, D., Fernandez-Korto, E. B., Garcia, C., & Jones, K. (in press). An investigation of the relationship between school counselor trainees' broaching behavior and their racial identity attitudes. *Journal of Counseling & Development*, 100(1), 3–13. https://doi.org/10.1002/jcad.12406

Day-Vines, N. L., Bryan, J., Brodar, J. R., & Griffin, D. (in press). Grappling with race: A national study of the broaching attitudes and behavior of school counselors, clinical mental health counselors, and counselor trainees. *Journal of Multicultural Counseling and Development, 50*(1), 25–34. https://doi.org/10.1002/jmcd.12231

Day-Vines, N. L., Bryan, J., & Griffin, D. (2013). The Broaching Attitudes and Behavior Survey (BABS): An exploratory assessment of its dimensionality. *Journal of Multicultural Counseling and Development, 41*(4), 210–223. https://doi.org/10.1002/j.2161-1912.2013.00037.x

Day-Vines, N. L., Cluxton-Keller, F., Agorsor, C., & Gubara, S. (2021). Strategies for broaching the subjects of race, ethnicity, and culture. *Journal of Counseling & Development, 99*(3), 348–357. https://doi.org/10.1002/jcad.12380

Day-Vines, N. L., Cluxton-Keller, F., Agorsor, C., Gubara, S., & Otabil, N. A. A. (2020). The Multidimensional Model of Broaching Behavior. *Journal of Counseling & Development, 98*(1), 107–118. https://doi.org/10.1002/jcad.12304

Day-Vines, N. L., Wood, S. M., Grothaus, T., Craigen, L., Holman, A., Dotson-Blake, K., & Douglass, M. J. (2007). Broaching the subjects of race, ethnicity, and culture during the counseling process. *Journal of Counseling & Development, 85*(4), 401–409. https://doi.org/10.1002/j.1556-6678.2007.tb00608.x

Livingston, R. (2021). *The conversation: How seeking and speaking the truth about racism can radically transform individuals and organizations.* Currency.

Zhang, N., & Burkard, A. W. (2008). Client and counselor discussions of racial and ethnic differences in counseling: An exploratory investigation. *Journal of Multicultural Counseling and Development, 36*(2), 77–87. https://doi.org/10.1002/j.2161-1912.2008.tb00072.x

CHAPTER 26

Cultural Considerations for Assessment, Diagnosing, and Treatment Planning

CAROLINE PERJESSY AND ANGIEMIL PÉREZ PEÑA

LEARNING OBJECTIVES

After reading this chapter, students will be able to:

- Discuss what it means to engage in thoughtful reflective practice as it relates to personal biases and values and how that shapes professional growth and development.
- Recognize how systemic racism has informed the diagnostic and assessment practice of the counseling profession.
- Describe ways counselors can practice culturally sensitive diagnostic and assessment practices with clients, including the understanding of how power, privilege, and social justice theories affect such practices.

SELF-REFLECTION QUESTIONS

1. How have historical and societal prejudice, bias, and assumptions hurt marginalized clients?
2. How do systemic racism and personal bias and values affect the counselor's ability to accurately conceptualize client concerns and presentations?
3. In what ways can culturally competent counselors use diagnosis and assessment ethically and effectively?

While this chapter is not meant to comprehensively explore how counselor training programs have prepared counseling graduates in diagnosing and treating people from marginalized communities and those from diverse cultures, this is an important area to pay attention to. Counseling graduate training programs, though evolving in their understanding of multicultural knowledge, skills, and awareness, are still criticized for not paying adequate attention to multicultural coverage (D. W. Sue & Sue, 2012). D. W. Sue and Sue (2012) suggest that each counseling course should contain several components, including (a) a consciousness-raising component, (b) an affective and experiential component, (c) a knowledge component, and (d) a skills component. The following sections relate to how the student in training, or novice counselor, can practice self-reflexivity in thoughtful, culturally sensitive, and informed work with clients.

THE COUNSELOR: EXPLORATION, INTROSPECTION, AND REFLECTION

In this section, we consider the different components of the counselor. Each therapeutic decision a counselor makes affects the diagnosis, treatment plan, and overall therapeutic approach. For that reason, this section focuses on *exploration*, *introspection*, and *reflection*, three different fundamental components of a counselor's self-awareness development. *Self-awareness*, the cornerstone of counseling—highly discussed albeit vaguely and in esoteric terms—refers to the ability (skill) and the process by which a counselor develops awareness (Pompeo & Levitt, 2014). The multicultural literature stresses that self-awareness is integral and the foundation on which multicultural competencies are developed. *Cultural auditing* is the practice of strategically considering the different conditions, beliefs, and components of one's culture that affect the working alliance between counselor and client (Collins et al., 2010). As Pompeo and Levitt (2014) astutely observe, self-awareness is enveloped by a certain vagueness that obscures the *how* of developing self-awareness. Liberation psychology, a key component of the social justice movement, also helps to develop counselor awareness of attitudes and beliefs through reflexivity (Aron & Corne, 1994). Therefore, throughout this chapter, we explore the necessary reflective practice that develops self-awareness.

Ethical Guidelines for Counselors

Before we consider how we may increase self-awareness, let us—novice and seasoned counselors alike—understand the importance and value of self-awareness. According to the American Counseling Association (ACA; 2014) *Code of Ethics*, there are several components of this subject or construct. Principally, as it relates to diagnosing and treatment planning, "[c]ounselors actively attempt to understand the diverse cultural backgrounds of the clients they serve. Counselors also explore their own cultural identities and how these affect their values and beliefs about the counseling process" (ACA, 2014, Section A). Further, the *ACA Code of Ethics* (2014, Section A.4.b) states that "Personal Values Counselors are aware of—and avoid imposing—their values, attitudes, beliefs, and behaviors." With these ethical guideposts, we posit that reflective practice is imperative for developing the self-reflection necessary to obtain and maintain effectiveness as a master counselor. After all, how can one "avoid imposing" what one is not aware of?

In accordance, the Council for the Accreditation of Counseling and Related Educational Programs (CACREP; 2016) Standards state that counselors must develop "strategies for personal and professional self-evaluation and implications for practice" (Section K). Self-evaluation, another component of self-awareness, is critical and established as essential to counseling training and counselor development. In other words, because counselors themselves are the instrument—*self-as-instrument*—one must be tuned. Developing self-awareness through a reflective practice, therefore, is not optional. It cannot be left to personality and the preferences of the counselor-in-training. Ivers et al. (2016) connected Multicultural Counseling Competencies (MCC) and mindfulness to this concept of self-reflective practice. They posited that MCC and mindfulness overlap in several tenets, including "self-awareness, compassion, non-judgment, empathy, acceptance, and emotional intelligence" (Ivers et al., 2016, p. 73). The authors' preliminary results based on this study revealed a relationship between MCC and mindfulness. Thus, all counselors have an ethical commitment to develop and maintain a reflective practice throughout their training and career.

Developing a Reflective Practice

Reflection examines the inherent dilemmas between theoretical and clinical practice. It moves students from an unclear understanding (e.g., personal values) to a clear understanding that allows them to be intentional in their clinical practice and the interventions utilized (López-de-Arana Prado et al., 2019). In considering the *what* and the *how* of reflective practice, like many things in counseling, theoretical definitions are available. For the purposes of this chapter, *reflective practice* refers to the intentional process of reflecting on professional problems, the self, and the overall counseling process to improve clinical effectiveness by increasing self-awareness (Rosin, 2015). Reflective practice remains an area where much is known, yet more understanding is needed within the counseling field (Collins et al., 2010).

In their work, Collins et al. (2010) identify the importance of an embedded reflective practice from the early onset of counselor development (i.e., training programs). *Reflective journals* are one example of a reflective practice that leads to increased self-awareness (Collins et al., 2010). An example of a reflective journal follows.

> I am still working on being authentic and letting the process unfold. I often feel more stuck when my supervisor is in the session than when I am alone. I still sometimes feel stuck about the direction I should take in the conversation with my clients. I still want to jump right to fixing things and giving advice, especially with those who are quiet. I enjoy watching my supervisor, though. She is very calm, asks great questions, and uses reflections of feelings, along with psychoeducation, very well. While I know I can't expect to be at her level so soon into practicum, as she has over 30 years of experience, it is a goal to find my authentic therapeutic self while utilizing some skills I see her use. I often feel pressured to be further in my skills and must remind myself that I just started practicum, which will take time. I realize that I must continue to educate myself, even outside of class, to learn more about subjects, skills, and treatment plans. This will take time, and I will develop my orientation and authentic self over time and with experience.

Insightfully, Collins et al. (2010) identify, within the counseling curriculum, the important role that the counselor-in-training's inner world plays. Nonetheless, often a counselor-in-training's internal psychology, culture, meaning-making, and values are not the main focus of training. Ultimately, as Collins et al. (2010) emphasize, it is impossible to train counselors to be clinically effective without teaching them how to engage in a reflective practice. A reflective practice examines their processes during sessions with clients and what concurrently occurs internally for them during and in between sessions.

Although a reflective practice provides a guidepost, it does not follow a prescribed step-by-step process. Nonetheless, López-de-Arana Prado et al. (2019) provide a conceptualization of reflective practice. The authors identify three levels of reflective practice. Level one focuses on the concrete description of the observation. Typically, this level is superficial, discrete, and focused on the external world (e.g., What do I see? What occurred in session?). Level two focuses on going deeper and bringing in previous knowledge of self, theory, and knowledge, and how that relates to the identified situation (e.g., How does my worldview affect the observed? Through my identified theoretical orientation, how do I organize and conceptualize the observed?). Finally, the third level focuses on understanding the underpinnings of the identified situation. This level highlights contradictions and complexities, bringing into the reflector's awareness their position with the observed and typically external situation from level one (e.g., What might be getting in my way of understanding? What previous lived experiences contradict the observed?; López-de-Arana Prado et al., 2019).

The López-de-Arana Prado et al. (2019) conceptual guideline toward a reflective practice is supported by other scholars' work, such as the DEAL model of reflection (Ash & Clayton, 2009). In their framework, Ash and Clayton (2009) organize reflection practice in three phases: description, analysis, and articulation. Additionally, Ziomek-Daigle (2017) suggests that a critical component of reflective practice is writing. Through writing, counselors can gain a greater understanding of self and begin the process of meaning-making (Cathro et al., 2017; Ziomek-Daigle, 2017). Similar to a counselor's expectation that clients create self-awareness through journaling and other creative interventions, these forms of reflective practice can also lead to a strengthening of self-awareness in counselors (Ziomek-Daigle, 2017). Ultimately, a reflective practice is a continuous and lifelong endeavor intended to create greater self-awareness and personal development (Rosin, 2015; Tansey & Kindsvatter, 2020).

Self-awareness increases by self-reflecting. It is essential to realize that we can only increase our awareness by intentionally reflecting on the process, ourselves, or the problem as it is in mindfulness practices. Rosin (2015) identifies two main domains upon which the reflective practice builds, the cognitive and affective domains. The *cognitive domain* refers to how one's worldview can change through the meaning-making process of reexamination and reflection. The *affective domain* refers to the collection of beliefs (unconscious) and feelings one has. Importantly, Rosin (2015) identifies a counselor's need to develop beyond their ideal self to their authentic self. Through the full integration of one's unconscious and consciousness, Rosin (2015) posited that counselors could achieve their highest functioning and master counselor self.

Through the consideration of increasing counselor self-reflective practices, we aim to increase overall counseling effectiveness. With self-as-instrument, the most critical skill to develop is attunement (self-awareness). In counseling, this mastery level is obtained through a fervent commitment to a reflective practice. Although further research is still needed in this area, it is commonly believed that counselors at a mastery level of practice have psychologically developed further than their counterparts (Rosin, 2015).

As we move forward, consider how you can increase your reflective practice, and in turn your counseling practice. Further, ask yourself what aspects of your cultural identity affect the conceptualization of your clients. Contemplate the subjectivity of client presentation and presenting problems as you respond to that question. For example, reflect on how you might respond to a Latin American client with traditional cultural values who holds strong principles deeply rooted in their family's values and overall family connectedness. Traditionally, this may result in a counselor's initial assessment of family enmeshment. Upon considering clinical assessment normativism, however, the Eurocentric underpinnings of the definition and assessments might lead to a possible misdiagnosis of enmeshment. What is not considered in this client scenario is the majority cultural assumption that individualization is the ultimate goal. We will discuss the topic of cultural considerations in diagnosis, assessment, and treatment, more in the next section.

CULTURAL INSENSITIVITY IN ASSESSMENT, DIAGNOSIS, AND TREATMENT PLANNING

While the profession of counseling has its roots deeply planted in wellness and prevention, the requirements of counselors to assess, diagnose, and treat clients are juxtaposed against the philosophical nature of the profession (Bonino & Hanna, 2018). However, for counselors to benefit from managed care reimbursements, utilizing the medical model—often pathologizing and limiting in nature—is a requirement when diagnosing and assessing. Thus, we will discuss some of the ways that cultural insensitivity occurs in assessment, diagnosis, and treatment planning, and how the counseling profession has attempted to mitigate these harmful systemic practices through more sensitive means.

The history of how cultural insensitivity manifested in assessment, diagnosis, and treatment planning can be traced to the origins of racism in America. It is not possible, in this single chapter, to adequately convey the magnitude of the impact of *scientific racism* (Thomas et al., 1972) on the development of the psychology and counseling professions. For further understanding of this phenomenon, we encourage you to read more about "genetically deficient models" and "culturally deficient models" to understand how systemic racism affected the counseling profession, particularly as it related to assessment, diagnosis and treatment planning (D. W. Sue & Sue, 2012; Thomas et al., 1972).

The experiences of people from marginalized communities are often conceptualized through the lens of White, Euro-American, middle-class perspectives, which constitute the majority of faculty and students within counseling training programs. This results in an overemphasis on creating modifications to traditional White models of therapy, along with a more embedded racist understanding of pathology. Further, because of this Eurocentric training model, traditional and legitimate forms of mental health support (e.g., church, social support, family, folk-healing methods) are not considered valid or worthy of consideration (D. W. Sue & Sue, 2012). Additionally, the training of mental health counselors in use of the *Diagnostic and Statistical Manual of Mental Disorders* (5th ed.; *DSM-5*; American Psychiatric Association [APA], 2013) lends itself to many cultural considerations. We will explore the implications of using the *DSM-5* and how it relates to client conceptualization. We conclude that there must be a thorough examination of how graduate counseling programs intentionally teach and train counselors to assess, diagnose, and treat clients of various cultures and backgrounds.

The *DSM*'s historical roots lie in a symptom-based system that is descriptive in nature and emphasizes the medical model of mental health (Bonino & Hanna, 2018). Davies (2017) identified research showing that the *DSM*, starting with the *DSM-III*, had little reliability and validity. Nonetheless, it is used by many medical and mental health professionals, including psychiatrists, clinical social workers, mental health counselors, and psychologists. Yet, the authors of the *DSM* are currently medical professionals from the field of psychology and do not represent counseling or counselor education (Bonino & Hanna, 2018). Considering that mental health counselors are one of the largest groups of consumers/users of the *DSM*, this leaves the voice of the profession missing from the creation of a manual that considers the cultural and developmental components of case conceptualization (Bonino & Hanna, 2018).

Counselor training programs strive to promote a professional identity consistent with empowering individuals, families, and other systems. This requires cultural and contextual knowledge and understanding of individuals and their concerns (Tomlinson-Clarke & Georges, 2014). As such, when teaching courses such as diagnosis and assessment, culture and meaning-making of individuals remains paramount; however, culture and meaning-making of client systems are pathologized and hardly considered in the *DSM* (Bonino & Hanna, 2018). Counselors face many challenging situations and cases, and, as articulated earlier, without careful consideration of self and a nuanced understanding of complex client concerns, counselor diagnostic skills may be impaired. Further, it is just as important to understand how bias in assessment and diagnosis manifests, which is discussed in the following sections.

Bias in Assessments

Biased assessment practices and improper use of instruments can have major implications for what constitutes pathology and treatment in counseling. Further, the manner in which clients participate in assessment and information gathering and the actual process of counseling may be antithetical to the values of culturally diverse individuals (D. W. Sue & Sue, 2013). The ways in which help-seeking behavior is addressed, how individuals convey strong emotion, and their comfort level with revealing personal information are all culturally bound phenomena. For example, in the Asian culture, restraint of strong feelings and difficulty asking for psychological help is widely known (Hays, 2016), yet a counselor who is uninformed of these cultural norms might misinterpret an Asian client's reluctance to freely reveal personal information as indicating pathology, and as a result might misdiagnose the client. Similarly, personality tests have characterized Black clients as mistrustful and paranoid of others; however, this characterization is propounded without consideration of the sociopolitical perspective. In their book *Black Rage*, Grier and Cobbs (1968) explained that in order for Black individuals to survive a racist society, they adopted a functional survival method to protect themselves against the potential for psychological and physical harm. Thus, skepticism and lack of trust are to be expected among the Black community; this is normative, and does not necessarily indicate pathology (Grier & Cobbs, 1968). A counselor who is assessing the needs of a Black client must understand how that client may experience intrusive questions about their family, history, and other past experiences. Another example of how a counselor's misunderstanding of cultural norms may lead to biased assessment practices is their expectation of insight-oriented behavior and self-disclosure. In some culturally diverse groups, these behaviors are not highly valued, and a counselor who assesses a client's level of insight based upon how much or little the client reveals may misinterpret the client without consideration of culture.

Counselors conducting a cross-cultural assessment may commit errors of omission and/or errors of commission (Kemp & Mallinckrodt, 1996). An *error of omission* occurs when the counselor fails to ask certain questions about the client's life, usually because the counselor is unfamiliar with the client's life and may hold dominant cultural beliefs about what is important to attend to and what is not. Conversely, an *error of commission* is committed when the counselor focuses on an area of exploration that is not particularly meaningful or important to the client. Again, this error stems from a counselor employing a dominant worldview of what is most important to diverse cultural groups.

Bias in Intelligence Assessments

Because many instruments have been constructed based upon White middle-class norms of what is considered healthy, pathological, and so on, the results obtained from these assessments may be considered invalid (D. W. Sue & Sue, 2012). The 10 most commonly used psychological tests, as surveyed by 74 clinical psychology doctoral programs, found that the vast majority were developed using European American worldviews and values (Ready & Veague, 2014). Further, the tests were developed by a panel of predominantly European American experts who validated the tests through correlation measures of other, related instruments. Thus, it has been suggested that standardized tests should not be used with ethnic clients and those of other minority cultures, as evidenced by the landmark case of *Larry P. v. Riles* (1979), in which the court ruled that psychologists must not use IQ tests to assess African American students for inclusion in special education courses. Over the years, counselors and others in the mental health professions have become aware of the inherent biases, especially as they relate to people who speak English as a second language (ESL). In the school systems, a partial resolution to identifying a specific learning disability (SLD) of ESL students has been through the use of language-reduced tests such as the Kaufman Assessment Battery (K-ABC; Kaufman & Kaufman, 2004), the Universal Nonverbal Intelligence Test (Bracken & McCallum, 2009), and others.

Researchers have attempted to seek alternatives to find solutions to testing bias. One way has been to establish separate norms for specific ethnic and cultural groups. However, there have been challenges associated with this as other factors, outside of culture, such as socioeconomic status, quality of education, and language proficiency, can affect testing outcomes (Cagigas & Manly, 2014). Additionally, researchers have constructed assessments from scratch, with consideration for the cultural norms of the group being tested. For example, researchers (Kathuria & Serpell, 1998) developed the Panga Munthu Test, which was specifically developed for assessing intelligence in Zambian children and incorporated information particular to the skill sets of Zambian children living in rural areas (Hays, 2016).

Another way researchers have attempted to address the bias within intelligence measurement instruments is through restandardized instruments (Hays, 2016). Restandardization includes collecting norms from samples that are more representative, and can assist researchers in revising or deleting original test questions that were found to be invalid across other cultures, and adding items or scales that are more culturally valid. This is another example of how assessment practices continue to change and evolve as multicultural awareness increases; however, much work remains to be done in identifying our cultural worldviews and how those permeate decisions, behaviors, and interactions with others.

APPROPRIATE ASSESSMENT AND TREATMENT TOOLS

Informed Consent

For counselors, culturally sensitive assessment practices begin with the conversation involving informed consent. For those working with clients from cultural backgrounds that are unfamiliar with counseling, taking extra time to explain the informed consent process is crucial. It is important not only to share what counseling entails, but also to understand what the client is expecting from counseling, which might take longer than one session due to language and cultural norms related to dialogue. Hays (2016) advised that informed consent conversations with clients from various cultural backgrounds may take longer than expected for the following reasons: the person does not have English fluency and the consent form is only in English; there is a disability that limits reading ability or ability to comprehend; the client is undocumented, a torture survivor, or has had other negative experiences with authority figures and is reluctant to sign; the client does not have insurance, does not believe government-provided health insurance will pay for services, or is unable to pay; or the client may not be familiar with counseling or might not believe in its effectiveness, thus highlighting the need for further conversations about informed consent.

Once informed consent is established, we can progress to the next steps of our work with clients, which is usually an intake assessment and mental status examination, while always keeping our self-reflective processes in mind.

Intake Assessments and Mental Status Evaluations

In conducting intake assessments and mental status examinations (MSEs), accurate knowledge of a client's cultural history is important for making valid interpretations based upon their results (Hays, 2016). For example, a non-native English speaking client will interpret questions such as "What state are we in?" differently, depending on their country of origin and what the term *state* means to them. Time is another culturally bound value that is regarded in varying ways, depending on the client's culture. Thus, someone who does not adhere to standard European American norms of keeping time, valuing time, and allocating time may need to have such questions framed differently, perhaps using life history charts and markers tied to significant events rather than dates (Manson and Kleinman [1998], as cited in Hays, 2016). Other aspects of the MSE include assessing eye contact, speech, motor activity, thought and perception, affect and mood, insight, and appearance. If we consider how other cultures demonstrate, value, or represent these areas, we can see what counselors need to be aware of as they conduct assessment practices.

Gathering information from clients of various backgrounds can look different, depending upon those clients' cultural identities. For example, various forms of communication can be expressed differently and require flexibility and knowledge on the part of the counselor to ensure that the therapeutic alliance is built before standard questions are asked. In the case of clients who grew up in generational poverty, for example, the client may respond to questions using responses that do not directly address the questions asked or are more story-telling in nature. This is described as a more casual language style, or *casual register*, that is typically used with family and friends and utilizes a smaller vocabulary, general words, and incomplete sentences (Payne, 2013). *Formal register* is a style of communication used in more formal settings, such as school and work, and is reinforced in middle-class homes (Payne, 2013). Those who come from generational poverty may never learn formal register and thus may use casual register even in formal settings because of their lack of experience and familiarity with any other form. It is also important that counselors remain cognizant of how many questions they are asking at once. For example, Native Americans are usually more reserved and may struggle with sharing personal information and might become overwhelmed with numerous questions (Payne, 2013). This may lead to them deciding not to return after the initial assessment. Additionally, understanding the cultural events of when and where the client was born and what was happening in their world at that time (e.g., historical events) and the subsequent experiences that shaped them is vital to assessment as well. The more the counselor knows about these historical events, the more accurate their conceptualization of the client will be.

During an intake assessment, inquiring about the client's educational history is common. If the client came from an educational system outside of the European American model, a counselor might consider using a cultural consultant. A *cultural consultant* is someone who is familiar with the client's culture and can speak to the meaning of what amount of education the client has and how that meaning is translated to the current circumstances (Hays, 2016). Similarly, when a counselor inquires about a client's career or employment history, the awareness of what *work* entails, from a cultural perspective, must be questioned and explored. In the majority U.S. culture, work is something often directly connected to one's identity, often consumes much of a person's time, and is a prioritized activity that identifies socioeconomic status, among other personal values. Hence, work and employment may mean very different things to those who do not share these values.

Being a culturally sensitive counselor requires assessing various components of a client's worldview and how that worldview informs diagnosis and treatment. White Kress et al. (2005) suggest that counselors *assess the client's worldview*, which includes their values, beliefs, and assumptions about the world, which will differ based upon the client's cultural, racial and ethnic, and religious background. Next, they suggest the counselor *assess the client's cultural identity* and what stage they may reside in within that identity. A client's cultural identity is informed by their levels of acculturation, which can be determined through questions focusing on religious beliefs, language development, educational status, employment, social status, and others. The researchers also recommend that the counselor *assess sources of cultural information relevant to the client* by educating themself on the culture of the client and engaging in professional development activities such as reading, visiting churches and other places of worship, and consulting with others who are from the same or a similar background as the client. Finally, they recommend *assessing the cultural meaning of a client's problem and symptoms*, which refers to understanding and exploring what the client believes the problem to be. The professionals find guidance through asking, "What are the client's views on the development of the problem, maintenance of it, and eventual treatment of it?" These suggestions allow for a more holistic and contextual assessment process, which is crucial to a less biased and more culturally sensitive assessment and diagnostic practice. This is especially important as we recognize how the diagnostic process is embedded within dominant Western values and thus promotes narrow and limited information in the diagnostic decision-making process.

The guidelines discussed here are akin to the liberation psychology theory of Ignacio Martín-Baró's liberation psychology theory (Aron & Corne, 1994), which encompasses four key tenets and can help counselors implement the Multicultural and Social Justice Counseling Competencies (MSJCC; Ratts et al., 2015). These tenets include: (a) realismo-critico, (b) recovering historical memory, (c) concientizacion, and (d) deideologized reality. Each area relates to how counselors can help clients move away from problems to focus on possible solutions, while emphasizing the need to recover historical memory and the client's community to aid and support the client's healing. Thus, counselors can work together with clients not only to develop awareness about the presenting concerns, but also to collaborate together on social justice advocacy efforts.

The *Diagnostic and Statistical Manual of Mental Disorders*

African American and Hispanic clients are more likely to be overdiagnosed and receive more diagnoses, and consequently experience less effective treatment than White clients (D. W. Sue & Sue, 2013). Further, a diagnosis, while providing some access to therapeutic treatment, can cause additional harm to a client by dictating medication management that does not address the underlying issue, or creates further challenges because of the medication's side effects. Clients of color who come from limited resources and means are financially limited in their ability to mitigate mental health conditions by using proactive, non-psychotropic practices (Hays, 2016). Therapeutic interventions such as developing a hobby could offer a client a valuable diversion and enhance their mental health, but lack of financial resources can prohibit this option. Recommending additional tutoring to a client who has a diagnosis of a learning disability could be a helpful course of action, but may not be realistic as it is cost-intensive. It may also be difficult to access individuals with the ability to provide such services. Thus, clients of various backgrounds often have to resort to medication management as the only recourse in their treatment because medication is usually covered by government-assisted health insurance.

The use of diagnostic labels can have both negative and positive consequences. For example, a child who requires special education services would gain benefit from an accurate learning disability diagnosis. However, positive psychology research confirms that negative diagnostic labels can affect motivation for change (Edwards et al., 2019). As we have discussed, limitations of the diagnostic system can lead to poorly contextualized diagnoses (Kress et al., 2014); thus, it is important that counselors consider their own internal biases and behaviors and how they influence the diagnostic process.

Consequently, multicultural counselor competencies in diagnosis are crucial skills to develop. D. Sue et al. (2016) developed a multipath model using four dimensions (i.e., psychological, biological, social, and social-cultural) to contextualize etiologies of abnormal behavior. Using this model, social, cultural, and economic variables must be considered when determining diagnosis and pathology. Differences in cultural norms and values lead those who are of different cultural backgrounds to misunderstand one another. Too often, this results in diagnosing and assigning a detrimental diagnosis to those demonstrating culturally congruent behaviors. In addition to the cultural considerations that are not recognized, the advent of managed care and its requirements for cost reimbursement has changed the field of psychology and counseling. As a result, *diagnostic inflation*, or overdiagnosis, can manifest, which, according to Wylie (2014), is influenced by

1. the *DSM*'s influential ability to make decisions about disability, courtroom verdicts, school placement, and so on;
2. the influence of pharmaceutical companies to profit from diagnosis and corresponding medication management;
3. insurance companies' requirement that a diagnosis be provided to cover payment and that a diagnosis be made before sufficient information is gathered; and
4. marketing by pharmaceutical companies to general medical providers that psychiatric disorders can be resolved through simplistic (and potentially adverse) medication management strategies.

The *DSM-5* (APA, 2013) received a much-needed update, reflecting an alignment with the *International Classification of Diseases*, Ninth Revision (*ICD-9*; World Health Organization, 1975), along with further clarification on how to *effectively communicate* clinical information, *implement effective* interventions, *predict* future needs and outcomes, and help clinicians *differentiate* disorders from non-disorders (First et al., 2015). These revisions resulted in several changes to the *DSM-5*, along with an increased emphasis on culture. One of the ways the *DSM-5* demonstrated a more holistic perspective, including culture, was through dimensional, as opposed to categorical, assessments (Tomlinson-Clarke & Georges, 2014). By using dimensional assessments, disorders are viewed on a continuum and can represent varying degrees of behavior (D. Sue et al., 2016). Using dimensional assessments also allows for more consideration of the influence of culture and race. The developers of the *DSM-5* attempted to integrate culture more systematically. For example, in the previous *DSM* edition "Specific Culture, Age, and Gender Features" consisted of a paragraph under some diagnoses, but not all. In the *DSM-5*, this section has been expanded into three separate paragraphs under most diagnoses: "Cultural Issues," "Developmental and Lifespan Considerations," and "Gender Differences" (Hays, 2016).

Multicultural considerations, one of the hallmarks of the *DSM* revision, resulted in a revised Cultural Formulation Interview (CFI), a derivative of the Outline for Cultural Formulation (OCF), which was introduced in the *DSM-IV* (APA, 1994). Despite goals of revising the diagnostic classification system to be "more clinically valuable and more biologically valid" (Nemeroff et al., 2013, p. 2) and to appreciate cultural variations in clients' expressions of their concerns, the *DSM-5* has been criticized for retaining many of the European American norms of pathology, although improvements have been made. Nonetheless, the CFI provides a way to specifically and intentionally incorporate culture into the *DSM*.

The *Diagnostic and Statistical Manual of Mental Disorders* Outline for Cultural Formulation

The OCF in the *DSM-IV* was a major milestone for cultural psychiatry, acknowledging the need to integrate culture into client conceptualization and treatment (Lewis-Fernández et al., 2014). The CFI, the subsequent revision of the OCF, was developed to accompany the *DSM-5*. The CFI is a 15- to 20-minute semi-structured interview that consists of a 16-item questionnaire. It is supplemented by 12 modules for further assessment and includes an informant version to obtain material from caregivers (APA, 2013). The modules assess topics or specific populations such as coping and help-seeking, refugees and immigrants, and spiritual or religious traditions and can help culturally competent counselors better understand their clients' worldviews (Dailey et al., 2014). The CFI may help counselors develop a relational connection with clients that can improve diagnostic decision-making (Kress et al., 2014). If a counselor chooses not to use the CFI, there are other less formal assessment practices that can inform culturally sensitive diagnosis. Castillo (1997) states that comprehensive cultural assessments are critical to the work of counselors, as culture affects both counselor perception and clinical presentation. Several considerations support the use of informal assessment practices, including (a) assessing the client's cultural identity, (b) identifying sources of relevant cultural information, (c) assessing the cultural meaning of client problems, (d) assessing for counselor biases, (e) planning collaborative treatment, and (f) exploring the impact of family, work, and stigma that may be associated with the mental illness (Castillo, 1997).

CURRENT RESEARCH AND CULTURALLY RESPONSIVE THERAPEUTIC INTERVENTIONS AND APPROACHES

While keeping the case of Mia in mind (see Clinical Case Scenario 26.1), let us consider how Jamie's decision-making relates to determining a culturally responsive diagnosis as supported by the literature. Hays (2016) offers several suggestions for diagnosing in a culturally responsive way. In addition to using the *DSM-5*, making a culturally responsive diagnosis involves thinking systematically and relationally, including cultural influences (Hays, 2016). One way to do this work is for the clinician to create a cultural profile which is guided by the acronym ADDRESSING (Hays, 2016). Next to each letter is the corresponding word that represents the most meaningful cultural components for the clients:

    Age and generational influence
    Developmental or other
    Disability
    Religious and spiritual orientation
    Ethical and racial identity
    Socioeconomic status
    Sexual orientation
    Indigenous heritage
    National origin
    Gender

This profile can continue to be expanded upon as the client and counselor work together, incorporating more of the client's culture as the counselor continues to learn about them.

Additionally, Hays (2016) suggests using caution when diagnosing personality disorders, because the criteria used to diagnose a personality disorder are often dependent upon the interpersonal skills and attitudes valued by a culture at any given point in time. When working with those with diagnosed personality disorders, care must be taken not to misinterpret normative emotional reactions to life events. For example, a clinician must be mindful of their own proclivity for and comfort with emotional expression, and what that reveals about their own biases. Naturally, other symptoms of personality disorders must also be carefully considered in the context of the clinician's and client's cultural backgrounds. Others have encouraged the use of "reframing" when considering personality diagnosis (Brown, 1992, as cited in Eriksen & Kress, 2008). Instead of administering a personality diagnosis that can have negative impacts on a client, reframing can help explain how the behavior manifested, given the circumstances, context, time, and so on. For example, a minoritized female abuse survivor who exhibits passivity, lacks a sense of self, and struggles with emotional self-regulation may be credited with harnessing personal power to tolerate the abuse, instead of obtaining a diagnosis of Borderline Personality Disorder. However, these decisions carry considerable implications, as diagnosis often determines treatment options.

In summary, Hays (2016) suggests that making a culturally responsive diagnosis requires transparency on the part of the counselor and integration of the components discussed here, along with a clear explanation of how the counselor arrived at the diagnosis and recommendation, both in the written report and directly to the client.

IMPLICATIONS FOR CLINICAL PRACTICE

Counselors are tasked with many competing responsibilities; they are often overwhelmed, overworked, and struggle with feeling competent regarding the treatment of clients from various cultures. The complexity of how culture manifests in individuals and how that is interpreted by the counselor is underscored by systemic racism, microaggressions, and biases that are sometimes not obvious to the counselor. Hence, using reflective practice, gaining additional professional development opportunities, and obtaining supervision and consultation are key tools for the multiculturally responsive counselor. Additionally, counselors also experience overwhelming feelings due to personal and professional experiences (e.g., microaggressions, societal messaging, cultural underpinnings). Therefore, it is imperative that counselors increase their self-awareness.

Identifying when a client is experiencing *microaggressions* (e.g., slights, oversights, assumptions) inside and outside of the therapy session is a crucial counseling skill (Johnson et al., 2018). The definition of microaggression includes a verbal component (Pierce et al., 1978) along with situational context, and is often what counseling focuses on. Some examples of microaggressions include: "When I look at you, I don't see color," "I'm not a racist, I have several Black friends," and so on. The microaggression may relate to any aspect of culture: race, gender, religion, and so on. However, researchers have identified that the nonverbals accompanying the communication largely convey the meaning of the message and are often considered more honest than the actual words spoken (Aviezer et al., 2012; Hickson et al., 2004). Over time, these microaggressions may stimulate a trauma response in the recipient (van der Kolk, 2014), but these responses are frequently vague and difficult to identify. Thus, clients may experience the painful emotion associated with the microaggression but cannot name or describe what happened. It is critical that counselors be able to identify microaggressions for the client when they think offenses have occurred.

In conducting a culturally responsive assessment, several areas must be attended to, including (a) continuous involvement in one's cultural self-assessment; (b) establishing a positive therapeutic alliance; (c) learning about diverse cultures, including the language, views, and colloquialisms; (d) exploring the client's specific identity and context; and (e) understanding how the client and counselor identities interact (Hays, 2016). Culturally responsive assessment involves actively looking for the strengths within clients and those that pertain to the client's system throughout the assessment process. This does not mean that the counselor asks the client direct questions about strengths; rather, the counselor is actively listening for strengths as the client shares their story. Then, later, the counselor may directly ask strengths-based assessment questions to hear the client expand upon what was shared through a different lens. This can then be reinforced by the counselor through their dialogue and reflection of feeling, meaning, and content.

Counselors can increase client agency and harness their internal strengths by highlighting and emphasizing client resourcefulness. Researchers have identified strengths-based perspectives to support client change when making a diagnosis (Tomlinson-Clarke & Georges, 2014). Using a strengths-based orientation can benefit clients by emphasizing character strengths and virtues that enhance well-being in all life areas. In using strengths-based exercises, counselors encourage the promotion of strength as part of their self-reflective practice. When using a strengths-based approach with clients from diverse backgrounds, counselors can tap into the spiritual, environmental, and social support systems of the clients. It is important to recognize that clients who have experienced oppression, marginalization, and other discriminatory practices have often developed strong resolve and resilience in the face of many obstacles. A strengths-based counselor will not only notice these characteristics, but also emphasize and reinforce them for the client, thus shifting the client narrative to one that is hopeful and positive.

CLINICAL CASE SCENARIO 26.1

Jamie is a middle-class, professional, White woman counselor-in-training at a community agency where there is a diverse group of clients ranging from emerging adults to late-in-life individuals. Jamie was assigned a client, Mia, a single White woman from a northeastern European country who, at 41 years old, is a nontraditional-aged college student. Clinical services at the agency where Jamie worked were promoted as part of an extra credit opportunity in one of Mia's psychology courses. Mia decided to sign up for the counseling services for extra credit. During Mia's initial intake session with Jamie, Mia references several traumatic events that had occurred in her lifetime. Jamie is mindful not to unpack trauma during the intake session, but instead validates Mia and collects further psychosocial information to inform her diagnosis. Based on the intake, Jamie provides an initial diagnosis of General Anxiety Disorder (300.02, F41.1; *DSM-5*; APA, 2013). Throughout several sessions, Mia reveals symptoms that also may indicate depression. Two months into their sessions, Mia seems to be decompensating and begins reporting suicidal ideation. Mia feels discouraged that she is not getting better, and says, "Nothing is going to make a difference. I am not going to have a baby next year. I am not going to be married." In addition,

(continued)

CLINICAL CASE SCENARIO 26.1 (CONTINUED)

Jamie begins to note symptoms of chronic feelings of emptiness and extreme shifts in moods. Jamie begins to consider a differential diagnosis of Borderline Personality Disorder (301.83, F60.3; *DSM-5*; APA, 2013). In their time together, Mia sometimes appears engaging and open, yet in other sessions seems withdrawn and despondent. After considering and engaging Mia in several courses of treatment, the result yields evidence of persistent depressive symptoms for Mia. Jamie begins to consider a more significant diagnosis. However, in considering a diagnosis, she goes back to her ethical duty to understand her client from a multiculturally responsive lens. She considers what differences may exist between herself and Mia. While both identify as White women, they are incredibly different in culture, background, and life experiences. Mia's family culture lacks emotional connection and depth of understanding of one another. Mia reports an absence of affection within her family dynamic and an unfair requirement of responsibility for her parents in their dysfunction, including witnessing and having to care for her mother when she attempted to harm herself. In addition, Mia has had to step in and take control of her father when he exhibited unhealthy behaviors. As Jamie learns more about Mia and begins to understand the complex trauma and cultural differences of this client, she feels the most accurate diagnosis is Persistent Depressive Disorder (PDD; 300.4, F34.1; *DSM-5*; APA, 2013). Upon examining her biases, Jamie recognizes that due to Mia's aloofness and emotional disconnection, Jamie has pathologized Mia's symptoms through her own cultural understanding and not that of the client. In addition, she considers the negative effect that carrying a more acute diagnosis could have for Mia due to cultural messages. Mia often speaks about being "crazy" and no one wanting to be with her because of her being "crazy." Jamie believes that with PDD criteria, Mia's symptoms are explained and can be best treated without a harmful impact.

CLINICAL CASE SCENARIO DISCUSSION QUESTIONS

1. What symptoms did Mia report (level 1)?
2. What knowledge did Jamie have about northeastern European culture?
3. What biases did Jamie have as a White American woman who was socialized in the normalcy of mental health practices (level 2)?
4. What diagnosis would best describe symptoms, guide treatment, and meet cultural needs (level 3)?

END-OF-CHAPTER RESOURCES

A robust set of instructor resources designed to supplement this text is located at http://connect.springerpub.com/content/book/978-0-8261-3953-5. Qualifying instructors may request access by emailing textbook@springerpub.com.

SUMMARY

More research is needed to understand the connection between therapeutic effectiveness and self-awareness. However, in general, counselors who are more reflective will consistently revisit sessions, ethical dilemmas, client presentations, and personal development; thereby being more likely to catch their errors and biases in their conclusions and treatment planning. In the worst of cases, they learn from their oversights to ensure that their counseling practice grows in affinity to support a multicultural and diverse clientele. In short, counseling is enhanced by the consistent practice of self-reflection and self-awareness (attunement).

DISCUSSION QUESTIONS

1. Identify time within your schedule to incorporate a reflective practice. What do you need to create or enhance your current reflective practice?
2. Is there something specific from this chapter that encourages or motivates you to incorporate reflective practice into your development?
3. How do systemic racism and personal bias and values affect the counselor's ability to accurately conceptualize client concerns and presentations?
4. In what ways can culturally competent counselors use diagnosis and assessment ethically and effectively?
5. How did this chapter resonate with you or provide a new perspective on your reflective practice?

KEY REFERENCES

Only key references appear in the print edition. The full reference list appears in the digital product on Springer Publishing Connect: https://connect.springerpub.com/content/book/978-0-8261-3953-5/part/part03/chapter/ch26

Bonino, J. L., & Hanna, F. J. (2018). Who owns psychopathology? The *DSM*: Its flaws, its future, and the professional counselor. *The Journal of Humanistic Counseling, 57*(2), 118–137. https://doi.org/10.1002/johc.12071

Hays, P. A. (2016). *Addressing cultural complexities in practice: Assessment, diagnosis, and therapy* (3rd ed.). American Psychological Association. https://doi.org/10.1037/14801-000

Kress, V. E., Barrio Minton, C. A. B., Adamson, N. A., Paylo, M. J., & Pope, V. (2014). The removal of the multiaxial system in the *DSM-5*: Implications and practice suggestions for counselors. *The Professional Counselor, 4*(3), 191–201. https://doi.org/10.15241/vek.4.3.191

Rosin, J. (2015). The necessity of counselor individuation for fostering reflective practice. *Journal of Counseling & Development, 93*(1), 88–95. https://doi.org/10.1002/j.1556-6676.2015.00184.x

Sue, D., Sue, D. W., Sue, D., & Sue, S. (2016). *Essentials of understanding abnormal behavior* (3rd ed.). Cengage Learning.

Sue, D. W., & Sue, D. (2012). *Counseling the culturally different: Theory and practice*. John Wiley & Sons.

Sue, D. W., & Sue, D. (2013). *Counseling the culturally diverse: Theory & practice* (6th ed.). John Wiley.

Tomlinson-Clarke, S. M., & Georges, C. M. (2014). *DSM-5*: A commentary on integrating multicultural and strength-based considerations into counseling training and practice. *The Professional Counselor, 4*(3), 272–281. https://doi.org/10.15241/stc.4.3.272

CHAPTER 27

Seeking and Receiving Culturally Responsive Supervision

TONYA DAVIS

LEARNING OBJECTIVES

After reading this chapter, students will be able to:

- Recognize what cultural responsiveness looks like in clinical supervision, and describe the various terminology (e.g., awareness, broaching, competence, humility).
- Describe the significance of exploration, introspection, and reflection within the supervisory relationship.
- Create a healthy working alliance within the clinical supervisory relationship.
- Compare the parallel process that occurs within the culturally responsive clinical supervisory relationship and that of their therapeutic relationship with clients.
- Combine ideas and concepts obtained in clinical supervision to construct and integrate meaningful treatment plans and strategies with clients.
- Interpret best practices from clinical supervision when drawing from the Multicultural and Social Justice Counseling Competencies (MSJCC) and liberation framework.

SELF-REFLECTION QUESTIONS

1. How do you define culturally responsive supervision?
2. What are the benefits of having a supervisor who can help you attend to contextual factors in your relationships with clients?
3. What challenges might you face addressing race and culture in supervision?
4. How will you overcome these challenges?

THE SUPERVISOR AND SUPERVISEE: EXPLORATION, INTROSPECTION, AND REFLECTION

Clinical supervision occurs when a more experienced or senior clinician oversees the professional clinical development of a novice counselor or counselor-in-training (CIT;

Bernard & Goodyear, 2019). Difficulties that develop within the clinical supervisory relationship can often be a result of the supervisor and supervisee having different ideas and needs (Borders, 2014). The hierarchy and power that exist within the clinical supervisory relationship have historically belonged to the supervisor (Murphy & Wright, 2005). As stated in the title of this chapter, a primary objective is to empower and equip supervisees to confidently seek and receive culturally responsive clinical supervision. Because supervisees may find themselves in a vulnerable position within this type of relationship, it can be helpful for personal and professional growth if supervisees can establish a healthy balance related to the interpersonal power that provides emotional and psychological safety (Ellis et al., 2014; Ivers et al., 2017; Murphy & Wright, 2005). Clinical supervisors must understand how to provide balanced and culturally responsive supervision, and how to develop ways to empower supervisees to advocate for themselves to get their supervisory needs met (American Psychological Association, 2015). Leong and Wagner (1994) share that cultural responsiveness in supervision occurs when supervisors are intentional about creating a supportive environment regarding the cultural needs of supervisees as well as knowing how to identify individualities between supervisor and supervisee. Having this understanding helps supervisors to be much more deliberate in providing culturally responsive supervision.

When considering cultural competence within clinical supervision, it is important to discuss how to provide culturally responsive supervision, and how to model and teach supervisees about the parallel process. Therefore, we explore concepts related to and in conjunction with multiculturalism and diversity (Ratts et al., 2016). A lack of cultural competence and culturally responsive supervision can distort supervisory relationships considerably and cause distress when individual cultural needs are not taken into account (Ellis, 2017). Multiculturally responsible supervision and its utilization is quite important because it is in direct alignment with professional and often personal supervisee development (Constantine, 1997; Crockett & Hays, 2015; Hird et al., 2001; Miville et al., 2005; Watkins, Hook, Owen, et al., 2019). The parallel process occurs within the clinical supervisory relationship when supervisees reconstruct matters of concern that occur within the counseling relationship within their clinical supervisory relationship (Tracey et al., 2012). This phenomenon requires an intentional awareness related to the clinical supervisor's multicultural competence (MCC) and how it affects the supervisor and supervisee relationship, and also the supervisee and client relationship (Sametband & Strong, 2013; Tracey et al., 2012). To reiterate, an early description of cultural awareness stems from Sue et al.'s work (1992) regarding the supervisor's conscious ability to recognize their cultural background, values, beliefs, worldview, and espoused biases held in relation or opposition to the lived experiences of supervisees. We consider best practices and the harm that may materialize if not broached or discussed within the clinical supervisory relationship (Day-Vines & Holcomb-McCoy, 2013; Jones & Branco, 2020; Sametband & Strong, 2013; Tracey et al., 2012). Cultural humility is also a large part of culturally responsive supervision (Jones & Branco, 2020; Watkins, Hook, Mosher, & Callahan, 2019; Watkins, Hook, Owen, et al., 2019). Watkins, Hook, Mosher, and Callahan (2019) discovered many descriptions of cultural humility, with one example being, "Accurately assessing one's own personal characteristics and achievements and being able to recognize one's own mistakes and limitations require using that very openness to then (a) look within, (b) see what emerges, and (c) act on that which is seen" (p. 60). This process of humility is described as the supervisor's ability to shift the focus from what is occurring from within or intrapersonally and externally or outside of self (Watkins, Hook, Mosher, & Callahan, 2019). It is the responsibility of clinical supervisors to intentionally practice humility and MCC so as to model appropriate characteristics of helping professionals. For example, modeling for supervisors can look like taking a stance of humility, being open to learning and understanding new concepts and ideas, self-reflective personal work, commitment toward ascertaining a working foundation of knowledge, willingness to consult, get supervision, seek counseling services, and the like. Combining humility with MCC can underscore what it means to be intentional about seeking an understating related to the generational, historical, and social context of their supervisees (Burkard et al., 2006). It is important to understand what is involved in establishing this relationship, and the many components that are required to make the supervisory relationship work. This relationship requires a willingness for both parties to actively engage in exploration, introspection, and reflection (Kelsey et al., 2018; Sametband & Strong, 2013). These described sets of skills can also be understood by the supervisee before and during their quest in seeking and receiving culturally responsive supervision.

WHAT MULTICULTURAL RESPONSIVENESS LOOKS LIKE IN CLINICAL SUPERVISION

When considering clinically relevant interactions, counselor and supervisor are drawing from best practices related to competence (Ratts et al., 2016). As stated in section F of the American Counseling Association (ACA) *Code of Ethics*, it is a supervisory obligation to strive toward increasing one's understanding of culture and all related matters (ACA, 2014). Supervisors and supervisees must also gain an understanding of how to begin accruing cultural competence. Watkins, Hook, Owen, et al. (2019) suggest that while cultural competence is essential, it may not be sufficient as a standalone aspect of development. As stated earlier, this is a lifelong personal and professional journey, not a destination at which we arrive once completed.

A final concept regarding the supervisor and supervisee relationship addresses how both parties can better understand their roles regarding the clinical supervisory relationship; seeking, receiving, and maintaining culturally responsive supervision; and establishing a working alliance. Schroeder et al. (2009) determined that the terms found in the literature (e.g., *multicultural*, *cross-cultural*, and *cross-racial supervision*) are frequently applied interchangeably (Constantine, 2003; D'Andrea & Daniels, 1997; Fukuyama, 1994; Leong & Wagner, 1994). Multicultural supervision occurs when supervisors and supervisees have a variety of demographic differences co-occurring at the same time (e.g., age, gender, religion, sexual orientation), whereas cross-cultural/racial supervision occurs when there is an explicit difference regarding lived experiences related to race or ethnicity among the supervisor, supervisee, and client (Constantine, 2003; D'Andrea & Daniels, 1997; Duan & Roehlke, 2001; Fukuyama, 1994; Leong & Wagner, 1994; Schroeder et al., 2009). Multicultural supervision looks at cultural themes or patterns that emerge in the scope of the supervisory relationship (Brown & Landrum-Brown, 1995). Cross-cultural/racial supervision distinguishes between the cultural or racial content that shows up in supervision, the process of creating a safe environment in which to broach a variety of difficult topics, and the creation of acceptable training outcomes specifically related to racial or ethnic differences espoused within the supervision relationship (Brown & Landrum-Brown, 1995).

FINDING AND ESTABLISHING A HEALTHY WORKING ALLIANCE WITHIN THE CLINICAL SUPERVISORY RELATIONSHIP

The distinction between supervisor and supervisee is the varying degree of clinical skill acquisition and development. Because supervisees can be negatively affected by the supervisory relationship, it is incumbent upon the supervisor to learn what is required of them within their role as supervisor, how *effectiveness* is defined, and how to convey this efficacy in their working relationships with supervisees (Falender & Shafranske, 2017; Gazzola et al., 2013). For supervisors to teach supervisees cultural awareness, they themselves must have an awareness or reckoning of their cultural upbringing related to worldview, values, and beliefs (Ratts et al., 2016). Supervisors cannot teach what they do not know, whether that is clinical knowledge or knowledge related to their personhood. Modeling a desire to stay current with personal cultural awareness of self is also seen within the parallel process related to the relationship between counselor and clients (Tracey et al., 2012). Because supervisors oversee individuals with less clinical insight, it behooves supervisors to be intentional when developing their own clinical skill set, understanding and knowledge, awareness of self and worldview, and a willingness to understand the worldview of others (Ratts et al., 2016; Tangen & Borders, 2016; Wallace et al., 2010). While it is a journey and not a destination, starting with a baseline of knowledge (i.e., knowing who you are as a racial being and having a clear understanding of your personhood) and awareness and building upon it models for supervisees what the journey toward becoming multiculturally competent might look like (Ratts et al., 2016). Kelsey et al. (2018) suggest there is a basic set of skills, knowledge, and competencies that supervisors need to attain before embarking upon a clinical supervisory relationship. Clinical supervisors are described as professionals who hold a set of skills, and because factors such as race, ethnicity, and culture are inescapable human dimensions, clinical supervisors must be intentional about knowing how these constructs show up in clinical supervision (Borders, 2014).

Supervisory Working Alliance

A strong supervisory working alliance is one of the requirements when striving to facilitate culturally responsive supervision. Such an alliance has multilayered historical influences, and isa phenomenon that has been studied for more than seven decades (Bhat & Davis, 2007; Watkins, Hook, Owen, et al., 2019). While it is important to note the many perspectives that have come before us, some of the challenges faced in today's clinical supervision speak directly to the lack of welcomed perspectives and inclusion of ideas (Ratts et al., 2016; Watkins, Hook, Mosher, & Callahan, 2019). Historically, there has been a lot of literature that discusses the structure and organization related to establishing a working alliance in the clinical supervisory relationship, and that has included the idea of increasing awareness of self, supervisees, and clients (Ratts et al., 2016; Watkins, Hook, Mosher, & Callahan, 2019). Also noteworthy is the connection between the development of a healthy and beneficial working alliance in supervision, and the intentional practice of mindfulness related to therapeutic outcomes (Kiyokawa et al., 2012; Tracey et al., 2012; Watkins, Hook, Owen, et al., 2019). Given the history of racism, discrimination, racial trauma, and civil unrest, it becomes an absolute necessity to know what it means to be a culturally competent and responsive supervisor (Comas-Díaz, 2012; Crockett & Hays, 2015; Ratts et al., 2016). This is why such topics of concern are broached or brought up within the clinical supervisory relationship.

For supervisors and supervisees to be effective in their clinical supervisory relationship, there must be an evolution in knowledge and skills, an awareness of self, an increase in self-efficacy, and an expanded aptitude in building the therapeutic alliance (Ratts et al., 2016; Watkins, Hook, Mosher, & Callahan, 2019). Efstation et al. (1990) created a tool to measure the working alliance within the clinical supervisory relationship called the Supervisory Working Alliance Inventory (SWAI). This tool can help supervisees and supervisors quantify their perceived working alliance. According to this inventory, higher scores suggest a stronger efficacy regarding the supervisory working alliance (Efstation et al., 1990). Seven of the 19 questions have been altered to include a culturally responsive point of view (Questions 2, 3, 5, 11, 13, 16, and 17). With humility, there is an understanding that while a power dynamic exists between supervisor and supervisee, it is essential to remember that no one person has power over the other (Jones & Branco, 2020; Watkins, Hook, Mosher, & Callahan, 2019; Watkins, Hook, Owen, et al., 2019). Finding and establishing this humility is a small portion of what it takes to develop trust as part of a healthy working alliance within the clinical supervisory relationship (Watkins, Hook, Mosher, & Callahan, 2019; Watkins, Hook, Owen, et al., 2019).

The Multicultural Supervision Inventory (MSI; Wong & Wong, 2000) has been an essential tool for supervisees to use when seeking, receiving, and maintaining culturally responsive supervision. The MSI captures all aspects of multicultural competencies, such as attitudes and beliefs, knowledge and understanding, skills and practices, and cross-racial supervision components within the clinical supervisory relationship (Ratts et al., 2016; Wong & Wong, 2000). The questions presented in the MSI are direct and succinct in navigating all essential target areas (i.e., attitudes and beliefs; knowledge and understanding; skills and practices; and relationship) that correlate with the establishment of culturally responsive supervision, particularly in cross-racial/ethnic/cultural supervision (Bernard & Goodyear, 2019; Borders, 2014; Constantine, 1997; Crockett & Hays, 2015; Ellis et al., 2014; Falender & Shafranske, 2017; Gazzola et al., 2013; Hird et al., 2001; Ivers et al., 2017; Miville et al., 2005; Watkins, Hook, Owen, et al., 2019). It is important to mention that the original questions have been altered to intentionally utilize inclusive language and pronouns which can be found in section 1 (labeled attitudes and beliefs), and are also listed in question 15 as well as in section 3 (labeled skills and practices), and listed in question 13.

By using inventories such as the SWAI or MSI to measure perceived working alliance, supervisors are deliberate about establishing a strong culturally responsive working alliance. Therefore, supervisees begin to develop confidence in identifying, understanding, addressing, and resolving the difficult matters that may emerge or exist within their clinical supervisory relationship. The goal of using the SWAI or MSI is for supervisees to be equipped and feel empowered to manage multicultural concerns as it relates to their therapeutic alliance with clients (Tracey et al., 2012). To a similar extent, supervisors can see where they may fall short in the process of establishing a working alliance with supervisees and ascertain a valuable outcome in course correction during the rupture and repair process (Borders, 2014). Something to consider is related to the types of adjustments that must be made when working toward an acceptable working alliance for both supervisor and supervisee. Both parties involved in this relationship will likely need a certain amount of comfort and safety, and that amount is operationalized solely by the supervisee and supervisor (Ellis et al., 2014; Ivers et al., 2017; Watkins, Hook, Mosher, & Callahan, 2019). Because there is the perception of power held by the supervisor within the clinical supervisory relationship, it is incumbent upon supervisors to be intentional when creating a space of comfort and safety so that the work (e.g., mental, emotional, psychological, multicultural, and culturally responsive) often involved with building a working alliance can be done (Ellis et al., 2014; Ivers et al., 2017; Ratts et al., 2016; Schroeder et al., 2009; Watkins, Hook, Mosher, & Callahan, 2019; Wong & Wong, 2000). The variables related to intrapersonal work involves intentional inclusivity, willingness to learn new information, an awareness and understanding of worldviews related to self and others, an acknowledgment that such a phenomenon exists, and the willingness to take ownership and responsibility for doing intrapersonal work (Efstation et al., 1990; Ratts et al., 2016; Wong & Wong, 2000).

IDENTIFYING THE POTENTIAL NEGATIVE IMPACT OF POWER AND RESPONSIBILITY HELD BY SUPERVISORS

A major responsibility in providing culturally responsive supervision is identification of the potential negative impacts on the clinical supervisory relationship, supervisees, and clients (Burkard et al., 2006; Tracey et al., 2012). Supervisees have a right to seek and receive culturally responsive supervision. Although the perception is that supervisors hold the power in the supervisory relationship due to their senior-level experience, supervisees should feel empowered to advocate for their needs and address them accordingly without concerns of repercussions or consequences (e.g., being graded poorly because students advocated for their own needs; losing opportunities to collaborate with clients, groups, or teams; experiencing a toxic supervisory relationship and environment). The responsibility to ensure that the space is free from these types of concerns rests within the clinical supervisor (Bernard & Goodyear, 2019). When formulating the clinical supervisory relationship, it would behoove supervisors to always consider and broach historical, generational, or cultural contexts (e.g., vicarious racial trauma, racism, sexism, colorism) that may be missing from the supervision space that may cause misunderstanding (Day-Vines & Holcomb-McCoy, 2013). Together, supervisors and supervisees can establish expectations and address requirements for a healthy, beneficial, and productive supervisory relationship. In turn, this paradigm teaches supervisees how to create healthy, beneficial, and productive therapeutic relationships (Tracey et al., 2012; Watkins, Hook, Mosher, & Callahan, 2019).

Power Dynamic

Culturally responsive supervisors pay close attention to the perception of power that supervisees may believe is held by their supervisors. This attentiveness coincides with addressing the concept of power (i.e., senior level versus junior level) within the supervisory relationship. Collaborating with and empowering supervisees, while acknowledging unchecked or undefined power, will prove most helpful (Day-Vines & Holcomb-McCoy, 2013; Murphy & Wright, 2005). Although no one holds power over another human, there is a power dynamic that accrues to supervisors related to the concept of choice when navigating authority, something that supervisees feel they often do not have (Murphy & Wright, 2005). Also present is an unspoken power that rests within the nature of supervision. This power and authority can work in one of two ways: (a) using this power to build healthy, beneficial, culturally responsive supervisory relationships, or (b) creating unhealthy and potentially harmful supervisory relationships (Beddoe, 2017; Bernard & Goodyear, 2019; Ellis, 2017; Ellis et al., 2014). Supervisors must have a clear and continual awareness and understanding of these two concepts, as it can make the difference between a healthy or unhealthy supervisory relationship.

Harmful Supervision

Ellis et al. (2014) distinguish between quality supervision and inadequate, moderately adequate, or harmful supervision. *Quality supervision* refers to situations where a supervisee may have a tough time navigating the difficult issues that emerge in supervision or struggles to process hard-hitting but helpful feedback and support received from the supervisor (Ellis et al., 2014). Ellis et al. (2014) share that harmful supervision is defined as "supervisory practices that result in psychological, emotional, and/or physical harm or trauma to the supervisee.... Harmful supervision can be through self-identification ... or occur when the supervisor's behavior (or inaction) meets specific criteria" (p. 440).

The objective is to help supervisors and supervisees make a distinction between respectful and useful supervisory actions and interactions regarding the boundaries found by supervisees. Another objective would be to establish well-intentioned actions that concentrate on helping supervisees develop proficient clinical skill acquisition, and to understand how this purpose differs from identifying what causes harm to supervisees, the supervisory relationship, and subsequently the possible relationship between supervisor and client (Ellis et al., 2014; Tracey et al., 2012). The concept of harmful supervision has been studied globally and the takeaway is that harmful supervision must be eradicated (Beddoe, 2017; Ellis et al., 2014; Ellis, 2017). This matter of concern can produce significant unease, but highlights the harm that might occur when culturally responsive supervision is missing from the clinical supervisory equation.

IMPORTANCE OF CULTURALLY RESPONSIVE SUPERVISION

The process of clinical supervision manages a variety of concerns simultaneously. Some of the concerns are related to conflict, tension, awareness, humility, broaching, and competencies or the lack thereof (Christiansen et al., 2011; Nelson et al., 2008). When investigating concepts involved in seeking, receiving, or providing culturally responsive supervision, we begin by defining some of the previously mentioned terms and how these concepts relate to culturally responsive supervision (e.g., culture, broaching, and competencies; Jones & Branco, 2020; Ratts et al., 2016; Watkins, Hook, Owen, et al., 2019). This will model for supervisees how to navigate these important matters (conflict, tension, awareness, humility, etc.) when broaching in their therapeutic relationships (Tracey et al., 2012).

Culture

A grasp of what culture means, and what its many components are, can bring about a personal awareness regarding the significance of culture and why such an understanding is required (Constantine, 2003). People have different lived experiences, and in many ways we are all shaped by these lived experiences. Simply, *culture* might be defined as the norms, values, and traditions one holds. When we include varied demographics, concepts of self, and the many subcultures that exist, the very definition of culture can be quite broad. Considering this awareness, it would be reasonable to state that all supervision is required to be culturally responsive supervision (Christiansen et al., 2011). Establishing cultural responsiveness in supervision begins with identifying that the need for culturally responsive supervision exists, making a commitment to understanding what it is, and being willing to choose and make necessary changes (Fong & Lease, 1997; Ivers et al., 2017; Leong & Wagner, 1994). It is important to note that the differences between the cultural background of the supervisee and that of the supervisor can be beneficial because they provide more context that can prove helpful for the client (i.e., parallel process; Tracey et al., 2012).

Broaching

There is a strong correlation between cultural humanity, broaching, competence, and how multicultural competence orientation for supervision (MCO-S) can increase the overall effectiveness of clinical supervisors (Jones & Branco, 2020; Watkins, Hook, Owen, et al., 2019). Day-Vines et al. (2013) define *broaching* as "the counselor's ability to consider the relationship of racial and cultural factors to the client's presenting problem, especially because these issues might otherwise remain unexamined during the counseling process" (p. 215). Broaching is also an active stance taken when the need to discuss matters of concern emerge (Jones & Branco, 2020).

In keeping with the need for multicultural and social justice competencies, supervisors should be aware that supervisees with cultural differences and additional identities that intersect with oppression and marginalization can be retraumatized should such problems emerge in supervision (Comas-Díaz, 2012; Crockett & Hays, 2015; Ratts et al., 2016). In knowing what culturally responsive supervision is, we can also comprehend its importance for the well-being of supervisees and the clinical supervisory relationship. It is important to assess the critical elements that the CIT will need to understand to navigate during their professional development in order to become a culturally responsive, humble, and empathic counselor and supervisor themself (Tracey et al., 2012).

BEST PRACTICES: DRAWING FROM THE MULTICULTURAL AND SOCIAL JUSTICE COUNSELING COMPETENCIES

Ethical Considerations

After talking about the difficulties experienced in being harmed by a negative impact, it could be helpful to take a brief analytical look at ethical considerations. The word *harm* (and variations thereof) is listed in the *ACA Code of Ethics* (2014) 44 times, across seven of nine sections. Harm is also listed in the preamble (i.e., nonmaleficence or to do no harm) and the *ACA Code of Ethics* list of terms. Based on the parallel process that occurs, both *nonmaleficence* and *serious and foreseeable harm* refer to all clinical interactions, whether the counselor–supervisee–client triad or the supervisor–supervisee dyad relationship (Tracey et al., 2012). Being intentionally mindful, aware, and willing to navigate the rupture and repair process related to harmful impacts in the supervisory relationship (see Section F of the *ACA Code of Ethics*) can be a good place to start in the reduction of harmful practices (Beddoe, 2017; Ellis et al., 2014; Ellis, 2017). There are many ethical dilemmas that supervisees might find themselves experiencing. For example, a supervisee of color has a supervisor who states that it is okay for the supervisee's family and friends to come to the site to receive counseling services from them since the site is experiencing a difficult time fulfilling their clinical caseload and needs. In this example, the supervisee is keenly aware of the ethical violation. In advocating for appropriate clinical training needs, the supervisee in this example shared section A.5 in the *ACA Code of Ethics* with the supervisor and felt confident about questioning such a suggestion. They both engaged in a dialogue regarding the need for the supervisee to speak up for themselves, as well as how to clearly address the ethical dilemma presented. In this case, the conversation was enough to get the desired result (i.e., avoid an ethical dilemma altogether).

Competence

The ACA, one of the counseling field's largest educational organizations and our governing body of accountability, ethics, and professional support, affirms that professional supervisors, counselors, and CITs seek and maintain competence in all its forms. Found in the supervisory relationship portion, Section F.11.c. states: "Multicultural/Diversity Counselor educators actively infuse multicultural/diversity competency in their training and supervision practices. They actively train students to gain awareness, knowledge, and skills in the competencies of multicultural practice" (ACA, 2014, p. 15). Borders (2014) noted that competencies summarize an essential understanding of what qualified supervisors are expected to know, and pointed out that *best practices* refers to a foundation where a "procedural knowledge" resides, describes how this knowledge is made applicable, and explains how supervisors navigate the process of supervision. Drawing from the Multicultural and Social Justice Counseling Competencies (MSJCC; Ratts et al., 2016), considerations are made for best practices and discussion regarding the harm that could emerge if culturally responsive supervision is not valued or prioritized within the clinical supervisory relationship.

The updated MSJCC have been referred to by schools, agencies, private practices, and the like. The MSJCC presents helpers (i.e., supervisors and supervisees) with a road map that adds to or broadens one's awareness and understanding of the many aspects of multicultural and social justice matters of concern that often emerge in the clinical supervisor or therapeutic relationship. Ratts et al. (2016) created the Multicultural and Social Justice Praxis as a visual representation of the many aspects and intersections related to identity and serves to further intentionality within the clinical supervisory or therapeutic relationship (Cook, 1994).

When considering the Multicultural and Social Justice Praxis, students can benefit from identifying the four quadrants and how each may directly affect their counseling and supervisory relationships. Students should be mindful of how this praxis might unfold within session with clients or within their clinical supervisory relationships.

CLINICAL CASE SCENARIO 27.1

Elaine identified as an Asian American woman in her mid-50s who had been fully licensed for more than 25 years, and was in her final semester in her counselor education and supervision doctoral program. Within this final semester, she received a new supervisor at her internship placement site. At a staffing session, Elaine was introduced to Bob, who identified as a White male, and scheduled their first supervision session at that time. She had a caseload of 12 adult clients, all of whom identified as Black, Indigenous, and People of Color (BIPOC). Her first impression of Bob was that he was profoundly rigid in his interactions with others (e.g., dismissive of others' time and ideas, rude, brief, inflexible). In speaking with other interns, Elaine discovered that Bob's interactions with BIPOC interns differed from his interactions with his White interns and peers. Bob was visibly much more patient, accepting, and very talkative with the latter. She initially brushed it aside because she had not personally seen this distinction within her working clinical supervisory relationship with Bob.

As the semester went on, Elaine noticed how dismissive Bob was regarding her thoughts about her caseload, and she could never seem to get anything right according to Bob. Elaine felt like Bob was attempting to make her feel inferior by saying things like "you wouldn't know that based on your current clinical skill acquisition." Bob would make insensitive and stereotyped comments about her clients, and eventually Bob began to microaggress Elaine frequently within their supervision. After consulting with her peers, Elaine decided to speak with Bob regarding her experience with him and how that was affecting their clinical supervisory relationship and her work with clients.

(continued)

CLINICAL CASE SCENARIO 27.1 (CONTINUED)

Although Elaine was concerned about her placement site and graduating on time, she decided to open up and share with Bob that she felt he was not able to provide acceptable clinical and culturally responsive supervision. The volume in Bob's voice grew loud as he stated, "Don't you dare pull the race card on me!" Elaine was upset and tried to continue expressing herself while standing firm. Unfortunately, Elaine was halted at every attempt by Bob. His rate of speech and the tone in his voice indicated his difficulty in regulating his emotions, and Elaine knew she was not getting anywhere. Bob stated to Elaine that if she did not like the type of clinical supervision he provided, she was "more than welcome to seek another supervisor or placement site."

Elaine was left with a lot of unanswered questions and uncertainty. She was sure that she could not move forward with Bob as her site supervisor. What Elaine was not sure about was whether her placement site would ask her to leave because of the power and position Bob felt he held over Elaine. She was also unsure if she could trust that the placement site would support her in this experience, or if she would be able to finish accruing the hours required for her to complete this portion of her doctoral program. Elaine scheduled an appointment with Marsha, the Director of Clinical Training at the site. Marsha identified as a White woman. Elaine candidly shared her experience and concerns related to identifying as Asian American, working with Bob, and if Marsha would believe her. To Elaine's surprise, Marsha validated Elaine's concerns and experiences. They spoke about the parallel process between Elaine's need for culturally responsive and competent supervision, and how seeing that modeled for her could empower and equip her to provide culturally responsive and competent counseling to her clients. Marsha shared with Elaine her views on the importance of providing culturally sensitive, responsive, and competent supervision. Marsha also shared what can happen to the therapeutic relationship and the ability to build an alliance with clients if supervisees are met with cultural incompetence within supervision. Marsha pointed out how negatively impactful the lack of awareness and cultural competence can be on supervisees, clients, and communities alike.

Soon thereafter, Elaine went back to have another conversation with Bob. Elaine was clear and unwavering in her communication with Bob regarding her disappointment in his poor treatment of her and his inability to accept feedback related to how she experienced him within their clinical supervisory relationship. Elaine also mentioned that she was concerned about his lack of cultural competence and how harmful that has been for her and will be should he not receive training to gain cultural competence and learn how to provide culturally responsive supervision. Unfortunately, Bob appeared uninterested, with his eyes focused elsewhere, and had little to say during the time Elaine shared her feedback. Elaine remained controlled in her resolve and left that

(continued)

CLINICAL CASE SCENARIO 27.1 (CONTINUED)

office knowing that she had been authentic in sharing her truth to Bob that day. For the remaining eight weeks of internship, Marsha agreed to supervise Elaine. During that time, they worked on how to be most effective when advocating for themselves or clients, and what self-care looks like for different people (e.g., practicing the intentional regulation of mental, emotional, or physical needs in a variety of ways). Lastly, Marsha and Elaine operationalized what it meant for Elaine to identify, understand, apply, and evaluate her personal and professional development on her journey to becoming a culturally responsive and competent counselor in her work with clients. In the final eight weeks, Marsha met with Elaine twice a week and was intentional about helping Elaine understand multicultural counseling and how to begin building cultural competence. When conceptualizing a client case, Elaine would consider all facets of her client's current needs, while also gathering historical and generational context to fully understand the client's lived experiences (e.g., navigating difficulties such as racism, poverty, education, social justice, healthcare, food and housing insecurities, and transportation). Elaine became more aware of the importance of understanding her clients as a whole and creating intentional spaces for clients to be seen and heard, and knew this was meaningful work. Marsha helped Elaine to understand that multicultural theory is about identifying the significance of looking at the overlap of systemic challenges experienced by BIPOC individuals and sharing authentic and empathetic responses to the intersectionality of these inequitable factors, which run deep and wide. Marsha also provided insight regarding why competence is essential in establishing a therapeutic alliance. Marsha described cultural competence as a lens through which counselors can see the worldview of clients, and how that worldview may look similar to self and the many ways it can look different. Marsha helped Elaine to understand what cultural awareness she has regarding herself and her clients, how to intentionally include the knowledge she had developed, and ways to incorporate intervention skills to help her clients.

CLINICAL CASE SCENARIO DISCUSSION QUESTIONS

1. What multicultural considerations exist between Bob and Elaine, and how would you attend to them?
2. Whose responsibility was it to acknowledge and address those multicultural factors?
3. If you were Elaine, would you have done anything differently?

END-OF-CHAPTER RESOURCES

A robust set of instructor resources designed to supplement this text is located at http://connect.springerpub.com/content/book/978-0-8261-3953-5. Qualifying instructors may request access by emailing **textbook@springerpub.com**.

SUMMARY

In this chapter, the major takeaway is being intentional about becoming informed, equipped, and empowered when seeking and receiving culturally responsive supervision. This chapter provided definitions for practical use within clinical supervision, a solid awareness, and the rationale behind the significance of cultural competence, as well as underlining the correlation between what occurs within the supervisory relationship and the counseling relationship in the parallel process. The goal in providing the reflection questions was to help create a space for intentional self-reflection and the construction of meaning through the case scenarios shared. In understanding the supervisor–supervisee relationship, the working alliance is operationalized, and we distinguished the major differences between multicultural supervision and cross-cultural and cross-racial supervision. The case scenarios provided insight regarding the importance of advocating for self and not avoiding the difficult conversations that may emerge as a result of identifying a need to advocate for oneself. By utilizing the SWAI (Efstation et al., 1990), supervisees can navigate their supervision and feel prepared and encouraged in their quest to receive culturally responsive supervision when completing the inventory with supervisors. The discussion of culturally responsive supervision also uncovered definitions for culture, what it means to broach difficult subject matter, and what the MCO-S looks like when incorporated within culturally responsive supervision. An important discussion covered the negative impact that poor supervision can have. This chapter dove into concepts like responsibility, power, harmful supervision, and who is impacted (i.e., supervisee, clinical supervisory relationship, and clients). This chapter took a deep dive into best practices related to MSJCC competencies and praxis to provide an in-depth look at the lived experiences that supervisors and supervisees bring into the clinical supervisory relationship from a contextual viewpoint. Lastly, we discussed the need for supervisors and supervisees to identify, understand, advocate, and promote all ethical considerations for recognizable reasons.

DISCUSSION QUESTIONS

1. What does multicultural responsiveness look like in clinical supervision?
2. Why might this exploration, introspection, and reflection within the supervisory relationship be an essential aspect of clinical supervision?
3. How might the clinical supervisory relationship be negatively affected if exploration, introspection, and reflection are not intentionally included at its onset and throughout?
4. What steps might you take when seeking and receiving culturally responsive supervision?
5. What tools and resources might you utilize that could help ensure a healthy working alliance within your clinical supervisory relationship?
6. Do you feel more confident about broaching difficult subject matter with your supervisor in supervision and in session with your clients? Why or why not?
7. How would you explain to your peers what multicultural and social justice counseling competencies and best practices for clinical supervision look like?

KEY REFERENCES

Only key references appear in the print edition. The full reference list appears in the digital product on Springer Publishing Connect: https://connect.springerpub.com/content/book/978-0-8261-3953-5/part/part03/chapter/ch27

American Psychological Association. (2015). Guidelines for clinical supervision in health service psychology. *The American Psychologist*, 70(1), 33–46. https://doi.org/10.1037/a0038112

Beddoe, L. (2017). Harmful supervision: A commentary. *The Clinical Supervisor*, 36(1), 88–101. https://doi.org/10.1080/07325223.2017.1295894

Bernard, J. M., & Goodyear, R. K. (2019). *Fundamentals of clinical supervision* (6th ed.). Pearson.

Bhat, C. S., & Davis, T. E. (2007). Counseling supervisors' assessment of race, racial identity, and working alliance in supervisory Dyads. *Journal of Multicultural Counseling and Development*, 35(2), 80–91. https://doi.org/10.1002/j.2161-1912.2007.tb00051.x

Borders, L. D. (2014). Best practices in clinical supervision: Another step in delineating effective supervision practice. *American Journal of Psychotherapy*, 68(2), 151–162. https://doi.org/10.1176/appi.psychotherapy.2014.68.2.151

Crockett, S., & Hays, D. G. (2015). The influence of supervisor multicultural competence on the supervisory working alliance, supervisee counseling self-efficacy, and supervisee satisfaction with supervision: A mediation model. *Counselor Education and Supervision*, 54(4), 258–273. https://doi.org/10.1002/ceas.12025

Day-Vines, N. L., & Holcomb-McCoy, C. (2013). Broaching the subjects of race, ethnicity, and culture as a tool for addressing diversity in counselor education classes. In J. West, D. Bubenzer, J. Cox, & J. McGlothlin (Eds.), *Teaching in counselor education: Engaging students in meaningful learning* (pp. 151–166). Association for Counselor Education and Supervision.

Ellis, M. V., Berger, L., Hanus, A. E., Ayala, E. E., Swords, B. A., & Siembor, M. (2014). Inadequate and harmful clinical supervision. *The Counseling Psychologist*, 42(4), 434–472. https://doi.org/10.1177/0011000013508656

Jones, C. T., & Branco, S. F. (2020). The interconnectedness between cultural humility and broaching in clinical supervision: Working from the multicultural orientation framework. *The Clinical Supervisor*, 39(2), 198–209. https://doi.org/10.1080/07325223.2020.1830327

Ratts, M. J., Singh, A. A., Nassar-McMillan, S., Butler, S. K., & McCullough, J. R. (2016). Multicultural and social justice counseling competencies: Guidelines for the counseling profession. *Journal of Multicultural Counseling and Development*, 44(1), 28–48. https://doi.org/10.1002/jmcd.12035

Watkins, C. E., Hook, J. N., Owen, J., DeBlaere, C., Davis, D. E., & Van Tongeren, D. R. (2019). Multicultural orientation in psychotherapy supervision: Cultural humility, cultural comfort, and cultural opportunities. *American Journal of Psychotherapy*, 72(2), 38–46. https://doi.org/10.1176/appi.psychotherapy.20180040

CHAPTER 28

Cultural Considerations for the Counseling Workplace

ADRIAN LIRA

LEARNING OBJECTIVES

After reading this chapter, students will be able to:
- Recognize culturally sensitive practices in the counseling workplace.
- Explain the three levels of care of the cultural care theory (CCT).
- Describe workplace environmental factors that affect counseling.
- Identify diversity and culture at the individual, family, organizational, and societal levels.

SELF-REFLECTION QUESTIONS

1. When you think about setting up your workplace, whose preferences do you think about first—yours or your clients'?
2. What contextual factors should you be aware of to ensure that every client feels welcome in your workplace?
3. How might ambient light be good for one client and poor for another?

Extending cultural considerations into the counseling workplace is an appropriate next step in the integration of the multicultural and social justice proficiencies that have been highlighted for more than 40 years (Ratts et al., 2016; Sue et al., 1982, 1992). The focus has often been placed on the client–counselor dyad, as well it should; however, the client experience is not limited to the therapeutic relationship. What the counseling workplace "says" to the client is as important as what is communicated by the therapist. From the first interaction the client has with the agency to the decision to terminate counseling, infusing multicultural sensitivity throughout the entire process is important. Thus, this concluding chapter addresses cultural considerations salient to the counseling workplace. We begin with a review of multicultural counseling before transitioning to discussing who the counseling office attracts.

MULTICULTURAL COUNSELING

A discussion of the culturally sensitive agency warrants an understanding of culture within the counseling workplace. Thus, framing cultural sensitivity within the multicultural competencies and ethical mandates of the mental health profession is crucial. After all, as mental health providers, our work with clients is guided by standards and principles that extend beyond the therapeutic alliance (American Association for Marriage and Family Therapy [AAMFT], 2015; American Counseling Association [ACA], 2014; American Psychological Association [APA], 2017; National Association of Social Workers [NASW], 2017). Included in these external factors is the counseling environment. But before discussing the workplace, we briefly turn our attention to culture-related terms, because defining these will set the stage for the discussion of cultural sensitivity within the counseling workplace.

According to Sue et al. (1982), multicultural counseling is a counseling relationship where two or more of the individuals differ in cultural background, values, and lifestyle. With that in mind, it becomes apparent that all interactions, in and out of the therapeutic relationship, are multicultural interactions. Furthermore, multicultural counseling includes practices that integrate culture-specific awareness, knowledge, and skills into the counseling interaction (Arredondo et al., 1996). The integration of multicultural awareness, knowledge, and skills into the counseling relationship improves the client's experience, especially among minority individuals who may approach counseling with some suspicion because of their uncertainty about the mental health system (Sue et al., 1992). That suspicion is not unwarranted. After all, early research on ethnically diverse and minority individuals considered many cultural differences to be cultural deficiencies, leading to feelings of distrust and a sense of oppression among minority individuals (Sue et al., 1982).

Even though counseling, psychology, and other mental health fields have highlighted the need to account for cultural differences within the therapeutic relationship (AAMFT, 2015; ACA, 2014; APA, 2017; NASW, 2017), the journey toward multiculturalism, or a focus on ethnicity, race, and culture, would extend for decades following its inception. The diversification of the United States has markedly increased during the past four decades (U.S. Census Bureau, 2001, 2011, 2021). Therefore, having a better understanding of the cultural background of clients is important. *Diversity*, within this context, refers to differences in age, gender, sexual orientation, religion, physical ability or disability, and other characteristics by which individuals self-define (Arredondo et al., 1996). These racial and cultural differences were often measured against the normative, Anglo-, Euro-Americans that have long held the majority status (Arredondo et al., 1996). Although strides have been made toward accounting for racial and cultural biases (Ratts et al., 2016), there is much room for improvement when considering the role of the counseling environment. Considering that much attention has gone to the client and counselor variables, it is crucial to consider less obvious, but also important, environmental factors that may influence the counseling process (Pressly & Heesacker, 2001).

It is important to consider the counseling environment to determine its overall impact on the counseling experience. It has been stated that the counseling setting is second in importance only to the counselor in establishing an effective therapeutic environment (Benton & Overtree, 2012). Moreover, the counseling environment has received minimal attention from the research community (Jeffreys & Zoucha, 2018; Pressly & Heesacker, 2001; Rogers et al., 2016) with even less attention being placed on culturally related environmental factors (Benton & Overtree, 2012). Therefore, this chapter examines multicultural factors within the counseling environment to address shortcomings in this area.

WHO DOES YOUR OFFICE ATTRACT?

Clients often scan for environmental cues to evaluate if providers understand what matters to them (Alegria et al., 2010). It is, therefore, important for counseling workplaces to consider both verbal and nonverbal messages sent to current and potential clients. By taking a look into the makeup of their clientele, workplaces can begin the process of tailoring marketing campaigns, paperwork, funding opportunities, staff representation, language needs, and services offered.

Equally important is having an awareness of the catchment area from which counseling workplaces attract clients for its services. But how are catchment areas analyzed? McMahon et al. (2013) recommend thinking of the catchment area in terms of distance. A realistic expectation is for clients to be targeted from a 2- to 5-mile radius for a densely populated area and from a 10- to 30-mile radius for rural locations. In terms of travel time, it should not take clients more than one hour to arrive for an appointment. In fact, travel time less than 30 minutes is highly encouraged.

Interestingly, the COVID-19 pandemic provided an increased opportunity to shift from physical to virtual catchment areas. These virtual catchment areas widened the reach of counseling and mental health services to otherwise underserved or never-served rural and marginalized areas. Expanding the reach of agencies to uncharted territories helped bridge metropolitan, suburban, and rural locations. Virtual catchment areas can, in extreme cases, span entire states. This is the case with recently popularized mental health service providers that focus solely on distance services. Their popularity reached an all-time high due to mental health advocacy campaigns provided by celebrities during a dire time in our history. Fortunately, most counseling workplaces will not have to consider statewide client residency; nevertheless, it is important to have an understanding of the areas from which they draw clients so as to understand client needs and determine continuity of care, should crisis situations arise.

As has been discussed, it is important to determine the area from which clients are drawn. But proximity is only one factor for counseling workplaces to consider. Mental health providers must also determine their branding and how the community at large perceives them. For example, an agency with specialized services aimed at children and adolescents may attract a larger percentage of that population even if they also serve individuals, couples, and families of all ages. Additionally, counseling workplaces with affiliations (e.g., religious, university, medical) may attract clients interested in that particular association while possibly alienating others. For instance, religious affiliations may be important for individuals seeking faith-based services, but individuals with reservations about religion, either because of personal experiences, beliefs, or fear, may shun such agencies despite those agencies' commitment to serve all.

Furthermore, the perception of the community is influenced by counselors and mental health providers themselves. That is, their race, ethnicity, gender, sexual orientation, and language fluency—among many other ascribed characteristics—play an integral part in whom the office attracts. In fact, matching a client with a therapist on identity measures creates a sense of understanding, comfort, and credibility within the therapeutic relationship (Ertl et al., 2019). Therefore, agencies should ensure that diversity among their employees is representative of the clients they serve.

Although there are innumerable factors that influence client attraction to counseling workplaces, it is important to begin by considering the perception of the community and staff representation. Fortunately, measures can be taken through marketing and advertising campaigns to address services and clarify misconceptions. These efforts are addressed in a subsequent section. The next step in determining who the counseling workplace attracts is to market or advertise services to target populations. However, before focusing on advertising services, counseling workplaces should center cultural sensitivity within their practices.

INTRODUCTION TO A CULTURALLY SENSITIVE AGENCY

Culturally sensitive agencies actively engage and promote culturally affirming practices. These practices not only incorporate the multicultural counseling competencies that have long guided the therapeutic relationship, but also address environmental factors that affect the counseling workplace. In order to obtain a more thorough understanding of these factors, a theoretical framework is integrated into this discussion. In their article, Jeffreys and Zoucha (2018) framed cultural congruence in the workplace through Leininger's cultural care theory (CCT). Madeleine Leininger, a nurse and theorist, pioneered the first transcultural nursing theory in the mid-1950s to increase the transcultural orientation of nurses in an increasingly multicultural world (Leininger, 1996). Through CCT, Leininger (1996) sought to expand knowledge about the dimensions of culture that were missing (e.g., language differences, social and cultural structure factors, and environmental factors) within the care model utilized by nurses. More specifically, the *cultural care* dimension of the CCT was designed to bring awareness to the influence of worldview, language, religion, social, political, educational, economic, technological, ethnohistorical, and environmental contexts of a particular culture. Although the information reviewed thus far on CCT is limited, further analysis on the theoretical underpinnings of the CCT will be provided through Jeffreys and Zoucha's (2018) investigation into a culturally congruent workplace.

In their manuscript, Jeffreys and Zoucha (2018) provided a contemporary view of multiculturalism within the workplace. They expanded their discussion of the CCT by addressing its three systems of caring: (a) *generic (folk) care*—culturally derived practices essential for growth, health, and human survival; (b) *professional care*—professional care practices that are learned through education and practice among professionals; and (c) *integrative care*—combining folk and professional care to provide culturally congruent care. Client recovery, health, and well-being are dependent on integrative care. That is, the integration of cultural factors into existing evidence-based practices ensures congruence with the cultural beliefs of individuals, families, and communities. Otherwise, culturally incongruent practices can result in cultural pain. Cultural pain can negatively affect client outcomes because of culturally incongruent workplace practices. For example, unfounded myths, politics, societal attitudes, racism, and stereotypes have contributed to health disparities, cultural invisibility, and marginalization among ethnic minorities. To prevent these misconceptions, Jeffreys and Zoucha (2018) encouraged zero tolerance to cultural incongruence in the workplace. This can be achieved in a contemporary workplace by creating a culturally safe environment where diversity is embraced. More so, implementing ongoing education focused on promoting multicultural workplace harmony provides the foundation for a safe workplace. Finally, a culturally sensitive workplace must also take employee well-being into account. Valuing and promoting diversity within the workforce can be achieved by measuring employee satisfaction; by offering opportunities for growth and promotions; and by publicizing employee and client rights, responsibilities, and written statements expressing zero tolerance for unacceptable verbal and nonverbal behaviors and actions within the workplace. Collectively, folk, professional, and integrative care provide the foundation for culturally sensitive practices that promote holistic care within the field of nursing.

The presence of Leininger's CCT has been expanded throughout the field of nursing. McFarland and Wehbe-Alamah (2019) proposed the following applications for CCT:

(a) research and practice—promoting culturally congruent nursing studies, including translation of findings; (b) education—as a guiding framework for undergraduate and graduate coursework; (c) health policy—as a way to guide and inform health policy initiative development; and (d) administration and leadership—helping administrators become culturally alert and use cultural care to address cultural clashes in the workplace. Given the various recommendations for the application of the CCT, it is possible to expand its use to other professions and settings, including within the field of mental health. Therefore, the CCT principles discussed thus far will be applied in an examination of the context of the counseling workplace.

The Physical Space

Despite early research examining the role of the counseling environment on the overall therapeutic experience, minimal attention has gone to investigating cultural factors within the counseling workplace or how these factors impact client outcomes. In 1976, Chaikin et al. (1976) investigated the influence of the physical space on the counseling process. They did so by varying the atmosphere of the counseling room from cold and distant to warm and intimate. Analyzing the differences in cold versus warm architecture was important because many institutional settings, including colleges, hospitals, prisons, and clinics, had cold architecture consisting of cinder-block walls, bright lights, concrete floors, and hard furniture. Therefore, the investigators were interested in analyzing the level of participant self-disclosure within both counseling atmospheres. The results from 52 undergraduate student participants (26 females, 26 males) supported investigators' hypothesis that the physical environment of the interview room affected the amount of client self-disclosure. Specifically, subjects disclosed more intimately when in the warm room. The warm, or intimate, room was the same one utilized in the cold condition, but it was decorated with a rug; had indirect light from floor and table lamps; contained framed pictures; offered upholstered seating, including cushioned armchairs; and contained other items such as magazines, ashtrays, a cigarette box, and a wicker wastebasket. Although the results from this study did not address cultural factors within the workplace, they shed light on the importance of the counseling environment for client outcomes. Of note is the lack of demographic information for the 52 participants. Other than gender, no other cultural demographic information was provided—perhaps signaling the lack of attention paid to matters of diversity during that time. Additionally, the results of the study fit into the professional care dimension of the CCT. That is, the results provide insight into the counseling, or professional, factors that affect client outcome. Next, we discuss research focusing on other environmental factors in the counseling workplace.

Pressly and Heesacker (2001) noted that early researchers focused on client and counselor variables while failing to recognize less obvious variables such as the influence of environmental factors. According to those authors, attributional error may have prevented scholars and clinicians from recognizing the influence of environmental factors. This recognition led Pressly and Heesacker to investigate the impact of the environment on both the client and the counselor. The environmental factors they addressed included accessories, color, furniture and room design, lighting, smell, sound, and thermal conditions.

Accessories, including artwork and personal items, were examined in inpatient and outpatient programs. It was discovered that inpatient clients preferred pictures of natural settings, such as those depicting animals, water, valleys, mountains, and farmlands, over images of people, urban scenes, and abstract compositions. The authors noted that inpatient clients may have preferred artwork that soothed them or helped them escape mentally from their current situation. Additionally, accessories that emphasized the counselor's personality and character were found to increase ownership of the counseling space and increase positive feelings among them. It is important to consider the experience of the counselor because counselors who are happy in their environment may transmit more positive attitudes and behaviors toward their clients (Pressly & Heesacker, 2001). It is necessary, however, to remain mindful of the message transmitted to clients by the chosen accessories, especially when showcasing personal items. For instance, displaying personal items and family pictures may elicit positive feelings from some clients while inadvertently offending other clients. This intersection between professional and personal factors provides opportunities for the integration of cultural sensitivities into the counseling workplace. Personal accessories provide opportunities for the integrative care mentioned within the CCT. Counselors and counseling workplaces can demonstrate cultural acceptance via the chosen accessories and create a warm environment that remains true to the personality of the counselor. Nevertheless, a balancing act must be implemented to ensure that personal or agency accessory preferences do not supersede or infringe upon the cultural identities and values of clients. Cultural sensitivity in the counseling workplace can promote feelings of acceptance and may provide positive client outcomes when environmental factors are carefully considered.

Wall color, furniture, lighting, smell, sound, and thermal conditions were found to be equal in importance to the accessories within the context of the workplace. Pressly and Heesacker (2001) reported that bright colors on walls were associated with positive emotions by clients and dark colors were linked to negative emotions. Colors on the cool spectrum, such as blue and violet, were found to be relaxing and decreased blood pressure, pulse, and respiration. In contrast, warm colors (e.g., orange and red) stimulated an opposite physiological response. Furniture and its placement within the office also provided opportunities within the counseling workplace. For example, cushioned seating with armrests provided a relaxed environment that increased client comfort (Pressly & Heesacker, 2001) and self-disclosure (Chaikin et al., 1976). Moreover, the placement of the seats—specifically, the spacing of the seating between the counselor and the client—also affected the client–counselor dyad. Women tend to have a smaller body buffer zone (the space required between them and another person to maintain comfort) than do men (Pressly & Heesacker, 2001). Further, male client–male counselor counseling dyads preferred larger body buffer zones than female–female or female–male dyads. Thus, the furniture placement provides a unique opportunity to increase cultural sensitivity within the counseling workplace. For instance, clients from close-contact cultures, such as Latin American countries, may prefer less distance in their interactions than individuals from noncontact cultures (i.e., European countries; Pressly & Heesacker, 2001).

Lighting was also found to play an important role within the counseling workplace. In fact, research has suggested that using soft and natural lighting was associated with greater self-disclosure (Pressly & Heesacker, 2001). Smell, sound, and thermal conditions also affect clients' counseling experience. Unpleasant smells were associated with retrieval of unpleasant memories in some clients, whereas pleasant smells triggered pleasant memories (Pressly & Heesacker, 2001). Although factors such as smell may be out of the counselor's control, counselors can attempt to intervene through other means. For example, counselors can attempt to mask sounds coming into and out of the counseling office by utilizing water sounds or other pleasant sounds. By doing so, the confidentiality of the counseling session can be ensured. Counselors and counseling agencies should also consider the thermal conditions of the workplace. Because room temperature has been found to influence the comfort and mental concentration of all in the counseling room, maintaining the temperature at a comfortable level is encouraged (Pressly & Heesacker, 2001).

The environmental factors reviewed thus far provide an opportunity for cultural sensitivity within the counseling workplace. More specifically, the choice of accessories, color, furniture and room design, lighting, smell, sound, and thermal conditions can not only affect overall treatment outcomes, but can also provide an opportunity for the integrative care dimension of the CCT. That is, by ensuring that professional evidence-based care is provided within the confines of culturally sensitive folk care, counselors and counseling agencies can begin to shift to culturally holistic practices. However, these practices make up only a portion of the agency's practices and efforts that lead to culturally sensitive care. Other agency workflow practices can be streamlined to incorporate culture into the workplace. The following section makes recommendations for such practices.

Culture in the Counseling Workplace

Too often, nonprofit agencies, including community mental health agencies, have an agency-based approach that focuses on equality. Client services are created around funding guidelines, accreditation mandates, and agency policies with the needs of the clients expected to fit into those predetermined categories and services (Joint Commission on Accreditation of Healthcare Organizations, n.d.; Siegel et al., 2000). Moreover, the often-used medical model imposed by the managed care and health insurance system places demands for diagnosis and treatment that makes individualization of services difficult to achieve (Joint Commission on Accreditation of Healthcare Organizations, n.d.). By focusing on treating all clients equally, counseling workplaces inadvertently fail to account for equitable treatment. It is through the provision of equitable services that cultural sensitivity can be incorporated. To overcome the expectations set by managed care and health insurance companies, independently licensed mental health professionals may decide against becoming credentialed managed care providers, thus turning to self-pay rates for their services. But, by not accepting insurance payments, counselors achieve two things: (a) they are able to individualize services without managed care demands, and (b) they focus care on individuals who can afford the out-of-pocket rates. The latter means not providing care for individuals who can only have access to services through managed care (e.g., Medicaid or Medicare). These situations create a conundrum that cannot be easily resolved.

Although the managed care and healthcare system will likely continue to mandate guidelines for the reimbursement of counseling services, steps can be taken at the agency level to attempt to ameliorate a possible impact on the individualization of services. According to Alegria et al. (2010), the mental health system has a unique opportunity to address diversity and culture at the individual, family, organizational, and societal levels within the counseling workplace. Culture is not an individual construct; rather, it is developed through interaction and is defined contextually. Yet, considering culture at the individual level acknowledges that individuals are embedded within cultural contexts that include ascribed characteristics, achieved characteristics, and experiences. Included within these ascribed and achieved characteristics are race, sex, and country of origin, and education, gender, and social position, respectively. Additionally, consideration of an individual's experiences and the aforementioned characteristics is important, but these may not be the most salient areas when addressing culture. For example, addressing the level of acculturation of an individual seeking asylum because of persecution for their minority sexual orientation may not adequately capture that person's most pressing concerns. In fact, the individual may be more inclined to address their sexual orientation than their racial or ethnic identity.

Therefore, having an adequate understanding of the client's worldview and their core beliefs, in conjunction with knowledge of salient characteristics, is important in addressing culture at the individual level within the counseling environment. In the previous example, it is important to consider the intersecting identities of the client (e.g., immigrant status, sexual orientations, trauma response resulting from displacement) to ensure that all relevant areas are addressed. Of course, receiving input from the client throughout the assessment and treatment process is vital to avoid misappraisals by mental health providers. Furthermore, considering culture at the family level includes obtaining a full understanding of the entire family's culture. This can be accomplished by considering family roles, determining expectations of family members, and, finally, assessing the fit between the family's culture and the prescribed treatment.

Moreover, Alegria et al. (2010) discussed addressing culture at the organizational level. This level includes the type of treatment practices and the use of evidence-based services. Other cultural practices at the organizational level include policies, supervisory practices, and referral procedures. This includes making sure that onboarding and training policies place culture front and center by highlighting its importance alongside diagnosis, treatment goals, and frequency of services. This can be accomplished by having clinical supervisors provide support and feedback to mental health providers following routine audits, consultation, and supervision to ensure that counselors are centering culture at the individual level. After all, culturally sensitive counseling workplaces ensure that these practices are addressed by implementing training, policies, assessment, services, and treatment plans with a cultural lens. Clients would also benefit from strong culturally informed collaborations between counseling workplaces and community partnerships. This would ensure that receiving agencies consider the client's ascribed and achieved characteristics. For example, referral sources should be able to accommodate the language needs and financial means of clients. Overlooking these, and other important sociocultural factors, can prevent clients from receiving much needed services.

Additionally, a strong link exists between a favorable organizational environment and a positive client experience (Alegria et al., 2010). For instance, increased collaboration between staff and clients led to higher client trust. However, the organizational environment can negatively affect the client's experience. This occurs when the organizational culture does not respect individuals and families, instead resorting to stereotypes and labels. Therefore, increased attention should be placed on supporting and uplifting diversity among families. A simple shift in practice can help achieve this. For example, referring to clients by their preferred names and respecting open expression of their gender identities is recommended.

Finally, the work of Alegria et al. (2010) addressed culture at the community and societal levels. They emphasized the inherent limitation associated with understanding the culture of others. To address this limitation, individuals tend to view other cultures through the lens of their own culture. When they do so, existing biases and personal values are likely to influence their understanding, and perhaps even cloud their judgement, leading to misattributions. This can have dire implications for service providers and agencies alike. Therefore, increasing awareness of other cultures and acquiring multicultural knowledge are crucial in understanding diversity (Alegria et al., 2010) and gaining skills to provide culturally sensitive services (Arredondo et al., 1996; Sue et al., 1992). Additionally, it is important to acknowledge the influence of sociopolitical factors. For instance, a shift in social norms is likely to have an impact at the community and societal cultural levels. Shifting norms and political climates should be acknowledged by the agency and, if clients are affected, addressed within the therapeutic relationship.

In sum, the counseling workplace is not free from external pressures that affect the provision of services. The expectations imposed by accreditation and managed care systems often emphasize equality over equity of services. Individualization of services by providers is one step to ensure cultural sensitivity within counseling workplaces. Specifically, addressing diversity and culture at the individual, family, organizational, and societal levels is needed to replace "one size fits all" treatment.

The Client's Experience

Infusing culturally informed services beginning at the client's initial point of contact and extending throughout treatment are opportunities to balance out mandates from accreditation and managed care systems. We start this section by discussing opportunities for infusing cultural sensitivity beginning with the initial contact by the client.

Initial Call

Seeking counseling services can be stressful (Chandrasekara, 2017; Goelitz & Stewart-Kahn, 2007; Hansen et al., 2021). The decision to contact a service provider and schedule an appointment takes courage. Thus, counseling workplaces can have a big impact on the client's experience during this first encounter. Cultural factors should be attended to within this initial call by meeting the client's language needs. This will ensure that the presenting problem for which the client sought services will be understood and addressed. In addition to meeting the client's language needs, the person doing the scheduling should inquire into and assess what family members or individuals will take part in the treatment. This will help with planning the session. For example, if more than one individual will take part in a session, the counselor can plan ahead and ensure adequate office space and seating options.

The factors discussed thus far incorporate the individual and family cultural levels discussed previously. To account for culture at the agency level, steps should be taken to ensure that clients are not inadvertently discriminated against. Although requesting certain demographic information may be customary, it is important to analyze whether such information is absolutely necessary. For instance, asking all clients to provide their social security number or citizenship status may seem customary, but these questions may cause suspicion and even panic in individuals who do not have a social security number or who may not hold a legal immigration status to reside in the United States. This is not to say that gaining such information is not possible or necessary, but to point out that obtaining such information at the onset may deter potential clients. The agency must be aware that certain sociopolitical conditions can create conditions that have a disproportionate impact on marginalized groups, thus creating service silos within agencies.

Admittedly, discussing all potential culture-related factors that may affect services during the initial contact/phone call is beyond the scope of this chapter. The examples provided in this section are meant to help stimulate further thought on the potential impact of the information requested from clients.

Assigning Clients

The relationship between the client and the therapist is an important therapeutic factor (Ardito & Rabellino, 2011). Special consideration should be made when matching a client with a therapist; however, many determinants influence this decision. For instance, counselor availability, managed healthcare credentialing, client language, and gender preference can all influence the assignment of a counselor. The diversity within the clinical staff is crucial in addressing these and other factors that may have an impact on the assignment of clients. Staff diversity contributes to cultural competence at the organizational level (Darnell & Kuperminc, 2006) and should be prioritized by counseling workplaces. In fact, the reason most frequently cited by clients for not starting therapy after making the initial appointment is wanting a different assigned therapist (Wang & Werbart, 2014). Clinical Case Scenario 28.1 continues this discussion by presenting a situation that may arise during the initial client session.

MARKETING MATERIALS

Marketing materials have the potential to reach untold numbers and types of individuals. Counseling agencies can also set the tone for the workplace culture through their marketing materials. Including individuals from diverse backgrounds would send a message of inclusivity. Creating marketing materials in the major languages spoken within the agencies' catchment area would further the aims of cultural sensitivity. In the age of smartphones and social media, marketing and advertising can be achieved at little to no cost. Facebook and YouTube are readily accessible to transmit psychoeducation and resources to the greater community. As the counseling world turned to telehealth for services during the COVID-19 pandemic, agencies reached out to their communities via social media to provide support and resources. These discussions also served to advertise counseling agencies. However, it is important to target individuals in their native languages. It may become a habit to address the English-speaking community, but outreach in other languages is strongly encouraged.

Moreover, the options described previously by McMahon et al. (2013) may result in referrals from other providers for services; this is an indirect method of obtaining clients. To do more direct outreach to clients, counseling workplaces can include their information on managed care and private healthcare provider lists. It would be helpful to include the hours of operations, a list of languages spoken by providers and staff members, a description of locale, and parking accessibility. The latter two are especially important to ensure that the physical abilities of clients are addressed.

Although not an exhaustive list, the following are additional advertising possibilities: (a) place the name of the counseling agency on a relevant community referral directory; (b) give talks at local organizations, clubs, and conferences; (c) encourage staff to join professional organizations; (d) write articles for newspapers or magazines; (e) provide informational leaflets about services rendered; and (f) create a website accessible in multiple languages (McMahon et al., 2013). Despite the most well-organized and well-intentioned advertising efforts, it may be difficult to ascertain how many potential clients are reached. An upside of a counseling workplace is that it is easier to publicize its services than it is for a private practice practitioner (McMahon et al., 2013), and this advantage should be capitalized upon.

INTAKE FORMS: READABILITY, TRANSLATION, PAPER AND PENCIL, AND USING COMPUTERS

Intake forms are a vital component of any counseling agency. These forms provide important information about the counseling process, grant consent for treatment, and provide authorization to bill health insurance providers for services. Utilizing handouts and other materials that are not in the language of minority cultures deters access to and utilization of services (Siegel et al., 2000). A lack of cultural sensitivity regarding the client's language needs not only creates challenges for clients, but also poses an ethical dilemma for mental health providers. A thorough informed consent is an integral part of the counseling relationship. Therefore, not meeting the language needs of clients poses a risk. In fact, the standards from the codes of ethics for the leading national mental health associations address the cultural needs of clients and mandate that services, informed consent, and forms be provided in the languages spoken by clients (AAMFT, 2015; ACA, 2014; APA, 2017; NASW, 2017). The chosen languages should match the demographics of the clients, which brings forth another challenge: Who is responsible for the translation of documents?

Translation websites and software that can provide these services abound. However, these services should be used with caution. In fact, translations obtained through these means should be reviewed by a person with fluency in the translated language because errors may exist and cultural nuances may be missed. With language being a complex, continually evolving construct (Hays, 2016), it is important to pay special attention to it throughout the client's experience. Language carries much more than spoken words and phrases (Hays, 2016); it also carries with it culture (Ivers & Villalba, 2015) and emotion (Delgado-Romero et al., 2018). Considering that communication is a key component in therapy, it is important to consider language within the context of the counseling relationship to ensure that culture at the individual and family levels is being addressed. Counseling workplaces cannot claim to be culturally responsive without first ensuring that the language needs of clients are met.

Moreover, agency forms should be readable and provided by means that are most convenient to the client. For instance, using a 12-point font and ensuring that the quality of the document is not degraded is important. Printed documents should be made available even if electronic versions are used because some clients may face challenges trying to navigate computers or tablets. Another important factor to consider is literacy. It should not be assumed that all individuals who seek counseling can read and write; thus, measures should be taken to provide assistance when these situations arise.

ACCESSIBILITY

As discussed previously, ensuring access to legible forms in the client's preferred language is important. Other areas should also be considered to promote accessibility within the counseling workplace. This section addresses accessibility and how to ensure that it is centered alongside other cultural factors.

A lack of awareness about addressing the physical needs of clients will likely alienate an entire subset of potential clientele. Specifically, individuals with mobility challenges may be further marginalized by not providing adequate access to parking, waiting areas, restrooms, and provider offices. In addition to ensuring accessibility in the areas mentioned, counseling workplaces should notify the public of efforts made to increase accessibility.

In addition to considering physical abilities, counseling workplaces should also consider the gender identities and sexual orientations of clients. For instance, having access to gender-neutral or family-style restrooms would ensure options for all, regardless of their gender identity and expression. It is important to note that many counseling workplaces will not have the ability to provide such accommodations; therefore, counselors and counselor supervisors should proactively have discussions about how to handle such situations. Moreover, creating an environment welcoming all sexual orientations can be accomplished by displaying images of LGBTQIA+ individuals. Incorporating images and language across all types of advertisements and flyers is important. In doing so, culturally affirming practices will be generalized to all being served and not compartmentalized to a subset of the population. Although brief, this section aimed to highlight the importance of acknowledging the role that accessibility plays in ensuring equitable services. Furthermore, in this day and age, accessibility extends beyond the physical space of the counseling workplace; it also includes access to reliable internet and technology to access distance counseling.

DISTANCE COUNSELING

Telehealth services have been in use since the turn of the 20th century (Reid, 1996). Telemental health services, a subset of telehealth medicine, is the use of technology to deliver mental health services, including assessment and treatment (Hilty et al., 2003). These distance services gained popularity following the COVID-19 pandemic that resulted in strict stay-at-home orders during most of 2020. These measures were taken to avoid the spread of the novel disease which placed at risk the lives of individuals across the globe. Telemental health, therefore, was instrumental in continuing to serve vulnerable, underserved, and marginalized communities (Murphy et al., 2020; Nielsen & Levkovich, 2020), as had been intended since its inception. However, challenges stemming from the use of distance counseling were also noted. Because of the quick shift from in-person, face-to-face services to distance counseling, mental health therapists were faced with having to learn this new way of providing counseling without previous experience or training (Murphy et al., 2020). Mental health therapists were left to navigate the challenges of therapeutic rapport via electronic means on their own while navigating the impact of the pandemic on their own lives. In addition to the challenges discussed thus far, the inequity of telehealth services was also highlighted. Many marginalized individuals did not have access to reliable internet or phone connection (Murphy et al., 2020), or even access to a private, confidential setting. Those who did have a reliable internet or phone connection and access to a private location were not free from problems. For instance, electronic versions of documents and signatures for intake forms became one of the biggest barriers faced when providing telehealth services (Murphy et al., 2020). Counseling workplaces, including community mental health agencies, were in uncharted territory.

Despite the challenges faced, telemental health provided many individuals access to much-needed treatment during one of the most challenging situations known in modern times. It became evident that telehealth services could, in fact, be effective when in-person sessions were not permissible or possible. Telemental health aligns with the professional care dimension of the CCT and also provides the foundation for integrative care that can lead to culturally sensitive treatment. The shift to distance counseling during the COVID-19 pandemic highlighted areas of opportunity and areas in need of attention. It demonstrated that telemental health was a viable alternative to in-person sessions, thus opening the door for the use of distance counseling. However, telemental health service delivery can further marginalize the most vulnerable populations, who may have unreliable internet service or limited access to technology. Finding solutions and alternative methods to address the challenges described thus far is instrumental in avoiding inequities in treatment. To ensure that culture is addressed at the individual, family, organizational, and societal levels, counseling workplaces have a responsibility to ensure equitable access to legible documents for clients in their native language. Moreover, use of physical and electronic documents should facilitate the client's experience, not impede it. Addressing culture at the organizational level is not limited to ethnic, gender, and language diversity; counseling workplaces should also focus on the messages they convey to the community. Otherwise, the opportunities to highlight the services provided may go unnoticed.

Are You Boxing Yourself In?

The mental health field and counseling workplaces alike have many opportunities to diversify their practices, the clients they serve, and the services they provide. The internet, telehealth, and social media have created opportunities for outreach to broader audiences, thereby addressing the needs of marginalized groups, extending the workplace mission throughout the community, and creating opportunities for linkage with other agencies. However, disregarding the opportunities made possible by technology may create blind spots for counseling workplaces. It may lead agencies to box themselves into only providing services typical for the majority of counseling agencies.

CLINICAL CASE SCENARIO 28.1

After two months of contemplating counseling services, Mr. Lopes contacted the Peace of Mind Community Counseling Center to discuss scheduling an appointment with a professional counselor. His call was answered by a friendly representative whom Mr. Lopes perceived to be warm, attentive, and empathetic. He was asked to discuss his "presenting problem" after identifying his full name, date of birth, address, phone number, and medical coverage information. He was advised that he should arrive at least 30 minutes before his scheduled appointment because he would have to fill out new client paperwork, including consents, historical and medical information, and other documents required by the agency. He was scheduled for an appointment with Juan Garcia, a bilingual professional counselor, specializing in addressing the needs of Spanish-speaking Latinx individuals and families. On the day of the appointment, Mr. Lopes arrived 15 minutes before his appointment. He apologized to the front desk personnel for his tardiness. He was greeted with a smile and was assured that there was nothing to worry about. He provided his identification card and his insurance card. He was handed the required forms, provided with a clipboard and pen, and advised to return the completed forms as soon as he was finished. Juan, the assigned counselor, made his way to the waiting area.

As Mr. Lopes began to fill out the form, he heard a male voice calling his name. Surprised, he immediately stood up and walked toward the male standing there wearing a button-down shirt, black slacks, and black dress shoes. As he approached, the man greeted Mr. Lopes in Spanish and introduced himself as Juan. Mr. Lopes paused for a second and advised Juan that he did not speak Spanish. Juan had a puzzled look and reviewed the documents in a manila folder. He immediately switched to speaking in English, apologized for the confusion, and advised Mr. Lopes that he could finish completing the forms after the session.

Juan summoned Mr. Lopes to his office, which was decorated with artwork depicting Latin American folklore. Mr. Lopes sat on a leather sofa in front of a single chair. Juan moved the chair back a few feet and proceeded to sit down, placing the manila folder on his lap. He reviewed a document describing the counseling process and advised Mr. Lopes that he would be asking more questions during the initial session than would typically be asked during a session. He began by asking Mr. Lopes about his thoughts about speaking to a male counselor, to which Mr. Lopes responded, "I'm okay with it. To be honest, I didn't know who I would be meeting with today." Juan then informed Mr. Lopes about his specialization in addressing the needs of the Latinx community, to which Mr. Lopes responded, "That is great, but I am not Latino. I mean, my father is from Brazil, but my mother is from Jamaica, where I was born. I moved to the United States after meeting my wife while she was on a trip to Jamaica. However, we are getting a divorce, which is why I decided to obtain counseling."

CLINICAL CASE SCENARIO DISCUSSION QUESTIONS

1. Explain the mishap in Mr. Lopes's case.
2. What should the agency do to address the incident?

END-OF-CHAPTER RESOURCES

A robust set of instructor resources designed to supplement this text is located at http://connect.springerpub.com/content/book/978-0-8261-3953-5. Qualifying instructors may request access by emailing **textbook@springerpub.com**.

SUMMARY

Cultural considerations within the counseling workplace provide a foundation for the therapeutic work between the client and the counselor. Cultural competencies are vitally important both in and out of the counseling session. Therefore, counseling workplaces have the responsibility to implement culturally sensitive practices. They can accomplish this by incorporating theoretical frameworks into their policies and practices. For example, Leininger's CCT brought awareness of cultural factors into the helping fields. Specifically, CCT addressed the generic (folk), professional, and integrative systems of caring. Together, these systems of care integrate cultural factors into evidence-based practices, thereby promoting a more holistic approach to treatment.

The physical space of the counseling workplace is an important factor to consider because it iaffects the counseling process. Additionally, the physical space of the office provides opportunities to integrate culture-sensitive practices. For instance, the client's perception of the office space as either warm or cold was found to influence self-disclosure. Environments that were perceived as warm resulted in higher levels of comfort and client self-disclosure. Office decor and accessories, wall color, lighting, smell, sound, and thermal conditions are all important environmental factors. These environmental factors can promote comfort, relaxation, acceptance, and overall positive feelings among clients when used in a culturally sensitive manner.

Incorporating culture into the workplace often means balancing the requirements set by the managed care system and accreditation bodies. Therefore, it is especially important that counseling workplaces address diversity and culture at the individual, family, organizational, and societal levels. To that end, counseling workplaces should ensure that clients' ascribed and achieved characteristics, as well as their worldview and core beliefs, are all considered. Additionally, the culture of the entire family should be acknowledged and addressed throughout treatment. Organizational policies and practices should support and uplift clients. Finally, incorporating salient social factors into service delivery and agency practices would address culture at the community and societal levels.

The client's experience of the counseling workplace begins at the initial call. The information that is requested from clients should be considered so as to minimize discomfort and avoid further marginalizing individuals. Steps should also be taken to ensure that staff and counselors are diverse and representative of the clientele. Many factors affect the assignment of clients (e.g., counselor availability, managed care credentialing, language, and gender), but attention should be placed on determining appropriate fit between client and counselor. Additionally, client forms should be legible and provided in the client's primary language. Although technology can be helpful, steps should be taken to address potential challenges. Technology has created the opportunity for distance counseling, which can provide opportunities for some clients while presenting barriers for others.

Comparatively, technology provides marketing and advertising opportunities for counseling workplaces. Cultural considerations should be given to incorporating diverse staff members fluent in languages spoken by the client community. Otherwise, agencies risk alienating clients.

The attitude and approach to the client are important. Counseling workplaces should prioritize the experience of the client and the messaging sent to the community; however, the bottom line is that the therapeutic relationship must be safeguarded. The client must feel that they are speaking to someone who cares. This has to be demonstrated both inside and outside of the counseling room. It should be a fundamental part of the counseling workplace's professional image (McMahon et al., 2013).

DISCUSSION QUESTIONS

1. What are the environmental factors that may affect the counseling experience for clients?
2. What are the three levels of caring of the CCT?
3. How can culture at the individual, family, agency, and society levels be addressed by counseling workplaces?
4. How can technology be incorporated into counseling workplace practices?

CULTURAL CONSIDERATIONS FOR THE COUNSELING WORKPLACE

Guest: Dr. Adrian Lira

https://connect.springerpub.com/content/book/978-0-8261-3953-5/part/part03/chapter/ch28

KEY REFERENCES

Only key references appear in the print edition. The full reference list appears in the digital product on Springer Publishing Connect: https://connect.springerpub.com/content/book/978-0-8261-3953-5/part/part03/chapter/ch28

Alegria, M., Atkins, M., Farmer, E., Stanton, E., & Stelk, W. (2010). One size does not fit all: Taking diversity, culture, and context seriously. *Administration and Policy in Mental Health and Mental Health Services Research*, 37(1–2), 48–60. https://doi.org/10.1007/s10488-010-0283-2

Chaikin, A. L., Derlega, V. J., & Miller, S. J. (1976). Effects of room environment on self-disclosure in a counseling analogue. *Journal of Counseling Psychology*, 23(5), 479–481. https://doi.org/10.1037/0022-0167.23.5.479

Jeffreys, M. R., & Zoucha, R. (2018). Cultural congruence in the workplace, health care, and academic settings for multiracial and multiheritage individuals. *Journal of Cultural Diversity*, 25(4), 113–126.

McFarland, M. R., & Wehbe-Alamah, H. B. (2019). Leininger's theory of culture care diversity and universality: An overview with a historical retrospective and a view toward the future. *Journal of Transcultural Nursing*, 30(6), 540–557. https://doi.org/10.1177/1043659619867134

McMahon, G., Palmer, S., & Wilding, C. (2013). *The essential skills for setting up a counselling and psychotherapy practice*. Routledge. https://doi.org/10.4324/9781315824581

Murphy, A. A., Karyczak, S., Dolce, J. N., Zechner, M., Bates, F., Gill, K. J., & Rothpletz-Puglia, P. (2020). Challenges experienced by behavioral health organizations in New York resulting from COVID-19: A qualitative analysis. *Community Mental Health Journal, 57*(1), 111–120. https://doi.org/10.1007/s10597-020-00731-3

Pressly, P. K., & Heesacker, M. (2001). The physical environment and counseling: A review of theory and research. *Journal of Counseling & Development, 79*(2), 148–160. https://doi.org/10.1002/j.1556-6676.2001.tb01954.x

Index

AADA. *See* Association of Adult Development and Aging
AAP. *See* American Academy of Pediatrics
AAPI communities. *See* Asian American and Pacific Islander communities
ableism. *See* people who live with disabilities
ACA Code of Ethics. See American Counseling Association *Code of Ethics*
Acceptance and Commitment Therapy (ACT), 138
acculturation
    Asian American clients, 80–81, 84
    European American descent, clients of, 146
    immigrant and refugee clients, 364–365
    Latin American clients, 93
    Native American descent, clients of, 114–117
Achieved Ethnic Identity, 73
ACLU. *See* American Civil Liberties Union
ACSA. *See* Advocacy Competencies Self-Assessment Survey
ACT. *See* Acceptance and Commitment Therapy
Adlerian therapy, 462
adolescents
    AAPI communities, 79–82
    European American descent, clients of, 142–145
    immigrant and refugee clients, 374–375
    Latin American clients, 100–101
    LGBQ++ clients, 184–185
    MENA and Muslim American clients, 288–287
    military service members and veterans, 395
    multiracial clients, 165
    multiracial identity development, 159
    Native American descent, clients of, 121–122
    people who live with disabilities (PWD), 353
    religion and spirituality, 260–262
    transgender clients, 200
    women clients, 227
adults
    European American descent, clients of, 145–148
    immigrant and refugee clients, 376
    Latin American clients, 101–102
    LGBQ++ clients, 185
    multiracial clients, 166–167
    Native American descent, clients of, 122–123
    older adult population, 329–330
    people who live with disabilities (PWD), 353–354
advocacy, 34
    African descent, clients of, 60
    AAPI communities, 76–79
    development of, 39–40
    European American descent, clients of, 141–142
    immigrant and refugee clients, 373–374
    Jewish descent, clients of, 285
    juvenile justice system, 39
    Latin American clients, 98–100
    LGBQ++ clients, 183–184
    men clients, 241–242
    military service members and veterans, 394–395
    multiculturalism, 41–43
    multiracial clients, 164
    Muslim and MENA American clients, 305–307
    Native American descent, clients of, 120–121
    older adult population, 325, 328–329
    people who live with disabilities (PWD), 347–378
    poor and affluent clients, 421
    readiness, 40–41
    religion and spirituality, 259–260
    transgender clients, 196, 198–200
    women clients, 225–227

Advocacy Competencies Self-Assessment
(ACSA) Survey, 40
advocates, 36–37
affectional identity, 191–192
affirmative therapy, polyamory communities
  assertive communication, 436
  avoidance behaviors, 435
  cognitive techniques, 436
  emotional awareness, regulation, and
    acceptance, 435
  minority stress, 435
  resilience, 436
  rewarding expressions, 437
  supportive relationships, 436
African American clients
  clinical case scenario, 65–66
  culture, 54–56
  family life, 54
  life expectancy and health, 54–55
  mental health, 52–53
  problem tolerance, 55
  religion and spirituality, 55–56
  slavery and segregation, 51–53
African descent, clients of
  adolescents and young adults, 61–62
  advocacy, 60
  African immigrants, 56–57
  Afro-Caribbean immigrant groups, 57–59
  America's Black/White binary paradigm,
    49–50
  Black children, 61
  client worldview, 59
  clinical practice, 63–65
  counseling relationship, 59–60
  counselor, 47–49
  counselor self-awareness, 59
  couples and families, 62–63
  cultural humility, 60
  culturally responsive practices, 59–60
  identity development, 50–51
  immigrants, 56–57
  life expectancy and health, 54–55
Afro-Caribbean immigrant groups
  1965 immigration reform, 58
  mental health, 58–59
  racial identity, 57–58
  stereotypes, 58
ageism, 316. *See also* older adult population
  ethical and counseling considerations, 323
  poor mental health, 323
  reverse, 322
ageist ageism, 322
agender, 176
AIES. *See* American Indian Enculturation Scale
AKSA. *See* attitudes and beliefs, knowledge,
  skills, and action

Ally Week, 202
AMCD. *See* Association for Multicultural
  Counseling and Development
American Academy of Pediatrics (AAP), 64
American Civil Liberties Union (ACLU), 199
American Counseling Association (ACA)
  Code of Ethics, 3, 5, 9, 12, 38, 48, 76, 78,
    97–99, 158, 172–174, 183, 225, 255, 259,
    298, 306, 348, 370, 371, 407, 480, 496, 501
American Indian Enculturation Scale (AIES),
  116–117
American Public Health Association (APHA),
  3, 393
Americanized Family, 71
America's Black/White binary paradigm,
  49–50
ancestors, clients of Native American descent,
  110
androgynous, 176
animals, clients of Native American descent,
  111
anorexia, women clients, 217
anti-Black racism, 47
anti-Catholic sentiments, 253
antisemitism, 278–280
anxiety, older adult population, 326
anxious attachment, 441
APHA. *See* American Public Health
  Association
appreciation stage, multiracial identity
  development, 159
artists, 455
asexual, 177
Asian American and Pacific Islander (AAPI)
  communities
  adolescents and young adults, 79–82
  advocacy agenda, 76–79
  children, 79–82
  clinical case scenario, 86
  collectivistic worldview, 70
  contextualized intersectionality, 85
  counselor, 69
  couples and families, 84
  cultural stigma, 74
  cultural strengths, 85
  culturally responsive practices, 75–76
  discrimination, 72
  emotional expression, 71
  family structure and parenting styles,
    70–71
  help-seeking, 74–75
  identity development, 73–74
  interpersonal societal issues, 69–72
  lack of health insurance coverage, 75
  mental health, 72
  microaggressions, 72

model minority, 72
queer communities, 83–84
racial discrimination, 74–75
racialized sexual harassment, 83
racism, 72
socioeconomic challenges, 72
sociopolitical challenges, 85
strengths-based approach, 85
within group differences, 84
AsianCrit theory framework, 76
assimilation, Latin American clients, 93
Association for Multicultural Counseling and Development (AMCD), 7
Association for Spiritual, Ethical, and Religious Values in Counseling Spiritual Competencies, 258–259
Association of Adult Development and Aging (AADA), 327
asylum-seekers, 362
attachment theory, 441–442
attitudes and beliefs, knowledge, skills, and action (AKSA), 133
attitudes and beliefs, transgender clients, 195
auditory disability, 340
Autonomy stage, WRID, 132
avoidant attachment, 441–442

behavioral familismo, 95
benevolent behaviors, 338
Bible, Jews, 270
Bicultural Asian American Family, 71
bigamy, 428, 433
bigender, 176
biomedical model, PWD, 340–341
BIPOC communities. *See* Black, Indigenous, and People of Color communities
bisexual, 177
Black Church theology, 264
Black Feminist methodological approach, 218
Black, Indigenous, and People of Color (BIPOC) communities, 2, 131
Black Liberation Theology (BLT), 264
blind culture and identity, 351–352
BLT. *See* Black Liberation Theology
Bohemian lifestyle, 427
border identity, 159
bravery, grandfather teaching, 109
broaching behavior
    assessment stage, 470–471
    clinical supervision, 500–501
    Continuum of Broaching Behavior, 467, 468
    delivery stage, 472
    joining stage, 470
    multidimensional model, 468–470
    organizational continuum, 473–476

preparation stage, 471
race and culture identities, 472–473
broaching model, 146
Brown Church theology, 265
burnout, 11

CACP model. *See* Culturally Adaptive Counseling Practice model
CACREP. *See* Council for the Accreditation of Counseling and Related Educational Programs
California Mental Health and Spirituality Initiative, 55
CALTAP. *See* Contextual Adult Life Span Theory for Adapting Psychotherapy
casual gamer, 452
casual register, 486
CBPR. *See* community-based participatory research
CCMP. *See* Competencies for Counseling the Multiracial Population
CCT. *See* cultural care theory
CFI. *See* Cultural Formulation Interview
child–parent psychotherapy, foreign-born youth, 375
children
    AAPI communities, 79–82
    European American descent, clients of, 142–145
    immigrant and refugee clients, 374–375
    Jewish descent, clients of, 285–286
    Latin American clients, 100–101
    LGBQ++ clients, 184–185
    military service members and veterans, 395
    Native American descent, clients of, 121–122
    people who live with disabilities (PWD), 352–353
    religion and spirituality, 260–262
    women clients, 227
Chinese Exclusion Act, 70
choice of group categorization, multiracial identity development, 158
chronosystem, AAPI communities, 79
cisgender, 176, 190, 213
class and classism, 403–404
    acknowledge realities, 408
    barriers removal, 409
    cultivating relationship, 408
    Grounded Theory Model, 409–411
    internally reflect, 408
    Social Class and Classism Consciousness (SCCC) Model, 412
clinical service provision, Muslim and MENA American clients, 306

clinical supervision
  broaching, 500–501
  clinical case scenario, 502–504
  competence, 501–502
  cultural competence, 495
  cultural responsiveness, 495
  culture, 500
  ethical considerations, 501
  healthy working alliance, 496–498
  humility, 495–496
  multicultural responsiveness, 496
  supervisory relationship, 495
cognitive disability, 340
collective exploration, 131
college/young adulthood stage, multiracial identity development, 159
colorblind approach, Latin American clients, 99–100
colorblindness, 5, 48–49
Combat Stress Control Teams, 383
comfort, clients of Native American descent, 124
communication, clients of Native American descent, 125
Community Cultural Wealth, 85
community-based participatory research (CBPR), 19
Competencies for Counseling the Multiracial Population (CCMP), 154
concrete operational stage, cognitive development, 143
Congressional Black Caucus report, 61
connection, Native American clients, 120
conscientization
  liberation psychology, 17
  military service members and veterans, 389
consonant acculturation, 81
context, transgender clients, 197
Contextual Adult Life Span Theory for Adapting Psychotherapy (CALTAP), 330
Continuum of Broaching Behavior, 468
coronavirus (COVID-19)
  AAPI communities, 72
  African Americans' mental health, 53
  social justice and advocacy, 37
  women clients, 217
cosplay, 454
Council for the Accreditation of Counseling and Related Educational Programs (CACREP), 3, 90, 154, 327, 480
counseling utilization
  multiracial clients, 161–163
  older adult population, 325–327
  people who live with disabilities (PWD), 344–347
counselors
  AAPI communities, 69
  people of African descent, 47–49
  privilege and marginalization, 75
  as researchers, 35–36
counselor's belief systems
  ACA Code of Ethics, 9
  countertransference, 9
  influences, 8
  transference, 8–9
  value conflict, 9
counselor's worldview
  cultural beliefs, 5
  cultural humility, 6
  implicit and explicit bias, 6
  Multicultural and Social Justice Counseling Competencies (MSJCC), 6–7
  stereotypes, 6
couple dynamics
  European American descent, clients of, 145–148
  immigrant and refugee clients, 376
  Latin American clients, 101–102
  LGBQ++ clients, 185
  multiracial clients, 166–167
  Muslim and MENA American clients, 208–209
  Native American descent, clients of, 123
  older adult population, 329–330
  people who live with disabilities (PWD), 354–355
  religion and spirituality, 262
  transgender clients, 204–205
  women clients, 227–228
COVID-19. *See* coronavirus
creative expression interventions, foreign-born youth, 375
Critical Race Theory (CRT), 42
cross-platform fandoms, 453
CRT. *See* Critical Race Theory
cultural auditing, 480
cultural beliefs, 5
cultural capital, 403
cultural care theory (CCT), 510–511
cultural comfort, 468
cultural competence, 10
Cultural Conflict Asian American Family, 71
cultural encapsulation, 4–5
Cultural Formulation Interview (CFI), 489
cultural humility, 6, 467
  AAPI communities, 76
  advocacy, systemic barriers, 26
  African descent, clients of, 60
  clinical case scenario, 28
  vs. cultural competence, 23
  cultural knowledge, 25
  European American descent, clients of, 141

immigrant and refugee clients, 361, 371–373
LGBQ++ clients, 182
liberatory framework, 24
lifelong self-exploration, 25
men clients, 240–241
mental health disparities, 216–218
Muslim and MENA American clients, 302–303
military service members and veterans, 393
multiracial clients, 163–164
Native American clients, 118–119
originators, 25
people who live with disabilities (PWD), 348–352
power dynamics and biases, 26
principles, 25–26
religion and spirituality, 257–259
self-care, 24
self-reflective questions, 25
and trustworthiness, 26
women clients, 216, 223–225
cultural immediacy, 473
cultural responsiveness
  barriers, 10
  cultural competence, 10
  cultural values, 10
  and social justice, 35–36
cultural stranglehold, 17
cultural tunnel vision, 4
Culturally Adaptive Counseling Practice (CACP) model, 372
culturally relevant models, African American clients
  Multisystemic Approach to Cultural and Disability Awareness (MACDA) model, 65
  Post Traumatic Slave Syndrome (PTSS), 64
  Racial Battle Fatigue (RBF), 65
  Segregation Stress Syndrome, 64–65
culturally responsive practices, 27–28
  African descent, clients of, 59–60
  Asian American and Pacific Islander communities, 75–76
  European American descent, clients of, 139–141
  immigrant and refugee clients, 371–373
  Jewish descent, clients of, 283–285
  Latin American clients, 96–98
  LGBQ++ clients, 182–183
  men clients, 240–241
  MENA and Muslim American clients, 298–304
  military service members and veterans, 393
  multiracial clients, 163–164
  Native American descent, clients of, 118–120
people who live with disabilities (PWD), 348–352
  poor and affluent clients, 419–422
  religion and spirituality, 257–259
  transgender clients, 195–198
  women clients, 223–225
culturally sensitive agencies
  accessories in physical space, 512–513
  client's experience, 515
  cultural care theory (CCT), 510–511
  culture, 513–514
  environmental factors, 512–513
  physical space, 511–513

dark fandoms, 457
deaf clients, 350–351
deideologizing, 303
demiromantic, 192
denaturalization, 17
depression
  European American descent, clients of, 144–145
  older adult population, 325–326
developmental disability, 340
diagnosis and assessment
  bias, 484–485
  clinical case scenario, 491–492
  cultural insensitivity, 483–485
  culturally responsive therapeutic interventions, 489–490
  Diagnostic and Statistical Manual of Mental Disorders (DSM), 487–489
  ethical guidelines, 480–481
  informed consent, 485
  intake assessments and mental status evaluations, 486–487
  microaggressions, 490–491
  reflective practice, 481–482
Diagnostic and Statistical Manual of Mental Disorders (DSM), 487–489
differently abled identity development models
  biomedical model, 340–341
  environmental model, 341
  functional model, 341
  sociopolitical model, 341–342
disability, 339–340. *See also* people who live with disabilities
  adaptation, 349–350
  identity, 349
disability-affirmative therapy, 349
discrimination
  AAPI communities, 72
  immigrant and refugee clients, 366–369
  Jewish descent, clients of, 278–280
  LGBQ++ clients, 179

discrimination (*cont.*)
  men clients, 239–240
  military service members and veterans, 393
  multiracial clients, 160–161
  people who live with disabilities (PWD), 342–344
  polyamory, kink, or taboo communities, 433–434
  religion and spirituality, 253–255
  transgender clients, 193–194
disengaged coping, 236
dissonant acculturation, 81
distance counseling, 517–518
domestic violence, Native Americans, 114
double jeopardy, 319
downward classism, 403
drapetomania, 2
drums, Native American culture, 111
DSM. *See Diagnostic and Statistical Manual of Mental Disorders*
dual diagnosis, 147

eagle feathers, Native American culture, 111
ecological models, multiracial identity development, 159–160
economic capital, 403
economic diversity, immigrant and refugee clients, 363–364
education, MENA Americans, 296
educational diversity, immigrant and refugee clients, 363
egalitarian therapeutic relationship, 219
elder abuse, Native Americans, 114
emotional expression, AAPI communities, 71
empathy. *See also* cultural humility
  client-centered approach, 27
  counseling setting, 26–27
  MENA and Muslim American clients, 304
  nonjudgmental approach, 27
enculturation, Latin American clients, 93
engaged coping, 236
enmeshment/denial stage, multiracial identity development, 158–159
entry to school stage, multiracial identity development, 159
environmental model, PWD, 341
Equal Justice Initiative, 51–52
ethical code location, 173
ethical consideration
  advice-giving, 11
  client's dignity, 11
  counselor's impairment, 11–12
  gatekeeping and supervision, 12–13
ethical non-monogamy, 428

ethnic identity development, Asian American and Pacific Islander communities, 73–74
Ethnic Identity Search, 73
Ethnic Minority Identity Development Model, 51
Euro-American Western mental health systems, 364
European American descent, clients of
  adults, 145–148
  advocacy agenda, 141–142
  Caucasian, 130–131
  children and adolescents, 142–145
  clinical case scenario, 149
  clinical practice, 148
  counseling utilization, 138–139
  culturally responsive practices, 139–141
  exploration, 131
  help-seeking, 138–139
  identity development, 135–138
  POC/BIPOC, 131
  White allyship, 133–135
  White racial identity, 131–133
  White supremacy, 130
evidence-based practice, military service members, 397–398
exosystem, AAPI communities, 79
exosystem, clients of European American descent, 142–143
explicit bias, 6

faith, 251–252
  development models, 260–261
  Fowler's stages, 261
  Genia's stages, 262
families
  European American descent, clients of, 145–148
  immigrant and refugee clients, 376
  Jewish descent, clients of, 287–288
  Latin American clients, 102
  LGBQ++ clients, 185
  multiracial clients, 166–167
  Muslim American clients, 296–297
  Native American descent, clients of, 123
  older adult population, 329–330
  people who live with disabilities (PWD), 355–356
  religion and spirituality, 262
  transgender clients, 206–207
  women clients, 227–228
familismo, 95
Family Advocacy Program (FAP), 383, 394
family structure and parenting styles, AAPI communities, 70–71
fandoms

INDEX | 529

children, adolescents, and young adults, 461
couples and families, 462
culturally responsive therapeutic interventions, 459–460
definition, 453
history, 453
identity, 457
subcultures, 453–454
fan-fiction creators, 455, 458
FAP. *See* Family Advocacy Program (FAP)
fatalismo, 103
feminist theory, polyamory communities
accountability, 438
client's well-being, 438
egalitarian relationship, 437
non-victim blaming, 438
revision, 438
fetishism, 429
forgiveness, people who live with disabilities (PWD), 354
formal operational stage, cognitive development, 143
formal register, 486
formalism, 103
fostering empowerment, women clients, 221–222
functional model, PWD, 341
furry community, 454
children, adolescents, and young adults, 461–462
culturally responsive therapeutic interventions, 460

GALA. *See* Gender Affirmative Lifespan Approach
gamer culture
categories, 452
children, adolescents, and young adults, 460–461
clinical practice, 463
counseling utilization and help-seeking, 458
couples and families, 462
culturally responsive therapeutic interventions, 458–459
history, 450–451
identity, 456
GAP. *See* Gay Affirmative Practices
gatekeeping, 12–13
gay, 177
Gay Affirmative Practices (GAP), 182
gender, 213
Gender Affirmative Lifespan Approach (GALA), 203
gender binary, 176
gender-expansive, 176

gender expression, 177
gender fluid, 176
gender identity, 176–177, 214
gender nonconforming, 176
gender roles
analysis, 220
Judaism, 275
genderqueer, 176
generic (folk) care, 510
Genia's Psychodynamic Spiritual Development, 259, 262
geriatrics, 318
Gideon's Developmental Model of Recovery, 148
give 'em hell script, men clients, 235
grandfather teachings, clients of Native American descent, 109–110
Grounded Theory Model
advocacy, 410–411
awareness, 409–410
knowledge, 410
skills, 410
training, 409
group work
multiracial clients, 156
women clients, 222

harmful supervision, 499–500
hate crimes, antisemitic, 278
healers, Native American culture, 110
hearing impaired, 350
Hebrew, 275
help-seeking behavior
Jewish descent, clients of, 282–283
LGBQ++ clients, 180–181
men clients, 237
military service members and veterans, 393–394
older adult population, 325–327
people who live with disabilities (PWD), 344–347
polyamory, kink, or taboo communities, 442
religion and spirituality, 262–263
Hindu Religious Coping Scale, 256
Hispanic culture, 90–91
historical memory recovery, liberation psychology, 17
holistic-wellness model, 77
honesty, grandfather teaching, 109
humility, grandfather teaching, 109

IARP. *See* International Anthropomorphic Research Project
I-CARE Model, 408–409, 413–415
IDEA. *See* Individuals with Disabilities Education Act

identity
  gamer culture, 456
  immigrant and refugee clients, 364–365
identity development
  AAPI communities, 73–74
  African descent, clients of, 50–51
  European American descent, clients of, 135–138
  Latin American clients, 92–94
  Muslim and MENA American clients, 304–305
IGDS9. *See* Internet Gaming Disorder Scale
IHS. *See* Indian Health Services
Immersion-Emersion stage, WRID, 132
immigrant and refugee clients
  acculturation and identity, 364–365
  adults, 376
  advocacy, 373–374
  children and adolescents, 374–375
  clinical case scenario, 377
  clinical practice, 376
  collectivism, 364
  communication difficulties, 371
  counseling intervention and advocacy, 361–362
  counseling relationship, 361
  counselor self-awareness, 361
  couples and families, 376
  cultural humility, 361
  culturally responsive practices, 371–373
  family-oriented culture, 364
  fear of deportation, 370
  foreign-born youth, 375
  immigration procedures, 370
  mental health and treatment, 369–370
  post-migration stressors, 367–369
  stressors and discrimination, 366–369
  United States, 362–364
Immigration and Nationality Act, 70
implicit bias, 6, 190
inclusive practices, transgender clients, 208
Indian Health Services (IHS), 118
Indigenous Environmental Network, 121
individual exploration, 131
individual identities, military service members and veterans, 392–393
individualism, clients of European American descent, 143
individualistic cultures, 364
individual-level advocacy, 198–199
Individuals with Disabilities Education Act (IDEA), 61
individuative-reflective faith, 261
informed consent, 485
integration, multiracial identity development, 159

integrative care, 510
interculturalism, 387
intergenerational trauma, 49
internalized antisemitism, Jews, 280
internalized classism, 403
internalized racism, 51
International Anthropomorphic Research Project (IARP), 458
Internet Gaming Disorder Scale (IGDS9), 459
Interracial Asian Family, 71
intersectionality theory, 42
intersex, 177
intra-counseling broaching dimensions, 469
intuitive-projective faith, 261
isolated coping, 236

Jewish descent, clients of
  adolescents and young adults, 288–287
  advocacy agenda, 285
  children, 285–286
  clinical case scenario, 288–289
  clinical practice, 288
  counseling considerations, 281–282
  culturally responsive practices, 283–285
  culture, 277
  discrimination, 280–281
  discrimination and stereotypes, 278–280
  families, 287–288
  help-seeking, 282–283
  identity development, 282
  individual identities, 269–278
  and Israel, 276
  multicultural framework, 269
  Shoah (Holocaust), 275–276
  stressors, 280–281
  worldviews and perspectives, 277–278
Jewish Religious Coping Scale, 256
Johari Window tool, 317
Judaism
  as chosen people, 273–274
  as civilization, 273
  denominations, 271–272
  ethnicity and culture, 272–273
  gender roles, 275
  languages, 275
  religious practices, 270–271
  United States, 269

kink communities
  fetishism, 429, 431
  homosexuality, 430
  LGBTQ+ community, 430–431
  sociopolitical influences, 429–432
  technology, 430–431
knowledge, transgender clients, 195–197

language
  immigrant and refugee clients, 363
  Judaism, 275
  Latino identity, 93
  transgender clients, 196
LARP community. *See* live-action role-play community
lateral classism, 403
Latino community
  adults and couples, 101–102
  advocacy, 98–100
  children and adolescents, 100–101
  clinical case scenario, 103–104
  culturally responsive practices, 96–98
  dichos work, 96
  families, 94–95, 102
  first-generation immigrants, 94
  help-seeking, 94–96
  Hispanic culture, 90–91
  identity development, 92–94
  institutional and linguistic obstacles, 95
  "Latinx" emergence, 91–92
  low socioeconomic status, 95
  mental health considerations and perceptions, 92
lawful permanent resident, 362
lesbian, 177
lesbian, gay, bisexual, queer++ (LGBQ++) clients
  adults, 185
  advocacy agenda, 183–184
  African descent, clients of, 63
  children and adolescents, 184–185
  clinical case scenario, 186
  clinical practice, 185–186
  couples and families, 185
  culturally responsive practices, 182–183
  discrimination, 179
  educational standards, 181–182
  exploration, 172
  gender expression, 177
  gender identity, 176–177
  help-seeking behaviors, 180–181
  intersectionality, 175
  introspection and reflection, 174–175
  kink communities, 430–431
  liberation psychology, 172
  oppression, 179–180
  prejudice, 179
  religion and sexual intersectionality, 178
  religious rejection, 254–255
  sexual orientation, 177
  stressors, 180
  young adults, 185
LGBQ++ clients. *See* lesbian, gay, bisexual, queer++ clients

liberation counseling
  military service members and veterans, 387–190
  and oppressed people, 19–20
  personal liberation, 16
  poor and affluent clients, 421–422
  psychology, 16–18
liberation framework, polyamory communities
  deideologized reality, 440
  methodological eclecticism, 440–441
  politico-social consciousness, 439
  preferential option, 440
  realismo-critico, 440
  social orientation principle, 439–440
Liberation Model, 36, 324
liberation psychology, 42–43
  LGBQ++ clients, 172
  military service members and veterans, 389–390
  Native American clients, 119
  older adult population, 320
liberation theory, 18–19
life-course perspective, military service
  empirically-based research, 391
  human agency, 392
  life structure, 390
  preschoolers, 391
  psychosocial development stages, 390
  social connections, 392
  timing, 392
  trust vs. mistrust, 390
  young adulthood phase, 390
life-course theory, 391–392
live-action role-play (LARP) community, 454–455, 457–458
Living in Two Worlds Survey (LTWS), 116
love, grandfather teaching, 109
LTWS. *See* Living in Two Worlds Survey

MACDA. *See* Multisystemic Approach to Cultural and Disability Awareness
macrosystem
  AAPI communities, 79
  European American descent, clients of, 143
major depressive disorder, clients of European American descent, 139
marginalized populations, 75, 318
masculinity, 234–235
MCC. *See* Multicultural Counseling Competencies
MCELFS. *See* Musical Chronology and Emerging Life Song
media, Muslim and MENA Americans, 306
medical conditions, 340
MEIM. *See* Multigroup Ethnic Identity Measure

men clients
- advocacy agenda, 241–242
- Black men, 237–238
- case conceptualization, 242
- clinical case scenario, 242–245
- clinical practice, 242
- contemporary issues and trends, 234–237
- counseling considerations, 239
- counseling relationship, 240
- culturally relevant clinical interventions, 244–245
- culturally responsive practices, 240–241
- discrimination, 239–240
- help-seeking behavior, 237
- RESPECTFUL model, 233–234
- scripts, internal
  - *give 'em hell*, 235
  - *playboy*, 235
  - *strong and silent*, 235
  - *tough guy*, 235
- self-awareness, 240
- stereotypes, 239
- stigmatization, 238–239
- strengths-based clinical interventions, 244–245
- stressors, 239
- worldviews and perspectives, 237–239

MENA American clients. *See* Middle Eastern/North African American clients

mental health
- AAPI communities, 72
- African American clients, 52–53
- African descent, clients of, 47–49
- African immigrants, 56–57
- Afro-Caribbean immigrant groups, 58–59
- counseling profession, 2–3
- European American descent, clients of, 139
- immigrant and refugee clients, 369–370
- Latin American clients, 92
- Native American descent, clients of, 113
- women clients, 216–218

mesosystems
- AAPI communities, 78–79
- European American descent, clients of, 142

mestizo, 91
metacognition, 90
metaphors, 462
microaggressions
- ableism, 343
- Asian American and Pacific Islander communities, 72

microsystems
- AAPI communities, 78
- European American descent, clients of, 142

Middle Eastern/North African (MENA) American clients
- advocacy agenda, 305–307
- Arab League countries, 293
- children and adolescents, 307–308
- clinical case scenario, 312–313
- couples and families, 208–209
- cultural humility, 302–303
- culturally responsive practices, 298–304
- education, 296
- family, 294–295
- gender, 295–296
- help-seeking, 298
- identity development, 304–305
- implications, 310–312
- liberation counseling, 303–304
- religion, 295
- U.S. Census, 294

migration stressors, immigrant and refugee clients, 366–369

Military and Family Life Counseling Program, 383

Military OneSource, 383

military service members and veterans
- advocacy agenda, 394–395
- children, adolescents, and young adults, 395
- clinical case scenario, 398–399
- clinical practice, 396–398
- culturally responsive practices, 393
- culture, 386–387
- deployment, 385
- exploration, 381–383
- help-seeking, 393–394
- individual identities, 392–393
- liberation counseling framework, 387–390
- life-course theory, 391–392
- moral injury, 387
- people who live with disabilities, 346–347
- reintegration, 385
- worldview and perspectives, 384–386

MIM. *See* Multiracial Identity Model
minority clients, 96
Minority Stress Theory, 238
model minority myth, Asian Americans, 80
modern Orthodox Jews, 271
modesty value, Native American clients, 119–120
moral injury, 387
MPM. *See* Multi-Phase Model
MSI. *See* Multicultural Supervision Inventory
MSJCC. *See* Multicultural and Social Justice Counseling Competencies
Multicultural and Social Justice Counseling Competencies (MSJCC), 6–7, 41, 42

AAPI communities, 75–76
European American descent, clients of, 140
immigrant and refugee clients, 371–373
men clients, 240–241
multiracial clients, 163–164
people who live with disabilities (PWD), 348–352
poor and affluent clients, 407, 420–421
religion and spirituality, 257–259
women clients, 223–225
multicultural awareness, MENA and Muslim American clients, 299
multicultural competency, 298
multicultural counseling approach
  ACA Code of Ethics, 3
  cultural encapsulation, 4–5
  cultural tunnel vision, 4
  culturally attentive counselor, 4
  ethical consideration, 11–13
  mental health counseling profession, 2–3
  positive therapeutic relationships, 4
  United States, 2
Multicultural Counseling Competencies (MCC), 41, 96–97
multicultural knowledge, MENA and Muslim American clients, 299–300
multicultural literacy, AAPI communities, 77–78
multicultural skills, MENA and Muslim American clients, 300–302
Multicultural Supervision Inventory (MSI), 498
multiculturalism, advocacy, 41–43
Multigroup Ethnic Identity Measure (MEIM), 51
Multi-Phase Model (MPM), 372
multiracial clients
  adolescents, 165
  adults, 166–167
  advocacy, 164
  assessment, 157
  career development, 156–157
  clinical case scenario, 168
  clinical practice, 167
  counseling utilization, 161–163
  couples and families, 166–167
  culturally responsive practices, 163–164
  group work, 156
  helping relationships, 155–156
  help-seeking, 161–163
  human growth and development, 154–155
  identity development, 158–160
  professional orientation and ethical practice, 158
  research and program evaluation, 157
  self-identified, 153
  social and cultural diversity, 155
  social construct, 153
  stressors and discrimination, 160–161
  United States, 153
multiracial identity development
  awareness, 160
  ecological models, 159–160
  stage models, 158–159
Multiracial Identity Model (MIM), 159
Multisystemic Approach to Cultural and Disability Awareness (MACDA), 65
Musical Chronology and Emerging Life Song (MCELFS), 263
Muslim American clients. See also Middle Eastern/North African American clients
  family, 296–297
  gender, 297
  help-seeking, 298
  religion, 297
mythic-literal faith, 261

National Latino and Asian American Study (NLAAS), 95
National Origin Act, 70
Native American descent, clients of
  acculturation, 114–117
  adults, 122–123
  advocacy agenda, 120–121
  children and adolescents, 121–122
  clinical case scenario, 125–126
  comfort, 124
  communication, 125
  context, 123–124
  counseling utilization, 117–118
  couples and families, 123
  cultural and spiritual values, 108–111
  cultural customs, 125
  culturally responsive practices, 118–120
  health disparities, 112–114
  help-seeking, 117–118
  historical background, 111–112
  storytelling practice, 108
  young adults, 121–122
naturalized citizens, 362
negritude, 2
NLAAS. See National Latino and Asian American Study
nonbinary people, 176, 214
Nonmedical Counseling Resources, 383
nonmonogamous relationships, 426–427
non-player characters (NPCs), 455
non-racist White identity, 132
NPCs. See non-player characters
nutrition, Native Americans, 113

OCF. *See* Outline for Cultural Formulation
older adult population
   advocacy, 325
   advocacy agenda, 328–329
   beliefs and thoughts, 316
   case vignette, 331–333
   clinical case scenario, 333–335
   clinical practice, 330–331
   competencies and cultural humility, 327–328
   counseling utilization, 325–327
   counselor educators, 324
   counselor training, 324
   couples and families, 329–330
   devaluation, 316
   group exercise, 317–318
   help-seeking, 325–327
   liberation counseling perspective, 316
   Liberation Model, 324
   personal/individual values, 317
   resilience, 318
   self-awareness, 317
   self-reflection, 316
   societal and cultural factors, 318–322
   transgender clients, 204
   us-versus-them phenomenon, 317
oppression, 18
   AAPI communities, 77
   lLGBQ++ clients, 179–180
   religion and spirituality, 253–255
Organizational Continuum of Broaching Behavior
   Avoidant organizations, 473
   clinical case scenario, 476
   Continuing/Incongruent organizations, 473
   empathy, 476
   Infusing organizations, 475
   Integrated/Congruent organizations, 475
   P-R-E-S-S framework, 475–476
   strategy stage, 476
Orthodox Judaism, 271
Outline for Cultural Formulation (OCF), 489

PAI. *See* Personality Assessment Scale
Pan-Hispanic identity, 91
pansexual, 177
paraphilias, 430
parental influences, Asian Americans, 81–82
PBE approach. *See* practice-based evidence approach
PCs. *See* player characters
People of Color (POC), 131
People of Color Racial Identity Model, 51
people who live with disabilities (PWD), 327
   adolescents, 353
   adults, 353–354
   advocacy, 347–378
   barriers for, 342–344
   benevolent behaviors, 338
   blind culture and identity, 351–352
   children, 352–353
   clinical case scenario, 357
   clinical practice, 356–357
   counseling utilization, 344–347
   counselor introspection, 339
   couples, 354–355
   culturally responsive practices, 348–352
   deaf, individuals who are, 350–351
   families, 355–356
   help-seeking, 344–347
   identity development models, 340–342
   military veterans, 346–347
   misconceptions, 340
   stressors and discrimination, 342–344
   substance use and addiction, 345–346
   suicide prevention, 339
   young adults, 353
personal cultural privilege, AAPI communities, 77
personal identity stage, multiracial identity development, 158
personal social justice compass, AAPI communities, 78
Personality Assessment Scale (PAI), 95
play therapy, foreign-born youth, 375
playboy script, men clients, 235
player characters (PCs), 455
POC. *See* People of Color
policies and laws related to Muslim and MENA Americans, 306–307
political countertransference, immigrant and refugee clients, 367–368
polyamorists, 428
polyamory, kink, or taboo communities
   affirmative therapy, 434–437
   allyship, 415
   attachment theory, 441–442
   clinical case scenario, 443–444
   clinical practice, 442–443
   counselor bias, 442–443
   feminist theory, 437–438
   help-seeking, 442
   heteronormative, 416
   liberation framework, 439–441
   oppression and challenges, 428
   vs. polygamy, 426–428
   psychoeducation, 443
   stigma and assumptions reduction, 442
   stressors and discrimination, 433–434
polyfidelity community, 428
polygamy, 426–428

poor and affluent clients
    best practices and counselor, 417–419
    class and classism, 408–413
    classism, 403–404
    clinical case scenario, 413–419
    culturally responsive counseling, 419–422
    ethical mandates, 407
    I-CARE Model, 413
    intersectionality, 405–407
    privilege and power, 404–405
    social class, 402
    Social Class Worldview Model–Revised (SCWM-R), 411–412
positive support couples therapy (PSCT), 355
Post Traumatic Slave Syndrome (PTSS), 64
post-migration stressors, immigrant and refugee clients, 367–369
Posttraumatic Growth (PTG), 397
posttraumatic stress disorder, women clients, 217
power analysis, women clients, 220–221
power dynamics, 17
practice-based evidence (PBE) approach, 19
praxis, 18
preadolescence stage, multiracial identity development, 159
prejudice, LGBQ++ clients, 179
preoperational stage, cognitive development, 143
primary spouse, 428
privilege and power, 404–405
problematization, 303
    liberation psychology, 17
    military service members and veterans, 389
professional advocacy, 164
professional care, 510
protean identity, 159
PSCT. *See* positive support couples therapy
Pseudo-Independence stage, WRID, 132
psychiatric disability, 339
psychoeducation
    Muslim and MENA Americans, 307
    polyamory, kink, or taboo communities, 443
psychology advocacy, 34
psychology, liberation, 16–18
PTG. *See* Posttraumatic Growth
PTSS. *See* Post Traumatic Slave Syndrome
public arena-level advocacy, 199–200
PWD. *See* people who live with disabilities

quality supervision, 499
queer, 176
queer communities, AAPI communities, 83–84
questioning, 178

race narrative questions, 48
racial and ethnic diversity, immigrant and refugee clients, 362–363
Racial Battle Fatigue (RBF), 65
racial complexity, 132
racial socialization, clients of European American descent, 136
racialized sexual harassment, AAPI communities, 83
racism, AAPI communities, 72
racism internalization, WRID, 132
radical empathy, 24
RBF. *See* Racial Battle Fatigue
RCT. *See* Relational Cultural Theory
Real Warriors, 394
realismo-critico, 440
recovering historical memory, 303
recovery-oriented systems of care, 226
reflective journal, 481
reflective practice, 481–482
refugee subjecthood, 74
refugees, 362
Relational Cultural Theory (RCT), 42
relationship dynamics, transgender clients, 206
religion and spirituality
    abuse, 254
    advocacy, 259–260
    African American clients, 55–56
    children and adolescents, 260–262
    clinical case scenario, 265–266
    consultation, 265
    coping assessment, 256
    counseling's history, 248–249
    couples and families, 262
    culturally responsive practices, 257–259
    definition, 250–251
    discrimination and oppression, 253–255
    faith, 251–252
    help-seeking behavior, 262–263
    immigrant and refugee clients, 364
    Musical Chronology and Emerging Life Song (MCELFS), 263
    personal history, 249
    rejection, 254–255
    spiritual bypass, 257
    spiritual genogram, 264
    strength sources, 255–256
    theory and theology, 264–265
    United States, 252–253
reorientation, liberation psychology, 17
researchers, 35–36
resilience
    older adult population, 318
    people who live with disabilities (PWD), 354

respect, grandfather teaching, 109
RESPECTFUL model, 7, 183, 233–234
reverse ageism, 322
Rosebud Personal Opinion Survey, 116

SAAB. *See* sex-assigned-at-birth
Sabbath, 270
same-gender loving, 178
sandplay, foreign-born youth, 375
SBS-13. *See* Spiritual Bypass Scale-13
Scale of Ethnocultural Empathy (SEE), 24
SCCC Model. *See* Social Class and Classism Consciousness Model
school- and community-level advocacy, 199
scientific racism, 483
SCWM-R. *See* Social Class Worldview Model–Revised
SEE. *See* Scale of Ethnocultural Empathy
Segregation Stress Syndrome, 64–65
selective acculturation, 81
self-awareness, 7–8, 41, 90, 240, 480
self-care, 12
self-compassion, PWD, 354
self-esteem, women clients, 217
sensorimotor stage, cognitive development, 143
sex, 213
sex-assigned-at-birth (SAAB), 190
sexism, 215
sexual orientation, 63, 177
Shoah (Holocaust), 275–276
sight loss, 351–352
singular identity, 159
SJARQ. *See* Social Justice Advocacy Readiness Questionnaire
skills
   Grounded Theory Model, 410
   transgender clients, 197
slacktivism, 38
smudging, Native American culture, 111
social and medical gender-affirming transitions, 196–197
social capital, 403
social class, 402
Social Class and Classism Consciousness (SCCC) Model, 412
social class bias, 404
Social Class Worldview Model–Revised (SCWM-R)
   classism, 412
   economic cultures, 411–412
   worldview, 412
Social Identity Theory, AAPI communities, 73–74
Social Justice Advocacy Readiness Questionnaire (SJARQ), 40
social justice and advocacy
   advocates, 36–37
   clinical case scenario, 43–44
   community-based work, 33
   cultural responsiveness, 34–38
   definition, 32
   Latin American clients, 98
   Liberation Model, 33–34
   Liberation Model Framework, 32
   multiculturalism, 32
   pandemic, 37
   poor and affluent clients, 420–421
   psychology advocacy, 34
   recurring wave, 32
   role oppression, 32
   social media, 38
social media, social justice, 38
socialization, clients of European American descent, 136
socioeconomic challenges, AAPI communities, 72
sociopolitical model, disability, 341–342
Solidarity Week, 202
Spiritual Bypass Scale-13 (SBS-13), 257
spiritual genogram, 264
spirituality, 250. *See also* religion and spirituality
   African American clients, 55–56
   Native American descent, clients of, 108–109
stereotypes, 6, 278–280
stress, men clients, 236
stressors
   immigrant and refugee clients, 366–369
   Jewish descent, clients of, 280–281
   LGBQ++ clients, 180
   men clients, 239
   military service members and veterans, 393
   multiracial clients, 160–161
   people who live with disabilities (PWD), 342–344
   polyamory, kink, or taboo communities, 433–434
   transgender clients, 193–194
strong and silent script, men clients, 235
Strong Black Woman Schema, 217
substance use and addiction
   European American descent, clients of, 139, 147–148
   Native Americans, 113
   people who live with disabilities (PWD), 345–346
suicide
   Black adolescents and young adults, 61–62
   Native Americans, 114

people who live with disabilities (PWD), 344
supervision, 12–13. *See also* clinical supervision
supervisor and supervisee, 494–496. *See also* clinical supervision
 harmful supervision, 499–500
 power dynamic, 499
supervisory working alliance, 497–498
swingers, 428
synthetic-conventional faith, 261

taboo culture, 432–433
telemental health, 354, 517–518
temporary migrants/visitors, 362
TGNC individuals. *See* transgender and gender nonconforming individuals
Torah, 270
tough guy script, men clients, 235
toxic masculinity, 147
Traditional Asian American Family, 71
traditional names, clients of Native American descent, 110
traditional values, clients of Native American descent, 119–120
transcendent identity, 159
transference, 8–9
transformative justice, 17
transgender individuals, 176–177, 213, 214
transgender and gender nonconforming (TGNC) individuals, 214
transgender clients
 adolescents, 200
 advocacy, 198–200
 clinical case scenario, 209
 coming-out process, 206
 consultation, supervision, and referrals, 208
 couples, 204–205
 culturally responsive practices, 195–198
 exploration, 190
 families, 206–207
 help-seeking behaviors, 194–195
 historical pathologizing, 201
 inclusive practices, 208
 intentionality, 208
 introspection and reflection, 190–191
 older adults, 204
 privacy and confidentiality, 201–202
 relationship dynamics, 206
 relationships and feelings, 202
 religion and sexual intersectionality, 192–193
 safety, 205
 social supports, 208
 stressors and discrimination, 193–194
 young adults, 200–201

transgender-affirmative care, 203
transition model, clients of European American descent, 146
transsexual person, 177
trauma-focused cognitive behavioral therapy, foreign-born youth, 375
trauma-informed care, 226
trauma-informed lens, 197
traumatic experiences, immigrant and refugee clients, 366–367
treatment barriers, 47–48
Tricare, 383
trustworthiness, 26
two-spirit, 177

ultra-Orthodox Jews, 271–272
undocumented immigrants, 362
undocumented Latino children, 101
universalizing faith, 261
upward classism, 403
us-versus-them phenomenon, 317

value conflict, 9
values and worldviews, clients of European American descent, 137–138
Veterans Crisis Line, 395
Veterans of Foreign Wars, 394
vicarious trauma, 11–12
vidders, 455, 458
video games, 452
violent crimes, Native Americans, 114
visual disabilities, 340

Ways of Religious Coping Scale, 256
wellness model, 396–397
West Indian immigrant identity, 58
White allyship
 coalition-building, BIPOC, 134
 Edwards's model, 134–135
 interrogation process, 133–134
 knowledge pursuit, 134
 self-awareness, 133
 self-reflexivity and self-exploration, 134
White privilege, 50–51
White Racial Identity Development Model (WRID), 51, 132–133
wisdom, grandfather teaching, 109
Womanism, 218
Womanist Theology, 264
women clients
 adolescents, 227
 advocacy, 225–227
 affirmative therapy, 216
 and aging, 321–323
 children, 227
 clinical case scenario, 229–230

clinical practice, 228
collaborative goal setting, 219
cultural humility, 216
cultural responsiveness, 216
culturally responsive counselors, 216
culturally responsive practices, 223–225
egalitarian therapeutic relationship, 219
external sources of distress, 219–220
family and couple dynamics, 227–228
fostering empowerment, 221–222
gender role analysis, 220
group work, 222
help-seeking behaviour, 223
intersectionality, 215
Native American descent, clients of, 110
power analysis, 220–221
resilience and activism, 222–223
women clients, 217
young adults, 227
work/career, men clients, 236–237
workplace
  accessibility, 517
  clinical case scenario, 519
  culturally sensitive agencies, 510–515
  distance counseling, 517–518
  intake forms, 516–517
  marketing materials, 516
  multicultural counseling, 508
  office attraction, 509
World Religion Calendar, 263
WRID. *See* White Racial Identity Development Model

xenophobic perceptions, immigrant and refugee clients, 368

Yiddish, 275
young adults
  AAPI communities, 79–82
  LGBQ++ clients, 185
  MENA and Muslim American clients, 288–287
  military service members and veterans, 395
  Native American descent, clients of, 122
  people who live with disabilities (PWD), 353
  religion and spirituality, 260–262
  transgender clients, 200–201
  women clients, 227

Zionist movement, 276